GET THE MOST FROM YOUR BOOK

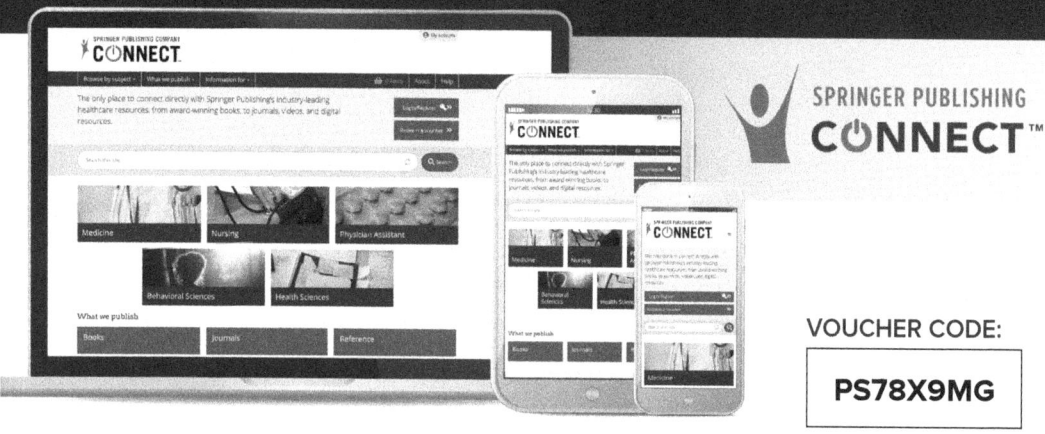

VOUCHER CODE:

PS78X9MG

Online Access

Your print purchase of *School Psychology, Second Edition*, includes **online access via Springer Publishing Connect**™ to increase accessibility, portability, and searchability.

Insert the code at https://connect.springerpub.com/content/book/978-0-8261-6344-8 today!

Having trouble? Contact our customer service department at cs@springerpub.com

Instructor Resource Access for Adopters

Let us do some of the heavy lifting to create an engaging classroom experience with a variety of instructor resources included in most textbooks SUCH AS:

Visit **https://connect.springerpub.com/** and look for the **"Show Supplementary"** button on your **book homepage** to see what is available to instructors! First time using Springer Publishing Connect?
Email **textbook@springerpub.com** to create an account and start unlocking valuable resources.

School Psychology

Sally L. Grapin, PhD, NCSP, is an associate professor of psychology in the College of Humanities and Social Sciences at Montclair State University. She received her PhD in school psychology from the University of Florida. Dr. Grapin has taught both lecture- and field-based graduate and undergraduate courses in school psychology, including academic assessment, psychotherapeutic interventions, diversity in education, and professional issues in school psychology. Her research focuses on the intersection of social justice and school psychology and has been funded by the American Psychological Foundation, National Association of School Psychologists, and Society for the Teaching of Psychology. She also has received awards from national organizations such as the American Psychological Association, Society for the Teaching of Psychology, and Trainers of School Psychologists, and she was the recipient of the Society for the Psychological Study of Social Issues Innovative Teaching Award in 2017. Dr. Grapin is the Editor-in-Chief of *School Psychology International* and has served on the editorial boards of several school psychology journals, including the *Journal of School Psychology*, *Psychology in the Schools*, *School Psychology*, and *School Psychology Review*.

John H. Kranzler, PhD, is Irving and Rose Fien Endowed Professor in Education and director of the American Psychological Association (APA)-accredited school psychology program in the School of Special Education, School Psychology, and Early Childhood Studies at the University of Florida. Dr. Kranzler's major area of scholarly interest concerns the nature, development, and assessment of human cognitive abilities. He has received a number of awards for his teaching and research, including the University of Florida Teaching Incentive Program award for undergraduate teaching, the Mensa Education and Research Foundation Award for Excellence in Research, and Article of the Year awards from *School Psychology Review* and *School Psychology Quarterly*. In 1997 and 2017, Dr. Kranzler received the University of Florida Research Foundation Professorship award for distinguished scholarship and was recently named a University of Florida Term Professor in 2019. He is a Fellow of the American Psychological Association and an elected member of the Society for the Study of School Psychology. Dr. Kranzler has served as associate editor of *School Psychology Quarterly* and the *International Journal of School and Educational Psychology* and currently serves on several editorial boards, including the *Journal of School Psychology*.

School Psychology
Professional Issues and Practices

SECOND EDITION

SALLY L. GRAPIN, PhD, NCSP

JOHN H. KRANZLER, PhD

Editors

Copyright © 2024 Springer Publishing Company, LLC

All rights reserved.

First Springer Publishing edition 2018 (978-0-8261-9473-2).

No part of this publication may be reproduced, stored in a retrieval system, or transmitted in any form or by any means, electronic, mechanical, photocopying, recording, or otherwise, without the prior permission of Springer Publishing Company, LLC, or authorization through payment of the appropriate fees to the Copyright Clearance Center, Inc., 222 Rosewood Drive, Danvers, MA 01923, 978-750-8400, fax 978-646-8600, info@copyright.com or at www.copyright.com.

Springer Publishing Company, LLC
www.springerpub.com
connect.springerpub.com

Acquisitions Editor: Mindy Okura-Marszycki
Compositor: S4Carlisle Publishing Services
Production Editor: Rachel Haines

ISBN: 978-0-8261-6343-1
ebook ISBN: 978-0-8261-6344-8
DOI: 10.1891/9780826163448

SUPPLEMENTS:

 A robust set of instructor resources designed to supplement this text is located at http://connect.springerpub.com/content/book/978-0-8261-6344-8. Qualifying instructors may request access by emailing textbook@springerpub.com.

LMS Common Cartridge: 978-0-8261-6348-6
Sample Syllabi: 978-0-8261-6346-2
Test Bank: 978-0-8261-6345-5
Instructor Chapter PowerPoints: 978-0-8261-6347-9

23 24 25 26 27 / 5 4 3 2 1

The author and the publisher of this Work have made every effort to use sources believed to be reliable to provide information that is accurate and compatible with the standards generally accepted at the time of publication. Because medical science is continually advancing, our knowledge base continues to expand. Therefore, as new information becomes available, changes in procedures become necessary. We recommend that the reader always consult current research and specific institutional policies before performing any clinical procedure or delivering any medication. The author and publisher shall not be liable for any special, consequential, or exemplary damages resulting, in whole or in part, from the readers' use of, or reliance on, the information contained in this book. The publisher has no responsibility for the persistence or accuracy of URLs for external or third-party internet websites referred to in this publication and does not guarantee that any content on such websites is, or will remain, accurate or appropriate.

Library of Congress Cataloging-in-Publication Data

Names: Grapin, Sally L., editor. | Kranzler, John H., editor.
Title: School psychology : professional issues and practices / editors, Sally L. Grapin, John H. Kranzler.
Other titles: School psychology (Springer Publishing Company)
Description: Second edition. | New York : Springer Publishing, 2024. | Includes bibliographical references and index.
Identifiers: LCCN 2023016385 (print) | LCCN 2023016386 (ebook) | ISBN 9780826163431 (cloth) | ISBN 9780826163448 (ebook)
Subjects: LCSH: School psychology—Study and teaching. | School psychologists—Training of. | School psychologists—In-service training. | School psychology.
Classification: LCC LB3013.6 .S29 2024 (print) | LCC LB3013.6 (ebook) | DDC 370.15—dc23/eng/20230413
LC record available at https://lccn.loc.gov/2023016385
LC ebook record available at https://lccn.loc.gov/2023016386

Contact sales@springerpub.com to receive discount rates on bulk purchases.

Publisher's Note: New and used products purchased from third-party sellers are not guaranteed for quality, authenticity, or access to any included digital components.

Printed in the United States of America by Hatteras, Inc.

*To my daughter, Brooke—you are the light of my life.
I will always love you.
—Sally L. Grapin*

*To the next generation of school psychologists—it has been my privilege to help in some small way with your training—you will make a difference.
—John H. Kranzler*

Contents

Contributors ix
Foreword xvii
Preface xxi
Acknowledgments xxvii
Springer Publishing Connect™ Resources xxix

SECTION I: FOUNDATIONS OF SCHOOL PSYCHOLOGY

1. **Introduction to School Psychology** 3
   Sally L. Grapin and John H. Kranzler

2. **Historical Foundations** 19
   Dan Florell

3. **Multicultural Foundations** 43
   Sherrie L. Proctor and Nakia M. Gray-Nicolas

4. **Antiracism and School Psychology** 61
   Prerna G. Arora, Celeste M. Malone, Olivia Khoo, and Tenisha S. Jones

5. **Ethical and Legal Foundations** 83
   Barbara Bole Williams and Laura W. Monahon

6. **Graduate Preparation and Credentialing** 101
   Eric Rossen, Natalie N. Politikos, and Joseph S. Prus

SECTION II: SERVICE DELIVERY IN SCHOOL PSYCHOLOGY

7. **Assessment** 121
   Nicholas F. Benson and Brandon S. Parker

8   Intervention Planning and Implementation   139
Erum Nadeem and Susan G. Forman

9   Academic Assessment and Intervention   155
Scott P. Ardoin, Stacy-Ann A. January, and Amy Trayers

10   Social, Emotional, and Behavioral Assessment and Intervention   171
Amy M. Briesch and Robert J. Volpe

11   Cognitive Assessment   189
John H. Kranzler and Randy G. Floyd

12   Consultation   203
William P. Erchul and Aaron J. Fischer

13   School Violence and Crisis Prevention and Intervention   221
Amanda B. Nickerson

14   Family, School, and Community Collaboration   233
Janise S. Parker, Tiffany C. Hornsby, Angelina Nortey, Ayanna Troutman, and Alana M. Parker

15   Systems Change and Program Evaluation   247
Amity L. Noltemeyer and Erin A. Harper

16   Research in School Psychology   263
Tai A. Collins, Alexis Blackmon, and Joseph S. Wang

SECTION III: LOOKING AHEAD

17   Internationality of School and Educational Psychology   283
John C. Begeny, Eui Kyung Kim, Jiayi Wang, Rahma Hida, KeAysia Jackson, and Kevin Han

18   Future of School Psychology   305
Lori E. Unruh, Kathleen M. Minke, and Eric Rossen

19   Preparing for a Career in School Psychology   329
Sarah Valley-Gray and Diana Joyce-Beaulieu

Glossary   345
Index   359

Contributors

Scott P. Ardoin, PhD, BCBA-D, is a professor of school psychology and codirector of the Center for Autism and Behavioral Education at the University of Georgia. He employs applied behavioral analysis to develop and evaluate classroom intervention and in his use of eye-tracking procedures to understand the processes and behaviors engaged in by students when completing reading comprehension tests as well.

Prerna G. Arora, PhD, is an assistant professor at Teachers College, Columbia University. She received her doctorate in school psychology at the University of Texas at Austin. Dr. Arora's research focuses on issues of access and quality of care for historically marginalized youth and adolescents.

John C. Begeny, PhD, is a professor of psychology at North Carolina State University. He is also the founder and executive director of Helps Education Fund, a nonprofit organization that offers various forms of free and research-based support for educators and families. His primary interests relate to issues of educational equity, such as trying to improve equity through academic supports, effective community–university partnerships, enhancing school-based systems, and internationalization.

Nicholas F. Benson, PhD, NCSP, is an associate professor of school psychology at Baylor University, where he serves as director of the PhD program in school psychology. His research interests focus on psychological and educational assessment, with an emphasis on examining the validity of interpretations and uses of test scores. Dr. Benson serves on the editorial boards of several journals and is an associate editor for the *Journal of School Psychology*.

Alexis Blackmon, BA, is a doctoral student in the school psychology program at the University of Cincinnati. Her research interests focus on culturally relevant interventions in schools.

Amy M. Briesch, PhD, is associate professor in the Department of Applied Psychology at Northeastern University. Her primary research interests involve the development of feasible and psychometrically sound measures for the assessment of student behavior in multitiered systems of support.

Tai A. Collins, PhD, BCBA-D, is an associate professor and coordinator of the school psychology program at the University of Cincinnati. Dr. Collins's research focuses on culturally relevant interventions and supports for Black students in urban schools.

William P. Erchul, PhD, ABPP, is a professor emeritus of psychology at North Carolina State University. His interests include processes and outcomes associated with school consultation as well as social influence and interpersonal communication. Dr. Erchul served as president of the American Academy of School Psychology and president of the Society for the Study of School Psychology, and he has received several national awards for his research and service to the field.

Aaron J. Fischer, PhD, BCBA-D, is the Dee Endowed Professor of School Psychology at the University of Utah. He directs the University of Utah Technology in Training, Education, and Consultation lab. His research focuses on the intersection of technology, behavior, and mental health; specifically, teleconsultation and telehealth applications to support students, caregivers, and educators.

Dan Florell, PhD, is a professor at Eastern Kentucky University and runs a private practice. Dr. Florell received his PhD in school psychology from Illinois State University and is a licensed psychologist and Nationally Certified School Psychologist (NCSP). He is the National Association of School Psychologists (NASP) Historian and has written several articles and book chapters on the history of school psychology.

Randy G. Floyd, PhD, is a professor of psychology and department chair in the Department of Psychology at The University of Memphis. His research focuses on understanding the measurement properties of psychological assessment techniques, including intelligence tests, and he is interested in understanding professional development processes supporting university-based faculty. He is the former editor of the *Journal of School Psychology*, and he serves on the editorial boards of the *Journal of Psychoeducational Assessment*, *Journal of School Psychology*, *School Psychology International*, and *School Psychology Training and Pedagogy*.

Susan G. Forman, PhD, is a university professor at Rutgers. She has published over 100 journal articles, book chapters, and books on factors that influence intervention implementation, interprofessional collaborative approaches to pediatric behavioral healthcare, and the effectiveness of cognitive behavioral interventions with children and adolescents. Her work has been supported by grants from the National Institutes of Health, the National Institute on Drug Abuse, the National Institute of Mental Health, the National Science Foundation, the U.S. Department of Education, and the American Psychological Association, as well as a number of corporate and family foundations. She is a fellow of the American Psychological Association and a member of the Society for the Study of School Psychology. She has served on the executive boards of the school psychology division of the American Psychological Association and the National Association of Psychologists, and as chair of the Council of Directors of School Psychology Programs.

Jon W. Goodwin, PhD, is an assistant professor at the University of California, Santa Barbara, where he also serves as the director of clinical training for the doctoral- and specialist-level school psychology programs. His research interests include the assessment of learning differences, psychoeducational services for students with advanced intellectual ability, and the scholastic functioning of children and adolescents with craniofacial disorders (e.g., clefts of the lip and/or palate). As a licensed psychologist and nationally certified school psychologist, he provides advanced training and supervision in psychoeducational assessment, counseling and psychotherapy, and the delivery of psychological services in schools.

Sally L. Grapin, PhD, NCSP, is an associate professor in the Psychology Department at Montclair State University. Her scholarly and professional interests center on the intersection of social justice and school psychology research and practice. She currently serves as Editor-in-Chief of *School Psychology International.*

Nakia M. Gray-Nicolas, EdD, is an assistant professor of educational leadership in the Department of Educational and Community Programs. Her scholarly research examines college access for and college readiness and persistence of traditionally marginalized students, distributed leadership and community engagement, and the intersectionality and experience of Black women in academia.

Kevin Han, BA, is a doctoral student in the school psychology program at the University of California, Riverside. His research interests include providing alternative interventions for English Language Learners in special education and implementing universal screening procedures in schools.

Erin A. Harper, PhD, is a Senior Research Scientist in the Center for Depression Research and Clinical Care at the University of Texas Southwestern Medical Center. Dr. Harper practiced school psychology in urban schools for 8 years. Her primary research interests include cocreating school-based preventive interventions with Black adolescent girls and school-based prevention of commercial sexual exploitation. Dr. Harper is an associate editor of *School Psychology International* and a member of the *Journal of Educational and Psychological Consultation* editorial board.

Rahma Hida, PhD, is a psychology fellow at Boston Children's Hospital and Harvard Medical School. Her clinical and research interests are broadly focused on providing quality behavioral health services to children and families historically underserved by the healthcare system, including racially and ethnically minoritized groups, culturally and linguistically diverse families, and pediatric patients with complex medical needs.

Tiffany C. Hornsby, PhD, NCSP, is an assistant professor of school psychology at James Madison University. Her scholarly and research interests include interprofessional collaboration, educational outcomes for culturally and linguistically diverse students, effective family–school–community partnerships, and professional issues in training and supervision regarding diversity, equity, and inclusion.

KeAysia Jackson, BA, is a doctoral student in the school psychology program at the University of California, Riverside. Her research interests include the disproportionality of Black students in special education, school-based prevention and intervention for children with adverse childhood experiences, and school-based mental health supports.

Stacy-Ann A. January, PhD, NCSP, is an assistant professor in the school psychology program at the University of South Florida. Her research focuses on improving data-based decision-making in schools and identifying evidence-based interventions that target children's academic skills.

Shane R. Jimerson, PhD, is a professor at the University of California, Santa Barbara. He has engaged in extensive scholarly and leadership efforts in the field of school psychology, including authoring over 400 publications (including more than 30 books) and serving as Editor-in-Chief of two major journals, *School Psychology Quarterly* and *School Psychology Review*. He has received the 2021 Lifetime Contributions Award from the California

Association of School Psychologists, the 2022 Senior Scientist Award from Division 16 of the American Psychological Association, and the 2023 Lifetime Achievement Award from the National Association of School Psychologists.

Tenisha S. Jones, MA, is a second-year doctoral student in school psychology at Howard University, Washington, D.C. She is primarily interested in the mental health and well-being of Black girls.

Diana Joyce-Beaulieu, PhD, is a scholar, psychologist and practica coordinator with the American Psychological Association (APA)-accredited school psychology program at the University of Florida. She has taught a range of graduate courses including developmental psychopathology, social–emotional assessment, counseling, and practica seminars. Her professional work includes five books as well as numerous chapters and journal articles, and she has been awarded nearly one million dollars in professional development grants to research training models for Response to Intervention (RtI) and multitiered systems of support.

Olivia Khoo, MA, EdM, is a PhD candidate in school psychology at Teachers College, Columbia University. Her research interests are in access to mental health services among racial and ethnic minority and immigrant-origin youth.

Eui Kyung Kim, PhD, is an assistant professor in the school psychology program at the University of California, Riverside. Her research interests focus on understanding the pathways to risk and resilience among children, families, and teachers from underrepresented backgrounds. Specifically, she conducts research on universal mental health screening, early identification and prevention services for children's social and emotional health, perceptions of school climate among racial minority teachers, and school readiness for children of international parents.

John H. Kranzler, PhD, is Irving and Rose Fien Endowed Professor in Education and director of the American Psychological Association (APA)-accredited school psychology program in the School of Special Education, School Psychology, and Early Childhood Studies at the University of Florida. Dr. Kranzler's major area of scholarly interest concerns the nature, development, and assessment of human cognitive abilities.

Celeste M. Malone, PhD, MS, is an assistant professor and coordinator of the school psychology program at Howard University. She received her PhD in school psychology from Temple University. Her primary research interest relates to multicultural and diversity issues embedded in the training and practice of school psychology.

Kathleen M. Minke, PhD, has worked as a school psychologist in Virginia, Indiana, and Maryland. From 1991 to 2018, she was a professor in the school psychology program at the University of Delaware. She currently serves as the National Association of School Psychologists' (NASP's) executive director.

Laura W. Monahon, PsyD, NCSP, is a licensed psychologist in New Jersey as well as a school psychologist. She currently maintains a private practice and also works as a consulting school psychologist. She has taught courses in school psychology ethics at the graduate level at Philadelphia College of Osteopathic Medicine.

Erum Nadeem, PhD, is an associate professor in the School Psychology Department at the Graduate School of Applied and Professional Psychology. Her work focuses on community-partnered research methods, implementation science to support the uptake of evidence-based practices in schools and community settings, and racial/ethnic disparities in children's educational and mental health outcomes. She has particular expertise in supporting schools to respond to the needs of children and adolescents exposed to trauma, and in the study of implementation strategies (e.g., coaching, consultation, learning collaboratives, continuous quality improvement).

Amanda B. Nickerson, PhD, is a professor of School Psychology and director of the Alberti Center for Bullying Abuse Prevention at the University at Buffalo, the State University of New York. Her research focuses broadly on school safety and building social–emotional strengths of youth, with a particular emphasis on bullying and other forms of violence and victimization.

Amity L. Noltemeyer, PhD, is a professor in the Department of Educational Psychology and associate dean of the Graduate School at Miami University. Dr. Noltemeyer is also consulting editor of *School Psychology International* journal, comanages several externally funded grants, is a past president of the Ohio School Psychologists Association, and previously served as a practicing school psychologist.

Angelina Nortey, PhD, LP, NCSP, is a clinical assistant professor at Yeshiva University. She is also the owner of a private therapy clinic in Alexandria, Virginia. Her primary research interests are in school discipline and early career school psychologists' social justice needs, with an emphasis in qualitative methodology.

Arlene Ortiz, PhD, is an assistant professor at the University of California, Santa Barbara. As a licensed psychologist and a nationally certified school psychologist, Dr. Ortiz has experience providing mental health services in English and Spanish to underserved children and their families. Dr. Ortiz is actively engaged in scholarship related to culturally responsive graduate training and assessment and early intervention for culturally and linguistically diverse students.

Alana M. Parker, MEd, has years of professional experience as a certified school psychologist providing individual and group psychotherapy, administration of comprehensive psychological assessments, school-based mental health consultation, and school-based behavioral support services. She works with adolescents, families, and young adults utilizing psychodynamic and cognitive behavioral therapeutic techniques to guide individuals toward increasing appropriate coping mechanisms, effective problem-solving, and improving overall psychological well-being.

Brandon S. Parker, MS, is a doctoral candidate in school psychology at Baylor University. His research interests focus on psychological assessment and multicultural competency in school psychology. Brandon was awarded Outstanding Graduate Student—Doctoral Level by the Texas Association of School Psychologists in 2020.

Janise S. Parker, PhD, LP, NCSP, is an assistant professor of school psychology at William & Mary. Her research focuses on (a) culturally responsive mental and behavioral health services, (b) sociocultural contexts and positive Black youth development, and (c) social–emotional and behavioral health implications for serving religiously and spiritually diverse youth from marginalized backgrounds.

Natalie N. Politikos, PhD, NCSP, is a professor at the University of Hartford and is currently the program director of the school psychology program. She is serving as the chair of the National Association of School Psychologists (NASP) Program Accreditation Board and served as the team colead for the revision of the NASP Standards for Graduate Preparation of School Psychologists (2020). She was the recipient of the 2019 and 2020 NASP Presidential Award.

Sherrie L. Proctor, PhD, is a professor of school psychology at Queens College, City University of New York. Her research is grounded in social justice and critical perspectives and explores issues related to Black students in K–12 and higher education. She is coeditor of *Critical Theories for School Psychology and Counseling: A Foundation for Equity and Inclusion in School-Based Practice* and *Best Practices in School Psychology, Seventh Edition*.

Joseph S. Prus, PhD, NCSP, is professor emeritus at Winthrop University, where he served as distinguished professor, director of the school psychology program, and chair of the Department of Psychology. He served as chair of the National Association of School Psychologists (NASP) Program Approval (now Accreditation) Board for 12 years and cochair of the NASP Graduate Education Committee and Accreditation Advisory Group. He was the 2015 recipient of the NASP Lifetime Achievement Award.

Eric Rossen, PhD, NCSP, is a nationally certified school psychologist, a licensed psychologist in Maryland, and a credentialed National Register Health Service psychologist. He has experience working in public schools, independent practice, and higher education. He is currently the director of professional development and standards for the National Association of School Psychologists (NASP).

Miriam E. Thompson, PhD, is an assistant professor at the University of California, Santa Barbara (UCSB). Her research and scholarship interests include training and professional issues in school psychology such as pedagogy, graduate student training, and the recruitment and retention of junior faculty of color in school psychology. Dr. Thompson is a licensed psychologist and nationally certified school psychologist as well as the director of the Mind and Behavior Assessment Clinic (MBAC) at UCSB. At the MBAC, she trains doctoral students in the administration of standardized psychological assessments. She also teaches courses on neuropsychological, cognitive, and personality assessment.

Amy Trayers, MA, is a school psychology graduate student at the University of South Florida. Her research interests are in the areas of facilitating multitiered systems of support (MTSS) implementation, academic assessments and interventions within a multitiered framework, and systems-level consultation to improve student outcomes.

Ayanna Troutman, MEd, is a doctoral student in the school psychology program at the University of Florida. Her research interests include the exploration of Black girls' experiences in the K–12 system; culturally responsive social, emotional, and behavioral (SEB) interventions for Black youth; and examining how Black youth engage in resistance and radicalism in their communities and schools.

Lori E. Unruh, PhD, has worked as a school psychologist in Kansas, Arizona, and North Carolina. She is currently an assistant professor in the school psychology program at Western Carolina University and served as program director for 15 years.

Sarah Valley-Gray, PsyD, ABPP, is a licensed psychologist, a board-certified school psychologist, a professor, and the director of the doctoral program in school psychology in the College of Psychology at Nova Southeastern University (NSU). She led the development of both the specialist and the doctoral programs in school psychology at NSU and is passionate about graduate education in school psychology, supervision, and the evaluation of competencies in school psychology curricula.

Robert J. Volpe, PhD, is professor and chair of the Department of Applied Psychology at Northeastern University. His research focuses on designing and evaluating behavioral and academic assessment and intervention systems for use in problem-solving models.

Jiayi Wang, PhD, is an assistant professor in the Department of Counseling and Educational Psychology at New Mexico State University. Her research interests focus on evidence-based intervention to support students' academic and social–emotional development, coaching to facilitate intervention fidelity, support for culturally and linguistically diverse graduate students in school psychology programs, as well as the internationalization of school psychology.

Joseph S. Wang, ES, is a doctoral student in the school psychology program at the University of Cincinnati. His research interests are in school social justice, academic interventions, and food insecurity.

Barbara Bole Williams, PhD, NCSP, is a professor and coordinator of the school psychology program at Rowan University, Glassboro, New Jersey. She was honored as the recipient of the 2011 Lifetime Achievement Award from the National Association of School Psychologists (NASP) conferred at the 2011 NASP Convention in San Francisco, California. She has previously served on the NASP Ethics Committee as the representative of the northeast region of the United States, chairs the Ethics Committee for the New Jersey Association of School Psychologists, and was a member of the writing team that developed the NASP 2020 revised ethics code.

Rondy Yu, PhD, is an assistant professor at the University of California, Riverside, where he is a core faculty member of the school psychology program and director of the applied behavior analysis program. He holds multiple advanced certifications, including licensure as a psychologist, national certification as a school psychologist, and board certification as a behavior analyst. Dr. Yu also serves on several journal editorial boards, including that of *School Psychology Review*. His research and teaching interests focus on cognitive and behavioral interventions for children and adolescents with emotional and behavioral disorders, building integrated systems of support, and advancing the field of implementation science.

Foreword

Positionality Statement: The authors of this foreword are early career and senior scholars in two research-intensive universities; several of us also have previous experiences as faculty in programs focusing on the preparation of practicing school psychologists at the master's or specialist levels. We have held numerous leadership positions in school psychology. Our scholarship and other professional activities span a range of topics in school psychology and have been informed and inspired by partnerships in a range of local, national, and international contexts. Our varied personal experiences, backgrounds, and tenures in the field of school psychology lend differing perspectives on the sociocultural and systemic factors addressed herein. As such, our perspectives are informed and bounded by our diverse personal and professional experiences, statuses, values, and aspirations, as are the perspectives of the contributors to the chapters in this book.

CONTEMPORARY CONTEXT FOR SCHOOL PSYCHOLOGISTS

The second edition of *School Psychology: Professional Issues and Practices* provides contemporary information pertinent to the present landscape of school psychology and education, including an emphasis on advancing social justice through preparing school psychologists who are effective advocates for children and families. This edition is particularly timely, as there has been an increasing emphasis in the field of school psychology on further advancing diversity, equity, inclusion, antiracism, social justice, and the reconceptualization of the field for the 21st century (see, for instance, García-Vázquez et al., 2020; Jimerson et al., 2021; Ortiz et al., 2023; Pham et al., 2022; Sabnis & Proctor, 2022; Song et al., 2020, 2021, 2022; Sullivan et al., 2022; Truong et al., 2021; Zhang et al., 2022). Individuals interested in pursuing a career that contributes to supporting (a) the social, emotional, behavioral, cognitive, and mental health development of children; (b) teachers, staff, and administrators; (c) families and communities; and (d) social justice, will find the information within the chapters of this book and the job of the school psychologist to be particularly rewarding. The following highlights important emphases and contributions featured within the second edition of *School Psychology: Professional Issues and Practices*.

SOCIAL JUSTICE AND SCHOOL PSYCHOLOGY

School psychology research, practice, and training around the world have increasingly prioritized social justice as a key focus (Noltemeyer & Grapin, 2021). In terms of service delivery, the adoption of a social justice lens can help school psychologists effectively identify and address issues of bias and discrimination in schools, advocate for the rights and needs of marginalized or disadvantaged groups of students, and contribute to more equitable and just policies and practices within schools, which in turn empower students (Leong et al., 2017). The field of school psychology stands out because of its dynamic and multifaceted nature and its potential to play a pivotal role in challenging inequitable systems and practices as well as pushing the needle forward in advancing social justice in education. The chapters of this book, including its new chapters, emphasize social justice considerations that are inclusive and respectful of all students across all aspects of service delivery.

FOUNDATIONS OF SCHOOL PSYCHOLOGY

The featured chapters of the *Foundations of School Psychology* section provide an overview of the profession, including its history, training, and credentialing standards. These chapters also discuss important topics such as multiculturalism, legal and ethical foundations, and the need for school psychologists to be knowledgeable about such considerations due to the diversity of students and families in communities. This foundational knowledge is essential for informing prospective school psychologists' understanding of the profession and its practice. In this updated edition, a new chapter has been included that examines the ways in which racism affects students in schools and opportunities for school psychologists to help combat racism and promote social justice.

SERVICE DELIVERY IN SCHOOL PSYCHOLOGY

School psychologists engage in a variety of activities in service of children and adolescents, teachers and school staff, and families and communities. One such activity involves using assessments to inform interventions that support students and teachers in schools. The book's emphasis on implementing multitiered systems of support (MTSS) for students reflects the importance of integrated, evidence-based assessment and intervention practices in school psychology. The chapters of the *Service Delivery in School Psychology* section cover the different types of assessments and interventions that school psychologists may use, including those that support all students in a classroom setting, small groups of students, and individual students. It also discusses the importance of consultation with teachers and families, systems-level service provision, and program evaluation for comprehensive school psychology service delivery. New chapters have been added to address important issues related to crisis prevention and intervention to promote safe and inclusive learning environments; family–school–community collaboration for addressing student needs and promoting equitable outcomes; program evaluation to support data-based decisions and systems-level change; and the current state of research in school psychology.

THE FUTURE AND PREPARING FOR A CAREER IN SCHOOL PSYCHOLOGY

The final section of the book explores potential developments and challenges in the field of school psychology, such as personnel shortages, lack of diversity among practitioners, virtual service delivery, and changes in professional organizations and standards. Recommendations are offered to support school psychologists in positively shaping the future of the field, including meeting the needs of an increasingly culturally and linguistically diverse student population. A chapter has also been added to provide an international perspective on the discipline of school psychology, including its status as a profession, the importance of recognizing cultural context and cross-cultural differences in promoting social justice, and current barriers and opportunities for internationalization.

Like its predecessor, the second edition of *School Psychology: Professional Issues and Practices* serves as a comprehensive resource for those interested in learning about the field of school psychology. It covers the history, roles, responsibilities, and preparation required for a career in this field as well as various social justice considerations relevant to school psychology. Written by leading experts in the field with diverse backgrounds and identities, the book's chapters provide a wealth of information for understanding the profession and highlight linkages to the National Association of School Psychologists' (2020) Practice Model. Collectively, chapter authors illustrate how school psychology offers a unique opportunity to make a positive impact on the well-being of children, families, schools, and communities and can be a rewarding career choice for those who are dedicated to helping others and advocating for social justice.

Shane R. Jimerson, Jon W. Goodwin,
Miriam E. Thompson, Rondy Yu,
and Arlene Ortiz

REFERENCES

García-Vázquez, E., Reddy, L., Arora, P., Crepeau-Hobson, F., Fenning, P., Hatt, C., Hughes, T. L., Jimerson, S., Malone, C., Minke, K., Radliff, K., Raines, T., Song, S., & Vaillancourt Strobach, K. (2020). School psychology unified anti-racism statement and call to action. *School Psychology Review, 49*(3), 209–211. https://doi.org/10.1080/2372966X.2020.1809941

Jimerson, S. R., Arora, P., Blake, J. J., Canivez, G. L., Espelage, D. L., Gonzalez, J. E., Graves, S. L., Huang, F. L., January, S.-A. A., Renshaw, T. L., Song, S. Y., Sullivan, A. L., Wang, C., & Worrell, F. C. (2021). Advancing diversity, equity, and inclusion in school psychology: Be the change. *School Psychology Review, 50*(1), 1–7. https://doi.org/10.1080/2372966X.2021.1889938

Leong, F. T. L., Pickren, W. E., & Vasquez, M. J. T. (2017). APA efforts in promoting human rights and social justice. *American Psychologist, 72*(8), 778–790. https://doi.org/10.1037/amp0000220

National Association of School Psychologists. (2020). *Model for comprehensive and integrated school psychological services.* https://www.nasponline.org/standards-and-certification/nasp-practice-model

Noltemeyer, A., & Grapin, S. L. (2021). Working together towards social justice, anti-racism, and equity: A joint commitment from school psychology international and journal of educational and psychological consultation. *School Psychology International, 42*(1), 3–10. https://doi.org/10.1177/01430343211070162

Ortiz, A., Sánchez Lizardi, P., Calvillo, O., D'Costa, S., Anguiano, R., Robinson-Zañartu, C., Ni, H., Jimerson, S. R., & Laija-Rodriguez, W. (2023). A collaborative journey to inform the development of Bilingual school psychology competencies in California. *Communiqué, 52*(1), 21–24. https://www.nasponline.org/resources-and-publications/periodicals/communiqu%C3%A9-volume-51-number-5-(january/february-2023)/a-collaborative-journey-to-inform-the-development-of-bilingual-school-psychology-competencies-in-california

Pham, A. V., Goforth, A. N. Aguilar, L. N., Burt, I., Bastian, R., & Diaków, D. M. (2022). Dismantling systemic inequities in school psychology: Cultural humility as a foundational approach to social justice. *School Psychology Review, 51*(6), 692–709. https://doi.org/10.1080/2372966X.2021.1941245

Sabnis, S. V., & Proctor, S. L. (2022). Use of critical theory to develop a conceptual framework for critical school psychology. *School Psychology Review, 51*(6), 661–675, https://doi.org/10.1080/2372966X.2021.1949248

Song, S. Y., Wang, C., Espelage, D. L., Fenning, P. A., & Jimerson, S. R. (2020). COVID-19 and school psychology: Adaptations and new directions for the field. *School Psychology Review, 49*(4), 431–437. https://doi.org/10.1080/2372966X.2020.1852852

Song, S. Y., Wang, C., Espelage, D. L., Fenning, P. A., & Jimerson, S. R. (2021). COVID-19 and school psychology: Contemporary research advancing practice, science, and policy. *School Psychology Review, 50*(4), 485–490. https://doi.org/10.1080/2372966X.2021.1975489

Song, S. Y., Wang, C., Espelage, D. L., Fenning, P. A., & Jimerson, S. R. (2022). COVID-19 and school psychology: Research reveals the persistent impacts on parents and students, and the promise of school telehealth supports. *School Psychology Review, 51*(2), 127–131. https://doi.org/10.1080/2372966X.2022.2044237

Sullivan, A. L., Worrell, F. C., & Jimerson, S. R. (2022). Reconceptualizing school psychology for the 21st century: The future of school psychology in the United States. *School Psychology Review, 51*(6), 647–660. https://doi.org/10.1080/2372966X.2022.2139131

Truong, D. M., Tanaka, M. L., Cooper, J. M., Song, S., Talapatra, D., Arora, P., Fenning, P., McKenney, E., Williams, S., Stratton-Gadke, K., Jimerson, S. R., Pandes-Carter, L., Hulac, D., & García-Vázquez, E. (2021). School psychology unified call for deeper understanding, solidarity, and action to eradicate anti-AAAPI racism and violence. *School Psychology Review, 50*(2–3), 469–483. https://doi.org/10.1080/2372966X.2021.1949932

Zhang, Y., Weber, M., Kaur, L., Mittelstet, A., & Jimerson, S. R. (2022). Toward a critical transactional ecological developmental theory: Informing and advancing practice and science. *Current Research in Psychology and Behavioral Science, 3*(2), 1041–1047. https://doi.org/10.54026/CRPBS/1041

Preface

This book provides a comprehensive introduction to the practice and profession of school psychology through a social justice lens. The term *social justice* has been defined in many ways by different scholars. In the context of school psychology, promoting social justice involves advocating for the well-being of all children and families and fostering school communities that reflect diverse values. We join many others in affirming that the goals of social justice and school psychology are inextricably linked. School psychologists strive to promote the welfare of all children and families, and in the absence of socially just learning environments, this goal cannot be fully achieved. Therefore, social justice issues must be studied in tandem with all areas of school psychological service delivery.

We believe that both *infusion* and *intentional* approaches are essential to the study of social justice. *Infusion* refers to the teaching of multicultural and social justice principles throughout the curriculum rather than as separate modules (Newell et al., 2010). In infusion approaches, social justice principles are integrated as core concepts across all areas of psychoeducational service delivery. We believe that an infusion approach is essential for encouraging students to draw clear connections between practice and advocacy across the curriculum.

Intentionality refers to the deliberate and visible emphasis of social justice issues in school psychology curricula. All too often, these issues are discussed as an afterthought, which reinforces a passive approach to addressing injustice. As we state in Chapter 1, continuing with routine practices is always easier and more comfortable than challenging the status quo. Thus, school psychologists must deliberately identify practices and policies that marginalize diverse students and take steps to dismantle these practices and policies in an intentional manner.

We believe that employing a combination of infusion and intentional approaches is the best way to prepare effective advocates for children and families. The structure of this book reflects these two approaches. Specifically, social justice principles are *infused* throughout the chapters as well as addressed clearly and explicitly (i.e., with *intentionality*).

FROM THE FIRST TO SECOND EDITIONS

Based on feedback from the first edition, the current status of the field, and anticipated future directions, we retained many of the book's original features for its second edition. We also are excited to introduce a number of new features to this edition. Below we describe features of the book that have been retained, enhanced, or added for the second edition.

New Chapters

All chapters from the previous edition have been retained; however, one of the most significant changes to this new edition is the addition of five new chapters addressing a wide range of important topics, including antiracism, globalization, research, and family–school–community collaboration. Chapters such as these address important shifts in the field toward more equitable and socially just practice, research, and training. For example, Chapter 4 (*Antiracism and School Psychology*) has been added to capture the field's evolving commitment to disrupting individual, systemic, and structural racism within and beyond school walls. This chapter is intentionally positioned in the book's first section, *Foundations of School Psychology*, to center antiracism as a critical pillar of the profession.

Other chapters have been added to capture a fuller spectrum of school psychologists' responsibilities. The addition of Chapters 13 (*School Violence and Crisis Prevention and Intervention*) and 14 (*Family, School, and Community Collaboration*) highlights the critical roles of school psychologists in building safe and supportive school environments and collaborating with vested partners, such as families and communities, to promote their engagement in educational decision-making and student learning. Moreover, Chapter 16 (*Research in School Psychology*) recognizes the key role of school psychologists in conducting and consuming research to support evidence-based, socially justice practice. Finally, the addition of Chapter 17 (*Internationality of School and Educational Psychology*) acknowledges the increasing globalization of the profession as well as the importance of international perspectives in meeting the needs of children with diverse cultural and geographic backgrounds. We believe that additions such as these allow readers to better understand the field's evolving context.

Social Justice Orientation

The social justice orientation of this book continues to be one of its most essential features. In Chapter 1, we provide a rationale for studying social justice and school psychology in tandem. By explicitly communicating this rationale at the beginning of the book, we reinforce the idea that social justice considerations should have a prominent and intentional presence in all areas of service delivery.

The remainder of the book addresses a range of social justice issues related to school psychology practice, including discriminatory assessment and disciplinary practices and the implementation of multitiered systems of support (MTSS) to promote equity in educational access. Such topics are featured in *Social Justice Connections* boxes, which appear in all of the book's chapters (with the exception of Chapter 1, which introduces key concepts in social justice). Each box poses a question related to the chapter's content and offers a thoughtful response. These responses are designed to provide concrete, actionable recommendations for aspiring advocates.

In line with its social justice focus, this book emphasizes the research and practice contributions of scholars and practitioners from racially, ethnically, and linguistically (REL) marginalized backgrounds. All too often, the history of psychology is told from a predominantly white, eurocentric perspective that omits and obscures the contributions of scholars with minoritized identities. One of our goals in developing this book was to illustrate the rich intellectual legacy of scholars from REL minoritized groups who have shaped the field of school psychology. This legacy is most clearly illustrated in Chapter 2, which describes the revolutionary contributions of scholars such as Drs. Albert Sidney Beckham, Kenneth Clark, Mamie Phipps Clark, Beverly Inez Prosser, Ena Vazquez-Nuttall, and Deborah Crockett. By featuring individuals such as these, we paint a more comprehensive and accurate picture of school psychology's past, present, and future.

Voices of Experts

Most introductory school psychology books are authored rather than edited books, meaning that they are written by, at most, several authors. This book, however, continues to be an edited one and comprises chapters from a range of authors. Whereas the first edition included 23 experts across 14 chapters, the second edition represents the perspectives of more than 40 faculty members, practitioners, and others across 19 chapters.

There are two primary advantages to the edited book format. First, producing an edited book has allowed us to leverage the wide range of backgrounds and orientations represented in school psychology. Our field is a complex one that thrives on this diversity of perspectives, and school psychologists may approach service delivery and social justice in many different ways. For example, some of the book's authors use lowercase in referring to white people (while using uppercase in referring to Black and Brown people) as an act of resistance to white supremacy (see Chapter 3 for an example). Still others have elected to capitalize the terms *White* and *Whiteness* in order to disrupt the privilege of racial invisibility granted to White people (see Chapter 17). In general, it is important for readers to understand how different perspectives shape advocacy, research, and practice in school psychology.

Second, an edited format allows readers to learn about theory, research, and practice in school psychology directly from experts in those areas. As illustrated in the brief biographies of contributors (presented in the Contributors section), we have recruited a group of highly regarded, accomplished, and prolific professionals to develop the various chapters of this book. The authors represented in this group include journal editors and editorial board members, principal investigators of major research grants, and leaders in school psychology's major professional associations. Rather than summarize their work, we connect readers directly to the experts.

Connections to Professional Standards

Chapters from the previous edition have also been updated substantially to reflect recent developments in school psychology. In 2020, the National Association of School Psychologists (NASP) published its revised and most recent professional standards, including its *Model for Comprehensive and Integrated School Psychological Services* (Practice Model). The NASP Practice Model is the most prominent and widely regarded model of school psychological service delivery in the United States and comprises 10 domains that illustrate the diverse roles and services that school psychologists perform. The 2020 Standards indicate NASP's increased emphasis on advocacy and social justice, which are also clearly reflected in the book's content and structure.

As in the first edition, the contents of this book continue to align with the NASP Practice Model; however, the second edition has been updated to reflect the 2020 revisions to this model. For each chapter, key domains are specified to orient readers to its relevance. In some cases, entire chapters are devoted to single domains, such as *Consultation and Collaboration* (Domain 2; Chapter 12) and *Academic Interventions and Instructional Supports* (Domain 3; Chapter 9); however, others (e.g., *Equitable Practices for Diverse Student Populations*; Domain 8) are integrated across several chapters. By drawing clear connections to the NASP Practice Model, we provide a comprehensive overview of the roles and functions of school psychologists as well as introduce readers to a widely applied framework of service delivery. Where applicable, chapters have also been updated to reflect recent revisions to other components of NASP's 2020 Standards, including its *Standards for Graduate Preparation of School Psychologists*, *Standards for the Credentialing of School Psychologists*, and *Principles for Professional Ethics*. Such changes are reflected in chapters such as Chapter 5 (*Ethical and Legal Foundations*), Chapter 6 (*Graduate Preparation and Credentialing*), and Chapter 18 (*Future of School Psychology*).

Learning Tools and Resources

As in the first edition, one of the goals of the second edition is to make school psychology accessible to a wide range of audiences. Its intended audiences are undergraduate and graduate students, related school personnel, and others who wish to explore the field. Thus, we have retained a number of features that are designed to facilitate the accessibility of content. Each chapter includes several Chapter Objectives as well as a brief introduction to orient readers to its main ideas. Additionally, several chapters review prerequisite concepts in psychological research and practice that are essential for understanding service delivery in school psychology. For example, concepts such as *reliability* and *validity* (introduced in Chapter 7) are important for understanding theory and practice in assessment. To bridge knowledge from previous coursework (e.g., introductory psychology and research methodology courses), the authors clearly explain foundational concepts and their relevance for school psychology practice. These bridges allow learners to better contextualize and integrate new ideas with previous learning.

As noted earlier, the second edition now includes explicit mappings of each chapter to the revised NASP Practice Model. In addition, we have included a number of new instructional features designed to enhance readers' comprehension of main ideas, specify applications of chapter content to professional activities, and provide directions for further study. For example, authors have identified and defined key terms, which has allowed for the development of a glossary comprising more than 200 entries. Moreover, authors have provided recommendations for further reading, which include a variety of seminal and recent resources to encourage further exploration of topical ideas.

For instructors who wish to use this book as the core text for an introductory school psychology course, a number of resources are available. At the end of each chapter, Discussion Questions are included, which can be used to facilitate both face-to-face and online discussion. These questions involve summarizing and applying key concepts from the text. Other resources include materials for fostering students' professional development, such as the curriculum vitae (CV) development checklist included in Chapter 19. Instructors can encourage students to use these resources in class or during independent assignments. Finally, updated sample syllabi are available to potential and current course instructors. **For more information regarding instructor resources, qualified adopters should contact textbook@springerpub.com.**

ORGANIZATION AND CONTENT

Like its first edition, the book's second edition is organized into three main sections: *Foundations of School Psychology* (Section I), *Service Delivery in School Psychology* (Section II), and *Looking Ahead* (Section III). The goals and rationale for each of these sections are described below.

Section I: Foundations of School Psychology

This section describes the foundations of school psychology, including the field's history and roots in multiculturalism, social justice, law, and ethics. These areas are described first because they permeate all areas of practice and therefore are integral to understanding the roles and functions of school psychologists. By covering issues of multiculturalism and antiracism within the first few chapters, we frame them as a primer for subsequent reading. Similarly, studying legal and ethical issues early on allows readers to consider the many ways in which school psychologists protect the rights and dignity of all children and families.

In Chapter 1, we present a general overview of the field of school psychology by introducing readers to the NASP Practice Model. We also describe the meaning of the term *social justice* and the value of studying school psychology through a social justice lens. Chapter 2 describes the history and development of the field. Only a little more than a century old, school psychology continues to be heavily influenced by its historical foundations. Knowledge of these foundations is critical for understanding contemporary practice and anticipating future directions. Recognizing that school psychology has undergone significant paradigm shifts in recent years, this book not only covers the field's early history but also advances and trends of the last 20 years (i.e., the early 2000s onward). To provide a comprehensive overview, this section of the book also includes chapters on multicultural foundations (Chapter 3), antiracism (Chapter 4), legal and ethical foundations (Chapter 5), and graduate preparation and credentialing (Chapter 6). Chapter 4 (*Antiracism and School Psychology*) is the newest addition to this section and describes essential connections between school psychology practice and efforts to disrupt individual, institutional, and structural racism.

Section II: Service Delivery in School Psychology

Whereas Section I describes the broad foundations of school psychology, Section II focuses on specific roles and functions of school psychologists. This section begins with an overview of two types of services that permeate all major areas of practice: *assessment* and *intervention*. Chapter 7 assumes a broad approach to conceptualizing assessment by considering its applications for planning (before intervention), monitoring (during intervention), and evaluating (after intervention) services. Chapter 8 describes foundational concepts in intervention, which are important prerequisites for understanding domain-specific interventions (e.g., academic, behavioral, social, and emotional interventions). Thus, Chapter 8 describes a number of essential terms, including *evidence-based intervention*, *randomized controlled trial*, and *random assignment*.

Chapter 9 describes academic assessment and intervention, and Chapter 10 describes social, emotional, and behavioral (SEB) interventions. These two chapters are written in similar formats (describing universal, targeted, and indicated interventions, respectively) to assist the reader in understanding how MTSS are applied in both academic and SEB domains. Chapter 11 describes intellectual assessment in school settings. The latter chapters of this section describe services for empowering school personnel, families, communities, and educational systems to better serve children. These services include consultation (Chapter 12); school violence and crisis prevention and intervention (Chapter 13); family, school, and community collaboration (Chapter 14); and systems change and program evaluation (Chapter 15). The section concludes with a chapter on research in school psychology (Chapter 16), another essential function of school psychologists that drives the development, availability, and delivery of evidence-based practices.

Section III: Looking Ahead

This section discusses the future of school psychology as well as considerations for preparing for a career in the field. Unlike similar books, the chapters in this section consider not only future directions for the field but also future professional pathways for the reader. Chapter 17 describes the increasing globalization of the profession, which has and will continue to foster international and cross-cultural collaboration among school psychologists around the world. Moreover, Chapter 18 describes emerging issues and anticipated future directions for the field. Topics include personnel shortages, virtual psychological service delivery, and the evolution of professional organizations and standards. Finally,

Chapter 19 describes considerations for pursuing a career in school psychology. It covers topics such as choosing specialization coursework, selecting mentors, and identifying potential career paths.

SUMMARY

We are pleased to present what we believe to be a comprehensive, inclusive, and justice-oriented overview of school psychology, a profession that clearly has immense potential for supporting the well-being of all school-age youth, their families, and their communities. It has been a tremendous privilege to work with each of the book's contributing authors (both new and returning) to portray the landscape of school psychology practice in the United States and beyond. We hope that this book will serve as a resource for undergraduate and graduate students, school personnel, and others who are invested in protecting the welfare of youth.

Sally L. Grapin
John H. Kranzler

REFERENCES

National Association of School Psychologists. (2020). *Professional standards of the National Association of School Psychologists.* https://www.nasponline.org/standards-and-certification/nasp-2020-professional-standards-adopted

Newell, M. L., Nastasi, B. K., Hatzichristou, C., Jones, J. M., Schanding, G. T., & Yetter, G. (2010). Evidence on multicultural training in school psychology: Recommendations for future directions. *School Psychology Quarterly, 25,* 249–278. https://doi.org/10.1037/a0021542

Acknowledgments

We would like to acknowledge the tremendous support we received from colleagues, family, and Springer Publishing Company. In particular, we are grateful to all of the authors who contributed chapters and the foreword for this book. It has been a privilege to work with each of them, and we immensely appreciate their expertise, incisive perspectives, eloquent writing, and willingness to share their work with us. Finally, we are grateful to Springer Publishing Company for their guidance and support throughout the publication process.

—*Sally L. Grapin and John H. Kranzler*

I would like to thank the many people who supported me during the development of this book. First, I am grateful to my coeditor, John Kranzler, for partnering with me on both editions and for providing ongoing support for this project and many others. I also appreciate the support of my wonderful colleagues at Montclair State University.

I would like to thank my parents for their unwavering support, especially as I balanced this project with the earliest months of parenthood. I am grateful to my mother, Julie Grapin, for being my first and greatest example of a committed and compassionate advocate for marginalized youth and families. I am grateful to my father, Larry Grapin, for his endless warmth, patience, and encouragement in supporting me both personally and professionally.

I am especially appreciative of the support I received from Scott Grapin, my brother and sounding board for discussing ideas related to equity and education. I am continually inspired by his passion for pursuing justice for multilingual learners in K–12 schools.

Finally, I am grateful to my wonderful husband, Peter Nurnberg, for all of his love, support, and advice. Thank you for the endless moments of joy and humor you bring to our family always and for being my rock and the loving companion I still cannot believe I was lucky enough to find.

—*Sally L. Grapin*

Springer Publishing Connect™ Resources

 A robust set of instructor resources designed to supplement this text is located at http://connect.springerpub.com/content/book/978-0-8261-6344-8. Qualifying instructors may request access by emailing textbook@springerpub.com.

- **LMS Common Cartridge With All Instructor Resources**
- **Sample Syllabi** containing two sample course syllabi (one for an Introduction to School Psychology course and one for a Professional Issues in School Psychology course) with course descriptions, course objectives, recommended and additional readings, course requirements, course schedules, and more.
- **Test Bank** with more than 150 multiple-choice and true/false questions (including full rationales) and more than 50 short-answer questions with sample answers.
- **Instructor Chapter PowerPoints**

SECTION I

Foundations of School Psychology

CHAPTER 1

Introduction to School Psychology

SALLY L. GRAPIN ■ JOHN H. KRANZLER

CHAPTER OBJECTIVES

After reading this chapter, you will be able to:

- Define *school psychology*.
- Describe the primary roles and employment contexts of school psychologists.
- Define *social justice* and *multiculturalism*.
- Describe the rationale for studying school psychology through a social justice lens.

NATIONAL ASSOCIATION OF SCHOOL PSYCHOLOGISTS PRACTICE MODEL CONNECTIONS

Domain 8: Equitable Practices for Diverse Student Populations
Domain 10: Legal, Ethical, and Professional Practice

INTRODUCTION

As compared with other areas of applied psychology, the profession of school psychology is relatively lesser known. For example, undergraduates typically report less exposure to school psychology relative to professions such as counseling and clinical psychology (Bocanegra et al., 2015). In some cases, even school staff, such as general and special education teachers, lack knowledge about the precise roles and job responsibilities of their school psychologist colleagues. As a result, they may infrequently call upon these colleagues to deliver essential services such as individual counseling, group counseling, and crisis intervention (Gilman & Medway, 2007). Overall, there is a critical need to educate school personnel, parents, legislators, and the general public about the value of school psychological services.

We begin this book on school psychology by providing a general orientation to the field. This chapter specifically addresses the practice of school psychology in the United States, although later chapters (e.g., Chapter 17) will address the practice of school psychology globally. First, we examine contemporary definitions of *school psychology*. Next, we provide a brief description of school psychologists' primary roles and employment contexts as well as the ways in which their roles differ from those of other related professionals (e.g., school counselors). Finally, we discuss the meaning of social justice and its relevance to the study of school psychology.

DEFINING SCHOOL PSYCHOLOGY

Although the field of *school psychology* has been defined in different ways over the years, definitions provided by the two most prominent national organizations representing school psychologists—the American Psychological Association (APA) and the National Association of School Psychologists (NASP)—are particularly important. *NASP* is a U.S. professional organization that represents school psychologists. As of the writing of this chapter, NASP comprises more than 25,000 members, including practitioners, graduate educators, graduate students, and others. Presently, it is the largest association of school psychologists in the United States and the world (NASP, n.d.-b). In response to the question "Who are school psychologists?" NASP (n.d.-d) provides the following answer on its website:

> School psychologists are uniquely qualified members of school teams that support students' ability to learn and teachers' ability to teach. They apply expertise in mental health, learning, and behavior, to help children and youth succeed academically, socially, behaviorally, and emotionally. School psychologists partner with families, teachers, school administrators, and other professionals to create safe, healthy, and supportive learning environments that strengthen connections between home, school, and the community. (para. 1)

Unlike NASP, *APA* is a professional organization that represents many different types of psychologists, including social, clinical, health, counseling, cognitive, and forensic psychologists. As of 2017, APA reported 117,321 members (most of whom were not school psychologists), including faculty, practitioners, and student members (Winerman, 2017). At this time, APA comprises more than 50 divisions, each of which represents a different area of psychology. Division 16 represents the profession of school psychology.

Since 1998, APA (2020b) has recognized school psychology as one of 18 approved specialty areas in professional psychology. A *specialty* is a defined area of professional psychological practice that requires advanced knowledge and skills acquired through an organized sequence of education and training (APA, 2020a). On its website, APA (2022) defines the specialty area of school psychology as follows:

> School Psychology, a general practice of Health Service Psychology,[1] is concerned with children, youth, families, and the schooling process. School psychologists are prepared to intervene at the individual and system levels, and develop, implement and evaluate programs to promote positive learning environments for children and youth from diverse backgrounds, and to ensure equal access to effective educational and psychological services that promote health development. (para. 1)

---

[1] According to APA (2018), *Health Service Psychology* refers to "the integration of psychological science and practice in order to facilitate human development and functioning" (p. 2).

What do the definitions provided by NASP and APA have in common? First, both definitions focus on the essential characteristics of school psychology rather than on specifying what school psychologists actually do or ideally should do. They describe school psychology as a profession whose activities facilitate the development of healthy environments to promote the psychological and educational well-being of children and youth. In addition, they indicate that school psychologists collaborate with professionals in schools and other settings to provide a range of psychological services to youth, families, and communities.

One of the main differences between these two definitions concerns the context within which school psychologists work. Although both emphasize the delivery of psychological services within educational systems, NASP's definition mentions only that school psychologists work as members of school-based teams. In contrast, APA's definition does not specify the settings in which these services are delivered, highlighting that school psychology is not a "place" but rather a profession that can be practiced in a variety of contexts. Despite their differences, however, both definitions describe school psychology as involving the delivery of psychological services that promote positive academic and mental health outcomes for youth.

SCHOOL PSYCHOLOGICAL PROFESSIONAL PRACTICES

As already stated, school psychologists work in schools and a variety of other settings. Within each of these settings, their professional practices are likely to vary as a function of the contexts in which they work. One widely accepted framework for describing the delivery of school psychological services is NASP's *Model for Comprehensive and Integrated School Psychological Services*, also known as the **NASP Practice Model** (NASP, 2020). This Practice Model is NASP's official policy statement on comprehensive service delivery in school psychology. It is meant to serve as a guide for the organization and delivery of services, with an emphasis on the delivery of school psychological services in the context of educational programs and settings.

The NASP Practice Model comprises two major parts: (a) Professional Practices and (b) Organizational Principles. The Professional Practices delineate the domains of knowledge and skill in which all school psychologists are expected to have competency. The Organizational Principles describe the structures and support systems that must be in place in school systems to facilitate effective service delivery. Because the purpose of this chapter is to describe the professional roles and functions of school psychologists, it focuses specifically on the Professional Practices part of the Practice Model.

Figure 1.1 displays a graphic representation of the NASP Practice Model. The model includes 10 practice domains that are organized into four major areas: (a) *Practices That Permeate All Services*, (b) *Direct Services: Student Level*, (c) *Indirect Services: Systems Level*, and (d) *Foundations of School Psychology Service Delivery*. In the following section, we briefly describe each of the domains within these four areas.

Practices That Permeate All Services

The first two domains of the Practice Model are categorized as *Practices That Permeate All Services*. Specifically, the two domains that constitute this area are *Data-Based Decision-Making* (Domain 1) and *Consultation and Collaboration* (Domain 2). These domains fall under this category because they are critical for providing a wide variety of direct and indirect services to students, families, and school systems.

FIGURE 1.1 NASP MODEL FOR COMPREHENSIVE AND INTEGRATED SCHOOL PSYCHOLOGICAL SERVICES.

Source: National Association of School Psychologists. (2020). *Model for comprehensive and integrated school psychological services.* Author. Reprinted/adapted with permission of the publisher. www.nasponline.org

Data-Based Decision-Making (Domain 1)

Data-based decision-making involves the use of individual, group, or school-wide data to make informed decisions regarding educational and psychological service delivery. According to the Practice Model, "School psychologists understand and utilize assessment methods for identifying strengths and needs; for developing effective interventions, services, and programs; and for measuring progress and outcomes" (NASP, 2020, p. 3). Examples of practices in this area include (a) collecting, analyzing, and interpreting data from caregivers, teachers, students, and other sources to understand student needs and make recommendations for evidence-based interventions (NASP, 2020) and (b) using "systematic, reliable, and valid data" to facilitate decision-making (NASP, 2020, p. 4).

Consultation and Collaboration (Domain 2)

Domain 2 refers to school psychologists' knowledge and skills in collaborating and communicating effectively with teachers, caregivers, administrators, community members, and others to facilitate positive outcomes for youth. School psychologists leverage such knowledge and skills to promote the implementation of high-quality, evidence-based services. Examples of practices in this area include (a) using "a consultative problem-solving process as a vehicle for planning, implementing, and evaluating academic and mental and behavioral health services" and (b) consulting and collaborating "at the individual, family, group, and systems levels" (NASP, 2020, p. 4).

Direct Services: Student Level

School psychologists provide a variety of direct services to their clients. *Direct services* are those in which the provider has firsthand client contact (typically face-to-face contact, although some services may be provided through other media). Common examples of direct services include individual and group counseling, in which the school psychologist interacts *directly* with the client. *Student-level services* are those that involve working with individuals or groups of students. The following describes direct, student-level domains of service delivery in the Practice Model.

Academic Interventions and Instructional Supports (Domain 3)

Domain 3 includes knowledge and skills related to supporting the academic success of students (e.g., success in areas such as reading, writing, math, and science). According to the Practice Model, "school psychologists understand the biological, cultural, and social influences on academic skills; human learning, cognitive, and developmental processes; and evidence-based curricula and instructional strategies . . . to implement and evaluate services that support academic skill development in children" (NASP, 2020, p. 5). Examples of practices in this area include (a) using "assessment data to inform evidence-based instructional strategies that are intended to improve student performance" and (b) working with "other school personnel to develop, implement, and evaluate effective interventions to improve learning engagement and academic outcomes" (NASP, 2020, p. 5).

Mental and Behavioral Health Services and Interventions (Domain 4)

Domain 4 describes school psychologists' role in supporting the social, emotional, and behavioral well-being of students. The Practice Model states that:

> School psychologists understand the biological, cultural, developmental, and social influences on mental and behavioral health; behavioral and emotional impacts on learning; and evidence-based strategies to promote social–emotional functioning. (NASP, 2020, p. 5)

> Examples of practices in this area include (a) facilitating the "design and delivery of curricula and interventions to help students develop effective social–emotional skills, such as self-regulation, self-monitoring, self-advocacy, planning/organization, empathy, positive coping strategies, interpersonal skills, and healthy decision-making" (NASP, 2020, pp. 5–6) and (b) providing "a continuum of developmentally appropriate and culturally responsive mental and behavioral health services, including individual and group counseling, behavioral coaching, classroom and school-wide social–emotional learning programs, positive behavioral supports, and parent education and support" (NASP, 2020, p. 6).

Indirect Services: Systems Level

The next set of domains are categorized as indirect, systems-level services. *Indirect services* are those in which the provider does not have firsthand contact with the client, but rather supports the client's functioning through contact with a third party. For example, school psychologists may provide support to school staff who subsequently deliver services to students. *Systems-level services* involve working with organizations (or specific organizational levels, such as a grade level) to impact client outcomes on a larger scale. Each of the domains in this category is described in the following.

School-Wide Practices to Promote Learning (Domain 5)

Domain 5 describes school psychologists' knowledge and skills in fostering respectful, supportive, and high-quality learning environments for all students. According to the Practice Model:

> School psychologists understand systems' structures, organization, and theory; general and special education programming; implementation science; and evidence-based school-wide practices that promote learning, positive behavior, and mental health . . . to develop and implement practices and strategies to create and maintain safe, effective, and supportive learning environments for students and school staff. (NASP, 2020, p. 6)

Examples of practices in this area include (a) promoting "high rates of academic engagement" and (b) working collaboratively "with other school personnel to create and maintain a multi-tiered system of services to support each student's attainment of academic, social–emotional, and behavioral goals" (NASP, 2020, p. 7).

Services to Promote Safe and Supportive Schools (Domain 6)

Domain 6 refers to competencies in identifying and promoting protective and adaptive factors that support healthy student development and functioning. The Practice Model states that:

> School psychologists understand principles and research related to social–emotional well-being, resilience, and risk factors in learning, mental and behavioral health, services in schools and communities to support multitiered prevention and health promotion, and evidence-based strategies for creating safe and supportive schools. (NASP, 2020, p. 7)

Examples of practices in this area include (a) "recognizing and addressing risk and protective factors that are vital to understanding and addressing systemic problems such as school failure, student disengagement, chronic absenteeism, school dropout, bullying, substance use, youth suicide and self-harm, and school violence," and (b) participating "in the implementation and evaluation of prevention programs that promote physically and psychologically safe and nonviolent schools and communities" (NASP, 2020, p. 7).

Family, School, and Community Collaboration (Domain 7)

Domain 7 refers to school psychologists' knowledge and skills in understanding, supporting, and forming robust partnerships with diverse families and communities. According to the Practice Model, "School psychologists understand principles and research related to family systems, strengths, needs, and cultures; evidence-based strategies to support positive family influences on children's learning and mental health; and strategies to develop collaboration between families and schools" (NASP, 2020, p. 8). Examples of practices in this area include (a) using "effective evidence-based strategies to design, implement, and evaluate effective policies and practices that promote family, school, and community partnerships to enhance learning and mental and behavioral health outcomes for children and youth" and (b) creating "linkages among schools, families, and community providers" to "coordinate services when programming for children involves multiple agencies" (NASP, 2020, p. 8).

Foundations of School Psychological Service Delivery

The remaining domains of the NASP Practice Model are situated as *Foundations of School Psychological Service Delivery* (see Figure 1.1). The domains within this section represent core areas of knowledge and skill that are essential for high-quality, socially just, ethical, and effective practice. The three domains in this section are *Equitable Practices for Diverse Student Populations* (Domain 8), *Research and Evidence-Based Practice* (Domain 9), and *Legal, Ethical, and Professional Practice* (Domain 10).

EQUITABLE PRACTICES FOR DIVERSE STUDENT POPULATIONS (DOMAIN 8)

Domain 8 of the Practice Model refers to school psychologists' knowledge and skills in applying principles of culturally responsive practice and social justice in serving youth, families, schools, and communities. Specifically, the Model states that:

> School psychologists understand principles and research related to diversity in children, families, schools, and communities, including factors related to child development, religion, culture and cultural identity, race, sexual orientation, gender identity and expression, socioeconomic status, and other variables . . . School psychologists recognize that equitable practices for diverse student populations, respect for diversity in development and learning, and advocacy for social justice are foundational to effective service delivery. (NASP, 2020, p. 8)

Notably, this domain distinguishes between *equity* and *equality*, with the former referring to children having the *same* access to services and the latter referring to children having access to services according to *need* (which can arise from ecological factors such as systemic discrimination). Examples of practices in this area include (a) acknowledging the impact of their own "subtle racial, class, gender, cultural, and other biases . . . and beliefs" and (b) promoting "equity and social justice in educational programs and services by ensuring that all children and youth learn in safe, supportive, and inclusive environments" (NASP, 2020, p. 9). Because school psychologists work with a diverse range of students, families, and school personnel, knowledge and skills in this area are critical for effective service delivery.

RESEARCH AND EVIDENCE-BASED PRACTICE (DOMAIN 9)

Domain 9 refers to knowledge and skills in applying research to facilitate the delivery of services that have empirical support. It also refers to knowledge and skill in assessing program outcomes through the use of sound analytic tools. According to the model:

> School psychologists have knowledge of research design, statistics, measurement, and varied data collection and analysis techniques sufficient for understanding research, interpreting data, and evaluating programs in applied settings. School psychologists evaluate and apply research as a foundation for service delivery and,

in collaboration with others, use various techniques and technology resources for data collection, measurement, and analysis to support effective practices at the individual, group, and/or systems levels. (NASP, 2020, p. 9)

Examples of practices in this area include (a) providing services to "evaluate, interpret, and synthesize a cumulative body of research findings and apply these as a foundation for effective service delivery" and (b) identifying and interpreting "evidence-based strategies that lead to meaningful school improvement through enhanced school climate, academic achievement, and sense of safety" (NASP, 2020, p. 9).

LEGAL, ETHICAL, AND PROFESSIONAL PRACTICE (DOMAIN 10)

Finally, Domain 10 encompasses professional behaviors, knowledge of the field of school psychology itself, and skills in applying legal and ethical principles to practice. Specifically, the Practice Model states that "school psychologists understand the history and foundations of school psychology; multiple service models and methods; ethical, legal, and professional standards; and other factors related to professional identity and effective practice as school psychologists" (NASP, 2020, p. 10). Examples of practices in this area include (a) practicing "in ways that are consistent with ethical, professional, and legal standards and regulations" and (b) using "professional supervision, peer consultation, and mentoring for effective practice" (NASP, 2020, p. 10).

Summary of the National Association of School Psychologists Practice Model

The NASP Practice Model provides a comprehensive framework for conceptualizing service delivery in school psychology. Collectively, the domains in this model describe the range of knowledge and skills that school psychologists use to support the well-being of children and families, especially in educational settings. Although this model illustrates the many services that school psychologists can provide, roles and responsibilities may vary considerably across employment contexts throughout the United States, as discussed in the next section.

PROFESSIONAL ACTIVITIES AND EMPLOYMENT OF SCHOOL PSYCHOLOGISTS

It has been estimated that more than 32,000 school psychologists are practicing in the United States (Jimerson et al., 2009). These individuals work in a variety of school and nonschool settings, including K–12 public and private schools, colleges and universities, independent practice, and hospital and medical settings. Some data have been published on the demographics, qualifications, and professional activities of school psychologists. Typically, these data are collected by individual research teams (e.g., scholars collaborating across higher education institutions) or professional organizations (e.g., NASP). For example, every five years, NASP surveys a random sample of its members regarding their training and professional activities. The most recent of these membership surveys was conducted in 2020 (Farmer et al., 2021; Goforth et al., 2021). Notably, NASP's survey includes only data from organizational members (and, therefore, is not necessarily representative of school psychologists who are not NASP members). Nevertheless, it provides some of the most comprehensive data available on the practice of school psychologists nationwide.

Employment Contexts and Professional Activities of School Psychologists

The 2020 NASP Membership Survey indicated that school psychologists serve in a variety of roles, including as practitioners (approximately 82%), university faculty (approximately 6%), administrators (approximately 4%), and other roles (approximately 6%; Goforth et al., 2021). Previous data have indicated that they also work in a variety of settings, including public schools, private schools, higher education institutions, and independent (private) practice (Walcott & Hyson, 2018).

Professional activities can vary significantly among school psychologists depending on their job titles (e.g., practitioner, administrator, faculty member) and employment contexts. Table 1.1 displays the professional activities of school-based practitioners as reported in the 2020 NASP Membership Survey. As shown in Table 1.1, the majority (more than 90%) of respondents reported conducting assessments (including initial evaluations and reevaluations) to determine students' eligibility for special education services. Other data from this survey indicated that NASP members spent a great deal of time participating in Individualized Education Program (IEP)[2] meetings (Farmer et al., 2021). Taken together, these data suggest that school psychologists frequently work with students with disabilities.

Many of the school psychologists represented in the 2020 NASP Membership Survey also provided mental and behavioral health services, although not as frequently as they did special education assessment and planning services. When asked how often they provided mental and behavioral health services, more than half (approximately 55%) of school-based practitioners indicated that they did so "often" or "very often" (Farmer et al., 2021). Specifically, many school psychologists reported providing individual counseling services to address mental and behavioral health concerns, with relatively smaller but substantial numbers of practitioners providing individual counseling to address academic issues and other areas, such as social skills development and family relationships (see Table 1.1; Farmer et al., 2021). Some school psychologists also reported providing group counseling services in areas such as mental and behavioral health, academics, and others (e.g., support for sexual and gender minoritized students as well as aspiring women leaders; Farmer et al., 2021).

TABLE 1.1 Professional Practices of Full-Time, School-Based School Psychologists

Professional Practice	Percentage of Respondents Engaging in Practice[a]
Reevaluations for special education	94
Initial evaluations for special education	91
Individual student counseling: Mental/behavioral health services	64
Individual student counseling: Academic services	37
Counseling groups: Mental/behavioral health services	31
Parent groups or presentations	13
Counseling groups: Academic services	9
Individual student counseling: Other	8
Counseling groups: Other	3

[a]Based on a sample of 827 school psychologists who responded to these items in the 2020 NASP Membership Survey.

Source: Farmer, R. L., Goforth, A. N., Kim, S. Y., Naser, S. C., Lockwood, A. B., & Affrunti, N. W. (2021). Status of school psychology in 2020, Part 2: Professional practices in the NASP Membership Survey. *NASP Research Reports*, *5*(3). https://www.nasponline.org/research-and-policy/research-center/nasp-research-reports

---

[2] IEPs are formal, individualized plans that specify the range of school-based services to which a student with a disability is entitled; these are discussed in Chapter 5.

Ultimately, the roles and functions of school psychologists are quite varied, and they can differ considerably across schools, districts, and states. Such variation may depend on the number of school psychologists available to serve the student population of a particular school or district (Farmer et al., 2021). For example, school psychologists who serve larger numbers of students may be more engaged in special education assessment activities but less engaged in mental and behavioral health intervention, crisis response, and school-wide programming to promote safe learning environments (Farmer et al., 2021). To ensure comprehensive, high-quality services for all youth, NASP (2020) recommends a ratio of one school psychologist for no more than 500 students (i.e., 1:500). Nevertheless, this ratio has not been attained by many school districts across the United States, and the average national practitioner-to-student ratio during the 2020–2021 school year was approximately 1:1,162 (Affrunti, 2022).

For many years, professional organizations and leaders in the field have advocated for the recruitment of more practitioners as well as the expansion of the school psychologist's role to routinely include a wide range of systems-level prevention and intervention activities (e.g., Dawson et al., 2004). While much work remains to be done, it is encouraging that many school psychologists generally perceive their work to be aligned with the NASP (2020) Practice Model (Farmer et al., 2021). Specifically, the majority of school psychologists who responded to the 2020 NASP Membership Survey reported that their roles were either "moderately consistent" (41%), "consistent" (29%), or "very consistent" (8%) with the 10 domains of the Practice Model (Farmer et al., 2021, p. 10).

SCHOOL PSYCHOLOGY AND RELATED PROFESSIONS

How does school psychology differ from other related fields in psychology? What makes the profession of school psychology unique? To some extent, the roles of school psychologists and other mental health providers overlap. For example, school psychologists, school counselors, and clinical psychologists are similar in that all three groups of professionals can provide counseling services to children and adolescents. Nevertheless, the training, credentialing, expertise, and roles of these professionals also differ in important ways.

How Is School Psychology Different From School Counseling?

School psychology and school counseling differ in several ways. First, school counselors typically require a minimum of two years of graduate education (including a 600-hour supervised internship), whereas school psychologists typically require a minimum of three years of training (including a 1,200-hour supervised internship). Second, school psychologists are more likely to have training in the areas of behavioral analysis, mental health diagnosis, research methods, and specific disability areas (NASP, n.d.-a).

In K–12 public schools, the roles of school counselors and school psychologists overlap to some extent but also differ in significant ways. Both school psychologists and school counselors are trained in mental health counseling, crisis prevention, and other intervention activities. In addition to these activities, school counselors typically work with all students in a school to assist with course scheduling, career planning, and family and academic problems (NASP, n.d.-a). Although school psychologists also provide supports to all students in a school building, they spend a considerable amount of time providing assessment and intervention services to students with disabilities (Farmer et al., 2021; NASP, n.d.-a). Finally, depending on their degrees and credentials, school psychologists may practice in a broader range of settings, including school-community mental health centers, hospitals, and residential facilities (NASP, n.d.-a).

How Is School Psychology Different From Child Clinical Psychology?

One of the primary distinctions between child clinical psychology and school psychology concerns the degrees required to practice in these fields. Whereas school psychologists may practice at either the doctoral or the nondoctoral level, the entry-level degree for independent practice as a child clinical psychologist is the doctoral degree. The majority of school psychologists are employed in K–12 school settings, although some are employed in hospitals, mental health centers, and other clinical settings. In contrast, clinical psychologists are less likely to be employed in elementary and secondary school settings and more likely to be found in hospitals, mental health clinics, and private clinics (NASP, n.d.-a).

While both clinical and school psychologists have training in child development, psychopathology, and other areas of psychology, school psychologists have expertise in issues that concern the intersection of education and psychology. Thus, as compared with clinical psychologists, school psychologists are much more likely to have skills in facilitating school change and organizational development, supporting classroom management, consulting with educators, and promoting students' academic success. School psychologists also are more likely to be knowledgeable about instruction, curriculum, and classroom behavior management (NASP, n.d.-a).

SOCIAL JUSTICE AND SCHOOL PSYCHOLOGY

As mentioned earlier, this book describes the practice and profession of school psychology through a social justice lens. We believe that all school psychologists must be well versed in the pervasive social, cultural, and political issues that impact children, families, teachers, special services staff, and the settings in which these individuals interact. These issues should be discussed in relation to all areas of practice, including each of the 10 domains of the NASP Practice Model. Why is it important to study school psychology through a social justice lens? To answer this question, we must first define the term *social justice*.

Defining Social Justice

Broadly, Bell (2013) defined ***social justice*** as the "full and equal participation of all groups in a society that is mutually shaped to meet their needs" (p. 21). This term has been defined in many ways by school psychologists and scholars and practitioners in related fields, but there are commonalities among these definitions. One of the most widely referenced definitions of social justice in school psychology was adopted by the NASP Board of Directors in 2017 and states:

> Social justice is both a process and a goal that requires action. School psychologists work to ensure the protection of the educational rights, opportunities, and well-being of all children, especially those whose voices have been muted, identities obscured, or needs ignored. Social justice requires promoting nondiscriminatory practices and the empowerment of families and communities. School psychologists enact social justice through culturally responsive professional practice and advocacy to create schools, communities, and systems that ensure equity and fairness for all children and youth. (NASP, n.d.-c, para. 4)

This definition highlights social justice not only as an aspirational goal but also a process by which school psychologists work to rectify historical harms and promote equitable service delivery for all youth. Moreover, it focuses on amplifying the perspectives of individuals and groups whose voices have been muted or ignored; thus, working toward social justice involves centering the experiences of people from traditionally marginalized backgrounds, such as people who identify with minoritized racial, ethnic, linguistic, gender, and other identities.

Numerous other scholars have conceptualized definitions of social justice; for example, Shriberg et al. (2008) investigated the meaning of the term by surveying a panel of cultural diversity experts. In two rounds of feedback, panelists were asked to define the term *social justice*, identify topics salient to this term, and describe the ways in which school psychologists can promote social justice. These experts most frequently generated definitions aligned with two primary categories: (a) ensuring the protection of rights and responsibilities for all and (b) assuming an ecological/systemic view (i.e., moving beyond the immediate school context to consider the larger impact of educational decision-making). When asked to rank the salience of various topics to social justice work, the panelists tended to assign the highest rankings to topics such as institutional power (e.g., dynamics of privilege and oppression in government) and advocacy. Many also agreed that social justice work is best characterized by a focus on issues of power, privilege, equity, and advocacy. *Advocacy* refers to the practice of proactively representing and supporting a cause or group of individuals. More specifically, social justice advocacy involves empowering and promoting the well-being of traditionally marginalized individuals and groups.

In this book, we embrace a broad view of social justice that incorporates concepts of equity, advocacy, and fairness. When applied to the field of school psychology specifically, social justice work involves building safe, supportive, and welcoming environments that promote the healthy development and educational success of all students. From this perspective, we acknowledge that pervasive injustices permeate the larger contexts in which schools are situated, including their cultural, social, economic, and political environments. Social justice advocacy involves recognizing and proactively addressing these injustices rather than simply accepting the status quo. Presently, a number of injustices impact children and families in schools, including the over- and underrepresentation of racial and ethnic minoritized students in certain categories of special education and related services (e.g., intellectual disability and giftedness), discrimination against gender and sexual minoritized youth, and disparities in disciplinary practices between racial and ethnic minoritized and nonminoritized students. This book addresses many of these issues in the context of school psychology practice.

Social Justice and Multiculturalism

To understand social justice, it is important to understand how this concept differs from *multiculturalism*. Multiculturalism is described extensively in Chapter 3. For now, however, we provide a basic definition of the term: a worldview that acknowledges and values diverse individuals and cultural backgrounds (Carroll, 2009). Multicultural knowledge, awareness, and skills are undoubtedly critical to effective psychological service delivery. Although inextricably linked, the terms *social justice* and *multiculturalism* have somewhat different meanings. More specifically, social justice is often described as the latest development in multicultural psychology (Ratts, 2011). Whereas multicultural competence generally refers to the awareness, knowledge, and skills needed to work effectively with diverse populations, social justice competencies center on recognizing and challenging systemic inequities, which often transcend the school context (Shriberg et al., 2008). Promoting social justice involves taking proactive measures to rectify pervasive societal inequalities and to promote equal access to educational opportunity for diverse groups (Shriberg et al., 2008).

To illustrate the differences between the terms *social justice* and *multiculturalism*, recall Shriberg and colleagues' (2008) findings regarding the meaning of *social justice*. Now, consider a similar study by Rogers and Lopez (2002), who also surveyed a panel of experts in providing culturally competent services to racial, ethnic, and linguistic minoritized populations. After conducting a comprehensive literature review and soliciting feedback from panelists, they identified 102 critical competency items across 14 major categories (e.g., *Assessment, Consultation, Counseling,* and *Organizational Skills*). Panelists were asked to rate competencies based on perceived importance, and average ratings for items were calculated for each category. Of the 14 categories, panelists assigned the highest mean ratings to competencies in the *Assessment* and *Report Writing* categories. Examples of highly rated items in these categories included the following: (a) "using instruments sensitive to cultural and linguistic differences"; (b) possessing "knowledge about non-biased assessment"; and (c) "incorporating information about family origins . . . into report." Conversely, *Working with Organizations* (i.e., competency related to organizational change) was ranked the second least important of the 14 categories. Overall, the multicultural experts in this study generally rated skills in culturally responsive service delivery (e.g., providing assessment and counseling services to diverse populations) as more central to cultural competence than skills in advocacy and facilitating organizational change.

Undoubtedly, Rogers and Lopez's (2002) and Shriberg and colleagues' (2008) studies suggest that there is considerable overlap in the meaning of the terms *multiculturalism* and *social justice*. For example, Rogers and Lopez's participants endorsed competencies in facilitating organizational change. Likewise, many of the experts in Shriberg and colleagues' (2008) study acknowledged the central role of cultural competence in social justice advocacy. Nevertheless, these studies also suggest that there are fundamental nuances that differentiate the two terms.

Despite their differences, multiculturalism and social justice clearly are inextricably linked. Concepts such as oppression and discrimination cannot be properly understood without first understanding multicultural principles. In fact, Ratts (2011) cautioned that engaging in social justice advocacy in the absence of multicultural competence may result in the selection of advocacy strategies that disregard important cultural variables. Developing multicultural competence is an essential prerequisite for promoting social justice; however, the latter term generally places greater emphasis on advocacy within and beyond school walls, as compared with the former.

Why Study School Psychology and Social Justice in Tandem?

Returning to our earlier question, why is it important to study school psychology through a social justice lens? Issues in school psychology and social justice should be studied in tandem for many reasons. In the following list, we describe several of these reasons, which provide an underlying rationale for the orientation and content of this book.

1. *Social justice advocacy is and must be regarded as a cornerstone of school psychology.* Professional organizations that represent school psychology are increasingly emphasizing the importance of social justice work. For example, NASP (2022) explicitly recognized *social justice* as one of its strategic goals through at least 2027. Generally, social justice principles are embedded in the core training and practice standards of school psychology's major professional organizations. By embracing a social justice orientation, school psychologists will be better prepared to accomplish the critical work their jobs necessitate and to align themselves with future directions for the field.
2. *Social justice issues must be studied with intentionality.* Social justice advocacy involves challenging both the overt and covert injustices that impact students and their families. Some injustices are seemingly less conspicuous, because they are part of the status quo, or the existing state of school affairs. For example, we noted

earlier that, assessment activities (typically special education assessments) often constitute a substantial part of school psychologists' daily routines. When school psychologists spend a great deal of time in assessment activities, they have less time to engage in prevention, intervention, and systems change work, which is vital for supporting our nation's most marginalized youth. The assessment-laden routine of the school psychologist can easily be overlooked because it is simply part of the typical practitioner's day (and ultimately, part of the status quo). As for all social justice issues, changing the status quo requires careful and intentional scrutiny of one's own practices and their impact on others. Thus, social justice issues must be studied with intentionality.

3. *We have a long way to go before the aspirational goals of social justice are realized.* This means that taking immediate steps to educate oneself about social justice issues is an imperative for all practitioners. Systems-level change in schools is a slow and painstaking process. As an example, the landmark court case that led to the racial integration of public schools (i.e., *Brown v. Board of Education*) was decided more than half a century ago (in 1954). However, well into the 21st century, U.S. public schools continue to proliferate many forms of racial injustice. For example, African American students are more likely to be subject to harsher disciplinary action in schools than their white peers (Skiba et al., 2011). Promoting social justice is a slow and laborious undertaking that will require the commitment and collaboration of a variety of vested partners. School psychologists are among these partners.

4. *School psychologists must possess knowledge and skill in the area of social justice advocacy to be effective in their work.* One of the authors of this chapter (SLG) often asks her students, "Is it necessary for school psychologists to become social justice advocates to be effective in their roles?" Most often, this question is met with a long, thoughtful pause followed by slow, tentative head nodding that gradually becomes more vigorous and self-assured. We believe these students are correct in answering this question affirmatively. As Shriberg (2012) noted, the goals of social justice are integrally linked with the goals of school psychology. School psychologists are ethically responsible for acting in the best interest of all students. At this time, many school-age youth face a range of injustices that compromise their overall well-being and opportunities for success. If school psychologists do not advocate vigorously for and with these students, they cannot fulfill their ethical and professional obligation to act in the best interest of all children.

For all of these reasons and others, this book describes the practice of school psychology through a social justice lens. To highlight social justice applications in each area of practice, every chapter includes a section on *Social Justice Connections*. The purpose of these sections is to encourage readers to consider the pervasive social justice issues that permeate school systems and to provide concrete strategies for addressing them.

SUMMARY AND CONCLUSIONS

This chapter provided an overview of the field of school psychology. In particular, it defined the profession, described the ways in which school psychology differs from other related professions, presented the 10 domains of the NASP Practice Model, and described the typical roles and functions of school psychologists in the schools. The NASP Practice Model is referenced frequently throughout the remainder of the book; thus, the figure provided in this chapter may assist readers in understanding how various components of practice are interrelated. Finally, this chapter defined the term *social justice* and presented a rationale for the orientation of this book. It is our sincere hope that readers will reflect on the social justice concepts presented throughout the remaining chapters and consider them in their future professional development and practice.

DISCUSSION QUESTIONS

1. What is school psychology? What makes the profession of school psychology unique?
2. What is the significance of the NASP Practice Model for the field of school psychology?
3. What are direct and indirect psychological services? Why are both types necessary for comprehensive school psychological service delivery?
4. Shriberg (2012) contended that the goals of school psychology and social justice are integrally linked. Do you agree or disagree? Why?
5. Identify three domains of the NASP Practice Model. How might each of these domains intersect with social justice principles?

RECOMMENDED READINGS

Biddanda, H., Shriberg, D., Ruecker, D., Conway, D., & Montesinos, G. (2019). Navigating the waters of social justice: Strategies from veteran school psychologists. *Contemporary School Psychology, 23*(4), 379–387. https://doi.org/10.1007/s40688-018-0187-9

Grapin, S. L., & Proctor, S. L. (in press). Social justice in school psychology. In P. Harrison, A. Thomas, & S. L. Proctor (Eds.), *Best practices in school psychology* (7th ed.). National Association of School Psychologists.

Malone, C. M., & Proctor, S. L. (2019). Demystifying social justice for school psychology practice. *Communiqué, 48*(1), 21–23. https://www.nasponline.org/publications/periodicals/communique/issues/volume-48-issue-1

National Association of School Psychologists. (2020). *The professional standards of the National Association of School Psychologists.* https://www.nasponline.org/standards-and-certification/nasp-2020-professional-standards-adopted

Sabnis, S. V., & Proctor, S. L. (2021). Use of critical theory to develop a conceptual framework for critical school psychology. *School Psychology Review, 51*(6), 661–675. https://doi.org/10.1080/2372966X.2021.1949248

A robust set of instructor resources designed to supplement this text is located at http://connect.springerpub.com/content/book/978-0-8261-6344-8. Qualifying instructors may request access by emailing textbook@springerpub.com.

REFERENCES

Affrunti, N. W. (2022). *Ratio of students to full-time equivalent (FTE) school psychologists in United States public elementary and secondary schools* [Research report]. National Association of School Psychologists.

American Psychological Association. (2018). *Standards of accreditation for health service psychology and accreditation operating procedures.* https://www.apa.org/ed/accreditation/about/policies/standards-of-accreditation.pdf

American Psychological Association. (2020a, August). *Principles for the recognition of specialties in professional psychology.* https://www.apa.org/about/policy/principles-recognition.pdf

American Psychological Association. (2020b, October). *Recognized specialties, subspecialties, and proficiencies in professional psychology.* https://www.apa.org/ed/graduate/specialize/recognized

American Psychological Association. (2022, May). *School psychology.* https://www.apa.org/ed/graduate/specialize/school

Bell, L. A. (2013). Theoretical foundations. In M. Adams, W. J. Blumenfeld, R. Castaneda, W. Hackman, M. L. Peters, & X. Zuniga (Eds.), *Readings for diversity and social justice* (3rd ed., pp. 21–26). Routledge.

Bocanegra, J. O., Gubi, A. A., Fan, C.-H., & Hansmann, P. R. (2015). Undergraduate psychology students' knowledge and exposure to school psychology: Suggestions for diversifying the field. *Contemporary School Psychology, 19*(1), 12–20. https://doi.org/10.1007/s40688-015-0046-x

Carroll, D. W. (2009). Toward multicultural competence: A practical model for implementation in the schools. In J. M. Jones (Ed.), *The psychology of multiculturalism in schools* (pp. 1–16). National Association of School Psychologists.

Dawson, M., Cummings, J. A., Harrison, P. L., Short, R. J., Gorin, S., & Palomares, R. (2004). The 2002 multisite conference on the future of school psychology: Next steps. *School Psychology Review, 33*(1), 115–125. https://doi.org/10.1080/02796015.2004.12086235

Farmer, R. L., Goforth, A. N., Kim, S. Y., Naser, S. C., Lockwood, A. B., & Affrunti, N. W. (2021). Status of school psychology in 2020, Part 2: Professional practices in the NASP Membership Survey. *NASP Research Reports, 5*(3). https://www.nasponline.org/research-and-policy/research-center/nasp-research-reports

Gilman, R., & Medway, F. J. (2007). Teachers' perceptions of school psychology: A comparison of regular and special education teacher ratings. *School Psychology Quarterly, 22*(2), 145–161. https://doi.org/10.1037/1045-3830.22.2.145

Goforth, A. N., Farmer, R. L., Kim, S. Y., Naser, S. C., Lockwood, A. B., & Affrunti, N. W. (2021). Status of school psychology in 2020: Part 1, Demographics of the NASP Membership Survey. *NASP Research Reports, 5*(2). https://www.nasponline.org/research-and-policy/research-center/nasp-research-reports

Jimerson, S. R., Stewart, K., Skokut, M., Cardenas, S., & Malone, H. (2009). How many school psychologists are there in each country of the world?: International estimates of school psychologists and school psychologist-to-student ratios. *School Psychology International, 30*(6), 555–567. https://doi.org/10.1177/0143034309107077

National Association of School Psychologists. (n.d.-a). *A career in school psychology: Frequently asked questions*. Retrieved May 25, 2023, from https://www.nasponline.org/about-school-psychology/selecting-a-graduate-program/a-career-in-school-psychology-frequently-asked-questions

National Association of School Psychologists. (n.d.-b). *About NASP*. Retrieved May 31, 2023, from https://www.nasponline.org/utility/about-nasp

National Association of School Psychologists. (n.d.-c). *Social justice*. Retrieved May 31, 2023, from https://www.nasponline.org/social-justice

National Association of School Psychologists. (n.d.-d). *Who are school psychologists?* Retrieved May 31, 2023, from https://www.nasponline.org/about-school-psychology/who-are-school-psychologists

National Association of School Psychologists. (2020). *The professional standards of the National Association of School Psychologists*. https://www.nasponline.org/standards-and-certification/nasp-2020-professional-standards-adopted

National Association of School Psychologists. (2022, September 17). *Strategic plan: 2022–2027*. https://www.nasponline.org/utility/about-nasp/vision-core-purpose-core-values-and-strategic-goals

Ratts, M. J. (2011). Multiculturalism and social justice: Two sides of the same coin. *Journal of Multicultural Counseling and Development, 39*(1), 24–37. https://doi.org/10.1002/j.2161-1912.2011.tb00137.x

Rogers, M. R., & Lopez, E. C. (2002). Identifying critical cross-cultural school psychology competencies. *Journal of School Psychology, 40*(2), 115–141. https://doi.org/10.1016/S0022-4405(02)00093-6

Shriberg, D. (2012). Graduate education and professional development. In D. Shriberg, S. Song, A. Miranda, & K. Radliff (Eds.), *School psychology and social justice: Conceptual foundations and tools for practice* (pp. 311–326). Routledge.

Shriberg, D., Bonner, M., Sarr, B. J., Walker, A. M., Hyland, M., & Chester, C. (2008). Social justice through a school psychology lens: Definition and applications. *School Psychology Review, 37*(4), 453–468. https://doi.org/10.1080/02796015.2008.12087860

Skiba, R. J., Horner, R. H., Chung, C., Rausch, M. K., May, S. L., & Tobin, T. (2011). Race is not neutral: A national investigation of African American and Latino disproportionality in school discipline. *School Psychology Review, 40*(1), 85–107. https://doi.org/10.1080/02796015.2011.12087730

Walcott, C. M., & Hyson, D. (2018). Results from the NASP 2015 Membership Survey, part one: Demographics and employment conditions. *NASP Research Reports, 3*(1). https://www.nasponline.org/research-and-policy/research-center/nasp-research-reports

Winerman, L. (2017). By the numbers: APA at its 125th anniversary: A snapshot of the association in its quasquicentennial year. *Monitor on Psychology, 48*(5), 80. https://www.apa.org/monitor/2017/05/numbers

CHAPTER 2

Historical Foundations

DAN FLORELL

CHAPTER OBJECTIVES

After reading this chapter, you will be able to:

- Define and describe the major epochs of school psychology's history (i.e., Hybrid and Thoroughbred Years).
- Describe foundations in psychology and education that prompted the inception of the field.
- Describe the development and contributions of school psychology's major professional associations.
- Describe influential legislation and court cases that shaped the development of school psychology.
- Describe the contributions of diverse individuals to the development of the field.

NATIONAL ASSOCIATION OF SCHOOL PSYCHOLOGISTS PRACTICE MODEL CONNECTIONS

Domain 8: Equitable Practices for Diverse Student Populations
Domain 10: Legal, Ethical, and Professional Practice

INTRODUCTION

Although relatively brief, the history of school psychology is brimming with innovation, missteps, successes, and challenges. Over the past 125 years, the profession of school psychology has been shaped by a number of influences, including developments in the fields of psychology and education, the changing sociopolitical environment of the United States, and, ultimately, the evolving contexts and needs of public schools. Many of these influences continue to be evident in contemporary practice.

Studying the history of school psychology is essential for understanding the current status of the field. In particular, knowledge of school psychology's history allows current scholars, practitioners, and graduate educators to avoid repeating past mistakes and to capitalize on opportunities for rectifying past injustices. This chapter describes important events and trends that contributed to the development of the field.

OVERVIEW OF SCHOOL PSYCHOLOGY'S HISTORY

According to Fagan (1986a), school psychology's roots can be traced back to the 1890s. The history of school psychology has been described as two periods: the **Hybrid Years** (1896–1969) and the **Thoroughbred Years** (1970–present). The term *hybrid* is used to describe a time in school psychology's history when the profession comprised a diverse range of practitioners in psychology and education who were loosely organized around the mission of providing psychoeducational services to school-age youth (Fagan & Wise, 2007). For the most part, these services centered on assessing children for the purpose of educational "sorting" or placement. The term *thoroughbred* refers to the period of time in which school psychology's professional identity became more cohesive and established. In particular, this time period saw a growing number of graduate preparation programs, school positions, and publication outlets specifically devoted to the practice and profession of school psychology. The turning point marking the transition from the Hybrid Years to the Thoroughbred Years was the formation of the National Association of School Psychologists (NASP), the profession's first national organization devoted specifically to the practice of school psychology. This chapter describes both time periods and the events and trends that shaped them.

THE HYBRID YEARS

The Emergence of Psychology in Europe and the United States

The foundations of school psychology began to take root only a few decades after the larger field of psychology was established. The field of psychology itself was a mixture of medicine and philosophy that emerged in Germany in the late 1800s. German pioneers of psychology, such as Herman von Helmholtz and Wilhelm Wundt, focused their work on understanding the human mind through **introspection** (i.e., the observation of one's own mental state and conscious thoughts) and the measurement of physiological reactions. Not long after the roots of psychology took hold in Europe, the United States began to contribute to the field as well. For example, William James, who studied under von Helmholtz in the late 1860s and later came to be regarded as "the Father of American Psychology," wrote one of the profession's most influential books, *The Principles of Psychology* (Angell, 1911; Evans, 1990). This work sparked great interest in the field of psychology among U.S. scholars. Inspired by James and his contemporaries, students in the United States and abroad began to specialize in the field of psychology.

The Changing Landscape of the Labor Force and Education

As the larger field of psychology began to take shape, the U.S. education system experienced significant changes as well. In the mid- to late 1890s, relatively few individuals enjoyed full access to formal education. The country was only a few decades removed from the Civil War, and racial and ethnic discrimination was rampant. For example, mandated racial segregation in public spaces resulted in Black students attending underresourced, inferior schools or their exclusion from public education altogether. Native Americans also were marginalized by the U.S. education system during this time. When Native American youth were included in schooling, it was often for the purpose of forced assimilation (Noltemeyer et al., 2012). Regardless of cultural background, financial circumstances prevented many children who worked in factories, mines, and other labor-intensive jobs from attending school (Rury, 2016).

As poor work conditions continued and concerns for children's rights mounted, social movements advocating for the formal education of youth gained momentum. According to Field (1976), these social movements were motivated by the desire for an educated workforce and the preservation of society's moral character and structure. State legislators became increasingly aware that child labor negatively impacted the workforce and therefore ought to be regulated. Organized labor unions and other social organizations were instrumental in many states to ban child labor. Early on, however, these laws often were not enforced (Siegel & White, 1982).

As various industries began to require a more highly skilled and educated workforce, states began to pass compulsory schooling legislation, which was more successful in removing children from the labor force. *Compulsory schooling* refers to the legal requirement that children of particular ages attend school for a designated period of time. The surge in compulsory schooling legislation between 1870 and 1890 was a major driving force in the development of school psychology, as it resulted in an influx of youth with diverse characteristics and needs into the U.S. public school system (Braden et al., 2001; Kaplan & Kaplan, 1985). As noted previously, however, many children (e.g., youth of color and youth with disabilities) continued to be routinely excluded from schools.

Child Study Movement

Among the many social movements of the late 1800s, the child study movement was the one that most directly facilitated the birth of school psychology (Fagan, 2000). During this time, scholars became increasingly aware that children were not simply "miniature adults," but rather were distinctly different in their mental and behavioral functioning. As a result, greater numbers of people and organizations committed to working with children. This increased interest was motivated by four primary goals: (a) the need to teach children about a community's shared beliefs and values; (b) the desire for partial regulation of the labor market; (c) the need to prepare children for adult economic roles; and (d) the desire to provide services and support for at-risk children (Siegel & White, 1982). These goals significantly influenced the development of social institutions that continue to serve and impact children.

The increasing diversity of the student population in public schools initially presented a number of new challenges for school personnel (Fagan, 1992; Hildreth, 1930). Many children who came to school were coping with a range of issues, including malnutrition, economic hardship, learning problems, and chronic disease. Whereas such problems previously had deterred these students from enrolling in public schools, compulsory schooling laws paved the way for their attendance. In response, schools developed special programs to address the needs of students who were experiencing learning problems (Siegel & White, 1982).

A number of psychologists contributed to the study of children's abilities, needs, and development. For example, Granville Stanley Hall was instrumental in drawing attention to the need for school-based services for children and adolescents. In 1880, Hall presented a series of lectures at Harvard University on the applications of psychology to education. Moreover, he studied the use of questionnaire methodology as a means for assessing the "common problems of school children" (Fagan, 1992, p. 238). Although Hall's questionnaire methodology was later discredited, he inspired other psychologists, such as Edward Thorndike, to pursue more scientifically rigorous studies of children (Ross, 1972). Ultimately, Hall's goal was to understand the basic nature of children and to apply this knowledge to the development of school programs (White, 1992).

Inspired by the child study movement, Lightner Witmer also made significant contributions to the study of children and schooling. In 1892, Witmer began teaching at the University of Pennsylvania, where he established the world's first applied psychological clinic in 1896 (Tulchin, 1956). Witmer focused on the assessment of schoolchildren who were referred by teachers, parents, and local community agencies (Fagan, 1992). Witmer's assessment techniques included interviews, naturalistic observations, record reviews, physical exams, and mental testing, all of which he used to ascertain the client's functioning while noting relevant environmental and social influences (Baker, 1988). He promoted a multidisciplinary approach centered on high-quality communication with parents and teachers to develop effective interventions (McReynolds, 1996; Routh, 1996). At the fifth annual meeting of the American Psychological Association (APA), Witmer (1897) emphasized the need for psychological experts "who [were] capable of treating the many difficult cases that resist the ordinary methods of the school room" (p. 117). Lightner Witmer is regarded as the founder of both school psychology and clinical psychology (Fagan, 1996; McReynolds, 1996).

Intelligence-Testing Movement

Interest in the measurement of individual differences in physiological and mental functioning significantly shaped the development of school psychology. Although many scholars contributed to the early development of intelligence testing, Alfred Binet, Victor Henri, and Theodore Simon are credited with the breakthrough in this area that most directly influenced school psychology. Commissioned by the French government to develop a measure that would identify students with intellectual disabilities, Binet, Henri, and Simon constructed the first modern intelligence test, the *Binet-Simon Intelligence Scale*, which was published in 1905 (Kaufman, 2000). As part of the development of this intelligence scale, Binet and colleagues identified age-related differences in children's cognitive development (Sattler, 2001).

Soon after the *Binet-Simon Intelligence Scale* was published in France, it was translated into English and distributed in the United States. Henry Goddard was the first to translate the test in 1908, and Lewis Terman followed with his own version in 1916. In his 1916 version, Terman introduced the concept of the intelligence quotient (Braden et al., 2001; Kehle et al., 1993). Between 1910 and 1920, other psychologists began to develop aptitude and achievement tests (Fagan, 2000; Kehle et al., 1993). Even though some school districts and child study bureaus embraced these tests, they were not well known by the general public.

Recognition of intelligence testing increased when the United States entered World War I. At the time, the U.S. military was relatively small and searching for a way to screen the intellectual and emotional functioning of soldiers. In response to this need, Robert Yerkes, who was the president of APA at the time the United States declared war, recruited several prominent psychologists, including Henry Goddard, to develop a group-administered intelligence test (Boake, 2002; Kaufman, 2000). These psychologists developed the Army Alpha intelligence test. They quickly realized, however, that not all recruits would be able to complete the test, due to cultural barriers, limited English proficiency, or illiteracy. Subsequently, the committee developed the Army Beta test, which emphasized nonverbal items to increase accessibility (Kaufman, 2000). The widespread use of the Army Alpha and Beta tests contributed to the legitimization of psychological testing in the public eye (Fagan, 1985). As these tests began to enter schools, they gradually ushered school psychologists into an assessment-focused role (Fagan & Wise, 2007).

The advent of intelligence testing legitimized the need for school staff with psychological training; however, it also created a haven for the proliferation of racial discrimination. Results from the Alpha tests indicated that, on average, whites performed better than members of other racial groups (e.g., African Americans) did. Some scholars who were influenced by Francis Galton's theory of *eugenics* used these findings as a vehicle for suggesting that whites were intellectually superior to African Americans and other minoritized racial groups (Brigham, 1922). In response, a number of psychologists of color, including Drs. Horace Mann Bond, Herman Canady, Martin Jenkins, George Sanchez, and Albert Sidney Beckham, set out to debunk these claims (Graves & Mitchell, 2011; Urban, 1989). For example, Albert Sidney Beckham, the first African American school psychologist, examined the impact of environmental variables (e.g., socioeconomic status) on intelligence test scores (Graves, 2009). Moreover, George Sanchez, the first Latino psychologist, argued against the validity of early intelligence tests for Mexican American children when these children did not have the same cultural experiences or English language proficiency as many of their white, non-Hispanic, English-speaking peers (on whom the tests were normed; Padilla & Olmedo, 2009). These individuals represent some of the field's earliest social justice advocates. Debate regarding the use of intelligence tests with diverse populations intensified in subsequent decades and would eventually become a source of heated controversy in state and federal courts.

An Emerging Profession

The confluence of sociopolitical forces and advances in child studies, intelligence testing, and other areas made it increasingly clear that school psychological services were necessary for supporting a diverse student body. As student populations continued to grow, public schools began conducting health screenings and providing preventive care to students. Many schools focused on assisting children with disabilities, including students with visual, auditory, physical, and intellectual impairments. These services required the expertise of specialists with multidisciplinary skill sets, and, consequently, laid the foundations of school psychology.

Organizations devoted to the welfare of children, such as the Illinois Society for Child Study (ISCS; established in 1894), contributed to the development of school-based services. For example, W. S. Christopher, who was a member of the Chicago Board of Education and the ISCS, assisted the Chicago Board of Education in establishing the nation's first *child study bureau* in 1899 (Slater, 1980). These child study bureaus conducted research on students to establish typical development and then identify students who were atypically developing so as to provide more appropriate educational services. Over the next few decades, the developments in Chicago began to spread to other urban school districts, which formed their own child study bureaus. Subsequently, child study bureaus were founded in major cities such as St. Louis, Baltimore, Cleveland, Los Angeles, New Haven, Louisville, and Detroit (Fagan, 1985; Hildreth, 1930; Wallin, 1920). Many of the psychologists in these bureaus devoted their time to measuring the physiological characteristics and mental aptitude of children (Gesell, 1921; Mullen, 1981; Slater, 1980). Employees in these bureaus also embraced the topic of teaching pedagogy, as teachers were becoming increasingly interested in learning effective techniques for educating students with a wide range of abilities.

Although pedagogical innovations were emerging, many students continued to struggle in the classroom. As a result, some school districts developed classification systems that would allow children to be targeted for specialized services. Parents and teachers referred students with a range of difficulties, including behavior problems and intellectual disabilities, for consideration for these services. Some districts even developed the earliest forms of special education services (Fagan, 2000).

The expansion of the child study bureaus and various student services led to an increase in the number of psychologists working with children in school settings. This trend eventually prompted the Connecticut State Board of Education to hire Arnold Gesell as the first school employee to hold the title of *school psychologist*. Gesell's role was to assist in mental examination case studies and to conduct survey research with students attending public schools. He also provided consultative services and in-service trainings to school staff (Fagan, 1987).

Growth of Training

Although increasing numbers of school psychologists were being hired by school districts, there was little consensus regarding the professional preparation necessary to serve in this role. Advances in training gained momentum in the 1920s, when New York University became the first higher education institution to offer a school psychology program (Trachtman, 1987). Other institutions began to offer specialized courses for students who were training to be school psychologists, and in the late 1930s, Pennsylvania State University established the first doctoral program in school psychology (Reynolds & Clark, 1984).

As more universities began offering courses related to school psychology, the need for literature and textbooks in this area arose. In 1930, Gertrude Hildreth wrote the first book on school psychology, *Psychological Service for School Problems*. This book presented a model of school psychological services and described the roles and functions of school psychologists. Additionally, Hildreth described the typical daily schedule of school psychologists, which included conferencing with staff and parents, conducting in-service trainings, and testing individual students. In many respects, the various activities described by Hildreth are similar to those performed by contemporary practitioners. Hildreth's textbook would stand alone for 25 years before the next book written specifically for school psychologists appeared, which was a summary of the Thayer Conference of 1954 (French, 1986). Ultimately, the availability of training programs and textbooks paved the way for the first state credentialing systems for school psychologists in New York and Pennsylvania. These systems were in place by the mid-1930s (Fagan & Wise, 2007).

While such advances fueled the expansion of school psychology's workforce, systemic racism in universities and other training settings led to the continued exclusion of school psychologists of color from graduate education. Many white university faculty believed that individuals from racial and ethnic minoritized backgrounds were incapable of advanced learning (Clewell & Anderson, 1995); thus, individuals of color were systematically excluded from school psychology training and higher education more broadly. As noted by Proctor (2022), the field of school psychology made virtually no effort in its earliest years to recruit or retain scholars and practitioners of color. Nevertheless, many school psychologists of color disrupted institutional racism in training, ultimately making indelible contributions to their field and building roadmaps for future psychologists of color. For example, John Henry Jackson (1922–2008), who practiced in the Milwaukee public schools for nearly 30 years, served as President of the American Board of School Psychology and became the first African American to be recognized with APA Division 16's Distinguished Service Award (Fagan, 2009). Moreover, Laura Hines (1922–2009), a African American school psychologist who also served as a supervisor for the New York Board of Education's Bureau of Child Guidance, ultimately became president of the New York School Psychology Association's School Division in 1983 (Fagan & Flanagan, 2012).

In many cases, minority-serving institutions (MSIs), such as historically Black colleges and universities (HBCUs), were powerhouses for propelling psychologists of color into the school psychology workforce; for instance, Albert Sidney Beckham (the first African American to hold the title of "school psychologist" in the United States) was a graduate of Lincoln University (the oldest HBCU in the United States; Graves, 2009), and Laura Hines was an alumna of Virginia State College (an HBCU now recognized as Virginia State University; Fagan & Flanagan, 2012). Throughout school psychology's history and presently, HBCUs and other MSIs have continued to yield a talented pipeline of diverse school psychologists who have been instrumental in shaping the profession (Grapin, 2022; Proctor, 2022).

Professional Organizations

As training programs and state credentialing systems populated the nation, professional organizations were slowly developing as well. Even though APA was established in 1893, it primarily emphasized academic psychology (i.e., research and scholarship) and placed relatively less emphasis on applied psychology (i.e., practice). As the number of applied psychologists grew, other psychological associations began to form. One of the most notable of these organizations was the American Association of Applied Psychologists (AAAP), which emerged in 1937 as APA's most significant competitor. AAAP represented four broadly defined specialties (i.e., clinical, educational, consulting, and business and industrial psychology), with school practitioners belonging predominantly to the clinical or educational sections. Despite the existence of these two national psychological associations, most school practitioners did not belong to either (Fagan & Wise, 2007).

APA and AAAP merged into one organization in 1945, and APA's subsequent reorganization led to the formation of its current division system. One of the original divisions established in 1945 was the Division for School Psychologists (Division 16). This was the first national organization devoted specifically to school psychologists. The division struggled to maintain a consistent membership for several years thereafter, but its establishment marked an important milestone in the formation of school psychology's professional identity (Fagan & Wise, 2007).

On the Brink of a Professional Identity

Impact of World War II

Similar to World War I, World War II had a significant impact on the development of the broader field of psychology. Whereas World War I introduced psychological assessment to the public, World War II increased public awareness of the ability of psychologists to provide counseling services. The atrocities of World II and the Holocaust (in which millions of Jews, individuals from racial, ethnic, and sexual minoritized groups, people with disabilities, and many others were executed in concentration camps) left many witnesses and victims deeply traumatized. It was at this point that applied psychologists began to focus on counseling as one of their primary functions.

Following World War II, the United States experienced a spike in its population as a result of the "baby boom." Between 1945 and 1961, more than 60 million children were born in the United States (Colby & Ortman, 2014) and flooded into the public school system. Consequently, even more psychologists were needed in schools to meet this demand. In response to the baby boom, the profession of school psychology experienced reciprocal growth, with the number of practitioners increasing from 500 to 5,000 between 1940 and 1970. There also was a corresponding increase in training programs from merely a handful to more than 100 programs that collectively enrolled more than 3,000 graduate students (Batsche et al., 1989; Reynolds & Clark, 1984). During this time, more states began to recognize the need for professional certification systems for school psychologists. The number of states implementing credentialing systems increased from 13 in 1946 to 23 in 1960. By 1970, the majority of states (approximately 40) had established credentialing systems for school psychologists.

IMPACT OF THE CIVIL RIGHTS MOVEMENT

Beginning in the early 1950s, simmering tensions regarding the education of racial and ethnic minoritized students came to a boil. During the first half of the 20th century, U.S. public schools operated in accordance with the doctrine "separate but equal," which emerged in 1896 from the infamous court case known as *Plessy v. Ferguson*. This landmark ruling upheld state laws requiring the racial segregation of public facilities (including schools) under the premise that "separate but equal" facilities would be provided to individuals from white and non-white backgrounds. As a result of this ruling, African American and other non-white students frequently were educated in schools with fewer resources and less qualified teachers than white students (Benjamin et al., 2005). When such schools were not accessible, many non-white students were excluded from the public school system altogether.

The *Plessy v. Ferguson* ruling sparked considerable debate among educators and psychologists regarding the best way to educate students from racial and ethnic minoritized backgrounds. In the 1930s, psychological research made a notable shift from focusing on racial differences (as a means of asserting superiority) to exploring the impact of racial prejudice (Samelson, 1978). For example, Inez Beverly Prosser, one of the first African American women to earn a doctorate in psychology, examined the relationship between school environment (i.e., racially segregated or mixed) and nonacademic variables (e.g., family relationships, personality characteristics, and social participation) in African American students. She found that African American students in racially mixed schools experienced higher levels of social maladjustment as well as less security and satisfaction in their social relations. Based on these findings, Prosser argued that segregated environments were preferable for supporting the healthy development of African American children, although she believed some students (depending on personality type) would fare well in mixed schools (Benjamin et al., 2005).

Others argued that school segregation would justify segregation in other aspects of society and would perpetuate misguided beliefs about African American inferiority (Benjamin et al., 2005). Advocates of this viewpoint included Kenneth Clark and Mamie Phipps Clark, a married couple who were among the first African American scholars to receive doctoral degrees in psychology. The Clarks studied African American children who attended either segregated or integrated schools and found that the students who attended segregated schools were more likely to internalize negative racial stereotypes (Gibbons & Van Nort, 2009).

In 1954, the U.S. Supreme Court rendered a decision in the landmark ***Brown et al. v. Board of Education of Topeka*** case that overturned the "separate but equal" doctrine that had emerged from *Plessy v. Ferguson* more than 50 years earlier. The 1954 ruling declared that state laws establishing separate schools for white and African American students were unconstitutional. This case was not only a significant victory for the public education system, but also a major milestone for the field of psychology. The research of the Clarks played a key role in the decision rendered in *Brown v. Board of Education* (1954) and was one of the first pieces of psychological research to be incorporated in a Supreme Court decision that effected monumental social change (Benjamin & Crouse, 2002; Jackson, 1998). The importance of this case cannot be overstated, as it not only desegregated schools but also incited a variety of subsequent lawsuits advocating for the rights of other marginalized populations (e.g., children with disabilities). The *Brown v. Board of Education* case and others would lead to immense change in the practice of school psychology, as described later in this chapter.

Thayer Conference

Following World War II and with the emerging need for diagnostic and therapeutic services, leaders in clinical psychology training and practice convened to discuss the roles, functions, and training standards for clinical psychologists. This meeting became known as the Boulder Conference of 1949 (held at the University of Colorado Boulder). At this conference, participants discussed specific directions for the proper training of clinical psychologists. These discussions led to the development of the *scientist-practitioner model* of training, which called for an emphasis on training in both research and clinical practice (Baker & Benjamin, 2000).

Unfortunately, the Boulder Conference was primarily focused on serving the adult population and provided little guidance on training standards for psychologists who specialized in serving children and schools. This omission prompted the organization of the **Thayer Conference**, which took place in West Point, New York, in 1954 (French, 1992). The Thayer Conference was one of the first professional gatherings exclusively focused on the professional practice of school psychologists. The main goals of the conference were to define the roles and functions of school psychologists and to specify training standards for the field. The proceedings of this conference were recorded in the second school psychology book to be published (25 years after Hildreth's book), *School Psychologists at Mid-Century: A Report of the Thayer Conference on the Functions, Qualifications, and Training of School Psychologists* (Cutts, 1955). Shortly following the publication of this book, several other school psychology books were published, including Stanley Marzolf's (1956) *Psychological Diagnosis and Counseling in the Schools* and W. D. Wall's (1956) *Psychological Services for the Schools* (French, 1986).

Formation of the National Association of School Psychologists and State Associations

Throughout the 1940s and 1950s, professional organizations representing school psychology continued to develop. Membership in APA's Division 16 rose to 601 members in 1956. Moreover, a number of state school psychological associations were formed throughout the 1950s and into the 1960s. In 1943, Ohio became the first state to develop an association for school psychologists (School Psychologists of Ohio, which was renamed the Ohio School Psychology Association in the early 1960s). California, Illinois, Massachusetts, New York, and New Jersey all followed suit in the 1950s. By the end of the 1960s, there were 17 state associations and a strong interest in forming a national association exclusively for school psychologists (Fagan et al., 1986).

Ohio's state association initiated efforts to increase communication among the various state associations. In 1968, leaders in school psychology convened the National Invitational Conference of School Psychologists in Ohio, which led to the resolution to form a national association devoted specifically to school psychologists. During the following year, the St. Louis planning convention was held, and NASP was officially established. At this time, it comprised more than 900 members. Pauline Alexander was elected the first president of NASP (Farling & Agner, 1979). The formation of NASP was particularly significant because it recentered school psychology's national representation. As noted by Fagan and Wise (2007), "Whereas Division 16 carried the national banner for school psychology from 1945 to 1970, NASP has carried it since" (p. 60).

As practicing school psychologists began to organize, a professional literature began to take hold. The journals *Psychology in the Schools*, *Journal of School Psychology*, and *Professional Psychology* were established in the 1960s, marking some of the first times that school psychologists had outlets devoted specifically to research in their field (Fagan & Jack, 2012). Around the same time, there was a corresponding increase in the number of school psychology books available, with approximately 13 being written between 1960 and 1969 (French, 1986). This growth in school psychology's literature would pave the way for tremendous growth in the number of graduate preparation programs.

THOROUGHBRED YEARS

As noted previously, the formation of NASP marked the transition from the Hybrid Years to the Thoroughbred Years. With the establishment of this national association, school psychology took a momentous step in its development and professionalization. As school psychology entered the Thoroughbred Years, many of the social changes and advances that took root in the Hybrid Years continued to gain momentum. These changes had a significant impact on the continued evolution of school psychology.

The Emergence of Federally Mandated Special Education Services

The ramifications of the *Brown v. Board of Education* ruling continued to reverberate throughout the 1960s and the civil rights movement. One of the widespread sentiments that emerged was the notion that all children and adolescents should have a right to public education and, in particular, a free and appropriate public education (FAPE). The emphasis on educational rights for all students spurred a series of court cases regarding the fair treatment of individuals with disabilities in school settings. The rationale for many of these cases was that children with disabilities were not being afforded equal protection under the law (as required in the 14th Amendment to the U.S. Constitution). For example, in 1972, the Pennsylvania Association for Retarded Children (PARC) challenged the state of Pennsylvania regarding its failure to provide equal access to public education for students with intellectual disabilities. Similarly, in the case of *Mills v. District of Columbia Board of Education* (1972), a class action suit was brought on behalf of a group of children with a variety of disabilities (e.g., behavioral and intellectual disabilities) who had been denied access to educational services due to their disability status. In both cases, students represented in these cases were granted numerous rights, including access to a free public education, documentation of an Individualized Education Program to support the students' success, and due process rights. Ultimately, these court decisions and others diversified the student population and expanded the range of services provided by public schools (Kurilott, 1975).

Increasing advocacy for the educational rights of students with disabilities led to several important pieces of legislation. In 1973, Congress passed the Rehabilitation Act, which prohibited institutions receiving federal funds (including schools) from discriminating against individuals with disabilities. In addition, Congress passed the Education for All Handicapped Children Act (EAHCA; Pub. L. No. [PL] 94-142) in 1975. This legislation required school districts to provide a FAPE to all students with disabilities ages 5 through 21 years. It also required schools to develop an Individualized Education Program (IEP) for each student with a disability who qualified for special education services. This IEP described the specific range of services to which a student was entitled and specific goals for educational progress. Ultimately, PL 94-142 marked the advent of widespread, federally mandated special education services for students with disabilities.

In 1986, PL 94-142 was reauthorized as PL 99-457. This reauthorization mandated states to expand services down to 3 years of age, thereby requiring schools to expand their services to include preschool and home-based services for infants and toddlers. This legislation and its subsequent iterations are discussed in greater detail in Chapter 5.

Both the EAHCA (reauthorized as the Individuals With Disabilities Education Act [IDEA] in 1990) and the Rehabilitation Act of 1973 had a significant impact on the roles and functions of school psychologists. For example, the 1986 reauthorization of the EAHCA (PL 99-457) prompted school psychologists to expand their range of competencies to include working with preschool-age children (McLinden & Prasse, 1991; Mowder et al., 1989). In particular, this series of legislation led school psychologists to adopt a wider range of roles, although most practitioners still were involved primarily in conducting evaluations, meeting with parents and teachers, and planning educational programs (Ramage, 1979).

Advances in Training and Practice

GRADUATE PROGRAMS AND PROFESSIONAL ACCREDITATION

As mentioned earlier, the growth of professional literature (including journals and books) in school psychology coincided with the proliferation of graduate training programs. By 1968, there were 96 school psychology training programs, and over the next three years this number rose to more than 150 (Fagan, 1986b). The increased capacity for training that resulted from program development directly impacted the number of practicing school psychologists, which rose to more than 5,000 nationwide by 1970 (Fagan & Wise, 2007).

Just as it impacted the roles of school psychologists, the advent of federal disability legislation affected the development of graduate programs. As school districts scrambled to meet the requirements imposed by this legislation, the demand for school psychologists increased, as did the demand for school psychology programs. By the late 1970s, there were more than 200 school psychology training programs and more than 10,000 school psychologists practicing in schools nationwide (Fagan, 1988).

As the number of graduate programs grew throughout the 1970s, national organizations representing the field of school psychology began to accredit programs that aligned with their standards for training and practice. APA began credentialing psychology graduate programs in 1971, during which time the University of Texas at Austin's PhD program became the first APA-accredited school psychology program in the nation. In 1976, NASP partnered with the National Council for Accreditation of Teacher Education (NCATE) to offer program approval in tandem with NCATE accreditation (Fagan & Wise, 2007). The emergence of these accreditation bodies and procedures resulted in the increased standardization of school psychology training, as many programs attempted to align with guidelines provided by national organizations. In 2022, NASP became recognized as an accrediting organization by the Council for Higher Education Accreditation (CHEA), a milestone that promises to afford graduate programs greater flexibility in navigating accountability processes (NASP, 2022). As will be discussed in Chapter 6, accreditation processes continue to shape the landscape of graduate training in school psychology.

THE SPRING HILL SYMPOSIUM AND OLYMPIA CONFERENCE

In response to legislation and litigation throughout the 1970s, leaders in school psychology recognized the need to provide guidance on the evolving roles and functions of school psychologists. With funding provided by the U.S. Department of Education, the National

School Psychology Inservice Training Network (NSPITN) was launched in 1978. This network had two primary goals: (a) to train school psychologists in innovative assessment and intervention practices consistent with those mandated by PL 94-142 and (b) to clarify the long-term goals, training needs, and roles of school psychologists. As part of its efforts, the NSPITN disseminated training modules on topics such as unbiased assessment, non–test-based assessment, and consultation for classroom teachers (Davis et al., 1984).

Collectively, the NSPITN and school psychology's two major national associations (APA's Division 16 and NASP) coordinated the Spring Hill Symposium, which took place in 1980 in Wayzata, Minnesota. At this symposium, 69 key constituents from 22 states, the District of Columbia, and Canada came together to discuss directions for the future of school psychology. As summarized by Ysseldyke (1982), participants at this conference raised issues related to the goals of school psychology practice, ethical and legal issues, the professionalization of school psychology, the content of training programs, and accountability for practice. The Spring Hill Symposium identified the broad overarching issues that the field needed to address, but specific details were left for discussion at a later time. One year later, the Olympia Conference was held in Wisconsin to develop specific strategies for achieving the vision laid out at the Spring Hill Symposium. The action plan for this conference was to address issues regarding legislation, practice, and the profession (Meyers et al., 1982). In addition, participants at the conference were encouraged to identify larger societal issues and their potential impact on future services (Brown & Cardon, 1982).

The NSPITN integrated many of the ideas generated during the Spring Hill Symposium and Olympia Conference in its subsequent publication of *School Psychology: A Blueprint for Training and Practice* (Ysseldyke et al., 1984) and the companion volume to this publication, *School Psychology: The State of the Art* (Ysseldyke, 1984). Together, these documents outlined various domains of competence and training for school psychologists.

Professional Regulation

In response to the changing landscape of schools throughout the 1960s and 1970s, professional regulation became a major priority for NASP. In 1974, NASP adopted its first professional code of ethics, the *Principles for Professional Ethics*. The purpose of this code was to protect recipients of school psychological services by ensuring that practitioners would implement empirically sound practices, respect the dignity of all parties involved in service delivery, and monitor their own behavior (NASP, 2010). By the end of its first decade (1979), NASP had issued standards for training, credentialing, practice, and field placements. These standards included the *Guidelines for the Provision of School Psychological Services* (1978). The guidelines were revised in 1984, 1992, and 1997. In 2000, NASP leaders decided that the standards would be revised every 10 years, setting the stage for the subsequent development of the 2010 and 2020 standards, respectively. The *Professional Standards of the National Association of School Psychologists* (i.e., the NASP Practice Model described in Chapter 1) represents the most recent iteration of these guidelines (NASP, 2020). The adoption of various standards ultimately allowed the profession to take ownership of its own regulation (Batsche et al., 1989; Curtis & Zins, 1989). As a result, external agencies (i.e., state and federal agencies) began to look to NASP and the broader profession for guidance on legislation and regulations.

One of NASP's landmark achievements was the establishment of its national credentialing system for practitioners. The National School Psychology Certification System (NCSP) was established in 1989 and approved the certification of more than 14,000 school psychologists in its first two years. Standards set forth by NASP for the NCSP were frequently adopted by state education agencies for credentialing purposes.

The advent of the NCSP is one example of how the profession began to drive its own regulation, rather than simply reacting to government requirements (Rossen & Williams, 2013).

APA also remained involved in the regulation of school psychology, although its professional positions sometimes clashed with those of NASP. Although the majority of school psychologists practiced at the nondoctoral level during the 1970s, APA contended that the doctoral degree should be the entry-level degree for any individual using the title of *psychologist*. In 1977, the APA Council passed a resolution affirming this position, which fueled tensions between the two organizations. In 1978, APA and NASP established an Inter-Organizational Committee to resolve their differences. Although tensions between APA and NASP abated in the 1990s, the Inter-Organizational Committee eventually was disbanded in 2002 due to a reprise of conflict (Fagan & Wise, 2007).

SOCIAL JUSTICE CONNECTIONS

How did the emergence of multicultural scholarship influence school psychology?

During the Thoroughbred Years, multicultural scholarship became increasingly prominent in the school psychology literature. Although psychological research addressed racial differences during the beginning of the 20th century, not all of this literature was beneficial for diverse youth. During the first few decades of the 20th century, a considerable body of psychological research centered on testing hypotheses of genetic inferiority, which proposed that racial and ethnic minoritized groups were inherently inferior to whites in a number of intellectual and psychosocial domains (Newell & Chavez-Korell, 2017). Toward the middle of the century, theories of cultural deprivation began to take hold. From this perspective, students from racial and ethnic minoritized backgrounds were believed to have poor academic, psychosocial, and economic outcomes due to inadequate exposure to European American values and norms (Newell & Chavez-Korell, 2017). Generally, individual differences among school-age youth were seen as a problem to be remedied rather than an asset to be embraced.

As social movements of the 1950s, 1960s, and 1970s emphasized respect for the rights and dignity of all children, psychologists began to recognize a need for multicultural competence. The Vail Conference of 1973, which examined the role of applied psychologists, was the first conference to directly address issues of diversity in psychology (Korman, 1974). Conference participants acknowledged a need for cultural diversity training among psychologists to promote ethically sound practice. When NASP published its first standards for school psychology training, it too addressed cultural issues related to service delivery.

Throughout the 1980s and 1990s, multicultural scholarship in psychology gained increasing momentum. Psychologists and others were beginning to embrace a cultural difference perspective, which acknowledged the legitimacy and value of diverse lifestyles, norms, beliefs, and customs (Newell & Chavez-Korell, 2017). Particularly in the 1990s, most of this scholarship focused on assessment practices, with relatively fewer articles addressing multicultural considerations for intervention (Miranda & Gutter, 2002). In school psychology, notable scholars who contributed to the field's emerging multicultural agenda included Ena Vazquez-Nuttall, Janine Jones, Antoinette Miranda, and Chieh Li. The work of these pioneers and many others would serve as the foundation for a subsequent wave of 21st century scholarship dedicated to social justice issues.

School Psychology's Evolving Agenda

The 1990s represented a period of quiet yet stable growth for school psychology (Fagan & Wise, 2007). Two additional school psychology organizations were established (the Society for the Study of School Psychology [SSSP] and the American Academy of School Psychology [AASP]), and the profession continued to enjoy increasing legitimacy. Despite this stability, the shortages in the number of available school psychologists became increasingly worrisome. Moreover, since the 1980s, it had been apparent that the demographic makeup of the school psychology workforce (which was predominantly white) did not reflect that of the U.S. student population. NASP leaders such as Deborah Crockett initiated efforts to remedy this problem through proactive efforts to recruit more professionals from racial and ethnic minoritized groups into school psychology. Crockett became the first African American president of NASP in 1997 and has continued to advocate for the recruitment of minoritized school psychologists (Crockett, 2004).

By the mid- to late 1990s, school psychologists began to fill a new role: *crisis intervention*. As will be discussed in greater detail in Chapter 13, crisis intervention refers to the provision of immediate, short-term psychological services to assist an individual in restoring problem-solving skills and employing coping strategies following an extremely or unusually stressful life event (Brock et al., 2014). A series of high-profile school shootings occurred in various locales including Jonesboro, Arkansas; Paducah, Kentucky; and Columbine, Colorado. These incidents drew attention to the need for schools to be able to deal with school violence, other traumatic events, and their aftermath.

Following the Oklahoma City bombing in 1995, NASP created the National Emergency Assistance Team (NEAT), which was composed of nationally certified school psychologists who had formal training in and direct experience with crisis situations (Heath et al., 2007). Scott Poland, Stephen Brock, and Bill Pfohl are notable school psychologists who served on NEAT during that time. Throughout the end of the decade and into the 2000s, school psychologists became more relied upon to assist students, teachers, parents, and administrators through various crisis events (NASP, 2012).

After several years of serving as a crisis resource for the nation, NASP decided to create a school crisis and intervention training for school-based professionals. The result was the PREPaRE training, which was developed in 2006 and continues to expand (NASP, 2012). The advent of PREPaRE and increased emphasis on crisis training at the graduate level has resulted in more school psychologists incorporating crisis prevention and intervention into their roles in schools.

The provision of crisis intervention services was just one indicator that the role of the school psychologist needed to undergo change. In the early 2000s, many school psychology leaders believed the field was at a crossroads. Whereas national associations and leaders emphasized roles in consultation, prevention, and intervention, many practitioners continued to find themselves mired in special education assessment activities (Cummings et al., 2004). Authors such as Sheridan and Gutkin (2000) cautioned that school psychologists were not actualizing their potential to fill a wider range of roles and that traditional models of assessment hindered school psychologists' ability to effectively meet the needs of all children. Specifically, many scholars advocated for the field to move away from the traditional medical model of assessment and diagnosis and toward an ecological model of service delivery. The traditional *medical model* focuses on identifying inherent "problems" within children through extensive diagnostic and assessment procedures. The *ecological model*, in contrast, focuses on person–environment interactions that give rise to academic and behavioral problems as well as emphasizes assessment for the purpose of designing interventions (rather than making diagnoses).

More than 20 years after the Spring Hill Symposium and Olympia Conference, the 2002 Conference on the Future of School Psychology was held. Sponsored by several of school psychology's major associations (e.g., NASP), the conference was motivated in part by a growing desire to reflect on the momentous changes in the profession and schools that had taken place during the previous two decades. At the 2002 Futures Conference, a number of broad themes emerged, including (a) a need to focus on prevention and early intervention, (b) a focus on evidence-based interventions, (c) a reduced emphasis on traditional assessment, (d) a greater emphasis on assessment for the purposes of intervention and accountability, and (e) an emphasis on systems-level functioning via the incorporation of public health approaches (Dawson et al., 2004).

The *public health model* is a population-based approach to addressing academic, health, and social problems that incorporates environmental factors as well as comprehensive, multilayered prevention and intervention efforts. This model served as the foundation for what eventually came to be known as the multitiered system of support (MTSS), which is described extensively in Chapter 8. Ultimately, the themes of the 2002 Futures Conference provided clear directions for the field's continued development. They also reflected trends in contemporary educational legislation, as described in the following.

Legislation of the 1990s and 2000s

The 1990s saw two reauthorizations of the EAHCA. In 1990, this legislation was reauthorized as IDEA. Among other changes, autism and traumatic brain injury were recognized as areas of disability. Moreover, the renaming of this act represented a shift away from the term *handicap* and toward the less pejorative and more widely accepted term *disability* (Bicehouse & Faieta, 2017). Subsequently, IDEA was reauthorized in 1997 and again in 2004. The 2004 reauthorization renamed this legislation the Individuals With Disabilities Education Improvement Act (IDEIA) and introduced other important changes. One of these changes was the requirement that states permit the use of Response to Intervention (RtI) methods for disability identification purposes. RtI is a form of MTSS that incorporates environmental and instructional factors in educational decision-making. Core features of these models include an emphasis on meeting the needs of all learners, an increased focus on prevention and intervention services in general education settings, and data-based decision-making. This legislation is discussed in further detail in Chapter 5.

The No Child Left Behind (NCLB) Act of 2001 was another critical piece of legislation that impacted the role of school psychologists. The goal of this legislation was to implement robust accountability systems that would hold schools responsible for measuring and supporting students' progress toward meeting rigorous academic standards. This focus on accountability meant that schools needed to aggregate and interpret large amounts of data. With the implementation of this legislation, schools increasingly called on school psychologists to support their data collection and accountability efforts. As explained in Chapter 5, NCLB is no longer in effect and was replaced by the Every Student Succeeds Act (ESSA) in 2015. Nevertheless, both the 2004 reauthorization of IDEIA and the 2001 implementation of NCLB were critical in supporting school psychology's emerging focus on evidence-based intervention and accountability for student outcomes.

Organizational Conflict in the 21st Century

While relations between APA and NASP were cordial throughout the 1990s, long-simmering issues became inflamed in 2007. In particular, APA and NASP continued to disagree regarding the appropriate entry-level degree for school psychologists. Tensions arose largely due to impending revisions to APA's *Model Licensure Act* (MLA), which represents the organization's formal recommendations to states regarding requirements for licensure in psychology. In its 1987 revision of the MLA, APA had included an exemption for nondoctoral-level school psychologists, which allowed these practitioners to retain the title of "school psychologist" when practicing in the context of schools and under the authority of a state certificate (NASP, 2009). In 2007, however, the MLA was revised and the exemption for school psychologists was removed in the initial draft. Advocacy efforts from school psychologists in both NASP and APA's Division 16 led to the subsequent revision of the MLA draft to include an exemption for nondoctoral school psychologists practicing in school settings. The collaborative efforts of NASP and APA's Division 16 during this time represent a milestone in the history of their relationship (Duncan & Bohmann, 2010; Nastasi, 2010).

Transitioning From the Past to the Present

In 2012, school psychology leaders held another conference to discuss future directions for the field. Like the 2002 conference, the 2012 School Psychology Futures Conference was sponsored jointly by a variety of professional organizations including NASP, APA's Division 16, AASP, and SSSP. The 2012 School Psychology Futures Conference was held in a virtual environment, which allowed for participation worldwide via live webinars. Its mission was to join school psychologists together to support the academic success and mental health of children and adolescents. The 2012 Conference had three themes: *leadership*, *critical skills*, and *advocacy*. Its emphasis on advocacy for school-age youth from diverse backgrounds was consistent with the field's emerging focus on social justice issues, which continues to permeate its work (Jarmuz-Smith et al., 2013). The conference speakers could not anticipate that in less than a decade, a global pandemic would spur unprecedented change in the field.

Shifting Ground: The Coronavirus 2019 Pandemic

In late March 2020, the arrival of the ***coronavirus 2019 (COVID-19) pandemic*** in the United States led to the shutdown of schools across the nation. To minimize the spread of the disease, schools transitioned to remote learning, leaving school psychologists to scramble to adapt their practice accordingly. Overall, the pandemic introduced new stressors and highlighted enduring injustices in society that continue to impact the well-being of youth and families today. There are two areas in particular that have significantly affected the practice of school psychology, namely: (a) the utilization of technology for remote services and (b) heightened attention to racial injustice.

In the immediate aftermath of school shutdowns, school psychologists needed to figure out how to continue to provide services remotely. Emerging technologies, such as remote assessment, were available; however, they were not yet widely used and raised a number of unaddressed ethical considerations (Florell, 2020b). Ultimately, the workhorse of remote services was videoconference software. It was quickly embraced by schools as the solution for holding classes, conducting special education meetings, and providing counseling services. In addition, efforts were made to conduct remote assessments through videoconferencing (Florell, 2020a). However, in the rush to provide services, many ethical considerations, such as privacy, security, and validity of test results, were pushed aside.

While many inevitable technological and ethical issues arose, the pandemic led to the widespread adoption of technologies in schools that will continue to impact school psychologists' work for years to come. Remote assessments were in their infancy when the pandemic emerged, and during the subsequent two years, test publishers prioritized making their tests and measurements usable online. Videoconference software quickly evolved to provide secure connections that allowed for remote classroom observations, virtual consultation, and virtual counseling (Florell, 2021). These innovations were addressed in the most recent update to NASP's (2020) code of ethics, which covered the use of technology much more extensively than previous iterations. Finally, these technologies have presented the opportunity for school psychologists to work remotely and thus to reduce their travel between schools. Fueled also by the overall shortage of school psychologists in the field, companies have emerged that contract with school districts to provide remote school psychological services. Such companies will likely continue to expand and provide new options for school psychologists looking for alternative practice arrangements.

With the onset of the pandemic also came heightened national attention to racial violence and other forms of racial injustice in the United States. In particular, the murders of Breonna Taylor and George Floyd, two Black Americans who were killed by police officers in Louisville, Kentucky (March 2020) and Minneapolis, Minnesota (May 2020), respectively, incited mass protests across the country calling for racial justice. The pandemic itself also highlighted pervasive structural racism across numerous social institutions (e.g., healthcare and education), with people from historically marginalized racial and ethnic groups being infected, hospitalized, and dying from COVID-19 at significantly higher rates than white people (Centers for Disease Control and Prevention, 2023). As the nation became increasingly attuned to deeply embedded structural oppression, calls for the larger field of psychology to assume responsibility for its contributions to these inequities intensified as well. For example, APA released several documents laying out the history of psychology's contributions to racial inequity (APA, 2023), apologizing for its own role in fueling this inequity (APA, 2021a), and committing to repairing harms moving forward (APA, 2021b, 2022). Although APA's efforts were acknowledged by other associations, they were deemed necessary but not sufficient for promoting justice (Association of Black Psychologists, 2021).

While some school psychologists had long been steeped in social justice work (e.g., Proctor, 2022), injustices evidenced in police brutality and the COVID-19 pandemic prompted the field as a whole to reckon with its complicity in racial injustice and to set up mechanisms to disrupt it moving forward. School psychology associations took various actions to better address racial inequity, inclusion, and (the lack of) cultural diversity within the profession. For instance, a number of school psychology leaders and professional organizations collaborated to develop the *School Psychology Unified Anti-Racism Statement and Call to Action* (García-Vázquez et al., 2020), which laid out a joint commitment to recognizing, interrogating, and disrupting racism in the field and in schools. Moreover, the Trainers of School Psychologists (n.d.) created race and diversity resources that included calls for cultural diversity in training and highlighted significant people of color in school psychology. NASP (2021) created a report on equity, diversity, and inclusion implementation which has since influenced several organizational actions, including its requirement of diversity training for every renewal cycle of a member's NCSP. As will be described in Chapter 4, school psychology's commitment to antiracist action is still evolving, and there is much work to be done to ensure its aspirations are fulfilled.

Overall, the pandemic era has had a powerful impact on school psychology. In particular, it has sparked the widespread adoption of technology in major areas of practice and spurred further action to promote equity, inclusion, and justice in the profession. The ramifications of this period will undoubtedly continue to influence the field for years to come.

SUMMARY AND CONCLUSIONS

The field of school psychology has undergone significant changes since its inception in the 1890s. As the public education system evolved to meet the needs of an increasingly diverse student population, so did the profession of school psychology. One recurrent theme throughout school psychology's history is an emphasis on consciousness raising in regard to a wide range of social, academic, and mental health issues that impact school-age youth. Reflecting on these changes, Ysseldyke (1982) commented, "Society increasingly expects schools to function as the major agent of social change. Society today does not place small demands on its schools. Schools are expected to bring about social equality and to eliminate poverty, unemployment, racism, and war" (pp. 547–548). Indeed, schools have become central institutions for addressing social issues and supporting diverse youth. As the future of the field begins to take shape, school psychologists should continue to make schools a primary venue for social change.

DISCUSSION QUESTIONS

1. How do the techniques used by Lightner Witmer in the United States' first psychological clinic reflect current practices in school psychology?
2. Identify a figure in school psychology's history who could be described as a social justice advocate. How did this individual disrupt injustice in the field?
3. The formation of NASP is believed to have marked the transition from the Hybrid Years to the Thoroughbred Years. Why was the formation of NASP such a monumental event in school psychology's history?
4. The professionalization of school psychology was greatly assisted by the formation of national organizations. What role did these organizations play in shaping the profession? What role do these organizations continue to play in shaping the profession?
5. Over time, a variety of social movements (e.g., civil rights movement) have influenced the field of school psychology. How did these movements influence the field's development? How do contemporary social concerns and values continue to shape school psychology's agenda?

RECOMMENDED READINGS

American Psychological Association. (2023, February). *Historical chronology: Examining psychology's contributions to the belief in racial hierarchy and perpetuation of inequality for people of color in U.S.* https://www.apa.org/about/apa/addressing-racism/historical-chronology

Fagan, T. K. (1992). Compulsory schooling, child study, clinical psychology, and special education: Origins of school psychology. *American Psychologist, 47*(2), 236–243. https://doi.org/10.1037/0003-066X.47.2.236

McReynolds, P. (1996). Lightner Witmer: A centennial tribute. *American Psychologist, 51*(3), 237–240. https://doi.org/10.1037/0003-066X.51.3.237

Trainers of School Psychologists. (n.d.). *Race and diversity resources*. Trainers of School Psychologists—Race & Diversity. https://tsp.wildapricot.org/Race-&-Diversity

Ysseldyke, J. E., Reynolds, M. C., & Weinberg, R. A. (1984). *School psychology: A blueprint for training and practice*. National School Psychology Inservice Training Network.

 A robust set of instructor resources designed to supplement this text is located at http://connect.springerpub.com/content/book/978-0-8261-6344-8. Qualifying instructors may request access by emailing textbook@springerpub.com.

REFERENCES

American Psychological Association. (2021a, December). *Apology to people of color for APA's role in promoting, perpetuating, and failing to challenge racism, racial discrimination, and human hierarchy in U.S.* https://www.apa.org/about/policy/racism-apology

American Psychological Association. (2021b, December). *Role of psychology and APA in dismantling systemic racism against people of color in U.S.* https://www.apa.org/about/policy/dismantling-systemic-racism

American Psychological Association. (2022, August). *Advancing health equity in psychology*. https://www.apa.org/about/policy/advancing-health-equity-psychology

American Psychological Association. (2023, February). *Historical chronology: Examining psychology's contributions to the belief in racial hierarchy and perpetuation of inequality for people of color in U.S.* https://www.apa.org/about/apa/addressing-racism/historical-chronology

Angell, J. R. (1911). William James. *Psychological Review, 18*(1), 78–82. https://doi.org/10.1037/h0067307

Association of Black Psychologists. (2021, November 24). *ABPSI's official statement to the APA apology*. https://abpsi.org/abpsis-official-statement-to-the-apa-apology

Baker, D. B. (1988). The psychology of Lightner Witmer. *Professional School Psychology, 3*(2), 109–121. https://doi.org/10.1037/h0090552

Baker, D. B., & Benjamin, L. T. (2000). The affirmation of the scientist-practitioner: A look back at Boulder. *American Psychologist, 55*(2), 241–247. https://doi.org/10.1037//0003-066x.55.2.241

Batsche, G. M., Knoff, H. M., & Peterson, D. W. (1989). Trends in credentialing and practice standards. *School Psychology Review, 18*(2), 193–202. https://doi.org/10.1080/02796015.1989.12085415

Benjamin, L. T., & Crouse, E. M. (2002). The American Psychological Association's response to *Brown v. Board of Education*: The case of Kenneth B. Clark. *American Psychologist, 57*(1), 38–50. https://doi.org/10.1037/0003-066X.57.1.38

Benjamin, L. T., Henry, K. D., & McMahon, L. R. (2005). Inez Beverly Prosser and the education of African Americans. *Journal of the History of the Behavioral Sciences, 41*(1), 43–62. https://doi.org/10.1002/jhbs.20058

Bicehouse, V., & Faieta, J. (2017). IDEA at age forty: Weathering Common Core Standards and data driven decision making. *Contemporary Issues in Education Research, 10*(1), 33–44. https://doi.org/10.19030/cier.v10i1.9878

Boake, C. (2002). From the Binet-Simon to the Wechsler–Bellevue: Tracing the history of intelligence testing. *Journal of Clinical and Experimental Neuropsychology, 24*(3), 383–405. https://doi.org/10.1076/jcen.24.3.383.981

Braden, J. S., DiMarino-Linnen, E., & Good, T. L. (2001). Schools, society, and school psychologists. *Journal of School Psychology, 39*(2), 203–219. https://doi.org/10.1016/S0022-4405(01)00056-5

Brigham, C. (1922). *A study of American intelligence*. Princeton University Press.

Brock, S. E., Reeves, M. A. L., & Nickerson, A. B. (2014). Best practices in school crisis intervention. In A. Thomas & J. Grimes (Eds.), *Best practice in school psychology* (Vol. 3, pp. 211–230). National Association of School Psychologists.

Brown, D. T., & Cardon, B. W. (1982). Synthesis and editorial comment. *School Psychology Review, 11*(2), 195–198. https://doi.org/10.1080/02796015.1982.12087334

Centers for Disease Control and Prevention. (2023, May 25). *Risk for COVID-19 infection, hospitalization, and death by race/ethnicity*. U.S. Department of Health and Human Services. https://www.cdc.gov/coronavirus/2019-ncov/covid-data/investigations-discovery/hospitalization-death-by-race-ethnicity.html

Clewell, B. C., & Anderson, B. T. (1995). African-Americans in higher education: An issue of access. *Humboldt Journal of Social Relations, 21*(2), 55–79. https://www.jstor.org/stable/23263010

Colby, S. L., & Ortman, J. M. (2014, May). *The baby boom cohort in the United States: 2012 to 2060* (Current Population Reports, P25-1141). U.S. Census Bureau. https://www.census.gov/history/pdf/babyboomers-boc-2014.pdf

Crockett, D. (2004). Critical issues children face in the 2000s. *School Psychology Review, 33*(1), 78–82. https://doi.org/10.1080/02796015.2004.12086232

Cummings, J. A., Harrison, P. L., Dawson, M. M., Short, R. J., Gorin, S., & Palomares, R. S. (2004). The 2002 conference on the future of school psychology: Implications for consultation, intervention, and prevention services. *Journal of Educational and Psychological Consultation, 15*(3–4), 239–256. https://doi.org/10.1080/10474412.2004.9669516

Curtis, M. J., & Zins, J. E. (1989). Trends in training and accreditation. *School Psychology Review, 18*(2), 182–192. https://doi.org/10.1080/02796015.1989.12085414

Cutts, N. E. (1955). *School psychologists at mid-century: A report of the Thayer Conference on the functions, qualifications, and training of school psychologists*. American Psychological Association.

Davis, T. F., Reynolds, M. C., Weinberg, R. A., & Ysseldyke, J. E. (1984). The National School Psychology Inservice Training Network (USA): A resource for change. *School Psychology International, 5*(2), 67–70. https://doi.org/10.1177/0143034384052002

Dawson, M., Cummings, J. A., Harrison, P. L., Short, R. J., Gorin, S., & Palomares, R. (2004). The 2002 multisite conference on the future of school psychology: Next steps. *School Psychology Review, 33*(1), 115–125. https://doi.org/10.1080/02796015.2004.12086235

Duncan, B., & Bohmann, J. (2010). APA Council of Representatives approves MLA, which retains the exemption for all school psychologists. *Communiqué, 38*(6), 7. https://www.nasponline.org/publications/periodicals/communique/issues/volume-38-issue-6

Evans, R. B. (1990). William James, "The Principles of Psychology," and experimental psychology. *American Journal of Psychology, 103*, 433–447. https://doi.org/10.2307/1423317

Fagan, T. K. (1985). Sources for the delivery of school psychological services during 1890–1930. *School Psychology Review, 14*(3), 378–382. https://doi.org/10.1080/02796015.1985.12085183

Fagan, T. K. (1986a). School psychology's dilemma: Reappraising solutions and directing attention to the future. *American Psychologist, 41*(8), 851–861. https://doi.org/10.1037/0003-066X.41.8.851

Fagan, T. K. (1986b). The historical origins and growth of programs to prepare school psychologists in the United States. *Journal of School Psychology, 24*(1), 9–22. https://doi.org/10.1016/0022-4405(86)90038-5

Fagan, T. K. (1987). Gesell: The first school psychologist Part II. Practice and significance. *School Psychology Review, 16*(3), 399–409. https://doi.org/10.1080/02796015.1987.12085302

Fagan, T. K. (1988). The historical improvement of the school psychology service ratio: Implications for future employment. *School Psychology Review, 17*(3), 447–458. https://doi.org/10.1080/02796015.1988.12085361

Fagan, T. K. (1992). Compulsory schooling, child study, clinical psychology, and special education. Origins of school psychology. *American Psychologist, 47*(2), 236–243. https://doi.org/10.1037//0003-066x.47.2.236

Fagan, T. K. (1996). Witmer's contributions to school psychological services. *American Psychologist, 51*(3), 241–243. https://doi.org/10.1037/0003-066X.51.3.241

Fagan, T. K. (2000). Practicing school psychology: A turn-of-the-century perspective. *American Psychologist, 55*(7), 754–757. https://doi.org/10.1037//0003-066x.55.7.754

Fagan, T. K. (2009). John Henry Jackson (1922–2008). *American Psychologist, 64*(1), 49. https://doi.org/10.1037/a0013716

Fagan, T. K., & Flanagan, R. (2012). Remembering Laura Hines, 1922–2009. *The School Psychologist, 66*(1), 30–31. https://apadivision16.org/wp-content/uploads/2015/12/TSP-Vol.-66-No.-1-January-2012.pdf

Fagan, T. K., Hensley, L. T., & Delugach, F. J. (1986). The evolution of organizations for school psychologists in the United States. *School Psychology Review, 15*(1), 127–135. https://doi.org/10.1080/02796015.1986.12085215

Fagan, T. K., & Jack, S. L. (2012). A history of the founding and early development of the *Journal of School Psychology*. *Journal of School Psychology, 50*(6), 701–735. https://doi.org/10.1016/j.jsp.2012.11.002

Fagan, T. K., & Wise, P. S. (2007). *School psychology: Past, present, and future* (3rd ed.). National Association of School Psychologists.

Farling, W. H., & Agner, J. (1979). History of the National Association of School Psychologists: The first decade. *School Psychology Review, 8*(2), 140–152. https://doi.org/10.1080/02796015.1979.12086480

Field, A. J. (1976). Educational expansion in mid-nineteenth-century Massachusetts: Human-capital formation or structural reinforcement? *Harvard Educational Review, 46*(4), 521–552. https://doi.org/10.17763/haer.46.4.127204p54638nm40

Florell, D. (2020a). Taking assessment online: Ready or not. *Communiqué, 49*(2), 36. https://www.nasponline.org/publications/periodicals/communique/issues/volume-49-issue-2

Florell, D. (2020b). The week we all became virtual school psychologists. *Communiqué, 48*(7), 36. https://www.nasponline.org/publications/periodicals/communique/issues/volume-48-issue-7

Florell, D. (2021). Tech lessons that stick after a virtual school year. *Communiqué, 50*(1), 34. https://www.nasponline.org/publications/periodicals/communique/issues/volume-50-issue-1

French, J. L. (1986). Books in school psychology: The first forty years. *Professional School Psychology, 1*(4), 267–277. https://doi.org/10.1037/h0090510

French, J. L. (1992). *The influence of school psychologists in APA on APA*. American Psychological Association.

García-Vázquez, E., Reddy, L., Arora, P., Crepeau-Hobson, F., Fenning, P., Hatt, C., Hughes, T., Jimerson, S., Malone, C., Minke, K., Radliff, K., Raines, T., Song, S., & Strobach, K. V. (2020). School psychology unified antiracism statement and call to action. *School Psychology Review, 49*(3), 209–211. http://doi.org/10.1080/2372966X.2020.1809941

Gesell, A. (1921). *Exceptional children and public school policy*. Yale University Press.

Gibbons, W., & Van Nort, S. C. (2009). Mamie Phipps Clark: The "other half" of the Kenneth Clark legacy. *Encounter: Education for Meaning and Social Justice, 22*(4), 28–32.

Grapin, S. L. (2022). Centering the contributions, perspectives, and experiences of Black school psychologists: Commentary on Proctor (2022). *School Psychology International, 43*(6), 560–567. https://doi.org/10.1177/01430343221111049

Graves, S., & Mitchell, A. (2011). Is the moratorium over? African American psychology professionals' views on intelligence testing in response to changes to federal policy. *Journal of Black Psychology, 37*(4), 407–425. https://doi.org/10.1177/0095798410394177

Graves, S. L. (2009). Albert Sidney Beckham: The first African American school psychologist. *School Psychology International, 30*(1), 5–23. https://doi.org/10.1177/0143034308101847

Heath, M. A., Ryan, K., Dean, B., & Bingham, R. (2007). History of school safety and psychological first aid for children. *Brief Treatment and Crisis Intervention, 7*(3), 206–223. https://doi.org/10.1093/brief-treatment/mhm011

Hildreth, G. H. (1930). *Psychological services for school problems* (1st ed.). World Book Company.

Jackson, J. P. J. (1998). Creating a consensus: Psychologists, the Supreme Court, and school desegregation, 1952–1955. *Journal of Social Issues, 54*(1), 143–177. https://doi.org/10.1111/j.1540-4560.1998.tb01211.x

Jarmuz-Smith, S., Harrison, P. L., & Cummings, J. A. (2013). The 2012 School Psychology Futures Conference: Accomplishments and next steps. *Communiqué, 41*(5), 6, 8. https://www.nasponline.org/publications/periodicals/communique/issues/volume-41-issue-5

Kaplan, M. S., & Kaplan, H. E. (1985). School psychology: Its educational and societal connections. *Journal of School Psychology, 23*(4), 319–325. https://doi.org/10.1016/0022-4405(85)90044-5

Kaufman, A. S. (2000). Intelligence tests and school psychology: Predicting the future by studying the past. *Psychology in the Schools, 37*(1), 7–16. https://doi.org/10.1002/(SICI)1520-6807(200001)37:1<7::AID-PITS2>3.0.CO;2-H

Kehle, T. J., Clark, E., & Jenson, W. R. (1993). The development of testing as applied to school psychology. *Journal of School Psychology, 31*(1), 143–161. https://doi.org/10.1016/0022-4405(93)90026-F

Korman, M. (1974). National conference on levels and patterns of professional training in psychology: The major themes. *American Psychologist, 29*(6), 441–449. https://doi.org/10.1037/h0036469

Kuriloff, P. (1975). Law, educational reform, and the school psychologist. *Journal of School Psychology, 13*(4), 335–348. https://doi.org/10.1016/0022-4405(75)90052-7

McLinden, S. E., & Prasse, D. P. (1991). Providing services to infants and toddlers under PL 99-457: Training needs of school psychologists. *School Psychology Review, 20*(1), 37–48. https://doi.org/10.1080/02796015.1991.12085531

McReynolds, P. (1996). Lightner Witmer: A centennial tribute. *American Psychologist, 51*(3), 237–240. https://doi.org/10.1037/0003-066X.51.3.237

Meyers, J., Brown, D. T., & Coulter, W. A. (1982). Analysis of the action plans. *School Psychology Review, 11*(2), 161–185. https://doi.org/10.1080/02796015.1982.12087330

Miranda, A. H., & Gutter, P. B. (2002). Diversity research literature in school psychology: 1990–1999. *Psychology in the Schools*, *39*(5), 597–604. https://doi.org/10.1002/pits.10051

Mowder, B. A., Widerstrom, A. H., & Sandall, S. (1989). School psychologists serving at-risk and handicapped infants, toddlers, and their families. *Professional School Psychology*, *4*(3), 159–171. https://doi.org/10.1037/h0090588

Mullen, F. A. (1981). School psychology in the USA: Reminiscences of its origin. *Journal of School Psychology*, *19*(2), 103–119. https://doi.org/10.1016/0022-4405(81)90053-4

Nastasi, B. K. (2010). Life after MLA: Message from Division 16 President. *Communiqué*, *38*(6), 7–8. https://www.nasponline.org/publications/periodicals/communique/issues/volume-38-issue-6

National Association of School Psychologists. (2009). Proposed APA Model Act for state licensure of psychologists: Implications for school psychological services. *Communiqué*, *37*(7). https://www.nasponline.org/publications/periodicals/communique/issues/volume-37-issue-7

National Association of School Psychologists. (2010). *Principles for professional ethics*. Author. https://www.nasponline.org/Documents/Standards%20and%20Certification/Standards/1_%20Ethical%20Principles.pdf

National Association of School Psychologists. (2012). *School safety and crisis preparedness and response NASP leadership: 1996–2011*. Author.

National Association of School Psychologists. (2020). *The professional standards of the National Association of School Psychologists*. https://www.nasponline.org/standards-and-certification/nasp-2020-professional-standards-adopted

National Association of School Psychologists. (2021). *Report of the NASP equity, diversity, and inclusion implementation task force*. Author.

National Association of School Psychologists. (2022, May 18). *NASP obtains Council for Higher Education Accreditation (CHEA) recognition as an accrediting organization*. https://www.nasponline.org/Documents/NASP%20CHEA%20Accreditation%20Press%20Release.pdf

Newell, M. L., & Chavez-Korell, S. (2017). Multiculturalism: An interdisciplinary perspective. In E. C. Lopez, S. G. Nahari, & S. L. Proctor (Eds.), *Handbook of multicultural school psychology* (pp. 3–17). Routledge.

Noltemeyer, A., Mujic, J., & Mcloughlin, C. S. (2012). The history of inequity in education. In A. Noltemeyer & C. S. Mcloughlin (Eds.), *Disproportionality in education and special education: A guide to creating more equitable learning environments* (pp. 3–15). Charles C. Thomas Publisher.

Padilla, A. M., & Olmedo, E. (2009). Synopsis of key persons, events, and associations in the history of Latino psychology. *Cultural Diversity and Ethnic Minority Psychology*, *15*(4), 363–373. https://doi.org/10.1037/a0017557

Proctor, S. L. (2022). From Beckham until now: Recruiting, retaining, and including Black people and Black thought in school psychology. *School Psychology International*, *43*(6), 545–559. https://doi.org/10.1177/01430343211066016

Ramage, J. C. (1979). National survey of school psychologists: Update. *School Psychology Review*, *8*(2), 153–161. https://doi.org/10.1080/02796015.1979.12086481

Reynolds, C. R., & Clark, J. H. (1984). Trends in school psychology research: 1974–1980. *Journal of School Psychology*, *22*(1), 43–52. https://doi.org/10.1016/0022-4405(84)90050-5

Ross, D. (1972). *G. Stanley Hall. The psychologist as prophet*. University of Chicago Press.

Rossen, E., & Williams, B. B. (2013). The life and times of the National School Psychology Certification System. *Communiqué*, *41*(7), 1, 28–30. https://www.nasponline.org/publications/periodicals/communique/issues/volume-41-issue-7

Routh, D. K. (1996). Lightner Witmer and the first 100 years of clinical psychology. *American Psychologist*, *51*(3), 244–247. https://doi.org/10.1037/0003-066X.51.3.244

Rury, J. L. (2016). *Education and social change: Contours in the history of American schooling* (5th ed.). Routledge.

Samelson, F. (1978). From "race psychology" to "studies in prejudice": Some observations on the thematic reversal in social psychology. *Journal of the History of the Behavioral Sciences*, *14*(3), 265–278. https://doi.org/10.1002/1520-6696(197807)14:3%3C265::aid-jhbs2300140313%3E3.0.co;2-p

Sattler, J. M. (2001). *Assessment of children: Cognitive applications* (4th ed.). Author.

Sheridan, S. M., & Gutkin, T. B. (2000). The ecology of school psychology: Examining and changing our paradigm for the 21st century. *School Psychology Review*, *29*(4), 485–502. https://doi.org/10.1080/02796015.2000.12086032

Siegel, A. W., & White, S. H. (1982). The child study movement: Early growth and development of the symbolized child. *Advances in Child Development and Behavior, 17,* 233–285. https://doi.org/10.1016/s0065-2407(08)60361-4

Slater, R. (1980). The organizational origins of public school psychology. *Educational Studies, 11*(1), 1–11. https://doi.org/10.1207/s15326993es1101_1

Trachtman, G. M. (1987). Bootstrapping it in the big apple: A history of school psychology at New York University. *Professional School Psychology, 2*(4), 281–296. https://doi.org/10.1037/h0090545

Trainers of School Psychologists. (n.d.). *Race and diversity resources.* Trainers of School Psychologists – Race & Diversity. https://tsp.wildapricot.org/Race-&-Diversity

Tulchin, S. H. (1956). In memoriam: Lightner Witmer. *American Journal of Orthopsychiatry, 27*(1), 200–201. https://doi.org/10.1111/j.1939-0025.1957.tb05211.x

Urban, W. J. (1989). The Black scholar and intelligence testing: The case of Horace Mann Bond. *Journal of the History of the Behavioral Sciences, 25*(4), 323–334. https://doi.org/10.1002/1520-6696(198910)25:4<323::aid-jhbs2300250403>3.0.co;2-j

Wallin, J. E. W. (1920). Problems confront a psycho-educational clinic in a large municipality. *Mental Hygiene, 4,* 103–136.

White, S. H. (1992). G. Stanley Hall: From philosophy to developmental psychology. *Developmental Psychology, 28*(1), 25–34. https://doi.org/10.1037/0012-1649.28.1.25

Witmer, L. (1897). The organization of practical work in psychology. *Psychological Review, 4,* 116–117.

Ysseldyke, J. E. (1982). The Spring Hill Symposium on the future of psychology in the schools. *American Psychologist, 37*(5), 547–552. https://doi.org/10.1037/0003-066X.37.5.547

Ysseldyke, J. E. (Ed.). (1984). *School psychology: The state of the art.* National School Psychology Inservice Training Network.

Ysseldyke, J. E., Reynolds, M. C., & Weinberg, R. A. (1984). *School psychology: A blueprint for training and practice.* Minneapolis, MN: National School Psychology Inservice Training Network.

CHAPTER 3

Multicultural Foundations

SHERRIE L. PROCTOR ■ NAKIA M. GRAY-NICOLAS

CHAPTER OBJECTIVES

After reading this chapter, you will be able to:

- Describe the demographics of school psychologists in the United States.
- Describe the importance of diversity in the profession.
- Describe the demographics of school-age youth.
- Discuss how the use of multiculturalism can guide school psychological service delivery.
- Describe recommendations for multiculturalism and social justice orientations to school psychology practice.

NATIONAL ASSOCIATION OF SCHOOL PSYCHOLOGISTS PRACTICE MODEL CONNECTIONS

Domain 6: Services to Promote Safe and Supportive Schools
Domain 8: Equitable Practices for Diverse Student Populations
Domain 10: Legal, Ethical, and Professional Practice

INTRODUCTION

No book on school psychology would be complete without a comprehensive discussion of factors related to human diversity and multicultural competence and cultural responsiveness. In this chapter, *diversity* is defined broadly as a spectrum of individual differences related to factors such as age, disability status, gender or gender identity, race, ethnicity, national origin, religion, sexual orientation, language, and socioeconomic status (SES). Culturally responsive school psychologists are intentional in accounting for human diversity in all aspects of their psychological service delivery (Parker et al., 2020).

The U.S. population has become more diverse in a number of ways. This diversification has implications for pre-K–12 schools as well as for society at large. Diversity within the student population provides educators with an important opportunity to teach students how to live in a pluralistic U.S. society and an increasingly global world (Proctor & Meyers, 2014; Proctor & Simpson, 2016). Nevertheless, educators, including school psychologists, who are predominantly white and monolingual, are sometimes challenged by how to provide culturally responsive and competent education and psychological services to diverse school-age populations and the adults who support them (Proctor & Meyers, 2014). This chapter explores the importance of school psychologists valuing and using a multicultural practice framework that extends to embracing principles of social justice. This is important because students from multicultural backgrounds, who are also often members of historically minoritized[1] communities, are sometimes prevented from reaching their full potential due to systemic barriers that school psychologists, through their service delivery, can prevent, interrupt, or disrupt.

MULTICULTURALISM, SOCIAL JUSTICE, AND INTERSECTIONALITY FOUNDATIONS

As discussed in Chapter 1, *multiculturalism* is a worldview that recognizes and values diverse learners, including their intersecting dimensions of individual identity and cultural backgrounds (Carroll, 2009). Many individuals who have attended public schools in the United States have experienced some aspect of "multicultural" education. **Multicultural education** refers to a wide variety of programs and practices designed to facilitate educational equity for individuals from all genders, racial and ethnic groups, language backgrounds, social classes, exceptionalities, and cultures (Banks, 2010). Banks (2010) underscored that multicultural education extends beyond curricular reform (e.g., including representation of diverse groups of people in the curriculum) to transforming all aspects of a school, including its culture, policies and politics, staff perceptions and beliefs, assessment and testing procedures, instructional materials, community participation, and so forth. Indeed, multiculturalism is a "practice movement" that has its roots in education, counseling, psychology, and the behavioral sciences (Carroll, 2009, p. 3).

In its most effective manifestation, multiculturalism permeates a school and results in educational policies, procedures, and practices that take into account the needs of students with a range of backgrounds and talents (Carroll, 2009). *Cultural responsiveness* is an extension of multiculturalism and is demonstrated by use of intentional practices that align with a person's beliefs, values, and culture (Parker et al., 2020). Proctor and Meyers (2014) have noted the importance of school psychologists understanding, valuing, and engaging a multicultural practice orientation as well as developing multicultural competence. Newell et al. (2010) described *multicultural competence* as the display of knowledge, attitudes, and behaviors that result in successful interactions with multicultural populations. Carroll (2009) explained that educators who apply a multicultural orientation to their practice "see learners, their families, and communities within the context of culture, race, ethnicity, gender, sexual orientation, and all those other cultural lenses that give meaning to students' daily learning experiences" (p. 5). Proctor and Meyers (2014) noted the importance of school psychologists understanding, valuing, and engaging in a multicultural practice orientation as well as developing multicultural competence and cultural responsiveness.

Some school psychologists who use multiculturalism to guide their practice may believe that providing culturally responsive psychological services is sufficient to support

---

[1] Refers to a person being forced into a group that is mistreated, faces prejudices, and/or is discriminated against because of situations outside of one's personal control.

minoritized learners. However, a more comprehensive view of multiculturalism in school psychology practice includes: (a) examining and challenging personal attitudes, perceptions, and beliefs about students and communities from diverse cultural backgrounds; (b) acquiring knowledge about students and communities from diverse cultural backgrounds; (c) understanding how systemic, school-wide issues (e.g., curriculum, policies, assessment and counseling practices) impact students from diverse cultural backgrounds; (d) engaging in advocacy for policies that promote equity for students from diverse cultural backgrounds who experience marginalization and oppression; and (e) acting in proactive ways that promote and proliferate the core values of multiculturalism (Carroll, 2009; Proctor & Meyers, 2014).

Indeed, school psychologists must acknowledge and value how culture plays a role in students' school-based experiences and must engage in advocacy that impacts systemic change for minoritized students—such as changes to oppressive school-based discipline policies (e.g., punitive policies that disproportionately penalize Black boys for subjective behaviors deemed disrespectful by administrators such as "talking back" or being "too loud"). A comprehensive definition of *social justice* is provided in Chapter 1; in addition, Linnemeyer et al. (2018) conceptualized social justice as the fair and equitable distribution of resources, rights, and treatment of individuals in society, particularly for people who do not possess equal power in society.

A critical concept for social justice is intersectionality. **Intersectionality** is a theoretical framework that elucidates how the simultaneous experience of social identities such as race, gender, SES, and sexual orientation overlap and intersect to create interdependent systems of power (e.g., white supremacy, patriarchy, heteronormativity) and oppression (e.g., racism, classism, sexism, heterosexism; Crenshaw, 1989). It is important to consider intersectionality because identity is complex and multidimensional and students can have different school experiences, including the experience of bias, prejudice, marginalization, and/or oppression, based on either one or a combination of their identities. (See Harris [2022] for insight into how intersectionality shapes Black girls' disciplinary experiences in U.S. public schools.) Furthermore, the most recent iteration of the American Psychological Association's (APA's) *Multicultural Guidelines* (2017) reflects a critical need to consider diversity and multicultural practice in all areas (i.e., practice, research, consultation, and education) of professional psychology while centering issues of intersectionality.

DEMOGRAPHICS OF SCHOOL PSYCHOLOGISTS

Since its beginning, school psychology has been a predominantly white profession, with few individuals from racially, ethnically, or linguistically minoritized backgrounds represented in its workforce (Castillo et al., 2013; Proctor & Romano, 2016). To ascertain the demographics of school psychologists, Goforth et al. (2021) surveyed a sample of National Association of School Psychologists (NASP) members during the 2019–2020 school year. Of the 1,308 respondents, 12% identified as male, 87% as female, and 0.1% as nonbinary. Regarding the racial and ethnic backgrounds of respondents, 86% identified as white; 3.9% as Black or African American; 2.5% as Asian; 7.6% as Hispanic; 0.5% as American Indian or Native Alaskan; 0.1% as Native Hawaiian or Other Pacific Islander; and 0.9% as Arab, Middle Eastern, or North African. The majority (92%) of school psychologists were monolingual English speakers, although the school psychologists surveyed reported fluency in a total of 24 different languages. American Sign Language, French, Italian, and Spanish were the most commonly endorsed languages in which school psychologists provided bilingual or multilingual psychological or educational services.

As becomes evident later in this chapter, there is a significant demographic mismatch between school psychologists and the student populations they serve. Yet, race, ethnicity, gender, linguistic preferences, religion, sexual orientation, and other dimensions of diversity in the school psychology workforce are critical for a number of reasons, some of which are described in the following text. Although NASP, APA, and other vested partners and organizations have striven to increase diversity in the profession for decades, the demographic composition of the field has remained stagnant (Castillo et al., 2013; Goforth et al., 2021). Given these difficulties, all school psychologists must be well versed in multiculturalism and principles of social justice to effectively meet the needs of today's student populations.

CHALLENGES ASSOCIATED WITH A HOMOGENEOUS WORKFORCE

The longstanding lack of racial, ethnic, and linguistic diversity in the school psychology workforce has resulted in a number of challenges both within and outside the profession itself. For example, it has had repercussions for both scholarship and innovations in school psychology. In both areas, a dearth of diversity among school psychologists may partially explain the profession's delayed focus on how school psychological practices impact diverse student populations (Newell et al., 2010; Proctor, 2022). Although studying multicultural issues is not, nor should be, the responsibility of racially, ethnically, and linguistically minoritized scholars, the historical underrepresentation and, at times, exclusion of minoritized scholars (and other scholars interested in multicultural issues) undoubtedly has impeded the field's development of a multicultural research base and its articulation of a social justice agenda (Miranda & Gutter, 2002; Newell et al., 2010; Shriberg et al., 2008; Speight & Vera, 2009).

Deficits in workforce diversity also have presented challenges in relation to practice. Notably, school psychology practitioners are key psychological service providers to students from diverse backgrounds (Curtis et al., 2012; Proctor & Truscott, 2012). As described in Chapter 1, a recent national survey of school psychologists noted that 77% were employed in public schools (Farmer et al., 2021). These school psychologists reported spending much of their time engaged in activities such as conducting evaluations to determine special education eligibility. Other job roles included conducting professional development and training for school staff and collecting and interpreting student data as part of school-based problem-solving teams and providing mental and behavioral health services to students (Farmer et al., 2021). All of the job roles in which school psychologists engage require attention to multicultural issues, especially given that most practitioners report serving diverse students (Curtis et al., 2012). Ultimately, a lack of diversity among school psychologists (in combination with a slowly emerging repository of multicultural scholarship) raises serious concerns regarding the field's preparedness to address the needs of minoritized students, their families, and communities (Proctor, 2022).

DEMOGRAPHICS OF U.S. PUBLIC SCHOOL STUDENTS

The U.S. public school student population has become notably more racially, ethnically, and linguistically diverse. During the 2018–2019 school year, the U.S. pre-K–12 public schools served 50.7 million students, of whom 47% were white, 27% were Hispanic, 15% were African American, 5% were Asian, less than 1% were Pacific Islander, 1% were American

Indian/Alaska Native, and 4% were two or more races or ethnicities (Irwin et al., 2021). During this same time, Hispanic students accounted for the largest percentage of the public school population in the West (42.7%) and the second largest percentage in the Northeast (21.1%) and South (27.0%), with white students representing the largest percentage of this population in the latter two regions. Although Black students have traditionally been one of the largest student demographics in the South, these data indicated that they were the third largest percentage in this region (22.8%). Asian/Pacific Islanders represented 9.2% of students in the West, 7.5% in the Northeast, 3.7% in the Midwest, and 3.8% in the South (National Center for Education Statistics [NCES], 2020).

Linguistic diversity also abounds, with more than 400 languages spoken in U.S. public schools (Irwin et al., 2021). Approximately five million students, or 10.2% of the total public school population, are English Language Learners (ELLs; Irwin et al., 2021). ELLs, or students who are in the process of developing English language proficiency, are a protected class of students under Title VI, a federal law that prohibits any organization that receives federal funding from discriminating on the basis of race, color, or national origin (Hakuta, 2011). While Spanish is the most common home language spoken by ELLs in the United States, other commonly used languages include Arabic, Chinese, Vietnamese, Somali, Russian, Portuguese, Haitian/Haitian Creole, and Hmong (Irwin et al., 2021). During the 2018–2019 school year, the ELL population was 10% or more of the student population in the following 10 states: Alaska, California, Colorado, Florida, Illinois, Massachusetts, Nevada, New Mexico, Texas, and Washington (Irwin et al., 2021). Additionally, 23 other states had ELL students representing between 6% and 10% of their student populations. Nationally, ELLs represent 14.9% of the student population in city schools, 9.8% in suburban schools, 6.9% in town schools, and 4.2% in rural schools (Irwin et al., 2021). These trends highlight the prevalence of racially, ethnically, and linguistically minoritized students in communities and public schools across the United States.

Students who attend U.S. public schools are also diverse in regard to SES and family structure (Lopez & Bursztyn, 2013). As compared with Asian and white children, higher percentages of Black, American Indian/Alaskan Native, Hispanic, Pacific Islander, and children of two or more races live in poverty, or low income and economic marginalization (LIEM; APA, 2019; Irwin et al., 2021). In fact, the prevalence of Black and American Indian/Alaska Native children living in poverty is approximately three times that of their Asian and white peers (Irwin et al., 2021). Moreover, data suggest that children who live in mother-only households have a higher rate of poverty than those who live in two-parent households (Irwin et al., 2021). Among children who live in mother-only households, poverty rates are higher for Black (42%), Hispanic (41%), and American Indian/Alaska Native (46%) children than they are for white (30%) and Asian (22%) children (Irwin et al., 2021).

In terms of understanding students' intersectional identities, school psychologists and other educators must also take into account how students identify in terms of religious affiliation and sexual orientation and gender identity. According to the 2014 Religious Landscape Study, approximately 70.6% of Americans identified with one of eight subgroups of Christianity, while others identified as Jewish (1.9%), Muslim (1.9%), Buddhist (0.7%), and Hindu (0.7%; Pew Forum on Religion and Public Life, 2014). Lopez and Bursztyn (2013) underscored the importance of understanding that differences exist within religious subgroups as well (e.g., the Protestant faith includes evangelical, mainline, and Black congregations).

Finally, according to the 2019 Youth Risk Behavior Survey (Centers for Disease Control and Prevention, 2020), 11.2% of high school students identified as lesbian, gay, or bisexual, and 4.5% of youth ages 13 to 18 were unsure of their sexual orientation. Further, the Williams Institute estimated that 0.7% of youth ages 13 to 17 identify as transgender based on state-level, population-based data (Herman et al., 2017). Altogether, the data suggest that 12% to 15% of high school students identify as lesbian, gay, bisexual, transgender, and queer (LGBTQ; Rivera et al., 2022). The percentage of LGBTQ elementary and middle-school students is much harder to estimate due to lack of population-based data and students' age and developmental stage (Rivera et al., 2022). As discussed later in this chapter, many students who identify as LGBTQ experience marginalization and oppression in U.S. public schools; moreover, their oppressive and discriminatory experiences are being systemically reinforced by anti-gay state legislation (e.g., anti-LGBTQ curriculum laws) across the United States that aims to limit how educators can support students who are members of the LGBTQ community.

CHALLENGES MINORITIZED STUDENTS FACE IN U.S. PUBLIC SCHOOLS

Students from minoritized racial, ethnic, linguistic, and socioeconomic backgrounds may face many challenges in their respective school environments. More specifically, they may encounter a range of systemic barriers (some of which are readily apparent and others that are seemingly "hidden") to academic, social, emotional, and behavioral success. The following describes several of these challenges.

Opportunity Gap

National data have long captured a discrepancy in academic outcomes, or the "achievement gap," between students of color and their white peers. For example, in 2019, 52% of Black fourth-graders scored below the basic level on the National Assessment of Educational Progress (NAEP) reading assessment, as compared to 23% of white fourth-graders (NCES, n.d.-b). This racial "achievement gap" is evidenced in higher grade levels as well. Specifically, 46% of Black eighth-graders scored below the basic level on the NAEP reading assessment as compared to 18% of white eighth-graders. The average NAEP math achievement score was 25 points lower for Black students than for white students in the fourth grade. This gap widened to 32 points lower for Black students than for white students in the eighth grade (NCES, n.d.-a). Further, findings from this assessment indicated that high percentages of students from American Indian/Alaska Native, Hispanic, and Native Hawaiian/Other Pacific Islander backgrounds also performed below basic levels in reading and math at both the fourth and eighth grade levels (NCES, n.d.-a, n.d.-b).

The often-referenced "achievement gap" highlights the aforementioned disparities in academic results between groups but does not fully acknowledge how these disparities are perpetuated by the inequitable distribution of resources and opportunities, or the *opportunity gap*. Framing the gap as an opportunity gap "shifts our attention from outcomes to inputs—to the deficiencies in the foundational components of societies, schools, and communities that produce significant differences in educational—and ultimately socioeconomic—outcomes" (Welner & Carter, 2013, p. 3). Here, it is important to note that opportunity gaps are also evident between fourth- and eighth-grade students from lower socioeconomic backgrounds and their peers from higher-income families. This is a particularly salient observation because children from historically minoritized racial and ethnic groups (e.g., Black, Hispanic, American Indian/Native Alaskan) experience higher rates of poverty (Albritton et al., 2016).

These data highlight the need for school psychologists and other educators to acknowledge and understand how the intersection of racial and socioeconomic identities can influence educational outcomes. Racial and socioeconomic opportunity gaps can result in specific groups of students (a) experiencing higher rates of grade retention, (b) having less access to higher-level classes, and (c) dropping out of school (Ford et al., 2016; Miranda, 2014).

Representation in Special Programming

Other concerning issues include the overrepresentation of racially and ethnically minoritized students in special education and, conversely, the underrepresentation of these students in gifted education (Ford et al., 2016; NASP, 2021; Sullivan & Proctor, 2016). Inaccuracies in special education identification in both directions (i.e., overidentification and underidentification) can be problematic for several reasons. For example, failure to identify students who truly have a disability may limit access to needed educational services. Conversely, identifying students as having a disability when, in fact, they do not have a disability may result in dire consequences, such as removal from inclusive settings and restricted access to the appropriate academic services. For example, some students who receive special education services receive limited preparation for college admissions and future employment (NASP, 2021; Proctor et al., 2012).

Specifically, studies frequently indicate that Black students are overidentified as having emotional disturbance and intellectual disabilities, whereas Indigenous students are overidentified as having learning disabilities. Conversely, Hispanic and Asian students often are disproportionately underidentified in most educational disability categories (Sullivan & Proctor, 2016). Unfortunately, years of research have suggested that Black students, in particular, often are identified in disability categories whose core criteria involve more subjective judgments (e.g., emotional disturbance, learning disabilities) rather than objective judgments (e.g., vision and hearing impairments; NASP, 2021; Sullivan & Proctor, 2016). To complicate matters further, when Black and Hispanic students are deemed eligible for special education services, they often are placed in more restrictive environments than their white peers (Sabnis & Proctor, 2022). Consequently, they may have less access to the general education curriculum and population.

In contrast, currently Black, Hispanic, and Indigenous students are underrepresented in gifted education in U.S. public schools. Black students make up just 10.33% of students enrolled in gifted and talented programs, despite representing 16% of the overall public-school student population. Additionally, Hispanic students constitute 18.75% of students enrolled in these programs, but make up 27% of students enrolled in public schools. Indigenous/Alaska Native students make up 1% of the total student population and 0.87% of those in gifted education programs (NCES, 2018). In light of the fact that Black and Hispanic students are enrolled in gifted programming at lower rates than they are enrolled in public schools altogether, it is clear that they are underrepresented in these programs. Conversely, white students (who, as noted previously, account for only 45% of the public school population) are overrepresented in gifted programs. The systematic underrepresentation of most groups of racially and ethnically minoritized students in gifted education is highly problematic, as these students are deprived of academic enrichment, a gateway to higher education classes, and preparation for college (Ford et al., 2016).

Discipline

Research indicates that racially and ethnically minoritized students are subject to more severe disciplinary practices for exhibiting similar or the same behaviors as their white, non-Hispanic peers. These disparate discipline practices (e.g., office disciplinary referrals, corporal punishment, and suspensions and expulsions) have been documented at the national level for American Indian/Alaska Native, Black, and Hispanic students (Blake et al., 2016; Gregory & Fergus, 2017; Skiba et al., 2011). Reliance on teacher, administrator, and school psychologists' subjective judgments about these behavioral infractions presents the opportunity for bias to be introduced in disciplinary procedures (Fergus, 2017; Skiba et al., 2011). Researchers have hypothesized that such bias occurs because of a cultural mismatch between majority white educators and ethnically and racially minoritized students (Fergus, 2017; Skiba et al., 2002, 2011).

For example, research indicates that many Black students are more likely to be disciplined for minor, subjective infractions classified as disruptive or insubordinate behavior (Skiba et al., 2002). Black students' suspension rates exceed their representation in the student population by twofold and for American Indian/Alaskan Native students, by fourfold (Blake et al., 2016). Researchers have also investigated other potential student variables (e.g., SES, disability status) that might relate to disparities in school-based discipline; however, they have found that these variables do not account for these differences (Blake et al., 2016). Thus, they have concluded that students' race is a significant predictor of overrepresentation in school-based discipline (Blake et al., 2016; Skiba et al., 2011).

National data indicate that disparate discipline practices along racial lines begin as early as pre-kindergarten. In 2017–2018, Black children made up 19.2% of all preschoolers but 43.3% of those receiving one or more out-of-school suspensions. Conversely, white children accounted for 43% of preschoolers but only 37% of those receiving one or more out-of-school suspensions (U.S. Department of Education, 2021). Although Black preschool girls were the only group of girls across all races and ethnicities with a disparity between enrollment rates and suspension rates, the percentage of Black male preschoolers receiving suspension was higher than that of Black preschool girls (U.S. Department of Education, 2021).

Disparate disciplinary practices constitute a major educational and social justice issue in U.S. public schools (Blake et al., 2016; Gregory & Fergus, 2017; NASP, 2021). These practices negatively impact individual students (e.g., loss of instructional time, academic failure, school dropout, involvement with juvenile justice system) as well as overall school climates (by rendering them less inviting, more alienating, and less welcoming and appreciative of racial diversity; NASP, 2021; Skiba et al., 2011).

SOCIAL JUSTICE CONNECTIONS

How can school psychologists work to eliminate racial disparities in student disciplinary practices?

As noted in this chapter, racial disparities in school-based disciplinary practices are alarming and undoubtedly call for urgent systems-level reform in schools. Clearly, traditional models of discipline that rely heavily on in-school and out-of-school suspension practices are ineffective approaches to fostering student success. What, then, are promising alternatives to these practices?

One such model is **school-based restorative justice** (SBRJ). Broadly defined, SBRJ is a systemic approach to discipline that engages all parties affected by a behavioral incident in proactive conflict resolution. The goals of SBRJ include teaching students to take

(continued)

> **SOCIAL JUSTICE CONNECTIONS (*continued*)**
>
> responsibility for their actions; fostering positive relationships among students, school personnel, and community members; and teaching alternatives to inappropriate and/or aggressive behaviors in an effort to prevent their recurrence. For example, one commonly employed mechanism of SBRJ is mediation. Through mediation, school psychologists and other educators can encourage students to consider questions such as the following (developed by Zehr, 2002, and recapitulated by Song & Swearer, 2016):
>
> 1. Who was harmed? What is the extent of the harm? (By contrast, a punitive approach asks which laws/rules were broken.)
> 2. What are the needs that gave rise to the event? (By contrast, a punitive approach asks who did it.)
> 3. How do we make this right? How do we ensure that harm is repaired, relationships are restored, and future harm is prevented? (By contrast, a punitive approach asks which punishments the perpetrator deserves; Song & Swearer, 2016, pp. 317–318)
>
> One reason that restorative justice may mitigate racial disparities in disciplinary practices is that it prevents disciplinary problems from escalating to the point of suspension, expulsion, and other severe consequences (which disproportionately impact racially minoritized youth). It also interrupts the harmful cycle of "offend, suspend, and reoffend" by helping students understand the consequences of their behaviors and encouraging them to engage in adaptive conflict resolution skills (von der Embse et al., 2009). For these reasons, SBRJ serves as a mechanism of both prevention and *intervention*.
>
> The implementation of SBRJ has been associated with a variety of positive student outcomes, including reductions in student suspensions and missed school days (e.g., Ashworth et al., 2008). Nevertheless, research on SBRJ practices is still emerging, and its implications for promoting racial justice have yet to be fully clarified. For example, Song and Swearer (2016) pose the following pressing questions regarding SBRJ:
>
>> Does RJ (restorative justice) need to incorporate practices that are explicit about race issues for it to be effective at promoting racial equity? Are there other benefits to being explicit about race that we have not thought about? What is compromised, if anything, when RJ is nonexplicit and indirect about race issues in schools? (p. 320)
>
> Answering each of these questions and others will be necessary for better understanding outcomes associated with SBRJ. Overall, these practices warrant further exploration and may be a promising alternative to traditional disciplinary practices.

Low Income and Economic Marginalization

LIEM is a broad conceptualization of poverty that incorporates many aspects of what it means to be economically oppressed, including limited access to financial resources and marginalization related to social class (APA, 2019). Living in circumstances of LIEM can also have a significant impact on the experiences and performance of diverse public school students (Barrett et al., 2019). This observation is particularly salient, as Black, Hispanic, American Indian/Alaska Native, and Native Hawaiian/Pacific Islander children are disproportionately represented in lower-income households (Irwin et al., 2021). For instance, students from lower-income backgrounds often begin school with less developed academic skills than their peers from middle- to upper-income backgrounds. As a result, opportunity gaps in achievement between these groups of students often persist throughout schooling (Albritton et al., 2016; Miranda, 2014; Proctor & Meyers, 2014). Regarding disciplinary outcomes, research findings documenting the experiences of students from LIEM backgrounds are less robust. Although students living in circumstances of LIEM are more likely to receive school-based discipline sanctions, research suggests that, even after controlling for SES, Black students are disciplined at a disproportionately higher rate as compared with students of other races (Skiba et al., 2011).

School Climate

Recent research has yielded concerning findings (e.g., increased levels of absenteeism, depression, and consideration of dropping out of school as well as lower self-esteem, grade-point average [GPA], and feelings of school belonging) regarding the experiences of students who identify as minoritized with respect to sex or gender (Kosciw et al., 2020). These findings are particularly relevant for LGBTQ students who attend unsafe schools in which they experience discrimination and victimization due to their sexual orientation and/or gender expression (Rivera et al., 2022). A national examination of the experiences of middle and high school students who identify as members of the LGBTQ community found that 68.7% experienced verbal harassment based on their sexual orientation, while 56.9% experienced verbal harassment based on their gender expression. Moreover, 25.7% and 21.8% were physically harassed due to sexual orientation and gender expression, respectively (Kosciw et al., 2020). Overall, 59.1% of the students sampled felt unsafe at school due to their sexual orientation, and 42.5% felt unsafe because of their gender expression. Results of this study also indicated that students who are ethnically or racially minoritized *and* sexually minoritized can face additional challenges. For instance, students of color who identified as LGBTQ reported higher frequencies of victimization (due to race) than white students who identified as LGBTQ (Kosciw et al., 2020). These findings underscore the salience of understanding how students' intersecting identities with respect to race, ethnicity, sexual orientation, and gender expression can affect their daily school experiences.

Unfortunately, research exploring school-based experiences of minoritized youth (including youth who are minoritized with respect to race, ethnicity, linguistic background, SES, gender, and sexual orientation) often engenders a deficit-oriented perspective rather than a strengths-based perspective (Baker & Rimm-Kaufman, 2014). In other words, these research findings are framed in a manner that attributes students' difficulties to within-person deficits, thereby de-emphasizing the contributions of environmental pressures and systemic obstacles. While the data presented here are certainly concerning, the intent is not to suggest that minoritized students have inherent deficits; in fact, they have a plethora of inherent strengths that enrich school environments. Rather, these data provide a foundation for understanding the variety of individual and systemic issues and injustices that minoritized students and their families may encounter in U.S. public schools. Ultimately, these issues highlight the need for multicultural and social justice perspectives to guide school psychological service delivery. Thus, the following section offers practice recommendations that are grounded in a multicultural and social justice–oriented approach.

RECOMMENDATIONS FOR ENHANCING MULTICULTURALISM AND SOCIAL JUSTICE IN SCHOOL PSYCHOLOGY PRACTICE

Develop Personal Awareness and Knowledge of Self as Intersectional

One of the first steps to implementing a multicultural framework is to acknowledge and understand one's own culture and recognize how it influences one's worldview (Miranda, 2014). It is also important to identify salient facets of one's identity (e.g., gender, gender identity, race, ethnicity, sexual orientation, religious affiliation) and the ways in which these facets intersect to influence one's view of the world (APA, 2017).

Self-examination with respect to cultural beliefs and worldview can be a difficult and arduous task. It involves, for example, considering one's own experiences with oppression and/or privilege. *Privilege* refers to the set of unearned benefits, advantages, and opportunities that are afforded to an individual simply due to their membership in a particular social group. In other words, while the oppression of some historically minoritized social groups (e.g., Indigenous populations) may be acknowledged, the corresponding advantages afforded to nonvictimized groups (e.g., white populations) typically go unrecognized. Generally, these privileges manifest in seemingly inconspicuous ways. Individuals from many types of social groups may hold privilege, including those who identify as white, cisgender, male, and heterosexual. In her seminal work, *White Privilege: Unpacking the Invisible Knapsack*, Peggy McIntosh (1989) provided numerous examples of white privilege. Writing from the perspective of a white person, McIntosh (1989) stated the following:

1. I can be sure that my children will be given curricular materials that testify to the existence of their race.
2. I am never asked to speak for all the people of my racial group.
3. I can take a job with an affirmative action employer without having coworkers on the job suspect that I got it because of race (p. 11).

While these privileges often go unrecognized on a daily basis, they play an important role in maintaining oppressive social structures and interpersonal dynamics that negatively impact the lives of those who are racially and ethnically minoritized.

Although a trying and, at times, daunting task, examining one's own experiences with oppression and privilege is key to becoming an effective school psychologist. This may be a challenge for some individuals who are not necessarily inclined to view themselves through an intersectional lens. Nevertheless, all humans possess personal identity features that influence their life experiences and the ways in which they make sense of the world. For example, most school psychologists identify as white and female. These two intersecting identities influence how many practitioners experience life in the United States (both inside and outside of schools) and can be associated with both privilege as a white person and, sometimes, oppression as a female.

How a white cisgender female school psychologist views the world is also influenced by other identity features, such as social class, religious affiliation, sexual orientation, immigration status, and so forth. Developing personal awareness of one's own identity features and how they intersect to influence personal assumptions, beliefs, and values can facilitate understanding of minoritized students and their experiences, perspectives, and behaviors. Gaining awareness and knowledge of self as an intersectional being requires self-reflection and can help school psychologists examine personal biases that might impact their service delivery, as described in the next section.

Identify and Challenge Biases

Although often difficult, and sometimes painful to admit, all people hold biases for and against certain groups. Such biases often arise as a result of our backgrounds, firmly held beliefs, life experiences, and exposure (or lack thereof) to those outside of our own groups. These biases have the potential to impede school psychologists' effective engagement with youth, families, and educators, thereby impacting the quality of services delivered. Moreover, harboring potential biases reduces the likelihood that the school psychologist will engage in advocacy behaviors at the systems level (e.g., school level). Personal biases can affect the way school psychologists approach virtually all job functions and areas of practice (e.g., disability identification, gifted identification, and disciplinary practices).

For instance, consider a school psychologist who is asked to provide counseling services to a student who identifies as bisexual. This school psychologist would need to critically examine any conscious or subconscious personal beliefs and/or biases about sexually minoritized youth, and in particular, bisexual youth. Using a multicultural approach to guide their practice, the school psychologist would attend to issues related to sexual orientation (if brought up and considered relevant by the student) and seek to understand how the student's experiences impact their overall well-being. In turn, the school psychologist would empower the individual to employ appropriate coping strategies, and when applicable, self-advocacy strategies. In considering the potentially larger social justice issues at play, the school psychologist should also advocate for school policies that seek to prevent victimization of and discrimination against LGBTQ students. Overall, identifying and challenging personal biases is an imperative and foundational step toward applying principles of multiculturalism and social justice.

Increase Knowledge of Minoritized Students and Multicultural Communities

School psychologists must also be knowledgeable about the challenges facing minoritized students and seek up-to-date information about educational and social issues that permeate school environments (Lopez & Bursztyn, 2013; Proctor & Meyers, 2014). This is important because it is difficult to provide culturally responsive school psychological services and/or to advocate for minoritized students without a clear understanding of issues that impact their access to quality educational experiences, safe school environments, and appropriate mental health supports. School psychologists can increase their knowledge about minoritized student groups by (a) attending professional development sessions focused on multicultural and minoritized populations at local and national conferences, (b) critically consuming current research about minoritized students and multicultural populations, and (c) seeking out community resources that enhance their multicultural knowledge (Newell et al., 2010). Notably, accessing local community resources can afford school psychologists invaluable insights into the cultural values, beliefs, and inherent strengths of the specific population(s) they serve. Further, Proctor and Meyers (2014) recommended that school psychologists join professional organizations that are dedicated to uplifting minoritized student populations (e.g., the National Black Child Development Institute), develop supportive networks with other professionals who are engaged in social justice work, and access resources (e.g., books, websites, videos) that address education and multicultural issues. Table 3.1 provides resources that may assist practitioners in increasing their knowledge of multicultural communities and minoritized student populations.

TABLE 3.1 Resources for Increasing Knowledge About Minoritized Student Populations

Name of Resource	Source	Content
Civil Rights Project at UCLA	civilrightsproject.ucla.edu	Effective educational practices for ELLs, long-term implications of U.S. demographic shifts, racial disparities in school discipline and special education
EdChange	www.edchange.org	Diversity awareness activities; diversity climate assessments for schools and organizations; journal articles, books, and essays on multicultural education and social justice
Gay, Lesbian, and Straight Education Network (GLSEN)	www.glsen.org	Research and evaluation on LGBTQ issues in K–12 education
National Center for Cultural Competence	www.nccc.georgetown.edu	Cultural competence checklists, cultural competence curricula for mental health providers, content related to specific subgroups
National Association of School Psychologists	www.nasponline.org	Information on minoritized students, social justice, disability rights, and school psychology roles and responsibilities
Southern Poverty Law Center	www.splcenter.org	Information on children at risk, immigrant justice, LGBTQ rights, and teaching tolerance

ELL, English Language Learner; LGBTQ, lesbian, gay, bisexual, transgender, and queer; UCLA, University of California, Los Angeles.

Share and Improve Skills Related to Working With Minoritized Students

School psychologists have a responsibility to enhance their skills in serving minoritized student populations and, when appropriate, to share these skills with other school professionals. For instance, school psychologists are sometimes called upon to help school-based problem-solving teams analyze and interpret school-wide data. In line with a social justice orientation, school psychologists participating in these teams can teach their colleagues how to examine data to determine whether educational injustices (e.g., racial disparities in discipline referrals) are present. If findings reveal that such disparities exist, school psychologists can share with staff skills they have developed in areas such as culturally responsive classroom management strategies, restorative justice practices (described in further detail in the *Social Justice Connections* section of this chapter), and collaborative problem-solving.

Engage in Social Justice Advocacy

Social justice advocacy involves working for and with marginalized populations to challenge institutional barriers and societal injustices (Linnemeyer et al., 2018). This often requires work at the local (i.e., school building) level. On a school-wide level, school psychologists can monitor school climate issues and work to make schools more welcoming and inclusive of minoritized students who experience schools as marginalizing spaces. For instance, school psychologists who serve schools with LGBTQ students can support the creation of a Gender and Sexuality Alliance (GSA) club. At the student level, school psychologists can advocate on behalf of LGBTQ students and other minoritized student populations to provide them—through trainings, for example—with skills to become self-advocates. School psychologists can also aim advocacy efforts at the systems level by working individually or collaboratively with others to eradicate institutional barriers that oppress and marginalize specific student demographics. For example, school psychologists can review special programming (e.g., special education and gifted education) referral and placement processes to determine whether disparities along racial, ethnic, and/or gender lines exist. When these disparities do exist, school psychologists can work with administrators to revise school-based policies that encourage fairness and justice for students. As Malone and Proctor (2019) noted, there are multiple entry points to social justice advocacy that provide opportunities for school psychologists to enact change within their spheres of influence.

The development of multicultural competence is a lifelong pursuit (Miranda et al., 2014), so school psychologists should continually strive to improve their own skills in serving minoritized students from multicultural backgrounds. In addition to employing the strategies described in the preceding text, school psychologists can seek consultation from other professionals who have expertise in working with particular populations. When and if it becomes apparent that school-wide professional development is needed, school psychologists can work with administrators to coordinate such activities.

SUMMARY AND CONCLUSIONS

In conclusion, school psychologists should consider diversity in all aspects of their service delivery. The use of multicultural and social justice frameworks provides a practice foundation for engaging minoritized clients. The ever-increasing diversity of the U.S. population necessitates school psychologists' critical attention to providing culturally relevant, competent, responsive, and effective school-based service delivery to minoritized children, families, and communities.

DISCUSSION QUESTIONS

1. How has the historical underrepresentation and exclusion of school psychologists with minoritized identities (e.g., race, ethnicity, ELLs) impacted the field?
2. What are some of the challenges minoritized students experience in U.S. public schools? How does oppression play out for minoritized students in U.S. public schools when their intersecting identities are taken into account?
3. How does the use of multiculturalism guide school psychologists' service delivery to minoritized students?
4. If you were a school psychologist, what are some of your intersecting identities that might influence, either positively or negatively, your service delivery to minoritized students? How might these identities influence your practice?
5. What are some actions school psychologists can take to increase their knowledge of and skills in working with minoritized student populations? How might school psychologists advocate for minoritized students?

RECOMMENDED READINGS

Jimerson, S. R., Arora, P., Blake, J. J., Canivez, G. L., Espelage, D. L., Gonzalez, J. E., Graves, S. L., Huang, F. L., January, S. A., Renshaw, T. L., Song, S. Y., Sullivan, A. L., Wang, C., & Worrell, F. C. (2021). Advancing diversity, equity, and inclusion in school psychology: Be the change. *School Psychology Review, 50*(1), 1–7. https://doi.org/10.1080/2372966X.2021.1889938

Malone, C. M., & Ishmail, K. Z. (2020). A snapshot of multicultural training in school psychology. *Psychology in the Schools, 57*(7), 1022–1039. https://doi.org/10.1002/pits.22392

Naser, S. C., Verlenden, J., Arora, P. G., Nastasi, B., Braun, L., & Smith, R. (2020). Using child rights education to infuse a social justice framework into universal programming. *School Psychology International, 41*(1), 13–36. https://doi.org/10.1177/0143034319894363

Proctor, S. L. (2020). Intersectionality as a prism for situating social justice at the intersection of marginalization and discrimination. *Communiqué, 49*(1), 30–32. https://www.nasponline.org/publications/periodicals/communique/issues/volume-49-issue-1

Proctor, S. L., & Rivera, D. P. (Eds.). (2022). *Critical theories for school psychology and counseling: A foundation for equity and inclusion in school-based practice*. Routledge.

A robust set of instructor resources designed to supplement this text is located at http://connect.springerpub.com/content/book/978-0-8261-6344-8. Qualifying instructors may request access by emailing textbook@springerpub.com.

REFERENCES

Albritton, K., Anhalt, K., & Terry, N. P. (2016). Promoting equity for our nation's youngest students: School psychologists as agents of social justice in early childhood settings. *School Psychology Forum: Research in Practice, 10*, 237–250. http://www.nasponline.org/publications/periodicals/spf/volume-10/volume-10-issue-3-(fall-2016)/promoting-equity-for-our-nations-youngest-students-school-psychologists-as-agents-of-social-justice-in-early-childhood-settings

American Psychological Association. (2019). *Guidelines for psychological practice for people with low-income and economic marginalization*. http://apacustomout.apa.org/commentPracGuidelines/Practice/LIEM_Guidelines.pdf

American Psychological Association. (2017). *Multicultural guidelines: An ecological approach to context, identity, and intersectionality*. http://www.apa.org/about/policy/multicultural-guidelines.pdf

Ashworth, J., Van Bockern, S., Ailts, J., Donelly, J., Erickson, K., & Woltermann, J. (2008). The National Restorative Justice Center: An alternative to school detention. *Reclaiming Children and Youth, 17*(3), 22–26. https://reclaimingjournal.com/node/89

Baker, C. E., & Rimm-Kaufman, S. E. (2014). How homes influence schools: Early parenting predicts African American children's classroom social–emotional functioning. *Psychology in the Schools, 51*(7), 722–735. https://doi.org/10.1002/pits.21781

Banks, J. A. (2010). Multicultural education: Characteristics and goals. In J. A. Banks & C. A. M. Banks (Eds.), *Multicultural education: Issues and perspective* (5th ed., pp. 3–26). Wiley.

Barrett, C., Kendrick-Dunn, T., & Proctor, S. L. (2019). Low-income and economic marginalization as a matter of social justice: Foundational knowledge. *Communiqué, 48*(2), 21–22. https://www.nasponline.org/publications/periodicals/communique/issues/volume-48-issue-2

Blake, J. J., Gregory, A., James, M., & Hasan, G. W. (2016). Early warning signs: Identifying opportunities to disrupt racial inequities in school discipline through data-based decision making. *School Psychology Forum: Research in Practice, 10*, 289–306. https://www.nasponline.org/publications/periodicals/spf/volume-10/volume-10-issue-3-(fall-2016)/early-warning-signs-identifying-opportunities-to-disrupt-racial-inequities-in-school-discipline-through-data-based-decision-making

Carroll, D. W. (2009). Toward multicultural competence: A practical model for implementation in the schools. In J. M. Jones (Ed.), *The psychology of multiculturalism in schools* (pp. 1–16). National Association of School Psychologists.

Castillo, J. M., Curtis, M. J., & Gelley, C. D. (2013). Gender and race in school psychology. *School Psychology Review*, 42(3), 262–279. https://doi.org/10.1080/02796015.2013.12087473

Centers for Disease Control and Prevention. (2020, August 20). *Youth risk behavior survey (YRBS)*. Retrieved April 1, 2021, from https://www.cdc.gov/healthyyouth/data/yrbs/feature

Crenshaw, K. (1989). Demarginalizing the intersection of race and sex: A Black feminist critique of antidiscrimination doctrine, feminist theory and antiracist politics. *University of Chicago Legal Forum*, 1989(1), 139–167. https://chicagounbound.uchicago.edu/uclf/vol1989/iss1/8

Curtis, M. J., Castillo, J. M., & Gelley, C. (2012). School psychology 2010: Demographics, employment, and the context for professional practice—Part 1. *Communiqué*, 40(7), 28–30. https://www.nasponline.org/publications/periodicals/communique/issues/volume-40-issue-7

Farmer, R. L., Goforth, A. N., Kim, S. Y., Naser, S. C., Lockwood, A. B., & Affrunti, N. W. (2021). Status of school psychology in 2020, Part 2: Professional practices in the NASP Membership Survey. *NASP Research Reports*, 5(3). https://www.nasponline.org/Documents/Research%20and%20Policy/Research%20Center/RR_NASP-2020-Membership-Survey-part-2.pdf

Fergus, E. (2017). *Solving disproportionality and achieving equity: A leader's guide to using data to change hearts and minds*. Corwin Press.

Ford, D. Y., Wright, B. L., Washington, A., & Henfield, M. S. (2016). Access and equity denied: Key theories for school psychologists to consider when assessing Black and Hispanic students for gifted education. *School Psychology Forum: Research in Practice*, 10(3), 265–277. https://www.researchgate.net/publication/312121099_Access_and_Equity_Denied_Key_Theories_for_School_Psychologists_to_Consider_When_Assessing_Black_and_Hispanic_Students_for_Gifted_Education

Goforth, A. N., Farmer, R. L., Kim, S. Y., Naser, S. C., Lockwood, A. B., & Affrunti, N. W. (2021). Status of school psychology in 2020: Part 1, Demographics of the NASP Membership Survey. *NASP Research Reports*, 5(2). https://www.nasponline.org/Documents/Research%20and%20Policy/Research%20Center/NRR_2020-Membership-Survey-P1.pdf

Gregory, A., & Fergus, E. (2017). Social and emotional learning and equity in school discipline. *Future of Children*, 27(1), 117–136. https://doi.org/10.1353/foc.2017.0006

Hakuta, K. (2011). Educating language minority students and affirming their equal rights: Research and practical perspectives. *Educational Researcher*, 40(4), 163–174. https://doi.org/10.3102/0013189X11404943

Harris, J. N. (2022). When they don't see us: Using intersectionality to examine the discipline experiences of Black girls. In S. L. Proctor & D. P. Rivera (Eds.), *Critical theories for school psychology and counseling: A foundation for equity and inclusion in school-based practice* (pp. 83–100). Routledge.

Herman, J. L., Flores, A. R., Brown, T. N. T., Wilson, B. D. M., & Conron, K. J. (2017). *Age of individuals who identify as transgender in the United States*. The Williams Institute.

Irwin, V., Zhang, J., Wang, X., Hein, S., Wang, K., Roberts, A., York, C., Barmer, A., Bullock Mann, F., Dilig, R., & Parker, S. (2021). *Report on the condition of education 2021* (NCES2021-144). U.S. Department of Education, National Center for Education Statistics. https://nces.ed.gov/pubs2021/2021144.pdf

Kosciw, J. G., Clark, C. M., Truong, T. L., & Zongrone, A. D. (2020). *The 2020 national school climate survey: The experiences of lesbian, gay, bisexual, transgender, and queer youth in our nation's schools*. GLSEN. https://www.glsen.org/research/2019-national-school-climate-survey

Linnemeyer, R. M., Nilsson, J. E., Marszalek, J. M., & Khan, M. (2018). Social justice advocacy among doctoral students in professional psychology programs. *Counselling Psychology Quarterly*, 31(1), 98–116. https://doi.org/10.1080/09515070.2016.1274961

Lopez, E. C., & Bursztyn, A. M. (2013). Future challenges and opportunities: Toward culturally responsive training in school psychology. *Psychology in the Schools*, 50(3), 212–228. https://doi.org/10.1002/pits.21674

Malone, C. M., & Proctor, S. L. (2019). Demystifying social justice for school psychology practice. *Communiqué*, 48(1), 21–23. https://www.nasponline.org/publications/periodicals/communique/issues/volume-48-issue-1

McIntosh, P. (1989). White privilege: Unpacking the invisible knapsack. *Peace and Freedom*, 10–12. https://psychology.umbc.edu/wp-content/uploads/sites/57/2016/10/White-Privilege_McIntosh-1989.pdf

Miranda, A. H. (2014). Best practices in increasing cross-cultural competency. In P. Harrison & A. Thomas (Eds.), *Best practices in school psychology: Foundations* (pp. 9–19). National Association of School Psychologists.

Miranda, A. H., & Gutter, P. B. (2002). Diversity research literature in school psychology: 1990–1999. *Psychology in the Schools, 39*(5), 597–604. https://doi.org/10.1002/pits.10051

Miranda, A. H., Radliff, K. M., Cooper, J. M., & Eschenbrenner, C. R. (2014). Graduate student perceptions of the impact of training for social justice: Development of a training model. *Psychology in the Schools, 51*(4), 348–365. https://doi.org/10.1002/pits.21755

National Association of School Psychologists. (2021). *Promoting just special education identification and school discipline practices* [Position statement]. https://www.nasponline.org/Documents/Research%20and%20Policy/Position%20Statements/PS_Just-Special-Ed-Identification-and-School-%20Discipline.pdf

National Center for Education Statistics. (n.d.-a). *NAEP report card: Mathematics: National average scores*. U.S. Department of Education, National Center for Education Statistics. https://www.nationsreportcard.gov/mathematics/nation/scores/?grade=4

National Center for Education Statistics. (n.d.-b). *NAEP report card: Reading: National achievement-level results*. U.S. Department of Education, National Center for Education Statistics. https://www.nationsreportcard.gov/reading/nation/achievement?grade=4

National Center for Education Statistics. (2018). *Number of public school students enrolled in gifted and talented programs, by sex, race/ethnicity, and state: Selected years, 2004 through 2013–14*. U.S. Department of Education, National Center for Education Statistics. https://nces.ed.gov/programs/digest/d19/tables/dt19_204.80.asp

National Center for Education Statistics. (2020, September). *Enrollment and percentage distribution of enrollment in public elementary and secondary schools, by race/ethnicity and region: Selected years, fall 1995 through fall 2029*. U.S. Department of Education, National Center for Education Statistics. https://nces.ed.gov/programs/digest/d20/tables/dt20_203.50.asp

Newell, M. L., Nastasi, B. K., Hatzichristou, C., Jones, J. M., Schanding, G. T., Jr., & Yetter, G. (2010). Evidence on multicultural training in school psychology: Recommendations for future directions. *School Psychology Quarterly, 25*(4), 249–278. https://doi.org/10.1037/a0021542

Parker, J. S., Castillo, J. M., Sabnis, S., Daye, J., & Hanson, P. (2020). Culturally responsive consultation among practicing school psychologists. *Journal of Educational and Psychological Consultation, 30*(2), 119–155. https://doi.org/10.1080/10474412.2019.1680293

Pew Forum on Religion & Public Life. (2014). *U.S. religious landscape survey*. Pew Research Center. https://www.pewresearch.org/religion/religious-landscape-study

Proctor, S. L. (2022). From Beckham until now: Recruiting, retaining, and including Black people and Black thought in school psychology. *School Psychology International, 43*(6), 545–559. https://doi.org/10.1177/01430343211066016

Proctor, S. L., Graves, S. L., Jr., & Esch, R. C. (2012). Assessing African American students for specific learning disabilities: The promises and perils of response to intervention. *Journal of Negro Education, 81*(3), 268–282. https://doi.org/10.7709/jnegroeducation.81.3.0268

Proctor, S. L., & Meyers, J. (2014). Best practices in primary prevention in diverse schools and communities. In P. Harrison & A. Thomas (Eds.), *Best practices in school psychology: Foundations* (pp. 33–47). National Association of School Psychologists.

Proctor, S. L., & Romano, M. (2016). School psychology recruitment research characteristics and implications for increasing racial and ethnic diversity. *School Psychology Quarterly, 31*(3), 311–326. https://doi.org/10.1037/spq0000154

Proctor, S. L., & Simpson, C. (2016). Improving service delivery to ethnic minority youth through improved program training. In S. L. Graves & J. Blake (Eds.), *Psychoeducational assessment and intervention for ethnic minority children: Evidence-based approaches* (pp. 251–265). American Psychological Association.

Proctor, S. L., & Truscott, S. D. (2012). Reasons for African American student attrition from school psychology programs. *Journal of School Psychology, 50*(5), 655–679. https://doi.org/10.1016/j.jsp.2012.06.002

Rivera, D. P., Proctor, S. L., Chen, Y.-C. C., & Gershon, P. (2022). Queer theory and school-based counseling for LGBTQ students. In S. L. Proctor & D. P. Rivera (Eds.), *Critical theories for school psychology and counseling: A foundation for equity and inclusion in school-based practice* (pp. 132–143). Routledge.

Sabnis, S. V., & Proctor, S. L. (2022). Use of critical theory to develop a conceptual framework for critical school psychology. *School Psychology Review, 51*(6), 661–675. https://doi.org/10.1080/2372966X.2021.1949248

Shriberg, D., Bonner, M., Sarr, B. J., Walker, A. M., Hyland, M., & Chester, C. (2008). Social justice through a school psychology lens: Definition and applications. *School Psychology Review, 37*(4), 453–468. https://doi.org/10.1080/02796015.2008.12087860

Skiba, R. J., Horner, R. H., Chung, C.-G., Rausch, M. K., May, S. L., & Tobin, T. (2011). Race is not neutral: A national investigation of African American and Latino disproportionality in school discipline. *School Psychology Review, 40*(1), 85–107. https://doi.org/10.1080/02796015.2011.12087730

Skiba, R. J., Michael, R. S., Nardo, A. C., & Peterson, R. L. (2002). The color of discipline: Sources of racial and gender disproportionality in school punishment. *Urban Review, 34*(4), 317–342. https://doi.org/10.1023/A:1021320817372

Song, S. Y., & Swearer, S. M. (2016). The cart before the horse: The challenge and promise of restorative justice consultation in schools. *Journal of Educational and Psychological Consultation, 26*(4), 313–324. https://doi.org/10.1080/10474412.2016.1246972

Speight, S. L., & Vera, E. M. (2009). The challenge of social justice for school psychology. *Journal of Educational and Psychological Consultation, 19*(1), 82–92. https://doi.org/10.1080/10474410802463338

Sullivan, A., & Proctor, S. L. (2016). The shield or the sword? Revisiting the debate on disproportionality in special education and implications for school psychologists. *School Psychology Forum: Research in Practice, 10*, 278–288. http://www.nasponline.org/publications/periodicals/spf/volume-10/volume-10-issue-3-(fall-2016)/the-shield-or-the-sword-revisiting-the-debate-on-racial-disproportionality-in-special-education-and-implications-for-school-psychologists

U.S. Department of Education. (2021). *An overview of exclusionary discipline practices in public schools for the 2017–18 school year.* https://www2.ed.gov/about/offices/list/ocr/docs/crdc-exclusionary-school-discipline.pdf

von der Embse, N., von der Embse, D., von der Embse, M., & Levine, I. (2009). Applying social justice principles through school-based restorative justice. *Communiqué, 38*(3), 18–19. https://www.nasponline.org/publications/periodicals/communique/issues/volume-38-issue-3

Welner, K. G., & Carter, P. L. (2013). Achievement gaps arise from opportunity gaps. In P. L. Carter & K. G. Welner (Eds.), *Closing the opportunity gap: What America must do to give every child an even chance* (pp. 1–10). Oxford University Press.

Zehr, H. (2002). *The little book of restorative justice.* Good Books.

CHAPTER 4

Antiracism and School Psychology

PRERNA G. ARORA ■ CELESTE M. MALONE ■
OLIVIA KHOO ■ TENISHA S. JONES

CHAPTER OBJECTIVES

After reading this chapter, you will be able to:

- Define *racism*.
- Describe the impact of racism on youth within the United States.
- Describe the role of racism in the field of school psychology.
- Describe antiracism efforts within the field of school psychology.

NATIONAL ASSOCIATION OF SCHOOL PSYCHOLOGISTS PRACTICE MODEL CONNECTIONS

Domain 8: Equitable Practices for Diverse Student Populations

INTRODUCTION

The United States has become an increasingly diverse society. Compared to 2010, the 2020 U.S. Census revealed that the population of racially/ethnically minoritized (REM) individuals grew considerably, with the categories of Black/African Americans growing by 5.6%, Hispanic/Latinos by 23%, Native Hawaiian/Other Pacific Islanders by 27.8%, Asian/Asian Americans by 35.5%, and American Indian/Alaska Natives by 160% within the last decade (U.S. Census Bureau, 2021). Moreover, the percentage of people who identified as "some other race" or multiple races accounted for 15.1% and 10.2% of the population, respectively, in 2020 (U.S. Census Bureau, 2021), underscoring the growing heterogeneity of the U.S. population in the past decade. These populations have been disproportionally impacted by disease, including diabetes, obesity, and asthma (National Center for Health Statistics, 2018); experience higher rates of mental health concerns (Miranda et al., 2008); and generally achieve poorer educational outcomes (Bohrnstedt et al., 2015) than their majority peers. Racism is a critical risk factor leading to these disparities, preventing many Americans from attaining their highest levels of health (Williams et al., 2019).

This chapter provides an overview of racism, including its definition, its impact on youth, and its connections to the field of school psychology. Further, it discusses critical antiracism efforts within the field to promote the health and well-being of the nation's most marginalized youth.

OVERVIEW OF RACISM

While varying definitions of *racism* exist (Paradies, 2006a), **racism** has been broadly defined as individual, structural, political, economic, and social forces that serve to discriminate against and disadvantage people of color based on their race for the purpose of maintaining white supremacy (Bell, 1992). The American Psychological Association (APA; 2021) has defined racism as a system of differential valuation of individuals based on phenotypic characteristics (e.g., skin color, hair texture) through interpersonal interactions or unequal access to educational, employment, or housing opportunities, whereby individuals belonging to marginalized racial groups are discriminated against and unfairly disadvantaged as compared to those from dominant racial groups.

To provide a structure to understand and operationalize racism, several characteristics of racism have been described, including its modes, forms, expressions, settings, perpetrators, and targets (Paradies, 2006b). First, modes of racism can be interracial or intraracial. Interracial racism occurs between actors of different races, whereas intraracial racism occurs between actors of the same race (Paradies, 2006b). Racism can also exist in a variety of forms, including (a) legal or illegal, (b) direct or indirect, (c) overt or covert, (d) blatant or subtle, and (e) intentional or unintentional, and through (f) action or inaction (Harrell, 2000; Krieger, 1999). Additionally, racism can be expressed through stereotypes (i.e., beliefs or cognitions), prejudice (i.e., emotions or affect), or discrimination (i.e., behaviors or actions; Jones, 2000). These expressions of racism can also occur in various settings, such as in educational, employment, media, justice, political, housing, health, recreational, or public settings (Krieger, 1999). Perpetrators and targets of racism may include the self, family, friends, acquaintances, employers, peers, strangers, officials, practices, policies, and laws, among many others (Paradies, 2006b).

Additionally, racism can occur on three distinct levels: (a) systemic/structural/institutionalized, (b) interpersonal/individual/personally mediated, and (c) internalized/intrapersonal (Harrell, 2000; Jones, 2000; Pincus, 1996). Definitions and examples of each of these levels are provided in Table 4.1. **Systemic racism** is defined as racism that is deeply embedded in and throughout systems, laws, policies, and practices that perpetuate prejudice or discrimination, as well as social inequities on a larger scale (Bailey et al., 2017). Though *systemic racism* and *structural racism* are often used interchangeably, systemic racism typically emphasizes the role of whole systems (e.g., education, healthcare), whereas structural racism emphasizes the laws, policies, or norms embedded within such systems (Bonilla-Silva, 1997).

Interpersonal racism is characterized by racist interactions between individuals in day-to-day interpersonal experiences (Essed, 2002). It reflects prejudice (i.e., irrational, negative assumptions about individuals from a specific social group; Friske et al., 2010) and discrimination (i.e., unjust treatment of people due to their legitimate or perceived group membership) imposed on racial groups by individuals or groups (Leventhal et al., 2018). REM youth who are victims of interpersonal racism have been found to experience higher rates of substance use, depression, and attention deficit hyperactivity disorder (ADHD) symptoms (Leventhal et al., 2018). Thus, interpersonal racism can result in detrimental effects on the behavioral and mental health outcomes of REM youth.

TABLE 4.1 Three Levels of Racism and Examples

Level of Racism	Examples
Systemic/structural/institutionalized	• Less insurance coverage (Alegria et al., 2015) • Greater transportation challenges (Alegria et al., 2015) • Limited availability of linguistically appropriate services (Alegria et al., 2015) • Limited availability of culturally competent mental health providers (Alegria et al., 2015)
Interpersonal/individual/personally mediated	• Verbal or physical attacks (Tynes et al., 2008) • Secondhand exposure to verbal or physical violence through in-person or virtual sources (Heard-Garris et al., 2018) • Lack of respect (e.g., provided poor service or denied service; Jones, 2000) • Suspicion (e.g., being met with increased vigilance or avoidance, such as street crossing and purse clutching; Jones, 2000) • Devaluation (e.g., expression of surprise at an individual's competence; Jones, 2000) • Scapegoating (e.g., blame for societal problems or crises, such as the coronavirus 2019 pandemic; Vasquez, 2020) • Dehumanization (e.g., police brutality, sterilization abuse, hate crimes; Jones, 2000) • Microaggressions (Sue et al., 2007)
Internalized/intrapersonal	• Embracing white norms of appearance as one's own standard of beauty (e.g., use of hair straighteners or face-lightening creams; Jones, 2000) • Self-devaluation (e.g., accepting racial slurs as nicknames, rejecting one's own culture; Jones, 2000) • Hopelessness (e.g., dropping out of school, failing to vote, engaging in risky health practices; Jones, 2000)

Internalized racism has been conceptualized as the acceptance of negative stereotypes about one's own racial or ethnic group (Cross, 1971); it also refers to the acceptance of prejudice toward one's own racial group by embracing the values and norms of the oppressive racial group (Pérez Huber et al., 2006). Bivens (1995) defined internalized racism as the support given by oppressed racial groups for maintaining attitudes, behaviors, social structures, and ideologies that privilege dominant racial groups. Internalized racism is also well encapsulated by the following definition: "the individual inculcation of the racist stereotypes, values, images, and ideologies perpetuated by the white dominant society about one's racial group, leading to feelings of self-doubt, disgust, and disrespect for one's race and/or oneself" (Pyke, 2010, p. 553).

RACISM IN K–12 EDUCATION

Systemic Racism in K–12 Schools

The education system within the United States has been identified as an oppressive institution that maintains the racial hierarchy of white supremacy (X & Haley, 1965). Prior to the

Supreme Court ruling in *Brown v. Board of Education* (1954; which, as described in Chapter 2, mandated school desegregation), racism in pre-K–12 schooling was exemplified by overtly discriminatory policies and practices. Though civil rights activism and subsequent legislation ultimately led to the desegregation of U.S. schools, experiences of racism within these schools remained. Specifically, numerous schools serving REM youth were closed, and REM youth were bussed to schools serving primarily white youth. This one-way school integration occurred due to the racist belief that schools serving REM communities were inferior, leaving mostly white teachers to educate REM youth (Bell, 2004). Further, schools that continued to predominantly serve REM youth were characterized by higher rates of unqualified teachers whose teaching styles were not culturally relevant to these youth (Delpit, 2006). Presently, racism is believed to persist in U.S. schools in a variety of ways at the systemic level, including (a) disproportionalities in special education placements; (b) inequitable access to quality instruction, educational facilities, and materials; and (c) the school-to-prison pipeline.

Disproportionality in Special Education

Disproportionality in special education services has been defined as the extent to which membership in a given group differentially affects the probability of being classified as having a disability and placed in special education services (Oswald et al., 1999). Disproportionality has been documented since the 1960s, at which time approximately 60% to 80% of students identified as having a disability were from REM households (Dunn, 1968). Since then, research has shown that Black students are overidentified as having emotional disturbances and intellectual disabilities; moreover, Native American students are overidentified with learning disabilities (Sullivan & Artiles, 2011), and Asian and Latinx students are underidentified in most disability categories (Sullivan et al., 2020). Although many consider special education to be a way for students from historically marginalized groups to access equitable education, the "paradox of special education" is that it also stigmatizes children from these groups and subjects them to curricula that further promote perceptions of inferiority because of lowered expectations (Donovan & Cross, 2002; Sullivan et al., 2008). Certainly, the disproportionate representation of REM youth promotes racialized ideas that these students are outsiders and perform at a lower standard (Pérez Huber, 2011). Given the misrepresentation of children from REM, immigrant, and low-income households in special education classrooms, special education is believed to result in further segregation, greater social stigma, higher dropout rates, and lower academic performance (Blanchett, 2006; Ferri & Connor, 2005).

Inequitable Access to Quality Instruction

Another way that racism persists in the education system is through inequitable access to quality instruction, educational facilities, and quality curriculum (Darling-Hammond, 2004). In one study of nationally representative data from the Early Childhood Longitudinal Study, researchers found that students who identified as Black, Hispanic, or Asian were more likely to attend schools characterized by scarce resources compared to non-Hispanic white students (Hibel et al., 2010). Further, data have shown that schools with predominantly REM youth spent $733 less per student than schools with predominantly white students (Spatig-Amerikaner, 2012). Findings on student–teacher ratios have also revealed that REM students are more likely to attend classes with 40 or more students, with Black students being three times as likely as white peers to be in large classrooms (Jacob et al., 2016). Additionally, schools with higher numbers of REM students were more likely to have teachers with lower levels of educational attainment and professional certification compared to schools with higher proportions of white students (Aud et al., 2010).

Given these findings, it is not surprising that REM students continue to face disparities in academic achievement compared to their white counterparts (National Center for Education Statistics [NCES], 2021). This disparity is typically referred to as the "achievement gap"; however, it is more accurately described as an "opportunity gap." According to the NCES (2019), REM students performed significantly poorer on standardized measures than non-Hispanic white students. Specifically, data from the NCES (2019) revealed that the achievement disparity between white and Black students in reading was 26 points and 25 points for fourth- and eighth-graders, respectively, while the white–Hispanic gap was 23 points and 19 points for fourth- and eighth-graders, respectively. Similarly, in regard to mathematics achievement, the differences in scores between white and Black students in fourth and eighth grades were 25 points and 32 points, respectively, while white and Hispanic students at fourth and eighth grades were similarly disparate at 19 points and 24 points, respectively. Overall, lower-resourced schools serving predominantly REM youth are more likely to have higher teacher–student ratios and lower-quality instruction, which in turn contribute to widening the racial opportunity gap and achievement disparities.

SCHOOL-TO-PRISON PIPELINE

Racism also presents in schools via zero-tolerance approaches that contribute to the "school-to-prison pipeline." This phenomenon can be described as the culmination of punitive treatment in schools, poor instruction, low academic achievement, restrictive special education placements, and repeated suspensions or expulsions that characterize many REM youth's school experiences and ultimately end in incarceration (Wald & Losen, 2003). Although federal civil rights laws prohibit discriminatory disciplinary measures in schools, data from the U.S. Government Accountability Office (Nowicki, 2018) and U.S. Department of Education (2016) have found that Black and American Indian students are overrepresented in student suspensions. For instance, Black children in grades K–12 are three times more likely to receive out-of-school suspension and 1.9 times more likely to be expelled than white students (U.S. Department of Education, 2016). Other data have shown that Black and Hispanic students are more likely to receive disciplinary removals (i.e., suspensions, expulsion) from schools than other groups of students (Bacher-Hicks et al., 2021; Office of Special Education Programs, 2021). Additionally, data from the NCES (2019) further showed that Black students had the highest suspension rate (13.7%), followed by Native Americans (6.7%), students of two or more races (5.3%), Hispanics (4.5%), and Pacific Islanders (4.5%). Meanwhile, only 3.4% of white students and 1.1% of Asian students experienced out-of-school suspensions in the same year (NCES, 2019).

REM students who attend schools with high suspension and expulsion rates are more likely to be held back a grade or drop out of high school (Fabelo et al., 2011), less likely to attend college, and more likely to experience future employment instability (Skiba et al., 2014). Additionally, these students may also be at risk of being arrested or repeatedly incarcerated as adults (Bacher-Hicks et al., 2021). Indeed, REM students are more likely to prematurely drop out of high school and/or experience practices that push students out of school compared to white students; specifically, Hispanic students ages 16 to 24 experience the highest likelihood of dropping out of high school (9%), followed by Black (6%) and white (5%) students (NCES, 2019). In sum, punitive disciplinary policies in schools exacerbate the rate at which disproportionate numbers of REM students face recurring suspensions and higher dropout (or "push-out") rates, which then lead to higher rates of future employment instability and repeated incarcerations.

Interpersonal Racism in K–12 Schools

In addition to systemic racism, REM youth in U.S. schools experience interpersonal racism in several ways, ranging from directly racist language (Graham & Erwin, 2011) to more subtle communications, such as racial microaggressions (i.e., statements or actions that communicate hostile, derogatory, or negative racial insults toward REM groups; Sue et al., 2007). Interpersonal racism experienced in the school setting may include instances of teacher bias against REM youth, such as lower expectations for graduating high school (Gershenson et al., 2016) or mispronouncing REM youth's names (Kohli & Solórzano, 2012). For instance, Black youth have been found to be more likely to receive worse ratings on behavior assessments from non-Hispanic white teachers than from Black teachers (Bates & Glick, 2013). Other research has demonstrated that non-Black teachers are more likely than Black teachers to predict that Black students will not finish high school (Gershenson et al., 2016). Indeed, teachers are highly likely to hold pro-white or anti-Black implicit racial bias (Starck et al., 2020). In contrast, overestimating the abilities of REM youth based on the model minority myth (i.e., the belief that Asian students are more successful and emotionally stable than students from other REM groups; Osajima, 2000) can also lead to harmful effects, as teachers may be less likely to acknowledge Asian Americans' academic challenges or needs and thus be less likely to identify them for special education services when appropriate (Empleo, 2006).

In general, studies show that the cumulative impact of racial microaggressions results in feelings of invisibility, devaluation, and interracial conflict, which can have a lasting and damaging effect on the self-perceptions of students (Allen, 2010). A sense of threat from teachers and peers may also cause REM youth to feel less connected to their school communities, thereby leading to higher truancy and lower graduation rates (McNulty & Bellair, 2003). Thus, interpersonal racism can be detrimental to the resilience and engagement of REM youth in schools.

Internalized Racism in K–12 Schools

Relative to research on systemic or interpersonal racism, fewer studies have examined internalized racism in schools (Kohli, 2008; Pérez Huber et al., 2006). Studies on REM adults suggest that those who experience greater systemic or interpersonal racism or are exposed to negative messages about their own race are more likely to exhibit higher levels of internalized racism (Graham et al., 2016). REM adults may also be less likely to agree that racism exists when they experience higher levels of internalized racism (Neville et al., 2005). Among the few studies that have investigated the impact of internalized racism, the results have shown that it significantly increases stereotype-confirming behaviors or intraracial hostility among REM youth (Bryant, 2011; Hwang, 2016). For instance, young Black males who self-reported higher rates of internalized racism had a higher likelihood of living in poverty, using drugs, and carrying a weapon (Bryant, 2011). Further, Asian youth who feel pressured to assimilate and give up their ethnic identity have been found to be more likely to victimize their less acculturated counterparts (Hwang, 2016).

Racism and Intersectionality in Schools

Certainly, the academic, behavioral, emotional, and social well-being of individuals cannot be fully understood considering race alone, as this approach does not account for the interlocking ways in which discrimination is experienced by members of multiple minoritized groups (Crenshaw, 1989). As described in Chapter 3, the intersection of students' multiple identities within social categories, such as ability, citizenship, class, culture, gender, gender identity, language, race, religion, and sexual orientation, and their interaction within academic and social settings must be considered (Proctor et al., 2017). Coupled with other common types of prejudice and discrimination against nondominant groups (e.g., classism, homophobia, sexism, xenophobia, etc.), intersectionality underscores the ways in which various social categories are experienced simultaneously and the additive or compounding effects of these experiences on individuals' outcomes (Cole, 2009). For instance, students who are Black and female are more likely to be suspended and expelled due to behaviors that both reinforce negative stereotypes about Black students and oppose traditional standards of femininity, thus illustrating the intersecting role of race and gender in informing disciplinary actions (Crenshaw et al., 2015). In sum, racism in K–12 education can only fully be understood and addressed when the intersection of students' multiple identities is considered.

RACISM AND SCHOOL PSYCHOLOGY

In October 2021, APA adopted a resolution apologizing for its and psychology's role in maintaining structural racism and human hierarchies. The resolution focused on psychology's contributions to scientific racism, including the use of scientific concepts and data to create and justify ideas of an enduring biologically based hierarchy (Winston, 2020). This was primarily done through the development and use of psychological tests and instruments to assess cognitive abilities, personality, and human performance. These measures, developed by white psychologists and normed on white samples, were used to compare the performance of REM and white individuals. The lower scores of REM individuals compared to white samples were used to allege the intellectual inferiority of REM individuals and to justify their exclusion from opportunities, education, and society more broadly. Using these assessments, psychologists reified the concept of race and provided scientific data to support the ideas of human hierarchy, biological differences between racial groups, and white superiority. In addition to this legacy of scientific racism, APA also acknowledged its and the profession's failure to respond to social harms to REM communities and to represent the voices, practices, and concerns of REM individuals within the field of psychology and within society (APA, 2021; Cummings Center for the History of Psychology [CCHP], 2021).

School psychology has also contributed to psychology's history of scientific racism. Through professional practices, most notably their involvement in special education evaluations, school psychologists have contributed to the disenfranchisement of and denial of educational opportunities for REM youth (National Association of School Psychologists [NASP], 2020a). To move toward antiracist practice in school psychology, it is important to consider how racial attitudes present in psychology and in society more broadly have influenced the development of school psychology and school psychologists' professional practices. While Chapter 2 provides a more detailed overview of school psychology's history, the following briefly reviews the field's origins in relation to the maintenance of racism in schools.

School Psychology's Origins and Early Development

As noted in Chapter 2, historians of the profession agree that school psychology began in 1896 when Lightner Witmer established the first psychoeducational clinic at the University of Pennsylvania (Fagan, 1992). There, he saw children who were referred to him because of developmental or educational concerns. In his practice, he applied principles of psychological science to study these children, provided clinical diagnoses, and developed remedial interventions (Fagan, 1992). School psychology was also heavily influenced by G. Stanley Hall, the founding president of APA. Hall advanced the child study movement, which utilized a questionnaire approach to study children and define normal child development (Brooks-Gunn & Duncan Johnson, 2006). He applied this knowledge to suggest education reforms that would address common problems of schoolchildren (Fagan, 1992).

Hall's concept of the normal child and Witmer's exploration of atypical child development influenced future psychology and school psychology practice. Notably, it is important to consider how their perspectives were influenced by the racial prejudicial beliefs prevalent at that time and by the use of psychological research to support the eugenics movement. For example, Witmer supported legislation in Pennsylvania that would have legalized the sterilization of males with severe intellectual disabilities (Thomas, 2009). In his writings, Hall described Indigenous people as childlike, with Indigenous adults being more similar to white children in their development (CCHP, 2021). He held similar beliefs about other REM groups and thus believed that Indigenous and other REM groups were hereditarily ill-equipped to handle civic responsibilities like voting or to benefit from the same education provided to white individuals (Brooks-Gunn & Duncan Johnson, 2006; Youniss, 2006). Witmer's and Hall's eugenicist views not only impacted their own practice and research but also likely influenced the psychologists whom they trained. Notably, Lewis Terman, one of Hall's students, created the Stanford-Binet Scale, one of the first cognitive assessments developed in the United States, and used racial differences on the scale to justify racially segregated school systems (CCHP, 2021). Arnold Gesell, another student of Hall and the first individual to use the title "school psychologist," endorsed eugenicist policies and promoted the use of testing to identify those students deemed too intellectually disabled to benefit from schooling (Harris, 2011).

School Psychology Professional Practices

The growth of school psychology as a profession is largely attributed to compulsory schooling laws enacted and increasingly enforced between 1890 and 1930 (Braden et al., 2001). These laws led to unprecedented growth in student enrollment and greater variability in the school population in regard to mental and physical health and educational needs. Schools created special classes to address the needs of children with mental and/or physical disabilities. The development of these special education classrooms led to an increased demand for school psychologists to assess students and determine their appropriate educational placements (Fagan, 1992). School psychologists typically used intelligence tests, such as the Stanford-Binet Scale developed by Terman, to assess students' cognitive functioning and determine if they were "educable." The Stanford-Binet, like other psychological assessments of that time, was normed on white samples. The lower scores REM students received on these measures were viewed as a validation of existing racial views of white superiority and were used to justify racially separate and substandard educational facilities for REM youth (CCHP, 2021; Washington et al., 2016).

As a result of biased intelligence tests, REM students, as well as bilingual students and economically marginalized students, were overidentified and labeled as intellectually disabled and placed in restrictive classroom settings (Dunn, 1968). The rate at which Black students were placed in special education was so concerning that in 1968 the Association of Black Psychologists called for a moratorium on the use of intelligence and aptitude tests until APA took action to address issues of bias in testing (Williams et al., 1980). Although APA acknowledged problems with testing, they concluded that these problems were caused by the misuse and misinterpretation of these tests as opposed to bias in the test itself (CCHP, 2021). The ongoing misuse of intelligence tests with Black and REM youth culminated in the *Larry P. v. Riles* ruling (1979), which found that Black children were being disproportionately placed in special education classes due to their performance on psychological tests. The ruling also prohibited schools in California from using intelligence tests for special education purposes. However, the use of intelligence tests is still permissible in other U.S. states, and special education assessment remains the primary job role of school psychologists (Farmer et al., 2021). Moreover, despite being knowledgeable about cultural bias in testing, school psychologists continue to use measures that are inappropriate for Black and REM youth (Aston & Brown, 2021).

School Psychology Research and Graduate Preparation

School psychologists' continued use of practices harmful to REM students is likely related to their graduate preparation. Although APA and NASP program accreditation standards require that graduate programs prepare their trainees to work with culturally, ethnically, and linguistically diverse populations (APA, 2015; NASP, 2020b), the quality of the training and coverage of diversity topics can vary significantly across programs. Not all school psychology programs require or even offer a multicultural-focused course (Gross & Malone, 2019). Most programs report using an integrated model of multicultural training in which relevant diversity content is incorporated across core school psychology courses (Malone & Ishmail, 2020). For this model to be successful, faculty must be knowledgeable in their respective content areas and possess the necessary competence to integrate multicultural content into core school psychology courses. However, fewer than two thirds of faculty have completed multicultural professional development postdegree (Malone & Ishmail, 2020). This calls into question the quality of multicultural training provided to school psychology graduate students and suggests that they may be insufficiently prepared to meet the needs of REM students. The lack of quality in graduate programs' multicultural training also reflects a broader pattern of lack of concern for REM communities and the care that they receive from school psychologists.

It does not help that there is a limited research base upon which to inform culturally responsive school psychology practice. A content analysis of school psychology research published between 1975 and 1990 found that only 9% of the articles reviewed focused on REM groups as study participants and/or addressed multicultural issues in school psychology (Wiese, 1992). Subsequent reviews of the school psychology literature have noted increases in multicultural research: specifically, 10.6% of articles published from 1990 to 1999 and 17% of articles published from 2000 to 2003 (Brown et al., 2007; Miranda & Gutter, 2002). Notably, most of the empirical multicultural research published from 1975 to 1999 focused on assessment and the school psychologist's role as a psychoeducational evaluator (Miranda & Gutter, 2002; Wiese, 1992). It was not until the early 2000s that a greater emphasis on intervention and prevention services emerged (Brown et al., 2007). In general, most psychological research on assessment focuses on individual differences in assessment outcomes and has been used to establish social hierarchies and determine access to opportunities. However, assessment research that focuses on individual differences without considering the impact of racism only serves to reify race, perpetuate deficit narratives about REM youth, and justify limited access to educational opportunities. Moreover, the limited availability of multicultural intervention and consultation research means that the profession has not been focused on generating solutions to remediate the challenges faced by REM youth.

School psychology has historically been silent or slow to respond on issues related to racial discrimination and prejudice that impact REM youth's school and life experiences

(NASP, 2020a). For example, in the official conference proceedings of the 1954 Thayer Conference, the professional conference which defined school psychology, there are no entries for the terms *culture, desegregation, discrimination,* or *minority* (Fagan, 2005). Even though the Thayer Conference occurred in the same year as the *Brown v. Board of Education* (1954) decision, there is no mention of this ruling in the conference proceedings (Fagan, 2005). This suggests that school psychology leaders did not perceive the cultural context as a key influence on school psychology's future standards. Subsequent professional conferences (i.e., Spring Hill Symposium, Olympia Conference) also failed to attend to issues of racial diversity and racial equity. While the 2002 Conference on the Future of School Psychology did include discussions about diversity, the need for change was directed externally, with an emphasis on school psychologists helping school communities address their own biases impacting REM students (Dawson et al., 2004); in other words, there was no recognition of the need for school psychology to explore how racial biases affect school psychologists' own professional practices. This lack of introspection is further evidenced by the paucity of multicultural research with school psychologists as study participants (Noltemeyer et al., 2013). In the absence of self-examination, school psychology will not be able to move forward with antiracist practice. Moreover, the ongoing exclusion of REM issues does not make school psychology an attractive profession for prospective REM graduate students.

Experiences of Racially/Ethnically Minoritized Individuals in School Psychology

From its inception, school psychology has been an overwhelmingly white profession with very little growth in racial/ethnic diversity over the past several decades. In the 2020 NASP Membership Survey, 86% of school psychologist respondents were white (Goforth et al., 2021). Because of the lack of racial/ethnic diversity in school psychology, a lot of emphasis is placed on the recruitment of REM professionals; however, far less attention is dedicated to understanding factors that contribute to the retention of REM individuals and their experiences in the profession (Proctor & Owens, 2019). The same racial biases that have influenced school psychology professional practices are reflected in the treatment of REM individuals in the profession. REM school psychologists and graduate students report ongoing challenges related to racism and racial bias. For example, REM graduate students often feel that representations of their respective racial/ethnic groups in psychology textbooks are grounded in stereotypes or are missing altogether, and they frequently report experiencing racial microaggressions from peers, faculty, and supervisors (Clark et al., 2012; Maton et al., 2011; Proctor & Truscott, 2012). Similarly, Black school psychology practitioners also report racial microaggressions from colleagues and parents suggesting that they are intellectually incompetent or ineffective at their jobs (Truscott et al., 2014). Experiences of microaggressions can leave REM school psychologists feeling isolated and disrespected and may push them out of the profession. For the sake of pre-K–12 students, as well as the field itself, school psychology needs to move toward antiracist practice to ensure that its workforce is well prepared to serve REM youth and that the profession remains relevant and viable.

ANTIRACISM IN SCHOOL PSYCHOLOGY

Antiracism has been defined as a system of equity on the basis of race that is built on and sustained by the interaction of psychological (e.g., equitable thoughts and actions) and sociopolitical (e.g., equitable laws, policies, and social norms) factors (Roberts & Rizzo, 2021). Antiracism thus attempts to deconstruct racism as a system of privilege and oppression (Basham, 2004) and reflects forms of thought and practices that seek to name, eradicate, or mitigate racism (Bonnett, 2000). Kendi (2019) describes the difference between racism and antiracism in the following:

> What's the problem with being "not racist"? It is a claim that signifies neutrality: "I am not a racist, but neither am I aggressively against racism." But there is no neutrality in the racism struggle. The opposite of "racist" isn't "not racist." It is "antiracist." What's the difference? One endorses either the idea of a racial hierarchy as a racist, or racial equality as an antiracist. One either believes problems are rooted in groups of people, as a racist, or locates the roots of problems in power and policies, as an antiracist. One either allows racial inequities to persevere, as a racist, or confronts racial inequities, as an antiracist. (pp. 18–19)

An antiracism approach may be considered a form of anti-oppressive practice (Butler et al., 2003) that directly seeks to address dynamics of power and privilege within social institutions as they relate to socially constructed racial categories (Bonnett, 1993). Within the field of mental health, antiracist frameworks have critically examined the impact of racism on the development of mental health concerns and the maintenance of mental health disparities (Corneau & Stergiopoulos, 2012; Hassen et al., 2021).

Antiracism efforts within the field of psychology have increased over the past two decades (Paradies, 2016), with a notable upsurge of focus within the past few years (Roberts & Rizzo, 2021). In response to the murders of George Floyd, Breonna Taylor, and many other unarmed Black individuals, as well as increasing global support for the Black Lives Matter movement, many within the field of psychology have drawn greater attention to the unjust experiences of Black people with law enforcement and the general role of systemic racism in the United States (Hargons et al., 2017). Calls from both scholars (Buchanan et al., 2021; Hargons et al., 2017) and students (Galán et al., 2021) have reiterated the need for all of psychology to engage in antiracist action to improve the production and dissemination of psychological science within the field.

Within school psychology, numerous efforts to integrate antiracism in research, practice, and training have been undertaken. The *School Psychology Unified Antiracism Statement and Call to Action*, in which representatives from APA's Division 16, the Trainers of School Psychologists (TSP), the Council of Directors of School Psychology Programs (CDSPP), the Society for the Study of School Psychology (SSSP), the American Board of School Psychology (ABSP), and NASP joined to reaffirm their commitment to antiracism within school psychology (García-Vázquez et al., 2020), was one such effort. In their call to action, they proposed eight main actions in pursuit of this goal. Additionally, in the wake of a national rise in anti-Asian hate crimes, several organizations (e.g., TSP and APA's Division 16) put forth the *School Psychology Unified Call for Deeper Understanding, Solidarity, and Action to Eradicate Anti-AAAPI Racism and Violence* (Truong et al., 2021). In this statement, these groups joined to reaffirm the field's commitment to antiracism by offering steps to promote equity for Asian/Asian American and Pacific Islander (AAAPI) youth, families, and communities.

Similarly, journals within the field, including the *Journal of Educational and Psychological Consultation* (Newman et al., 2021, 2022), *School Psychology International* (Noltemeyer & Grapin, 2020, 2022), *School Psychology Review* (Jimerson et al., 2021), and *School Psychology* (Codding et al., 2020), have expressed their commitment to antiracism, outlining actionable steps for editors, associate editors, and editorial boards within their respective journals. Moreover, many have put forth special issues or special topic sections dedicated to antiracism-focused scholarship (e.g., the *Journal of School Psychology*'s special issue on "Promoting Equitable and Socially Just School Climates for Minoritized and Marginalized Students"; *School Psychology Review*'s special topic section on "Theory, Methods, and Practice to Advance Equity in School Psychology"). Several organizations further demonstrated their commitment to antiracism via their establishment of financial support for related research (e.g., SSSP's Diversity, Equity, and Inclusion Research Award; APA Division 16's Outstanding Commitment to Anti-Racism Scholarship Award).

Notably, several conferences dedicated to antiracism have recently been held. The *Uprooting School Psychology: 2021 School Psychology Anti-Racism Unconference*, a participant-driven gathering with the goal of disrupting school psychology practices that perpetuate systems of racism and oppression, was one such example. Others, including the *Academics for Black Survival and Wellness Anti-Racism Training* and the *Decolonizing Psychology Conference* held in 2020 and 2021, respectively, engaged members of the school psychology community.

Bringing together members of the larger school psychology community, in 2020 NASP held its first antiracism-focused town hall with the goal of stimulating dialogue about and promoting action against systemic racism (NASP, 2020a). This was followed by NASP's *Resolution Committing to Antiracism Action*, which highlighted the historical role of school psychology in sustaining racism within the field. Similarly, TSP sought to join the school psychology training community in pursuing antiracist education within the field by calling on graduate training programs to adopt an antiracism training stance (Williams et al., 2021) and by developing and maintaining a list of diversity, equity, and inclusion (DEI) focused resources on their web page, among many other critical efforts.

Despite these numerous advances, many of which would have seemed unimaginable several years ago, there remains significant work to be done to put into action the aspirations outlined in the various calls to the field over the last several years. Indeed, in response to these recent shifts, many have received backlash for their comments and calls to disrupt the field via antiracism efforts (Lim et al., 2021). It is imperative that the field of school psychology continue to engage in the previously proposed antiracist actions, ensuring the safety and amplifying the voices of its most marginalized members.

SOCIAL JUSTICE CONNECTIONS

What is critical consciousness? How can Youth Participatory Action Research be used to foster critical consciousness among Black youth?

As racism plays a significant role in the everyday lives and future endeavors of Black children, it is critical that they learn how race affects their interpersonal interactions and environment (Hope et al., 2015). Black children are aware of racial discrimination as early as third grade (Rowley et al., 2010). Because Black children spend a significant amount of time in schools, school psychologists can help students navigate complex emotions evoked by racial discrimination by implementing interventions to promote positive racial socialization, the process by which Black students can develop a positive self-concept and learn to cope in racist and sometimes hostile environments (Malone et al., 2021; Paasch Anderson & Lamborn, 2014; Thomas et al., 2010).

To promote positive racial socialization, schools should provide Black students with the opportunity to develop critical consciousness. Paulo Freire (1970) described **critical consciousness** as the ability and commitment to recognize, analyze, and act against systems of inequality. Critical consciousness involves (a) critical reflection, or the ability to understand social problems through the lens of oppression; (b) political efficacy, or one's confidence to enact social change; and (c) critical action, or individual or collective actions taken to challenge oppression (Watts et al., 2011). Research also suggests that a critical consciousness of racism can empower Black students to resist oppressive forces and disprove mainstream stereotypes by persisting in school and achieving in academics (Carter, 2008). Thus, critical consciousness can serve as a gateway to academic motivation and achievement for students affected by racism.

(continued)

SOCIAL JUSTICE CONNECTIONS (*continued*)

Without developing critical consciousness, Black children who experience racial discrimination may experience feelings of invisibility and devaluation, which can have damaging effects on their self-perception (Allen, 2010). Furthermore, Black students may feel disenfranchised and unable to evoke change, as they are typically excluded from crucial conversations on schooling inequities, especially school policies and practices that affect their well-being (Rodríguez & Brown, 2009). Thus, it is necessary to adopt a multilevel approach to empowerment that allows students to reorganize the environment they are most affected by (Schulz et al., 1995). To help with this process, schools should implement curricula that help students develop racial socialization by improving their critical consciousness and interrogating complex issues like race, discrimination, and oppression (Hope et al., 2015).

The critical exploration of race embedded in **Youth Participatory Action Research** (YPAR) serves as a form of racial socialization by providing Black youth with the necessary tools to construct and deconstruct messages they received about being Black from their experiences in schools and communities (Hope et al., 2015). YPAR is a process in which youth investigate social inequities to improve their lives and communities, as well as the institutions intended to serve them (Cammarota & Fine, 2008; Ozer & Piatt, 2017). This social justice youth-led approach allows youth to dismantle oppressive systems by creating a space where youth are encouraged to reflect, analyze, and challenge injustices alongside supportive adults (Sprague Martinez et al., 2020). Youth develop a more nuanced understanding of how research can influence policies and impact systemic change alongside supportive adults. Power sharing in YPAR allows youth to exert power over key aspects of the research process, such as problem identification, data collection, data analysis, and action steps (Ozer & Douglas, 2012). Examples of antiracist YPAR projects include Black high school students performing a critical analysis of the lack of racial diversity in curricular offerings (Hope et al., 2015) and Black male students in a suburban high school exploring the perception of race, identity, and oppression in their school (Smith & Hope, 2020). Black youth who actively participated in YPAR exhibited growth in sociopolitical skills, academic achievement, and increased motivation to participate in schools and communities (Carter, 2008; Ginwright, 2010; Watts et al., 2011).

When implemented with integrity, YPAR is congruent with antiracist principles and practices (Toraif et al., 2021). School psychologists can engage in the following practices for implementing an intentionally antiracist YPAR (Toraif et al., 2021):

1. Prioritizing youth of color (YOC) in YPAR by not only advocating for their rights but also allowing YOC to lead the project and respond to questions with practice and policy implications relevant to them.
2. Creating discussion spaces for youth to confront racialized dynamics, name racism and microaggressions, and create strategies for proactively and directly responding to these inequalities.
3. Engaging youth and facilitators in ongoing preparation and continuing education on racism and microaggression, shared decision-making, and power dynamics.
4. Promoting continuous community building through ongoing dialogue and reflections to build trust, rapport, and community with adult allies and other youth members.

In this context, youth viewed trust building as an essential component of discussing sensitive issues and adopting an antiracist framework within YPAR projects (Toraif et al., 2021). Ideally, when school psychologists implement YPAR projects, students gain safe spaces to have authentic conversations about racism, amplify their voices, and enact change within their communities (Arora et al., in press). The future of social justice work in the field of school psychology calls for YPAR projects to dismantle oppressive systems by empowering students to create new systems that better serve their needs.

SUMMARY AND CONCLUSIONS

School psychologists are uniquely positioned to help eradicate racism in schools. With the goal of supporting the field's antiracism efforts, this chapter defined and described the role of racism in schools and its impact on youth. Further, it outlined the historical and current role of racism within the field of school psychology, providing examples of the ways in which school psychologists have engaged in antiracism work. At the core of all antiracism work is a deep integration of one's critical consciousness, historical understanding of racial inequalities, and willingness to advocate against socially unjust practices. As the demographics of school-age children continue to diversify, it remains imperative that school psychologists reflect on and commit to antiracism as they serve the needs of the nations' diverse students, their families, and their communities.

DISCUSSION QUESTIONS

1. What are the various ways in which racism exists in U.S. school systems?
2. Thinking about your personal experiences in school, have you seen examples of racism?
3. What are some examples of antiracist efforts that have taken place within the field of school psychology?
4. How are antiracism practices implemented into your psychology graduate program curriculum coursework?
5. What is one action you can take to promote antiracism in school psychology?

RECOMMENDED READINGS

Kendi, I. X. (2019). *How to be an antiracist.* One World.
Pollock, M. (Ed.). (2008). *Everyday antiracism: Getting real about race in school.* The New Press.
Saad, L. F. (2020). *Me and white supremacy: Combat racism, change the world, and become a good ancestor.* Sourcebooks, Inc.
Saini, A. (2020). *Superior.* Fourth Estate.
Singh, A. A. (2019). *The racial healing handbook: Practical activities to help you challenge privilege, confront systemic racism, and engage in collective healing.* New Harbinger Publications.

A robust set of instructor resources designed to supplement this text is located at http://connect.springerpub.com/content/book/978-0-8261-6344-8. Qualifying instructors may request access by emailing textbook@springerpub.com.

REFERENCES

Alegria, M., Green, J. G., McLaughlin, K. A., & Loder, S. (2015). *Disparities in child and adolescent mental health and mental health services in the U.S.* https://wtgrantfoundation.org/wp-content/uploads/2015/09/Disparities-in-Child-and-Adolescent-Mental-Health.pdf
Allen, Q. (2010). Racial microaggressions: The schooling experiences of Black middle-class males in Arizona's secondary schools. *Journal of African American Males in Education, 1*(2), 125–143. https://jaamejournal.scholasticahq.com/article/18400-racial-microaggressions-the-schooling-experiences-of-black-middle-class-males-in-arizona-s-secondary-schools

American Psychological Association. (2015). *Standards of accreditation for health service psychology.* Author. https://www.apa.org/ed/accreditation/about/policies/standards-of-accreditation.pdf

American Psychological Association. (2021, October). *Apology to people of color for APA's role in promoting, perpetuating, and failing to challenge racism, racial discrimination, and human hierarchy in U.S.* https://www.apa.org/about/policy/resolution-racism-apology.pdf

Arora, P. G., Staubi, K., Khoo, O., & Lim, K. (in press). Action research as a tool for social justice. In L. Parris & C. Malone (Eds.), *Oxford handbook of social justice in school psychology.* Oxford University Press.

Aston, C., & Brown, D. L. (2021). Progress or setback: Revisiting the current state of assessment practices of Black children. *Contemporary School Psychology, 25*(2), 140–148. https://doi.org/10.1007/s40688-020-00308-7

Aud, S., Hussar, W., Planty, M., Snyder, T., Bianco, K., Fox, M. A., Frohlich, L., Kemp, J., Drake, L., Ferguson, K., Nachazel, T., & Hannes, G. (2010). *The Condition of Education 2010* (NCES 2010-028). U.S. Department of Education, National Center for Education Statistics. https://nces.ed.gov/pubs2010/2010028.pdf

Bacher-Hicks, A., Billings, S., & Deming, D. (2021). Proving the school-to-prison pipeline: Stricter middle schools raise the risk of adult arrest. *Education Next, 21*(4), 52–57. https://www.educationnext.org/proving-school-to-prison-pipeline-stricter-middle-schools-raise-risk-of-adult-arrests

Bailey, Z. D., Krieger, N., Agénor, M., Graves, J., Linos, N., & Bassett, M. T. (2017). Structural racism and health inequities in the USA: Evidence and interventions. *Lancet, 389*(10077), 1453–1463. https://doi.org/10.1016/S0140-6736(17)30569-X

Basham, K. (2004). Weaving a tapestry: Anti-racism and the pedagogy of clinical social work practice. *Smith College Studies in Social Work, 74*(2), 289–314. http://doi.org/10.1080/00377310409517717

Bates, L. A., & Glick, J. E. (2013). Does it matter if teachers and schools match the student? Racial and ethnic disparities in problem behaviors. *Social Science Research, 42*(5), 1180–1190. https://doi.org/10.1016/j.ssresearch.2013.04.005

Bell, D. (2004). *Silent covenants:* Brown v. Board of Education *and the unfulfilled hopes for racial reform.* Oxford University Press.

Bell, D. A. (1992). *Faces at the bottom of the well: The permanence of racism.* Basic Books.

Bivens, D. (1995). *Internalized racism: A definition.* The Women's Theological Center. https://www.ci.tumwater.wa.us/home/showpublisheddocument/23133/637672320616270000

Blanchett, W. J. (2006). Disproportionate representation of African American students in special education: Acknowledging the role of white privilege and racism. *Educational Researcher, 35*(6), 24–28. https://doi.org/10.3102/0013189X035006024

Bohrnstedt, G., Kitmitto, S., Ogut, B., Sherman, D., & Chan, D. (2015). *School composition and the Black–white achievement gap* (NCES 2015-018). U.S. Department of Education, National Center for Education Statistics. https://nces.ed.gov/nationsreportcard/subject/studies/pdf/school_composition_and_the_bw_achievement_gap_2015.pdf

Bonilla-Silva, E. (1997). Rethinking racism: Toward a structural interpretation. *American Sociological Review, 62*(3), 465–480. https://doi.org/10.2307/2657316

Bonnett, A. (1993). The formation of public professional radical consciousness: The example of anti-racism. *Sociology, 27*(2), 281–297. https://doi.org/10.1177/0038038593027002007

Bonnett, A. (2000). *Anti-racism* (1st ed.). Routledge.

Braden, J. S., DiMarino-Linnen, E., & Good, T. L. (2001). Schools, society, and school psychologists: History and future directions. *Journal of School Psychology, 39*(2), 203–219. https://doi.org/10.1016/S0022-4405(01)00056-5

Brooks-Gunn, J., & Duncan Johnson, A. (2006). G. Stanley Hall's contribution to science, practice and policy: The child study, parent education, and child welfare movements. *History of Psychology, 9*(3), 247–258. https://doi.org/10.1037/1093-4510.9.3.247

Brown v. Board of Education, 347 U.S. 483 (1954).

Brown, S. L., Shriberg, D., & Wang, A. (2007). Diversity research literature on the rise? A review of school psychology journals from 2000 to 2003. *Psychology in the Schools, 44*(6), 639–650. https://doi.org/10.1002/pits.20253

Bryant, W. W. (2011). Internalized racism's association with African American male youth's propensity for violence. *Journal of Black Studies, 42*(4), 690–707. https://doi.org/10.1177/0021934710393243

Buchanan, N. T., Perez, M., Prinstein, M. J., & Thurston, I. B. (2021). Upending racism in psychological science: Strategies to change how science is conducted, reported, reviewed, and disseminated. *American Psychologist, 76*(7), 1097–1112. https://doi.org/10.1037/amp0000905

Butler, A., Elliott, T., & Stopard, N. (2003). Living up to the standards we set: A critical account of the development of anti-racist standards. *Social Work Education, 22*(3), 271–282. https://doi.org/10.1080/0261547032000083469

Cammarota, J., & Fine, M. (2008). *Revolutionizing education: Youth participatory action research in motion.* Routledge.

Carter, D. J. (2008). Cultivating a critical race consciousness for African-American school success. *Educational Foundations, 22*(1–2), 11–28. https://files.eric.ed.gov/fulltext/EJ839495.pdf

Clark, C. R., Mercer, S. H., Zeigler-Hill, V., & Dufrene, B. A. (2012). Barriers to the success of ethnic minority students in school psychology graduate programs. *School Psychology Review, 41*(2), 176–192. http://doi.org/10.1080/02796015.2012.12087519

Codding, R. S., Collier-Meek, M., Jimerson, S., Klingbeil, D. A., Mayer, M. J., & Miller, F. (2020). School Psychology reflections on COVID-19, antiracism, and gender and racial disparities in publishing. *School Psychology, 35*(4), 227–232. http://doi.org/10.1037/spq0000399

Cole, E. R. (2009). Intersectionality and research in psychology. *American Psychologist, 64*(3), 170–180. https://doi.org/10.1037/a0014564

Corneau, S., & Stergiopoulos, V. (2012). More than being against it: Anti-racism and anti-oppression in mental health services. *Transcultural Psychiatry, 49*(2), 261–282. http://doi.org/10.1177/1363461512441594

Crenshaw, K. (1989). Demarginalizing the intersection of race and sex: A Black feminist critique of antidiscrimination doctrine, feminist theory, and antiracist politics. *University of Chicago Legal Forum, 1989*(1), 139–167. https://chicagounbound.uchicago.edu/cgi/viewcontent.cgi?article=1052&context=uclf

Crenshaw, K., Ocen, P., & Nanda, J. (2015). *Black girls matter: Pushed out, overpoliced, and underprotected.* Center for Intersectionality and Social Policy Studies, Columbia University.

Cross Jr., W. E. (1971). The negro-to-black conversion experience. *Black World, 20*(9), 13–27.

Cummings Center for the History of Psychology. (2021). *Examining psychology's contributions to the belief in racial hierarchy and perpetuation of inequality for People of Color in the United States.* Cummings Center for the History of Psychology (proposed for vote to receive in Council of Representatives meeting scheduled for October 2021).

Darling-Hammond, L. (2004). The color line in American education: Race, resources, and student achievement. *Du Bois Review, 1*(2), 213–246. http://doi.org/10.1017/S1742058X0404202X

Dawson, M., Cummings, J. A., Harrison, P. L., Short, R. J., Gorin, S., & Palomares, R. (2004). The 2002 multisite conference on the future of school psychology: Next steps. *School Psychology Review, 33*(1), 115–125. https://doi.org/10.1080/02796015.2004.12086235

Delpit, L. (2006). *Other people's children: Cultural conflict in the classroom.* The New Press.

Donovan, M. S., & Cross, C. (2002). *Minority students in special and gifted education.* National Academies Press.

Dunn, L. M. (1968). Special education for the mildly retarded—Is much of it justifiable? *Exceptional Children, 35*(1), 5–22. https://doi.org/10.1177/001440296803500101

Empleo, A. C. (2006). Disassembling the model minority: Asian Pacific Islander identities and their schooling experiences. *Multicultural Perspectives, 8*(3), 46–50. https://doi.org/10.1207/s15327892mcp0803_8

Essed, P. (2002). Everyday racism: A new approach to the study of racism. In P. Essed & D. Goldberg (Eds.), *Race critical theories: Texts and contexts* (pp. 176–194). Oxford.

Fabelo, T., Thompson, M. D., Plotkin, M., Carmichael, D., Marchbanks, M. P., & Booth, E. A. (2011). *Breaking schools' rules: A state-wide study of how school discipline relates to students' success and juvenile justice involvement.* Council of State Governments Justice Center.

Fagan, T. K. (1992). Compulsory schooling, child study, clinical psychology, and special education: Origins of school psychology. *American Psychologist, 47*(2), 236–243. https://doi.org/10.1037/0003-066X.47.2.236

Fagan, T. K. (2005). The 50th anniversary of the Thayer Conference: Historical perspectives and accomplishments. *School Psychology Quarterly, 20*(3), 224–251. https://doi.org/10.1521/scpq.2005.20.3.224

Farmer, R. L., Goforth, A. N., Kim, S. Y., Naser, S. C., Lockwood, A. B., & Affrunti, N. W. (2021). Status of school psychology in 2020, Part 2: Professional practices in the NASP Membership

Survey. *NASP Research Reports, 5*(3), 1–17. https://www.nasponline.org/research-and-policy/research-center/nasp-research-reports#:~:text=Volume%205,%20Issue%203

Ferri, B. A., & Connor, D. J. (2005). In the shadow of *Brown*: Special education and overrepresentation of students of color. *Remedial and Special Education, 26*(2), 93–100. https://doi.org/10.1177/07419325050260020401

Freire, P. (1970). *Pedagogy of the oppressed.* Continuum International Publishing Group.

Friske, S. T., Gilbert, D. T., & Gardner, L. (Eds.). (2010). *Handbook of social psychology* (5th ed.). John Wiley & Sons.

Galán, C. A., Bekele, B., Boness, C., Bowdring, M., Call, C., Hails, K., McPhee, J., Mendes, S. H., Moses, J., Northrup, J., Rupert, P., Savell, S., Sequeira, S., Tervo-Clemmens, B., Tung, I., Vanwoerden, S., Womack, S., & Yilmaz, B. (2021). Editorial: A call to action for an antiracist clinical science. *Journal of Clinical Child & Adolescent Psychology, 50*(1), 12–57. https://doi.org/10.1080/15374416.2020.1860066

García-Vázquez, E., Reddy, L., Arora, P., Crepeau-Hobson, F., Fenning, P., Hatt, C., Hughes, T., Jimerson, S., Malone, C., Minke, K., Radliff, K., Raines, T., Song, S., & Strobach, K. V. (2020). School psychology unified antiracism statement and call to action. *School Psychology Review, 49*(3), 209–211. https://doi.org/10.1080/2372966X.2020.1809941

Gershenson, S., Holt, S. B., & Papageorge, N. W. (2016). Who believes in me? The effect of student–teacher demographic match on teacher expectations. *Economics of Education Review, 52*(1), 209–224. https://doi.org/10.1016/j.econedurev.2016.03.002

Ginwright, S. A. (2010). *Black youth rising: Activism and radical healing in urban America.* Teacher's College Press.

Goforth, A. N., Farmer, R. L., Kim, S. Y., Naser, S. C., Lockwood, A. B., & Affrunti, N. W. (2021). Status of school psychology in 2020: Part 1, Demographics of the NASP Membership Survey. *NASP Research Reports, 5*(2), 1–17. https://www.nasponline.org/Documents/Research%20and%20Policy/Research%20Center/NRR_2020-Membership-Survey-P1.pdf

Graham, A., & Erwin, K. (2011). "I don't think Black men teach because of how they get treated as students": High achieving Black boys' perceptions of teaching as a career option. *The Journal of Negro Education, 80*(3), 398–416. https://diversity.utexas.edu/black-male-education-research/2016/11/i-dont-think-black-men-teach-because-how-they-get-treated-as-students-high-achieving-african-american-boys-perceptions-of-teaching-as-a-career-option

Graham, J. R., West, L. M., Martinez, J., & Roemer, L. (2016). The mediating role of internalized racism in the relationship between racist experiences and anxiety symptoms in a Black American sample. *Cultural Diversity and Ethnic Minority Psychology, 22*(3), 369–376. https://doi.org/10.1037/cdp0000073

Gross, T. J., & Malone, C. M. (2019). Examination of multicultural coursework across school psychology training programs. *Contemporary School Psychology, 23*(2), 179–189. https://doi.org/10.1007/s40688-018-00221-0

Hargons, C., Mosley, D., Falconer, J., Faloughi, R., Singh, A., Stevens-Watkins, D., & Cokley, K. (2017). Black Lives Matter: A call to action for counseling psychology leaders. *The Counseling Psychologist, 45*(6), 873–901. https://doi.org/10.1177/0011000017733048

Harrell, S. P. (2000). A multidimensional conceptualization of racism-related stress: Implications for the well-being of people of color. *American Journal of Orthopsychiatry, 70*(1), 42–57. https://doi.org/10.1037/h0087722

Harris, B. (2011). Arnold Gesell's progressive vision: Child hygiene, socialism and eugenics. *History of Psychology, 14*(3), 311–334. https://doi.org/10.1037/a0024797

Hassen, N., Lofters, A., Michael, S., Mall, A., Pinto, A. D., & Rackal, J. (2021). Implementing anti-racism interventions in healthcare settings: A scoping review. *International Journal of Environmental Research and Public Health, 18*(6), 1–15. http://doi.org/10.3390/ijerph18062993

Heard-Garris, N. J., Cale, M., Camaj, L., Hamati, M. C., & Dominguez, T. P. (2018). Transmitting trauma: A systematic review of vicarious racism and child health. *Social Science & Medicine, 199*(1), 230–240. https://doi.org/10.1016/j.socscimed.2017.04.018

Hibel, J., Farkas, G., & Morgan, P. L. (2010). Who is placed into special education? *Sociology of Education, 83*(4), 312–332. https://doi.org/10.1177/0038040710383518

Hope, E. C., Skoog, A. B., & Jagers, R. J. (2015). "It'll never be the white kids, it'll always be us": Black high school students' evolving critical analysis of racial discrimination and inequity in schools. *Journal of Adolescent Research, 30*(1), 83–112. https://doi.org/10.1177/0743558414550688

Hwang, W. (2016). *Culturally adapting psychotherapy for Asian heritage populations: An evidence-based approach*. Elsevier.

Jacob, B., Crespin, R., Libassi, C. J., & Dynarski, S. M. (2016). *Class size in Michigan: Investigating the risk of being in very large classes*. Education Policy Initiative. https://edpolicy.umich.edu/sites/epi/files/uploads/class-size-policy-brief-revised.pdf

Jimerson, S. R., Arora, P., Blake, J. J., Canivez, G. L., Espelage, D. L., Gonzalez, J. E., Graves, S. L., Huang, F. L., January, S.-A. A., Renshaw, T. L., Song, S. Y., Sullivan, A. L., Wang, C., & Worrell, F. C. (2021). Advancing diversity, equity, and inclusion in school psychology: Be the change. *School Psychology Review, 50*(1), 1–7. https://doi.org/10.1080/2372966X.2021.1889938

Jones, C. P. (2000). Levels of racism: A theoretic framework and a gardener's tale. *American Journal of Public Health, 90*(8), 1212–1215. https://doi.org/10.2105/ajph.90.8.1212

Kendi, I. X. (2019). *How to be an antiracist* (1st ed.). One World.

Kohli, R. (2008). Breaking the cycle of racism in the classroom: Critical race reflections from future teachers of color. *Teacher Education Quarterly, 35*(4), 177–188. https://www.jstor.org/stable/23479180

Kohli, R., & Solórzano, D. G. (2012). Teachers, please learn our names!: Racial microaggressions and the K–12 classroom. *Race, Ethnicity and Education, 15*(4), 441–462. https://doi.org/10.1080/13613324.2012.674026

Krieger, N. (1999). Embodying inequality: A review of concepts, measures, and methods for studying health consequences of discrimination. *International Journal of Health Services, 29*(2), 295–352. https://doi.org/10.2190/M11W-VWXE-KQM9-G97Q

Larry P. v. Riles, 495 F. Supp. 926 (N.D. Cal. 1979).

Leventhal, A. M., Cho, J., Andrabi, N., & Barrington-Trimis, J. (2018). Association of reported concern about increasing societal discrimination with adverse behavioral health outcomes in late adolescence. *JAMA Pediatrics, 172*(10), 924–933. https://doi.org/10.1001/jamapediatrics.2018.2022

Lim, K., Salazar, L. G., Dvorak, E., Parr, K., & Phansalkar, E. (2021). SASP student corner: How to be antiracist: A school psychology starter pack. *The School Psychologist, 75*(1), 20–26. https://apadivision16.org/wp-content/uploads/2021/03/TSP-Spring-2021.pdf

Malone, C. M., & Ishmail, K. Z. (2020). A snapshot of multicultural training in school psychology. *Psychology in the Schools, 57*(7), 1022–1039. https://doi.org/10.1002/pits.22392

Malone, C. M., Wycoff, K., & Turner, E. A. (2021). Applying a MTSS framework to address racism and promote mental health for racial/ethnic minoritized youth. *Psychology in the Schools, 59*(12), 2438–2452. https://doi.org/10.1002/pits.22606

Maton, K. I., Wimms, H. E., Grant, S. K., Wittig, M. A., Rogers, M. R., & Vasquez, M. J. (2011). Experiences and perspectives of African American, Latina/o, Asian American, and European American psychology graduate students: A national study. *Cultural Diversity and Ethnic Minority Psychology, 17*(1), 68–78. https://doi.org/10.1037/a0021668

McNulty, T. L., & Bellair, P. E. (2003). Explaining racial and ethnic differences in serious adolescent violent behavior. *Criminology, 41*(3), 709–747. https://doi.org/10.1111/j.1745-9125.2003.tb01002.x

Miranda, A. H., & Gutter, P. B. (2002). Diversity research literature in school psychology: 1990–1999. *Psychology in the Schools, 39*(5), 597–604. https://doi.org/10.1002/pits.10051

Miranda, J., McGuire, T. G., Williams, D. R., & Wang, P. (2008). Mental health in the context of health disparities. *American Journal of Psychiatry, 165*(9), 1102–1108. https://doi.org/10.1176/appi.ajp.2008.08030333

National Association of School Psychologists. (2020a). *Resolution on antiracism action* [Resolution]. Author.

National Association of School Psychologists. (2020b). *The professional standards of the National Association of School Psychologists*. Author.

National Center for Education Statistics. (2019). *Status and trends in the education of racial and ethnic groups 2018* (NCES 2019-038). U.S. Department of Education. https://nces.ed.gov/pubs2019/2019038.pdf

National Center for Education Statistics. (2021). *The condition of education, 2020*. U.S. Department of Education. https://nces.ed.gov/pubs2020/2020144.pdf

National Center for Health Statistics. (2018). *Health, United States, 2018.* U.S. Department of Health and Human Services, Centers for Disease Control and Prevention. https://www.cdc.gov/nchs/data/hus/hus18.pdf

Neville, H. A., Coleman, M. N., Falconer, J. W., & Holmes, D. (2005). Color-blind racial ideology and psychological false consciousness among African Americans. *Journal of Black Psychology, 31*(1), 27–45. https://doi.org/10.1177/0095798404268287

Newman, D. S., Albritton, K., Barrett, C., Fallon, L., Moy, G. E., O'Neal, C., & VanMeter, S. (2021). Working together towards social justice, anti-racism, and equity: A joint commitment from *Journal of Educational and Psychological Consultation and School Psychology International. Journal of Educational and Psychological Consultation, 31*(1), 8–12. https://doi.org/10.1080/10474412.2020.1848313

Newman, D. S., Albritton, K., Barrett, C. A., Fallon, L., Moy, G. E., O'Neal, C., & VanMeter, S. (2022). Working together toward social justice, anti-racism, and equity: One-year reflections on the joint commitment from *Journal of Educational and Psychological Consultation and School Psychology International. Journal of Educational and Psychological Consultation, 32*(1), 1–5. https://doi.org/10.1080/10474412.2021.2015645

Noltemeyer, A., & Grapin, S. L. (2020). Working together towards social justice, anti-racism, and equity: A joint commitment from *School Psychology International* and *Journal of Educational and Psychological Consultation. School Psychology International, 42*(1), 3–10. https://doi.org/10.1177/0143034320977618

Noltemeyer, A., & Grapin, S. L. (2022). Working together towards social justice, anti-racism, and equity: One-year reflections on the joint commitment from *School Psychology International* and *Journal of Educational and Psychological Consultation. School Psychology International, 43*(1), 3–11. https://doi.org/10.1177/01430343211070162

Noltemeyer, A. L., Proctor, S. L., & Dempsey, A. (2013). Race and ethnicity in school psychology publications: A content analysis and comparison to publications in related disciplines. *Contemporary School Psychology, 17*(1), 129–142. https://doi.org/10.1007/BF03340994

Nowicki, J. M. (2018). *K–12 education: Discipline disparities for Black students, boys, and students with disabilities.* Report to congressional requesters (GAO-18-258). U.S. Government Accountability Office.

Office of Special Education Programs. (2021, August 9). *OSEP fast facts: Race and ethnicity of children with disabilities served under IDEA part B.* Individuals With Disabilities Education Act. https://sites.ed.gov/idea/osep-fast-facts-race-and-ethnicity-of-children-with-disabilities-served-under-idea-part-b

Osajima, K. (2000). Asian Americans as the model minority. In M. Zhou & J. V. Gatewood (Eds.), *Contemporary Asian America: A multidisciplinary reader* (pp. 449–458). New York University Press.

Oswald, D. P., Coutinho, M. J., Best, A. M., & Singh, N. N. (1999). Ethnic representation in special education: The influence of school-related economic and demographic variables. *The Journal of Special Education, 32*(4), 194–206. https://doi.org/10.1177/002246699903200401

Ozer, E. J., & Douglas, L. (2012). Assessing the key processes of youth-led participatory research: Psychometric analysis and application of an observational rating scale. *Youth & Society, 47*(1), 29–50. https://doi.org/10.1177/0044118x12468011

Ozer, E. J., & Piatt, A. A. (2017). *Adolescent participation in research: Innovation, rationale and next steps.* https://www.semanticscholar.org/paper/adbaa96bcab2ee253113d1dc568e316f80b1988f

Paasch-Anderson, J., & Lamborn, S. D. (2014). African American adolescents' perceptions of ethnic socialization and racial socialization as distinct processes. *Journal of Adolescent Research, 29*(2), 159–185. https://doi.org/10.1177/0743558413510969

Paradies, Y. (2006a). A systematic review of empirical research on self-reported racism and health. *International Journal of Epidemiology, 35*(4), 888–901. https://doi.org/10.1093/ije/dyl056

Paradies, Y. C. (2006b). Defining, conceptualizing and characterizing racism in health research. *Critical Public Health, 16*(2), 143–157. https://doi.org/10.1080/09581590600828881

Paradies, Y. (2016). Whither anti-racism? *Ethnic and Racial Studies, 39*(1), 1–15. https://doi.org/10.1080/01419870.2016.1096410

Pérez Huber, L. (2011). Discourses of racist nativism in California public education: English dominance as racist nativist microaggressions. *Educational Studies, 47*(4), 379–401. https://doi.org/10.1080/00131946.2011.589301

Pérez Huber, L., Johnson, R. N., & Kohli, R. (2006). Naming racism: A conceptual look at internalized racism in US schools. *Chicano/Latino Law Review, 26*(1), 183–206. https://doi.org/10.5070/C7261021172

Pincus, F. L. (1996). Discrimination comes in many forms: Individual, institutional, and structural. In M. Adams, W. J., Blumenfelt, R. Castaneda, H. W. Hackman, M. L. Peters, & X. Zuniga (Eds.), *Readings for diversity and social justice* (pp. 31–34). Routledge.

Proctor, S. L., & Owens, C. (2019). School psychology graduate education retention research characteristics: Implications for diversity initiatives in the profession. *Psychology in the Schools, 56*(6), 1037–1052. https://doi.org/10.1002/pits.22228

Proctor, S. L., & Truscott, S. D. (2012). Reasons for African American student attrition from school psychology programs. *Journal of School Psychology, 50*(5), 655–679. https://doi.org/10.1016/j.jsp.2012.06.002

Proctor, S. L., Williams, B., Scherr, T., & Li, K. (2017). Intersectionality and school psychology: Implications for practice. *National Association of School Psychologists, 46*(4), 1, 19. https://www.nasponline.org/resources-and-publications/resources-and-podcasts/diversity-and-social-justice/social-justice/intersectionality-and-school-psychology-implications-for-practice

Pyke, K. D. (2010). What is internalized racial oppression and why don't we study it? Acknowledging racism's hidden injuries. *Sociological Perspectives, 53*(4), 551–572. https://doi.org/10.1525/sop.2010.53.4.551

Roberts, S. O., & Rizzo, M. T. (2021). The psychology of American racism. *American Psychologist, 76*(3), 475–487. https://doi.org/10.1037/amp0000642

Rodríguez, L. F., & Brown, T. M. (2009). From voice to agency: Guiding principles for participatory action research with youth. *New Directions for Youth Development, 2009*(123), 19–34. https://doi.org/10.1002/yd.312

Rowley, S., Kurtz-Coates, B., & Cooper, S. (2010). The schooling of African American children. In J. L. Meece & J. S. Eccles (Eds.), *Handbook of research on schools, schooling, and human development* (pp. 275–292). Routledge.

Schulz, A. J., Israel, B. A., Zimmerman, M. A., & Checkoway, B. N. (1995). Empowerment as a multi-level construct: Perceived control at the individual, organizational and community levels. *Health Education Research, 10*(3), 309–327. http://doi.org/10.1093/her/10.3.309

Skiba, R. J., Arredondo, M. I., & Williams, N. T. (2014). More than a metaphor: The contribution of exclusionary discipline to a school-to-prison pipeline. *Equity & Excellence in Education, 47*(4), 546–564. https://doi.org/10.1080/10665684.2014.958965

Smith, C. D., & Hope, E. C. (2020). "We just want to break the stereotype": Tensions in Black boys' critical social analysis of their suburban school experiences. *Journal of Educational Psychology, 112*(3), 551–566. https://doi.org/10.1037/edu0000435

Spatig-Amerikaner, A. (2012). *Unequal education: Federal loophole enables lower spending on students of color*. Center for American Progress. https://eric.ed.gov/?id=ED535549

Sprague Martinez, L., Tang Yan, C., McClay, C., Varga, S., & Zaff, J. F. (2020). Adult reflection on engaging youth of color in research and action: A case study from five U.S. cities. *Journal of Adolescent Research, 35*(6), 699–727. https://doi.org/10.1177/0743558420906086

Starck, J. G., Riddle, T., Sinclair, S., & Warikoo, N. (2020). Teachers are people too: Examining the racial bias of teachers compared to other American adults. *Educational Researcher, 49*(4), 273–284. https://doi.org/10.3102/0013189X20912758

Sue, D. W., Capodilupo, C. M., Torino, G. C., Bucceri, J. M., Holder, A. M., Nadal, K. L., & Esquilin, M. (2007). Racial microaggressions in everyday life: Implications for clinical practice. *American Psychologist, 62*(4), 271–286. https://doi.org/10.1037/0003-066X.62.4.271

Sullivan, A. L., & Artiles, A. J. (2011). Theorizing racial inequity in special education: Applying structural Inequity theory to disproportionality. *Urban Education, 46*(6), 1526–1552. http://doi.org/10.1177/0042085911416014

Sullivan A., Kozleski, E. B., & Smith, A. (2008, March). *Understanding the current context of minority disproportionality in special education: Federal response, state activities, and implications for technical assistance.* Paper presented at the American Educational Research Association Annual Meeting, New York, New York.

Sullivan, A. L., Kulkarni, T., & Chhuon, V. (2020). Making visible the invisible: Multistudy investigation of disproportionate special education identification of U.S. Asian American and Pacific Islander students. *Exceptional Children, 86*(4), 449–467. https://doi.org/10.1177/0014402920905548

Thomas, A. J., Speight, S. L., & Witherspoon, K. M. (2010). Racial socialization, racial identity, and race-related stress of African American parents. *Family Journal, 18*(4), 407–412. https://doi.org/10.1177/1066480710372913

Thomas, H. (2009). Discovering Lightner Witmer: A forgotten hero of psychology. *Journal of Scientific Psychology*, 3–13. http://www.psyencelab.com/uploads/5/4/6/5/54658091/discovering_lightner_witmer.pdf

Toraif, N., Augsberger, A., Young, A., Murillo, H., Bautista, R., Garcia, S., Sprague Martinez, L., & Gergen Barnett, K. (2021). How to be an antiracist: Youth of color's critical perspectives on antiracism in a youth participatory action research context. *Journal of Adolescent Research, 36*(5), 467–500. https://doi.org/10.1177/07435584211028224

Truong, D. M., Tanaka, M. L., Cooper, J. M., Song, S., Talapatra, D., Arora, P., Fenning, P., McKenney, E., Williams, S., Stratton-Gadke, K., Jimerson, S. R., Pandes-Carter, L., Hulac, D., & García-Vázquez, E. (2021). School psychology unified call for deeper understanding, solidarity, and action to eradicate anti-AAAPI racism and violence. *School Psychology Review, 50*(2–3), 469–483. http://doi.org/10.1080/2372966X.2021.1949932

Truscott, S. D., Proctor, S. L., Albritton, K., Matthews, Y., & Daniel, K. (2014). African American school psychologists' perceptions of the opportunities and challenges of practicing in southeastern United States. *Psychology in the Schools, 51*(4), 366–383. https://doi.org/10.1002/pits.21753

Tynes, B. M., Giang, M. T., Williams, D. R., & Thompson, G. N. (2008). Online racial discrimination and psychological adjustment among adolescents. *Journal of Adolescent Health, 43*(6), 565–569. https://doi.org/10.1016/j.jadohealth.2008.08.021

U.S. Census Bureau. (2021, August 21). *2020 census illuminates racial and ethnic composition of the country*. https://www.census.gov/library/stories/2021/08/improved-race-ethnicity-measures-reveal-united-states-population-much-more-multiracial.html

U.S. Department of Education, Office for Civil Rights. (2016). *2013–2014 civil rights data: A first look*. https://www2.ed.gov/about/offices/list/ocr/docs/2013-14-first-look.pdf

Vasquez, M. (2020, March 12). *Calling COVID-19 the "Wuhan Virus" or "China Virus" is inaccurate and xenophobic*. Yale School of Medicine. https://medicine.yale.edu/news-article/calling-covid-19-the-wuhan-virus-or-china-virus-is-inaccurate-and-xenophobic/

Wald, J., & Losen, D. J. (2003). Defining and redirecting a school-to-prison pipeline. *New Directions for Youth Development, 2003*(99), 9–15. https://doi.org/10.1002/yd.51

Washington, K., Malone, C., Briggs, C., & Reed, G. K. (2016). Testing and African Americans: Testing monograph from the association of Black psychologists. In F. T. L. Leong & Y. S. Park (Eds.), *Testing and assessment with persons and communities of color* (pp. 3–11). American Psychological Association.

Watts, R. J., Diemer, M. A., & Voight, A. M. (2011). Critical consciousness: Current status and future directions. *New Directions for Child and Adolescent Development, 2011*(134), 43–57. https://doi.org/10.1002/cd.310

Wiese, M. R. R. (1992). Racial/ethnic minority research in school psychology. *Psychology in the Schools, 29*(3), 267–272. https://doi.org/10.1002/1520-6807(199207)29:3<267::AID-PITS2310290309>3.0.CO;2-G

Williams, D. R., Lawrence, J. A., & Davis, B. A. (2019). Racism and health: Evidence and needed research. *Annual Review of Public Health, 40*(1), 105–125. https://doi.org/10.1146/annurev-publhealth-040218-043750

Williams, R. L., Dotson, W., Don, P., & Williams, W. S. (1980). The war against testing: A current status report. *The Journal of Negro Education, 49*(3), 263–273. https://doi.org/10.2307/2295085

Williams, S. A. S., Cooper, J. M., & Shriberg, D. (2021). Social justice, antiracism and school psychology: Reconciling with our past to build an equitable future. *School Psychology Training and Pedagogy, 38*(1), 1–10. https://www.researchgate.net/publication/357033487_Social_justice_anti-racism_and_school_psychology_Reconciling_with_our_past_to_build_an_equitable_future

Winston, A. S. (2020). Why mainstream research will not end scientific racism in psychology. *Theory & Psychology, 30*(3), 425–430. https://doi.org/10.1177/0959354320925176

X., Malcolm, & Haley, A. (1965). *The autobiography of Malcolm X* (pp. 402–415). Harvard University Press.

Youniss, J. (2006). G. Stanley Hall and his times: Too much so, yet not enough. *History of Psychology, 9*(3), 224–235. https://doi.org/10.1037/1093-4510.9.3.224

CHAPTER 5

Ethical and Legal Foundations

BARBARA BOLE WILLIAMS ■ LAURA W. MONAHON

CHAPTER OBJECTIVES

After reading this chapter, you will be able to:

- Define and differentiate between law, ethics, and applied professional ethics.
- Understand the similarities and differences between various codes of ethics in professional school psychology.
- Describe the four broad principles encompassed in the National Association of School Psychologists' *Principles for Professional Ethics*.
- Describe the impact that legislation, including federal and state education and civil rights laws, has had on professional school psychology, both historically and currently.
- Illustrate applications of a problem-solving model to solve ethically challenging situations or dilemmas.

NATIONAL ASSOCIATION OF SCHOOL PSYCHOLOGISTS PRACTICE MODEL CONNECTIONS

Domain 10: Legal, Ethical, and Professional Practice

INTRODUCTION

Domain 10 of the National Association of School Psychologists (NASP; 2020) Practice Model dictates that school psychologists should be knowledgeable about ethical, legal, and professional standards for practice. Moreover, they must be competent in delivering services in accordance with these standards and engage in responsible ethical and legal decision-making. As described previously, Domain 10 is one of three domains in the NASP Practice Model identified as *Foundations of Service Delivery*, meaning that professional knowledge and skills in this area are essential for supporting practice in all other domains. Indeed, legal and ethical issues underlie all types of service delivery in school psychology, and practitioners must be mindful to operate within the parameters of state and federal laws and local school policies, as well as professional codes of ethics. This chapter describes the nature of legal and ethical codes that govern school psychology service delivery. Moreover, it presents a model for ethical decision-making and describes its applications.

DEFINING LAW AND ETHICS

One might ask, "How are law and ethics related?" and "Why should law and ethics be studied in tandem?" To answer these questions, one must first consider the definitions of the terms *law, ethics,* and *applied professional ethics*. According to Jacob et al. (2021), **law** is defined as "a source of control that is external to the profession" of school psychology (p. ix). These same authors define **ethics** as "a system of principles of conduct that guide the behavior of an individual" (p. 1). Finally, **applied professional ethics** refers to the application of such broad ethical principles and specific rules to problems that arise in professional practice (Beauchamp & Childress, 2001). More simply stated, *laws* are rules of conduct prescribed by the government that have binding legal force, and *ethics* comprise a range of acceptable (or unacceptable) social and personal behaviors, from rules of etiquette to more fundamental rules of society (Jacob et al., 2021). In the context of this chapter, we focus primarily on *applied professional ethics* in school psychology, or the ways in which professional codes of ethics are applied in practice.

Returning to our earlier question, why should ethics and law be studied in tandem? One answer is that ethics and law are closely related and both provide a form of quality control over school psychologists' professional interaction with others, including students, parents and guardians, teachers, principals, and other school personnel. In essence, ethics and law comprise procedures for school psychology practice and, therefore, guide school psychologists' professional behavior.

The relationship between ethics and law becomes particularly evident when situations arise that require a school psychologist to look to both areas for guidance in problem-solving. Situations like these are often referred to as dilemmas, which implies that the presenting problem does not have one clear-cut solution, but rather many alternatives that should be considered carefully before arriving at a plan of action. In these situations, a school psychologist must look to both ethical and legal guidelines to solve the problem. According to Jacob et al. (2016), professional codes of ethics are "generally viewed as requiring decisions that are 'more correct or more stringent' than required by law" (p. 22). Further, Jacob and colleagues recommend that if ethical responsibilities of school psychologists conflict with law, school psychologists should clarify the nature of the conflict and attempt to resolve it in a responsible manner.

One of the hallmarks of a profession is the development of a code of ethics that helps to guide the behavior of professionals. A *code of ethics* is a body of principles and guidelines (typically developed and endorsed by a professional organization or other entities) for engaging in equitable and morally sound professional behaviors that ensure the well-being of affected parties. Additionally, in school psychology, Williams et al. (2008) posited that codes of ethics are developed for the purposes of: (a) protecting the public and maintaining public trust, (b) showing the profession's commitment to self-regulation, (c) enhancing the prestige of the profession, (d) educating professionals and assisting them in monitoring their own behavior, and (e) providing guidelines for adjudicating complaints.

For school psychologists, three primary ethical codes may govern the practice of school psychology: the American Psychological Association's (APA's; 2017) *Ethical Principles of Psychologists and Code of Conduct*; NASP's (2020) *Principles for Professional Ethics* (NASP-PPE); and the International School Psychology Association's (ISPA's;

2011) *Code of Ethics*. Whereas APA's ethical codes apply to professional psychologists in many areas (e.g., clinical psychologists, counseling psychologists, school psychologists), the ethical codes of ISPA and NASP focus exclusively on the practice of school psychology. Each of these ethical codes is described in the following sections.

ETHICAL GUIDELINES OF THE AMERICAN PSYCHOLOGICAL ASSOCIATION

The *Ethical Standards of Psychologists* was initially adopted by APA in 1952 and subsequently has been revised and amended 10 times (Fisher, 2017). APA's current code of ethics, *Ethical Principles of Psychologists and Code of Conduct* (heretofore referred to as the APA Ethics Code), includes both aspirational goals and enforceable rules for conduct (APA, 2017). The code's aspirational principles (i.e., broad, guiding principles) mirror those developed by Ross (1930) and include: (a) beneficence and nonmaleficence, (b) fidelity and responsibility, (c) integrity, (d) justice, and (e) respect for people's rights and dignity (Knapp & VandeCreek, 2005). The enforceable rules for conduct provide more specific guidelines for behavior across a variety of professional activities.

While the adoption of the original APA Ethics Code in 1952 represented a breakthrough in the field of psychology in terms of ethical standards and codes of conduct, it soon became clear that there was a need for specific disciplines within the field of professional psychology to develop specialized ethical guidelines and codes of conduct. In 1974, NASP addressed emerging ethical and legal issues in school psychology in a special issue of *School Psychology Digest* (now *School Psychology Review*; Kaplan et al., 1974). Proponents of a specialized code of ethics and conduct for school psychology felt that the existing APA Ethics Code (which, at that time, had been most recently revised in 1963) could not be readily applied to practitioners who worked within a school system (Trachtman, 1974). In addition, the existing APA Ethics Code did not address issues that were critical to professional school psychologists. These issues included balancing the interests of children with the rights of parents, including students in educational and mental health decision-making processes, defining boundaries of confidentiality within a school setting, and ensuring fair and valid assessments of students from diverse cultural and linguistic backgrounds (Jacob, 2008). In addition to these issues, another topic central to decision-making in the profession of school psychology remained largely unaddressed: namely, the resolution of conflicts that resulted from serving in the dual roles of child advocate and school employee (Bersoff, 1983; Jacob et al., 2021; Trachtman, 1974). To address these issues, NASP developed and adopted the first iteration of its *Principles for Professional Ethics* (NASP-PPE) in 1974. Since then, the NASP code of ethics has been revised six times, most recently in 2020.

THE NATIONAL ASSOCIATION OF SCHOOL PSYCHOLOGISTS PRINCIPLES OF PROFESSIONAL ETHICS

As previously described, the APA Ethics Code was developed for psychologists trained in a variety of specialty areas and settings, including private practice, industry, hospitals and clinics, public schools, postsecondary institutions, and research settings (APA, 2017; Williams & Armistead, 2010). NASP developed and adopted its *Principles for Professional Ethics* to address specifically the practice of school psychology (NASP, 2020). Williams and Armistead (2010) describe the NASP-PPE as the ethical guidelines most school psychologists use as a resource to guide their practice.

When school psychologists join NASP, they agree to abide by the guidelines set forth in the NASP-PPE in all professional interactions with consumers of school psychological services (e.g., students, parents, school personnel, and colleagues). Some school psychologists may seek membership in both NASP and APA, in which case they are beholden to apply both the NASP-PPE and the APA Ethics Code in their professional practice. Jacob (2005) further notes that school psychology students and practitioners should be familiar with both ethics codes, as doing so will likely bolster their knowledge of ethical principles and standards more generally. This knowledge can, in turn, increase their ability to anticipate and possibly prevent ethical problems from occurring. Further, if a challenging situation does arise, this knowledge prepares the practitioner to make ethically and legally sound choices (Jacob, 2005).

Like the APA Code of Ethics, the NASP-PPE encompasses and endeavors to codify the "moral duties" outlined by Ross (1930), including nonmaleficence, fidelity, beneficence, justice, and autonomy (NASP, 2020). The NASP-PPE also provides a framework (i.e., a code of conduct) for the application of these moral duties within the scope of professional duty (i.e., applied professional ethics). The NASP-PPE includes two fundamental underlying principles that are introduced at the outset of the document. First, school psychologists consider the interests and rights of children and youth to be their highest priority in decision-making. Second, school psychologists act as advocates for all students (NASP, 2020). The NASP-PPE also addresses four broad themes regarding professional ethical competence: (a) respecting the dignity and rights of all persons, (b) professional competence and responsibility, (c) honesty and integrity in professional relationships, and (d) responsibility to schools, families, communities, the profession, and society (NASP, 2020). Each of these areas is further discussed in this chapter.

Respecting the Dignity and Rights of All Persons

As outlined in the NASP-PPE, a fundamental responsibility of school psychology practitioners is to engage only in those practices that promote and maintain the dignity of all individuals. Inherent in this principle is the need for school psychologists to consider the constructs of personal autonomy, self-determination, and privacy when working with individuals and their families (Jacob et al., 2021). Additionally, all professional school psychologists have an ethical responsibility to uphold "a commitment to just, equitable, and fair treatment of all persons" (NASP, 2020, p. 42).

Informed consent is one method by which school psychologists seek to maintain a client's self-determination and autonomy. *Autonomy* refers to the ability to self-govern and assert responsible control over one's life, including the freedom of choice and action. Put simply, professional school psychologists must ensure that individuals with whom they work have a "voice and a choice" in all decision-making processes (Jacob et al., 2021, p. 9). Not all professional services provided by a school psychologist, however, require informed consent. For example, when school psychologists serve on a multidisciplinary team or make recommendations to a classroom teacher regarding an intervention that is within the scope of a typical classroom intervention, they are not required to obtain informed consent from the parent(s) of the child or children who may be recipient(s) of the consultative services (Burns et al., 2008; Corrao & Melton, 1988; Jacob et al., 2021). This example underscores the need for an ethical code of conduct specific to school psychologists, as their professional duties frequently are shaped by their work settings. It also reinforces the notion that practicing school psychologists must be knowledgeable about their code of professional ethics and its application in a variety of situations.

NASP recognizes that school psychologists often are required to advocate for students within the school system in which they are employed. Similarly, it is important to acknowledge that school psychologists must maintain relationships with a variety of individuals, groups, and systems across the scope of their professional duties. Generally speaking, school psychologists must strive to develop relationships that improve the quality of the life of children, their families, and the school community (Williams & Armistead, 2010). At times, however, negotiating the best interests of all parties can be a challenging task. For example, when school psychologists employed by a school board make professional decisions regarding students in their district, they are obligated to maintain knowledge and respect for these students' rights under both state and federal law (NASP, 2020). While, on the surface, this task seems straightforward, school psychologists must be able to balance the authority of parents to participate in educational decision-making with the needs and rights of children. To complicate matters further, all decisions must be made considering the "purposes and authority" of the school system (NASP, 2020, p. 39). Although the NASP-PPE recognizes that it can be difficult to balance the wishes of involved parties while observing school, state, and federal policies, the responsibility to resolve these types of situations in an ethically and legally sound manner clearly rests on the school psychologist. To illustrate this point, the introductory section of the NASP-PPE states, "It is expected that school psychologists will make careful, reasoned, and principled ethical choices based on knowledge of [the] code, recognizing that responsibility for ethical conduct rests with the individual practitioner" (NASP, 2020, p. 39).

Discussion of the first broad theme, *representing the dignity and rights of all persons*, leads directly to a better understanding of social justice and its implications for the practice of school psychology. According to Shriberg and Moy (2014), social justice is something school psychologists *do*; in other words, principles of social justice are woven into the practice of school psychology. As advocates for students and agents of educational change, school psychologists share the belief that they can make a positive impact on the lives of students. These authors subscribe to a definition of social justice that "reflects equitable distribution of resources and respectful, culturally responsive practice" (p. 22). Included in this definition is the protection of educational rights and opportunities as well as nondiscriminatory practices that are the basis of much of federal educational law.

Shriberg and Moy (2014) noted that social justice within the context of school psychology has a strong grounding in both ethics and law. Citing the NASP-PPE 2010, they referred to terms found in this ethics code such as *fairness, justice,* and *creating school climate that is safe and welcoming to all persons* regardless of "race, ethnicity, color, religion, ancestry, national origin, immigration status, socioeconomic status, primary language, gender, sexual orientation, gender identity, gender expression, disability, or any other distinguishing characteristics" (NASP, 2010, pp. 5–6).

Professional Competence and Responsibility

Beneficence, or responsible caring, is a common theme across many professional ethical codes of conduct. In the field of school psychology, beneficence is achieved through engaging in actions that are likely to benefit others, practicing within the boundaries of professional competence, using evidence-based knowledge to guide decision-making, and accepting responsibility for professional decisions (Jacob et al., 2021; Welfel & Kitchener, 1992). Complementary to the concept of beneficence is **nonmaleficence**, or the obligation to act in a manner that does not inflict harm on others. As it relates to professional competence, nonmaleficence involves meeting a standard of care provision that minimizes or avoids risk.

The NASP-PPE further stipulates that school psychologists act as advocates for children across every facet of their practice (NASP, 2020). This requires school psychologists to be knowledgeable about best practices across the various types of services they provide. For example, consider a case in which a school psychologist is asked to evaluate a student and share assessment results with relevant vested partners (i.e., the student, the student's parents, and appropriate school personnel). Under the guidelines of the NASP-PPE, the practitioner must select appropriate, empirically supported, valid, and reliable assessment measures, as well as administer them in the standardized manner outlined in the test materials. Next, the school psychologist must report assessment results using language that is understandable and meaningful (NASP, 2020). Moreover, according to the NASP-PPE, all relevant data must be reported in a manner that best serves the school psychologist's primary client (i.e., the student) and must be shared only with those individuals who will be actively involved in the development, delivery, and monitoring of subsequent interventions (e.g., parents/guardians and appropriate school personnel). As illustrated in this example, the NASP-PPE not only provides aspirational goals for professional service delivery but also delineates the proper procedures for specific activities (NASP, 2020).

Honesty and Integrity in Professional Relationships

In addition to beneficence, school psychologists must demonstrate fidelity in all professional duties (Jacob et al., 2021). Bersoff and Koeppl (1993) define *fidelity* as continuing faithfulness to the truth and to one's professional duties. As such, school psychologists must be honest about the boundaries of their competence and must accurately represent the services they are able to provide based on their training and credentials (NASP, 2020). They also must be able to explain the scope of their services to clients and families in a clear and straightforward manner. In the same vein, school psychologists must be respectful of the participation and competencies of other professionals who are involved with clients and their families (NASP, 2020).

Included in the principle of honesty and integrity is the directive that school psychology practitioners abstain from any activity in which their own personal problems might interfere with their professional effectiveness (Williams & Armistead, 2010). If such a situation should arise, school psychologists should seek assistance from supervisors and/or colleagues and make every effort to resolve conflicts in an ethically sound manner (Jacob et al., 2021). Finally, to maintain the highest standards of professional competence, the NASP-PPE indicates that school psychologists must be responsible for knowing and actively applying the code within their practice (NASP, 2020). As Williams and Armistead (2010) summarize, "ignorance of the ethical code is no excuse" (p. 18).

Responsibility to Schools, Families, Communities, the Profession, and Society

As members of a helping profession, school psychologists must promote healthy school, family, and community environments (Jacob et al., 2021). In addition to acting in ways that maintain safe and healthy environments for all clients and families, the NASP-PPE further charges school psychologists with the duty of assuming a proactive role in counteracting social injustices that affect children and schools (NASP, 2020). While school psychologists must work on an individual level to ensure that the students and families under their direct care are treated fairly and justly, they also should strive to be a part of systems-level change to secure socially just environments for all.

CODE OF ETHICS OF THE INTERNATIONAL SCHOOL PSYCHOLOGY ASSOCIATION

ISPA, founded in 1982, adopted an international code of ethics in 2011 (ISPA, 2011). ISPA's Code of Ethics contains six principles that constitute aspirational behaviors. The six principles that form the basis of ISPA's Code of Ethics are: (a) beneficence and nonmaleficence, (b) competence, (c) fidelity and responsibility, (d) integrity, (e) respect for people's rights and dignity, and (f) social justice. In addition, the ISPA Code of Ethics contains four professional standards: (a) professional responsibilities, (b) confidentiality, (c) professional growth, and (d) professional limitations. Finally, it comprises three professional practices: (a) professional relationships, (b) assessment, and (c) research. As written, the ISPA Code of Ethics is not intended to supersede national codes of ethics but rather to reflect principles and standards from an international perspective.

PUBLIC LEGISLATION RELEVANT TO THE PRACTICE OF SCHOOL PSYCHOLOGY

To trace the influence of legislation relevant to the practice of school psychology, one must begin with the U.S. Constitution. Considered the "supreme law of the land" and adopted in 1787, the U.S. Constitution outlines the federal government's role as the protector of the rights and liberties of the people. The U.S. Constitution does not guarantee the provision of education to U.S. citizens; however, the 10th Amendment to the Constitution indicates that this responsibility rests with individual states. Moreover, the U.S. Constitution and the 14th Amendment provide the basis for contemporary special education law through the equal protection clause and due process rights (Jacob et al., 2016). The *equal protection clause* prohibits states from denying any individual in its territory equal protection under the law. *Due process* requires government officials to afford all individuals fair and equal treatment through the judicial system. So, while the provision of education is a matter of individual states' rights, the Supreme Court of the United States becomes involved in and arbitrates states' jurisdiction over public education when it is believed that one or more civil rights guaranteed under the Constitution have been violated.

Individuals With Disabilities Education Improvement Act

In 1975, the U.S. Congress passed Public Law No. 94-142, which, among other mandates, ensures that all children with disabilities are entitled to a free and appropriate public education (FAPE). The legislation also mandates that such an education must be provided in the least restrictive environment appropriate to meet students' needs. The *least restrictive environment* (LRE) refers to the environment, educational setting, or placement in which the child is educated with peers without disabilities to the maximum extent possible. In 1977, Congress reauthorized this legislation under the new title of the Education for All Handicapped Children Act (EHA). In 1990, EHA was again reauthorized under the Individuals With Disabilities Education Act (IDEA; 1990, 1997), which was subsequently revised and reauthorized under the *Individuals With Disabilities Education Improvement Act* (IDEIA) of 2004 (IDEIA, 2004). Under Part B of IDEIA (2004), the federal government allocates funds to those states that provide assurances that all students with disabilities ages 3 to 21 years are provided FAPE. According to the National Center for Education Statistics (NCES; 2022), during the 2020–2021 academic year, there were approximately 7.2 million students with disabilities between the ages of 3 and 21 years in the United States who received services through IDEIA.

This series of statutes forms the basis for federal education law that governs special education and directly impacts the professional practice of school psychology. Murdick et al. (2007) outline six basic principles of special education legislation. These principles require that a child with a disability be provided (a) FAPE; (b) the guarantee of a nondiscriminatory assessment process for identifying any potential disabilities; (c) an IEP (defined in the following text) to ensure that the entitled instruction and services are provided to the student with a disability; (d) the right to be educated within the LRE (e.g., inclusion in general education classes to the greatest extent possible); (e) the right to procedural due process, should there be a disagreement between parties; and (f) the assurance of parents' rights and procedural safeguards to facilitate their participation in educational decision-making. As already mentioned, an **Individualized Education Program** (IEP) is a comprehensive plan detailing the specific disability services to which a student is entitled to support their access to the curriculum and participation in the school community. Such services may include psychological counseling, speech and language therapy, occupational therapy, academic support services, and testing accommodations. IEPs also document goals for student growth and are developed jointly by parents, teachers, special services staff (e.g., school psychologists), and students (when they are old enough to participate in the process).

Section 504 of the Rehabilitation Act of 1973

Section 504 of the **Rehabilitation Act of 1973** is a section of civil rights legislation that prohibits discrimination against individuals with disabilities (Jacob et al., 2016). This law applies to all schools that receive federal funding. Jacob et al. (2016) assert that a contemporary interpretation of Section 504 requires schools to address three types of potential discrimination. First, it prohibits public schools from excluding students from participating in school programs solely on the basis of their disability. Second, it requires schools to take steps to prevent harassment on the basis of students' disability. Third, it requires schools to provide "reasonable" accommodations for students with disabilities, such that they have equal opportunity to benefit from programs that are also provided to students without disabilities. Thus, under this civil rights law, students who are identified as having a disability (as interpreted by Section 504) are entitled to an accommodation plan, often referred to as a **504 Plan**. Like an IEP, a 504 Plan stipulates the services and accommodations to which a student with a disability is entitled in school. Unlike services provided to students under IDEIA (via an IEP), however, the federal government does not contribute funds to assist with the cost of services provided under Section 504.

DIFFERENCES BETWEEN THE INDIVIDUALS WITH DISABILITIES EDUCATION IMPROVEMENT ACT AND SECTION 504

One important distinction between Section 504 of the Rehabilitation Act and IDEIA concerns the way in which these two laws define the term *disability*. Under IDEIA, Part B, students suspected of having a disability must be evaluated in accordance with procedures outlined in Part B and, subsequently, must be deemed eligible for special education and related services under one of 13 categories of disability. These 13 IDEIA categories (in alphabetical order) are as follows: autism spectrum disorders, deaf–blindness, deafness, emotional disturbance, hearing impairment, intellectual disability, multiple disabilities, orthopedic impairment, other health impaired, specific learning disability, speech or language impairment, traumatic brain injury, and visual impairment including blindness (34 C.F.R. § 300.8). Under IDEIA, determining special education eligibility requires a two-pronged approach; in addition to meeting criteria for one of the 13 disability categories, the student must demonstrate a *need* for special education services (i.e., the disability impedes the student's access to the general curriculum; Reschly, 2000).

Under Section 504, the definition of a *disability* is broader and more open-ended than under IDEIA (Jacob et al., 2016). This legislation defines a disability as a "physical or mental impairment that substantially limits one or more of major life activities" (28 C.F.R. § 35.104). Major life activities include, but are not limited to: caring for oneself, performing manual tasks, seeing, hearing, eating, sleeping, walking, standing, lifting, bending, speaking, breathing, learning, reading, concentrating, thinking, communication, and working (28 C.F.R. § 35.104). Overall, from a school psychologist's perspective, understanding the eligibility requirements for receiving services under either IDEIA or Section 504 is important for daily assessment and intervention activities.

Family Educational Rights and Privacy Act of 1974

Another piece of federal legislation that governs the provision of educational services to students in U.S. public schools is the *Family Educational Rights and Privacy Act* of 1974 (FERPA). Also known as the Buckley Amendment, FERPA protects and safeguards the rights of parents by guaranteeing privacy and confidentiality of student educational records. Educational records are defined under FERPA as records, files, documents, and other materials that contain information directly related to a student or are maintained by an educational agency (34 C.F.R. § 99.3). Such records may include report cards, class schedules, psychoeducational reports, and attendance records, among other student information. Under FERPA, any educational agency (e.g., school) that receives federal funds must develop policies and procedures that require written parental consent to release education records. The only potential exceptions to this include release of information to employees in the student's school system who have "legitimate educational interest," authorized officers of state or federal agencies, and/or members of certain judicial and law enforcement agencies (FERPA, 20 U.S.C. § 1232g; 34 C.F.R. Part 99). An educator or other school employee has "legitimate educational interest" in reviewing a student's education records when, for example, access to such data is necessary for carrying out essential job assignments or the individual is called upon to provide direct or indirect services to benefit the student.

No Child Left Behind Act and Every Student Succeeds Act

In 2001, Congress passed legislation known as the No Child Left Behind (NCLB) Act. These statutes were heavily focused on accountability and, to that end, mandated the implementation of state-wide student-performance assessment systems. Specifically, NCLB required each state to adopt academic content standards for mathematics, reading or language arts, and science. Additionally, states were required to develop and administer yearly state-wide achievement tests to gauge students' progress toward meeting academic standards. School districts or individual schools whose standardized test results did not meet the predetermined levels of acceptable performance were labelled as *low-performing* or *failing* and consequently subject to remedial sanctions (Jacob et al., 2016).

In December 2015, President Barack Obama signed into law the *Every Student Succeeds Act* (ESSA), which replaced NCLB Act. According to Jacob et al. (2016), ESSA attempts to maintain an emphasis on high performance expectations for students, while also correcting the overreliance on state-wide achievement test scores to determine school effectiveness. As its name implies, ESSA emphasizes the provision of high-quality educational services to *all* students. NASP (2021) has identified several essential school-based practices that school psychologists should strive to implement and that are consistent with ESSA's goals:

1. Use of data in an effective, coordinated manner that informs instruction, student outcomes, and school outcomes and accountability
2. Provision of comprehensive, rigorous curricula to all students
3. Coordination of effective services across systems and within schools

4. Provision of comprehensive learning supports that are evidence-based
5. Integration of comprehensive school mental health and behavioral health services into learning supports
6. Integration of safety and school climate efforts into school improvement
7. Provision of high-quality and relevant professional development
8. Implementation of comprehensive accountability systems

ESSA emphasizes high-quality instruction, professional development for educators, and comprehensive learning supports that are responsive to the unique needs of school communities (NASP, 2021). Furthermore, ESSA provides states and districts with greater flexibility to blend federal funding streams in order to achieve these goals, and encourages states and districts to use the funds to implement multitiered systems of supports (MTSS). Broadly defined, MTSS is a multilevel framework of evidence-based prevention and intervention services for supporting the academic, behavioral, social, and emotional well-being of all students (NASP, 2016). MTSS is explored in greater detail in Chapter 8.

With the advent of ESSA, advocates for school psychological services (e.g., NASP) have highlighted the "goodness of fit" between the goals of this legislation and the skills of school psychologists. ESSA language uses two terms whose definitions explicitly reference school psychologists: (a) school-based mental health services providers, or professionals who are qualified under state law to provide mental health services to children and adolescents; and (b) specialized instructional support personnel, or school-based professionals who are qualified to provide assessment, diagnosis, counseling, educational, therapeutic, and other related services. As outlined in the NASP Practice Model, school psychologists are highly qualified to guide schools in meeting the goals of ESSA, as they have expertise in improving academic achievement, facilitating effective instruction, supporting behaviorally and socially successful students, supporting diverse learners, and creating safe, positive school climates (NASP, 2020).

A MODEL FOR LEGAL AND ETHICAL DECISION-MAKING

Returning to our earlier discussion of law and ethics, school psychologists must be able to integrate and apply legal and ethical principles to their professional practice so as to make morally sound decisions. Although critical to effective practice, this process can be trying. To guide school psychologists in resolving potential dilemmas, Williams et al. (2008) advocate for the use of a decision-making model in which ethical and legal issues are examined in a critical and logical fashion. Based on the earlier work of Koocher and Keith-Spiegel (2008), this decision-making model employs a sequential, step-by-step approach to evaluating dilemmas and formulating an action plan. These steps are described in Table 5.1 and are as follows: (a) state objectively the problem situation and its controversies; (b) carefully define the potential ethical–legal issues from multiple perspectives; (c) consult available ethical–legal guidelines; (d) consult with supervisors and valued colleagues; (e) evaluate the rights, responsibilities, and welfare of all affected parties; (f) consider alternative solutions and consequences of making each decision; and (g) make a decision and take responsibility for it.

Williams et al. (2008) contended that following this decision-making model may increase the likelihood that actions taken to resolve ethical dilemmas will be principled and reasoned (as well as potentially applicable to other similar situations). Rather than relying on intuition, it is imperative that school psychologists use critical–evaluative decision-making, especially when faced with complex and sometimes emotionally charged dilemmas. Overall, the decision-making model of Williams et al. may assist school psychologists in arriving at more proactive and reflective solutions to ethical issues.

TABLE 5.1 Ethical and Legal Decision-Making Model

Model of Ethical and Legal Decision-Making in School Psychology
1. Describe the problem situation.
Focus on available information and attempt to gather and objectively state the issues or controversies. Breaking down complex, sometimes emotionally charged situations into clear, behavioral statements is helpful.
2. Define the potential ethical–legal issues involved.
Enumerate the ethical and legal issues in question. Again, state these as clearly and accurately as possible, without bias or exaggeration.
3. Consult available ethical–legal guidelines.
Research the issues in question using reference sources, such as NASP's *Principles for Professional Ethics*, IDEA 2004, state guidelines governing special education, textbooks on ethics and legal issues in school psychology (e.g., Jacob et al.'s *Ethics and Law for School Psychologists* [7th ed., 2016]), job descriptions, school board policies, and other appropriate sources.
4. Consult with supervisors and colleagues.
Talk with your supervisor and trusted colleagues who are familiar with the legal and ethical guidelines that apply to school psychology. On a need-to-know basis, share information specifically about the issues you have identified. Brainstorm possible alternatives and consequences, and seek input from those whose opinions you value.
5. Evaluate the rights, responsibilities, and welfare of all affected parties.
Consider the "big picture" rather than focusing on the isolated details of the controversy. Consider implications for students, families, teachers, administrators, other school personnel, and yourself. How will the various alternative courses of action affect each party involved? Remember two basic assumptions underlying NASP's *Principles for Professional Ethics*: (a) school psychologists act as advocates for their student-clients and (b) at the very least, school psychologists will do no harm.
6. Consider alternative solutions and the consequences of making each decision.
Carefully evaluate, in a step-by-step manner, how each alternative solution will impact the involved parties. Who will be affected and how will they be affected? What are the positive and negative outcomes of each alternative? Weigh the pros and cons. Step back and carefully consider the information you have gathered.
7. Make the decision and take responsibility for it.
Once all the steps are completed, make a decision that is consistent with ethical and legal guidelines and one that you feel confident is the best choice. Take responsibility for following through on that decision, attend to the details, and attempt to bring closure to the scenario.

IDEA, Individuals With Disabilities Education Act; NASP, National Association of School Psychologists.

Source: Koocher, G. P., & Keith-Spiegel, P. (2008). *Ethics in psychology and the mental health professions: Standards and cases.* Oxford University Press. Source for adapted table: Williams, B. B., Armistead, L., & Jacob, S. (2008). *Professional ethics for school psychologists: A problem-solving model casebook.* National Association of School Psychologists.

As discussed earlier in this chapter, the practice of school psychology within the context of social justice often intersects with school psychology's ethics and relevant education laws. Ethical school psychologists advocate for parity in opportunities for students' academic and mental health wellness. For example, during the coronavirus 2019 pandemic, in-person classroom learning was frequently replaced with virtual instruction. As a result, students experienced a loss of face-to-face instructional time, which many believe has had a negative impact on students' academic achievement as well as on their mental health. Consider the following ethical dilemma in *Social Justice Connections* that illustrates some of these issues.

SOCIAL JUSTICE CONNECTIONS

How can practitioners advocate for social justice in their legal and ethical decision-making?

Social justice, legal, and ethical issues regularly intersect. Thus, models of ethical decision-making may assist practitioners in bringing school-based social issues to light and provide guidance when advocating for marginalized populations. The following case example illustrates the application of the Williams et al. (2008) model of decision-making in an ethical dilemma concerning the rights and opportunities of students with disabilities.

1. **Describe the problem situation.**
   Mr. Jones is a special education teacher in a large, urban high school who teaches secondary-level science to students with learning disabilities. Mr. Jones is finding it challenging to provide these students with science instruction that follows the goals and objectives outlined in the students' Individualized Education Programs (IEPs) and would like to enhance the students' exposure to hands-on science experiments. To further complicate matters, during the 2020–2021 school year, amidst the coronavirus 2019 pandemic, it became necessary to switch the students' science class from traditional face-to-face instruction to online learning. Now that school has reopened for in-person instruction, Mr. Jones consults with the school psychologist to consider what additional options are available to his students to accommodate their learning differences and their loss of in-person instruction. Mr. Jones and Ms. Green, the school psychologist, confer and decide that one option would be to schedule a period each day in one of the school's science labs. When Mr. Jones contacts the administrator responsible for scheduling the science lab, he is told that, according to school policy, special education classes are not permitted to use the science lab because the students may damage the expensive science equipment. What should Mr. Jones and Ms. Green do?
2. **Define the potential ethical–legal issues involved. Review guidelines. Consult others as needed.**
   Ms. Green offers to research both legal and ethical guidelines related to this problem situation. She recalls from her Professional School Psychology course in graduate school that there are several laws that might pertain to this issue. She refers to Jacob et al. (2016) and finds that, under Section 504 of the Rehabilitation Act of 1973 (a civil rights law), public schools are prohibited from excluding students from participating in school programs and activities solely on the basis of a disability (p. 151). Ms. Green believes this school policy of prohibiting students with disabilities from using the science lab is a violation of Section 504.

   Ms. Green now must consider how to approach the school administrator who cited school policy as a reason not to allow students with disabilities to use the science lab. Ms. Green reviews the National Association of School Psychologists' *Principles for Professional Ethics* and finds that it is her ethical responsibility to advocate for these students to have access to the science lab. According to NASP (2020), "school psychologists consider the interests and rights of children and youth to be their highest priority in decision-making, and act as advocates for all students" (p. 39). Furthermore, Ms. Green reads the following: "To meet the needs of children and youth and other clients most effectively, school psychologists cooperate with other psychologists and professionals from other disciplines in relationships based on mutual respect" (Principle III.3.1; NASP, 2020, p. 51).

   Contemplating both the legal and ethical guidelines relevant to this issue, Ms. Green confers with her supervisor, who is an experienced school psychologist, to discuss her

(continued)

SOCIAL JUSTICE CONNECTIONS (*continued*)

options. How should she approach the school administrator who conveyed the school policy regarding students with disabilities being prohibited from using the science lab? Ms. Green and her supervisor discuss various strategies and options.

3. **Evaluate the rights, responsibilities, and welfare of all affected parties.**
   Based upon review of legal and ethical guidelines, the *students with disabilities* have a right to use the science lab (i.e., have equal opportunity to gain the same benefit as other students) as part of their science instruction. *Parents of students with disabilities* also have the right for their children to benefit from equal opportunity to be instructed in the science lab. Mr. Jones, the *special education teacher*, has the responsibility to provide students with disabilities with the same benefit as general education students in having access to the hands-on experiences in the science lab to help students meet the objectives outlined in their IEPs. Ms. Green, *the school psychologist*, has the responsibility to understand the legal aspects of the situation and to support her colleagues (both Mr. Jones and the school administrator) in making a well-informed choice regarding the students' access to the lab (i.e., a choice that is both legally and ethically sound).

4. **Consider alternative actions and the consequences of each action.**
   Ms. Green has several alternative actions to consider:
   a. Meet with her union representative to gain the association's support in her fight to overturn the school policy of not allowing students with disabilities access to the science lab. (Consequence: The situation may quickly become adversarial.)
   b. Attend a Board of Education meeting to testify during the public portion of the session to express her disagreement with the school policy that prevents students with disabilities from accessing the science lab. (Consequence: The Board of Education members have an expectation that these types of issues would have been discussed previously with the administrative staff, including the school superintendent.)
   c. Make an appointment to meet with the school administrator to discuss her concerns related to the policy and express her willingness to work on a draft of the school policy to bring it in line with Section 504. (Consequence: This action is consistent with the NASP-PPE, which recommends that school psychologists approach problem-solving with mutual respect.)
   d. Inform parents of the students with disabilities of this injustice and ask for their support to protest this school policy. (Consequence: This action may become necessary if the option of working within the system with school administrators is not effective.)
   e. Do nothing and comply with the school administrator's interpretation of the school policy. (Consequence: Nothing will change.)

5. **Make the decision and take responsibility for it. Monitor outcomes.**
   Ms. Green decides to begin by requesting a meeting with the school administrator to discuss her concerns related to the school policy of not allowing students with disabilities access to the science lab. She plans to discuss the legal implications of the policy and to explain her ethical obligation to advocate for students with disabilities to have parity with other general education students whose science instruction includes exposure to laboratory science experiments. Fortunately, her supervisor agrees to accompany her to this meeting to offer her support. Ms. Green is hopeful that, by working within the system to correct the misinterpretation of this legislation, the school's policy can be revised. She believes she has "done her homework" and is well prepared to openly discuss the issues. She is willing to volunteer to work with a committee of her

(*continued*)

> **SOCIAL JUSTICE CONNECTIONS (*continued*)**
>
> colleagues to draft a proposal to the school superintendent and ultimately to the Board of Education to formally revise the existing policy. Fortunately, during her meeting with the school administrator and her supervisor, the three agree that the school policy regarding the use of the science lab should be reviewed and revised to be compliant with both legal and ethical standards. As a result of their discussion, an action plan is developed to begin the process. If Ms. Green had not been able to effect change via this approach, she was prepared to consider other methods to attempt to resolve the issue.

CONSEQUENCES OF ETHICAL VIOLATIONS

While consequences of legal violations fall under the purview of the government, consequences of ethical violations are addressed by the organizations that develop and enforce professional codes of ethics. As noted earlier, school psychologists are beholden to the ethical codes of professional organizations in which they are members. Thus, for example, members of NASP and/or those who hold the organization's hallmark credential of Nationally Certified School Psychologist (NCSP) are responsible for abiding by the NASP-PPE. Likewise, APA members are responsible for upholding the APA Ethics Code, and members of both NASP and APA are beholden to both codes.

As part of their organizational structures, NASP, APA, and other professional organizations (e.g., state school psychology associations) typically establish a standing committee for ethics and professional practices that provides ongoing support and education for organizational members. These committees also respond to informal inquiries regarding ethical dilemmas and assist members in resolving them. State-level ethics committees often provide an educative function and may serve as the first-level contact for members inquiring about ethical and professional matters. The majority of state school psychology associations adopt the NASP-PPE rather than a state-specific code of ethics. Through the local application of these principles, many ethical concerns and legal questions are resolved at the state level, without further escalation to the national level.

The NASP-PPE provides valuable guidance for school psychologists who believe that colleagues in the profession are acting in an unethical manner. Before filing a formal complaint, NASP members are encouraged to consider this guidance. In its *Principle IV.3. Maintaining Public Trust by Self-Monitoring and Peer Monitoring*, the NASP-PPE suggests potential responses to these situations: "When a school psychologist suspects that another school psychologist has engaged in unethical practices, they attempt to resolve the suspected problem through a collegial problem-solving process, if feasible" (NASP, 2020, p. 55).

This standard recommends an informal approach to resolving potential problems and puts the onus on the school psychologist to broach these issues in an unofficial manner with the colleague in question. (Remember Ms. Green's decision to first meet with the school administrator to discuss her concerns about the school policy regarding access to science labs.) If, however, this action is not successful, Standard IV.3.2 states that the following action is appropriate:

> If a collegial problem-solving process is not possible or productive, school psychologists take further action appropriate to the situation, including discussing the situation with a supervisor in the employment setting, consulting state association ethics committees, and, if necessary, filing a formal ethical violation complaint with state associations, state credentialing bodies, or the NASP Ethical and Professional Practices Board in accordance with their procedures. (NASP, 2020, p. 55)

When necessary, and presumably following interaction with the state school psychology association, a school psychologist who is also a member of NASP may refer a concern to the NASP Ethical and Professional Practices Committee (EPPC) for formal consideration and possible adjudication. Specific procedures are available on the NASP website. Once a complaint is heard by the EPPC, possible sanctions suggested by the committee may include mandated professional development or peer supervision and, in more severe cases, probation, suspension, or termination of NASP membership or revocation of the NCSP credential.

Ultimately, problems may be less likely to arise when school psychologists are knowledgeable about relevant legal and ethical codes and, therefore, able to adhere to them closely. Engaging in best practices in promoting ethical behavior involves remaining abreast of new developments in ethics and law through activities such as reading professional publications and attending state and national conferences. By becoming well versed in ethical and legal issues, school psychologists can strive for excellence in this area, rather than merely meeting minimum standards for acceptable behavior.

SUMMARY AND CONCLUSIONS

Within the NASP Practice Model, Domain 10 requires school psychologists to be knowledgeable about ethical, legal, and professional standards of practice. Armed with this knowledge, school psychologists are better equipped to deal effectively with professional dilemmas that arise in the delivery of school-based services. These dilemmas may involve a school psychologist's interactions with students, parents and guardians, teachers, administrators, and other school personnel. School psychologists rely upon codes of ethics (e.g., the NASP-PPE), educational laws (e.g., ESSA), and other types of regulations to guide their behavior. For example, two important fundamentals underlying ethical principles embedded within the NASP-PPE are: (a) school psychologists consider the interests and rights of children and youth to be their highest priority in decision-making, and (b) school psychologists act as advocates for all students (NASP, 2020). When implemented effectively, the legal and ethical decision-making model outlined in this chapter helps school psychologists examine issues on a critical–evaluative level to arrive at ethically and legally sound decisions.

DISCUSSION QUESTIONS

1. Best practices suggest that coursework in ethics and law should be introduced to students early on in their school psychology graduate preparation. Why is early exposure to this content important?
2. Unlike the APA Ethics Code, the NASP-PPE specifically addresses school-based practice. Provide examples of how each of the four broad ethical themes of the NASP-PPE relates to school-based practice for school psychologists.
3. Pub. L. No. 94-142 (now known as IDEIA) was the first legislation to mandate educational services for students with disabilities throughout the United States. How do you think this legislation has affected the practice of school psychology?
4. How does ESSA specifically address the role of the school psychologist?
5. What are some of the advantages of using a decision-making model when examining ethical and legal dilemmas?

> **RECOMMENDED READINGS**
>
> Jacob, S. (2014). Best practices in ethical school psychological practice. In P. L. Harrison & A. Thomas (Eds.), *Best practices in school psychology* (6th ed., pp. 437–448). National Association of School Psychologists.
> Jacob, S., Decker, D. M., & Lugg, E. T. (2016). *Ethics and law for school psychologists* (7th ed.). Wiley.
> Jacob, S., Williams, B. B., & Armistead, L. D. (2021). *Professional ethics for school psychologists* (3rd ed.). National Association of School Psychologists.
> National Association of School Psychologists. (2020). *National Association of School Psychologists principles for professional ethics*. https://www.nasponline.org/Documents/Standards%20and%20Certification/Standards/1_%20Ethical%20Principles.pdf
> Shriberg, D., & Moy, G. (2014). Best practices in school psychologists acting as agents of social justice. In P. L. Harrison & A. Thomas (Eds.), *Best practices in school psychology* (6th ed., pp. 21–32). National Association of School Psychologists.

A robust set of instructor resources designed to supplement this text is located at http://connect.springerpub.com/content/book/978-0-8261-6344-8. Qualifying instructors may request access by emailing textbook@springerpub.com.

REFERENCES

American Psychological Association. (2017). Ethical principles of psychologists and code of conduct. *American Psychologist, 57*, 1060–1073. https://www.apa.org/ethics/code/ethics-code-2017.pdf
Beauchamp, T., & Childress, J. (2001). *Principles of biomedical ethics* (5th ed.). Oxford University Press.
Bersoff, D. N. (1983). Children as participants in psychoeducational assessment. In G. B. Melton, G. P. Koocher, & M. J. Sakes (Eds.), *Children's competence to consent* (pp. 149–177). Plenum Press.
Bersoff, D. N., & Koeppl, P. M. (1993). The relation between ethical codes and moral principles. *Ethics &Behavior, 3*(3–4), 345–357. https://doi.org/10.1080/10508422.1993.9652112
Burns, M. K., Jacob, S., & Wagner, A. R. (2008). Ethical and legal issues associated with using response-to-intervention to assess learning disabilities. *Journal of School Psychology, 46*(3), 263–279. https://doi.org/10.1016/j.jsp.2007.06.001
Corrao, J., & Melton, G. B. (1988). Legal issues in school-based behavior therapy. In J. C. Witt, S. N. Elliot, & F. M. Gresham (Eds.), *Handbook of behavior therapy in education* (pp. 131–144). National Association of School Psychologists.
Family Educational Rights and Privacy Act. (1974). *Family Educational Rights and Privacy Act of 1974*, 20 U.S.C. § 1232g.
Fisher, C. B. (2017). *Decoding the ethics code* (4th ed.). Sage.
Individuals With Disabilities Education Act. (1990). *Individuals With Disabilities Education Act*, Pub. L. No. 101-476, 104 Stat. 1142.
Individuals With Disabilities Education Act. (1997). *Individuals With Disabilities Education Act of 1997*, Pub. L. No. 105-17, 105 Stat. 37.
Individuals With Disabilities Education Improvement Act. (2004). *Individuals With Disabilities Education Improvement Act of 2004*, Pub. L. No. 108-446.
International School Psychology Association. (2021). *International School Psychology Association code of ethics*. https://www.ispaweb.org/wp-content/uploads/2021/07/ISPA-Code-of-Ethics-2021.pdf
Jacob, S. (2005). *Ethics and law update for school psychologists*. Presentation at the NASP 2005 Summer Conference, Philadelphia, Pennsylvania.
Jacob, S. (2008). Best practices in developing ethical school psychological practice. In A. Thomas & J. Grimes (Eds.), *Best practices in school psychology: V* (pp. 1921–1932). National Association of School Psychologists.

Jacob, S., Decker, D. M., & Lugg, E. T. (2016). *Ethics and law for school psychologists* (7th ed.). Wiley.
Jacob, S., Williams, B. B., & Armistead, L. D. (2021). *Professional ethics for school psychologists* (3rd ed.). National Association of School Psychologists.
Kaplan, M. S., Crisci, P. E., & Farling, W. (1974). *School Psychology Digest*, Vol. 3 (Special Issue). National Association of School Psychologists.
Knapp, S. J., & VandeCreek, L. D. (2005). *Practical ethics for psychologists: A positive approach*. American Psychological Association.
Koocher, G. P., & Keith-Spiegel, P. (2008). *Ethics in psychology and the mental health professions: Standards and cases*. Oxford University Press.
Murdick, N. L., Gartin, B. C., & Crabtree, T. L. (2007). *Special education law* (2nd ed.). Merrill Publishing.
National Association of School Psychologists. (2010). *National Association of School Psychologists principles for professional ethics*. https://www.nasponline.org/Documents/Standards%20and%20Certification/Standards/1_%20Ethical%20Principles.pdf
National Association of School Psychologists. (2016). *ESSA and multitiered systems of supports for school psychologists*. http://www.nasponline.org/research-and-policy/current-law-and-policy-priorities/policy-priorities/the-every-student-succeeds-act/essa-implementation-resources/essa-and-mtss-for-school-psychologists
National Association of School Psychologists. (2020). *Professional standards of the National Association of School Psychologists*. https://www.nasponline.org/x55315.xml
National Association of School Psychologists. (2021). *Leveraging essential school practices, ESSA, MTSS, and the NASP practice model: A crosswalk to help every school and student succeed* [Policy brief]. https://www.nasponline.org/Documents/Research%20and%20Policy/ESSA/ESSA%20PM%20Crosswalk.Nov.2021.pdf
National Center for Education Statistics. (2022, May). *Students with disabilities*. Condition of Education. U.S. Department of Education, Institute of Education Sciences. https://nces.ed.gov/programs/coe/indicator/cgg
Reschly, D. J. (2000). Assessment and eligibility determination in the Individuals With Disabilities Education Act of 1997. In C. F. Telzrow & M. Tankersley (Eds.), *IDEA amendments of 1997* (pp. 65–104). National Association of School Psychologists.
Ross, W. D. (1930). *The right and the good*. Claredon Press.
Shriberg, D., & Moy, G. (2014). Best practices in school psychologists acting as agents of social justice. In P. L. Harrison & A. Thomas (Eds.), *Best practices in school psychology* (6th ed., pp. 21–32). National Association of School Psychologists.
Trachtman, G. M. (1974). Ethical issues in school psychology. *School Psychology Digest*, 3(1), 4–15. https://doi.org/10.1080/02796015.1974.12086299
Welfel, E. R., & Kitchener, K. S. (1992). Introduction to the special section: Ethics education: An agenda for the '90s. *Professional Psychology: Research and Practice*, 23(3), 179–181. https://doi.org/10.1037/0735-7028.23.3.179
Williams, B. B., & Armistead, L. (2010). Applying law and ethics in professional practice. In T. M. Lionetti, E. P. Snyder, & R. W. Christener (Eds.), *A practical guide to building professional competencies in school psychology* (pp. 209–225). Springer.
Williams, B. B., Armistead, L., & Jacob, S. (2008). *Professional ethics for school psychologists: A problem-solving model casebook*. National Association of School Psychologists.

CHAPTER 6

Graduate Preparation and Credentialing

ERIC ROSSEN ■ NATALIE N. POLITIKOS ■ JOSEPH S. PRUS

CHAPTER OBJECTIVES

After reading this chapter, you will be able to:

- Identify differences in degree types among school psychology graduate preparation programs.
- Describe the national context and value of program approval and accreditation.
- Specify relevant aspects of accreditation/approval bodies.
- Differentiate among various credentials relevant to school psychology.
- Identify different credentialing pathways based on degree or setting.

NATIONAL ASSOCIATION OF SCHOOL PSYCHOLOGISTS PRACTICE MODEL CONNECTIONS

Domain 10: Legal, Ethical, and Professional Practice

INTRODUCTION

School psychologists care for the well-being of our nation's most vulnerable youth and families, so it is critical that they deliver high-quality and ethically sound psychological services. A number of organizations work to ensure that school psychologists are appropriately qualified to provide psychological and educational services to youth and families. These entities include both professional organizations (e.g., American Psychological Association [APA] and National Association of School Psychologists [NASP]) and government organizations (e.g., state education agencies and licensing boards). Collectively, guidelines delineated by professional organizations and government agencies help to ensure that our nation's school psychologists receive high-quality graduate preparation, demonstrate appropriate qualifications when entering the workforce, and pursue continuing education on a regular basis. To illustrate these concepts, this chapter describes the current landscape of accreditation and pathways of graduate preparation and credentialing for school psychologists.

PROFESSIONAL STANDARDS

To ensure the quality of service delivery, professional psychology organizations (e.g., NASP and APA) develop *professional standards*, or benchmarks that delineate expectations for preparation, practice, and continuing education among professionals. Standards may govern a wide range of professional preparation and practice activities, including graduate education, field experiences, professional practice, ethical behavior, and continuing education. Moreover, they serve as an important tool for communicating and advocating among vested partners, policy makers, and other professional groups at the national, state, and local levels. Overall, standards help define contemporary practices and lay the foundation for future advancements and directions in a field. They are revised regularly to account for changes in contemporary practices and the evolving contexts within which services are provided.

The professional organizations that generate standards most relevant to the practice of school psychology include APA, the International School Psychology Association (ISPA), and NASP. Of these three organizations, NASP maintains standards most directly tailored to the diverse roles of school psychologists practicing in the United States. NASP's (2020b) professional standards consist of its: (a) *Model for Comprehensive and Integrated School Psychological Services* (practice); (b) *Standards for Graduate Preparation of School Psychologists* (graduate education); (c) *Standards for the Credentialing of School Psychologists* (certification and licensure); and (d) *Principles for Professional Ethics* (ethics). These four sets of standards are developed concurrently and provide a comprehensive, cohesive, and unified set of national principles to guide the field.

Similar to NASP, APA maintains related but independently developed standards, such as the *Ethical Principles of Psychologists and Code of Conduct* (APA, 2017), *Standards of Accreditation for Health Service Psychology* (SoA; APA, 2015), and the *Model Act for State Licensure of Psychologists* (APA, 2010). Unlike NASP's professional standards, these documents are designed to address all practice specialties within psychology (e.g., clinical, counseling, school, and pediatric psychology). Thus, they are written broadly and are less tailored for the practice of school psychology specifically. Moreover, APA has differed historically from NASP in advocating for the doctoral degree to be the entry-level degree for professional psychologists; therefore, its standards for graduate program accreditation and professional and ethical practice primarily address doctoral-level psychologists. However, APA has recently drafted standards for the accreditation of master's-level programs in health service psychology (APA, 2020).

Finally, ISPA maintains a code of ethics for school psychologists internationally (ISPA, 2011) as well as the *International Guidelines for the Preparation of School Psychologists* (Cunningham & Oakland, 1998). These graduate preparation guidelines are described in further detail later in this chapter. Although ISPA accreditation has been pursued by some U.S. programs that emphasize an international focus, ISPA guidelines are likely to be more beneficial to programs located in countries that do not possess separate standards at the national level.

Professional standards confer a number of benefits on a field. Specifically, they offer a consistent set of expectations for the profession as well as widely accepted benchmarks for quality. Consistency in professional expectations is highly important (especially for the field of school psychology), as variability in the quality and types of services provided would create substantial challenges for ensuring that all youth have equal access to appropriate supports. Additionally, such inconsistencies have the potential to create confusion among the recipients of school psychological services, such that a school psychologist in one school may serve a different role than the school psychologist in another. However, the need for consistency is also problematic in some ways. For example, standards development teams often grapple with the challenge of crafting language that is adequately specific to ensure clarity while also accommodating potential future directions for the field and natural variations in the school psychologist's role based on their unique and evolving context. At times, the desire to foster professional consistency may result in standards that inadvertently undermine innovation or stifle potential advances in the profession.

As noted previously, both professional standards and state legislation shape pathways to becoming a school psychologist. Generally, these pathways involve completing a graduate preparation program, obtaining relevant credentials, and maintaining credentials through ongoing professional development. The next few sections of this chapter describe procedures and requirements for graduate preparation, credentialing, and continuing education in school psychology. Standards documents relevant to each section are described or referenced throughout.

GRADUATE PREPARATION IN SCHOOL PSYCHOLOGY

Degree Types

In the United States, there are approximately 267 universities with established programs that offer *school psychology preparation*, or the coursework and supervised field experiences required to earn a graduate degree in school psychology (Gadke et al., 2022). School psychology programs (SPPs) may offer a variety of degrees, and different types of degrees are associated with different preparation requirements, employment outcomes, and credentialing standards. Generally, school psychology degrees can be divided into two broad categories: *nondoctoral* (e.g., specialist-level) *degrees* and *doctoral degrees*.

Nondoctoral Degrees

According to NASP standards, the *specialist-level degree* is the entry-level degree for school psychologists, meaning that it represents the minimum level of education required to become a certified/licensed school psychologist. Generally, these types of degrees require a *minimum* of 3 years of full-time graduate study (or the equivalent) beyond the bachelor's degree, involving at least 60 graduate semester or 90 graduate quarter hours. In addition to coursework, these degrees require a yearlong internship consisting of at least 1,200 clock hours of supervised practice, 600 of which must be completed in a school setting (NASP, 2020b).

Different institutions or programs may refer to nondoctoral school psychology degrees by different names. For example, some SPPs grant a specialist degree (e.g., Educational Specialist [EdS] or Specialist in Psychology [PsyS]), whereas others award a 60-credit-hour master's degree or some combination of a master's degree *and* certificate of graduate study. For example, in some parts of the country, students obtain both a master's degree in school psychology (approximately 30 credits) and a Certificate of Advanced Graduate Study/Studies (CAGS; approximately 30 credits). All of these would still meet the definition of a specialist-level degree, even if the name of the degree itself does not include the word *specialist*.

Conversely, master's degree programs in school psychology that constitute fewer than 60 graduate credit hours generally have been phased out by U.S. graduate institutions. In a few states, terminal master's degrees of fewer than 60 credit hours may allow individuals to obtain a credential as an educational or psychoeducational diagnostician (who provides a limited range of assessment services), but rarely as a school psychologist. Although APA has approved the development of standards for the accreditation of master's programs in health service psychology (which by definition includes school psychology), specific credit-hour requirements have yet to be established as of the writing of this chapter, leaving some questions about the standards' potential impact on the scope of graduate preparation in school psychology.

This variation in degrees can cause confusion among prospective program applicants. Most important, however, candidates ideally complete a program of at least 60 graduate hours with curriculum and internship requirements consistent with national standards developed by NASP. It is also important to be properly supervised by a credentialed school psychologist or, for any setting outside of the schools, a psychologist who has obtained the appropriate credential for practice in that particular setting.

The majority of school psychologists (68.5%) hold a specialist degree or CAGS, and 9% hold a master's degree (many of whom possess a master's degree that required 60 graduate credit hours or more; Goforth et al., 2021). Thus, overall, 78% of school psychologists practice at the nondoctoral level, which is not surprising given that no state or U.S. territory requires a doctoral degree to work as a school psychologist. Individuals may opt to pursue a specialist-level degree for a variety of reasons, including the desire to become school-based practitioners who work directly with children, families, and educational systems; the desire for a broad, generalist training; and the freedom to pursue employment sooner (i.e., sooner than doctoral-level candidates). However, in many states, practitioners with nondoctoral degrees have fewer employment opportunities, especially in nonschool settings, than those with a doctoral degree.

Doctoral Degrees

Approximately 22% of school psychologists hold a doctoral degree (Goforth et al., 2021). The number of necessary credit hours for a doctorate varies by program (although NASP requires 90 semester hours), as does the specific emphasis. For example, some doctoral programs emphasize clinical preparation over research preparation, and vice versa. Moreover, some programs provide options to pursue an area of specialization, such as school neuropsychology or pediatric school psychology. Doctoral programs may be accredited by NASP, APA, and/or ISPA.

Doctoral programs in school psychology may confer several different degree types, such as Doctor of Philosophy (PhD), Doctor of Education (EdD), or Doctor of Psychology (PsyD) degrees. For doctoral programs approved or accredited by NASP, candidates must accrue a minimum of 90 graduate semester hours and complete a 1,500-hour internship (NASP, 2020b). Faculty positions in higher education institutions and, in some instances, research and policy jobs within school psychology typically require candidates to have earned a doctoral degree. Factors that may contribute to an individual's decision to pursue a doctoral degree include aspirations to enter academia, the desire for "prestige," and the desire to pursue increased expertise and skill level (often in a specialized area of practice; Laurent et al., 2008).

Content and Structure

The content and structure of graduate preparation programs are often linked closely to standards issued by professional organizations. This alignment is largely attributable to efforts by many programs to achieve accreditation, which is described later in this chapter. As already noted, three primary organizations provide guidance on the content and structure of SPPs: NASP, APA, and ISPA. Standards for program content for each of these organizations are listed in Table 6.1 and described in further detail in this section.

NATIONAL ASSOCIATION OF SCHOOL PSYCHOLOGISTS GRADUATE PREPARATION STANDARDS

NASP has been developing graduate preparation standards since its 1972 *Guidelines for Training Programs in School Psychology*. Since that time, the organization has revised its standards approximately every 10 years, and each successive revision has introduced several changes. The most recent revision of NASP's (2020b) *Standards for Graduate Preparation of School Psychologists* retains much of the structure that was already present and organizes the standards into five main areas:

1. School Psychology Program Context/Structure
2. Domains of School Psychology Graduate Education and Practice
3. Practica and Internships in School Psychology
4. Program Assessment and Accountability
5. School Psychology Program Support/Resources

Notably, the 10 domains of practice in the NASP (2020b) Practice Model are the same as those described in the Domains of School Psychology Graduate Education and Practice. These domains describe the necessary content to be taught and reinforced in graduate preparation programs, which then translate to practice. The 10 domains are reiterated in Table 6.1.

AMERICAN PSYCHOLOGICAL ASSOCIATION STANDARDS FOR HEALTH SERVICE PSYCHOLOGY

In 2015, APA (2015) passed the *Standards of Accreditation for Health Service Psychology* (SoA), which came into effect on January 1, 2017 and were revised in 2018 and 2019. These standards continue to be outcome oriented, allowing each program to define its model of preparation, goals, competencies, and student outcomes. Each program also must monitor individual student performance and conduct ongoing program evaluation. The SoA includes five broad standards:

1. Institutional and Program Context
2. Aims, Competencies, Curriculum, and Outcomes
3. Students
4. Faculty
5. Communication Practices

Each of these standards has specific requirements that must be addressed by the program. Several structural items (e.g., residency requirements), program processes (e.g., annual written evaluation of all students), program assessment and quality improvement mandates (e.g., systematic program self-assessment), and public disclosure issues are also required. Additionally, Standard II (B) includes nine distinct areas that must be addressed in the program's curriculum. These nine areas are listed in Table 6.1.

INTERNATIONAL SCHOOL PSYCHOLOGY ASSOCIATION TRAINING STANDARDS

ISPA's Professional Development and Practice Committee initially developed key standards for accreditation in 2001, which were substantially updated in 2014 (ISPA, 2017). ISPA identifies six broad goals and standards for SPPs. These goals designate skills and competencies that emerging professionals should attain to become successful school psychologists (ISPA, 2017). The goals and standards listed in Table 6.1 have many similarities to NASP's standards, with the exception of Goal 3 (i.e., transnational/multicultural standard).

TABLE 6.1 Areas of Competency for Program Accreditation

National Association of School Psychologists	American Psychological Association	International School Psychology Association
Domain 1: Data-Based Decision-Making	1. Research	*Goal 1: Core Knowledge in Psychology and Education*
Domain 2: Consultation and Collaboration	2. Ethical and legal standards	1.1 Cognition and Learning
		1.2 Social and Emotional Development
Domain 3: Academic Interventions and Instructional Supports	3. Individual and cultural diversity	1.3 Individual Differences
	4. Professional values, attitudes, and behaviors	*Goal 2: Professional Knowledge and Skills in Assessment and Intervention*
Domain 4: Mental and Behavioral Health Services and Interventions		2.1 Evidence-Based Decision-Making and Accountability
	5. Communication and interpersonal skills	2.2 Prevention, Mental Health Promotion and Crisis Intervention
Domain 5: School-Wide Practices to Promote Learning	6. Assessment	2.3 School and Systems Organization, Policy Development and Implementation
Domain 6: Services to Promote Safe and Supportive Schools	7. Intervention	2.4 Home–School–Community Collaboration
Domain 7: Family, School, and Community Collaboration	8. Supervision	*Goal 3: Transnational/Multicultural School Psychology*
	9. Consultation and interprofessional/ interdisciplinary skills	3.1 Role and functions of school psychologists nationally and internationally
Domain 8: Equitable Practices for Diverse Student Populations		3.2 Working with children and families from culturally diverse communities
Domain 9: Research and Evidence-Based Practice		*Goal 4: Professional Practice of School Psychologists*
Domain 10: Legal, Ethical, and Professional Practice		4.1 Legislation that impacts on education policy and practice
		4.2 Ethical issues in professional practice
		4.3 Report writing
		Goal 5: Interpersonal Skills
		5.1 Self-awareness and reflexivity
		5.2 Interviewing
		5.3 Consultation
		Goal 6: Research Methods
		6.1. Research design and implementation
		6.2 Analysis and interpretation of research findings

Sources: American Psychological Association. (2015). *Standards of accreditation for health service psychology.* http://www.apa.org/ed/accreditation/about/policies/standards-of-accreditation.pdf; International School Psychology Association. (2017). *The accreditation of professional training programs in school psychology.* https://www.ispaweb.org/accreditation; and National Association of School Psychologists. (2020). *Standards for the graduate preparation of school psychologists.* Author.

> **SOCIAL JUSTICE CONNECTIONS**
>
> *How can school psychology programs (SPPs) prepare effective agents of social justice?*
>
> Over time, NASP and SPPs across the United States have increasingly recognized the importance of integrating social justice throughout the curriculum and teaching advocacy skills to preservice school psychologists. The 2020 NASP graduate preparation standards describe the need for school psychologists to "have knowledge of individual differences, abilities, disabilities, and other diverse characteristics and the impact they have on development and learning" and to "recognize that equitable practices for diverse student populations, respect for diversity in development and learning, and advocacy for social justice are foundational to effective service delivery" (p. 32). In addition, NASP has identified the promotion of social justice as one of its strategic goals, highlighting the need to address social justice within preparation programs, professional organizations, and the field as a whole. Other professional organizations also address social justice issues in their mission statements and professional standards. For example, APA's *Standards of Accreditation (SoA) for Health Service Psychology* call for programs and their constituents to engage in actions that promote respect for cultural diversity and individual differences.
>
> How can SPPs teach skills in social justice advocacy? As noted by Shriberg (2012), "best practices" in preparing future social justice advocates are still emerging; however, scholars in school, clinical, and counseling psychology have made attempts to tackle this question. For example, Goodman et al. (2004) identified six core competencies related to the practice of social justice advocacy: (a) engaging in ongoing self-examination; (b) sharing power (i.e., among practitioners, students, families, and others); (c) giving voice (i.e., empowering students and families to share their perspectives and participate in educational decision-making); (d) facilitating consciousness raising (e.g., helping children and families become more aware of social injustices in society); (e) building on strengths; and (f) leaving clients with the tools to work toward social change. Notably, several of these competencies center on empowering clients to actively participate in service delivery and educational decision-making processes. Others are more practitioner centered and require the psychologist to reflect meaningfully on their own personal beliefs and attitudes. Principles such as those described by Goodman et al. (2004) provide a strong foundation for preparing effective social justice advocates and have slowly begun to permeate the curricula of SPPs across the nation (e.g., Grapin, 2017; Miranda et al., 2014; Moy et al., 2014). Finally, evidence suggests that increasing the diversity of racially and ethnically minoritized students and faculty can enhance discourse and development related to cultural competence and humility (Schilling et al., 2021).

GRADUATE PROGRAM ACCREDITATION

Broadly, higher education *accreditation* is "a system for recognizing educational institutions and professional programs affiliated with those institutions for a level of performance, integrity, and quality which entitles them to the confidence of the educational community and the public they serve" (Chernay, 1990, p. 1). Generally, government regulations related to accreditation focus on institutional/university or program infrastructure and student outcomes, and rely on professions to more specifically dictate the skills and knowledge required for competency in that field. In other words, the profession itself determines an appropriate set of standards and behaviors that govern the field, and private, nonprofit organizations (e.g., NASP, APA) conduct external reviews of program quality (Eaton, 2012). One of the main goals of accreditation is to provide the public with assurance that the institutions or programs under scrutiny are meeting or exceeding established professional standards.

APA began accrediting doctoral clinical psychology programs in 1946, and by 1973 it had adopted criteria for the accreditation of professional psychology, regardless of specialty (Prus & Strein, 2011). APA is recognized by both the U.S. Department of Education and the Council on Higher Education Accreditation (CHEA; a nonprofit association that evaluates and recognizes accrediting bodies in higher education) to accredit doctoral programs in psychology. As mentioned earlier, it is currently developing standards for the accreditation of master's programs in health service psychology, although as of the writing of this chapter, the exact title of such programs and credentials that graduates might qualify for are yet to be determined (APA, 2020).

Historically, NASP developed the ability to review and "approve" programs through its affiliation with the National Council for Accreditation of Teacher Education (NCATE), which began in 1976 (Fagan & Wells, 2000). In 2010, NCATE merged with the Teacher Education Accreditation Council (TEAC) to become the Council for the Accreditation of Educator Preparation (CAEP; Prus & Strein, 2011). Programs recognized by NASP through its affiliation with NCATE and then CAEP were considered to be "NASP-approved." However, beginning in 1988, NASP also reviewed programs independently of NCATE and then CAEP. Such programs were, and are, considered to be "NASP-accredited." In May 2022, NASP achieved CHEA recognition for the independent accreditation of specialist-level degree programs and doctoral-level degree programs in school psychology.

Importantly, accreditation is "voluntary," meaning that universities may or may not choose to pursue this marker of program quality (Prus & Strein, 2011). However, some state departments of education require applicants for school psychology state certification or licensure to be graduates of NASP-approved or accredited programs or to hold the Nationally Certified School Psychologist (NCSP) credential (described in the following section). In doing so, they are seeking to ensure that graduate preparation has taken place in line with standards identified by the profession. Additionally, states may utilize this external review from organizations such as NASP to minimize the need for their own internal review of a candidate's graduate preparation. This means that programs in those states must secure NASP approval or accreditation in order to produce candidates who are qualified to practice within the state. Likewise, some state licensing boards either require or encourage applicants for the title of "licensed psychologist" to be graduates of APA-accredited programs. This incentivizes doctoral programs in these states to seek APA accreditation. In general, accreditation in a specialized professional field increases the legitimacy of the credentials awarded to program graduates. Moreover, although nonapproved or nonaccredited programs may indeed provide high-quality preparation, accreditation signals to prospective applicants that a program is subject to quality control by an independent, external agency (Prus & Strein, 2011).

Over time, there has been a shift in higher education accreditation from focusing on program operations to focusing on accountability for student outcomes (Nelson & Messenger, 2003). Essentially, in addition to asking, "Do programs contain the necessary components determined by organizational and national standards?", accreditation agencies are increasingly asking the question "Are students actually learning what they are supposed to be learning?" As a result, there is relatively less emphasis on scrutinizing program structure and supports (i.e., inputs) and greater emphasis on assessing candidate performance (i.e., outcomes). The question "Are students actually learning what they are supposed to be learning?" can be answered through performance assessments (e.g., measures of both knowledge and skill in psychological service delivery) throughout the various stages of graduate preparation. It is for this reason that programs often must have at least one full student cohort complete all coursework and requirements in their entirety prior to consideration for approval or accreditation.

CREDENTIALING IN SCHOOL PSYCHOLOGY

Credentialing generally describes the process of establishing qualifications and authorizing individuals to practice professionally. In the context of school psychology, *credential* is a generic, umbrella term that includes both *certification* and *licensure*. From a national perspective in school psychology, the terms are generally interchangeable, as they both refer to a process of a state agency (typically the state department of education) granting permission to practice under that agency's authority. Certification is often mistakenly assumed to refer only to school-based practice, whereas licensure is sometimes considered a term exclusively dedicated to credentialing for psychological services provided outside of school settings, such as independent practice, hospitals, and clinics. Indeed, many states use those terms in this manner (i.e., certification for school practice; licensure for independent practice). However, in some states, credentials for school-based practice are officially called licenses or endorsements; therefore, such global distinctions in terminology are potentially misleading. Ultimately, each state agency will identify the title of any credentials it may oversee.

Additional differences exist between practice and nonpractice credentials. **Practice credentials** are awarded by a government agency (e.g., state education agency [SEA]) and are required for an individual to practice psychology legally in a specified range of settings (e.g., K–12 schools). These credentials also identify settings where services can be provided (e.g., K–12 school settings, early childhood and pre-K settings, private and charter schools) and the scope of practice (i.e., the range of allowable services) in these settings. Individuals who do not hold a valid credential are generally not permitted to serve in the role of school psychologist in schools.

By comparison, **nonpractice credentials** are issued by nongovernment agencies (e.g., professional organizations such as NASP). These credentials are desirable because they are markers of high-quality or specialized training. Additionally, the majority of states acknowledge or recognize the NCSP as partially or fully meeting eligibility requirements for the state school psychology credential. In other words, showing evidence of the NCSP alone is sometimes sufficient for a state agency to award its own credential (in lieu of requiring candidates to complete a lengthier application process). Some states are also *requiring* either the NCSP or completion of a NASP-approved or -accredited program. However, holding the NCSP credential alone without a credential from the state agency would not be sufficient to authorize the provision of services. Holding the NCSP also signals to employers that the individual has met NASP's rigorous graduate preparation standards and maintains a commitment to ongoing professional growth. Ultimately, it is common for practitioners to hold more than one credential (although usually not required by law within the United States).

Practice Credentials at the State Level

Credentialing for the purposes of professional practice in school psychology is a state-level function. In other words, each state maintains independent credentialing laws, regulations, and requirements. In nearly every state and territory, the credential for school psychological practice is issued by the state department of education or SEA; Texas and Hawaii represent the only exceptions. The Texas State Board of Examiners of Psychologists (i.e., board of psychology) oversees the credentialing of school psychology practitioners in Texas. As of the writing of this chapter, in Hawaii, no state-level agency has oversight over the credentialing of school psychologists, though the state board of education offers general descriptions and minimum qualifications for districts to use in the hiring process. Given that SEAs largely oversee the credentialing of school psychologists, the requirements and expectations are generally more affected by educational rather than psychological norms. Updated information on state requirements can be found at www.nasponline.org/standards-and-certification/state-school-psychology-credentialing-requirements.

CREDENTIALING FOR PRACTICE IN SCHOOLS

States vary considerably in their credentialing requirements with respect to a range of factors, including: (a) basic eligibility requirements (e.g., graduate preparation, supervised field experiences, exams); (b) title (e.g., "school psychologist"); (c) setting where services can be provided (e.g., schools, hospitals); and (d) scope or range of services. As of the writing of this chapter, no states maintain an official reciprocity agreement for school psychologists; in other words, holding a school psychology credential in one state does not automatically qualify an individual to work in another state (though some states consider out-of-state credentials or the NCSP as part of their application process). Thus, any school psychologist who is considering work in more than one state, at any point in time, should become familiar with the various requirements and pursue experiences that allow for eligibility in as many states as possible. Unfortunately, a study of 216 school psychology students found that only 34% of those who had planned to pursue multiple credentials had actively researched the requirements to obtain them (Hall et al., 2007).

Eligibility and Education

Although eligibility requirements for the practice of school psychology vary by state, they typically include criteria related to education (e.g., degree), supervised field experiences, and, in some states, examination. Generally, these requirements should be completed as part of a school psychology degree or program of study. Most states require a degree specifically in school psychology and a minimum of a specialist-level degree as the entry-level requirement. A specialist-level degree is typically defined as 60 semester hours (or 90 quarter hours) of graduate study packaged under various degree titles including, but not limited to, EdS, PsyS, Master of Arts (MA), Master of Science (MS), MA with CAGS, or MA with Certificate of Advanced Study (CAS). Some, however, allow for degrees in fields other than school psychology or for fewer credit hours; for example, Washington, D.C., requires only 42 graduate semester hours in school, educational, or clinical psychology. Some state requirements are broader or have additional requirements that go beyond national standards. Others specify unique requirements within their degree criteria, such as North Dakota, which requires candidates to complete a three-credit course in Native American and multicultural studies. Notably, *no state requires a doctoral degree for the school psychology credential for practice in schools*, and there is no indication that we will see any significant trend toward requiring a doctoral degree in the foreseeable future.

Additionally, some states require that candidates come from a school psychology graduate program that held NASP or APA approval/accreditation at the time of their graduation (or that the individual hold the NCSP). Thus, an individual who has worked as a practitioner for many years in one state could potentially not be eligible to work in another state if they did not attend an approved or accredited program.

Supervised Field Experiences

Supervised field experiences in SPPs are comprised of both practicum and internship experiences. Although terminology varies across graduate programs, a ***practicum*** (plural: *practica*) is a field-based experience that generally occurs during the early-to-middle years of graduate preparation, exposes students to professional settings, and builds skills in psychological and educational service delivery through close supervision. Very few states have specific requirements related to practica for the purposes of certification or licensure, though some exist (e.g., specified hours working with certain populations or in certain settings).

In SPPs, an ***internship*** is a culminating field experience that typically requires the integration of skills developed during practica and, in many cases, greater independence (although interns continue to be closely supervised by their appointed field-based and university-based supervisors). The internship is the culminating experience in school psychology graduate preparation and thus typically occurs in the final year of the program. Many states require a 1,200-hour internship experience, and some go on to stipulate that at least 600 of those hours take place in a school setting, which aligns with the NASP (2020b) credentialing standards. No state requires *more* than 1,200 hours of internship. However, some states require certain types of experiences (e.g., working with minoritized students or students with emotional/behavioral disabilities) or specify requirements for intern supervisors.

Examinations

Approximately half of all states require candidates to achieve a passing score on the School Psychologist Praxis exam (#5403), which is administered by the Educational Testing Service (ETS). Some states, however, utilize different exams that assess basic skills in reading, writing, and math or have adopted a school psychology exam administered by other test publishers. In addition, albeit rarely, a state may require a state-specific exam; for example, Nevada requires an exam demonstrating knowledge of both the U.S. and Nevada constitutions. No SEA requires the Examination for Professional Practice in Psychology (EPPP) for a school psychology credential (although this exam is often a requirement for a general psychology credential from a state board of psychology). The EPPP is described briefly later in this chapter.

Title

A credential identifies a professional title and/or a scope of practice. In the vast majority of states, the school psychology credential allows use of the title "school psychologist" in professional settings. Some states may have expanded titles; for example, Maine's credential specifies whether the school psychologist holds a specialist or doctoral degree. Other states do not have "school psychologist" in the name of the credential and instead confer titles such as School Specialist License (e.g., Kansas). The majority of these states, however, do not prohibit use of the title "school psychologist" among individuals who have obtained these credentials. The exception is Arkansas, as explicit restrictions within this state prohibit the use of "psychologist" in any title without a general psychologist credential (reserved for doctoral-level psychologists only). Thus, the Arkansas credential confers the title of School Psychology Specialist (SPS).

Setting and Scope of Services

Credentials typically specify the services that can be provided, the recipients of those services, and the settings in which service delivery can take place. Most state regulations allow qualified practitioners (i.e., those who hold the school psychology credential) to provide a general, nonspecific range of school psychological services. In other words, states rarely restrict specific psychological services or techniques and instead define the practice of school psychology broadly. Broad language allows for the continuous improvement and evolution of practice and the provision of services based on contextual need. This broad language also allows school psychologists to provide services within the scope of their competencies.

Some SEA credentials may restrict service delivery to students from pre-K to grade 12 only, whereas others extend these parameters to include college students and children ages birth through 5 years. Such distinctions are not made clear in many states. Credentials may also identify the settings in which services can be provided. For those with the SEA school psychology credential, the majority of states restrict service delivery to schools, which typically include public, charter, and private schools (including contractual services). Sometimes, states do not specify which agency has regulatory authority over the credentialing of school psychologists employed in private/independent schools (i.e., schools privately funded that are not administered by local, state, or federal governments), leaving hiring decisions to the independent schools themselves. A school psychologist with the SEA credential working outside of an approved setting may be considered as operating outside of the scope of the credential.

ALTERNATIVE, PROVISIONAL, OR TEMPORARY CREDENTIALING

The field of school psychology has faced workforce shortages for decades, such that the supply of personnel has not met the demand (Bocanegra et al., 2017). Some settings or areas of the country experience more severe shortages than others do; for example, many rural districts report difficulties filling vacant positions, particularly in states where very few school psychology graduate programs exist. As a result, some states have created alternative credentialing practices that allow for temporary or emergency credentials (e.g., a 2-year temporary and nonrenewable credential while fulfilling other requirements) in an effort to fill gaps in service delivery. Often, these credentials have less strict criteria related to graduate preparation, field experiences, and exams, which, in turn, may undermine the quality and consistency of services provided. Some states also require school psychology interns to obtain a provisional or temporary credential to complete an internship in the schools. The NASP 2020 Professional Standards provide additional guidance on provisional credentialing, indicating recommendations such as: (a) issuing a 2-year, nonrenewable credential that clearly indicates "temporary" or "provisional" in its official title; and (b) permitting such credentials to be issued to retired school psychologists or those holding the NCSP who have not had the opportunity to complete the full credentialing process with the SEA.

RESPECIALIZATION AND PROFESSIONAL RETRAINING

The NASP 2020 Professional Standards included specific guidance and definitions to clarify *respecialization and professional retraining* (RPR). Specifically, RPR refers to a process of institutions enrolling students from related fields or backgrounds in *nondegree-seeking programs* that lead to state certification or licensure only. In other words, an individual engaged in RPR may complete a compressed program of study that leads to the issuance of a license or certification to practice in a particular state; however, they would not be granted a degree and likely would have difficulty obtaining any other credential for their efforts. RPR is considered a form of alternative credentialing. This usually requires a partnership and agreement between institutions and SEAs and is often born out of a shortage of school psychologists.

Conversely, many programs may accept students from related fields or backgrounds into a degree-seeking program by reviewing previous graduate preparation and waiving certain coursework. These students may obtain a degree from that program and thus would not be considered to be pursuing RPR. See NASP's (2020a) *Guidance for Respecialization and Professional Retraining* for more information.

Related Credentials

Some states issue credentials that allow for a limited scope of services, such as conducting only assessments for special education evaluations in school settings. These credentials may have titles such as *educational diagnostician*, *psychometrist*, or even *school psychology assistant* and often require less graduate preparation than credentials for school psychologists. Such credentials often appear in order to address shortages of providers; however, school psychologists, local agencies, and state agencies should recognize that individuals with these related credentials cannot replace school psychologists, given their limited scope of services. Instead, such individuals ideally would supplement the role of the school psychologist. NASP does not set standards for these types of credentials, as they are not considered to be for school psychologists.

Credentialing for Practice Outside of Schools

The majority (89%) of NASP members maintain an active SEA credential, whereas few hold credentials with the state board of psychology (13%; Goforth et al., 2021). Despite this minority, some have anticipated a rise in the number of school psychologists pursuing secondary employment outside of schools, either due to burnout or due to the need to supplement income (Rossen, 2011). Generally, to practice psychology outside of schools, one must obtain a credential from the state board of psychology (though specific names of state boards or agencies vary) or other relevant agencies. Credentials to practice independently (i.e., outside of schools without supervision) typically require a doctoral degree in either school, clinical, or counseling psychology; however, there are many states that allow for nondoctoral-level practitioners to practice outside of schools in some capacity and under different titles.

Doctoral Practice

In most states, practicing psychology outside of schools requires a doctoral degree in school, clinical, or counseling psychology, a passing score on the EPPP (described later in this chapter), and the completion of supervised field experiences. Some states also require a state-level jurisprudence exam or oral exam, postdoctoral supervision hours (i.e., field supervision *after* the completion of doctoral studies and formal internship), a doctoral degree from an APA-accredited graduate program, and/or the completion of an APA-accredited or Association of Psychology and Postdoctoral Internship Center (APPIC) internship. APPIC is an organization that sets quality standards for internships, postdoctoral positions, and fellowships in professional psychology and facilitates matches between applicants and approved training sites. Many states do not require candidates to complete accredited degree programs or internships to qualify for the psychology license (meaning that candidates may graduate from nonapproved or nonaccredited programs and complete internships outside of the APPIC network). Candidates should continually check the credentialing requirements in the states in which they plan to live and work; alternatively, they may attempt to meet the most stringent of these requirements if they are unsure as to where they will eventually practice.

As noted earlier, many states require that candidates achieve a passing score on the EPPP exam. Developed by the Association of State and Provincial Psychology Boards (ASPPB), the EPPP has historically been a knowledge-based exam of a variety of areas pertinent to the practice of professional psychology, including topics such as biological, social, and cultural bases of behavior; growth and life-span development; assessment, diagnosis, prevention, and treatment practices; research methods; and legal and ethical issues. However, the EPPP consists of two parts: The EPPP Part 1 (Knowledge) and the EPPP Part 2 (Skills). A beta version of the skills portion of the test was launched in early 2021 in three U.S. states and two Canadian provinces that were "early adopters" (ASPPB, 2021). It remains to be seen if and how state boards will utilize the skills portion of the exam. The choice to include or require Part 2 remains up to each individual state board or agency.

Nondoctoral Practice

Some states allow for the delivery of psychological services by nondoctoral school psychologists outside of schools. In many instances, separate credentials have been developed for which school psychologists may qualify, though often the credential does not include "school psychologist" as a professional title. For example, Massachusetts confers the title of *Educational Psychologist*, and South Carolina and California confer the titles of *Licensed Psycho-Educational Specialist* and *Licensed Educational Psychologist*, respectively; each of these allows for some amount of practice outside of schools. An even greater number of states have credentials for nondoctoral professionals that allow for practice under the supervision of a licensed psychologist. The requirements, scope of practice, titles, and agencies that maintain oversight over all of these credentials vary significantly across states.

Finally, depending on their preparation and supervised experience, school psychologists often qualify for other credentials in related professions that may allow for practice outside of schools. These may include, but are not limited to, *Licensed (Clinical) Professional Counselor* or *Licensed Mental Health Counselor/Therapist*. Each credential specifies preparation requirements, the professional title to be used when operating under that credential, the scope of practice, and the settings in which services can be provided.

Maintenance and Renewal of Credentials

The majority of credentials (both practice and nonpractice credentials) require some form of periodic renewal, although a few exceptions exist where no renewal or maintenance is required. In fact, an analysis found that eight out of 51 SEAs (including the District of Columbia) do not require or mandate any continuing professional development (CPD) or continuing education (CE) for renewal (Rossen et al., 2019). Those requiring renewal typically mandate a process for CE or CPD in the form of a certain number of clock or credit hours (e.g., 75 clock hours) over a specified period of time (e.g., 3 years). On average, SEAs require approximately 20 CPD/CE hours per year, with an average renewal period of approximately 5 years. In contrast, state psychology boards tend to most frequently have a 2-year renewal cycle, with a range of 9 to 30 hours required per year (Rossen et al., 2019). Some state agencies require that a portion of these hours cover specific topics (e.g., ethics; legal regulation; or diversity, equity, and inclusion) or be obtained from specific types of providers (NASP- or APA-approved providers). As with all components of credentialing, the specific requirements vary from state to state and often evolve over time.

Nonpractice Credentials

Recall that the conferral of practice credentials is primarily a state-level function, such that one must possess an appropriate state-level credential to legally provide services. Nonpractice credentials (as described earlier), however, often are conferred at the national level. Although nonpractice credentials alone typically do not afford regulatory authority to provide services, they can provide a great deal of professional benefit to practitioners. To name a few, these credentials include the Diplomate in School Psychology, Diplomate in School Neuropsychology, and NCSP (as mentioned toward the beginning of this chapter). Of particular relevance among nonpractice credentials, is the NCSP.

Nationally Certified School Psychologist Credential

The NCSP credential, while considered a nonpractice credential, does provide a number of benefits. First, the credential is recognized by more than 30 states as either partially or fully meeting the criteria to earn an SEA credential. This means that, although holding the NCSP alone does not allow for legal practice, possession of this credential provides a facilitated path to obtaining the state credential. This recognition allows for greater mobility among school psychologists who wish to relocate or practice in more than one state. As of the writing of this chapter, a few states require candidates either to hold the NCSP or to complete a NASP-approved or APA-accredited program to obtain a state practice credential.

Some school districts, and a few states, offer an additional annual stipend to any school psychologists holding the NCSP credential. Aside from the more tangible benefits, the NCSP also provides professional credibility and demonstrates that the individual has met national standards for practice. Approximately two thirds of all NASP members presently hold the NCSP (Goforth et al., 2021), and there are more than 17,000 active NCSPs as of the writing of this chapter. To qualify for this credential, one must meet NASP credentialing standards (NASP, 2020b) and basic eligibility requirements, including the following:

- Completion of an organized program of study that is officially titled "School Psychology" that consists of at least 60 graduate semester/90 quarter hours
- Completion of a sequence of supervised experiences that occurred prior to and exclusive of the internship is required (i.e., practica)
- Successful completion of a 1,200-hour internship in school psychology, of which at least 600 hours must be in a school setting
- A passing score on the Praxis School Psychologist Exam

The NCSP credential also requires completion of a NASP-accredited or approved program or the equivalent (i.e., a program that does not have NASP accreditation or approval but upholds the graduate preparation standards set forth for the NCSP). Graduates of programs *not* approved or accredited by NASP are eligible to apply for the NCSP, but they must demonstrate that they have attained the knowledge and skills represented in NASP standards by providing more extensive documentation of their preparation. Graduates of NASP-accredited or approved programs submit relatively less documentation because their programs have already been deemed aligned with NASP standards and have documented candidate outcomes. The NCSP credential also has an NCSP-Inactive status (e.g., those on a leave of absence) as well as an NCSP-Retired status. More information can be found at www.nasponline.org/certification.

SUMMARY AND CONCLUSIONS

Regulation of professional preparation and practice in school psychology is critical for ensuring that students, families, and other vested partners in schools receive high-quality services. A number of organizations and agencies, including both government and nongovernment organizations, confer credentials for school psychologists that attest to the quality and depth of their preparation for practice. As the field of school psychology continues to evolve in response to the ever-changing landscape of education and mental health service delivery, regular review and revision of professional standards and credentialing requirements must be undertaken. These revisions should be responsive to changes in the field (e.g., use of technology, virtual service delivery) as well as the increasingly diverse and challenging social context in which youth live. This ongoing process of responsive reflection allows for the continuous improvement of approaches to preparing and supporting highly qualified and effective professionals.

DISCUSSION QUESTIONS

1. What are the benefits of accreditation to consumers, including prospective graduate students? What might be some drawbacks of accreditation?
2. NASP and all U.S. states view the specialist-level degree as the entry-level degree for school psychology, as opposed to the doctoral degree. What might be some consequences for the field of shifting to a doctoral-only profession?
3. States largely maintain oversight of school psychology credentialing, despite the existence of a national certification procedure. Why is state oversight important?
4. As noted in the chapter, one state (Arkansas) chooses not to allow specialist-level school psychology practitioners to use the title "school psychologist." Do you agree with this restriction? Why or why not?
5. What are some advantages and disadvantages of alternative and temporary credentialing options? Should more graduate programs consider creating pathways leading to credentialing (without conferral of degree) as a way to reduce school psychologist shortages? Why or why not?

RECOMMENDED READINGS

National Association of School Psychologists. (2020). *Graduate educators: Guidance for respecialization and professional retraining.* https://www.nasponline.org/Documents/Standards%20and%20Certification/Standards/NASP_Guidance_RPR.pdf

Prus, J., & Strein, W. (2011). Issues and trends in the accreditation of school psychology programs in the United States. *Psychology in the Schools, 48*(9), 887–900. https://doi.org/10.1002/pits.20600

Rossen, E. (2011). Essential tools for prospective and early career school psychologists: Credentialing for school and independent practice. *Communiqué, 40*(1), 28–30. https://www.nasponline.org/publications/periodicals/communique/issues/volume-40-issue-1

Rossen, E., Guiney, M., Peterson, C., & Silva, A. (2019). Alignment of CPD/CE requirements for credential renewal with best practices for professional learning in psychology and school psychology. *Professional Psychology: Research and Practice, 50*(2), 87–94. https://doi.org/10.1037/pro0000231

Shriberg, D. (2012). Graduate education and professional development. In D. Shriberg, S. Song, A. Miranda, & K. Radliff (Eds.), *School psychology and social justice: Conceptual foundations and tools for practice* (pp. 311–326). Routledge.

 A robust set of instructor resources designed to supplement this text is located at http://connect.springerpub.com/content/book/978-0-8261-6344-8. Qualifying instructors may request access by emailing textbook@springerpub.com.

REFERENCES

American Psychological Association. (2010). *Model act for state licensure of psychologists.* https://www.apa.org/about/policy/model-act-2010.pdf

American Psychological Association. (2015). *Standards of accreditation for health service psychology.* http://www.apa.org/ed/accreditation/about/policies/standards-of-accreditation.pdf

American Psychological Association. (2017). *Ethical principles of psychologists and code of conduct.* http://apa.org/ethics/code/index.aspx

American Psychological Association. (2020, March). *Master's level accreditation: A status update from the master's accreditation work group.* https://www.apa.org/ed/accreditation/newsletter/2020/03/masters-accreditation

Association of State and Provincial Psychology Boards. (2021). *Beginning in January 2020 the EPPP will consist of two exams: The EPPP (Part 1-Knowledge) and the EPPP (Part 2-Skills).* https://www.asppb.net/page/EPPPPart2-Skills

Bocanegra, J. O., Grapin, S. L., Nellis, L. M., & Rossen, E. (2017). Remediating the shortages crisis through the creation of a resource guide. *Communiqué, 45*(6), 16–18. https://www.nasponline.org/publications/periodicals/communique/issues/volume-45-issue-6

Chernay, G. (1990). *Accreditation and the role of the Council on Postsecondary Accreditation.* Council on Postsecondary Education.

Cunningham, J., & Oakland, T. (1998). International School Psychology Association guidelines for the preparation of school psychologists. *School Psychology International, 19,* 19–30. https://doi.org/10.1177/0143034398191002

Eaton, J. (2012, August). *An overview of U.S. accreditation.* http://www.chea.org/pdf/Overview%20of%20US%20Accreditation%202012.pdf

Fagan, T. K., & Wells, P. D. (2000). History and status of school psychology accreditation in the United States. *School Psychology Review, 29*(1), 28–51. https://doi.org/10.1080/02796015.2000.12085996

Gadke, D. L., Valley-Gray, S., & Rossen, E. (2022). NASP report of graduate education in school psychology: 2019–2020. *NASP Research Reports, 6*(3), 1–10. https://www.nasponline.org/research-and-policy/research-center/nasp-research-reports

Goforth, A. N., Farmer, R. L., Kim, S. Y., Naser, S. C., Lockwood, A. B., & Affrunti, N. W. (2021). Status of school psychology in 2020: Part 1, Demographics of the NASP Membership Survey. *NASP Research Reports, 5*(2), 1–17. https://www.nasponline.org/research-and-policy/research-center/nasp-research-reports

Goodman, L. A., Liang, B., Helms, J. E., Latta, R. E., Sparks, E., & Weintraub, S. R. (2004). Training counseling psychologists as social justice agents: Feminist and multicultural principles in action. *Counseling Psychologist, 32*(6), 793–837. https://doi.org/10.1177/0011000004268802

Grapin, S. (2017). Social justice training in school psychology: Applying principles of organizational consultation to facilitate change in graduate programs. *Journal of Educational and Psychological Consultation, 27*(2), 173–202. https://doi.org/10.1080/10474412.2016.1217489

Hall, J. E., Wexelbaum, S. F., & Boucher, A. P. (2007). Doctoral student awareness of licensure, credentialing, and professional organizations in psychology: The 2005 National Register International Survey. *Training and Education in Professional Psychology, 1,* 38–48. https://doi.org/10.1037/1931-3918.1.1.38

International School Psychology Association. (2011). *Code of ethics.* https://www.ispaweb.org/wp-content/uploads/2020/07/The_ISPA_Code_of_Ethics_2011.pdf

International School Psychology Association. (2017). *The accreditation of professional training programs in school psychology.* https://www.ispaweb.org/accreditation

Laurent, J., Steffey, L., & Swerdlik, M. (2008). *Why students pursue a specialist or doctoral degree in school psychology.* Poster presented at 40th annual convention of the National Association of School Psychologists, New Orleans, Louisiana.

Miranda, A. H., Radliff, K. M., Cooper, J. M., & Eschenbrenner, C. R. (2014). Graduate student perceptions of the impact of training for social justice: Development of a training model. *Psychology in the Schools, 51*(4), 348–364. https://doi.org/10.1002/pits.21755

Moy, G., Briggs, A., Shriberg, D., Jackson, K., Smith, P., & Tompkins, N. (2014). Developing school psychologists as agents of social justice. *Journal of School Psychology, 52(3)*, 323–341. https://doi.org/10.1016/j.jsp.2014.03.001

National Association of School Psychologists. (2020a). *Graduate educators: Guidance for respecialization and professional retraining.* https://www.nasponline.org/Documents/Standards%20and%20Certification/Standards/NASP_Guidance_RPR.pdf

National Association of School Psychologists. (2020b). *The professional standards of the National Association of School Psychologists.* https://www.nasponline.org/standards-and-certification/nasp-2020-professional-standards-adopted

Nelson, P. D., & Messenger, L. C. (2003). Accreditation is psychology and public accountability. In E. M. Altmaier (Ed.), *Setting standards in graduate education: Psychology's commitment to excellence in accreditation* (pp. 7–37). American Psychological Association.

Prus, J., & Strein, W. (2011). Issues and trends in the accreditation of school psychology programs in the United States. *Psychology in the Schools, 48*(9), 887–900. https://doi.org/10.1002/pits.20600

Rossen, E. (2011). Essential tools for prospective and early career school psychologists: Credentialing for school and independent practice. *Communiqué, 40*(1), 28–30. https://www.nasponline.org/publications/periodicals/communique/issues/volume-40-issue-1

Rossen, E., Guiney, M., Peterson, C., & Silva, A. (2019). Alignment of CPD/CE requirements for credential renewal with best practices for professional learning in psychology and school psychology. *Professional Psychology: Research and Practice, 50*(2), 87–94. https://doi.org/10.1037/pro0000231

Schilling, E. J., Malone, C. M., Bocanegra, J. O., & Barrett, C. (2021). *Recruitment and retention of racial and ethnic minoritized students in school psychology graduate programs* [Technical assistance brief]. National Association of School Psychologists. https://www.nasponline.org/x58026.xml

Shriberg, D. (2012). Graduate education and professional development. In D. Shriberg, S. Song, A. Miranda, & K. Radliff (Eds.), *School psychology and social justice: Conceptual foundations and tools for practice* (pp. 311–326). Routledge.

SECTION II

Service Delivery in School Psychology

CHAPTER 7

Assessment

NICHOLAS F. BENSON ■ BRANDON S. PARKER

CHAPTER OBJECTIVES

After reading this chapter, you will be able to:

- Define *assessment* in the context of school-based service delivery.
- Describe essential features of assessment.
- Describe purposes and applications of assessment in school settings.
- Describe commonly used assessments in school psychology.
- Describe integration and reporting of assessment results.
- Describe multicultural considerations in assessment.

NATIONAL ASSOCIATION OF SCHOOL PSYCHOLOGISTS PRACTICE MODEL CONNECTIONS

Domain 1: Data-Based Decision-Making
Domain 3: Academic Interventions and Instructional Supports

INTRODUCTION

In psychology and education, ***assessment*** is a methodical process that involves the collection, evaluation, integration, and application of information to guide decision-making and to achieve professional objectives (e.g., instructional decision-making, diagnosis, and treatment planning). One common misconception about the process of assessment is that it is synonymous with tests and testing. Although tests are typically an integral part of this process, tests are only one of several types of assessment methods. Moreover, assessment often focuses on multiple domains of functioning (e.g., academic, behavioral, and emotional domains), occurs on multiple occasions, and includes collection of information from multiple sources.

There is a strong demand for assessment in school settings. In fact, most of the assessment practices utilized in other settings originated from applications in schools (Fagan, 1996).

Assessment is routinely used to help promote desired outcomes and address problems that hinder students' psychological and educational functioning. This chapter highlights the importance, foundations, and applications of assessment in the practice of school psychology.

IMPORTANCE OF ASSESSMENT IN THE PRACTICE OF SCHOOL PSYCHOLOGY

People display individual differences in the extent to which they successfully execute various tasks (e.g., reading and writing) and participate in life activities (e.g., interacting with peers and engaging in daily routines). Understanding individual differences in students' functioning is essential for providing appropriately matched services and, ultimately, to the educational process. Thus, information gleaned from assessments is invaluable for fostering students' strengths and preventing and/or remediating difficulties.

Assessments conducted by school psychologists have traditionally focused on determining students' eligibility for special education and related services. While it continues to be important to identify students in need of these services, the role of the school psychologist has broadened. For example, many school psychologists are now involved in universal screenings of academic skills and behavior to identify students in need of early interventions (Albers et al., 2007). To help ensure that students make adequate progress in meeting academic and behavioral expectations, school psychologists must engage in assessment *for* intervention (i.e., assessment aimed at evaluating the need for and focus of an intervention), assessment *during* intervention (i.e., assessment that monitors a student's progress during intervention), and assessment *of* intervention (assessment that evaluates the outcomes of the intervention; Albers et al., 2015). The purpose of these assessment activities is to develop customized interventions for individual students and to guide decisions regarding whether these interventions should be continued, terminated, or modified.

OVERVIEW OF ASSESSMENT PROCESSES

Assessments typically involve interactions between a person or an agency (e.g., caregiver or school) that arranges for an assessment, one or more professionals with competency in testing and assessment (e.g., school psychologist), and an individual or group (e.g., all students in a classroom or school) that is the subject of the assessment. For example, a parent or teacher may refer a student for an assessment, and a variety of school-based professionals may engage in assessment activities to identify the student's strengths and weaknesses. The assessment process is often interdisciplinary, meaning that it involves a team of professionals who possess complementary areas of expertise. This interdisciplinary assessment team assumes varied roles in the collection, evaluation, and utilization of data. In schools, school psychologists may collaborate with several individuals, including school social workers, behavior interventionists, guidance counselors, teachers, and others, to coordinate assessment activities.

The collection process involves gathering historical data as well as data regarding current functioning. This information is used to clarify a referral question and refine assessment goals. The referral question, or **reason for referral**, indicates the reason or purpose for which an assessment is undertaken. Theoretically, there can never be too much information collected during an assessment; however, it is important for practitioners to be efficient in their data collection practices. Excessive data collection can detract from students' instructional time, which can ultimately interfere with their learning.

ESSENTIAL FEATURES OF TESTS: PSYCHOMETRIC PROPERTIES

For school psychologists to hone competencies in assessment, they must first understand the features of high-quality assessments. As previously noted, the assessment process is often interdisciplinary. Nonpsychological staff may have minimal training in measurement and assessment issues (Reynolds, 1986); thus, it is imperative that school psychologists immerse themselves in this literature to ensure the quality of assessment services.

Psychometrics refers to the study of psychological measurement. Psychometricians (and ultimately, school psychologists) are concerned with the extent to which psychological instruments accurately and consistently measure the phenomenon, or *construct*, they are designed to measure. **Constructs** are conceptual abstractions of phenomena that are not directly observable but are theorized to influence observable behaviors (MacCorquodale & Meehl, 1948). For example, some constructs that school psychologists may evaluate among youth include intelligence and self-esteem. While not observable to the human eye, these latent attributes can be measured using psychological tests. A comprehensive review of psychometrics and measurement is beyond the scope of this chapter; however, some key concepts are reviewed here.

Validity

Validity is the most fundamental consideration in selecting and evaluating tests and other assessment techniques. Broadly defined, *validity* refers to the weight of evidence supporting proposed interpretations and uses of test-derived scores. Validity is not a property of a test per se; rather, it pertains to specific interpretations and uses of test scores. In other words, the validity of an instrument cannot be evaluated without considering the purpose and context of the instrument's use and interpretation. For example, a test of reading comprehension cannot be deemed either universally "valid" or "invalid" across all contexts; rather, it may have some degree of established validity for a particular purpose or interpretation (e.g., measurement of third-grade students' end-of-year reading competence). Evidence of validity is needed to support the interpretation and use of test scores, and tests should not be administered in the absence of sufficient evidence to support proposed interpretations or uses.

Test developers, school psychologists, and others can evaluate validity evidence in several ways. For example, experts in a particular domain can examine the content of the assessment (e.g., whether it addresses the full range of reading comprehension skills targeted for measurement). They can also evaluate the internal structure of the test (e.g., relations among test items) as well as its relations with other similar and dissimilar tests (e.g., correlations with other measures of reading comprehension). Importantly, school psychologists should also consider validity evidence based on test consequences, meaning the intended or unintended consequences of test use. Although evidence may suggest that a test is an excellent measurement tool, it is inappropriate to use test scores to drive policy unless there is sufficient evidence to indicate that this use leads to acceptable outcomes. For example, while there is ample evidence to support the reliability and validity of scores from most state-wide achievement tests, research suggests that teacher identity explains less than 20% of variance in student achievement outcomes (e.g., Hanushek et al., 1998). Although student achievement data are commonly used to evaluate teachers and inform policy decisions such as the provision of merit pay, little to no evidence exists to support the consequential validity of such practices (Welner, 2013).

Test fairness is an important element of validity for school psychologists to consider, especially when utilizing measures to assess a latent trait (such as cognitive ability) in students from diverse backgrounds. Fairness includes (a) equitable treatment of examinees by the examiner and test standardization; (b) lack of measurement bias as determined by procedures such as differential item functioning, which assesses whether individuals with identical abilities have different likelihoods of answering items correctly due to group differences; (c) accessibility to the measured construct, which may require testing accommodations; and (d) valid interpretations and uses of test scores (American Educational Research Association et al., 2014).

Reliability

Classical test theory posits that an examinee's observed scores on a particular test or measure comprise the examinee's true score and error. The examinee's true score, or the score that best represents the examinee's true skills or abilities, is masked by some degree of error. Error in scores arises for several reasons, including mistakes in administration or scoring, chance distractions during the testing process, or guessing on the part of the examinee. Because error is pervasive and unavoidable, test administrators can never know an examinee's true score definitively; they can only observe the score that the examinee obtains during test administration, known as the *observed score*.

Reliability refers to the extent to which measures yield consistent scores and are free from error. The goal of estimating reliability is to determine how much of the variability in test scores reflects meaningful individual differences as opposed to measurement error. When considering a test's psychometric properties, school psychologists should consider several types of reliability, including internal consistency and test–retest reliability. *Internal consistency* refers to the average interitem correlation among test items—in other words, the interrelatedness of items. Reliability coefficients range from .00 (perfectly unreliable) to 1 (perfectly reliable). *Test–retest reliability* refers to the temporal stability of test scores, or the extent to which scores can be replicated across measurement occasions. For example, a test that generally yields highly similar scores when administered to the same individuals at different points in time may be considered to have high test–retest reliability.

FORMATIVE AND SUMMATIVE ASSESSMENT

Traditionally, assessments of student learning have been categorized as formative or summative based on their purpose and actions. *Formative assessment* refers to the collection and use of information to monitor students' progress over the course of intervention. This type of assessment aims to improve students' learning and attainment of intervention objectives by providing ongoing information that can be used for instructional decision-making (Black & Wiliam, 1998; Shepard, 2006). *Summative assessment* also focuses on the collection and use of information to evaluate students' learning and attainment of instructional objectives, but it is conducted after the curricular content addressing these objectives has already been delivered. That is, it provides a summary of the students' outcomes in the intervention.

The distinction between formative and summative assessments is important but is not always clear, as some argue that assessments can serve both formative and summative functions. For example, results from end-of-year, state-wide achievement tests are commonly used for summative accountability purposes. Such results are used to evaluate the effectiveness of instructional practices and to hold school districts accountable for student outcomes. However, these results also assist with the identification of students who fail to meet academic proficiency standards and students who do not display adequate yearly progress. Thus, end-of-year results can be used formatively to plan instruction for the upcoming school year. Such dual functions (i.e., using results both to evaluate instructional effectiveness and to monitor student progress) have blurred the distinction between formative and summative assessment (Dixson & Worrell, 2016; Hattie & Leeson, 2013).

PURPOSES OF ASSESSMENT IN SCHOOLS

There are multiple financial, pragmatic, legal, ethical, and professional reasons for providing assessment services in schools. Assessment procedures most utilized in school settings are those that "address student learning, psychoeducational interventions, and intervention implementation mediated via consultation" (Braden, 2003, p. 262). As previously noted, school psychologists may engage in assessment for intervention, during intervention, and of intervention (Albers et al., 2015).

Assessment for Intervention

Assessing for intervention centers on several goals, including (a) identifying students who may require further assessment and intervention services, and (b) clarifying areas of need and potential targets for intervention. These assessments reveal information that allows school psychologists to target students' needs efficiently and effectively. Two ways that school psychologists typically assess for intervention are through screening and disability identification.

SCREENING

Many schools conduct **universal screening** of academic skills and behavior, meaning that an entire population of students (e.g., all students at a grade level within a school or school district) is assessed to identify individuals in need of additional academic or mental health supports (Albers et al., 2007). Universal screening is a preventative assessment technique that fits within a multitiered system of support (MTSS) framework (described in greater detail in Chapter 8). It involves identifying students who show early warning signs of academic and behavioral difficulties. Students who do not meet the performance criterion on a school's screener(s) may receive additional interventions to prevent difficulties from escalating into more severe problems.

Because screening measures are administered to all students for the purpose of identifying individuals who are at risk for various types of difficulties, they must be both efficient and psychometrically defensible. Thus, screening procedures rely on brief tests and other assessment procedures to provide information regarding students' academic and behavioral functioning. A variety of tests, rating scales, and other procedures can be used in screening systems aimed at identifying students who are at risk for problems in a wide range of areas (e.g., early reading skills, early numeracy skills, social functioning, or emotional functioning). Screening systems typically include decision criteria for taking action. For example, school personnel may decide that students identified on a screener as experiencing "some risk" will receive moderately intensive services, whereas students identified as experiencing "high risk" will receive the most intensive services. In this manner, screeners can guide schools in utilizing their limited resources more efficiently.

DIAGNOSIS/ELIGIBILITY DETERMINATION

Classification involves assigning things to categories based on common features. *Diagnosis* is a special case of classification that involves using *nosology* to group individuals into taxonomies of proposed syndromes, diseases, or disabilities. Diagnoses are made based on properties that provide meaningful distinctions, such as etiology (i.e., cause), pathogenesis (i.e., onset, course, and underlying mechanisms), or syndromes (i.e., patterns of signs and symptoms). Diagnoses and disability identifications often provide valuable information that sets the stage for intervention and treatment planning.

It is important to note that nondoctoral school psychologists employed in pre-K–12 settings do not diagnose students per se. Rather, they identify students as eligible or not eligible to receive special education and related services based on criteria associated with 13 broad disability categories (e.g., emotional and behavioral disabilities, specific learning disabilities, and autism spectrum disorders). These broad disability categories derive from the Individuals With Disabilities Education Improvement Act (IDEIA) of 2004 (described in Chapter 5) as well as specific eligibility criteria developed by individual states. Evaluations must be sufficiently comprehensive to identify the need for any special education or related services and must utilize a variety of technically sound assessment tools and strategies (34 C.F.R. § 300.304). Eligibility determinations must be made by a multidisciplinary team that includes a parent or guardian, teachers, a school administrator, an assessment specialist who assists with the interpretation of assessment data (e.g., a school psychologist), and other relevant educational professionals. A student is considered eligible for special education and related services if the team determines that the student is a child with a disability (as defined by one or more of the 13 disability categories) and, because of their disability status, needs special education and related services (34 C.F.R. § 300.306).

School psychologists who have secured the appropriate state-level credentials and who are employed in settings other than pre-K–12 schools (e.g., private practice and hospital settings) often make mental health diagnoses. Mental health professionals in the United States utilize the *Diagnostic and Statistical Manual of Mental Disorders*, which is currently in the text revision of its fifth edition (*DSM-5-TR*; American Psychiatric Association, 2022), to diagnose mental disorders. The *DSM-5-TR* contains descriptive text and diagnostic criteria for each disorder, as well as diagnostic codes used for billing service providers and data collection purposes. In school settings, *DSM-5-TR* classifications are often used to gain third-party (e.g., Medicaid or private healthcare insurers) reimbursement for psychological services (Tobin & House, 2016). *DSM-5-TR* diagnoses are used ubiquitously in the United States to determine the need for and allow access to mental health and rehabilitation services.

Assessment During Intervention

It is critical that school psychologists assess not only *prior to* and *following* intervention, but also *during* intervention. These types of assessments allow school personnel to monitor student growth in response to interventions as these services are being delivered. Failure to periodically monitor student progress may result in the continued delivery of interventions that are not accomplishing their intended objectives. This wastes valuable instructional time as well as coveted school resources. Conversely, having more regular data available allows school psychologists to make more immediate adjustments to interventions that can enhance their efficiency and impact.

Progress monitoring involves measuring the student's rate of change using a time-series design (i.e., data are collected at several successive, equally spaced measurement occasions). Progress monitoring may focus on an array of academic, social, and emotional behaviors, although in schools it is most associated with the assessment of academic development (Fuchs & Fuchs, 2010). Progress monitoring involves formative assessment, meaning that the results are used to inform instructional or interventional efforts. Specifically, frequent (e.g., weekly, or biweekly) measurements are collected at the level of individual students with verified academic problems and the resulting time-series data are analyzed to guide decisions regarding responsiveness to intervention. Responsiveness to intervention is evaluated relative to the expected rate of change (improvement) and informs decisions regarding the continuation, modification, or discontinuation of intervention.

Assessment of Intervention

Assessment of intervention, or **outcome assessment**, refers to the assessment that takes place following an intervention. Unlike progress monitoring, it involves summative assessment. Outcome assessment focuses on change in students' skills and functioning that occurs after instruction or intervention. Broadly, such assessments are used to inform evaluations of efficacy (i.e., how well an intervention works under ideal circumstances) and effectiveness (i.e., how well the intervention works when replicated across implementers, populations, and settings). Outcome assessment can occur at a variety of levels (e.g., national, state-wide, school-wide, classroom, or individual students). Academic achievement is undoubtedly the most measured outcome in school settings, although a variety of systems-level (e.g., school climate) and individual (e.g., social–emotional adjustment) outcomes may be measured.

State-wide assessments of academic achievement are among the most common types of outcome assessments. The Every Student Succeeds Act (ESSA; 2015; described in Chapter 5) mandates that state achievement tests align with state content and performance standards. This allows student achievement to be evaluated relative to these standards. More generally, these assessments focus on the extent to which learning objectives or performance standards were attained. Attainment may be judged relative to norm-referenced or criterion-referenced standards. Norm-referenced and criterion-referenced standards are discussed in more detail in the next section of this chapter. Numerous outcomes can be assessed beyond academic outcomes. For example, outcome assessment may focus on the results of interventions aimed at improving emotional, social, or other behavioral outcomes. These measures are discussed in greater detail in Chapter 10.

ASSESSMENT TECHNIQUES

Testing

Testing can be defined as a method used to examine the presence of some phenomenon (VandenBos, 2015). This method involves the observation and measurement of behavioral samples. The aim of testing may be to measure manifest behaviors (e.g., behaviors that are easily observed, such as skills in complete single-digit addition problems) or to make inferences about traits that are not directly observable (i.e., intelligence or personality). Performance on formal tests can be evaluated using norm-referenced, criterion-referenced, or qualitative interpretations. Informal tests also may be used to collect supplemental information. For example, teachers will sometimes create informal tests to measure attainment of classroom learning objectives. Notably, there are many informal procedures that are not tests (e.g., school records and referral documents).

Norm-Referenced and Criterion-Referenced Comparisons

School psychologists commonly administer tests that use two types of comparisons: norm-referenced comparisons (NRCs) and criterion-referenced comparisons (CRCs).

A test that uses NRCs is one in which an individual's test performance is compared to that of a larger reference group, or normative sample. The normative sample typically comprises a large number of individuals who have previously taken the test and who are similar to the examinee in some way (typically same-age peers or same-grade peers who speak the same language). When considering tests to use within an evaluation, it is important to consider whether the student being assessed is represented in the normative sample. For example, the Woodcock-Johnson, Fourth Edition, Tests of Achievement (WJIV-TA; Schrank et al., 2014) is a widely administered norm-referenced test of academic achievement that includes both age-based and grade-based norms. It allows the examiner to identify the percentile rank at which the examinee scored, or the percentage of individuals in the normative sample who achieved an equal or lower score.

Norm-referenced tests are standardized, meaning that procedures for administering (e.g., giving directions and delivering test items) and scoring the test are precisely delineated and must be executed in a consistent manner. Standardization ensures the validity of assessment results by providing equal opportunities for test takers to display the construct being assessed. To minimize the possibility of administration and scoring errors (e.g., Hopwood & Richard, 2005; Ramos et al., 2009), it is important to become proficient in administering and scoring a test before using it in practice. Having an experienced practitioner who is deeply familiar with a particular test observe administration and provide corrective feedback is one strategy that is effective in reducing administration and scoring errors (Roberts & Davis, 2015).

Unlike NRCs, CRCs (Glaser, 1963) use a content domain as a frame of reference, focusing on what an examinee can do rather than where the examinee's performance ranks relative to a normative comparison group. Often, performance levels are compared to specific and absolute standards, or criteria, that demonstrate mastery of a content domain. For example, performance on state-mandated tests of academic achievement may be interpreted relative to cut scores that reflect preestablished criteria for grade-level proficiency within a particular academic content area (e.g., reading or mathematics). Like norm-referenced tests, many criterion-referenced tests are standardized (e.g., curriculum-based measures, which are discussed in greater detail in Chapter 9).

Qualitative Interpretations

Qualitative interpretations of test performance can focus on a variety of behaviors, including test-taking strategies, patterns of error, and behaviors that are likely to facilitate or hinder test performance (e.g., attention/inattention, compliance/resistance, interest/indifference, and persistence/unresponsiveness). Observations of test session behavior provide insights into how an examinee approached and responded to test stimuli. Moreover, test session behavior can provide a means of cross-checking the validity of score interpretations (Glutting et al., 1989). Specifically, observations can be used to judge the appropriateness of the testing conditions and the extent to which test session behaviors suggest that observed test scores are likely to provide accurate estimates of an examinee's true scores.

Reviews of Historical Records

A student's current functioning must be evaluated against the backdrop of their history and sociological contexts. Knowledge of the incidence of physical and mental illness and other genetically linked diseases in first- and second-degree relatives is important, given familial-related proclivity for these conditions. The potential impact of cultural and sociological factors should also be considered. Different dimensions of diversity that school psychologists may consider are described by Hays's (2016) ADDRESSING framework, which highlights key facets of cultural identity, including: *A*ge and generational influences; *D*evelopmental or other *D*isability; *R*eligion and spiritual orientation; *E*thnicity and race; *S*ocioeconomic status; *S*exual orientation; *I*ndigenous heritage; *N*ational origin; and *G*ender identity (Hays, 2016).

Other records that tend to be useful include those from medical, psychiatric, neurological, neuropsychological, psychological, legal, and educational sources. In reviewing students' educational records, school psychologists may be particularly interested in previous intervention data, previous psychoeducational reports, attendance records, course grades, standardized test scores, and, if applicable, records from special education services (e.g., Individualized Education Plan documents). On many occasions, practitioners will find that historical records are less comprehensive than desired and have to be supplemented with interview data.

Historical information may be particularly important for students who have experienced disease or trauma that negatively affects their current functioning. In fact, premorbid functioning is best established by review of historical records (Reynolds, 1997). Of course, school psychologists must make determinations about the relative value of historical records for informing the assessment process. For example, relying on course grades as indicators of academic achievement can be problematic due to variability in grading criteria, which often incorporate nonacademic criteria (e.g., class participation). Moreover, assessments used to determine course grades (e.g., unit tests and quizzes) are often informal, tend to be unstandardized, and rarely apply principles of good measurement (Allen, 2005).

School psychologists should consider both strengths and weaknesses in assessing the skill sets of their clients. **Strengths-based assessments** focus on personal competencies (e.g., emotional and behavioral skills) that enhance coping, promote development in domains such as academic achievement and social functioning, and allow individuals to set and accomplish goals (Jimerson et al., 2004). It is also important to consider strengths originating from the student's cultural background (e.g., coping skills based on religious belief; Jones, 2008). Thus, when reviewing historical records, it is important to focus on past accomplishments and identify assets and skills that facilitated success. Moreover, numerous measures have been developed to measure assets and skills such as optimism, gratitude, empathy, prosocial behavior, student engagement, and life satisfaction (Furlong et al., 2014).

Behavioral Observations

Observations are used to elucidate patterns of behavior. Observations may be indirect or direct. *Indirect observation* relies on the observations of others and includes methods such as rating scales (described in further detail in the following text), whereas *direct observations* require assessors to directly view and record the behaviors themselves. Direct observation "requires careful attention to specifying what and how long the behaviors are observed, where and how observations are made, and how they are recorded" (Benson, 2010, p. 74).

Behavioral observations can be qualitative or quantitative. For example, a practitioner may use qualitative observations, such as writing a narrative of behavioral and classroom events, to form a general impression of cooperation and motivation during testing. When quantifying behaviors, school psychologists can attend to several observable characteristics of the behavior (Salvia et al., 2017), including its frequency and duration. To illustrate the concepts of duration and frequency, consider a school psychologist who wishes to observe a student's tantrum behaviors. The school psychologist could measure the frequency, or number of occurrences of a behavior during a fixed period of time, by counting the number of tantrums that occur in one class period. The frequency of a behavior can be measured only if the target behavior has a clear beginning and end and does not occur at such a high frequency that it is difficult to count. The school psychologist could also quantify the behavior's duration, or the length of time for which a behavior occurs, by measuring the number of minutes during which the tantrum lasts.

School psychologists often use behavioral observations to identify environmental events that predict and maintain behaviors. For example, *antecedents* (i.e., stimuli that precede a target behavior) and *consequences* (i.e., behavior or event that occurs subsequent to a target behavior) are controlling variables that maintain behavior. In the case of a student experiencing tantrums, one or more antecedents may trigger the behavior (e.g., receiving a poor grade on a test), while consequences can affect whether a behavior continues and/or is likely to occur again in the future (e.g., receiving teacher and peer attention as a result of the tantrum). Observations can be used to identify controlling variables that can be manipulated to promote the desired behavior and reduce the problem behavior, as well as to monitor changes in the target behaviors that occur as a result of manipulating environmental variables.

Rating Scales

Rating scales are commonly used as part of the assessment process because they are an efficient way to acquire information. Behavior rating scales contain a limited set of items that measure the frequency with which relevant behaviors are displayed. (These types of rating scales are discussed in further detail in Chapter 10.) Ratings are an indirect measure that summarize the behaviors an informant observes over an extended period. Benefits of rating scales include efficiency, ease of administration and scoring, and relatively low cost. Moreover, rating scales feature normative samples that allow comparisons with representative samples of same-age peers.

Numerous rating scales are available for a large range of problems. Some rating scales are narrow-band instruments, meaning that they measure a specific construct (e.g., depression, attention, and anxiety); others are broad-band instruments, meaning that they measure several constructs. A broad-band rating scale that is widely used in educational settings is the Behavior Assessment System for Children, Third Edition (BASC-3; Reynolds & Kamphaus, 2015). The BASC-3 system includes self-report, parent, and teacher rating forms, each of which measures several areas (e.g., adaptive skills, externalizing problems, internalizing problems, school problems, clinical scales measuring specific constructs such as anxiety and aggression). A commonly used narrow-band rating scale is the Revised Children's Manifest Anxiety Scale (RCMAS; Reynolds & Richmond, 2008), which measures various signs and symptoms associated with anxiety (e.g., physiological anxiety, worry, social anxiety).

School psychologists often request multiple raters, or informants (e.g., students, teachers, and parents), to complete rating scales so that they can gain multiple perspectives on behavior. In many cases, raters may not agree in their scoring. Likely causes of disagreement between raters include systematic differences in (a) what is observed, (b) access to information other than observations of performance (e.g., conversations with parents and staff), and (c) expertise in interpreting what is observed (e.g., knowledge of developmental milestones; Achenbach et al., 1987). When using information from multiple informants, it is important to examine assessment results for discrepancies among raters. Nevertheless, it remains beneficial to administer assessment tools to multiple informants to gain valuable information on the student in varying settings (i.e., within school and outside of school; De Los Reyes et al., 2015).

Interviews

Interviews are purposeful and planned encounters intended to obtain information about a person's behaviors, preferences, experiences, strengths, and areas of need. They also offer an opportunity for the clinician to observe the interviewee's verbal and nonverbal behavior. Additionally, interviews can help build rapport and trust with the interviewee, and specific questions (such as those found in the *Jones Intentional Multicultural Interview Schedule*, for example) can facilitate interpersonal connections and help clinicians conceptualize cases through a multicultural lens (Jones, 2014). In educational assessments, interviews are most commonly conducted with students, teachers, and parents. Like rating scales, interviews can be used to gather information from multiple informants.

The content of interviews varies depending on the interviewer's goals. Practitioners may use a variety of interview instruments, including structured, semistructured, and unstructured interviews. Structured diagnostic interviews are characterized by standardized formats and explicit guidelines on how responses are to be scored and followed up (Frick et al., 2020). They provide relevant information regarding symptom presentation and functional impairments associated with these symptoms (Loney & Frick, 2003). This information closely relates to *DSM-5-TR* criteria and typically is not obtained using other assessment methods such as rating scales. Semistructured interviews are similar to structured interviews in that they comprise a predetermined list of questions; however, responses may be open-ended and can be followed up with clarifying questions as deemed appropriate by the interviewer. Finally, unstructured interviews are open-ended interviews that lack a specific set of questions and afford the interviewer full flexibility in following up on the interviewee's responses. When compared to unstructured interviews, semistructured and structured interviews demonstrate superior reliability (McClellan & Werry, 2000). However, structured interviews are, by definition, considerably more rigid and do not allow the interviewer to deviate from the preset question list.

INTEGRATING AND REPORTING ASSESSMENT RESULTS

Integration of assessment results is essential to accomplishing professional objectives. Given that school psychologists typically use several different techniques to evaluate students' functioning in several domains, the assessment process often yields a plethora of data. These data often conflict, as information is typically acquired using multiple methods, from multiple settings on multiple occasions, and from multiple informants. Thus, it is necessary to (a) assign relative weights to data based on evidence of reliability, validity, and utility; (b) look for themes and patterns in assessment data; (c) develop testable alternative hypotheses and the means of testing these hypotheses when possible; and (d) determine the probability that various inferences and impressions are accurate.

Further, when describing an examinee, it is important to provide a balanced discussion of strengths (i.e., positive characteristics that might be built upon and contribute to success) and weaknesses that ostensibly contribute to problems. As Weiner (2013) notes, "psychological assessment has often addressed mainly what is wrong with people while giving insufficient attention to their adaptive capacities, positive potentials, and admirable qualities" (p. 20).

Assessment results are typically reported to others both orally and in written format. Typically, reports are written first, then shared, summarized orally, and discussed with vested partners (e.g., students, parents, teachers, multidisciplinary teams). When needed, school psychologists may need to call upon skilled interpreters to help transmit assessment data to families (Arroyos et al., 2018). Psychoeducational reports contain integrated assessment information that describes the examinee, informs the question that led to referral for assessment, and informs planning of instruction and intervention. Psychoeducational reports generally include the following components: identifying information (e.g., student's name and chronological age), description of the referral question, a list of the assessment procedures utilized, background information, observations of test session behavior, assessment results, summary, and recommendations. However, the components of reports vary depending on the purpose of the assessment.

MULTICULTURAL CONSIDERATIONS IN ASSESSMENT

It is important for school psychologists to ensure that their practices are culturally responsive. Recall from Chapter 3 that *cultural responsiveness* involves appreciating differences in language, values, customs, and experiences, and implementing practices that are sensitive to these differences (Sullivan, 2010). There are ethical, legal, demographic, and empirical rationales for culturally responsive practices.

As described in Chapter 3, the U.S. student population is becoming increasingly diverse. Specifically, more than 50% of children in the United States identify as members of racial or ethnic minoritized groups, and representation of traditionally marginalized youth is projected to increase in the coming decades. Moreover, it has been projected that, by 2030, international migration will be the main driver of population growth in the United States (Vespa et al., 2020). The number of English Language Learners (ELLs) in the United States also continues to increase. In 2018, five million children enrolled in public schools were identified as ELLs (National Center for Education Statistics, 2020). Overall, continued demographic shifts in the United States require that school psychologists be aware, knowledgeable, and skilled in regard to multicultural considerations in assessment.

Sue and colleagues' (1982) seminal tripartite model of multicultural competence in psychological practice describes three fundamental pillars: (a) *awareness*, which refers to a clinician's awareness of how their and their clients' beliefs, attitudes, and worldview impact practice; (b) *skill*, which refers to the use and implementation of culturally sensitive and responsive best practices in a clinical setting; and (c) *knowledge*, which involves nonjudgmentally learning about other cultures and how multicultural factors influence behaviors (Sue et al., 1982, 1992). Recent additions to conceptualizations of multicultural competency include an awareness of systemic barriers to equitable care and intentional efforts to eliminate these obstacles (e.g., social justice). As described in Chapter 1, advocacy entails the promotion of change. School psychologists may advocate for change when states, school systems, or individual practitioners utilize inappropriate assessment practices or interpret and use test scores in unfair ways. According to Sullivan (2010), school psychologists "have an ethical responsibility to speak up against practices that are potentially biased, not based on research, and/or that contribute to undesirable outcomes" (p. 26). Therefore, it is imperative that school psychologists be culturally sensitive and responsive at every stage of the assessment process and in every aspect of assessment described in this chapter.

School psychologists should be skilled in working with students and families from diverse backgrounds, and a substantial body of scholarship has discussed assessment practices for ELLs in particular. Depending on the practitioner's linguistic background, essential skills may include: (a) assessing students' language proficiency; (b) conducting evaluations in the language in which students are most proficient; (c) collaborating with multilingual school psychologists to conduct evaluations; (d) working with skilled interpreters to facilitate communication with students and families; and (e) determining levels of acculturation through interviews and observations (Arroyos et al., 2018; Clinton & Olvera, 2014; Schon et al., 2008). School psychologists should also have an understanding of processes involved in native and second language acquisition (Clinton & Olvera, 2014; Schon et al., 2008). Importantly, school psychologists should have an understanding of how testing accommodations (such as the use of interpreters) may influence the psychometric properties of a measure, thereby impacting the interpretability of scores (Arroyos et al., 2018). Psychometric limitations can be addressed by utilizing integrated assessment techniques and various methods of data collection. Specifically, Olvera and Gómez-Cerrillo (2014) noted, "When assessing ELLs, it is important to use an integrated approach to assessment that incorporates nondiscriminatory, nonbiased, and ecological frameworks in order to determine whether any presenting academic difficulties are due primarily to a language/cultural difference and/or a disability" (p. 200).

Finally, continued professional development is essential for school psychologists engaged in culturally competent assessment. Continuous professional development involves acquiring and maintaining knowledge of best practices in working with diverse populations and promoting equity in the assessment process. It can also involve remaining abreast of trends in policy, practice, and research that impact culturally responsive assessment, such as updates to legislation in school settings (e.g., Individuals With Disabilities Education Improvement Act, 2004), ethical codes and professional standards and relevant professional literature. Additionally, continued professional development involves receiving supervision and feedback as needed to ensure multicultural competence in the delivery of assessment services.

SOCIAL JUSTICE CONNECTIONS

How can school psychologists promote socially just assessment practices?

Generally, the field of school psychology has generated a considerable amount of literature related to test bias as well as culturally responsive and nondiscriminatory assessment practices. Even so, there is a need for more scholarship that explores assessment processes through a social justice lens. Many of the challenges that racial, ethnic, and linguistic minoritized students face (e.g., inappropriate educational placements and excessively harsh discipline) can be addressed, in part, by promoting socially just assessment practices.

As described in this chapter, it is imperative that school psychologists employ culturally responsive assessment practices. However, in and of itself, displaying cultural sensitivity is not sufficient to rectify deep-rooted injustices in school-based practices. The following general recommendations are appropriate when employing a social justice approach to the broad process of assessment.

1. ***Assume an ecological, strengths-based approach.*** As noted in Chapter 2, a traditional medical model of assessment and diagnosis posits that evaluators should seek to identify "problems" within individuals and subsequently propose solutions for eliminating

(continued)

> **SOCIAL JUSTICE CONNECTIONS** (*continued*)
>
> those problems. For school psychologists, this approach is problematic for two reasons. First, it assumes that problems reside solely within individuals rather than in the person–environment interactions that shape their experiences. Second, it implores practitioners to focus on clients' "inherent problems" and weaknesses at the expense of recognizing their strengths. A more constructive approach to assessment is one that proactively seeks to identify both the within-person and environmental variables that impact student functioning as well as strengths that are likely to serve as the foundation for future successes. This type of approach can provide clear avenues for effective intervention as well as reduce the likelihood that teachers and other personnel will perceive children as "problem students."
>
> 2. ***Advocate for holistic and comprehensive assessment practices.*** Recognize that test scores alone cannot provide a comprehensive picture of a child's strengths and weaknesses. Multimethod approaches that incorporate test scores, parent and teacher interviews, classroom observations, and other sources of data will provide the most well-rounded information about students' and their school experiences.
> 3. ***Advocate for valid assessment practices.*** It is easier for schools to default to discriminatory assessment practices (often unintentionally) when time, money, and resources are scarce. In some cases, school psychologists may need to find creative ways to access the right assessment tools and training opportunities. For example, many academic progress monitoring measures are available to users online free of charge. Connecting with colleagues in neighboring districts and local professional organizations may allow practitioners to share or borrow resources when necessary. Finally, connecting with nearby universities and scholars who are involved in high-quality research can afford access to training opportunities and assessment procedures that might not be otherwise feasible (although school psychologists should ensure that the practices to be implemented have some established evidence base).

SUMMARY AND CONCLUSIONS

School psychologists spend much of their time conducting assessments. While the identification and implementation of effective interventions are essential to student outcomes, the efficiency and effectiveness of instruction and intervention are unquestionably enhanced by assessment. Assessment allows educators and other professionals to engage in data-based decision-making. It also informs many important decisions such as eligibility for and allocation of services, instructional planning, and selection and implementation of intervention services. Moreover, intentionally incorporating the cultural and sociological backgrounds of students in the assessment process yields a more comprehensive understanding of a student's current functioning as well as a stronger foundation for subsequent decision-making around placement or intervention. Ultimately, assessment is a critical function of school psychologists, as is demonstrated throughout the remaining chapters of this book.

DISCUSSION QUESTIONS

1. As noted in this chapter, school psychologists conduct assessments *for* intervention, *during* intervention, and *of* intervention. What are the purposes of each of these types of assessments?
2. Describe at least three reasons why diversity and multicultural factors are important to consider in the assessment process. How can you build or improve upon your command of culturally responsive assessment practices?
3. For classroom observations, which types of student behaviors are best quantified by measuring frequency? Why? Which types of behaviors are best quantified by measuring duration? Why?
4. A school psychologist administers a broad-band rating scale (i.e., BASC-3) to a student, two of the student's teachers, and one of the student's parents. Upon scoring the protocols, it is found that the student's and teachers' results indicate elevated levels of anxiety and depression; however, results from the parent's rating scale do not indicate that the student is experiencing any anxiety or depression. Why might this situation arise? In this situation, what steps might the school psychologist take next? What other data might the school psychologist choose to collect?
5. Describe at least three important considerations for communicating assessment results to parent and teachers.

RECOMMENDED READINGS

Frick, P. J., Burns, C., & Kamphaus, R. W. (2020). *Clinical assessment of child and adolescent personality and behavior* (4th ed.). Springer.

Kranzler, J. H., & Floyd, R. G. (2020). *Assessing intelligence in children and adolescents: A practical guide for evidence-based assessment* (2nd ed.). Rowman & Littlefield.

Sattler, J. M. (2018). *Assessment of children: Cognitive foundations and applications* (6th ed.). Jerome M. Sattler, Publisher.

Sattler, J. M. (2022). *Foundations of behavioral, social, and clinical assessment of children* (7th ed.). Jerome M. Sattler, Publisher.

Sellbom, M., & Suhr, J. A. (Eds.). (2020). *The Cambridge handbook of clinical assessment and diagnosis*. Cambridge University Press.

A robust set of instructor resources designed to supplement this text is located at http://connect.springerpub.com/content/book/978-0-8261-6344-8. Qualifying instructors may request access by emailing textbook@springerpub.com.

REFERENCES

Achenbach, T. M., McConaughy, S. H., & Howell, C. T. (1987). Child/adolescent behavioral and emotional problems: Implications of cross-informant correlations for situational specificity. *Psychological Bulletin, 101*(2), 213–232. https://doi.org/10.1037/0033-2909.101.2.213

Albers, C. A., Elliott, S. N., Kettler, R. J., & Roach, A. T. (2015). Evaluating intervention outcomes within problem-solving-based assessment. In R. Brown-Chidsey, K. J. Andren, R. Brown-Chidsey, & K. J. Andren (Eds.), *Assessment for intervention: A problem-solving approach* (2nd ed., pp. 344–360). Guilford Press.

Albers, C. A., Glover, T. A., & Kratochwill, T. R. (2007). Where are we, and where do we go now? *Journal of School Psychology, 45*(2), 257–263. https://doi.org/10.1016/j.jsp.2006.12.003

Allen, J. D. (2005). Grades as valid measures of academic achievement of classroom learning. *Clearing House: A Journal of Educational Strategies, Issues and Ideas, 78*(5), 218–223. https://doi.org/10.3200/TCHS.78.5.218-223

American Educational Research Association, American Psychological Association, & National Council on Measurement in Education (Eds.). (2014). *Standards for educational and psychological testing*. American Educational Research Association.

American Psychiatric Association. (2022). *Diagnostic and statistical manual of mental disorders* (5th ed., text rev.). https://doi.org/10.1176/appi.books.9780890425787

Arroyos, E., Diaz, D., & Torres, I. (2018). Best practices in collaborating with interpreters: Lessons learned. *Communiqué, 46*(5), 29–30. https://www.nasponline.org/publications/periodicals/communique/issues/volume-46-issue-5

Benson, N. (2010). Types of tests and assessments. In E. Mpofu & T. Oakland (Eds.), *Assessment in rehabilitation and health* (pp. 72–90). Allyn & Bacon.

Black, P., & Wiliam, D. (1998). Assessment and classroom learning. *Assessment in Education: Principles, Policy and Practice, 5*(1), 7–74. https://doi.org/10.1080/0969595980050102

Braden, J. P. (2003). Psychological assessment in school settings. In J. R. Graham, J. A. Naglieri, J. R. Graham & J. A. Naglieri (Eds.), *Handbook of psychology: Assessment psychology* (Vol. 10, pp. 261–290). John Wiley & Sons.

Clinton, A. B., & Olvera, P. (2014). Norm-referenced assessment and bilingual populations. In S. G. Little & A. Akin-Little (Eds.), *Academic assessment and intervention* (pp. 102–113). Routledge.

De Los Reyes, A., Augenstein, T. M., Wang, M., Thomas, S. A., Drabick, D. A. G., Burgers, D. E., & Rabinowitz, J. (2015). The validity of the multi-informant approach to assessing child and adolescent mental health. *Psychological Bulletin, 141*(4), 858–900. https://doi.org/10.1037/a0038498

Dixson, D. D., & Worrell, F. C. (2016). Formative and summative assessment in the classroom. *Theory into Practice, 55*(2), 153–159. https://doi.org/10.1080/00405841.2016.1148989

Every Student Succeeds Act, Pub. L. No. 114-95, § 1177 (2015).

Fagan, T. K. (1996). Witmer's contributions to school psychological services. *American Psychologist, 51*(3), 241–243. https://doi.org/10.1037/0003-066X.51.3.241

Frick, P. J., Burns, C., & Kamphaus, R. W. (2020). *Clinical assessment of child and adolescent personality and behavior* (4th ed.). Springer.

Fuchs, L. S., & Fuchs, D. (2010). Progress monitoring. In P. Peterson, E. Baker, & B. McGaw (Eds.), *Encyclopedia of education* (3rd ed., Vol. 4, pp. 102–111). Elsevier.

Furlong, M. J., Gilman, R., & Huebner, E. S. (2014). *Handbook of positive psychology in schools* (2nd ed.). Routledge, Taylor & Francis Group.

Glaser, R. (1963). Instructional technology and the measurement of learning outcomes: Some questions. *American Psychologist, 18*(8), 519–521. https://doi.org/10.1037/h0049294

Glutting, J. J., Oakland, T., & McDermott, P. A. (1989). Observing child behavior during testing: Constructs, validity, and situational generality. *Journal of School Psychology, 27*(2), 155–164. https://doi.org/10.1016/0022-4405(89)90003-4

Hanushek, E. A., Kai, J. F., & Rivken, S. J. (1998). *Teachers, schools, and academic achievement*, NBER working paper 6691. http://www.cgp.upenn.edu/pdf/Hanushek_NBER.PDF

Hattie, J., & Leeson, H. (2013). Future directions in assessment and testing in education and psychology. In K. F. Geisinger, B. A. Bracken, J. F. Carlson, J. C. Hansen, N. R. Kuncel, S. P. Reise, & M. C. Rodriguez (Eds.), *APA handbook of testing and assessment in psychology, Vol. 3: Testing and assessment in school psychology and education* (pp. 591–622). American Psychological Association. https://doi.org/10.1037/14049-028

Hays, P. A. (2016). *Addressing cultural complexities in practice: Assessment, diagnosis, and therapy* (3rd ed.). American Psychological Association. https://doi.org/10.1037/14801-000

Hopwood, C. J., & Richard, D. C. (2005). Graduate student WAIS-III scoring accuracy is a function of Full Scale IQ and complexity of examiner tasks. *Assessment, 12*(4), 445–454. https://doi.org/10.1177/1073191105281072

Individuals With Disabilities Education Improvement Act, Pub. L. No. 108-446 (2004).

Jimerson, S. R., Sharkey, J. D., Nyborg, V., & Furlong, M. J. (2004). Strength-based assessment and school psychology: A summary and synthesis. *California School Psychologist*, 9(1), 9–19. https://doi.org/10.1007/BF03340903

Jones, J. M. (2008). Best practices in multicultural counseling. In A. Thomas & J. Grimes (Eds.), *Best practices in school psychology* (5th ed., Vol. 5, pp. 1771–1783). National Association of School Psychologists.

Jones, J. M. (2014). Best practices in providing culturally responsive interventions. In P. Harrison & A. Thomas (Eds.), *Best practices in school psychology: Foundations* (pp. 1–12). National Association of School Psychologists.

Loney, B. R., & Frick, P. J. (2003). Structured diagnostic interviewing. In C. R. Reynolds, R. W. Kamphaus, C. R. Reynolds & R. W. Kamphaus (Eds.), *Handbook of psychological and educational assessment of children: Personality, behavior, and context* (2nd ed., pp. 235–247). Guilford Press.

MacCorquodale, K., & Meehl, P. E. (1948). On a distinction between hypothetical constructs and intervening variables. *Psychological Review*, 55(2), 95–107. https://doi.org/10.1037/h0056029

McClellan, J. M., & Werry, J. S. (2000). Introduction to special section: Research psychiatric diagnostic interviews for children and adolescents. *Journal of the American Academy of Child and Adolescent Psychiatry*, 39(1), 19–27. https://doi.org/10.1097/00004583-200001000-00013

National Center for Education Statistics. (2020). *Digest of education statistics*. U.S. Department of Education, Institute of Education Sciences. https://nces.ed.gov/programs/digest/

Olvera, P., & Gómez-Cerrillo, L. (2014). Integrated intellectual assessment of the bilingual student. In A. B. Clinton (Ed.), *Assessing bilingual children in context: An integrated approach* (pp. 109–135). American Psychological Association. https://doi.org/10.1037/14320-006

Ramos, E., Alfonso, V. C., & Schermerhorn, S. M. (2009). Graduate students' administration and scoring errors on the Woodcock–Johnson III Tests of Cognitive Abilities. *Psychology in the Schools*, 46(7), 650–657. https://doi.org/10.1002/pits.20405

Reynolds, C. R. (1986). The elusive professionalism of school psychology: Lessons from the past, portents for the future. *Professional School Psychology*, 1(1), 41–46. https://doi.org/10.1037/h0090499

Reynolds, C. R. (1997). Postscripts on premorbid ability estimation: Conceptual addenda and a few words on alternative and conditional approaches. *Archives of Clinical Neuropsychology*, 12(8), 769–778. https://doi.org/10.1016/S0887-6177(97)00051-6

Reynolds, C. R., & Kamphaus, R. W. (2015). *Behavior assessment system for children* (3rd ed., p. BASC-3). Pearson.

Reynolds, C. R., & Richmond, B. O. (2008). *Revised children's manifest anxiety scale* (2nd ed.; RCMAS-2) *manual*. WPS Publishing.

Roberts, R. M., & Davis, M. C. (2015). Assessment of a model for achieving competency in administration and scoring of the WAIS-IV in post-graduate psychology students. *Frontiers in Psychology*, 6, 641. https://doi.org/10.3389/fpsyg.2015.00641

Salvia, J., Ysseldyke, J. E., & Witmer, S. (2017). *Assessment in special and inclusive education* (13th ed.). Cengage Learning.

Schon, J., Shaftel, J., & Markham, P. (2008). Contemporary issues in the assessment of culturally and linguistically diverse learners. *Journal of Applied School Psychology*, 24(2), 163–189. https://doi.org/10.1080/15377900802089395

Schrank, F. A., Mather, N., & McGrew, K. S. (2014). *Woodcock-Johnson IV tests of achievement*. Riverside.

Shepard, L. A. (2006). Classroom assessment. In R. L. Brennan (Ed.), *Educational measurement* (pp. 623–646). Praeger.

Sue, D. W., Arredondo, P., & McDavis, R. J. (1992). Multicultural counseling competencies and standards: A call to the profession. *Journal of Multicultural Counseling and Development*, 20(2), 64–88. https://doi.org/10.1002/j.2161-1912.1992.tb00563.x

Sue, D. W., Bernier, J. B., Durran, M., Feinberg, L., Pedersen, P., Smith, E., & Vasquez-Nuttall, E. (1982). Position paper: Cross-cultural counseling competencies. *Counseling Psychologist*, 10, 45–52.

Sullivan, A. L. (2010). Preventing disproportionality: A framework for culturally responsive assessment. *Communiqué*, 39(3), 1 and 24. https://www.nasponline.org/publications/periodicals/communique/issues/volume-39-issue-3

Tobin, R. M., & House, A. E. (2016). DSM-5 *diagnosis in the schools*. Guilford Press.
VandenBos, G. R. (2015). *APA dictionary of psychology* (2nd ed.). American Psychological Association.
Vespa, J., Medina, L., & Armstrong, D. M. (2020, February). *Demographic turning points for the United States: Population projections for 2020 to 2060*. United States Census Bureau. https://www.census.gov/content/dam/Census/library/publications/2020/demo/p25-1144.pdf
Weiner, I. B. (2013). The assessment process. In I. B. Weiner, J. R. Graham, J. A. Naglieri, J. R. Graham, J. A. Naglieri, & I. B. Weiner (Eds.), *Handbook of psychology: Assessment psychology* (pp. 3–25). Wiley.
Welner, K. G. (2013). Consequential validity and the transformation of tests from measurement tools to policy tools. *Teachers College Record: The Voice of Scholarship in Education, 115*(9), 1–6. https://doi.org/10.1177/016146811311500902

CHAPTER 8

Intervention Planning and Implementation

ERUM NADEEM ■ SUSAN G. FORMAN

CHAPTER OBJECTIVES

After reading this chapter, you will be able to:

- Describe the multitiered systems of support framework for service delivery.
- Describe how screening, assessment, and progress monitoring are used in data-based decision-making.
- Define a data-based problem-solving model for use in decision-making about services and programs.
- Discuss the importance of research evidence in selecting interventions.
- Introduce the process of implementation and the importance of using implementation strategies to support successful intervention use.

NATIONAL ASSOCIATION OF SCHOOL PSYCHOLOGISTS PRACTICE MODEL CONNECTIONS

Domain 1: Data-Based Decision-Making
Domain 4: Mental and Behavioral Health Services and Interventions
Domain 5: School-Wide Practices to Promote Learning

INTRODUCTION

The primary goal of schools is to provide students with the educational services that they need to become well-adjusted and productive members of society. This means that schools should provide high-quality programs and services that promote students' academic development as well as their social, emotional, and behavioral (SEB) well-being. In addition to specific social–emotional learning programs (Taylor et al., 2017), recent efforts in districts across the country have focused their SEB efforts on school and classroom climate (Charlton et al., 2021; Wang et al., 2020), positive behavioral supports (Horner & Monzalve-Macaya, 2018), trauma-informed systems (Chafouleas et al., 2016), and culturally responsive sustaining education (Johnston et al., 2017). Ultimately, these approaches are designed to ensure that students are meeting appropriate milestones and to prevent problems from arising. When problems do arise, school personnel must respond appropriately before they escalate further.

Prevention refers to those services that foster student competencies (e.g., academic and social skills) so as to promote healthy development and avoid the onset of long-term problems. *Intervention* refers to services that address problems that have already become apparent. Schools can deliver prevention and intervention services in a number of ways, and both types of services are fundamental for supporting the success of all students. The goal of this chapter is to discuss broadly how prevention and intervention services may be structured, delivered, and evaluated in schools. In subsequent chapters, we address specific types of prevention and intervention services in academic and SEB domains.

MULTITIERED SYSTEMS OF SUPPORT

Among other organizations, the National Association of School Psychologists (NASP; 2016) endorses a framework of service delivery commonly referred to as multitiered systems of support. Broadly defined, ***multitiered systems of support*** (MTSS) are comprehensive service delivery frameworks that provide a continuum of prevention and intervention services to meet the needs of all students. The goal of MTSS is to promote successful academic or SEB development for all students in a school building. The framework is predicated on the assumption that all students can learn when provided with the appropriate instruction. Prevention and intervention services represented in this continuum must be evidence-based, meaning that they must have acceptable levels of research support. MTSS can be implemented at various organizational levels, including the individual school, district, and state levels. For consistency and clarity, this chapter describes MTSS implementation at the individual school level.

One of the core features of MTSS is its ecological (i.e., environmentally focused) approach to conceptualizing and addressing student problems. In MTSS, student problems are conceptualized as a mismatch between student variables (e.g., previous knowledge and motivation) and environmental variables (e.g., instructional strategies and classroom routines), rather than as inherent problems that lie within students themselves. Thus, the primary mechanism by which academic and behavioral skill problems are resolved is the alteration of environmental and intervention variables to better match individual students' needs. This ecological approach is beneficial because it requires educators to move away from "blaming" students for academic and behavioral problems and instead to focus on environmental variables that impact instruction.

Overview of the Tiered System

In MTSS, a continuum of supports is provided through a tiered system. While many MTSS models comprise three tiers of support, others include four or even as many as seven tiers. Collectively, tiered services provide an integrated system of school-wide, classroom-wide, and individual learning and behavioral supports for students with a range of needs. As struggling students progress upward through these tiers, the intervention services they receive become increasingly intensive. When and if their difficulties are remediated, students also may progress downward through the tiers, meaning that the services are removed or gradually become less intensive.

Services provided within the tiered system range from school-wide preventive programs for all students to intensive interventions for students with identified problems. One common misconception about MTSS is that it is designed to be a remedial framework for supporting only those students who are struggling behaviorally or academically. In reality, MTSS is a comprehensive service delivery framework for supporting *all* students, including those who are meeting academic and behavioral standards as well as those who are not. Furthermore, this tiered system is based on the assumption that, in many cases, problems in academic and SEB functioning can be prevented if they are identified and addressed early on (Cook et al., 2015). In addition, recent calls have been made to implement MTSS in ways that promote inclusion and racial equity in schools (Fallon et al., 2021).

The following subsections provide an overview of MTSS. The descriptions presented here are based on a three-tiered model, as such models are mostly commonly referenced in the school psychology literature. Figure 8.1 depicts the three tiers and their core features.

Tier 1

Tier 1 services and interventions are also called *primary*, *universal*, or *preventive* services. As already noted, MTSS is designed to support the progress of all students in a school. Tier 1 constitutes those services that are provided to *all* students at the classroom, school, or district level. For example, with respect to academic learning, Tier 1 services would consist of an effective, evidence-based core curriculum that is aligned with state and school district learning goals. With respect to SEB learning, Tier 1 interventions may consist of clearly

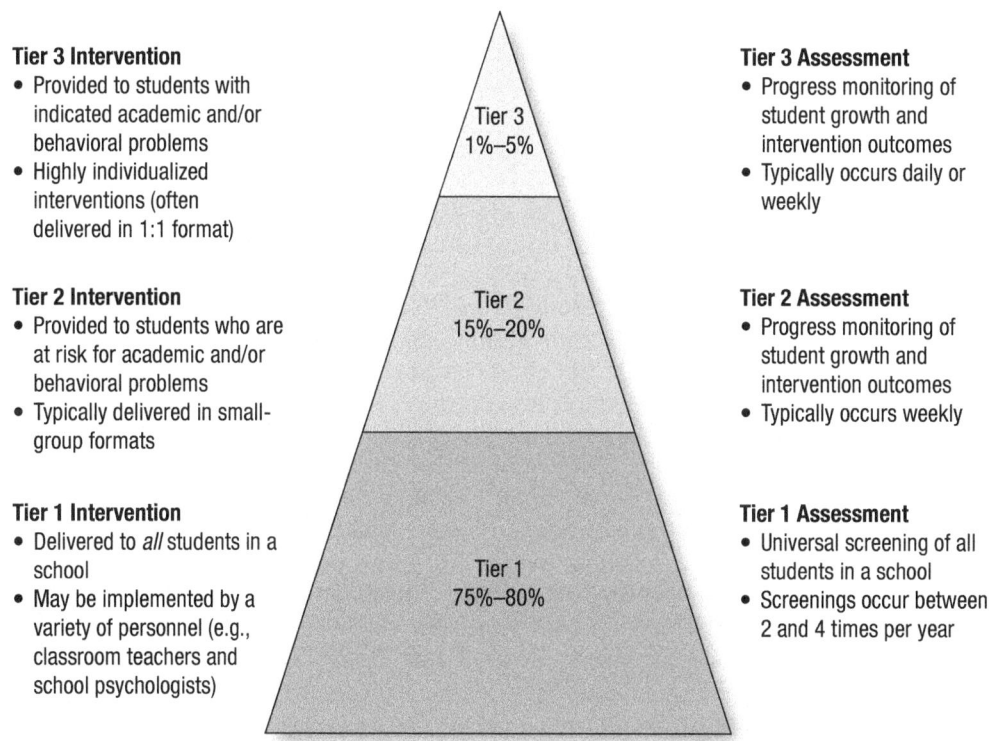

FIGURE 8.1 ASSESSMENT AND INTERVENTION IN MULTITIERED SYSTEMS OF SUPPORT (MTSS).

communicated school-wide behavioral expectations (e.g., positively stated school rules) and school-wide instruction in areas such as conflict resolution, bullying prevention, emotional coping, and self-regulation. Because they are designed to reach all students, Tier 1 interventions tend to be large-group programs conducted with whole classrooms or in multiple classrooms. Moreover, they may be implemented by a variety of personnel who interact regularly with students, including teachers, guidance counselors, and school psychologists. For example, Tier 1 academic interventions are implemented by classroom teachers, as they deliver the whole-group instruction that all students receive in their classrooms on a daily basis. Tier 1 interventions in the SEB domain may be implemented by teachers or, alternatively, by school psychologists or school counselors in collaboration with the classroom teacher.

One of the goals of providing Tier 1 services is to decrease the need for students to accelerate to higher tiers for further, more intensive interventions. Generally, it is expected that the majority of students in a school will be able to meet academic standards when receiving Tier 1 services only. More specifically, Tier 1 services aim to comprehensively meet the needs of between 75% and 80% of students (Stoiber & Gettinger, 2016). If fewer than 75% to 80% of students are meeting performance expectations while receiving Tier 1 supports alone (meaning that more than approximately 20% of students demonstrate need of higher tiers of intervention), there is likely a problem with the design or delivery of the school's universal supports. This observation would suggest a need for teachers, school psychologists, and other personnel to consider the design and delivery of core instruction and to make necessary changes such that the majority of students will be successful in response to these supports.

TIER 2

One critical assumption of the MTSS framework is that not all students learn in exactly the same way and that some will require more intensive instruction than others do to meet academic and behavioral standards. Students who struggle, despite access to Tier 1 services, may demonstrate need of *Tier 2* services, which are also called *secondary, targeted*, or *selective* interventions. Interventions in this tier are provided to students who are deemed to be at risk for academic or SEB problems. Further information about how these students are identified as being "at risk" is provided in subsequent sections of this chapter.

Because it is expected that fewer students will demonstrate a need for Tier 2 supports, these interventions tend to be conducted in small groups. Smaller group sizes allow students to receive more frequent and immediate feedback from instructors as well as more individualized attention. It is important to note that Tier 2 services do not replace Tier 1 services, which are consistently delivered to all students. Instead, these secondary services are intended to supplement Tier 1 interventions, thereby accelerating the student's rate of learning. For example, they may involve more exposure to targeted material and more opportunities for guided practice. Tier 2 interventions typically are delivered for 6 to 20 weeks, and sometimes longer. Like Tier 1 interventions, they may be implemented by a variety of school personnel, including teachers, school psychologists, social workers, and others.

Because the majority of learners should be accommodated by Tier 1 services, a relatively smaller number of students will demonstrate a need for Tier 2 services—specifically, approximately 15% to 20% of students. Like Tier 1 services, Tier 2 interventions are designed to prevent students from demonstrating need for even more intensive supports (i.e., Tier 3 interventions).

TIER 3

Tier 3 services are also called *tertiary, indicated*, or *intensive* interventions. They are provided to students with identified academic or SEB problems (i.e., students who are considered to have the highest risk for long-term problems). Tier 3 interventions are customized and delivered individually or in small groups (i.e., smaller groups than those seen in Tier 2).

Tier 3 interventions typically require extensive resources, professional involvement, and time beyond what is provided in Tiers 1 and 2. Because students who need Tier 3 interventions have severe difficulties, multicomponent services may be needed. Tier 3 interventions typically are implemented by highly skilled special services staff (e.g., school psychologists) as well as by community-based behavioral health professionals, as necessary. They tend to be longer in duration than Tier 2 programs, sometimes extending to multiple years (Sanetti & Collier-Meek, 2015).

As compared with Tiers 1 and 2, it is expected that an even smaller percentage of students will demonstrate a need for Tier 3 services. Tier 3 services serve approximately 1% to 5% of students who need services beyond what is provided in the first two tiers (Center for Mental Health in Schools, 2011; Stoiber & Gettinger, 2016). Often, students receiving Tier 3 interventions have been identified as individuals in need of special education. Generally, if more than 5% of students in a given school demonstrate a need for Tier 3 supports, it may be necessary for school staff to review and modify the Tier 1 and Tier 2 services, such that the majority of student needs are met at those intervention levels.

Screening, Assessment, and Progress Monitoring in Multitiered Systems of Support

After reading these sections, one might wonder: *How do school personnel identify students who are at risk or who have identified problems?* In other words, how do educators determine which students are in need of which tiers of support? Moreover, how do they assess student progress at each tier, and how do they determine whether students should be escalated or de-escalated to and from different tiers of intervention?

Data-based decision-making is a critical feature of MTSS implementation and allows personnel to answer these questions in a reliable and valid manner. As described in Domain 1 of the NASP (2020) Practice Model, **data-based decision-making** refers to the use of any number of assessment or data collection strategies to inform the design, implementation, and evaluation of services and programs. When executed properly, data-based decision-making allows school psychologists to accurately identify student- and systems-level needs, match those needs to the appropriate interventions and services, and monitor related outcomes. Thus, it is an essential component of MTSS implementation.

Data-based decision-making relies heavily on the use of reliable and valid assessment procedures (as described in Chapter 7). Assessments may be similar or different across tiers, depending on the school's MTSS model and selected procedures. Generally, assessments are administered more frequently at higher tiers of intervention, although assessment schedules vary across schools with different MTSS models. Common assessment procedures implemented at the different tiers are described in further detail in the following subsections.

Tier 1

At Tier 1, assessment objectives are twofold: (a) to determine whether the majority of students (i.e., between 75% and 80% of individuals) are meeting grade-level expectations with Tier 1 supports alone and (b) to identify students who are at risk for academic and behavioral problems and therefore demonstrate need for higher tiers of intervention. These objectives are accomplished through universal screening for all students. *Universal screening* (a concept first introduced in Chapter 7) involves the administration of brief measures of target skills and behaviors. Often, screeners are selected based on their validity for predicting later student outcomes (e.g., state test performance and long-term mental health outcomes).

In MTSS, screenings typically occur between two and four times per year. Some screeners directly measure students' skills (e.g., students complete a brief reading task), whereas others measure skills and behaviors indirectly (e.g., the parent or teacher completes a rating scale reporting the student's behaviors). Often, screening procedures incorporate multiple measures and are supplemented by other types of data, such as grades and attendance records. At times, risk factors or problems identified during screening are followed by more intensive assessment to determine the nature of the problem and to develop appropriate intervention goals. More information about academic and SEB screening is provided in Chapters 9 and 10, respectively.

Universal screening is an essential part of the process for linking students with appropriate services and interventions. Students are identified either as at risk or not at risk based on their screening performance and other factors (e.g., teacher and parent input). School teams may analyze screening data several times per year. In particular, schools analyze data for two primary purposes: (a) to ensure that the majority of students (approximately 75% to 80%) are meeting academic and behavioral expectations with Tier 1 supports alone and (b) to differentiate those students who need additional interventions (i.e., Tier 2 and Tier 3 interventions) from those who do not. In other words, universal screening allows educators to evaluate their school-wide programming and to identify candidates for receiving more intensive interventions. The availability of intervention services is essential for universal screening to be useful.

TIERS 2 AND 3

Once students in need of interventions beyond Tier 1 are identified, further data must be collected for decision-making purposes. As described in Chapter 7, *progress monitoring* allows for the periodic assessment of student progress and intervention effectiveness and is essential for ensuring that students are benefiting from interventions. Moreover, progress monitoring data are key for determining whether interventions should be continued, terminated, or changed.

Progress monitoring is a type of formative assessment, meaning that it provides ongoing information about student progress so as to guide instructional decision-making. Assessment schedules may vary depending on the characteristics of the intervention, skills and behaviors observed, and the progress monitoring instruments themselves. For example, progress monitoring may occur on a monthly, weekly, or daily basis. In many cases, more intensive interventions are associated with more frequent progress monitoring, as they are more resource intensive and intended for higher-risk students. Thus, data must be collected frequently to ensure that instructional resources are used judiciously.

When evaluating progress, students' performance during and following an intervention can be compared to predetermined criteria, or benchmarks, that are based on local or national samples of same-grade or same-age students. Based on these criteria, educators may continue an intervention, provide a modified intervention within the same tier, or escalate or de-escalate to a different tier. For example, if a student were to catch up to same-age or same-grade peers over the course of a Tier 2 intervention, that student might either return to Tier 1 or continue with the Tier 2 intervention, depending on whether the intervention was deemed necessary to sustain skill growth over time. In contrast, if a student continued to struggle despite receiving Tier 2 intervention services, they might be escalated to Tier 3.

Pyle and Vaughn (2012) suggested four decision-making rules for evaluating progress monitoring to determine whether students should be escalated from Tier 2 to Tier 3:

1. If the student has participated in two rounds of Tier 2 intervention and has not made sufficient progress, they should be escalated to Tier 3.
2. If the student has participated in one round of Tier 2, but shows a marked lack of progress, they should be moved to Tier 3.
3. If the student has received less than one round of Tier 2, but intensive intervention is indicated to accelerate skill development and prevent further problem development, they should be escalated to Tier 3.
4. If the student has previously received Tier 3 services, they should reenter Tier 3 as needed.

PROBLEM-SOLVING MODEL

The preceding sections have provided a number of considerations for selecting interventions and monitoring student progress. School psychologists and others must consider a number of factors in their decision-making about service delivery within and across tiers. These pieces of information allow them to identify student needs, select appropriate intervention services, determine whether those services should be continued and/or modified, and evaluate the intervention's effectiveness in achieving predetermined goals.

School psychologists may implement a *problem-solving* model to gather and synthesize information in a logical manner and, subsequently, to make educational decisions that best serve students and school systems. The problem-solving model is a systematic process used "to make decisions about continuously improving educational programs and services" (Pluymert, 2014, p. 25). Problem-solving relies heavily on data-based decision-making procedures. Typically, a problem-solving model is conceptualized as involving four primary steps. Each of these steps is described in the following text and depicted in Figure 8.2.

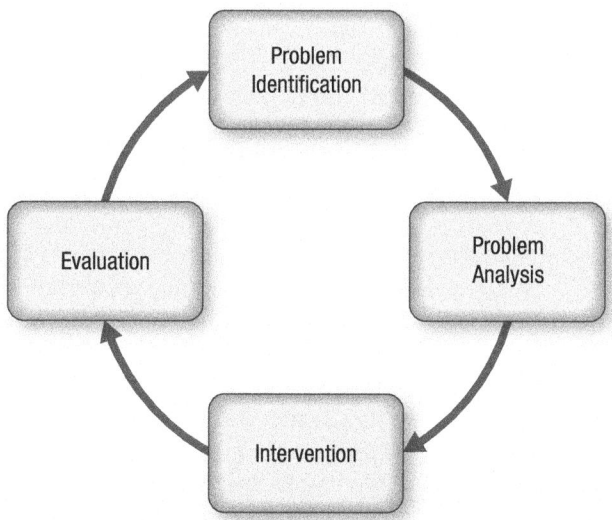

FIGURE 8.2 PROBLEM-SOLVING MODEL.

1. *Problem identification.* In this stage, the school psychologist develops a clear and measurable definition of the problem to be remediated. **Gap analysis** quantifies the difference between current performance and targeted (desired) performance. For example, simply identifying a student as being a "slow reader" would not constitute a clear and measurable definition of a reading problem. Instead, a school psychologist might measure the student's reading rate and accuracy by calculating the number of words the student can read correctly in 1 minute. Subsequently, the school psychologist would identify a target reading rate for the student based on grade-level standards and local or national norms. By comparing these two quantities, the school psychologist is able to more clearly and concisely state the problem. An example of a clear, well-defined problem statement is as follows: "Suzanne reads 84 words correct per minute from grade-level passages. On average, Suzanne's same-grade peers read 123 words correct per minute from the same passages." This statement suggests that Suzanne must increase her reading rate by 39 words correct per minute and paves the way for the development of clear and concrete reading intervention goals.
2. *Problem analysis.* Problem analysis involves identifying the causes of the student's or system's difficulties. One of the key assumptions of this stage is that identifying the cause of the problem facilitates the development of appropriate and successful interventions (Burns & Gibbons, 2008; Pluymert, 2014). Through various assessment methods (e.g., observation, brief testing, and record review), the school psychologist may seek to clarify a number of questions. For example, is Suzanne's slow reading attributable to a deficit in core reading skills (a *skill problem*)? Or is Suzanne's reading hindered by other factors, such as attention difficulties or shyness (a *performance problem*)? Knowledge of the various factors contributing to Suzanne's slow reading would assist school personnel in developing the intervention best suited to her needs. The problem analysis phase culminates in the formation of a hypothesis that describes the root cause of the problem.
3. *Plan development and implementation.* This third step involves the development of an intervention plan to remediate the problem defined in the first step. First, the school psychologist must define clear intervention goals or clear criteria for desirable performance. These criteria must be easily measured (e.g., by counting Suzanne's number of words read correctly in 1 minute). The intervention itself should be aligned with the hypothesized cause of the problem identified during problem analysis. Moreover, the intervention should be research based, and procedures for progress monitoring and measuring achievement outcomes should be clearly delineated.
4. *Plan evaluation.* The final phase of the problem-solving process involves determining whether the intervention has successfully remediated the problem at hand. This involves reviewing progress-monitoring data and comparing the student's level of performance at the end of the intervention to the performance criteria stated in the intervention goals. Based on this information, the school psychologist and others can determine whether the intervention should be continued, modified, terminated, or replaced by a different intervention.

The four phases of the problem-solving model are intended to be recursive rather than linear, meaning that the school psychologist may revert to previous stages as necessary. For example, if the school psychologist reaches the plan evaluation phase only to find that the problem has not been remediated, it may be necessary to return to previous steps to reformulate the problem definition or hypothesis and, ultimately, the intervention plan. Overall, the problem-solving model allows the school psychologist to develop a methodical and practical approach to addressing student- and systems-level problems.

SELECTING INTERVENTIONS: THE IMPORTANCE OF EVIDENCE

As described in the MTSS framework and problem-solving models, selecting interventions that are likely to be effective in addressing student-specific and school-wide problems is an essential role of the school psychologist. Key considerations for selecting an appropriate intervention are the goals for the client(s) and the evidence base for the intervention. *Evidence-based interventions* (EBIs) are interventions that are likely to produce positive outcomes for clients because they are supported by high-quality research indicating that such outcomes are probable. Various authors, federal agencies, and professional associations have offered different definitions of the term *evidence-based*, though these definitions all share some commonalities. Generally, EBIs are interventions that are supported by an appropriate number of well-designed research studies, such that they meet Kazdin and Weisz's (2010) six criteria:

1. The support includes two or more research studies in which there has been specification of the target population.
2. Random assignment of participants to conditions (e.g., treatment and control groups in the experiment) is utilized in these supporting studies.
3. Supporting studies report utilizing intervention manuals that specify intervention procedures in detail (which facilitates the replicability of the intervention).
4. Supporting studies use multiple outcome measures, including measures of the target problem.
5. These studies report statistically significant differences between the intervention group and a comparison group after treatment.
6. Research findings regarding the intervention have been replicated, ideally, by independent investigators.

In intervention research, the "gold standard" for research design is the randomized controlled trial. A *randomized controlled trial* (RCT) involves the comparison of at least two groups of participants: an experimental group (i.e., a group of participants who receive the intervention under investigation) and a control group (i.e., a comparison group of participants who do not receive the intervention). Although RCTs share a number of core features, one quintessential feature is random assignment. **Random assignment** refers to the process of sorting participants into treatment comparison groups based on chance (i.e., each participant is equally likely to be assigned to any one particular group). Researchers can use a variety of tools for carrying out random assignment, including random number generators (i.e., electronic mechanisms in which each participant is assigned a number at random that corresponds with membership in a particular group). Random assignment is expected to ensure that participant groups are comparable with respect to both observable and nonobservable characteristics, meaning that treatment effects can be identified in a valid manner.

Many EBIs have been introduced for treating academic and mental health problems among children and adolescents. School psychologists can identify these interventions through individual studies, research reviews published in peer-reviewed journals, and reports from national and international organizations that vet research on academic and SEB prevention and intervention programs. Examples of these organizations include the U.S. Department of Education's What Works Clearinghouse (https://ies.ed.gov/ncee/wwc); the Blueprints for Healthy Youth Development (www.blueprintsprograms.org); the California Evidence-Based Clearinghouse for Child Welfare (www.cebc4cw.org); the National Institute on Drug Abuse (www.drugabuse.gov);

the Collaborative for Academic, Social, and Emotional Learning (http://casel.org); and the Effective Child Therapy website (http://effectivechildtherapy.com), developed by the Society of Clinical Child and Adolescent Psychology (Division 53 of the American Psychological Association).

Best practices indicate that an intervention that is supported by well-designed research should be chosen over one that does not have this type of empirical support. Unfortunately, EBIs do not currently exist for all problems and needs. In the absence of strong evidence, it may sometimes be necessary to use an intervention with emerging empirical support or to rely on empirical evidence and interventions that are indirectly linked to client and school needs.

The common-elements approach to intervention has been used to tailor an SEB intervention to client and setting characteristics. Reviews of the research literature on child and adolescent SEB interventions have found that practice elements, such as cognitive restructuring, problem-solving, relaxation, and psychoeducation, are common across evidence-based manualized interventions (Chorpita & Weisz, 2009). Common elements are the components that have been found across EBIs for specific SEB problems, and are thought to be the fundamental ingredients that underlie effective prevention and treatment. Use of common elements can be individualized and flexible according to client needs and setting resources and has been found to be effective for a range of SEB problems (Chorpita et al., 2013, 2017; Weisz et al., 2012).

SOCIAL JUSTICE CONNECTIONS

How do school psychologists adapt interventions to serve culturally diverse clients?

The children and adolescents with whom school psychologists work are diverse in many respects. In some cases, a student's responsiveness to an intervention may be influenced by the degree to which the intervention aligns with the student's cultural background. **Cultural adaptation** describes the process of modifying an intervention to ensure that it is congruent with the patterns, meanings, and values of a client's culture.

When an intervention is modified from its original form as described in research studies, client outcomes may also be different (i.e., the outcomes documented in previous research may not be reproduced). On the one hand, while cultural adaptations can be key for maximizing client–intervention fit, practitioners must be careful that these adaptations do not disrupt key intervention mechanisms that are believed to lead to positive client change. On the other hand, when executed properly, cultural adaptation can enhance the success of an intervention (see Barrera et al., 2013, 2017). There is considerable debate in the literature regarding the types and degree of adaptation that are appropriate, although there is general agreement that core components of an intervention should not be violated.

Typical adaptations to an intervention include additions, deletions, or modifications of intervention components; changes in the manner of delivery or intensity of components; and cultural modifications based on local circumstances (McKleroy et al., 2006; Ngo et al., 2008). Language translations and use of culturally relevant examples are frequently employed to enhance the match between interventions and clients. Other types of adaptations may include involving families and other significant individuals, changing the setting of the intervention, and incorporating cultural values in intervention content (Barrera et al., 2013). Ultimately, successful cultural adaptation requires practitioners to consider the individual characteristics and needs of their clients as well as to demonstrate knowledge of intervention design principles.

INTERVENTION IMPLEMENTATION

Selecting an appropriate intervention based on research evidence is only an initial step in the process of successful intervention use. The process of incorporating a program or practice at the individual, group, or organizational level is called *implementation*. Implementation involves a set of strategies and activities designed to put a program into use in a specific setting, such as a classroom or school. The mere act of selecting EBIs will not necessarily lead to successful implementation. Rather, specific steps must be taken to ensure that the individual receiving the intervention (client), those who are invested in the intervention (vested partners), and the larger organizational setting are supportive. Good intentions related to delivering an intervention will not guarantee its success unless appropriate measures are taken during planning and implementation. The larger systems-change process in schools is discussed in depth in Chapter 15; concepts related to intervention implementation are introduced and described here.

Implementation Components and Stages

The implementation process is characterized by several components and stages. Important components of the implementation process include (a) an *innovation*—a new program or practice to be instituted, such as an intervention; (b) a *communication process*—mechanisms by which those who have knowledge about the intervention exchange information with those who do not; (c) a *social system*—the social/organizational setting in which implementation takes place; (d) a *change agent*—the individual who assumes primary responsibility for the implementation process; (e) *vested partners*—all individuals who are invested in the delivery and outcome of the intervention; and (f) *implementers*—individuals who either conduct the intervention or play an essential role in its delivery to clients. Primary implementers are those who directly conduct the intervention, whereas secondary implementers are those who have an essential role in supporting intervention delivery.

For example, consider a school psychologist who is well versed in the Life Skills Training program (Botvin & Griffin, 2004) and is interested in implementing this program in their middle school as means of decreasing substance use. In this scenario, Life Skills Training is the *innovation* because although it is not a newly developed program, it is new to the middle school. The *communication process* includes presentations, meetings, and informal discussions between the school psychologist, who is knowledgeable about Life Skills Training, and other staff and administrators who are less familiar with this preventive program. The *social system* for this intervention is the school as well as larger systems that affect educational settings, such as the community and state and federal agencies. The *change agent* is the school psychologist, who is assuming primary responsibility for bringing this new prevention program to the middle school. *Primary implementers* for this program are the health teachers who will conduct the program in their classes, and *secondary implementers* are individuals such as the principal and assistant principal, who will arrange for the purchase of manuals, workbooks, and teacher training. *Vested partners* include teachers, administrators, counselors, parents, police, and others, all of whom have an interest in school operations and the overall well-being of students. Recognizing each of these components and the roles they play in contributing to the success of the intervention is a fundamental part of the implementation process. Successful implementation hinges on leadership support, a favorable implementation climate, strong fit between the intervention and the setting, and feedback loops between different types of vested partners (Aarons et al., 2011; Fixsen et al., 2009).

As noted earlier, the implementation process also can be conceptualized as a series of stages or phases in which the intervention is introduced and put into practice. These phases include (a) *dissemination*—the dispersal of information about the intervention to potential users; (b) *adoption*—the collective decision to use the intervention; (c) *implementation*—the delivery of the intervention to clients; and (d) *sustainability*—the continued use of the intervention after its first full implementation (Durlak & DuPre, 2008). During each stage, the change agent must take different steps to support the successful implementation of the intervention. Notably, success in one stage will not necessarily lead to success in a subsequent stage. For example, the decision to use an intervention will not necessarily lead to a successful first full implementation, unless the change agent works to ensure the development of a supportive context. Actions on the part of the change agent that can facilitate a smooth progression through each of the stages include developing implementer and vested partner support, providing training and technical assistance, developing organizational support, and leveraging external systems (Forman, 2015).

Selecting Interventions: Maximizing Contextual Fit

In addition to examining the evidence base for an intervention (as described previously), it is important to consider other characteristics of an intervention to maximize the fit of the intervention with an implementing organization such as a school. Several intervention characteristics, as perceived by vested partners, have been identified as influencing implementation success (Durlak & DuPre, 2008; Greenhalgh et al., 2004; Rogers, 2003): (a) *relative advantage*—the degree to which a new intervention is perceived as better than what currently exists; (b) *compatibility*—the degree to which an intervention is perceived as consistent with the values, beliefs, experiences, and needs of vested partners; (c) *complexity*—the degree to which an intervention is perceived as difficult to use; (d) *trialability*—the degree to which an intervention may be tried on a limited basis; (e) *observability*—the degree to which results of an intervention are visible; (f) *riskiness*—the perceived degree to which an intervention use may bring about unwanted consequences; (g) *task relevance*—the degree to which the intervention is seen as having the potential to improve the vested partner's work performance; and (h) *flexibility*—the degree to which the intervention is viewed as adaptable to the unique client and organization aspects and needs.

These intervention characteristics are *perceived* characteristics, meaning that they reflect vested partners' personal understanding of and beliefs about the intervention. Perceptions of interventions may be based on previous experiences with similar types of programs; beliefs about the capabilities, roles, and responsibilities of oneself and others; and other personal and individual factors. Notably, perceptions are changeable. As change agents, the school psychologist and leadership team members can take action to establish positive perceptions and dispel negative perceptions of an intervention. Such action can include discussion, consultation, presentations, workshops, and email communications that frame the intervention in positive terms with respect to the characteristics previously described.

Providing Training and Technical Assistance

Implementers must acquire an understanding of the principles, content, and processes of an intervention as well as skill in delivering it. Other vested partners also need to acquire knowledge about an intervention that will encourage their support for the implementation process. Training and technical assistance are the means through which implementers and other vested partners learn about an intervention. Training through presentations and workshops can be used to increase knowledge about an intervention, while technical assistance or coaching can increase an individual's skill in delivering the intervention to clients.

Presentations and workshops can provide information about the rationale, philosophy, theory, and research related to an intervention. These methods can introduce vested partners to the components and key practices of an intervention. They can also provide a venue for implementers to begin to practice new skills. Effective workshop training for implementers takes place over multiple sessions and includes written materials and participant goal setting, modeling, participant practice opportunities, and feedback (Joyce & Showers, 2002). In addition, it is important for workshop training for implementers to focus on acceptable forms of adaptation that can be used to tailor interventions to the characteristics of their clients and organization.

Workshop training alone is rarely sufficient to result in sustainable changes in the skills of those who will be delivering the intervention to clients (Lochman et al., 2009). Thus, technical assistance or coaching after initial training sessions is used to develop sustained implementer skills. This coaching and technical assistance process is well aligned with the school psychologist's role as consultant (described in Chapter 12). In this role, the school psychologist observes the use of the intervention, provides performance feedback that addresses implementation barriers, adapts the intervention to specific client needs and characteristics, and supports the implementer's self-efficacy (Han & Weiss, 2005).

Evaluating Implementation Outcomes: The Importance of Fidelity

In any effort to implement an EBI, it is important to evaluate both implementation and client/student outcomes. When evaluating interventions, psychologists have historically focused on intervention outcomes—that is, the effects of the intervention on the client. For example, in the example presented earlier describing the Life Skills Training program, intervention outcomes measured by the school psychologist and others may center on students' substance use behaviors, self-regulation, and emotional coping skills. However, implementation outcomes, which are indicators of whether an intervention is delivered properly and as intended, are also important. Implementation evaluation can provide information about how an intervention is being delivered, so that adjustments can be made, if necessary, regarding the quality or features of the intervention. Implementation evaluation serves to document what is provided to clients and, therefore, can assist in meeting accountability requirements. Implementation evaluation also allows intervention outcomes or client change to be attributed to the intervention. Implementation outcomes include indicators of whether the social and organizational context for the intervention is supportive. The most frequently used implementation outcome is typically related to *fidelity*.

Intervention fidelity (also referred to as program fidelity or treatment integrity) refers to the extent to which an intervention is delivered as planned or conceptualized (Sanetti & Kratochwill, 2009). Positive client outcomes have been consistently associated with high intervention fidelity (Durlak & DuPre, 2008). Fidelity is usually measured using direct observation of the delivery of an intervention. In this process, an observer checks the occurrence (or nonoccurrence) of operationally defined essential components of the intervention. The observation can occur in vivo or through the use of audio or video clips. A percentage of essential components implemented is derived by summing the number of components observed to have been implemented and dividing this number by the total number of components that should have been implemented. Direct observations can be used to measure adherence to core intervention components (i.e., the extent to which intervention components are present or not present) as well as quality of delivery (i.e., the implementer's skill in delivering each of these core components; Dane & Schneider, 1998).

SUMMARY AND CONCLUSIONS

School psychologists have an integral role in school-based intervention planning and implementation. Although there are many ways in which school psychologists and other personnel can structure intervention services, MTSS is a particularly promising approach, due to its ecological orientation and its focus on outcomes for all students. Moreover, MTSS promotes early intervention and increases the likelihood that student problems will be remediated in a timely fashion (or avoided altogether). Within MTSS, using EBIs is essential for ensuring the potential for positive student outcomes. Ultimately, considerable planning and action are needed to build competency and support among vested partners as well as to support the implementation of EBIs in MTSS. The school psychologist has the potential to be a key leader in facilitating this process and in promoting effective and equitable school services for all students.

DISCUSSION QUESTIONS

1. As a school psychologist, which challenges might you face in assisting a school to implement MTSS for the first time?
2. Which methods can be used to determine if Tier 2 or Tier 3 services are appropriate for a student?
3. Which activities does a school psychologist engage in when using a data-based problem-solving model to make educational decisions about students?
4. Which issues should be considered in selecting interventions for students?
5. What are some barriers to implementing EBIs in schools? Which activities does a school psychologist engage in to ensure that an intervention will be implemented successfully?

RECOMMENDED READINGS

Aarons, G. A., Hurlburt, M., & Horwitz, S. M. (2011). Advancing a conceptual model of evidence-based practice implementation in public service sectors. *Administration and Policy in Mental Health and Mental Health Services Research, 38*(1), 4–23. https://doi.org/10.1007/s10488-010-0327-7

Barrera, M., Berkel, C., & Castro, F. G. (2017). Directions for the advancement of culturally adapted preventive interventions: Local adaptations, engagement, and sustainability. *Prevention Science, 18*(6), 640–648. https://doi.org/10.1007/s11121-016-0705-9

Durlak, J. A., & DuPre, E. P. (2008). Implementation matters: A review of research on the influence of implementation on program outcomes and the factors affecting implementation. *American Journal of Community Psychology, 41*, 327–350. https://doi.org/10.1007/s10464-008-9165-0

Fixsen, D. L., Blase, K. A., Naoom, S. F., & Wallace, F. (2009). Core implementation components. *Research on Social Work Practice, 19*(5), 531–540. https://doi.org/10.1177/1049731509335549

Forman, S. G. (2015). *Implementation of mental health programs in schools: A change agent's guide*. American Psychological Association.

 A robust set of instructor resources designed to supplement this text is located at http://connect.springerpub.com/content/book/978-0-8261-6344-8. Qualifying instructors may request access by emailing textbook@springerpub.com.

REFERENCES

Aarons, G. A., Hurlburt, M., & Horwitz, S. M. (2011). Advancing a conceptual model of evidence-based practice implementation in public service sectors. *Administration and Policy in Mental Health and Mental Health Services Research, 38*(1), 4–23. https://doi.org/10.1007/s10488-010-0327-7

Barrera, M., Berkel, C., & Castro, F. G. (2017). Directions for the advancement of culturally adapted preventive interventions: Local adaptations, engagement, and sustainability. *Prevention Science, 18*(6), 640–648. https://doi.org/10.1007/s11121-016-0705-9

Barrera, M., Jr., Castro, F. G., Strycker, L. A., & Toobert, D. J. (2013). Cultural adaptations of behavioral health interventions: A progress report. *Journal of Consulting and Clinical Psychology, 81*(2), 196–205. https://doi.org/10.1037/a0027085

Botvin, G. J., & Griffin, K. W. (2004). Life skills training: Empirical findings and future directions. *Journal of Primary Prevention, 25*(2), 211–232. https://doi.org/10.1023/B:JOPP.0000042391.58573.5b

Burns, M. K., & Gibbons, K. A. (2008). *Implementing response-to-intervention in elementary and secondary schools*. Routledge.

Center for Mental Health in Schools. (2011, February). *Moving beyond the three tier intervention pyramid: Toward a comprehensive framework for student and learning supports*. http://smhp.psych.ucla.edu/pdfdocs/briefs/threetier.pdf

Chafouleas, S. M., Johnson, A. H., Overstreet, S., & Santos, N. M. (2016). Toward a blueprint for trauma-informed service delivery in schools. *School Mental Health, 8*(1), 144–162. https://doi.org/10.1007/s12310-015-9166-8

Charlton, C. T., Moulton, S., Sabey, C. V., & West, R. (2021). A systematic review of the effects of schoolwide intervention programs on student and teacher perceptions of school climate. *Journal of Positive Behavior Interventions, 23*(3), 185–200. https://doi.org/10.1177/1098300720940168

Chorpita, B. F., Daleiden, E. L., Park, A. L., Ward, A. M., Levy, M. C., Cromley, T., Chiu, A. W., Letamendi, A. M., Tsai, K. H., & Krull, J. L. (2017). Child STEPs in California: A cluster randomized effectiveness trial comparing modular treatment with community implemented treatment for youth with anxiety, depression, conduct problems, or traumatic stress. *Journal of Consulting and Clinical Psychology, 85*(1), 13–25. https://doi.org/10.1037/ccp0000133

Chorpita, B. F., & Weisz, J. R. (2009). *Modular approach to therapy for children with anxiety, depression, trauma, or conduct problems (MATCH-ADTC)*. PracticeWise.

Chorpita, B. F., Weisz, J. R., Daleiden, E. L., Schoenwald, S. K., Palinkas, L. A., Miranda, J., Higa-McMillan, C. K., Nakamura, B. J., Austin, A. A., Borntrager, C. F., Ward, A., Wells, K. C., Gibbons, R. D., & Research Network on Youth Mental Health. (2013). Long-term outcomes for the Child STEPs randomized effectiveness trial: A comparison of modular and standard treatment designs with usual care. *Journal of Consulting and Clinical Psychology, 81*(6), 999–1009. https://doi.org/10.1037/a0034200

Cook, C. R., Lyon, A. R., Kubergovic, D., Wright, D. B., & Zhang, Y. (2015). A supportive beliefs intervention to facilitate the implementation of evidence-based practices within a multi-tiered system of supports. *School Mental Health, 7*(1), 49–60. https://doi.org/10.1007/s12310-014-9139-3

Dane, A. V., & Schneider, B. H. (1998). Program integrity in primary and early secondary prevention: Are implementation effects out of control? *Clinical Psychology Review, 18*(1), 23–45. https://doi.org/10.1016/S0272-7358(97)00043-3

Durlak, J. A., & DuPre, E. P. (2008). Implementation matters: A review of research on the influence of implementation on program outcomes and the factors affecting implementation. *American Journal of Community Psychology, 41*(3–4), 327–350. https://doi.org/10.1007/s10464-008-9165-0

Fallon, L. M., Veiga, M., & Sugai, G. (2021). Strengthening MTSS for behavior (MTSS-B) to promote racial equity. *School Psychology Review*, 1–16. https://doi.org/10.1080/2372966X.2021.1972333

Fixsen, D. L., Blase, K. A., Naoom, S. F., & Wallace, F. (2009). Core implementation components. *Research on Social Work Practice, 19*(5), 531–540. https://doi.org/10.1177/1049731509335549

Forman, S. G. (2015). *Implementation of mental health programs in schools: A change agent's guide*. American Psychological Association.

Greenhalgh, T., Robert, G., Macfarlane, F., Bate, P., & Kyriakidou, O. (2004). Diffusion of innovations in service organizations: Systematic review and recommendations. *Milbank Quarterly, 82*(4), 581–629. https://doi.org/10.1111/j.0887-378X.2004.00325.x

Han, S. S., & Weiss, B. (2005). Sustainability of teacher implementation of school-based mental health programs. *Journal of Abnormal Child Psychology, 33*(6), 665–679. https://doi.org/10.1007/s10802-005-7646-2

Horner, R. H., & Monzalve-Macaya, M. (2018). A framework for building safe and effective school environments: Positive behavioral interventions and supports (PBIS). *Pedagogická Orientace, 28*(4), 663–685. https://doi.org/10.5817/PedOr2018-4-663

Johnston, E., D'Andrea Montalbano, P., & Kirkland, D. E. (2017). *Culturally responsive education: A primer for policy and practice*. Metropolitan Center for Research on Equity and the Transformation of Schools. New York University.

Joyce, B. R., & Showers, B. (2002). *Student achievement through staff development* (3rd ed.). Association for Supervision and Curriculum Development.

Kazdin, A. E., & Weisz, J. R. (2010). Introduction: Context, background, and goals. In A. E. Kazdin & J. R. Weisz (Eds.), *Evidence-based psychotherapies for children and adolescents* (pp. 3–9). Guilford Press.

Lochman, J. E., Boxmeyer, C., Powell, N., Qu, L., Wells, K., & Windle, M. (2009). Dissemination of the Coping Power program: Importance of intensity of counselor training. *Journal of Consulting and Clinical Psychology, 77*(3), 397–409. https://doi.org/10.1037/a0014514

McKleroy, V. S., Galbraith, J. S., Cummings, B., Jones, P., Harshbarger, C., Collins, C., Gelaude, D., Carey, J. W., & ADAPT Team. (2006). Adapting evidence-based behavioral interventions for new settings and target populations. *AIDS Education & Prevention, 18*(4 Suppl. A), 59–73. https://doi.org/10.1521/aeap.2006.18.supp.59

National Association of School Psychologists. (2016). *Every Student Succeeds Act opportunities: Multi-tiered systems of supports*. https://www.nasponline.org/Documents/Research%20and%20Policy/ESSA_MTSS_Members.pdf

National Association of School Psychologists. (2020). *Model for comprehensive and integrated school psychological services*. https://www.nasponline.org/standards-and-certification/nasp-practice-model

Ngo, V., Langley, A., Kataoka, S. H., Nadeem, E., Escudero, P., & Stein, B. D. (2008). Providing evidence-based practice to ethnically diverse youths: Examples from the Cognitive Behavioral Intervention for Trauma in Schools (CBITS) program. *Journal of the American Academy of Child and Adolescent Psychiatry, 47*(8), 858–862. https://doi.org/10.1097/CHI.0b013e3181799f19

Pluymert, K. (2014). Problem-solving foundations for school psychological services. In P. L. Harrison & A. Thomas (Eds.), *Best practices in school psychology: Data-based and collaborative decision making* (pp. 25–39). National Association of School Psychologists.

Pyle, N., & Vaughn, S. (2012). Remediating reading difficulties in a response to intervention model with secondary students. *Psychology in the Schools, 49*(3), 273–284. https://doi.org/10.1002/pits.21593

Rogers, E. M. (2003). *Diffusion of innovations*. Free Press.

Sanetti, L. M. H., & Collier-Meek, M. A. (2015). Data-driven delivery of implementation supports in a multi-tiered framework: A pilot study. *Psychology in the Schools, 52*(8), 815–828. https://doi.org/10.1002/pits.21861

Sanetti, L. M. H., & Kratochwill, T. R. (2009). Toward developing a science of treatment integrity: Introduction to the special series. *School Psychology Review, 38*(4), 445–459. https://www.proquest.com/docview/219656532

Stolber, K. C., & Gettinger, M. (2016). Multi-tiered systems of support and evidence-based practices. In S. R. Jimerson, M. K. Burns, & A. M. VanDerHeyden (Eds.), *Handbook of response to intervention* (pp. 121–141). Springer.

Taylor, R. D., Oberle, E., Durlak, J. A., & Weissberg, R. P. (2017). Promoting positive youth development through school-based social and emotional learning interventions: A meta-analysis of follow-up effects. *Child Development, 88*(4), 1156–1171. https://doi.org/10.1111/cdev.12864

Wang, M.-T., Degol, J. L., Amemiya, J., Parr, A., & Guo, J. (2020). Classroom climate and children's academic and psychological wellbeing: A systematic review and meta-analysis. *Developmental Review, 57*, 100912. https://doi.org/10.1016/j.dr.2020.100912

Weisz, J. R., Chorpita, B. F., Palinkas, L. A., Schoenwald, S. K., Miranda, J., Bearman, S. K., Daleiden, E. L., Ugueto, A. M., Ho, A., Martin, J., Gray, J., Alleyne, A., Langer, D. A., Southam-Gerow, M. A., Gibbons, R. D., & Research Network on Youth Mental Health. (2012). Testing standard and modular designs for psychotherapy treating depression, anxiety, and conduct problems in youth: A randomized effectiveness trial. *Archives of General Psychiatry, 69*(3), 274–282. https://doi.org/10.1001/archgenpsychiatry.2011.147

CHAPTER 9

Academic Assessment and Intervention

SCOTT P. ARDOIN ■ STACY-ANN A. JANUARY ■ AMY TRAYERS

CHAPTER OBJECTIVES

After reading this chapter, you will be able to:

- Describe the nature of academic skills in the areas of reading, mathematics, and written language.
- Describe an ecologically oriented approach to academic assessment.
- Name and describe the assessments that educators use to measures students' academic skills.
- Illustrate academic assessment and intervention procedures within multitiered systems of support (MTSS).
- Describe the relevance of social justice in implementing academic MTSS.

NATIONAL ASSOCIATION OF SCHOOL PSYCHOLOGISTS PRACTICE MODEL CONNECTIONS

Domain 1: Data-Based Decision-Making
Domain 3: Academic Interventions and Instructional Supports
Domain 5: School-Wide Practices to Promote Learning

INTRODUCTION

One of the primary functions of the K–12 education system is to prepare children to be ready for college or a career. Central to college and career readiness is students' proficiency in three key academic skill areas: reading, mathematics, and writing. Although most students acquire the necessary skills when taught by teachers, some students need additional support in the form of academic interventions. Given the importance of academic skills, a core skill for school psychologists is the ability to collect and use assessment data that informs the development of interventions that address the academic skill needs of individual students. This chapter reviews the essential components of academic assessment and intervention and couches them within a multitiered system of support (MTSS).

DEFINITIONS AND PREVALENCE OF ACADEMIC SKILL PROBLEMS

Reading

Many students in grades K–12 in the United States struggle with reading. Data from the National Assessment of Educational Progress (NAEP), an annual assessment of academic achievement that is administered to a nationally representative sample of public and private school students in the United States, indicate that only 35% of fourth-grade students and 34% of eighth-grade students who completed this assessment in 2019 performed at or above the Proficient level (i.e., demonstrated adequate competency) in the subject of reading (U.S. Department of Education, 2020b). These data are even more alarming when examining the proportions of racially and ethnically minoritized fourth-grade students who are proficient in reading (e.g., 18% of Black or African American students, 23% of Hispanic or Latine students, 19% of American Indian or Alaskan Native students). It is important to note that these differences are a result of factors (e.g., racism, discrimination) that influence educational opportunities for children (i.e., opportunity gaps) and do not indicate inherent achievement differences among groups of students. Nonetheless, the current status of reading achievement in the United States indicates a need for widespread improvements in reading instruction that promotes equitable outcomes for students who have been and are currently marginalized in the education system.

Proficient readers read with accuracy, speed, and appropriate expression, and comprehend what they read. In the early elementary grades, there is a focus on teaching students to read, as this is fundamental to being able to read for understanding across all content areas (e.g., science, social studies) in late elementary, middle, and high school. The process of reading relies on a number of basic and advanced skills, including phonological awareness, decoding, fluency, vocabulary, and comprehension (National Reading Panel, 2000). *Phonological awareness* refers to the understanding that words are composed of smaller units of sound (e.g., the understanding that the word *cat* comprises three sounds—namely /c/, /a/, and /t/). *Decoding* refers to knowledge and skill in applying sound–letter correspondences (e.g., knowledge that the letter *c* corresponds with the sound /c/). *Reading fluency*, which is discussed later in this chapter, refers to the rate, accuracy, and prosody of an individual's reading. Students who lack fluency because they struggle with reading individual words generally have difficulty comprehending text because they must allocate their attention to reading the words of the text instead of understanding its meaning (LaBerge & Samuels, 1974). *Vocabulary* refers to the student's knowledge of individual words in text, which is important for reading comprehension. Finally, *reading comprehension* refers to the construction of meaning from text. Providing students with effective instruction in each of these five component areas is essential to the development of skilled readers (National Reading Panel, 2000).

Mathematics

Recent results from the NAEP in math are comparable to those in reading, with only 41% of fourth-grade students and 34% of eighth-grade students having performed at or above the Proficient level in this area in 2019 (U.S. Department of Education, 2020a). As in the area of reading, opportunity gaps in math achievement exist for students with marginalized identities. Indeed, there is a significant need for nationwide improvement in students' math performance.

Proficiency in math is multifaceted and includes the ability to perform basic computations, understand key mathematical concepts, and solve problems. One of the earliest skills that young children must acquire to become competent in math is number sense

(Shapiro, 2011). *Number sense* refers to an individual's general facility with numerical concepts. For example, a student who observes two different-size piles of candy and identifies the larger pile without counting individual pieces of candy is displaying number sense (and specifically the abstract concepts of *more* and *less*). In the early elementary grades, students must also master basic computational skills, such as addition, subtraction, and multiplication. As in reading, students must develop proficiency in basic math skills to complete complex multistep math problems (Shapiro, 2011).

Written Language

The 2011 results of the NAEP Writing Assessment (the most recent data available) indicated that only 27% of eighth-grade and 12th-grade students performed at or above the Proficient level on this test (U.S. Department of Education, 2017). Proficient writers plan and compose writing that communicates one or more ideas clearly and in an organized manner. Just as basic addition and subtraction skills are necessary for students to become proficient in complex mathematics, spelling and handwriting (and potentially typing) are necessary skills to become proficient writers. Students who must exert substantial cognitive resources to write letters and spell words will have fewer cognitive resources to expend on the meaning of the text that they are trying to write (Shapiro, 2011). Other important writing skills that must be taught include generating ideas and topics, producing written text fluently (i.e., producing viable content at an appropriate pace), writing in response to a variety of demands, structuring information, revising, and applying appropriate punctuation and grammar.

OVERVIEW OF ACADEMIC ASSESSMENT

As noted in Chapter 7, assessment for, during, and after intervention is critical for determining individual students' instructional needs to promote academic success. School psychologists use assessment data to learn about students' overall achievement, strengths, and needs as well as to monitor the effects of intervention on students' academic outcomes. The following subsections review methods commonly used for assessing students' learning in reading, math, and written language.

Assessing the Environment

When evaluating a student's academic skills for the purpose of informing intervention, it is critical to understand the contexts in which the child is functioning. Academic skill deficits, or discrepancies between what a student knows and what the student needs to know to be academically successful, are best understood as a mismatch between the child and the environment rather than a deficit that lies within the child. According to ecological systems theory (Bronfenbrenner, 1977; Bronfenbrenner & Morris, 1998), children grow and develop within a series of nested contexts, and it is the interaction between the child and these contexts that facilitates the child's learning. Assessing the contexts in which the child lives and learns provides the most complete picture of their academic functioning, which better informs intervention strategies. The most proximal of those contexts are the home environment and the classroom environment.

Children's learning is not isolated to the classroom, as learning also takes place in the home setting and through interactions with caregivers and friends. Thus, it is not surprising that features of the home environment may be informative for better understanding of the student's functioning at school. For example, parenting practices and the quality of the instructional environment predict children's academic skills and functioning in school (Baker & Rimm-Kaufman, 2014; Brennan et al., 2013). To assess the home environment, one can conduct an interview with parents/caregivers. Caregivers can provide information about the resources available at home to support learning (e.g., access to the internet) or the student's academic strengths and opportunities for growth (e.g., books). They may also provide information about when/if the child met developmental milestones (e.g., first words and steps) that may be relevant for understanding the child's current academic functioning.

In school, the *instructional environment* refers to the location, items, people, and curriculum used where students' academic learning occurs. Considering the direct association between the instructional environment and students' academic skills, it is essential that academic assessment include evaluations of the classroom ecology. To assess the instructional environment, one would (a) interview the teacher, (b) review the student's classroom work and prior records, (c) conduct observations of the student in the classroom, and (d) interview the student. First, it is essential that school psychologists obtain an understanding of the curriculum to which the student is exposed. More specifically, they need to identify the skills that have and have not been taught. Although curriculum standards exist for each grade level, they do not guarantee that the student was actually instructed in those skills. The second purpose of assessing the instructional environment is to understand the difference between what the child is *able to do* and what the child is *expected to be able to do* at their grade level. This information can be obtained via interview with the teacher, with a review of the student's classroom work, or through direct assessment methods (described later in this chapter).

Measuring Academic Skills

In addition to assessing the instructional environment, school psychologists must assess students' academic skill levels. The most common assessments for measuring the academic skills of students are curriculum-based measurement, *computer adaptive interim tests* (CATs), *norm-referenced tests* (NRTs), *criterion-referenced tests* (CRTs), and state-mandated tests. Each type of assessment has its own purpose, strengths, and weaknesses.

CURRICULUM-BASED MEASUREMENT

Curriculum-based measurement (CBM) refers to a standardized set of brief assessments that measure students' accuracy and speed (i.e., fluency) in performing academic skills in reading, mathematics, writing, and spelling. They are often described as a *general outcome measure*, meaning that it requires the integration of several component skills that make up an academic task and, therefore, can be used as a measure of student performance across an academic year (Hosp et al., 2016). There are a number of publishers of CBM assessments, such as aimswebPlus (www.aimsweb.com), DIBELS (https://dibels.uoregon.edu), Acadience Reading (https://acadiencelearning.com), EasyCBM (https://easycbm.com), and FastBridge Learning (www.renaissance.com/products/fastbridge). Although the specific materials that each of these companies distributes differ, they share several common features: namely, standardized procedures for administration, tasks that measure students' speed and accuracy, and relatively cost-efficient materials (as compared to other measures). They also are quick to administer and allow for a student's gains to be graphed across time so that progress can be assessed. CBM is most commonly used to assess skills in reading, math, writing, and spelling.

Reading Curriculum-Based Measures

Some of the most commonly used measures are curriculum-based measures of oral reading (CBM-R), nonsense word fluency (NWF), and word identification fluency (WIF). CBM-R is a timed, individually administered measure of students' oral reading rate with accuracy. To administer CBM-R, the examiner has two copies of the grade-level passage: one student probe and one corresponding examiner score sheet. After providing the student with a copy of the passage, the examiner reads a set of standardized instructions aloud to the student. These instructions inform the student where to begin reading, to read aloud, to do their best reading, and that, if they do not know a word, the examiner will provide that word.

After providing the instructions and answering any questions the student may have, the examiner says "Begin," and starts a 1-minute timer when the student reads the first word. While the student is reading, the examiner follows along, noting any errors (e.g., skipped words, substitutions, or misread words), and providing unknown words after the student hesitates for 3 seconds. At the end of 1 minute, the examiner instructs the student to stop reading. The probe is then scored by subtracting the number of words read with errors from the total number of words read. The resulting number is the final score, or the words read correctly per minute (WRCM). Decades of research evaluating the technical characteristics of scores from CBM-R support its reliability and provide evidence that WRCM is a strong indicator of reading achievement and reading comprehension skills (January et al., 2016; Reschly et al., 2009).

Because it is important to catch students with academic needs early in their academic careers, and because not all struggling readers can read text, other CBM procedures are available to assess reading skills that are prerequisites to text reading. Two measures frequently used with early readers, or older students who are struggling to read, are NWF and WIF. NWF assesses a student's ability to identify and blend a list of vowel–consonant and consonant–vowel–consonant nonwords, directly measuring beginning readers' alphabetics and phonics skills (i.e., letter–sound correspondence and decoding skills). In contrast to NWF, WIF is a task in which students read a list of real words. WIF probes include decodable words, which are words that can be sounded out (e.g., cat and car), and/or high-frequency words, which are words that appear often in texts (e.g., *the* and *or*). As with CBM-R, administration of NWF and WIF is done individually. As the student completes the task, the examiner makes a slash through incorrect words or sounds. After 1 minute has elapsed, a close bracket is used to mark the student's last word or sound. The number of incorrect sounds or words is then subtracted from the total number of sounds or words read to obtain the correct letter sounds or WRCM. NWF and WIF measures continue to be used widely, and extensive evidence exists supporting their use for identifying students with instructional needs and monitoring such students' progress; however, research supports the use of WIF and CBM-R over NWF (Clemens et al., 2011; January & Klingbeil, 2020; Van Norman et al., 2018).

Math Curriculum-Based Measurement

In mathematics, CBM tools fall into one of two categories: (a) computation or (b) concepts and applications. CBM math computation probes measure the skills of addition, subtraction, multiplication, and division; they can measure skills in one or more of these areas. For example, a multiple-skill computation probe for second grade may include one- or two-digit addition and subtraction facts with and without regrouping. CBM math concepts and applications probes typically measure a range of skills such as number concepts, money, graphs and charts, and word problems. The specific skills assessed at each grade level vary and are aligned with grade-level expectations for academic performance. Although specific instructions may vary across publishers, when administering CBM math probes, the examiner generally explains the task and asks students to start with the first problem, working in order from left to right and showing their work. Students may skip problems but are encouraged to try to complete each problem. The time allotted for probes varies by publisher and grade level/skills but generally is shorter for computation (e.g., 2–4 minutes) and longer for concepts/applications (e.g., 10–15 minutes or untimed). Math CBM probes are typically scored based on the number and/or percentage of items completed correctly. Research on the technical properties of CBM math generally supports its reliability and relation to mathematics achievement (Anselmo et al., 2021; Foegen et al., 2007).

Writing Curriculum-Based Measurement

Within the area of writing, CBM typically involves asking students to complete a brief writing task in response to a prompt (e.g., "Write about a time you experienced something surprising."). These prompts vary in difficulty by grade level. Students are asked to write a response to the prompt for 3 minutes. There are various ways to score these types of probes, such as counting total words written (TWW), total words spelled correctly (WSC), or total number of correct word sequences (CWS). TWW methods do not account for accuracy of spelling, punctuation, or grammar, whereas WSC methods account for spelling but not grammar, punctuation, or context. CWS methods, however, account for both spelling and grammar. A CWS is defined as two adjacent words that are grammatically congruent (e.g., use correct verb tense or exhibit subject–verb agreement) and that are spelled correctly. Often, comparing scores derived via multiple methods can provide useful information about a student's writing skills. For example, using a combination of all three methods may allow the examiner to identify students who produce an appropriate volume of writing but who have difficulty spelling or sequencing words accurately. As with other CBM methods, research supports the reliability and validity of these procedures for assessing and predicting students' writing skills (McMaster & Espin, 2007). Nevertheless, unlike for other CBM tools, sex differences may exist such that females produce more writing, whereas males may be more accurate (Jewell & Malecki, 2005). The exact reasons for these differences are unclear.

Spelling Curriculum-Based Measurement

Spelling CBM differs from other types of written language CBM in that it focuses on writing individual words correctly rather than producing connected text. To conduct a spelling CBM, the examiner provides the student with a blank sheet of lined paper and instructs them to write a series of dictated words on the sheet. After reading the instructions, the examiner dictates a list of words to the student at intervals of 7 to 10 seconds (depending on the student's grade level). This occurs for 2 minutes, and the student is instructed to proceed with the next word, even if they have not completed the previous one (Shinn, 1989). During this task, the examiner says each word twice. Scoring of spelling measures typically involves counting the total number of WSC and/or the number of correct letter sequences (CLSs) in each word. A CLS refers to two adjacent letters (or adjacent initial and final letters and their adjacent spaces) that are written in the correct order (Hosp et al., 2016). For example, the word *psychology* would have 11 possible CLSs.

Computer Adaptive Interim Tests

CATs are computer-administered assessments that may cover a range of academic skills, but are most often available in the areas of reading and mathematics. CATs present students with a set of multiple-choice test items that are tailored to their skill level. The first item of a CAT is of moderate difficulty, and subsequent items are presented to the student based on their accuracy with the previous item that was presented. That is, if the student gets the item correct, they are presented with a more difficult question. Conversely, if the student gets the item incorrect, they get an easier question. As such, items on a CAT are adapted to student performance, with the goal of obtaining a precise estimate of a student's skills in a certain area. An advantage of administering CATs is that these tests typically have a very large bank of items, which results in more precise estimates of the academic skills of lower-performing and higher-performing students, as compared with traditional NRTs. The large item bank also means that CATs can be administered multiple times per year. In comparison to CBM probes, which may be obtained for free, CATs are relatively expensive and require a computer lab for their administration. Independent research on CATs is emerging and supports their technical adequacy (Boorse & Van Norman, 2021; Thomas & January, 2021).

Norm-Referenced and Criterion-Referenced Tests

Many schools choose to administer NRTs, such as the Iowa Assessments (Dunbar & Welch, 2015), to students each year. As one might expect, NRTs rely on norm-referenced comparisons (described in Chapter 7), meaning that they are useful for understanding how a student's academic achievement compares to that of same-age peers. This information is useful for making decisions about special education eligibility, such as whether a student has a specific learning disability. However, the information provided by these tests does not necessarily allow for (a) determining which specific skills a student has or has not mastered and need to be targeted through intervention or (b) monitoring a student's progress to examine whether an intervention is effective. Thus, schools may also choose to administer CRTs to their students. These types of tests rely on *criterion-referenced comparisons* (also described in Chapter 7), meaning that they measure student performance as compared with specific criteria, such as a state's grade-specific content learning standards. Results from CRTs may be useful for understanding the extent to which a student has mastered the skills that were expected to be taught during the academic year. Unfortunately, scores from CRTs cannot be used to inform instruction or monitor students' responsiveness to intervention. This is due in part to the fact that some CRTs are typically administered at the end of the year, when it is too late to make changes in the instructional practices to which students are exposed. Some schools do, however, administer CRTs on a regular basis to determine whether students have mastered skills and whether particular students are ready to progress to the next skill or need additional instruction. Such data can be used to examine the amount of instruction individual students need in comparison to their peers and can aid in evaluating whether supplemental instruction is sufficient for an individual student.

State-Mandated Tests

In all states, schools must administer one or more state-mandated tests each year, often beginning in third grade. These state-mandated tests are criterion-referenced and/or norm-referenced, may be computer adaptive (e.g., the Partnership for Assessment of Readiness for College and Careers), and are administered near the end of the academic year. Potential benefits of these tests are that they can be better aligned with students' curriculum than NRTs and are useful for understanding the extent to which a student has mastered the curriculum that was taught during the academic year. Despite these benefits, some limitations weaken their utility when assessing academic skills for the purpose of intervention. First, like NRTs, they are not designed to be administered multiple times per year, so they cannot be used to measure growth. Second, the results do not provide information regarding which skills a student has or has not mastered. Further, because the tests are administered at the end of the year, results are not timely in identifying the skills in which students may need additional support. Due to their limited utility for academic assessment and intervention, state-mandated tests are most useful for accountability purposes. That is, states use results from these tests as part of their accountability systems for identifying schools that may need improvement or may benefit from additional support (Every Student Succeeds Act, 2015).

In summary, each of the assessment tools described here has distinct purposes, benefits, and weaknesses. However, to measure the academic skills of students for the purpose of informing instruction, it is most useful to directly measure students' academic skills in the context of the curriculum. The most appropriate tools with which to accomplish this goal are CBM instruments.

ADDRESSING ACADEMIC SKILL PROBLEMS THROUGH MULTITIERED SYSTEMS OF SUPPORT

Chapter 8 broadly described the general framework of MTSS. This section, in contrast, describes the applications of this framework to the delivery of academic assessment and intervention services. MTSS offers a promising model for academic service delivery because it is prevention oriented, focused on outcomes for all students, and heavily reliant on data-based decision-making. In particular, the sections that follow provide examples of assessment and intervention procedures at each of the three tiers.

Tier 1 Assessment and Intervention

A properly implemented MTSS process takes into consideration a student's instructional environment by assessing Tier 1 instruction (Ardoin et al., 2016). Tier 1 instruction is the instruction to which all students in a building are exposed. As part of the MTSS model, Tier 1 services are evaluated through the universal screening of all students within a school building. Consistent with the MTSS model described in Chapter 8, universal screening at Tier 1 generally involves all students in a school being administered one or more academic assessment measures (e.g., CBM, CAT) three times annually and the comparison of the resulting assessment data to national and/or local norms. National norms are estimates of how students at a particular age or grade level perform. They are determined by averaging student performance data for a particular age or grade level across the nation. Testing companies provide these national norms, which are specific to each test. Local norms are based on the average performance of students at a specific age or grade level within the individual school or district. Administration of academic measures multiple times across the school year allows schools to evaluate both the level of performance and the rate of change for both groups and individual students. Prior to the advent of MTSS, few schools conducted universal screening, and even fewer did so on a triannual basis.

To assess the environment in which a student is learning, universal screening data must be evaluated by comparing the performance of groups of students (e.g., students in a specific grade within a specific school, performance disaggregated by race or ethnicity). This allows personnel to determine whether the quality of instruction provided to students in the school/district is sufficient for supporting adequate gains. If the environment (i.e., classroom, school, school district) in which a student is receiving instruction does not promote equitable and adequate gains for most students, it is unreasonable to expect that any given student will demonstrate achievement at a level commensurate with national norms (Ardoin et al., 2016). Thus, universal screening data should be examined to determine whether the average achievement level and rate of gain of students within the district, individual schools, and classrooms are at expected levels. If the answer to any of these questions is "no," or if marginalized and minoritized students perform at significantly lower levels than their peers, then instructional changes must be made. Failure to consider the environment in which a student is receiving instruction and whether that environment is providing equitable, quality instruction has the potential for an individual student to be blamed for their failure to achieve, when in actuality the student's poor achievement is largely due to the environment. In the absence of Tier 1 universal screening data, schools are more likely to attribute student deficits to a disability within the student than to a deficit in the quality of the instruction being provided by the school (Fien et al., 2021).

Tier 2 Assessment and Intervention

After considering the quality of Tier 1 instruction being provided to students, universal screening data should be examined to determine which students might need supplemental or Tier 2 intervention. Recall from Chapter 8 that Tier 2 intervention is instruction that is supplemental to Tier 1 instruction. It should provide students with extra opportunities to practice skills, more explicit instruction, and/or instruction that targets skills the student has not yet mastered but that other students within the instructional environment have already learned.

When selecting students in need of Tier 2 intervention services, several factors must be taken into consideration. First, although universal screening data should be used as a primary source of information, it should not be the only source of information used in selecting students for such services. It is essential that all reliable and valid data are considered when making decisions regarding the educational services that will or will not be provided to a student. Decisions about the educational services provided to a student should never be made based on a single source of data. Although school psychologists are not always called upon to be part of the MTSS decision-making process at Tier 2, they should work closely with schools to ensure that multiple quality sources of data are used as the basis for making educational decisions and that equity and social justice are always considered. The education that school psychologists receive regarding test development, test evaluation, and standardized administration procedures makes them uniquely suited for helping schools in evaluating their assessment tools (Fenning et al., 2015).

Another important factor to consider when selecting students for Tier 2 services is that individual student achievement must be evaluated in the context of the environment in which the student has received instruction. Unfortunately, some schools mistakenly select students for Tier 2 services based solely on how each student's scores compare to national norms, thereby failing to take into consideration the context in which students have received instruction. Students should generally be selected for Tier 2 services by comparing their performance to local norms. Selecting students based on national norms can not only result in students being considered as needing Tier 2 instruction when the problem is Tier 1 instruction, but also lead to more students being identified as needing Tier 2 intervention than a school has the resources to provide. For instance, if the performance of 30% of students in a school is in the bottom 15% of students nationally, it is unlikely the school would have the resources to provide quality Tier 2 intervention services to that many students. In such situations, the school should (a) consider the changes that should be made to Tier 1 instruction/behavior management to ensure that more students are making significant gains, (b) make the necessary changes, and (c) provide supplemental Tier 2 intervention to students whose achievement is discrepant from peers within that environment.

A final factor to consider when selecting students for Tier 2 services is that students should be considered for these services when they are discrepant from peers, regardless of whether their performance is significantly lower or significantly higher than their peers'.

Although this chapter focuses on assessment and intervention for students who are struggling academically, universal screening data are useful for assessing whether schools are meeting the instructional needs of all students, including high-achieving students (McCallum et al., 2013).

Tier 2 instructional services vary within and across districts in regard to where and by whom they are provided. Such services also vary within and across school districts in terms of their quality, intensity, fidelity of implementation, and the extent to which the instruction meets the individual needs of the students being provided with Tier 2 intervention. For instance, some schools provide students with what they deem to be Tier 2 interventions but that are, in truth, simply surface-level changes to assessment procedures (e.g., providing students with extra time to complete assignments) or classroom structure (e.g., reducing lengths of assignments, changing a student's seat location) and theoretically would not be expected to improve student learning. When these types of so-called interventions are implemented, it is important that school psychologists inform the school's MTSS team that such interventions would not be expected to change a student's rate of growth and, therefore, cannot be considered Tier 2 interventions. Other schools provide students with standardized evidence-based interventions that theoretically could improve students' learning but do not necessarily target specific instructional needs. For instance, in some schools, all students identified as having a reading deficit are provided with the same computer-based reading intervention, despite the differing reasons for student deficits. For example, whereas some students may lack skills in decoding, others may lack vocabulary skills or specific reading comprehension skills. Providing the same intervention to all students, regardless of their individual deficits, often occurs when schools lack the resources to provide different interventions or lack the knowledge to determine which academic deficits a student might have. Although such interventions might prove to be successful when they happen to address a student's needs, students are more likely to benefit most when interventions are selected that target their specific skill deficits (Hall & Burns, 2018; Martens et al., 2015).

Finally, some schools do their best to successfully provide interventions that match the instructional needs of their students. Schools that match interventions to students' instructional needs must assess those needs, as universal screening data do not generally provide the necessary information. Assessment of a student's instructional needs involves first conducting a task analysis. A *task analysis* is used to determine which skills a student needs to meet academic expectations and identify the student's proficiency in each of those skills. CBM assessment procedures are generally helpful for these purposes, as they provide information related to both accuracy and fluency. However, CBM probes must be developed that assess single (as opposed to multiple) skills. For instance, a task analysis of second-grade math word problems would reveal that, to be successful in completing these problems, students must have the skills to do the following: (a) read the words that make up each problem with accuracy and fluency; (b) determine whether the problem requires addition or subtraction of numbers; and (c) add and subtract two-digit by two-digit numbers with accuracy and fluency. CBM reading and math probes composed of each of these skills could be developed and administered to the Tier 2 student using CBM assessment procedures. The same reading and math probes would also be administered to a sample of same-age peers who are considered to be successful in completing the second-grade math word problems. The performance of the student receiving Tier 2 services would then be compared to the average performance of the same-age peers in each skill area to determine skills in which the student requires further instruction. Intervention could then be developed to target the skill(s) for which intervention is needed. Subsequently, data regarding the student's response to the developed intervention(s) would provide information regarding the type of intervention the student may need if they are deemed eligible for special education (Mellott & Ardoin, 2019).

When examining student data and determining which skills should be targeted for intervention, it is essential to consider a student's accuracy, fluency, and ability to generalize each skill. Attending to accuracy alone (e.g., percentage of items answered correctly) fails to acknowledge the importance of developing mastery of basic skills that facilitate the learning and mastery of more complex skills (Shapiro, 2011). Haring and Eaton's (1978) Instructional Hierarchy provides schools with a framework for both developing effective intervention and monitoring the effects of intervention. According to the Instructional Hierarchy, accuracy must be targeted before developing students' fluency. *Accuracy interventions* must include modeling of how to complete the skill correctly, multiple opportunities to practice the skill, immediate performance feedback for students regarding response accuracy, and reinforcement for accurate completion. Interventions targeting response accuracy include cover–copy–compare, listening passage preview, and incremental rehearsal (Klingbeil et al., 2020; Mellott & Ardoin, 2019). The effects of accuracy-based interventions should be measured by assessing the student's response accuracy. Once these data indicate that the student can consistently complete the skill with accuracy, instruction should target response fluency. Fluent responding is the performance of a task with both speed and accuracy. When students are able to perform the basic component tasks of a complex skill with fluency, they do not have to dedicate as much attention to its smaller components and can place greater focus on the more complex tasks. *Fluency interventions* must include the provision of multiple opportunities to practice the task, with reinforcement provided for fast and accurate responding. Examples of interventions targeting skill fluency regularly employed within schools include repeated readings, flash card drills, and taped problems (Ardoin et al., 2018). The effects of fluency interventions should be assessed by measuring the number of problems/items that the student completes in a given time frame.

Throughout the Tier 2 intervention, it is important that generalization of skills be programmed through providing students with the opportunity to respond to multiple exemplars. *Multiple exemplars* offer the opportunity to practice a skill across varying contexts, situations, or variations of the skill. For example, when teaching students sight words, teachers might use flash cards. When developing response accuracy, the teacher might first read (i.e., model) the sight words to the students and then have students immediately practice reading the words aloud. Fluency instruction might then involve timing students' reading of the words for which accuracy was established during the accuracy intervention. Generalization of this skill might then be programmed by having students read previously learned words when presented in texts or by having students read compound words containing previously taught words. In these examples, the students would be required to respond to the same words, but the words are presented in different settings and/or the student must read the words combined with other words (Ardoin et al., 2018).

Districts and schools within districts also vary in the level of instructional intensity that they provide to students receiving Tier 2 interventions. In fact, most states require that prior to identifying a student as needing special education services, multiple interventions of increasing intensity be implemented and their impact on student growth be evaluated. *Instructional intensity* is often defined by the amount of intervention time provided to a student (e.g., four 30-minute sessions per week versus five 45-minute sessions per week) or the number of students per intervention group. These two variables are expected to affect the number of opportunities that students have to respond—and number of opportunities to respond is believed to be a key determinant in predicting gains made by students (Martin et al., 2018).

In addition to using universal screening data to identify students in need of Tier 2 intervention, conducting task analyses to determine for which skills students need to be provided instruction, and developing interventions that appropriately target those skills, schools must monitor the impact of Tier 2 interventions on students' academic progress.

Typically, schools use CBM progress monitoring procedures to monitor student gains. These procedures involve administering CBM probes associated with the skill on which instruction is being provided on a regular basis (two to eight times per month) and plotting the resulting data on a graph that has time on the x-axis and student performance on the y-axis. After several weeks of data are collected, schools use those data to determine whether the student's observed rate of growth indicates adequate achievement (Ardoin et al., 2013; Van Norman & Parker, 2018). If the rate of growth is not adequate, intervention intensity should be increased and the effects of intervention continually monitored. Should it be determined that the level of intervention intensity necessary for the student to make adequate growth exceeds that which can be provided through regular education services, the resulting data should be used as evidence that the student may need special education services.

When interpreting progress monitoring data and deciding whether a student has achieved adequate growth, it is important to consider that Tier 2 instruction is supplemental to Tier 1 instruction. The majority of instruction that a Tier 2 student receives should be provided in the Tier 1 environment with the student's peers. Thus, when determining what an adequate rate of growth for a specific student is, the rate of growth being made by the student's peers who are receiving the same Tier 1 instruction should be considered (Ardoin & Sayeski, 2019; Joseph et al., 2016). Such procedures assure that the assessment properly considers the environment in which instruction is taking place.

Tier 3 Assessment and Intervention

If students are identified as candidates for Tier 3 instruction, it is essential that many of the practices employed during Tier 2 instruction be continued. For instance, Tier 3 services should involve (a) frequent task analyses of the skills a student needs to perform, (b) determination of the level of fluency possessed by Tier 1 students who are proficient in the skills, (c) assessment of the student's level of proficiency in each of the skills, and (d) the matching of instruction to the student's instructional needs. The effects of the intervention on student progress should also be continually evaluated to determine whether instructional intensity should be modified. Students' instructional needs are not static, but rather are constantly changing; in turn, continual assessment is always necessary. Tier 3 students do not need different types of instruction; rather, they need instruction to be made more explicit and they need more opportunities to respond to stimuli than do students who require only Tier 1 instruction.

> **SOCIAL JUSTICE CONNECTIONS**
>
> *How is academic MTSS consistent with a social justice agenda?*
>
> The goals and design of academic MTSS are consistent with social justice principles in a number of ways. First, a primary aim of academic MTSS is to ensure that all students receive evidence-based core instruction (i.e., Tier 1 instruction). Ensuring high-quality reading instruction for youth who have been systematically marginalized in schools contributes to advancing social justice, given the history of some populations being restricted from learning to read.
>
> When schools use universal screening data to evaluate the quality of their Tier 1 instruction, they increase the likelihood that all students will receive a quality education.

(continued)

> **SOCIAL JUSTICE CONNECTIONS (*continued*)**
>
> This will, however, occur only if educators not only examine the extent to which Tier 1 instruction impacts growth across all students but also how it impacts growth within groups of students (i.e., examine data separately by grade level, gender, race, language, special education status). If Tier 1 data suggest that instruction is not promoting adequate gains for all students, changes to instruction must be made. Thus, these data can be monitored regularly to ensure that students from diverse groups are meeting performance benchmarks. Further, data-based decision-making should promote equity by reducing subjectivity in the evaluation of student progress (Kressler et al., 2020).
>
> Academic MTSS also promotes social justice in that it helps to increase the probability that students in need of intervention will be identified early. The earlier that students are identified as needing intervention, the greater the likelihood that such intervention will be effective (Diamond et al., 2013). Conversely, failure to build students' foundational academic skills increases the probability that those students will later need special education services (Lonigan et al., 2013). Moreover, students who lack foundational skills may be more likely to engage in disruptive behavior, as they may have difficulty participating in classroom instruction (Darney et al., 2013; Reynolds et al., 2017). Thus, teaching students the skills they need to succeed academically is key to promoting social justice. Overall, as suggested by Artiles et al. (2010), MTSS implementation promises to improve the distribution of school resources by promoting early identification and increasing the quality of universal instruction.

SUMMARY AND CONCLUSIONS

This chapter introduced readers to (a) the importance of evaluating the environment in which a student is receiving instruction, (b) assessment instruments used within schools for identifying and monitoring the progress of students with academic intervention needs, and (c) the three tiers of MTSS. After reading this chapter, readers should better appreciate the importance of the school psychologist not simply asking why a student is not learning, but rather asking whether the student's environment supports learning and which aspects of that environment might have to be altered so that the student can learn and develop the skills necessary for academic and life success.

DISCUSSION QUESTIONS

1. Why is CBM valuable for monitoring academic outcomes?
2. What are the differences in the purposes for which schools might employ CBM, CRTs, and NRTs?
3. When assessing academic strengths and weaknesses, why is it important to consider the environment in which a student's learning has taken place?
4. How does the MTSS model facilitate the evaluation of both student and environmental variables?
5. What are the ways in which MTSS can be leveraged as a tool for promoting social justice?

RECOMMENDED READINGS

Ardoin, S. P., & Sayeski, K. (2019). Assessing and promoting the choice of academic engaged time during reading instruction. In J. Fredrick, A. Reschly, & S. Christenson (Eds.), *Handbook of student engagement interventions: Working with disengaged students* (pp. 135–150). Elsevier Academic Press.

Daly III, E. J., Martens, B. K., Barnett, D., Witt, J. C., & Olson, S. C. (2007). Varying intervention delivery in response to intervention: Confronting and resolving challenges with measurement, instruction, and intensity. *School Psychology Review, 36*(4), 562–581. https://journals.sagepub.com/doi/10.1177/1063426616649162

Harbour, K. E., Evanovich, L. L., Sweigart, C. A., & Hughes, L. E. (2015). A brief review of effective teaching practices that maximize student engagement. *Preventing School Failure, 59*(1), 5–13. https://doi.org/10.1080/1045988X.2014.919136

Kruger, A. M., Strong, W., Daly III, E. J., O'Connor, M., Sommerhalder, M. S., Holtz, J., Weis, N., Kane, E. J., Hoff, N., & Heifner, A. (2016). Setting the stage for academic success through antecedent intervention. *Psychology in the Schools, 53*(1), 24–38. https://doi.org/10.1002/pits.21886

Spear-Swerling, L. (Ed.). (2022). *Structured literacy interventions: Teaching students with reading difficulties, grades K–6*. Guilford Press.

A robust set of instructor resources designed to supplement this text is located at http://connect.springerpub.com/content/book/978-0-8261-6344-8. Qualifying instructors may request access by emailing textbook@springerpub.com.

REFERENCES

Anselmo, G. A., Yarbrough, J. L., & Tran, V. V. N. (2021). To screen or not to screen: Criterion-related validity of math and reading curriculum-based measurement in relation to high-stakes math scores. *Journal of Psychoeducational Assessment, 39*(2), 153–165. https://doi.org/10.1177/0734282920950141

Ardoin, S. P., Binder, K. S., Zawoyski, A. M., & Foster, T. E. (2018). Examining the maintenance and generalization effects of repeated practice: A comparison of three interventions. *Journal of School Psychology, 68*, 1–18. https://doi.org/10.1016/j.jsp.2017.12.002

Ardoin, S. P., Christ, T. J., Morena, L. S., Cormier, D. C., & Klingbeil, D. A. (2013). A systematic review and summarization of the recommendations and research surrounding curriculum-based measurement of oral reading fluency (CBM-R) decision rules. *Journal of School Psychology, 51*(1), 1–18. https://doi.org/10.1016/j.jsp.2012.09.004

Ardoin, S. P., & Sayeski, K. (2019). Assessing and promoting the choice of academic engaged time during reading instruction. In J. Fredrick, A. Reschly, & S. Christenson (Eds.), *Handbook of student engagement interventions: Working with disengaged students* (pp. 135–150). Elsevier Academic Press.

Ardoin, S. P., Wagner, L., & Bangs, K. E. (2016). Applied behavior analysis: A foundation for response to intervention. In S. R. Jimerson, M. K. Burns, & A. M. VanDerHeyden (Eds.), *Handbook of response to intervention: The science and practice of multi-tiered systems of support* (2nd ed., pp. 29–42). Springer.

Artiles, A. J., Bal, A., & King Thorius, K. A. (2010). Back to the future: A critique of response to intervention's social justice views. *Theory into Practice, 49*(4), 250–257. https://doi.org/10.1080/00405841.2010.510447

Baker, C. E., & Rimm-Kaufman, S. E. (2014). How homes influence schools: Early parenting predicts African American childrens' classroom social–emotional functioning. *Psychology in the Schools, 51*(7), 722–735. https://doi.org/10.1002/pits.21781

Boorse, J., & Van Norman, E. R. (2021). Modeling within-year growth on the Mathematics Measure of Academic Progress. *Psychology in the Schools, 58*(11), 2255–2268. https://doi.org/10.1002/pits.22590

Brennan, L. M., Shelleby, E. C., Shaw, D. S., Gardner, F., Dishion, T. J., & Wilson, M. (2013). Indirect effects of the family check-up on school-age academic achievement through improvements in parenting in early childhood. *Journal of Educational Psychology, 105*(3), 762–773. https://doi.org/10.1037/a0032096

Bronfenbrenner, U. (1977). Toward an experimental ecology of human development. *American Psychologist, 32*(7), 513–531. https://doi.org/10.1037/0003-066x.32.7.513

Bronfenbrenner, U., & Morris, P. A. (1998). The ecology of developmental processes. In W. Damon & R. M. Lerner (Eds.), *Handbook of child psychology, Vol. 1: Theoretical models of human development* (5th ed., pp. 993–1023). John Wiley & Sons.

Clemens, N. H., Shapiro, E. S., & Thoemmes, F. (2011). Improving the efficacy of first grade reading screening: An investigation of word identification fluency with other early literacy indicators. *School Psychology Quarterly, 26*(3), 231–244. https://doi.org/10.1037/a0025173

Darney, D., Reinke, W. M., Herman, K. C., Stormont, M., & Ialongo, N. S. (2013). Children with co-occurring academic and behavior problems in first grade: Distal outcomes in twelfth grade. *Journal of School Psychology, 51*(1), 117–128. https://doi.org/10.1016/j.jsp.2012.09.005

Diamond, K. E., Justice, L. M., Siegler, R. S., & Snyder, P. A. (2013). *Synthesis of IES research on early intervention and early childhood education* (NCSER 2013-3001). National Center for Special Education Research, Institute of Education Sciences, U.S. Department of Education. https://ies.ed.gov/ncser/pubs/20133001/pdf/20133001.pdf

Dunbar, S., & Welch, C. (2015). *The Iowa assessments, forms E and F*. Riverside Publishing.

Every Student Succeeds Act. (2015). *Every Student Succeeds Act*, Pub. L. No. 114–95, § 1177.

Fenning, P., Diaz, Y., Valley-Gray, S., Cash, R. G., Spearman, C., Hazel, C. E., Grunewald, S., Riccio, C., & Harris, A. (2015). Perceptions of competencies among school psychology trainers and practitioners: What matters? *Psychology in the Schools, 52*(10), 1032–1041. https://doi.org/10.1002/pits.21877

Fien, H., Nelson, N. J., Smolkowski, K., Kosty, D., Pilger, M., Baker, S. K., & Smith, J. L. M. (2021). A conceptual replication study of the enhanced core reading instruction MTSS-reading model. *Exceptional Children, 87*(3), 265–288. https://doi.org/10.1177/0014402920953763

Foegen, A., Jiban, C., & Deno, S. (2007). Progress monitoring measures in mathematics: A review of the literature. *Journal of Special Education, 41*(2), 121–139. https://doi.org/10.1177/00224669070410020101

Hall, M. S., & Burns, M. K. (2018). Meta-analysis of targeted small-group reading interventions. *Journal of School Psychology, 66*, 54–66. https://doi.org/10.1016/j.jsp.2017.11.002

Haring, N. G., & Eaton, M. D. (1978). Systematic procedures: An instructional hierarchy. In N. G. Haring, T. C. Lovitt, M. D. Eaton, & C. L. Hansen (Eds.), *The fourth R: Research in the classroom* (pp. 23–40). Merrill.

Hosp, M. K., Hosp, J. L., & Howell, K. W. (2016). *The ABCs of CBM: A practical guide to curriculum based measurement* (2nd ed.). Guilford Press.

January, S.-A. A., Ardoin, S. P., Christ, T. J., Eckert, T. L., & White, M. J. (2016). Evaluating the interpretations and use of curriculum-based measurement in reading and word lists for universal screening in first and second grade. *School Psychology Review, 45*(3), 310–326. https://doi.org/10.17105/SPR45-3.310-326

January, S.-A. A., & Klingbeil, D. A. (2020). Universal screening in grades K-2: A systematic review and meta-analysis of early reading curriculum-based measures. *Journal of School Psychology, 82*, 103–122. https://doi.org/10.1016/j.jsp.2020.08.007

Jewell, J., & Malecki, C. K. (2005). The utility of CBM written language indices: An investigation of production-dependent, production-independent, and accurate-production scores. *School Psychology Review, 34*(1), 27–44. https://doi.org/10.1080/02796015.2005.12086273

Joseph, L. M., Alber-Morgan, S., & Neef, N. (2016). Applying behavior analytic procedures to effectively teach literacy skills in the classroom. *Psychology in the Schools, 53*(1), 73–88. https://doi.org/10.1002/pits.21883

Klingbeil, D. A., January, S.-A. A. & Ardoin, S. P. (2020). Comparative efficacy and generalization of two word-reading interventions with English learners in elementary school. *Journal of Behavioral Education, 29*(3), 490–518. https://doi.org/10.1007/s10864-019-09331-y

Kressler, B., Chapman, L. A., Kunkel, A., & Hovey, K. A. (2020). Culturally responsive data-based decision making in high school settings. *Intervention in School and Clinic, 55*(4), 214–220. https://doi.org/10.1177/1053451219855737

LaBerge, D., & Samuels, S. J. (1974). Toward a theory of automatic information processing in reading. *Cognitive Psychology, 6*(2), 293–323. https://doi.org/10.1016/0010-0285(74)90015-2

Lonigan, C. J., Purpura, D. J., Wilson, S. B., Walker, P. M., & Clancy-Menchetti, J. (2013). Evaluating the components of an emergent literacy intervention for preschool children at risk for reading difficulties. *Journal of Experimental Child Psychology, 114*(1), 111–130. https://doi.org/10.1016/j.jecp.2012.08.010

Martens, B. K., Daly III, E. J., & Ardoin, S. P. (2015). Applications of applied behavior analysis to school-based instructional intervention. In H. S. Roane, J. E. Ringdahl, & T. S. Falcomata (Eds.), *Clinical and organizational applications of applied behavior analysis* (pp. 125–150). Elsevier.

Martin, B., Sargent, K., Van Camp, A., & Wright, J. (2018). *Intensive intervention practice guide: Increasing opportunities to respond as an intensive intervention*. Office of Special Education Programs, U.S. Department of Education. https://files.eric.ed.gov/fulltext/ED591076.pdf

McCallum, R. S., Bell, S. M., Coles, J. T., Miller, K. C., Hopkins, M. B., & Hilton-Prillhart, A. (2013). A model for screening twice-exceptional students (gifted with learning disabilities) within a response to intervention paradigm. *Gifted Child Quarterly, 57*(4), 209–222. https://doi.org/10.1177/0016986213500070

McMaster, K., & Espin, C. (2007). Technical features of curriculum-based measurement in writing: A literature review. *The Journal of Special Education, 41*(2), 68–84. https://doi.org/10.1177/00224669070410020301

Mellott, J. A., & Ardoin, S. P. (2019). Using brief experimental analysis to identify the right math intervention at the right time. *Journal of Behavioral Education, 28*(4), 435–455. https://doi.org/10.1007/s10864-019-09324-x

National Reading Panel. (2000). *Teaching children to read: An evidence-based assessment of the scientific research literature on reading and its implications for reading instruction* (NIH Publication No. 00-4754). National Institute of Child Health and Human Development.

Reschly, A. L., Busch, T. W., Betts, J., Deno, S. L., & Long, J. D. (2009). Curriculum-based measurement oral reading as an indicator of reading achievement: A meta-analysis of the correlational evidence. *Journal of School Psychology, 47*(6), 427–469. https://doi.org/10.1016/j.jsp.2009.07.001

Reynolds, A. J., Ou, S. R., Mondi, C. F., & Hayakawa, M. (2017). Processes of early childhood interventions to adult well-being. *Child Development, 88*(2), 378–387. https://doi.org/10.1111/cdev.12733

Shapiro, E. S. (2011). *Academic skills problems: Direct assessment and intervention* (4th ed.). Guilford Press.

Shinn, M. R. (Ed.). (1989). *Curriculum-based measurement: Assessing special children*. Guilford Press.

Thomas, A. S., & January, S.-A. A. (2021). Evaluating the criterion validity and classification accuracy of universal screening measures in reading. *Assessment for Effective Intervention, 46*(2), 110–120. https://doi.org/10.1177/1534508419857232

U.S. Department of Education, Institute of Education Sciences, & National Center for Education Statistics. (2017). *National Assessment of Educational Progress (NAEP): 2011 writing assessments*. https://www.nationsreportcard.gov/writing_2011

U.S. Department of Education, Institute of Education Sciences, & National Center for Education Statistics. (2020a). *NAEP Report Card: 2019*. NAEP Mathematics Assessment. https://www.nationsreportcard.gov/highlights/mathematics/2019

U.S. Department of Education, Institute of Education Sciences, & National Center for Education Statistics. (2020b). *NAEP Report Card: 2019*. NAEP Reading Assessment. https://www.nationsreportcard.gov/highlights/reading/2019

Van Norman, E. R., Nelson, P. M., & Parker, D. C. (2018). A comparison of nonsense-word fluency and curriculum-based measurement of reading to measure response to phonics instruction. *School Psychology Quarterly, 33*(4), 573–581. https://doi.org/10.1037/spq0000237

Van Norman, E. R., & Parker, D. C. (2018). A comparison of common and novel curriculum-based measurement of reading decision rules to predict spring performance for students receiving supplemental interventions. *Assessment for Effective Intervention, 43*(2), 110–120. https://doi.org/10.1177/1534508417728695

CHAPTER 10

Social, Emotional, and Behavioral Assessment and Intervention

AMY M. BRIESCH ■ ROBERT J. VOLPE

CHAPTER OBJECTIVES

After reading this chapter, you will be able to:

- Provide an understanding of the need for social, emotional, and behavioral supports in schools.
- Describe the most common forms of universal behavioral support (i.e., Positive Behavioral Interventions and Supports; social and emotional learning).
- Highlight available screening approaches for the proactive identification of students who demonstrate some level of social, emotional, or behavioral risk.
- Explain how more intensive behavioral intervention and assessment supports may be provided at the Tier 2 level while maintaining efficiency.
- Discuss how diagnostic data may be used to develop individualized behavioral supports at the Tier 3 level.

NATIONAL ASSOCIATION OF SCHOOL PSYCHOLOGISTS PRACTICE MODEL CONNECTIONS

Domain 4: Mental and Behavioral Health Services and Interventions
Domain 5: School-Wide Practices to Promote Learning
Domain 6: Services to Promote Safe and Supportive Schools

INTRODUCTION

In recent years, there have been notable changes in the way in which schools conceptualize student success. Student success is no longer seen simply as ensuring that students master skills in reading, writing, and math. Rather, schools have taken on the additional responsibility of developing students' social, emotional, and behavioral (SEB) skills and preparing them to become healthy and productive members of society. In this chapter, we describe the types and prevalence of SEB challenges that school-age youth may experience.

We also describe how these SEB skill deficits affect students in educational settings. Finally, we present a multitiered model of service delivery, including intervention and assessment strategies, for supporting students' SEB wellness in schools.

SOCIAL, EMOTIONAL, AND BEHAVIORAL PROBLEMS: DEFINITIONS AND PREVALENCE

The term *social, emotional, and behavioral (SEB) skills* refers to a broad range of interrelated skills in self-regulating emotion and behavior as well as in interacting with others. *Social skills* are those skills that involve communicating and interacting with others. In schools, students must be able to interact competently with peers, teachers, administrators, parents, and others (e.g., community members) who contribute to educational activities. *Emotional skills* are those skills involved in recognizing, regulating, and expressing one's emotions in a safe and healthy manner. *Behavioral skills* refers to both interpersonal and task-related skills needed to be successful in a given environment (e.g., attending to class instruction and raising one's hand to participate in class). Notably, there is considerable overlap among the definitions and skills associated with each of these areas, which often are addressed jointly in schools. For example, suppressing a tantrum requires a student to exhibit emotional and behavioral regulation skills as well as to consider alternative approaches for interacting effectively with others. Thus, many prevention and intervention programs target a wide range of SEB skills to promote student success.

Students with SEB skill deficits may experience problems in a number of domains and daily activities. For example, many students struggle with following directions, managing their anger or frustration, attending to class instruction, resolving interpersonal conflicts, and expressing emotions. Others struggle with displaying empathy, asking for help, acting responsibly, or ignoring peer distractions.

Students can struggle to develop or display SEB skills for a number of reasons. In some cases, students may struggle with SEB skills as a result of genetic or biological factors. However, significant life events, such as losing a family member or transitioning to a new school or neighborhood, can also precipitate SEB difficulties for shorter or more extended periods of time. Additionally, research has shown student mental health to be significantly related to various environmental conditions, including the presence of bullying (e.g., Woods et al., 2009), perceived school safety (e.g., Nijs et al., 2014), and experiences of racial discrimination (Priest et al., 2012). Regardless of the underlying causes, population surveys have suggested that as many as 25% of youth in the United States may meet diagnostic criteria for a mental health disorder and that roughly 10% of youth may suffer from some type of emotional disturbance (Williams et al., 2018). Lifetime prevalence rates (i.e., having the problem at any time in one's life) are even higher, indicating that between the ages of 13 and 18 years, 46% of youth experience some mental health disorder, with about 21% of youth experiencing a severe disorder (Merikangas et al., 2010). The most common disorder in school-age children is attention deficit hyperactivity disorder (ADHD; between 8% and 9%), followed by anxiety disorders (approximately 8%), behavioral or conduct problems (approximately 7%), and depression disorders (approximately 3%; see Bitsko et al., 2022). According to data collected through the 2017 Youth Behavior Risk Survey (YRBS), 31.5% of high school students reported experiencing persistent feelings of sadness or hopelessness and 17.2% seriously considered suicide in the past year (Centers for Disease Control and Prevention [CDC], 2019). Given rising prevalence statistics compounded by the coronavirus 2019 pandemic, the American Academy of Pediatrics, American Academy of Child and Adolescent Psychiatry, and Children's Hospital Association declared a national emergency in children's mental health in 2021.

Although these statistics may sound worrisome enough on their own, what makes them even more concerning is the fact that only one in five youth who exhibit a diagnosable mental health disorder receives mental healthcare (Burns et al., 1995; CDC, 2004; U.S. Department of Health and Human Services, 1999). Furthermore, research has shown significant disparities in access, with Black and Latinx youth less likely to receive mental healthcare than their white peers (Marrast et al., 2016). When youth exhibiting SEB skill difficulties do not receive the appropriate care, the impact is far reaching, affecting not only the students themselves but also their larger communities. For example, when asked about their primary concerns in the classroom, teachers have repeatedly ranked students with emotional and behavioral problems very high on their lists (Bushaw & Lopez, 2010; Langdon & Vesper, 2000). In fact, many teachers have even cited student behavior problems as a central reason for leaving the teaching profession (U.S. Department of Education, 2004).

MULTITIERED SYSTEMS OF SUPPORT FOR SOCIAL, EMOTIONAL, AND BEHAVIORAL FUNCTIONING

Schools can play an incredibly important role in supporting the SEB well-being of all youth, given that most children and adolescents spend nearly 1,200 hours per year in educational settings. In fact, research has shown that schools are one of the most common points of entry for accessing care, with more than one in five youth struggling with mental health challenges receiving needed services in schools (Duong et al., 2021). A general overview of multitiered systems of support (MTSS) was provided in Chapter 8; in Chapter 9, applications of MTSS to academic service delivery were described. In this chapter, we discuss the applications of MTSS for enhancing students' SEB functioning. As described in Chapter 8, one of the primary goals of MTSS is to provide each student with the level of support they need to be successful. As in Chapter 9, both intervention and assessment practices are described for supporting students at Tiers 1, 2, and 3, respectively.

Tier 1

INTERVENTION

Tier 1 intervention focuses on teaching those skills that *all* students in a given population are expected to demonstrate. Generally, in the academic domain, there is widespread agreement regarding expectations for skill development. These expectations are delineated in learning standards, which explicitly describe the knowledge and skills that students are expected to demonstrate at each grade level. Although the specific content of learning standards varies across the country, every state has a published set of standards for each of the primary academic areas, including language arts, math, science, and social studies.

In contrast, a review by Eklund and colleagues (2018) found that only 11 states had adopted standards for students' SEB development. This suggests that there is far less consensus regarding the SEB skills students should be able to demonstrate than there is regarding the academic skills. As a result, universal instruction within the SEB domain varies considerably across schools.

Universal instruction typically has been conceptualized within either a Positive Behavioral Interventions and Supports framework or a social and emotional learning framework (see Durlak et al., 2011); however, these approaches are not necessarily mutually exclusive. Although somewhat different, both are accessible to all students, evidence-based, and grounded in the belief that students learn best in safe and supportive school environments. Moreover, they focus on developing similar types of skill and student competencies.

Positive Behavioral Interventions and Supports

Positive Behavioral Interventions and Supports (PBIS) is a problem-solving framework for providing a continuum of evidence-based behavioral supports that are designed to facilitate the academic and behavioral success of all students (Technical Assistance Center on Positive Behavioral Interventions and Supports, 2015). At the universal level (i.e., Tier 1), one core tenet of PBIS is that all students should receive explicit instruction regarding behavioral expectations. Although school personnel often expect students to know how to act or behave in particular contexts (e.g., classrooms, playgrounds, and cafeterias), the reality is that not all students have been taught how to do so. Just as we would not expect students to teach themselves to read on their own, so we should not expect students to figure out how to conduct themselves without clear instruction and expectations. In PBIS, behavioral skills are taught to students in the same manner as academic skills—namely, by explicitly defining the skill, modeling its implementation, and providing practice opportunities and feedback regarding skill application (Sugai & Horner, 2002). Consistent with other forms of Tier 1 instruction, the ultimate goal of teaching and reinforcing prosocial behaviors is to reduce the number of students who exhibit more severe challenging behaviors and, in turn, require additional, more intensive supports.

Although the explicit teaching of behavioral expectations is a critical component of PBIS implementation, scholars and educators do not necessarily agree as to what these expectations should entail. Generally, however, it is recommended that schools establish a set of three to five expectations that meet three criteria: (a) They are positively stated (e.g., "be respectful" as opposed to "don't talk back"); (b) they are easy for students and staff to remember (e.g., not too long or wordy); and (c) they are socially valid (i.e., address those behaviors that the school community believes are important to change; Warren et al., 2006). School-wide expectations often utilize global or broad wording, such that they are applicable to a wide range of behaviors across school settings (e.g., classroom, lunchroom, playground). For example, common school-wide expectations include the following: Be Responsible (e.g., clean up after self, follow directions, participate in class); Be Respectful (e.g., listen to others, take turns, use kind words); Be Ready/Prepared (e.g., arrive at class on time, come to school with appropriate materials, do your best work); and Be Safe (e.g., keep hands and feet to self, stay in assigned area, walk in the hallways). School staff regularly reference, review, and model expected prosocial behaviors for students, who are rewarded for engaging in behaviors consistent with the school-wide expectations. Typically, students are awarded tokens or coupons for demonstrating expected prosocial behaviors, which can be exchanged for prizes and privileges. When possible (and safe to do so), negative behaviors are ignored.

Social and Emotional Learning

Whereas PBIS at the universal level focuses on the teaching, practice, and reinforcement of positive behavioral expectations, the aims of social and emotional learning are somewhat different. Broadly, ***social and emotional learning*** (SEL) is the process by which individuals acquire the knowledge, attitudes, and skills necessary to recognize, regulate, and express emotions, set positive goals, and maintain positive relationships with others (Collaborative for Academic, Social, and Emotional Learning [CASEL], 2022a). CASEL (2022a) identifies five core competencies that have been shown to lead to positive life outcomes: self-awareness, self-management, responsible decision-making, relationship skills, and social awareness. CASEL (2022a) offers the following definitions of each of these five core competencies. ***Self-awareness*** refers to the individual's skills in recognizing personal strengths, weaknesses, thoughts, and emotions, whereas ***self-management*** refers to skills in regulating those thoughts and emotions (e.g., impulse control and goal setting). *Social awareness* refers to the individual's recognition of the perspectives of others (e.g., displaying empathy) and social norms that dictate acceptable behaviors. *Relationship skills* are those skills necessary for communicating, cooperating, and interacting appropriately with others. Finally, *responsible decision-making* refers to balancing concerns regarding social norms, others' perspectives, ethical considerations, and personal goals to make choices about one's own actions.

Often, SEL competencies are taught explicitly to students within the context of freestanding lessons, such as those that are part of established curricula. For example, elementary-level programs such as PATHS and Second Step may be used to teach younger students how to identify feelings and make appropriate personal and social decisions. Secondary-level programs such as Responding in Peaceful and Positive Ways can be used to teach older students essential problem-solving and conflict-resolution skills for preventing violent behavior (CASEL, 2022b). SEL can also be promoted through teachers' use of instructional practices that foster supportive and engaging classroom environments. As one example, the Responsive Classroom program emphasizes the use of 10 teaching practices and strategies (e.g., rule creation, positive teacher language, and collaborative problem-solving) to foster a nurturing classroom environment that is responsive to the cognitive, social–emotional, and physical needs of students (CASEL, 2022b). Overall, SEL has a strong, well-established evidence base. In reviewing the results of four meta-analyses focused on the use of universal SEL programs with K–12 students, Mahoney et al. (2018) found that those students who received SEL instruction not only experienced increases in prosocial behaviors and decreases in problem behavior but also made considerable gains in academic achievement.

Class-Wide Behavioral Interventions

Regardless of whether a school chooses to implement PBIS, SEL, or both frameworks, Tier 1 behavioral interventions also can be implemented on a class-wide basis by individual teachers. One example of a class-wide behavioral intervention is the Good Behavior Game (GBG), the use of which was first reported in the late 1960s (Barrish et al., 1969). In the GBG, the teacher divides the classroom into two teams and explicitly teaches both teams the classroom rules as well as the actions that constitute rule violations. Teams are then given points for any rule violations (e.g., getting out of one's seat at the inappropriate time or talking out of turn). Typically, the team with the fewest points at the end of the game wins some predetermined reward (e.g., extra break time or access to a preferred activity). Alternatively, both teams may earn some privilege if they reach a predetermined point criterion (i.e., fewer than 5 points total). Although punitively awarding points for misbehavior is a typical component of the GBG, several variations have focused on rewarding points for positive behaviors (e.g., Wright & McCurdy, 2012). The GBG is relatively easy to implement, and it has been demonstrated to have a positive impact on a wide array of classroom behaviors, including oppositional behavior, out-of-seat behaviors, and work completion (Flower et al., 2014). Research indicates that it has a strong impact on disruptive behaviors and on-task behaviors, particularly for students with emotional and behavior disorders (Bowman-Perrott et al., 2016).

Assessment

As you may recall from Chapter 8, the implementation of high-quality, evidence-based Tier 1 behavior interventions should be effective in supporting the academic and behavioral needs of approximately 75% to 80% of the student population. However, regardless of how powerful or well supported Tier 1 interventions may be, approximately 15% to 20% of students are likely to continue to require additional, more intensive supports. Thus, schools must utilize efficient and effective procedures for identifying these students and ensuring their timely access to needed services. Although many students struggling with SEB skill deficits may exhibit behaviors that are easily identified by personnel (e.g., tantrums and physically aggressive behaviors), others may not be recognized as easily. One factor that may determine how easily or quickly an at-risk behavior is identified concerns its topography, or the manner in which it is expressed. *Externalizing behaviors* refer to behaviors that manifest outwardly, such as throwing tantrums, hitting, and biting. *Internalizing behaviors* refer to problems that manifest within individuals, such as elevated levels of anxiety and depression. Generally, students who exhibit externalizing behaviors are more readily identified as being at risk than students who experience internalizing behaviors.

As in academic MTSS, school personnel who implement social, emotional, and behavioral MTSS (SEB MTSS) conduct universal screenings to identify students with a wide variety of difficulties. These procedures assist personnel in proactively identifying at-risk students, such that Tier 2 and Tier 3 interventions can be implemented to prevent problems from intensifying or becoming more resistant to remediation over time.

Within an SEB MTSS, schools can employ several different screening approaches, depending on their objectives. In some cases, the goal of screening may be to identify those students who currently have—or are at risk for developing—a mental health disorder or emotional/behavioral disorder. To accomplish this goal, the screening instrument selected must be capable of quantifying symptoms or indicators of a particular diagnosis or area of concern. Most typically, this type of screening involves the use of *behavior rating scales* (introduced in Chapter 7), which are designed to assess the perceptions of relevant vested partners (i.e., teachers, parents, and students themselves) regarding student behaviors. A teacher may be asked, for example, to rate the frequency with which a student has exhibited a particular behavioral indicator (e.g., "easily distracted by peers") over the past month using a 4-point scale (i.e., 0 = *never*, 3 = *almost always*). When used as a universal screening tool, this type of rating scale would be completed for each student in the classroom. Subsequently, students whose scores exceeded an established threshold would be targeted for further assessment and/or intervention.

In other cases, the goal of screening may be to identify those students whose behavior is impeding their success in school, regardless of their diagnostic status. Thus, rather than highlighting the presence of particular symptoms, the screening process is focused on identifying students who exhibit SEB skill deficits as measured by contextual, school-based indicators. These indicators may include attendance, incidents of suspension or expulsion, and office discipline referrals. Typically, these types of indicators can be examined using existing data (and therefore do not warrant additional data collection). Schools that implement PBIS commonly utilize school-based indicators to screen students for SEB problems. In these settings, a school-based team meets periodically to review attendance, disciplinary, and other records so as to identify students in need of additional supports. General guidelines suggest that students who have received between two and five office discipline referrals may require Tier 2 support, whereas students who have received six or more referrals may need Tier 3 support (McIntosh et al., 2009). Although relatively easy to collect and use, there are several limitations to the use of these extant data; for example, they are less likely to capture students with internalizing behaviors. Moreover, the disproportionate use of both office discipline referrals (e.g., Bradshaw et al., 2010) and suspensions/expulsions (e.g., Office of Civil Rights, 2016) across white students and students of color has been repeatedly documented in the literature.

Regardless of which screening approach is used to identify those students believed to be at risk, the overarching goal remains the same: to ensure that students receive needed

SEB supports in a timely fashion. Thus, it is recommended that school-wide screening be conducted between two and three times per year, with the first administration occurring within the first month or two of the school year (Parisi et al., 2014). The data collection process should be followed by an immediate, formal review of data (often by a school-based decision-making team). This immediacy allows the team to act quickly upon the information obtained and to place students who need higher tiers of support as quickly as possible.

Tier 2

Intervention

Tier 2 intervention provides a select group of students who are deemed to be at risk for SEB problems with *supplementary* and *targeted* supports. These supports are *supplementary* because they are provided to students in addition to (rather than in place of) Tier 1 supports, which are provided to all students regardless of their risk status. These supports also are *targeted* because they are matched closely with specific student needs identified through Tier 1 screening.

In some cases, Tier 2 supports may best be provided by specialized personnel (e.g., school psychologists or school social workers) outside of the regular classroom setting. Small-group interventions often are delivered in a pull-out fashion (i.e., outside of the classroom) and can be used to address the needs of students with similar types of difficulties. Often, these interventions are **manualized**, meaning that their content and procedures are both explicit and highly structured. As an example, the Anger Coping Program (Lochman et al., 1981) is a manualized program designed to reduce aggressive and disruptive behaviors in elementary and middle school students. Administered to groups of between four and six students across a total of 18 1-hour sessions, the program uses a combination of didactic instruction, group discussion, and activities to teach students skills such as problem-solving, recognizing emotions, and managing conflicts. The Social Skills Intervention Guide (Elliot & Gresham, 2008) is another example of a manualized intervention that can be used with small groups of students who struggle with social skills. The 43 scripted lessons in this intervention focus on teaching skills related to cooperation, assertion, responsibility, empathy, and self-control through a four-step model of *tell* (i.e., explain the skill), *show* (i.e., model the skill), *do* (i.e., role-play use of the skill), and *practice* (i.e., have the student rehearse the skill).

In other situations, it is possible for teachers (rather than specialized staff) to provide supplementary, targeted supports within the regular classroom setting. One example of a Tier 2 classroom intervention is the Daily Behavior Report Card (DBRC). The DBRC serves as both an intervention and a progress monitoring tool and can be used to address a wide array of classroom behavior problems (see Volpe & Fabiano, 2013). In a DBRC intervention, students earn points for working toward a set of predetermined behavioral goals. Typically, the DBRC form itself lists three to five goals (e.g., starts work with fewer than two reminders; follows directions on work assignments; and keeps hands and feet to self), and teachers record whether the student has met each goal at various intervals (e.g., at the end of each class period). Throughout the day, teachers provide feedback and encouragement to the student as they work toward the goals. At the end of the day, the teacher tallies the number of points the student earned, and the student receives a reward for reaching an established criterion (as applicable). Ideally, these rewards are provided by caregivers in the home setting but often are provided at school.

Another example of a Tier 2 classroom intervention concerns self-monitoring (see Briesch & Chafouleas, 2009). *Self-monitoring* refers to both a skill and a type of intervention. Broadly, self-monitoring (the skill) refers to tracking, management, and regulation of one's own behaviors (Bruhn et al., 2015). In self-monitoring (the intervention), a student rates, reflects on, and/or scores their own behavior (e.g., proportion of time on task). Typically, some kind of prompt (e.g., timer) is used to indicate to the student when they should complete the evaluation. Although the only individual who needs to complete the form is the student, often the student is asked to compare their evaluation to one completed by the teacher (see Cole & Bambara, 1992). In such cases, students typically are rewarded for rating their behavior accurately (e.g., within a point of the teacher rating). They also may be rewarded for reaching a preestablished criterion for the behavior ratings.

Assessment

All interventions within MTSS should be evidence-based. However, an intervention or strategy that is identified as *evidence-based* will not necessarily work for *all* students in *all* contexts. As a result, it is necessary to collect ongoing progress monitoring data to examine whether Tier 2 supports have been successful in meeting the needs of individual students. If students do not respond to the services available in Tier 2, they may demonstrate need for the more intensive supports offered in Tier 3. As in academic MTSS, the frequency of assessment in Tier 2 is greater than that in Tier 1. Whereas screening assessments can be likened to a "one-time snapshot" picture of a child's functioning, progress monitoring assessments are better characterized as moving pictures that depict a student's response to intervention. Tier 2 assessments can take many forms; however, given that these assessments involve repeated measurement, they must be carefully vetted for technical adequacy (e.g., reliability and validity) and feasibility (e.g., length of assessment and obtrusiveness; see Briesch & Volpe, 2007).

Systematic Direct Observation

A decade ago, there was heavy reliance on systematic direct observation to track students' response to school-based interventions. **Systematic direct observation** (SDO) is a form of direct behavioral observation that involves having a trained observer enter the classroom to examine and record in real time the occurrence of a small number of preselected student behaviors. In SDO, each behavior must have a clear set of defining criteria to ensure the reliability of the data recorded. School psychologists commonly conduct SDOs; however, teachers can also conduct them for certain low-frequency, discrete behaviors (e.g., cursing, throwing objects, and biting) that can be tallied easily via a recording sheet or frequency clicker. There are several advantages to using SDOs, as they are sensitive to small or incremental changes in student behavior. Moreover, because they follow a predetermined set of criteria for coding behavior, they are less prone to subjectivity than are other, less structured forms of observation (see Briesch et al., 2018). Although SDO continues to be a common assessment method for monitoring students' intervention response, the extensive training and lengthy, frequent observation sessions needed to obtain reliable and valid data may be barriers to its widespread use.

Rating Scales

Among the progress monitoring methods most commonly used today are brief rating scales that may be completed one or more times per week. Rating scales designed for behavioral screening typically are fairly long (i.e., 30 or more items) because they are administered relatively infrequently (i.e., two to three times per year). Rating scales designed for progress monitoring, however, tend to be much shorter (i.e., 10 or fewer items), because they often are administered on a weekly or biweekly basis. Scale developers or publishers create shorter versions of full-length rating scales by selecting the best (i.e., psychometrically strongest) items from the original, longer measure using statistical procedures.

Direct Behavior Rating

A hybrid of SDO and rating scales, Direct Behavior Ratings are administered one or more times each day (see Briesch et al., 2016). *Direct Behavior Ratings* (DBRs) are teacher ratings of student behavior that are completed at the end of a predetermined observation period (e.g., literacy block) and within a natural context (e.g., classroom). DBR can look very much like rating scales; however, unlike traditional rating scales, they are designed for rating behaviors over a much smaller window of observation (an instructional period or, at most, a school day). A common approach to implementing DBR is to use a single-item scale. In single-item DBR, a definition of the behavior category (e.g., disruptive behavior) is provided to the rater (typically a teacher), who is asked to record the proportion of time that the behavior was exhibited by the target student. To record this information, raters are provided with a line representing the entirety of the observation interval and asked to mark the appropriate proportion (ranging from 0% of the time to 100% of the time). Multi-item approaches to DBR also have received considerable attention in recent years. In these approaches, raters record multiple, specific behaviors (e.g., calling out) and can sum item scores to yield measures of broader behavior categories (e.g., disruptive behavior; see Volpe & Briesch, 2012, 2015). Although early work on the development of DBR was limited to a small number of problem behaviors, this method has been expanded to cover a wide range of behaviors typically targeted in classroom interventions (see Briesch et al., 2022; Daniels et al., 2019: Volpe et al., 2019).

Permanent Products

In some cases, permanent products can be used for progress-monitoring purposes. In the context of school-based assessment, *permanent products* are the material entities that result from a given action or task that provide insight into the processes associated with those activities. By their nature, permanent products are naturally occurring sources of data in the classroom. For example, when a teacher takes attendance and records it in a ledger, their notes constitute a permanent product. If the teacher were interested in determining whether their classroom interventions were resulting in improved student attendance, they could use this existing record to monitor changes in attendance. For example, they might track the number of days on which a particular student attended school on time.

Other examples of permanent products include office disciplinary referral forms, completed (or incomplete) work assignments, and records of homework completion. These measures can be useful because they capitalize on existing data rather than burdening teachers with additional data collection responsibilities. At the same time, however, they lack the breadth, depth, and, in many cases, psychometric defensibility of the other measures described in this chapter (e.g., behavior rating scales). Nonetheless, permanent products can be quite useful when their resulting data are well matched with intervention goals.

Tier 3

Tier 3 intervention and assessment efforts can be differentiated from those at Tier 2 with respect to their degree of intensity and individualization. Tier 3 interventions are more likely to be delivered in individualized (i.e., one-to-one) formats. Moreover, they often are developed after a detailed assessment of the presenting problem has been undertaken. When progress monitoring data indicate that Tier 2 supports are insufficient to meet an individual student's needs, more intensive and individualized assessment is conducted to develop interventions in Tier 3. Generally, this type of assessment is diagnostic in nature, meaning that it is intended to identify the specific strengths and weaknesses in the student's skill set. Because diagnostic assessments often precede intervention in Tier 3, they are described first.

Assessment

Functional Behavior Assessment

Within SEB MTSS, the most typical form of diagnostic assessment is functional behavior assessment. *Functional behavior assessment* (FBA) is a data collection process for developing hypotheses regarding the factors that precipitate, maintain, or deter behaviors of interest (i.e., target behaviors). Recall from Chapter 7 the terms *antecedent* and *consequence*. Antecedents are events or cues that are believed to trigger or increase the likelihood that a student will exhibit a particular target behavior. For example, a student may be more likely to engage in a target behavior when they are asked to complete a task that they do not enjoy (e.g., completing a math worksheet independently) or when seated near a particular peer. *Consequences*, in contrast, are events or cues that follow a target behavior and either increase or decrease its likelihood of recurring in the future. Identifying the sequences of cues and events that take place both before and after a target behavior occurs can assist school psychologists in better understanding the nature and mechanisms of the behavior.

Reinforcement occurs when consequences lead to the increased recurrence of a target behavior. For example, consider a student (Molly) who tells a joke during class that prompts her peers to laugh and smile. If Molly comes to class the next day armed with a new arsenal of jokes, the peer attention she received after telling the first joke likely reinforced her behavior. *Punishment*, by comparison, refers to consequences that lead to the decreased recurrence of target behaviors. Consider Molly's situation again; however, this time, she is verbally reprimanded by her teacher. Following this event, Molly stops telling jokes in class. In this scenario, the teacher's verbal reprimand likely served as a punishing consequence, rendering her behavior less likely to occur in the future.

The goal of conducting an FBA is to identify the most likely antecedents and consequences of a target behavior and to develop a corresponding intervention plan. A school psychologist may gather this information indirectly by asking a classroom teacher to identify the most likely antecedents and consequences of a student's behavior. Semistructured interviews such as the Functional Assessment Checklist for Teachers and Staff (FACTS; March et al., 2000) and rating scales such as the Problem Behavior Questionnaire (PBQ; Lewis et al., 1994) can be used to guide this process. Alternatively, information concerning antecedents and consequences may be gathered directly by conducting observations of the student in the classroom or other relevant settings. During these observations, the school psychologist documents behaviors of interest and proximal environmental events as they arise, thereby allowing them to identify the most probable antecedents and consequences of the target behaviors.

The final step in conducting an FBA is to use the information obtained to develop a hypothesis regarding the function of the target behavior, or the reason why the behavior is occurring. Within the context of an FBA, there are believed to be two primary functions of problem behaviors: (a) to get or obtain something or (b) to avoid or escape something. Common behavioral functions include obtaining or avoiding items, activities, or attention from peers or adults. Based on the data collected, the school psychologist incorporates their best guess as to the likely function of a student's behavior into a hypothesis statement. Typically, a hypothesis statement is written in the following form: *When [an antecedent occurs], Student X is likely to [exhibit a target behavior] so as to [function of behavior].* For example, returning to the example presented earlier, a potential hypothesis statement might be as follows: *When the class is asked to listen quietly during whole-group instruction, Molly is likely to tell jokes so as to obtain peer attention.* This hypothesis statement can then be used to guide the selection of appropriate Tier 3 intervention strategies.

Other Forms of Diagnostic Assessment

Although FBAs are commonly used at Tier 3, other assessment tools can provide diagnostic information beyond that related to behavioral function. For example, narrow-band rating scales are instruments designed to obtain a detailed report from a particular informant (e.g., parent, teacher, or the student) of a student's functioning within a specific area. One commonly used narrow-band measure is the Children's Depression Inventory 2 (CDI-2; Kovacs, 2014). The CDI-2 self-report form contains 28 items, all of which are designed to assess symptoms of depression in children and adolescents ages 7 to 17 years. Responses to the items are used to generate both an overall score of depressive symptomatology and four subscale scores that gauge negative mood, negative self-esteem, ineffectiveness, and interpersonal problems.

Clinical interviews may also be used to gather diagnostic information. Whereas rating scales typically ask a respondent to provide a global judgment of a student's behavior over a period of time (e.g., past 2 weeks or past month), interviewing allows the practitioner to obtain more detailed information about particular behaviors, such as when they emerged, how long they have been occurring, and the degree of impairment they have caused. School psychologists most typically use *semistructured interviews* (as described in Chapter 7) to gather information regarding student functioning. In a semistructured interview, the examiner starts with a set of preestablished questions and then generates additional questions during the course of the interview to obtain clarifying information. Unlike semistructured interviews, *structured interview schedules* (also described in Chapter 7) use very specific wording, coding, and item ordering, such that their administration is highly standardized across respondents. Structured interview schedules often are used to determine whether a student meets diagnostic criteria for a particular disorder or disability. One example of a structured interview schedule is the Diagnostic Interview Schedule for Children Version IV (DISC-IV; Shaffer et al., 2000), which can be used to assess more than 30 psychiatric diagnoses in youth ages 6 to 18 years.

INTERVENTION

Whereas multiple students often receive the same intervention at Tier 2, intervention strategies at Tier 3 are highly individualized in nature. Among the most common intervention approaches at Tier 3 are the use of behavior intervention plans and therapeutic interventions. These approaches are described in further detail in the following text.

Behavior Intervention Plans

When an FBA is conducted at Tier 3, the data from this assessment directly inform the development of a behavior intervention plan (see Figure 10.1). A ***behavior intervention plan*** (BIP) provides strategies for preventing problem behavior from occurring as well as for teaching and reinforcing students for engaging in alternative, more appropriate behaviors.

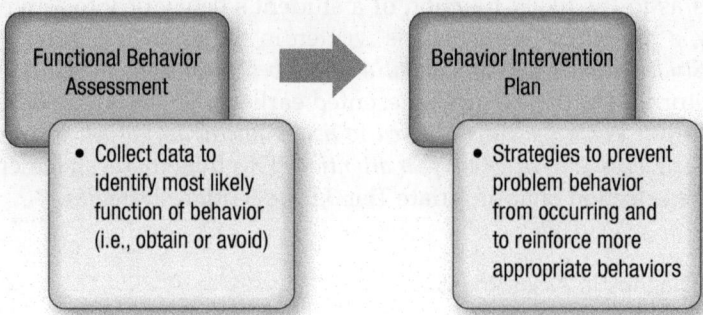

FIGURE 10.1 RELATIONSHIP BETWEEN FUNCTIONAL BEHAVIOR ASSESSMENT AND BEHAVIOR INTERVENTION PLAN.

Generally, strategies described in the BIP are integrally linked to each component of the hypothesis statement generated in the FBA. First, *antecedent strategies* involve altering the environment in which the behavior typically occurs in an effort to prevent the behavior from occurring. Suppose, for example, that the results of an FBA suggest that the presentation of a particular task demand (e.g., reading aloud to a peer) was the most likely antecedent of a student's (Marco's) verbally aggressive behavior. One possible antecedent strategy for decreasing this behavior might involve modifying the task demand, such as offering Marco a choice between two or more tasks (e.g., reading aloud to peer or reading aloud to a teaching assistant), rather than insisting that he complete one in particular.

The second group of strategies within a BIP includes those that aim to teach the student replacement behaviors. *Replacement behaviors* are behaviors that serve the same or a similar function as the problem behavior but are considered to be more appropriate than the current problem behavior. In other words, exhibiting a replacement behavior allows the student to achieve the same outcome (i.e., obtaining or avoiding something) as the problem behavior but in a more appropriate or acceptable manner. For example, returning to our earlier example of the student with verbally aggressive behavior, teaching replacement behaviors may help reduce the recurrence of this problem behavior. If each time the student responds to the peer reading task with verbally aggressive behavior, they are sent out of the classroom (and thus do not have to complete the task), task avoidance would be a likely function of the behavior. One possible replacement behavior for this student might involve telling the teacher privately that they do not want to read aloud in front of a peer and requesting an alternative task (e.g., reading aloud with a teaching assistant). This behavior would be more appropriate than verbal aggression but would achieve the same desired outcome (i.e., avoiding the task).

Finally, *consequence strategies* are those that target outcomes and responses to both problem and replacement behaviors. One common and effective consequence strategy for reducing problem behavior is to eliminate the potential reinforcers of that behavior. For example, continuing with the earlier example, it would be important for Marco's BIP to specify that he should not be able to avoid the peer reading task by engaging in verbally aggressive behavior. Instead, the teacher might wait until Marco has calmed down before presenting him with the same task again. Consequence strategies should also be used to reinforce Marco for engaging in the appropriate replacement behavior. Each time that Marco asks politely to read with a teaching assistant, the task demand of reading with a peer should be reliably removed. In addition, Marco may receive other desirable consequences, such as verbal praise, for demonstrating the replacement behavior.

Therapeutic Interventions

Tier 3 interventions may also include manualized interventions to treat individual students with internalizing problems, such as anxiety or depression. One example of a manualized intervention for treating anxiety in children and adolescents is Coping Cat (Kendall & Hedtke, 2006). Coping Cat is an evidence-based cognitive behavioral intervention that helps students recognize and understand their emotional and physical reactions to anxiety and critically examine personal thoughts and feelings that arise during anxiety-inducing situations (Kendall et al., 2008). It is designed to help students develop plans for effectively coping with anxiety, evaluate the degree to which they use coping strategies, and reward themselves for implementation. Typically, Coping Cat is administered individually in 50-minute weekly sessions over 16 weeks, but it also can be used effectively in small groups of four or five students (Flannery-Schroeder et al., 2005). During each session, students are introduced to particular concepts and strategies; in between sessions, they complete related homework assignments. Procedures for implementation are clearly delineated in the Coping Cat manual. These well-defined procedures minimize training demands and increase the likelihood that the intervention will be delivered with fidelity (i.e., as designed).

> **SOCIAL JUSTICE CONNECTIONS**
>
> *How can school psychologists apply an equity-centered approach to social and emotional learning to support racially/ethnically minoritized youth in schools?*
>
> Forces of institutional oppression can negatively impact the mental health of minoritized youth, including youth of color. For example, a systematic review conducted by Priest et al. (2012) found that perceived racial discrimination was significantly associated with higher levels of anxiety and depression as well as lower levels of self-esteem among children and youth. School psychologists must work to deconstruct systemic barriers (e.g., racism) that impact the social, emotional, and behavioral outcomes of youth in schools. They must also focus on elevating student voice, agency, strengths, and assets.
>
> As described previously, SEL encompasses a range of competences related to self-awareness, self-management, social awareness, relationship skills, and decision-making. However, traditional conceptualizations of these five domains have not accounted for structural racism and other forces of oppression that impact racial and ethnic minoritized youth (e.g., Jagers et al., 2018, 2019). For example, although the domain of *self-awareness* involves being cognizant of one's emotions and personal strengths, interventions in this area have often overlooked facets of self-knowledge such as awareness of one's racial identity and personal prejudices (Jagers et al., 2018).
>
> Critiques of the traditional model have paved the way for advances in equity-focused, culturally responsive SEL practices, or *transformative SEL* (Jagers et al., 2018). These practices position SEL as a lever for promoting justice in educational service delivery and student outcomes (Schlund et al., 2020). Across all five areas of SEL, school psychologists can promote wellness by encouraging students to understand themselves as cultural beings as well as engaged, justice-oriented members of their school communities. As described by Jagers et al. (2018), examples of key skills in each of the five domains are as follows:
>
> - **Self-awareness:** (a) understanding one's intersecting sociocultural identities (e.g., racial identity); (b) examining personal values and prejudices
> - **Social awareness:** (a) understanding norms for social behavior in diverse settings; (b) taking the perspectives of people with similar and different cultural backgrounds

(continued)

> **SOCIAL JUSTICE CONNECTIONS (*continued*)**
>
> - ***Self-management:*** (a) understanding how personal biases impact interactions with others; (b) coping with prejudice, discrimination, and acculturative stress
> - ***Relationship skills:*** (a) building supportive friendships with individuals with diverse identities; (b) culturally responsive conflict resolution
> - ***Responsible decision-making:*** (a) evaluating consequences of interpersonal and institutional actions; (b) building classroom and school communities that value members' diverse identities
>
> Research on transformative SEL is continually emerging and suggests that the aforementioned skills are important for promoting students' well-being. For example, Griffin et al. (2020) found that, among Black high school students, active coping with race-related stress (i.e., self-management) was positively associated with efforts to master academic material. Overall, supporting equity-centered SEL practices represents an important way that school psychologists can advance social justice and promote positive outcomes for all youth.

SUMMARY AND CONCLUSIONS

In this chapter, we described a multitiered model of service delivery for supporting students' SEB success in schools (i.e., SEB MTSS). Within a multitiered framework, school psychologists and other personnel can provide high-quality, evidence-based supports that are appropriately matched to the type and intensity of students' needs. MTSS also allows schools to make the most efficient use of their potentially limited mental health and behavioral support resources.

Although this chapter has surveyed a variety of common assessment and intervention methods at each tier, specific strategies vary considerably across schools. Notably, the literature on school-based SEB assessment and intervention is expansive, and practitioners should be well versed in this research before selecting procedures for their unique school contexts. Ultimately, there is much work to be done to meet the needs of students who are experiencing SEB concerns and to address institutional barriers to students' well-being, particularly for marginalized youth. Fortunately, schools are an ideal context for identifying students in need of services and for providing them with the supports they need to be successful in a variety of settings.

> **DISCUSSION QUESTIONS**
>
> 1. In SEB MTSS, what are some purposes of universal screening?
> 2. What are some key differences between PBIS and SEL? How are these frameworks alike?
> 3. Tier 2 SEB interventions may be provided by teachers within the regular classroom setting or in a pull-out fashion by specialized personnel. What might be the advantages of providing such supports in the classroom? What might be the disadvantages?
> 4. The data gathered through an FBA are used to develop a hypothesis regarding the function of the problem behavior. How does understanding the function of a behavior help us to develop more appropriate interventions for students?
> 5. As noted in the chapter, Tier 3 assessment procedures tend to be diagnostic in nature and are highly linked to intervention design. Why is this necessary at Tier 3 in particular?

RECOMMENDED READINGS

Burns, M. K., Riley-Tillman, T. C., & Rathvon, N. (2017). *Effective school interventions: Evidence-based strategies for improving student outcomes* (3rd ed.). Guilford.

Collins, T. A., Dart, E. H., & Arora, P. G. (2019). Addressing the internalizing behavior of students in schools: Applications of the MTSS model [Special issue]. *School Mental Health, 11*. https://link.springer.com/article/10.1007/s12310-018-09307-9

Fallon, L. M., Veiga, M., & Sugai, G. (2021). Strengthening MTSS for Behavior (MTSS-B) to promote racial equity. *School Psychology Review*. https://doi.org/10.1080/2372966X.2021.1972333

Jagers, R. J., Rivas-Drake, D., & Williams, B. (2019). Transformative social and emotional learning (SEL): Toward SEL in service of educational equity and excellence. *Educational Psychologist, 54*(3), 162–184. https://doi.org/10.1080/00461520.2019.1623032

Saeki, E., Jimerson, S. R., Earhart, J., Hart, S. R., Renshaw, T., Singh, R. D., & Stewart, K. (2011). Response to intervention (RtI) in the social, emotional, and behavioral domains: Current challenges and emerging possibilities. *Contemporary School Psychology, 15*, 43–52. https://files.eric.ed.gov/fulltext/EJ934705.pdf

A robust set of instructor resources designed to supplement this text is located at http://connect.springerpub.com/content/book/978-0-8261-6344-8. Qualifying instructors may request access by emailing textbook@springerpub.com.

REFERENCES

American Academy of Pediatrics (AAP), American Academy of Child and Adolescent Psychiatry, & Children's Hospital Association. (2021). *AAP-AACAP-CHA declaration of a national emergency in child and adolescent mental health*. Author.

Barrish, H. H., Saunders, M., & Wolf, M. M. (1969). Good behavior game: Effects of individual contingencies for group consequences on disruptive behavior in a classroom. *Journal of Applied Behavior Analysis, 2*, 119–124. https://doi.org/10.1901/jaba.1969.2-119

Bitsko, R. H., Claussen, A. H., Lichstein, J., Black, L. I., Jones, S. E., Danielson, M. L., Hoenig, J. M., Jack, S. P. D., Brody, D. J., Gyawali, S., Maenner, M. J., Warner, M., Holland, K. M., Perou, R., Corsby, A. E., Blumberg, S. J., Avenevoli, S., Kaminski, J., & Ghandour, R. M. (2022). Mental health surveillance among children—United States, 2013-2019. *MMWR Surveillance Summaries, 71*(2), 1–42. https://doi.org/10.15585/mmwr.su7102a1

Bowman-Perrott, L., Burke, M. D., Zaini, S., Zhang, N., & Vannest, K. (2016). Promoting positive behavior using the Good Behavior Game: A meta-analysis of single-case research. *Journal of Positive Behavior Interventions, 18*, 180–190. https://doi.org/10.1177/1098300715592355

Bradshaw, C. P., Mitchell, M. M., O'Brennan, L. M., & Leaf, P. J. (2010). Multilevel exploration of factors contributing to the overrepresentation of Black students in office disciplinary referrals. *Journal of Educational Psychology, 102*, 508–520. https://doi.org/10.1037/a0018450

Briesch, A. M., & Chafouleas, S. M. (2009). Review and analysis of literature on self management interventions to promote appropriate classroom behaviors (1988–2008). *School Psychology Quarterly, 24*, 106–118. https://doi.org/10.1037/a0016159

Briesch, A. M., Chafouleas, S. M., & Riley-Tillman, T. C. (2016). *Direct behavior rating: Linking assessment, communications, and intervention*. Guilford Press.

Briesch, A. M., & Volpe, R. J. (2007). Selecting progress monitoring tools for evaluating social behavior. *School Psychology Forum, 1*, 59–74.

Briesch, A. M., Volpe, R. J., & Floyd, R. G. (2018). *School-based observation: A practical guide to assessing student behavior*. Guilford Press.

Briesch, A. M., Donaldson, A. R., Matta, M., Volpe, R. J., Daniels, B., & Owens, J. S. (2022). Development of brief rating scales for progress monitoring internalizing behavior. *Journal of Emotional and Behavioral Disorders, 30*(3), 199–209. https://doi.org/10.1177/10634266211039761

Bruhn, A., McDaniel, S., & Kreigh, C. (2015). Self-monitoring interventions for students with behavior problems: A systematic review of current research. *Behavioral Disorders, 40,* 102–121. https://doi.org/10.17988/BD-13-45.1

Burns, B. J., Costello, E. J., Angold, A., Tweed, D., Stangl, D., Farmer, E. M., & Erklani, A. (1995). Children's mental health service use across service sectors. *Health Affairs, 14,* 147–159. https://doi.org/10.1377/hlthaff.14.3.147

Bushaw, W. J., & Lopez, S. J. (2010). Highlights of the 2010 Phi Delta Kappa/Gallup Poll. *Phi Delta Kappan, 92,* 8–26. http://www.pdkintl.org/kappan/docs/2010_Poll_Report.pdf

Centers for Disease Control and Prevention. (2004). *National Center for Health Statistics: National health interview survey.* Author.

Centers for Disease Control and Prevention. (2019). *Youth risk behavior survey: Data summary and trends 2007–2017.* https://www.cdc.gov/healthyyouth/data/yrbs/pdf/trendsreport.pdf

Cole, C. L., & Bambara, L. M. (1992). Issues surrounding the use of self-management interventions in schools. *School Psychology Review, 21,* 193–201. https://doi.org/10.1080/02796015.1992.12085606

Collaborative for Academic, Social, and Emotional Learning. (2022a). *Fundamentals of SEL.* http://www.casel.org/fundamentals-of-sel

Collaborative for Academic, Social, and Emotional Learning. (2022b). *Program guide.* https://pg.casel.org/

Daniels, B., Briesch, A. M., Volpe, R. J., & Owens, J. S. (2019). Content validation of Direct Behavior Rating multi-item scales for assessing problem behaviors. *Journal of Emotional and Behavioral Disorders, 29*(2), 71–82. https://doi.org/10.1177/1063426619882345

Duong, M. T., Bruns, E. J., Lee, K., Coifman, J., Mayworm, A., & Lyon, A. R. (2021). Rates of mental health service utilization by children and adolescents in schools and other common service settings: A systematic review and meta-analysis. *Administration and Policy in Mental Health, 48,* 420–439. https://doi.org/10.1007/s10488-020-01080-9

Durlak, J. A., Weissberg, R. P., Dymnicki, A. B., Taylor, R. D., & Schellinger, K. B. (2011). The impact of enhancing students' social and emotional learning: A meta-analysis of school-based universal interventions. *Child Development, 82,* 405–432. https://doi.org/10.1111/j.1467-8624.2010.01564.x

Eklund, K., Kilpatrick, K. D., Kilgus, S. P., & Haider, A. (2018). A systematic review of state-level social-emotional learning standards: Implications for practice and research. *School Psychology Review, 47,* 316–326. https://doi.org/10.17105/SPR-2017.0116.V47-3

Elliot, S., & Gresham, F. (2008). *Social Skills Improvement System (SSIS) intervention guide.* Pearson.

Flannery-Schroeder, E., Choudhury, M. S., & Kendall, P. C. (2005). Group and individual cognitive-behavioral treatments for youth with anxiety disorders: 1-year follow-up. *Cognitive Therapy and Research, 29,* 253–259. https://doi.org/10.1007/s10608-005-3168-z

Flower, A., McKenna, J. W., Bunuan, R. L., Muething, C. S., & Vega, R. (2014). Effects of the Good Behavior Game on challenging behaviors in school settings. *Review of Educational Research, 84,* 546–571. https://doi.org/10.3102/0034654314536781

Griffin, C. B., Gray, D. L., Hope, E. C., Metzger, I. W., & Henderson, D. X. (2020). Do coping responses and racial identity promote school adjustment among Black youth? Applying an equity-elaborated social-emotional learning lens. *Urban Education, 57*(2), 198–223. https://doi.org/10.1177/0042085920933346

Jagers, R. J., Rivas-Drake, D., & Borowski, T. (2018, November). Equity & social and emotional learning: Acultural analysis. *CASEL Assessment Work Group Brief Series.* https://casel.org/wp-content/uploads/2020/04/equity-and-SEL-.pdf

Jagers, R. J., Rivas-Drake, D., & Williams, B. (2019). Transformative social and emotional learning (SEL): Toward SEL in service of educational equity and excellence. *Educational Psychologist, 54*(3), 162–184. https://doi.org/10.1080/00461520.2019.1623032

Kendall, P. C., & Hedtke, K. (2006). *The Coping Cat workbook* (2nd ed.). Workbook Publishing.

Kendall, P. C., Hudson, J. L., Gosch, E., & Flannery-Schroeder, E. (2008). Cognitive-behavioral therapy for anxiety disordered youth: A randomized clinical trial evaluating child and family modalities. *Journal of Consulting and Clinical Psychology, 76,* 282–297. https://doi.org/10.1037/0022-006X.76.2.282

Kovacs, M. (2014). *Children's depression inventory* (2nd ed.). Multi-Health Systems.

Langdon, C. A., & Vesper, N. (2000). The sixth Phi Delta Kappa poll of teachers' attitudes toward the public schools. *Phi Delta Kappan, 81*, 607–611. http://www.jstor.org/stable/20439737

Lewis, T. J., Scott, T. M., & Sugai, G. (1994). The problem behavior questionnaire: A teacher-based instrument to develop functional hypotheses of problem behavior in general education settings. *Diagnostique, 19*, 103–115. https://doi.org/10.1177/073724779401900207

Lochman, J. E., Nelson, W. M., & Sims, J. P. (1981). A cognitive behavioral program for use with aggressive children. *Journal of Clinical Child Psychology, 13*, 146–148. https://doi.org/10.1080/15374418109533036

Mahoney, J. L., Durlak, J. A., & Weissberg, R. P. (2018). An update on social and emotional learning outcome research. *Phi Delta Kappan, 100*(4), 18–23. https://doi.org/10.1177/0031721718815668

March, R. E., Horner, R. H., Lewis-Palmer, T., Brown, D., Crone, D., Todd, A. W., & Carr, E. G. (2000). *Functional assessment checklist: Teachers and staff (FACTS)*. Educational and Community Supports.

Marrast, L., Himmelstein, D. U., & Woolhandler, S. (2016). Racial and ethnic mental health care for children and young adults: A national study. *International Journal of Health Services, 46*, 810–824. https://doi.org/10.1177/0020731416662736

McIntosh, K., Campbell, A. L., Carter, D. R., & Zumbo, B. D. (2009). Concurrent validity of office discipline referrals and cut points used in schoolwide positive behavior support. *Behavioral Disorders, 34*, 100–113. http://www.jstor.org/stable/43153806

Merikangas, K. R., He, J. P., Burstein, M., Swanson, S. A., Avenevoli, S., Cui, L., Benjet, C., Georgiades, K., & Swendsen, J. (2010). Lifetime prevalence of mental disorders in US adolescents: Results from the National Comorbidity Survey Replication—Adolescent Supplement (NCS-A). *Journal of the American Academy of Child & Adolescent Psychiatry, 49*, 980–989. https://doi.org/10.1016/j.jaac.2010.05.017

Nijs, M. M., Bun, C. J. E., Tempelaar, W. M., de Wit, N. J., Burger, H., Plevier, C. M., & Boks, M. P. M. (2014). Perceived school safety is strongly associated with adolescent mental health problems. *Community Mental Health Journal, 50*, 127–134. https://doi.org/10.1007/s10597-013-9599-1

Parisi, D. M., Ihlo, T., & Glover, T. A. (2014). *Screening within a multitiered early prevention model: Using assessment to inform instruction and promote students' response to intervention*. American Psychological Association.

Priest, N., Paradies, Y., Trenerry, B., Truong, M., Karlsen, S., & Kelly, Y. (2012). A systematic review of studies examining the relationship between reported racism and health and wellbeing for children and young people. *Social Science & Medicine, 95*, 115–127. https://doi.org/10.1016/j.socscimed.2012.11.031

Schlund, J., Jagers, R. J., & Schlinger, M. (2020). *Advancing social and emotional learning (SEL) as a lever for equity and excellence*. https://drc.casel.org/uploads/sites/3/2020/09/CASEL-Equity-Insights-Report.pdf

Shaffer, D., Fisher, P., Lucas, C., Dulcan, M., & Schwab-Stone, M. (2000). NIMH Diagnostic Interview Schedule for Children, Version IV (NIMH DISC-IV): Description, differences from previous versions, and reliability of some common diagnoses. *Journal of the American Academy of Child and Adolescent Psychiatry, 39*, 28–38. https://doi.org/10.1097/00004583-200001000-00014

Sugai, G., & Horner, R. (2002). The evolution of discipline practices: School-wide positive behavior supports. *Child & Family Behavior Therapy, 24*, 23–50. https://doi.org/10.1300/J019v24n01_03

Technical Assistance Center on Positive Behavioral Interventions and Supports. (2015). *Implementation blueprint*. U.S. Department of Education, Office of Special Education Programs.

U.S. Department of Education Office for Civil Rights. (2016). *2015-2016 civil rights data collection: School climate and safety*. https://www2.ed.gov/about/offices/list/ocr/docs/school-climate-and-safety.pdf

U.S. Department of Education, Policy and Program Studies Service. (2004). *State education indicators with a focus on Title I, 2000–01*. Author.

U.S. Department of Health and Human Services. (1999). *Mental health: A report of the surgeon general*. U.S. Department of Health and Human Services, Substance Abuse and Mental Health Services Administration, Center for Mental Health Services, National Institutes of Health, National Institute of Mental Health.

Volpe, R. J., & Briesch, A. M. (2012). Generalizability and dependability of single item and multiple item direct behavior rating scales for engagement and disruptive behavior. *School Psychology Review, 41*, 246–261. https://doi.org/10.1080/02796015.2012.12087506

Volpe, R. J., & Briesch, A. M. (2015). Multi-item direct behavior ratings: Dependability of two levels of assessment specificity. *School Psychology Quarterly, 30,* 431–442. https://doi.org/10.1037/spq0000115

Volpe, R. J., Chaffee, R. K., Yeung, T. S., & Briesch, A. M. (2019). Initial development of multi-item direct behavior rating measures of academic enablers. *School Mental Health, 12,* 77–87. https://doi.org/10.1007/s12310-019-09338-w

Volpe, R. J., & Fabiano, G. A. (2013). *Daily behavior report cards: An evidence-based system of assessment and intervention.* Guilford Press.

Warren, J. S., Bohanon-Edmonson, H. M., Turnbull, A. P., Sailor, W., Wickham, D., Griggs, P., & Beech, S. E. (2006). School-wide positive behavior support: Addressing behavior problems that impede student learning. *Educational Psychology Review, 18,* 187–198. https://doi.org/10.1007/s10648-006-9008-1

Williams, N. J., Scott, L., & Aarons, G. A. (2018). Prevalence of serious emotional disturbance among U.S. children: A meta-analysis. *Psychiatric Services, 69,* 32–40. https://doi.org/10.1176/appi.ps.201700145

Woods, S., Done, J., & Kalsi, H. (2009). Peer victimisation and internalising difficulties: The moderating role of friendship quality. *Journal of Adolescence, 32*(2), 293–308. https://doi.org/10.1016/j.adolescence.2008.03.005

Wright, R. A., & McCurdy, B. L. (2012). Class-wide positive behavior support and group contingencies: Examining a positive variation of the Good Behavior Game. *Journal of Positive Behavior Interventions, 14,* 173–180. https://doi.org/10.1177/1098300711421008

CHAPTER 11

Cognitive Assessment

JOHN H. KRANZLER ■ RANDY G. FLOYD

CHAPTER OBJECTIVES

After reading this chapter, you will be able to:

- Define intelligence.
- Describe the structure of intelligence.
- Describe how intelligence is measured.
- Describe the use of intelligence tests in the schools.
- Discuss issues of social justice pertaining to intelligence test use.

NATIONAL ASSOCIATION OF SCHOOL PSYCHOLOGISTS PRACTICE MODEL CONNECTIONS

Domain 1: Data-Based Decision-Making
Domain 9: Research and Evidence-Based Practice

INTRODUCTION

The "existence of individual differences in cognitive aptitude for learning from instruction is the most longstanding, well-established fact in educational psychology" (Snow & Lohman, 1984, p. 347). Indeed, in virtually every classroom, it is common for teachers to observe that some students struggle to acquire certain knowledge and skills, whereas others learn that same material quickly and with ease. While at least some academic skill deficits are best viewed as a mismatch between the child and the instructional environment, individual differences in the ability to learn from instruction can also stem from differences in intelligence. Such differences present a challenge for teachers, because they require adaptions to instruction to promote the attainment of common instructional objectives for all students.

Intelligence tests were originally developed to improve educational efficiency by identifying children and youth who were at risk for educational failure (Chapman, 1988). Such tests were used to classify students to fixed educational structures on the basis of general intellectual ability, where they would either succeed or drop out. After the Education for All Handicapped Children Act was passed in 1975 (as described in Chapters 2 and 5), however, public school systems were mandated to provide an appropriate education for all students, including those with disabilities who had previously been excluded from the education system. Society's commitment to equal educational opportunity for all necessitates that instructional accommodations be made to address the wide range of aptitudes for learning. As Braden and Shaw (2009) have stated, today intelligence tests are administered "to students who are experiencing academic difficulties in school under the assumption that doing so will help stakeholders (e.g., educators, support services personnel, and parents) find ways to help students overcome their difficulties" (p. 106).

This chapter reviews the current status of intelligence testing in the schools. We begin by defining intelligence, its structure, and distribution. Next, we discuss the origins of individual differences in intelligence and its malleability. We then examine how intelligence is measured and briefly describe the most widely administered intelligence test with children and youth, the Wechsler Intelligence Test for Children, Fifth Edition (WISC-V; Wechsler, 2014). Finally, we discuss how tests of intelligence are used in the schools. We conclude with a discussion of intelligence testing and social justice.

WHAT IS INTELLIGENCE?

Despite the fact that tests of intelligence have been used for more than 100 years, a consensus on the definition of *intelligence* has not been reached (e.g., Kranzler & Floyd, 2020). The fact that intelligence can be conceptualized from several different perspectives is one reason why a consensus definition has been so elusive (cf. Eysenck, 1998). One conception of intelligence, *biological intelligence*, refers to the biological functioning of the brain that is involved in all thought and action. Biological intelligence is influenced by genes, because they are related to brain structure and its physiological and biochemical functioning (Haier, 2018). The second conception of intelligence, *psychometric intelligence*, refers to the behaviors that are measured on intelligence tests. Performance on intelligence tests is related not only to one's biological functioning but also to the environment in which one was raised. Important environmental influences on intelligence test performance include family background and level and quality of education, among others (Gottfredson, 2008; Jensen, 1998). The third and final conception of intelligence is *social intelligence*. Social intelligence refers to what is considered "intelligent" behavior in specific contexts, such as school or work. Moreover, the behaviors that are seen as intelligent may differ across cultures (e.g., Gottfredson, 2008). Thus, what is considered "real-world intelligence" is determined in part by one's biological functioning and in part by one's background and experience, as well as by numerous noncognitive factors (e.g., personality, nutrition, and motivation).

Given that intelligence can be defined from these different perspectives, it is perhaps not surprising that a consensus definition is lacking; it is important to note, however, that these different conceptualizations of intelligence do overlap in important and meaningful ways. In fact, most researchers vigorously studying intelligence agree that it involves the ability to reason abstractly, solve complex problems, and acquire new knowledge. Intelligence, therefore, reflects more than "book learning" or "test-taking skill"; that is, it incorporates a larger capacity for comprehending and reasoning (Eysenck, 1998; Gottfredson, 2002; Neisser et al., 1996).

THE STRUCTURE OF INTELLIGENCE

One important discovery in the history of psychology is called the positive manifold. The positive manifold refers to the fact that all intelligence tests are positively intercorrelated. Thus, persons who perform well on one kind of test (e.g., a verbal test) tend to do well on every other kind of test (e.g., a spatial test and a reasoning test), and vice versa. The positive manifold indicates that individual differences on all tests of intelligence have something in common. Charles Spearman (1904) developed a sophisticated statistical analysis called factor analysis to measure the degree to which different tests of intelligence are related to a common source of individual differences, which he called the general factor, or psychometric g. In factor analysis, a *factor* is an underlying variable that accounts for the correlations among test scores. In his two-factor theory, Spearman hypothesized that every test of cognitive ability measures psychometric g and another factor that is unique to that specific test. Soon after the development of factor analysis, however, Spearman and other pioneers in this method discovered the existence of group factors. Group factors are different from psychometric g in that they are common only to certain groups of tests that require similar content (e.g., verbal, numerical, or spatial) or cognitive processes (e.g., memory). Factor analysis revealed that intelligence, as measured by intelligence tests, is both general in a sense and specific to subsets of tests.

Over the past 100 years, numerous theories about the number of factors and their relations with one another have been postulated (e.g., Cattell, 1971; Thurstone, 1938). At present, the most widely accepted theory of the structure of factors from intelligence tests is the Cattell-Horn-Carroll (CHC) theory (e.g., Schneider & McGrew, 2018). The CHC theory is an integration of two different theories: Carroll's (1993) three-stratum theory and Horn-Cattell's fluid and crystallized (Gf-Gc) theory (Horn & Noll, 1997). According to the CHC theory, intelligence is structured hierarchically, with three levels that differ in how general or narrow they are. At Stratum III, the apex of the hierarchy, is psychometric g, the most general factor. Every test of cognitive ability measures g to some extent. At the next level of generality, Stratum II, there are eight to 10 broad group factors (e.g., Fluid Reasoning, Comprehension–Knowledge, and Short-Term Memory). Finally, at Stratum III, there are more than 80 narrow group factors, including those representing differences in map-reading ability, vocabulary knowledge, and accuracy in learning people's names. What, then, is intelligence? The vast literature on human cognitive abilities clearly indicates that it is multidimensional, which means that intelligence cannot be fully captured by any single factor or intelligence test score.

When Alfred Binet and Théodore Simon invented the first intelligence test, they began with the assumption that children become more intelligent with age. They developed and administered a set of questions and tasks to children at 1-year intervals between 3 and 15 years of age. Within each age group, Binet and Simon then grouped the test items based on the percentage of children who got each item correct. For example, if the average child at the age of 10 years correctly answered a particular item, then that item had an age level of 10 years. Thus, children who could solve this item were said to have a mental age (MA) of 10 years. At each age level, these researchers selected five items so that they could measure MA in months as well as years. By comparing a child's MA to their chronological age (CA), Binet and Simon were able to determine whether a child's intelligence was above or below average in comparison to same-age peers.

Wilhelm Stern was the first to describe intelligence by the ratio of MA by CA to derive a "mental quotient," a term that was later changed to "intelligence quotient" (IQ). When this ratio is multiplied by 100 to remove the decimal point, IQ = MA/CA × 100. Thus, for example, an 8-year-old child with an MA equivalent to that of the average 10-year-old would have an IQ of 125 (10/8 × 100). Despite its appeal, it quickly became apparent that the new IQ scale was not useful after about 16 years of age, given that intellectual skills do not continue to develop steadily after that age. For adults, this method is clearly inappropriate, because their MA would remain relatively constant, while their CA would constantly increase with time. For this reason, all intelligence tests now use a different method for calculating IQs, called a point scale. Using this method, the number of points an individual earned on the test (called a *raw score*) is converted statistically to an IQ based on that individual's relative standing in relation to a normative sample of same-age peers. The average score at each age is set at 100, with a standard deviation (*SD*) of 15. The point scale more accurately measures intelligence in comparison to others of the same age.

Intelligence tests have been increasingly developed based on theories as described previously. CHC theory, in particular, has been used in this manner, or it has been referenced as an interpretative option (Keith & Reynolds, 2010). For example, the individually administered intelligence tests such as the Kaufman Assessment Battery for Children, Second Edition (Kaufman & Kaufman, 2004), and the Woodcock-Johnson IV Tests of Cognitive Abilities (Schrank et al., 2014) are explicitly based on CHC theory. They were designed to measure five to seven CHC broad group factors in addition to psychometric *g*. In contrast, the intelligence test called the Wechsler Intelligence Scale for Children, Fifth Edition (WISC-V; Wechsler, 2014) was not explicitly developed based on CHC theory. However, it measures five CHC broad group factors in addition to psychometric *g* (cf. Canivez et al., 2016).

The broad group factors that are measured at Stratum II of CHC theory are not always the same across intelligence tests, so different intelligence tests may not measure all of the same abilities. Nevertheless, all of the most widely used measures of intelligence tests correlate substantially with each other, with the average correlation being approximately +.80. This finding results from the fact that they all largely measure the same thing: psychometric *g*. Factor analysis has revealed that psychometric *g* is the largest factor underlying individual differences on intelligence tests, typically explaining a greater proportion of individual differences than all of the group factors that are measured *combined*. On the WISC-V, for example, psychometric *g* explains more than 80% of all individual differences. In addition, research has shown that the psychometric *g* measured by different tests of intelligence is essentially the same (Floyd et al., 2013).

The best measure of psychometric *g* is the overall IQ score on intelligence tests. Many important social outcomes—such as academic achievement, years of education, social status, and income, among others—are predicted better by IQ than they are by any other measurable psychological variable independent of IQ (e.g., Gottfredson, 2008). Nevertheless, despite the fact that IQs are quite predictive of a number of important social criteria, their prediction is far from perfect. As Gottfredson (1997) has noted, "The effects of intelligence—like other psychological traits—are probabilistic, not deterministic. Higher intelligence improves the *odds* of success in school and work. It is an advantage, not a guarantee. Many other things matter" (p. 551, original emphasis). Noncognitive factors such as *conscientiousness*, *ambition*, and *openness to experience*, among others, may be equally important for real-life success.

THE DISTRIBUTION OF INTELLIGENCE

Like many characteristics in the social and behavioral sciences, individual differences in intelligence closely approximate the normal distribution, which is sometimes called a *bell curve*. An idealized normal distribution of intelligence test scores (IQs) is shown in Figure 11.1. As can be seen in this figure, the mean of the distribution of intelligence tests is typically 100 and the *SD* is 15. The overall score on intelligence tests for most individuals

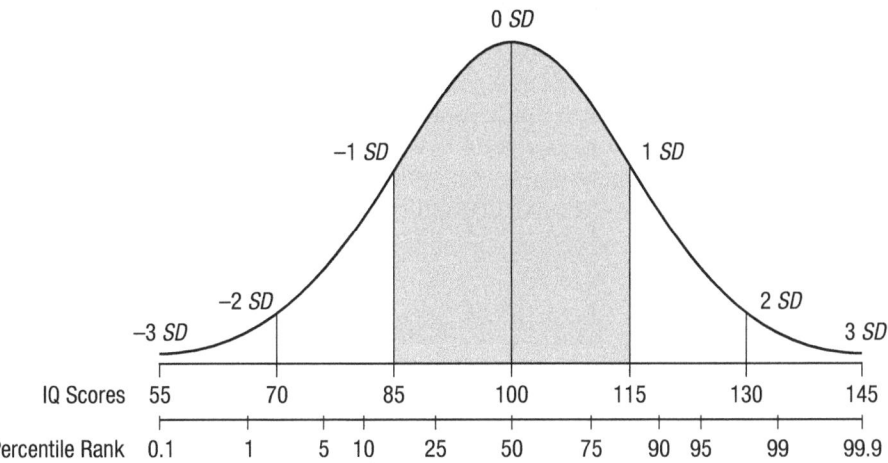

FIGURE 11.1 DISTRIBUTION OF INTELLIGENCE TEST SCORES.

Source: Adapted from Kranzler, J. H., & Floyd, R. G. (2013). *Assessing intelligence in children and adolescents: A practical guide.* The Guilford Press.

falls near the mean, with increasingly fewer scores at the high and low tails of the distribution. Approximately 68% of all people have IQs that are within one *SD* above and below the mean (i.e., IQs = 85–115), and about 95% have scores that fall within two *SD*s from the mean (i.e., 70–130). For the middle 95% of the population, the normal distribution is a reasonably accurate model of the distribution of intelligence. When the remaining 5% of scores at the extreme tails of the distribution are included, the normal distribution is not perfectly accurate. One reason is that there is a greater proportion of individuals with very low IQs at the extreme low end of the distribution (i.e., IQs < 50) than on a normal curve.

INTERPRETATION OF INTELLIGENCE TESTS

The first intelligence tests, such as the Stanford-Binet Intelligence Scale (Terman, 1916), yielded only a single score (the IQ) as an estimate of psychometric *g*. Since the publication of intelligence tests in the 1930s that measured psychometric *g* and a number of broad and narrow abilities (e.g., Wechsler, 1939), psychologists have conducted intra-individual analyses (or *ipsative analyses*) of an individual's test scores to identify cognitive strengths and weaknesses. In intra-individual analyses, the primary focus of clinical interpretation is on the scores that reflect certain group factors, rather than on psychometric *g*. The aim of this approach is to maximize the effectiveness of instructional interventions by pairing them with particular profiles of intelligence test scores (e.g., Flanagan et al., 2010).

Results of a survey by Kranzler et al. (2020) found that most practicing school psychologists (80%) interpret the overall score on intelligence tests, which is a positive sign given that the overall cognitive ability score is the most reliable and valid score for most uses of intelligence tests in the schools (e.g., Nisbett et al., 2012). In addition, 64% reported that they regularly interpret index score profiles, particularly with a focus on the interpretation of population-relative (or normative) strengths and weaknesses in an individual's index scores. Last, Kranzler et al. (2020) found that, despite the fact that the interpretation of subtest scores is consistently discouraged by many researchers due to their relatively poor psychometric properties, nearly 70% of respondents reported that they also interpreted subtest profiles.

Despite its potential utility, intra-individual analysis of intelligence test scores has not been shown to yield the kinds of results that were anticipated. Identified cognitive strengths and weaknesses tend not to be consistent across time, and there is little scientific evidence that links these strengths and weaknesses to more accurate diagnoses of disabilities or effective interventions designed to treat learning problems (see Watkins, 2003). Based on the weak evidence base supporting the utility of intra-individual analysis, some (e.g., Canivez, 2013; Kranzler & Floyd, 2020) have called for a return to a narrower focus on a single score (the IQ).

INTELLIGENCE TESTING IN THE SCHOOLS

In the early 1900s, intelligence tests were initially used in schools to sort students by instructional level or educational track (i.e., vocational or college bound). From then until the 1970s, the practice of testing and grouping students was a common practice in the schools. Throughout this period, however, the use of intelligence tests for "ability grouping" or "tracking" was strongly criticized, resulting in a number of legal challenges related to school admissions, tracking, and determining eligibility for special education. In *Hobson v. Hansen* (1967), for example, the court ruled that the administration of intelligence tests for tracking purposes "deprived students from racial/ethnic minoritized groups and students from families of low socioeconomic status of educational opportunity, because they were disproportionately placed in lower ability tracks that were substantially different from and inferior to higher ability tracks" (Kranzler et al., 2016, p. 277). As a result, the system for tracking students based on intelligence was abolished.

In 1975, the U.S. Congress passed a federal law called the Education for All Handicapped Children Act (Pub. L. No. [PL] 94-142), which mandated that all public school systems provide a free and appropriate public education to children and youth with disabilities. PL 94-142 was reauthorized in 2004 as the Individuals With Disabilities in Education Improvement Act (IDEIA). IDEIA has explicit guidelines for the use of intelligence tests in the schools to determine eligibility for special education and related services. Under IDEIA, intelligence tests are mandated in most states for the identification of intellectual disabilities, intellectual giftedness, and specific learning disabilities (as described in more detail in the following sections). Intelligence tests may be used as a benchmark against which to compare students' current academic achievement, but the specific requirements for use of intelligence tests vary across states. IQ tests may be required for the identification of certain disabilities in some states but not in others (e.g., Maki et al., 2015).

Many medical conditions (i.e., diseases, illnesses, and injuries) share the same or similar symptoms, and some present in different ways. To differentiate between two or more possible causes of an individual's condition, medical doctors and other clinicians (e.g., licensed psychologists) engage in a process known as *differential diagnosis*. The goal of this process is to narrow down the list of possible causes to arrive at a diagnosis. Diagnoses are essentially hypotheses that organize and explain an array of clinical data. They facilitate communication among those providing patient care, provide an understanding of the condition's etiology and prognosis, guide treatment selection, and, in some cases, can be useful for prevention. The *Diagnostic and Statistical Manual of Mental Disorders*, Fifth Edition, Text Revision (*DSM-5-TR*; American Psychiatric Association, 2022), is the nosological system used by mental health professionals and researchers to classify mental disorders.

IDEIA is the nation's federal special education law which ensures that public schools provide a free and appropriate education (FAPE) to all children and youth with disabilities. To qualify, a student must be found to have a disability that requires special education and related services (e.g., counseling or speech therapy) designed to meet their unique educational needs. Schools do not diagnose the causes of learning and other difficulties, however. Rather, they determine whether a student is eligible or ineligible based on the criteria for 13 categories of disability under IDEIA. In the next section, we discuss the main uses of intelligence tests for identifying disabilities in the schools.

Intellectual Disability

Intellectual disability (ID) is defined in IDEIA as "significantly subaverage general intellectual functioning, existing concurrently with deficits in adaptive behavior and manifested during the developmental period that adversely affects a child's educational performance" (Office of Special Education and Rehabilitative Services, Department of Education, 2006, p. 46756). This definition addresses two primary criteria: (a) general intellectual functioning as measured by intelligence tests and (b) adaptive behavior. As of late 2014, in 75% of states, special education eligibility for ID required very low intellectual functioning as reflected in an IQ result from a comprehensive intelligence test that is about two *SD*s below the mean when compared to age-based norms (McNicholas et al., 2017). *Adaptive behavior* refers to "the level of everyday performance of tasks that is required for a person to fulfill typical roles in society, including maintaining independence and meeting cultural expectations regarding personal and social responsibility" (VandenBos, 2006, p. 18). Similar deficits in adaptive functioning are also required for a diagnosis of ID, but most states do not specify exactly which scores (e.g., total or domains scores) should be used to identify these deficits (McNicholas et al., 2017). Thus, intelligence tests are important when identifying children and adolescents with ID.

Intellectual Giftedness

Intellectual giftedness is defined in IDEIA as being present in those persons who give evidence of high achievement capability in areas such as intellectual, creative, artistic, or leadership capacity, or in specific academic fields, and who need services or activities not ordinarily provided by the school in order to fully develop those capabilities (20 U.S.C. § 7801(22)).

At present, most conceptualizations of giftedness view intelligence as a central feature, although all of them expand upon the historical conception of giftedness as an all-purpose, inherited quality of the individual that is identified primarily by an intelligence test (for reviews, see Kranzler & Floyd, 2020; Sternberg & Davidson, 2005). Approximately 90% of states include intelligence as an area or category of giftedness, and one third require the assessment of intelligence as part of the identification process (McClain & Pfeiffer, 2012). In addition to other criteria, such as rating scales of gifted characteristics, most states require consideration of IQs, but only 36% of states specify a particular score marker (e.g., IQ >125). Again, intelligence tests yield useful information in the assessment of giftedness.

Specific Learning Disabilities

Specific learning disability (SLD) is defined in IDEIA as "a disorder in one or more of the basic psychological processes involved in understanding or in using language, spoken or written, which disorder may manifest itself in an imperfect ability to listen, speak, write, spell, or do mathematical calculations" (Pub. L. No. 108–446, § 300.8[c]).

There is much disagreement surrounding the definition and diagnosis of SLD, and no consensus definition of SLD exists. Nevertheless, all current definitions of SLD (a) specify that individuals with SLD experience difficulty with school learning and (b) require that certain criteria be ruled out (e.g., inadequate educational background, sensory impairment, and ID). The biggest point of disagreement among the most widely used definitions of SLD is the need for assessment of intelligence to make the SLD diagnosis (see Kranzler & Floyd, 2020).

SLD was originally conceptualized as unexpected underachievement (Kirk, 1962). In the IQ–achievement discrepancy approach, SLD is identified when an individual's level of performance or rate of skill acquisition in a particular academic area falls substantially below the level one would predict based on the person's intelligence. SLD is identified when a significant discrepancy between IQ and academic achievement is observed, after ruling out exclusionary criteria. As late as 2013, more than two thirds of states allowed for use of the intelligence–achievement discrepancy method for identifying SLD (Maki et al., 2015). Critics of this approach (e.g., Francis et al., 2005) have argued that intelligence tests do not differentiate between students with SLD and slow learners in terms of their cognitive profiles or response to intervention, which makes these tests irrelevant. Some critics (e.g., Vaughn & Fuchs, 2003) refer to the IQ–achievement discrepancy model as supporting a "wait-to-fail" approach, because it is often difficult to determine a severe discrepancy between intelligence and achievement until as late as the third grade.

Given these criticisms, the most recent authorization of IDEIA allows for the identification of SLD on the basis of significant low achievement and lack of Response to Intervention (RtI) within a multitiered service delivery system, as discussed by Kovaleski et al. (2013). Although methods of identification vary, nonresponders to intervention are defined by academic performance that falls below a predetermined level in comparison to school, district, or national norms and an absence of growth in targeted skills (e.g., oral reading) across time despite intensive, evidence-based interventions. Within a multitiered service delivery system emphasizing RtI, intelligence tests are not typically administered, but they may be included as part of a comprehensive assessment designed to eliminate the hypothesis that ID is the cause of academic problems. Results of a study by Kranzler et al. (2020) support Reynolds's (2009) contention that use of an RtI model results in a fundamental shift in the conceptualization of SLD from unexpected underachievement to expected underachievement, that is, difficulty with academic achievement in general. As of 2013, approximately two thirds of all states allowed for use of the RtI approach to SLD identification (Maki et al., 2015).

The third approach to SLD identification is referred to as the pattern of strengths and weaknesses (PSW) approach (e.g., Flanagan et al., 2013). The PSW approach defines SLD as unexpected underachievement as well as corresponding weaknesses in broad or narrow abilities measured by intelligence tests. Although based on the widely accepted CHC theory, very little empirical evidence supports the use of the PSW approaches to SLD identification (e.g., Kranzler et al., 2016a, 2016b, 2019). As of 2013, only one fourth of all states allowed for the use of this approach for SLD identification.

INTELLIGENCE AND SOCIAL JUSTICE

Despite more than 100 years of research into intelligence and its measurement, these topics continue to be frequently debated and remain controversial in the fields of psychology and education and in the broader society, including politics. One reason is the frequent finding of group differences, across racial and ethnic groups of children, adolescents, and adults, in average performance on intelligence tests (Nisbett et al., 2012). Another reason is the finding of disproportionate representation of students from minoritized racial and ethnic groups in special education classes. This disproportionality is particularly prominent in categories for which intelligence tests play a central role. For example, African American and Hispanic students are overrepresented in identifications of ID and SLD and underrepresented in identifications of giftedness (Musu-Gillette et al., 2016; National Center for Education Statistics, 2023; U.S. Department of Education, Office of Special Education and Rehabilitative Services, 2016). This chapter's *Social Justice Connections* box suggests some potential strategies for addressing these systemic problems.

SOCIAL JUSTICE CONNECTIONS

How do school psychologists promote social justice for students from minoritized racial/ethnic groups and other marginalized groups?

We see five strategies as necessary. First, researchers should continue to conduct research to explain group differences and develop methods to reduce them (e.g., through interventions reducing health disparities and early childhood education; Helms, 2007). Second, test authors, test publishers, and independent researchers should continue to evaluate potential bias in intelligence tests at the item level and the score level (Reynolds & Carson, 2005).

Third, professionals who administer intelligence tests (school psychologists and others) should complete assessments that are informed by scientific research and that target not only students' intelligence, knowledge, and skills but also the most salient risk and protective factors predicting success in school and community settings. In particular, they should select tests that are likely to minimize measurement error (and presumed bias) while tapping into different facets of intelligence (Kranzler & Floyd, 2020) as well as consider socioeconomic status and richness of early childhood experiences, which intersect with risk and protective factors (Ford et al., 2016).

Fourth, during testing, school psychologists and other professionals should be aware of confounding influences on performance during testing. In particular, students from minoritized racial and ethnic backgrounds may perform more poorly on intelligence tests due to the influence of **stereotype threat**, which is "being at risk of confirming, as self-characteristic, a negative stereotype about one's group" (Steele & Aronson, 1995, p. 797). Careful planning of, relationship building during, and monitoring of negative emotions, such as anxiety, during testing are important in each individual assessment case and vital for assessing students from minoritized racial and ethnic backgrounds.

Finally, professionals in psychology and education should carefully examine their own beliefs and expectations that may bias their interactions and lead to harmful or otherwise discriminatory actions. Ford et al. (2016), in referring to assessment for giftedness, stated that

> school psychologists must be self-reflective and consult and collaborate with other educators. It is especially critical to collaborate with educators of color when making gifted education assessments and decisions to decrease cultural misunderstanding in all aspects and phases of assessment and decision making. (pp. 270–271)

SUMMARY AND CONCLUSIONS

In conclusion, we encourage readers to consider the balanced approach offered by Nisbett et al. (2012):

> The measurement of intelligence is one of psychology's greatest achievements and one of its most controversial. Critics complain that no single test can capture the complexity of human intelligence, all measurement is imperfect, no single measure is completely free from cultural bias, and there is the potential for misuse of scores on tests of intelligence. There is some merit to all these criticisms. But we would counter that the measurement of intelligence—which has been done primarily by IQ tests—has utilitarian value because it is a reasonably good predictor of grades at school, performance at work, and many other aspects of success in life. . . . It is important to remain vigilant for misuse of scores on tests of intelligence or any other psychological assessment and to look for possible biases in any measure, but intelligence test scores remain useful when applied in a thoughtful and transparent manner. (p. 131)

DISCUSSION QUESTIONS

1. What is intelligence? Is intelligence one thing or many?
2. What is psychometric *g*, and why is it particularly important?
3. How are intelligence tests used in the schools today?
4. Describe some of the approaches used to identify SLD in schools. Why do you think that identification of this particular disability has become such a contentious topic in school psychology?
5. Which social justice issues are related to the use of intelligence tests in the schools?

RECOMMENDED READINGS

Ford, D. Y., Wright, B. L., Washington, A., & Henfield, M. S. (2016). Access and equity denied: Key theories for school psychologists to consider when assessing Black and Hispanic students for gifted education. *School Psychology Forum, 10,* 265–277. https://www.nasponline.org/publications/periodicals/spf/volume-10/volume-10-issue-3-(fall-2016)/access-and-equity-denied-key-theories-for-school-psychologists-to-consider-when-assessing-black-and-hispanic-students-for-gifted-education

Haier, R. J. (2017). *The neuroscience of intelligence.* Cambridge University Press.

Kaufman, A. S. (2009). *IQ testing 101.* Springer Publishing Company.

Kranzler, J. H., & Floyd, R. G. (2020). *Assessing intelligence in children and adolescents: A practical guide for evidence-based assessment* (2nd ed.). Rowman & Littlefield.

Schneider, W. J., & McGrew, K. S. (2018). The Cattell-Horn-Carroll theory of cognitive abilities. In D. P. Flanagan & E. M. McDonough (Eds.), *Contemporary intellectual assessment: Theories, tests, and issues* (4th ed., pp. 73–162). Guilford Press.

 A robust set of instructor resources designed to supplement this text is located at http://connect.springerpub.com/content/book/978-0-8261-6344-8. Qualifying instructors may request access by emailing textbook@springerpub.com.

REFERENCES

American Psychiatric Association. (2022). *Diagnostic and statistical manual of mental disorders* (5th ed., text rev.). https://doi.org/10.1176/appi.books.9780890425787

Braden, J. P., & Shaw, S. R. (2009). Intervention validity of cognitive assessment: Knowns, unknowables, and unknowns. *Assessment for Effective Intervention, 34*, 106–115. https://doi.org/10.1177/1534508407313013

Canivez, G. L. (2013). Psychometric versus actuarial interpretation of intelligence and related aptitude batteries. In D. H. Saklofske, C. R. Reynolds, & V. L. Schwean (Eds.), *The Oxford handbook of child psychological assessments* (pp. 84–112). Oxford University Press.

Canivez, G. L., Watkins, M. W., & Dombrowski, S. C. (2016). Factor structure of the Wechsler Intelligence Scale for Children—Fifth Edition: Exploratory factor analyses with the 16 primary and secondary subtests. *Psychological Assessment, 28*, 975–986. https://doi.org/10.1037/pas0000238

Cattell, R. B. (1971). *Abilities: Their structure, growth, and action*. Houghton Mifflin.

Chapman, P. D. (1988). *Schools as sorters: Lewis M. Terman, applied psychology, and the intelligence testing movement, 1890–1930*. New York University Press.

Eysenck, H. J. (1998). *Intelligence: A new look*. Transaction.

Flanagan, D. P., Fiorello, C. A., & Ortiz, S. O. (2010). Enhancing practice through application of Cattell-Horn-Carroll theory and research: A "third method" approach to specific learning disability identification. *Psychology in the Schools, 47*, 739–760. https://doi.org/10.1002/pits.20501

Flanagan, D. P., Ortiz, S. O., & Alfonso, V. C. (2013). *Essentials of cross-battery assessment* (3rd ed.). Wiley.

Floyd, R. G., Reynolds, M. R., Farmer, R. L., & Kranzler, J. H. (2013). Are the general factors from different child and adolescent intelligence tests the same? Results from a five-sample, six-test analysis. *School Psychology Review, 42*, 383–401. https://doi.org/10.1080/02796015.2013.12087461

Ford, D. Y., Wright, B. L., Washington, A., & Henfield, M. S. (2016). Access and equity denied: Key theories for school psychologists to consider when assessing Black and Hispanic students for gifted education. *School Psychology Forum, 10*, 265–277. https://www.nasponline.org/publications/periodicals/spf/volume-10/volume-10-issue-3-(fall-2016)/access-and-equity-denied-key-theories-for-school-psychologists-to-consider-when-assessing-black-and-hispanic-students-for-gifted-education

Francis, D. J., Fletcher, J. M., Stuebing, K. K., Lyon, R. L., Shaywitz, B. A., & Shaywitz, S. E. (2005). Psychometric approaches to the identification of LD: IQ and achievement scores are not sufficient. *Journal of Learning Disabilities, 38*, 98–108. https://doi.org/10.1177/00222194050380020101

Gottfredson, L. S. (1997). Why g matters: The complexity of everyday life. *Intelligence, 24*, 79–132. https://www1.udel.edu/educ/gottfredson/reprints/1997whygmatters.pdf

Gottfredson, L. S. (2002). g: Highly general and highly practical. In R. J. Sternberg & E. L. Grigorenko (Eds.), *The general factor of intelligence: How general is it?* (pp. 331–380). Erlbaum.

Gottfredson, L. S. (2008). Of what value is intelligence? In A. Prifitera, D. Saklofske, & L. G. Weiss (Eds.), *WISC-IV applications for clinical assessment and intervention* (2nd ed., pp. 545–563). Elsevier.

Haier, R. J. (2018). The parieto-frontal integration theory: Assessing intelligence from brain images. In D. P. Flanagan & E. M. McDonough (Eds.), *Contemporary intellectual assessment: Theories, tests, and issues* (4th ed., pp. 219–224). Guilford Press.

Helms, J. E. (2007). Implementing fairness in racial-group assessment requires assessment of individuals. *American Psychologist, 62*, 1083–1085. https://doi.org/10.1037/0003-066X.62.9.1083

Hobson v. Hansen, 269 F. Supp. 401 (D.D.C. 1967).

Horn, J. L., & Noll, J. (1997). Human cognitive capabilities: Gf-Gc theory. In D. P. Flanagan, J. L. Genshaft, & P. L. Harrison (Eds.), *Contemporary intellectual assessment: Theories, tests, and issues* (pp. 53–91). Guilford Press.

Individuals With Disabilities Education Improvement Act, Pub. L. No. 108–446. (2004).

Jensen, A. R. (1998). *The g factor: The science of mental ability*. Praeger.

Kaufman, A. S., & Kaufman, N. L. (2004). *Kaufman assessment battery for children* (2nd ed.). American Guidance Service.

Keith, T. Z., & Reynolds, M. R. (2010). Cattell-Horn-Carroll theory and cognitive abilities: What we've learned from 20 years of research. *Psychology in the Schools, 47*(7), 635–650. https://psycnet.apa.org/record/2010-15383-002

Kirk, S. A. (1962). Diagnosis and remediation of learning disabilities. *Exceptional Children, 29*, 73–78. https://doi.org/10.1177/001440296202900204

Kovaleski, J. F., VanDerHeyden, A. M., & Shapiro, E. S. (2013). *The RTI approach to evaluating learning disabilities*. Guilford Press.

Kranzler, J. H., Benson, N., & Floyd, R. G. (2016). Intellectual assessment of children and youth in the United States of America: Past, present, and future. *International Journal of School and Educational Psychology, 4*, 276–282. https://doi.org/10.1080/21683603.2016.1166759

Kranzler, J. H., & Floyd, R. G. (2020). *Assessing intelligence in children and adolescents: A practical guide for evidence-based assessment* (2nd ed.). Rowman & Littlefield.

Kranzler, J. H., Floyd, R. G., Benson, N., Zaboski, B., & Thibodaux, L. (2016a). Cross-battery assessment pattern of strengths and weaknesses approach to the identification of specific learning disorders: Evidence-based practice or pseudoscience? *International Journal of School and Educational Psychology, 3*, 146–157. https://doi.org/10.1080/21683603.2016.1192855

Kranzler, J. H., Floyd, R. G., Benson, N., Zaboski, B., & Thibodaux, L. (2016b). Classification agreement analysis of cross-battery assessment in the identification of specific learning disorders in children and youth. *International Journal of School and Educational Psychology, 3*, 124–136. https://doi.org/10.1080/21683603.2016.1155515

Kranzler, J. H., Gilbert, K., Robert, C. R., Floyd, R. G., & Benson, N. F. (2019). Further examination of a critical assumption underlying the dual-discrepancy/consistency approach to specific learning disability identification. *School Psychology Review, 48*(3), 207–221. https://doi.org/10.17105/SPR-2018-0008.V48-3

Kranzler, J. H., Yaraghchi, M., Matthews, K., & Otero-Valles, L. (2020). Does the response-to intervention model fundamentally alter the traditional conceptualization of Specific Learning Disability? *Contemporary School Psychology, 24*, 80–88. https://doi.org/10.1007/s40688-019-00256-x

Maki, K. E., Floyd, R. G., & Roberson, T. (2015). State learning disability eligibility criteria: A comprehensive review. *School Psychology Quarterly, 30*, 457–469. https://doi.org/10.1037/spq0000109

McClain, M.-C., & Pfeiffer, S. (2012). Identification of gifted students in the United States today: A look at state definitions, policies, and practices. *Journal of Applied School Psychology, 28*(1), 59–88. https://doi.org/10.1080/15377903.2012.643757

McNicholas, P. J., Floyd, R. G., Woods, I. L., Singh, L. J., Manguno, M. S., & Maki, K. E. (2017). State special education criteria for identifying intellectual disability: A review following revised diagnostic criteria and Rosa's Law. *School Psychology Quarterly, 33*(1), 75–82. https://doi.org/10.1037/spq0000208

Musu-Gillette, L., Robinson, J., McFarland, J., KewalRamani, A., Zhang, A., & Wilkinson-Flicker, S. (2016). *Status and trends in the education of racial and ethnic groups 2016* (NCES 2016-007). U.S. Department of Education, National Center for Education Statistics. https://nces.ed.gov/pubs2016/2016007.pdf

National Center for Education Statistics. (2023). *Racial/ethnic enrollment in public schools: Condition of education*. U.S. Department of Education, Institute of Education Sciences. Retrieved June 4, 2023, from https://nces.ed.gov/programs/coe/indicator/cge

Neisser, U., Boodoo, G., Bouchard, T. J. Jr., Boykin, A. W., Brody, N., Ceci, S. J., Halpern, D. F., Loehlin, J. C., Perloff, R., Sternberg, R. J., & Urbina, S. (1996). Intelligence: Knowns and unknowns. *American Psychologist, 51*, 77–101. http://psych.colorado.edu/~carey/pdfFiles/IQ_Neisser2.pdf

Nisbett, R. E., Aronson, J., Blair, C., Dickens, W., Flynn, J., Halpern, D. F., & Turkheimer, E. (2012). Intelligence: New findings and theoretical developments. *American Psychologist, 67*, 130–159. https://doi.org/10.1037/a0026699

Office of Special Education and Rehabilitative Services, Department of Education. (2006). *Federal Register: Assistance to states for the education of children with disabilities and preschool grants for children with disabilities, final rule*. 34 C.F.R. Parts 300 and 301.

Reynolds, C. R. (2009). RTI, neuroscience, and sense: Chaos in the diagnosis and treatment of learning disabilities. In E. Fletcher-Janzen & C. R. Reynolds (Eds.), *Neuropsychological perspectives on learning disabilities in the era of RtI: Recommendations for diagnosis and intervention* (pp. 14–27). Wiley.

Reynolds, C. R., & Carson, A. D. (2005). Methods for assessing cultural bias in tests. In C. Frisby & C. R. Reynolds (Eds.), *Comprehensive handbook of multicultural school psychology* (pp. 795–823). Wiley.

Schneider, W. J., & McGrew, K. S. (2018). The Cattell-Horn-Carroll theory of cognitive abilities. In D. P. Flanagan & E. M. McDonough (Eds.), *Contemporary intellectual assessment: Theories, tests, and issues* (4th ed., pp. 73–162). Guilford Press.

Schrank, F. A., McGrew, K. S., & Mather, N. (2014). *Woodcock-Johnson IV tests of cognitive abilities*. Riverside.

Snow, R. E., & Lohman, D. F. (1984). Toward a theory of cognitive aptitude for learning from instruction. *Journal of Educational Psychology, 76*, 347–376. https://doi.org/10.1037/0022-0663.76.3.347

Spearman, C. E. (1904). "General intelligence" objectively determined and measured. *American Journal of Psychology, 15*, 201–293. https://doi.org/10.2307/1412107

Steele, C. M., & Aronson, J. (1995). Stereotype threat and the intellectual test performance of African Americans. *Journal of Personality and Social Psychology, 69*, 797–811. https://doi.org/10.1037//0022-3514.69.5.797

Sternberg, R. J., & Davidson, J. (Eds.). (2005). *Conceptions of giftedness* (2nd ed.). Cambridge University Press.

Sternberg, R. J., & Kaufman, S. B. (Eds.). (2011). *The Cambridge handbook of intelligence*. Cambridge University Press.

Terman, L. M. (1916). *The measurement of intelligence*. Houghton & Mifflin.

Thurstone, L. L. (1938). *Primary mental abilities*. University of Chicago Press.

U.S. Department of Education, Office of Special Education and Rehabilitative Services. (2016). *Racial and ethnic disparities in special education: A multi-year disproportionality analysis by state, analysis category, and race/ethnicity.* https://www2.ed.gov/programs/osepidea/618-data/LEA-racial-ethnic-disparities-tables/disproportionality-analysis-by-state-analysis-category.pdf

VandenBos, G. R. (2006). *APA dictionary of psychology*. American Psychological Association.

Vaughn, S., & Fuchs, L. S. (2003). Redefining learning disabilities as inadequate response to instruction: The promise and potential problems. *Learning Disabilities Research & Practice, 18*, 137–146. https://doi.org/10.1111/1540-5826.00070

Watkins, M. W. (2003). IQ subtest analysis: Clinical acumen or clinical illusion? *Scientific Review of Mental Health Practice, 2*, 118–141. http://edpsychassociates.com/Papers/ClinicalIllusion.pdf

Wechsler, D. (1939). *The measurement of adult intelligence*. Williams & Wilkins.

Wechsler, D. (2014). *Wechsler intelligence scale for children* (5th ed.). Pearson Assessment.

CHAPTER 12

Consultation

WILLIAM P. ERCHUL ■ AARON J. FISCHER

CHAPTER OBJECTIVES

After reading this chapter, you will be able to:

- Define consultation within the contemporary practice of school psychology.
- Describe several models and modalities of consultation practiced by school psychologists.
- Consider consultation as fundamentally a problem-solving process.
- Present the evidence base for the effectiveness of school consultation.
- Describe selected multicultural issues and social justice advances within school consultation.

NATIONAL ASSOCIATION OF SCHOOL PSYCHOLOGISTS PRACTICE MODEL CONNECTIONS

Domain 1: Data-Based Decision-Making
Domain 2: Consultation and Collaboration
Domain 7: Family, School, and Community Collaboration

INTRODUCTION

Providing consultative services in schools is a fundamental role of the school psychologist, and consultation as we view it today began in a formal sense in the 1960s (Erchul & Sheridan, 2014). In addition, the National Association of School Psychologists (NASP; 2020) identifies *Consultation and Collaboration* as a core domain of practice that "permeates all aspects of service delivery" (pp. 3–4). Finally, whereas previous chapters have described how school psychologists can work directly with children and adolescents to support their well-being, this chapter describes how school psychologists engage in cooperative partnerships with parents, educators, and administrators to influence outcomes for youth.

The primary purpose of this chapter is to offer an introduction to many fundamental concepts in consultation, with the intent that readers gain a basic understanding of key aspects of the important role of school psychologists serving as consultants. After presenting some widely recognized models/modalities of consultation and an overview of the typical process, we turn our attention to its evidence base. We then discuss multicultural considerations within consultation and present two studies that deal with social justice issues. In keeping with the goal of this book, we hope that this chapter illustrates some clear ways in which school psychologists are uniquely positioned to serve as agents of social justice for students, parents, and school staff (cf. Li & Vazquez-Nuttall, 2009).

DEFINING CONSULTATION

Given the range of professional settings and contexts in which consultants may deliver services, the term *consultation* has many definitions. Two definitions that are particularly relevant to the field of school psychology, however, are as follows. First, Zins and Erchul (2002) defined *consultation* as

> a method of providing preventively oriented psychological and educational services in which consultants and consultees form cooperative partnerships and engage in a reciprocal, systematic problem-solving process guided by ecobehavioral principles. The goal is to enhance and empower consultee systems, thereby promoting clients' well-being and performance. (p. 626)

In a similar vein, Erchul and Martens (2012) defined *school consultation* as

> a process for providing psychological and educational services in which a specialist (consultant) works cooperatively with a staff member (consultee) to improve the learning and adjustment of a student (client) or group of students. During face-to-face interactions, the consultant helps the consultee through systematic problem solving, social influence, and professional support. In turn, the consultee helps the client(s) through selecting and implementing effective school-based interventions. In all cases, school consultation serves a remedial function and has the potential to serve a preventive function. (pp. 12–13)

Several aspects of these definitions should be reinforced. First, the key participants in the consultative process are the consultant, consultee, and client. The ***consultant*** is an individual (e.g., school psychologist) who provides guidance and expertise to another individual, group, or system (i.e., consultee), which in turn directly delivers the recommended services to a third party (i.e., client). Thus, the ***consultee*** is the person or entity that implements the action plan resulting from consultation, and the ***client*** is the recipient of the subsequent services delivered by the consultee. Various models of consultation conceptualize the roles of consultants, consultees, and clients differently; however, this basic constellation generally characterizes the nature of school-based consultation services.

Second, in contrast to the direct service activities described in Section II of this book, consultation is considered an *indirect service* (as defined in Chapter 1). That is, the school psychologist typically works directly with the consultee only, who in turn works directly with the client. In fact, depending on the nature of the case, a consultant may never even meet with the client. One advantage of working in this manner is that the school psychologist's "reach" or sphere of influence is expanded and, as a result, problems occurring throughout schools stand a better chance of being detected earlier (and perhaps prevented altogether). A second advantage is that consultees benefit from the direct support they receive from the consultant. In particular, consultees have opportunities to develop skills that benefit both the target client and future students and families. As emphasized in the preceding definitions, the success of consultation hinges largely on the quality of the relationship that develops between the consultant and the consultee.

MAJOR MODELS/MODALITIES OF CONSULTATION

Several models of consultation are commonly employed in schools. Each model tends to be based on a particular scientific theory (although some are more theory based than others). We describe four models in the text: (a) mental health consultation, (b) behavioral consultation, (c) conjoint behavioral consultation, and (d) organization development consultation. Additionally, the *Social Justice Connections* box presents a fifth model known as advocacy consultation. Although many other consultative models exist (e.g., collaborative, instructional, Adlerian, process, rational–emotive), they are not presented here because they share many key characteristics with the aforementioned models. We then present two modalities of consultative practice: team-based consultation and teleconsultation. The distinction between a model and a modality is that a modality is not necessarily based on a single formal theory but rather describes a format for offering consultation (e.g., serving multiple consultees, communicating via computer tablet). In other words, some models of consultation can be delivered via multiple modalities.

Mental Health Consultation

The primary development of **mental health consultation** (MHC) may be traced to the work of community psychiatrist Gerald Caplan. Caplan (1970) proposed that a consultee's professional effectiveness could be improved through a process involving collegial case discussion and problem-solving with a consultant. Importantly, within MHC a consultant must strive to maintain a coordinate, nonhierarchical relationship and never cross boundaries by acting as a psychotherapist to the consultee. In other words, the consultant's overt focus clearly should be on professional issues rather than personal problems. Caplan also urged consultants to examine the strengths, weaknesses, capacity, and so forth, of the consultee's organization, as well as to consider the importance of relationships among people in the larger organization. Although Caplan's name is nearly synonymous with MHC, he is credited with broader contributions, including those related to primary prevention, social support, and crisis intervention (Erchul, 2009).

MHC is influenced by Freudian psychoanalytic theory, which accounts for its strong emphasis on more intrapersonal/person-centered issues and unconscious motivations for behavior. Along these lines, a mental health consultant often targets consultee-related factors (e.g., lack of objectivity) as a focus for change (Caplan, 1970). For example, with great finesse and subtlety, a mental health consultant might help a third-grade teacher overcome their difficulty in teaching a student to read by having the teacher make the connection between the present situation and their negative experience with the student's brother, whom they taught 5 years earlier.

There are four overlapping types of MHC: client-centered case consultation, consultee-centered case consultation, program-centered administrative consultation, and consultee-centered administrative consultation (Caplan, 1970). These types differ in regard to whether their focus is on individual cases or programs and vary in terms of emphasizing prevention or remediation. Consultee-centered case consultation, for instance, is concerned with "elucidating and remedying the shortcomings in the consultee's professional functioning . . . [so as to] lead to an improvement in the consultee's professional planning and action, and hopefully to improvement in the client" (Caplan & Caplan, 1999, p. 101). MHC offers a rich conceptualization of how to consult; however, when subjected to rigorous standards, it has been found to have minimal empirical support, in part due to a lack of consensus regarding core definitions and constructs (Kratochwill & Pittman, 2002). Consultee-centered consultation (Newman & Ingraham, 2017), by comparison, holds promise as an updated variation of MHC, as its proponents have adapted many of Caplan's basic principles for specific use in schools.

Behavioral Consultation

Behavioral consultation (BC) is based on theories of learning and behavioral psychology, although more recently ecological and social learning theories have been incorporated into the model. Seminal works on BC (e.g., Bergan & Kratochwill, 1990), however, tend to focus on proximal environmental variables that influence learning and behavior and give far less weight to more distal events and systems issues. Considered largely a client-centered approach, BC targets observable client problems (e.g., student frequency of outbursts) as the object of change.

As in the problem-solving model described in Chapter 8, problems most often are defined as a discrepancy between current and desired behavior, and evidence-based interventions (EBIs) are implemented to reduce the observed discrepancy (Erchul & Martens, 2012). In Bergan and Kratochwill's (1990) approach to BC, clearly defined problem-solving steps embedded in structured interviews address problem identification, problem analysis, plan implementation, and problem evaluation. Later in the chapter, we see how an expansion of these four basic steps constitutes a predominant approach to effective consultation within school psychology. Today BC is commonly referred to as *problem-solving consultation* (Frank & Kratochwill, 2014). We believe this is the case because of BC's (a) longstanding association with the general problem-solving model and its steps, (b) incorporation of influences outside of behavioral psychology over time, and (c) prominence as a model of school consultation.

A primary contribution of BC/problem-solving consultation is its adherence to methodological rigor and scientific precision. For this reason, the majority of the research on consultation in schools has focused on this model and found it to be effective (e.g., Sheridan et al., 1996). It also has been touted as a viable means of delivering psychoeducational services in schools through contemporary multitiered systems of support (MTSS) models (Erchul & Ward, 2016).

Conjoint Behavioral Consultation

Conjoint behavioral consultation (CBC) is an expansion of BC/problem-solving consultation that is conducted with parents and teachers together, over time, and across settings. CBC is defined as:

> a strength-based, cross-system problem-solving and decision-making model wherein parents, teachers, and other caregivers or service providers work as partners and share responsibility for promoting positive and consistent outcomes related to a child's academic, behavioral, and socio-emotional development. (Sheridan & Kratochwill, 2008, p. 25)

CBC considers school, family, and, frequently, community factors, and is therefore an ecologically based model (i.e., one that considers person–environment interactions in understanding development and behavior; Bronfenbrenner, 1977).

CBC often assumes that a child's problem presents similarly both in school and at home. Thus, a CBC consultant typically progresses through a variation of the four stages of BC (Bergan & Kratochwill, 1990) with the child's teacher(s) and parent(s) concurrently. For instance, if a child's problem behavior is identified as frequent tantrums, the consultant would need to identify how specifically the behavior presents itself at school and home (e.g., examine the frequency, duration, and/or intensity of the behavior), develop goals for improvement in each setting, select and help to implement an EBI in each setting, and evaluate its impact (Sheridan & Kratochwill, 2008). CBC is an excellent example of how school psychologists can coordinate their efforts as consultants to educators, families, and systems.

Organization Development Consultation

Consultation in schools that is intended to have an impact on large groups, targeted layers within a school, an entire school, or a school system (e.g., school district) falls into the category of *organization development consultation* (ODC). Some school psychologists utilize ODC because it has the clear advantage of allowing them to share their skills and knowledge with a greater number of individuals and, therefore, to extend their impact. Contemporary examples of situations in which ODC might be applied in schools include systems-level efforts to implement MTSS (Forman & Crystal, 2015), school-wide mental health screening systems (Dowdy et al., 2015), and school-wide restorative justice interventions (Mayworm et al., 2016).

ODC draws on many different theoretical perspectives, ranging from general systems theory (von Bertalanffy, 1968) to theories specifically developed for use in human services organizations (e.g., French & Bell, 1999). In general, ODC lacks a unified identity and theoretical basis (Illback, 2014). However, the overall approach to ODC involves a planned, systemic process of introducing new principles and practices into an organization with the goal of effecting organizational improvement, effectiveness, and competence (Castillo & Curtis, 2014).

Despite the promise of ODC for effecting change across systems, the typical school psychologist reports spending only 6% of their time on organizational/system-focused consultation (Castillo et al., 2012). We believe school psychologists could increase their impact on positive outcomes for children if they devoted more time to facilitating systems-level change; however, role and setting constraints mentioned in earlier chapters may limit opportunities to engage in such activities.

SOCIAL JUSTICE CONNECTIONS

What is advocacy consultation?

In addition to the consultation models previously described, another model holds promise for practitioners who are interested in advancing a social justice agenda: **advocacy consultation** (AC; Conoley, 1981; Conoley & Conoley, 1982). An advocacy consultant is someone who partners with disenfranchised individuals and groups, engaging in roles such as activist, organizer, negotiator, and, of course, advocate. A common role of an advocacy consultant in schools is to assist parents of children who have been placed in, or are being considered for, special education programming.

An example of AC is as follows: A consultant (Dr. Smith) arrives at a school-based meeting to help the mother (Ms. Gonzalez) of a second-grade student (Guillermo) who has a moderate hearing impairment. Ms. Gonzalez believes that Guillermo has not been

(continued)

> **SOCIAL JUSTICE CONNECTIONS (*continued*)**
>
> receiving adequate help from the school community to address specific goals in his Individualized Education Program (IEP), but his teachers have decided Guillermo will be retained next year due to low achievement scores. Operating within the role of advocacy consultant, Dr. Smith partners with the Gonzalez family to seek clarification, define/elaborate on the problem, reinforce the requirements of federal law, engage in problem-solving, and generate shared goals for moving forward.
>
> According to Conoley and Conoley (1982), advocacy consultants need to develop additional knowledge and skills in the areas of law, community organization, event organization, media utilization, negotiation, and parent partnerships, above and beyond the expected skill set possessed by other human services consultants. At this time, the empirical examination of and support for AC is still emerging within the consultation literature. However, the goals and core tenets of AC render it a promising form of service delivery that warrants further investigation.

A complementary way to look at school consultation is to consider some modalities of practice that are not uniquely linked to a particular theoretical base. Next, we consider the modalities of team-based consultation and teleconsultation.

Team-Based Consultation

If an advantage of consultation is that it increases the consultant's sphere of influence to help more clients, why not meet with multiple consultees simultaneously? This reasoning is foundational to team-based consultation. Notably, an interest in conducting group-based consultation dates back nearly 60 years (e.g., Altrocchi et al., 1965). Within K–12 education generally and school psychology specifically, team-based consultation was evident in prereferral intervention teams popular in the 1980s and 1990s, and it remains present in MTSS approaches implemented currently. In fact, much of consultation in the schools today occurs in the context of teams rather than the traditional consultant/consultee dyad (Dowd-Eagle & Eagle, 2014).

Newman and Morrison (2019) noted the importance of ***team-based consultation*** as it commonly plays out in the practice of MTSS. Recall from Chapter 8 that MTSS is built around providing a continuum of EBIs, including low-intensity universal supports for all (Tier 1), targeted interventions for students at-risk or with mild to moderate problems (Tier 2), and intensive, individualized interventions for students with moderate to severe problems (Tier 3). Given this backdrop, Newman and Morrison suggested how a consultant may function within the following nested team structures to implement MTSS:

1. *Individual student-level and problem-solving teams*—At this level, a school psychologist may consult with individual students and teachers or address student-level problems as a member of a school-based problem-solving team.
2. *Classroom and grade-level teams*—A school psychologist may serve on and consult with teams comprised of educational personnel (e.g., teachers, instructional assistants, support staff) who work in the same classroom or at the same grade level.
3. *School leadership teams*—A school psychologist may serve on and consult with administrators and other leaders on building-level teams that oversee, implement, and evaluate MTSS services.
4. *School district leadership teams*—A school psychologist may consult with higher-level administrators who sanction and maintain the overall integrity of MTSS services at the district level.

The preceding description suggests that any of the consultation models presented previously could be adapted for use with teams (though some models may be more appropriate for some teams than others). The description also hints at the complexity of working with multiple consultees simultaneously to provide effective team-based consultation. Noting this complexity, Dowd-Eagle and Eagle (2014) concluded that there is a "need for research targeting efficient, sustainable, and consistently applied team-based problem-solving models to ensure decisions made within the context of teams are valid" (p. 468).

Teleconsultation

In contrast to team-based consultation, which has been practiced for decades, teleconsultation is a relatively new development that emerged around 2008. *Teleconsultation* may be defined as the process of providing consultative services through telecommunication technology (e.g., videoconferencing, telepresence robots; King et al., 2022). Teleconsultation is made possible due to advances in videoconferencing technology and collaboration software; increasing availability of high-bandwidth internet connections; and access to smartphones, tablets, and desktop computers. A clear advantage of teleconsultation is that it provides school consultants with the ability to interact with teachers and students who are in remote and/or underserved schools (Fischer et al., 2018). Consultants with long commutes also can benefit from teleconsultation due to reduced travel time and the potential to serve a greater number of teachers and students. Teleconsultation has been in use for quite some time now; however, the coronavirus 2019 global pandemic's broad impact on schools and schooling (e.g., Nickerson & Sulkowski, 2021) has greatly raised awareness of its utility.

School psychologists have effectively used teleconsultation with teachers and paraprofessionals in special and general education settings (Kennedy, Rowely, Crosby, & Fischer, 2021). For example, early teleconsultation studies focused primarily on improving outcomes for students with disabilities by training teachers to conduct behavioral assessment procedures (e.g., functional behavior assessments) to inform individualized intervention plans (e.g., Frieder et al., 2009; Gibson et al., 2010; Machalicek et al., 2009). More recently, investigations that applied problem-solving consultation models have shown teleconsultation to be effective at reducing body rocking and disruptive behavior as well as increasing on-task behavior (Bice-Urbach & Kratochwill, 2016; Fischer et al., 2017). Moreover, several studies have found that teachers who participate in teleconsultation find it to be an acceptable modality for receiving consultation services (e.g., Bice-Urbach & Kratochwill, 2016; Fischer et al., 2017).

Whereas the preceding studies used videoconferencing as the modality to conduct teleconsultation, some of the most recent research in this area has augmented videoconferencing with telepresence robots. For instance, Fischer, Bloomfield, and colleagues (2019) implemented problem-solving teleconsultation to address noncompliance in three students receiving special education services. Fischer et al. used a telepresence robot (i.e., a computer tablet on a mobile device controlled remotely) to conduct interviews, observe classrooms, and collect data. With a telepresence robot, consultants were not only able to interact with consultees but also to dynamically move and look around the environment from a distance. The study results showed an increase in student compliance with teacher instructions, moderate levels of treatment integrity, and high ratings of acceptability of the process and technology associated with teleconsultation.

It is clear that teleconsultation in schools has arrived and is here to stay. Importantly, school psychologists who choose this modality of consultation must be well versed in related legal and ethical issues and take appropriate steps to ensure student confidentiality and maintain data security. This is particularly important for teleconsultants' compliance with the provisions of legislation such as the Family Educational Rights and Privacy Act (FERPA; 1974; see also Chapter 5).

CONSULTATION AS A PROBLEM-SOLVING PROCESS

To reinforce an earlier point, "[p]roblem-solving is the essence of consultation" (Zins & Erchul, 2002, p. 631). Given this assumption, the consultative process incorporates a sequence of steps that exemplify problem-solving. Similar to the problem-solving process described in Chapter 8, this sequence of steps focuses on identifying, analyzing, and addressing problems in a data-driven manner. Specifically, the steps are as follows: (a) relationship development, (b) identification and analysis of the problem, (c) intervention development/selection, (d) intervention implementation, (e) evaluation of intervention effectiveness, and (f) follow-up (Erchul & Martens, 2012). Furthermore, it is necessary for the school psychologist to engage in multiple levels of problem analysis and intervention development during consultation. Because consultation is an indirect service (i.e., focused on delivering services to clients through an intermediary), it requires that changes be achieved on more than just the individual student level. Accordingly, it is essential to monitor the link between changes in the environment or in teachers' behavior and changes in the target student(s) (Truscott et al., 2012). Finally, it should be noted that, although consultation in schools can involve multiple consultants, consultees, and organizational levels, the primary focus here is on the work and contributions of individual consultants, consultees, and students. The following section contains some content presented previously (i.e., Erchul & Fischer, 2018; Erchul & Martens, 2012; Erchul & Young, 2014; Zins & Erchul, 2002).

Relationship Building/Establishing a Cooperative Partnership

Prerequisites to effective problem-solving within consultation include refined *interpersonal skills* and the development of a trusting, cooperative partnership. Relationship building is an essential element of consultation, beginning with initial entry into the school and/or classroom and continuing throughout the process. When a school psychologist consultant and a consultee meet initially, each participant tries to become better acquainted with the other, and together they strive to establish an atmosphere of mutual respect and trust. They discuss and negotiate a working contract, which is a mutually agreed-upon oral or written understanding of what will happen during consultation. The contract minimally specifies the roles and responsibilities of each participant, the expected activities, and the anticipated timeline for the consultation (Zins & Erchul, 2002). Additional interpersonal skills that are critical throughout consultation include active listening (e.g., acknowledging, reflecting, paraphrasing, summarizing, clarifying, elaborating) and giving/receiving feedback (Conoley & Conoley, 1982).

Identifying and Clarifying the Problem

Once problem-solving begins, the first activity is to identify or clarify the problem and seek agreement on the definition of the problem (Bergan & Kratochwill, 1990). To the greatest extent possible, problems should be defined in clear, concise, objective, and measurable terms so that progress toward solving them can be assessed. It is an unfortunate reality that consultees do not always have clear conceptualizations of problems and, therefore, may describe a problem initially in vague, global terms. Through the consultant's careful questioning and active listening, however, many aspects of the problem can be discussed and subsequently defined in clearer terms. Once a problem is defined satisfactorily, participants can then generate specific goals to address it.

If accurate problem identification does not occur, effort may be wasted in attempts to solve the wrong problem. Conversely, once a problem is identified accurately, this action meets the necessary, but not always the sufficient, conditions of solving a problem or promoting some desired goal (Zins & Erchul, 2002).

Analyzing the Problem

During this phase, the consultant and consultee try to understand the forces that are causing and maintaining the problem as well as those resources that may be applied to solve it. They attempt to develop the best possible hypotheses about why the problem exists, collect baseline data (e.g., frequency, duration, and intensity), and identify antecedent and consequent events that may be contributing to it. Taking a broader ecological systems perspective is important because problems usually are the result of a complex interaction of multiple factors. Unless a larger array of factors is considered, it is likely that an overly simplistic and unsuccessful solution will be implemented. All resources that potentially could be utilized in the development and implementation of interventions should be explored at this step. These considerations include student strengths, system or setting characteristics that help the student be successful in other situations, and material and human resources (e.g., teachers, parents, peer and volunteer tutors, and community support systems) available for intervention (Zins & Erchul, 2002).

During problem analysis, it has become increasingly important and common for school psychology consultants to employ curriculum-based measurement (described in Chapter 9), functional behavior assessment (described in Chapter 10), and/or brief experimental analysis, rather than to depend largely on the verbal reports and observations of consultees (Erchul & Young, 2014). *Brief experimental analysis* refers to the systematic process of quickly assessing the relative effects of two or more interventions on a target behavior (e.g., computational or oral reading fluency) so as to determine which approach is likely to be most successful (Burns & Wagner, 2008). These procedures allow the consultant and/or consultee to utilize direct measures of skill and intervention response to inform decision-making.

Selecting an Intervention

Moving toward problem resolution, it is important to carefully consider appropriate EBIs. Resources such as comprehensive reviews in scientific journals, *What Works Clearinghouse*, *Intervention Central*, and the Collaborative for Academic, Social, and Emotional Learning (CASEL) are helpful in locating EBIs. Once a list of suitable EBIs is generated, participants need to assess each option regarding its feasibility, acceptability, cost, likelihood of success, consequences, and so forth. In an earlier time, an intervention's *acceptability* (i.e., judgments about whether a treatment is fair, reasonable, or intrusive) was perhaps the top consideration in intervention selection. However, because the hypothesized positive association between acceptability and implementation has not been demonstrated consistently in research (Noell & Gansle, 2014), factors related to intervention effectiveness are now a much higher priority (Erchul & Young, 2014).

A key element in the intervention selection and implementation process is obtaining the consultee's buy-in (i.e., commitment to implementing an EBI). Because a consultant holds no administrative authority over a consultee (Martin, 1978), a consultant cannot simply "tell the consultee what to do" and expect positive results (Erchul & Martens, 2012). Instead, persuasive strategies—drawn, for example, from Raven's (1993) Power/Interaction Model of Interpersonal Influence—may be used to increase consultee buy-in. In particular, social influence strategies stemming from the noncoercive, soft bases of expert power and referent power may be effective in achieving consultee behavior change (Kennedy, Rowley, & Crosby, 2021). *Expert power* depends on a consultee's positive perception of the consultant's knowledge and expertise; based on this perception, the consultee may be more willing to commit to intervention selection and implementation. *Referent power* hinges on a consultee's favorable identification with the consultant (e.g., likeability);

given this identification, the consultee may be more willing to follow through with intervention implementation (Erchul et al., 2014). Owens et al. (2017) documented the significance of expert and referent power by showing that teachers who needed classroom management consultation and who reported being influenced by soft power bases exhibited better management skills following consultation than other teachers who reported not being influenced by soft bases.

Clarifying Implementation Procedures and Responsibilities

A common obstacle to achieving success in consultation is that intervention implementation procedures are not always specified in sufficient detail. Subsequently, the intervention may be carried out inconsistently. In these situations, even a highly recommended EBI may fail to produce the desired results. To remedy this situation, it is advised that the consultant develop a written plan of action that clearly specifies the steps of the intervention, plans for follow-up after intervention implementation is complete, and strategies for monitoring the implementation process. In particular, there should be a plan to monitor treatment integrity (Sanetti & Kratochwill, 2014), also known as *intervention fidelity*, and defined as the degree to which the intervention has been implemented as planned (Noell & Gansle, 2014). Finally, it is advised that the consultant model the intervention for consultees and/or directly train them on implementation procedures (Erchul & Young, 2014).

Implementing the Intervention

The selected EBI now can be implemented according to the plans and timelines developed. Although the consultee is typically responsible for intervention implementation, consultants need to be available to assist in the event that unforeseen problems arise or there are any changes in setting or context. Consultants provide ongoing feedback and support for consultees' efforts (especially in the early stages of intervention, when client improvement may not be particularly discernible). Additionally, the consultant facilitates the assessment of intervention integrity using strategies such as direct observation, self-report, and/or reviews of permanent products (e.g., student work products). It is well established that treatment integrity can improve considerably when consultants give performance feedback (e.g., Sanetti et al., 2013). Moreover, the consistency of this effect appears to be strengthened when data are presented to consultees in graph formats (Noell & Gansle, 2014).

Evaluating Intervention Effectiveness and Follow-Up

The evaluation and follow-up phase involves several interrelated tasks, including determining intervention effectiveness and facilitating the client's generalization of new skills. First, the same data collection procedures that were initially used to measure the client's baseline functioning typically are used again at the end of the intervention to facilitate a pre/post (i.e., before and after) comparison. The results of this evaluation likely will indicate one of two outcomes: (a) the intervention resulted in the client's attainment of desired goals, thereby indicating that follow-up monitoring and/or generalization are needed; or (b) the intended outcomes were not entirely attained, suggesting the need to cycle back through earlier steps of the problem-solving process (Zins & Erchul, 2002).

During this final phase of the consultation process, facilitating client generalization is important. In consultation, *generalization* refers to the student's application of a new skill or behavior learned in one context to other, different contexts. For example, consider a student who receives an intervention designed to increase appropriate class participatory behaviors (e.g., hand raising). This student receives the intervention during math class only. If, during or following the intervention, the student demonstrated the target behavior (i.e., hand raising) during other classes (e.g., science or physical education), they would be generalizing the learned behavior.

Generalization of new skills and behaviors may be facilitated in several ways. First, when possible, the intervention should take place in several settings using multiple tasks and teachers. Second, students (and, when appropriate, parents) should assume an active role in intervention selection and implementation, and efforts should be made to assist them in understanding the intervention's purpose and relevance to their own lives. Moreover, opportunities to confront and deal positively with failure or mistakes should be incorporated into intervention procedures (Zins & Erchul, 2002).

It is important to remember that following the aforementioned problem-solving steps during consultation is often necessary but is rarely sufficient for ensuring favorable outcomes. Effective consultants need not only to include key ingredients in the consultation process (e.g., problem-solving stages) but also to maintain open, collegial, and culturally sensitive consultative relationships. Next, we turn our attention to outcomes of school consultation.

EFFECTIVENESS OF CONSULTATION

Does consultation work? In other words, is there empirical evidence indicating that positive outcomes result when a school psychologist consults with one or more consultees, who then work directly with one or more clients? Before addressing this fundamental question, it is important to step back and recognize that consultation research is difficult to conduct and, unfortunately, many studies are conceptually and methodologically flawed (Erchul & Sheridan, 2014). In other words, because consultation reflects an effort to help a third party (e.g., student client) through the assistance of a second party (e.g., teacher consultee), it often is not possible to determine whether client changes have resulted from consultant efforts or other variables. Despite these shortcomings, evidence from literature reviews, meta-analyses, and randomized controlled trial research on consultation indicates it often results in improved outcomes for consultee and client participants.

With respect to literature reviews, Sheridan et al. (1996) completed a thorough analysis of 46 school consultation outcome studies published between 1985 and 1995. They found that consultation resulted in positive effects in 67% of the studies reviewed, while 28% resulted in neutral effects and 5% resulted in negative effects. Moreover, meta-analytic research has yielded positive results in regard to consultation in the school setting. A *meta-analysis* is a study that employs a quantitative method for summarizing the effects of a treatment across large numbers of original research studies that investigated that treatment. Meta-analyses are especially useful for evaluating treatment outcomes, because they allow for the summarization of results across a number of studies, many of which may have divergent findings. Often, results are summarized in the form of an *effect size*, or standardized measure of the magnitude of an effect (What Works Clearinghouse, 2017). With respect to consultation research, Sibley (1986, reported in Gresham & Noell, 1993) found large before–after effect sizes for consultees and even larger effect sizes for clients across 63 studies of school consultation. Smith et al. (2021) conducted a meta-analysis of "consultation-based family-school engagement" (considered here as CBC but with a broader focus). They found significant client effects of consultation on children's social–behavioral competence, mental health, and academic achievement. Significant consultee effects for consultation on parent practices, parent attitudes, and relational outcomes also were revealed.

Recall from Chapter 8 that randomized controlled trials (RCTs) are considered the "gold standard" of treatment research, as they rely on random assignment of participants to conditions and pay careful attention to experimental control. RCTs of school consultation (e.g., Cappella et al., 2012; Sheridan et al., 2017) have produced positive outcomes, and these types of studies, which employ a more rigorous methodology, support the use of consultation as an evidence-based practice in schools (Erchul & Sheridan, 2014). Taken together, our conclusion is that outcome research on consultation as conducted by school psychologists over many decades has documented its overall effectiveness.

MULTICULTURAL CONSIDERATIONS

As described in Chapter 1, before the term *social justice* was commonly found in the school psychology literature, a similar, though broader, term used by scholars was *multiculturalism*. Several definitions of *multiculturalism* have been offered throughout this book, and we offer another, namely: "a general commitment to recognizing, understanding, and valuing cultural diversity, as well as striving to promote equal opportunities for all individuals" (Parker et al., 2020, p. 121). There is no doubt that multicultural elements are critical to consider within the realm of school psychology, and particularly within the consultant role. For example, it is essential for a consultant to acknowledge the powerful influence of culture in its many forms (e.g., race, ethnicity, language, socioeconomic status, sexual orientation, gender, age, religious/spiritual beliefs) and to realize the potential impact of these factors on the consultative process (Erchul & Young, 2014).

We do not consider *multicultural consultation* to be a separate model of consultation but rather an essential element of the models and modalities of consultation described earlier. This perspective underscores the notion that cultural variables are central aspects of the consultation process and, therefore, must be given appropriate attention (Ingraham, 2014). Cultural differences may exist between and among the consultant, consultee, and client, and culture can have a significant influence on environmental and interpersonal dynamics (e.g., among family, classroom, school, community). Therefore, it is important for a consultant to be able to discern the extent to which cultural variables are affecting significant processes and outcomes of consultation and to provide responsive services to achieve desired results. Similarly, a consultant must be able to distinguish between the impact of individual differences and the effects of group cultural variables (Erchul & Young, 2014).

Ingraham's (2000) multicultural consultation framework describes some aspirational competencies for understanding and applying multicultural considerations in consultation. First, as described in Chapter 3, consultants must have some personal awareness of their own cultural background, worldview, and biases. The consultant must also be knowledgeable about the cultural context in which the consultative process will be situated and understand how interpersonal and environmental factors will affect relationships among participants and intervention implementation. Specifically, consultants should consider how values, norms, and traditions permeate relationships and impact consultative dynamics. This often involves reflecting on how privilege and oppression can moderate power dynamics among students, families, and school personnel.

Second, consultants should consider not only their own awareness of personal and contextual variables, but also the consultee's awareness. The consultation process offers an important opportunity to improve the consultee's knowledge, skills, objectivity, and self-confidence in relation to multicultural service delivery. In the consultation relationship, *objectivity* refers to the perception of client problems in a manner that is free from judgment, bias, and other psychological interference. Lack of objectivity on the part of the consultee—sometimes the result of the consultee's cultural biases—may be a barrier to accurately defining and addressing client problems through consultation (Caplan, 1970). When appropriate, the consultant should strive to improve the consultee's understanding of diversity and appreciation of multiculturalism (Erchul & Young, 2014).

SOCIAL JUSTICE IN CONSULTATION: TWO STUDIES

Bell (2013) defined *social justice* as "the full and equal participation of all groups in a society that is mutually shaped to meet their needs" (p. 21). This book promotes a social justice perspective, and the present chapter has attempted to describe and apply related principles to the practice of school consultation. To do so, we refer to a concept previously introduced in Chapter 3, *restorative justice* (RJ). Recall that RJ:

> is a broad term that encompasses a growing social movement to institutionalize non-punitive, relationship-centered approaches for avoiding and addressing harm, responding to violations of legal and human rights, and collaboratively solving problems.... In the school setting, RJ often serves as an alternative to traditional discipline, particularly exclusionary disciplinary actions such as suspension or expulsion. RJ proponents often turn to restorative practices out of concern that exclusionary disciplinary actions may be associated with harmful consequences for children. (Fronius et al., 2019, p. 1)

Understandably, restorative justice is a complex concept that defies a universally accepted definition (Fronius et al., 2019). However, one strength of RJ appears to be its potential to address racial inequity issues in schools (e.g., disproportionate exclusionary discipline practices across race; Song & Swearer, 2016). In this final section of the chapter, we examine two empirical studies that demonstrate how consultants acted in the service of restorative justice and, more broadly, social justice.

The first investigation (Ingraham et al., 2016) focused on developing, implementing, and evaluating the impact of RJ practices in a culturally and linguistically diverse pre-K–fifth-grade elementary school. The targeted school was located in an urban community of San Diego that had very high rates of violence, poverty, domestic violence, trauma, and immigration. Importantly, 100% of enrolled students qualified for compensatory education (Title I services, which are designed to support students from economically marginalized backgrounds).

Across a 3-year period Ingraham et al. (2016) employed a problem-solving approach and emphasized the importance of developing communication skills, creating positive relationships, improving school climate, and building empathy between and among the teachers, staff, students, families, and members of the community associated with the school. Some specific RJ activities that were introduced included classroom discussion circles, modeling of conflict mediation, and practice in repairing previous harm done. Consultants made conscious efforts to reduce power differentials among parties, use strengths-based approaches to show respect for participants' expertise and assets, and recognize and respect cultural values and family obligations. As a part of the overall process, the researchers also expended considerable effort in having vested partners identify and personalize goals, design and implement specific interventions, and assess outcomes.

In Ingraham et al.'s (2016) mixed method research design, participant data were collected mainly through focus groups, surveys, and direct observation. Comparing project year 1 to year 3, some key quantitative findings included: (a) student referrals to the principal's office for behavior problems decreased by 85%; (b) the percentage of parents concerned about their children graduating decreased from 67% to 47%; and (c) parent and community engagement increased. Important qualitative results included: (a) teachers expressing surprise over students' depth of understanding and endorsement of an RJ philosophy; and (b) parents raising questions about their own discipline/punishment practices, with some wanting to learn how to eliminate intergenerational patterns of violence.

The second study (McIntyre et al., 2022) is remarkable because consultants not only served Latinx consultees in their native Spanish language but also delivered their services remotely in a group format via teleconsultation (due to the coronavirus 2019 pandemic, which shut down U.S. schools beginning in March 2020). Before describing this study, however, we must clarify that McIntyre et al. acted as behavioral parent trainers rather than consultants per se (although the lines between consultation and education/training are often blurred; Gallessich, 1982). Therefore, unlike some other examples of school consultation described earlier, parents rather than teachers were the consultees in this study.

McIntyre et al. (2022) provided group-based behavioral parent training (BPT) across 10 sessions to 42 monolingual Spanish-speaking Latinx parents who had preschool children with documented developmental delays. The children exhibited delays in physical, cognitive, communication, social, emotional, and/or adaptive development, and about half also qualified for an autism diagnosis. The BPT was based on the Incredible Years Parent Training (Webster-Stratton, 2001) and emphasized skill building in the activities of play, praise, rewards, limit setting, and handling challenging behaviors. Operationalizing teleconsultation using Zoom Video Communications, two group leaders facilitated the sessions entirely in Spanish and incorporated discussion, modeling, and feedback techniques. A variety of implementation outcomes (Proctor et al., 2011) suggested that the effort was successful in regard to its acceptability, adoption, appropriateness, feasibility, treatment fidelity, and implementation cost. Overall, this study represents an outstanding example of delivering family-centered interventions to support students from traditionally marginalized backgrounds.

Taken together, these studies show us that social justice-oriented consultants need to consider the larger systems of support for the students they serve. Consultants also should engage caregivers and educators in cooperative partnerships to support all students, particularly those from disadvantaged backgrounds.

SUMMARY AND CONCLUSIONS

This chapter emphasized the importance of consultation in school psychology by providing definitions of fundamental concepts, introducing conceptual models and modalities of practice, delineating the steps of a problem-solving approach to consultation, reviewing evidence of the effectiveness of consultation, and considering how multicultural and social justice issues frame contemporary practice. One clear message is that consultation provides a vehicle for school psychologists to address client problems by working with consultees to select, implement, and evaluate EBIs. Another message is that school psychologists, acting in a consultant role, are uniquely positioned to serve as agents of social justice. When knowledgeable about foundational aspects of the consultation role, future school psychologists will be better able to serve all children, educators, and caregivers.

DISCUSSION QUESTIONS

1. How does consultation differ from traditional direct service delivery models, and what are the benefits of working in a consultant role?
2. How are the various consultation models and modalities described in this chapter similar? How are they different?
3. Why does consultation lend itself well to a problem-solving framework?
4. Which interpersonal skills does a school consultant need to be effective?
5. Recall the discussion of legal and ethical principles presented in Chapter 5. Which ethical and legal issues may be associated with the use of consultation?

RECOMMENDED READINGS

Crothers, L. M., Hughes, T. L., Kolbert, J. B., & Schmitt, A. J. (2020). *Theory and cases in school-based consultation: A resource for school psychologists, school counselors, special educators, and other mental health professionals* (2nd ed.). Routledge.

Erchul, W. P., & Martens, B. K. (2012). *School consultation: Conceptual and empirical bases of practice* (3rd ed.). Springer.

Fischer, A. J., Collins, T. A., Dart, E. H., & Radley, K. C. (Eds.). (2019). *Technology applications in school psychology consultation, supervision, and training*. Routledge.

King, H. C., Bloomfield, B. S., Wu, S., & Fischer, A. J. (2022). A systematic review of school teleconsultation: Implications for research and practice. *School Psychology Review, 51*(2), 237–256. https://doi.org/10.1080/2372966X.2021.1894478

Miranda, A. H. (Ed.). (2016). *Consultation across cultural contexts: Consultee-centered case studies*. Routledge.

A robust set of instructor resources designed to supplement this text is located at http://connect.springerpub.com/content/book/978-0-8261-6344-8. Qualifying instructors may request access by emailing textbook@springerpub.com.

REFERENCES

Altrocchi, J., Spielberger, C. D., & Eisendorfer, C. (1965). Mental health consultation with groups. *Community Mental Health Journal, 1*, 127–134. https://doi.org/10.1007/BF01435201

Bell, L. A. (2013). Theoretical foundations. In M. Adams, W. J. Blumenfeld, C. Castañeda, H. W. Hackman, M. L. Peters, & X. Zúñiga (Eds.), *Readings for diversity and social justice* (3rd ed., pp. 21–26). Routledge.

Bergan, J. R., & Kratochwill, T. R. (1990). *Behavioral consultation and therapy*. Plenum.

Bice-Urbach, B., & Kratochwill, T. R. (2016). Teleconsultation: The use of technology to improve evidence-based practices in rural communities. *Journal of School Psychology, 56*, 27–43. https://doi.org/10.1016/j.jsp.2016.02.001

Bronfenbrenner, U. (1977). Toward an experimental ecology of human development. *American Psychologist, 32*, 513–531. https://doi.org/10.1037/0003-066X.32.7.513

Burns, M. K., & Wagner, D. (2008). Determining an effective intervention within a brief experimental analysis for reading: A meta-analytic review. *School Psychology Review, 37*, 126–136. https://doi.org/10.1080/02796015.2008.12087913

Caplan, G. (1970). *The theory and practice of mental health consultation*. Basic Books.

Caplan, G., & Caplan, R. B. (1999). *Mental health consultation and collaboration*. Waveland Press.

Cappella, E., Hamre, B. K., Kim, H. Y., Henry, D. B., Frazier, S. L., Atkins, M. S., & Schoenwald, S. K. (2012). Teacher consultation and coaching within mental health practice: Classroom and child effects in urban elementary schools. *Journal of Consulting and Clinical Psychology, 80*, 597–610. https://doi.org/10.1037/a0027725

Castillo, J. M., & Curtis, M. J. (2014). Best practices in systems-level change. In P. L. Harrison & A. Thomas (Eds.), *Best practices in school psychology—6: Systems-level services* (pp. 11–28). National Association of School Psychologists.

Castillo, J. M., Curtis, M. J., & Gelley, C. D. (2012). School psychology 2010: Part 2: School psychologists' professional practices and implications for the field. *Communiqué, 40*(8), 4–6. https://www.nasponline.org/publications/periodicals/communique/issues/volume-40-issue-8

Conoley, J. C. (1981). Advocacy consultation: Promises and problems. In J. C. Conoley (Ed.), *Consultation in schools: Theory, research, procedures* (pp. 157–178). Academic Press.

Conoley, J. C., & Conoley, C. W. (1982). *School consultation: A guide to practice and training*. Pergamon.

Dowd-Eagle, S., & Eagle, J. (2014). Team-based school consultation. In W. P. Erchul & S. M. Sheridan (Eds.), *Handbook of research in school consultation* (2nd ed., pp. 450–472). Routledge.

Dowdy, E., Furlong, M., Raines, T. C., Bovery, B., Kauffman, B., Kamphaus, R. W., Dever, B. V., Price, M., & Murdock, J. (2015). Enhancing school-based mental health services with a preventive and promotive approach to universal screening for complete mental health. *Journal of Educational and Psychological Consultation, 25*, 178–197. https://doi.org/10.1080/10474412.2014.929951

Erchul, W. P. (2009). Gerald Caplan: A tribute to the originator of mental health consultation. *Journal of Educational and Psychological Consultation, 19*, 95–105. https://doi.org/10.1080/10474410902888418

Erchul, W. P., & Fischer, A. J. (2018). Consultation. In S. L. Grapin & J. H. Kranzler (Eds.), *School psychology: Professional issues and practices* (pp. 181–195). Springer Publishing Company.

Erchul, W. P., Grissom, P. F., Getty, K. C., & Bennett, M. S. (2014). Researching interpersonal influence within school consultation: Social power base and relational communication perspectives. In W. P. Erchul & S. M. Sheridan (Eds.), *Handbook of research in school consultation* (2nd ed., pp. 349–385). Routledge.

Erchul, W. P., & Martens, B. K. (2012). *School consultation: Conceptual and empirical bases of practice* (3rd ed.). Springer.

Erchul, W. P., & Sheridan, S. M. (2014). Overview: The state of scientific research in school consultation. In W. P. Erchul & S. M. Sheridan (Eds.), *Handbook of research in school consultation* (2nd ed., pp. 3–17). Routledge.

Erchul, W. P., & Ward, C. S. (2016). Problem-solving consultation. In S. R. Jimerson, M. K. Burns, & A. M. VanDerHeyden (Eds.), *Handbook of response to intervention: The science and practice of multi-tiered systems of support* (2nd ed., pp. 73–86). Springer. https://doi.org/10.1007/978-1-4899-7568-3_6

Erchul, W. P., & Young, H. L. (2014). Best practices in school consultation. In A. Thomas & P. L. Harrison (Eds.), *Best practices in school psychology—6: Data-based and collaborative decision making* (pp. 449–460). National Association of School Psychologists.

Family Educational Rights and Privacy Act. (1974). *Family Educational Rights and Privacy Act of 1974*, 20 U.S.C. § 1232g.

Fischer, A. J., Bloomfield, B. S., Clark, R. R., McClelland, A. L., Thompson, M. C., & Erchul, W. P. (2019). Increasing student compliance with teacher instructions using telepresence robot problem-solving teleconsultation. *International Journal of School & Educational Psychology, 7*, 158–172. https://doi.org/10.1080/21683603.2018.1470948

Fischer, A. J., Dart, E. H., Radley, K. C., Richardson, D., Clark, R., & Wimberly, J. (2017). An evaluation of the effectiveness and acceptability of teleconsultation. *Journal of Educational and Psychological Consultation, 27*(4), 437–458. https://doi.org/10.1080/10474412.2016.1235978

Fischer, A. J., Erchul, W. P., & Schultz, B. K. (2018). Teleconsultation as the new frontier in educational and psychological consultation [Special issue]. *Journal of Educational and Psychological Consultation, 28*(3). https://doi.org/10.1080/10474412.2018.1425880

Forman, S. G., & Crystal, C. D. (2015). Systems consultation for multitiered systems of supports (MTSS): Implementation issues. *Journal of Educational and Psychological Consultation, 25*, 276–285. https://doi.org/10.1080/10474412.2014.963226

Frank, J. L., & Kratochwill, T. R. (2014). School-based problem-solving consultation: Plotting a new course for evidence-based research and practice in consultation. In W. P. Erchul & S. M. Sheridan (Eds.), *Handbook of research in school consultation* (2nd ed., pp. 18–39). Routledge.

French, W., & Bell, C. H. (1999). *Organization development: Behavioral science interventions for organization improvement* (6th ed.). Prentice-Hall.

Frieder, J. E., Peterson, S. M., Woodward, J., Crane, J., & Garner, M. (2009). Teleconsultation in school settings: Linking classroom teachers and behavior analysts through web-based technology. *Behavior Analysis in Practice, 2*, 32–39. https://doi.org/10.1007/BF03391746

Fronius, T., Darling-Hammond, S., Persson, H., Guckenburg, S., Hurley, N., & Petrosino, A. (2019). *Restorative justice in U.S. schools: An updated research review*. WestEd. https://www.wested.org/resources/restorative-justice-in-u-s-schools-an-updated-research-review

Gallessich, J. (1982). *The profession and practice of consultation: A handbook for consultants, trainers of consultants, and consumers of consultation services*. Jossey-Bass.

Gibson, J. L., Pennington, R. C., Stenhoff, D. M., & Hopper, J. S. (2010). Using desktop videoconferencing to deliver interventions to a preschool student with autism. *Topics in Early Childhood Special Education, 29*, 214–225. https://doi.org/10.1177/0271121409352873

Gresham, F. M., & Noell, G. H. (1993). Documenting the effectiveness of consultation outcomes. In J. E. Zins, T. R. Kratochwill, & S. N. Elliott (Eds.), *Handbook of consultation services for children: Applications in educational and clinical settings* (pp. 249–273). Jossey-Bass/Wiley.

Illback, R. J. (2014). Organization development and change facilitation in school settings: Theoretical and empirical foundations. In W. P. Erchul & S. M. Sheridan (Eds.), *Handbook of research in school consultation* (2nd ed., pp. 276–303). Routledge.

Ingraham, C. L. (2000). Consultation through a multicultural lens: Multicultural and cross-cultural consultation in schools. *School Psychology Review, 29*, 320–343. https://doi.org/10.1080/02796015.2000.12086018

Ingraham, C. L. (2014). Studying multicultural aspects of consultation. In W. P. Erchul & S. M. Sheridan (Eds.), *Handbook of research in school consultation* (2nd ed., pp. 323–348). Routledge.

Ingraham, C. L., Hokoda, A., Moehlenbruck, D., Karafin, M., Manzo, C., & Ramírez, D. (2016). Consultation and collaboration to develop and implement restorative practices in a culturally and linguistically diverse elementary school. *Journal of Educational and Psychological Consultation, 26*, 354–384. https://doi.org/10.1080/10474412.2015.1124782

Kennedy, E., Rowley, J., & Crosby, E. (Hosts), & Fischer, A. J. (Guest). (2021, November). *Conversations on consultation: Using teleconsultation to support educators and caregivers* [Audio podcast]. Tavistock and Portman NHS Foundation Trust, Tavistock Centre, London, United Kingdom. https://rss.com/podcasts/conversationsaboutconsultation

Kennedy, E., Rowley, J., & Crosby, E. (Producers). (2021, June). *Conversations about consultation: Relationships, communication and influence in consultation with Professor Bill Erchul* [Audio podcast]. Tavistock and Portman NHS Foundation Trust, Tavistock Centre, London, United Kingdom. https://soundcloud.com/user-136428403/relationships-communication-and-influence-in-consultation

King, H. C., Bloomfield, B. S., Wu, S., & Fischer, A. J. (2022). A systematic review of school teleconsultation: Implications for research and practice. *School Psychology Review, 51*(2), 237–256. https://doi.org/10.1080/2372966X.2021.1894478

Kratochwill, T. R., & Pittman, P. (2002). Defining constructs in consultation: An important training agenda. *Journal of Educational and Psychological Consultation, 13*, 69–95. https://doi.org/10.1207/S1532768XJEPC1301&2_07

Li, C., & Vazquez-Nuttall, E. (2009). School consultants as agents of social justice for multicultural children and families. *Journal of Educational & Psychological Consultation, 19*, 26–44. https://doi.org/10.1080/10474410802462769

Machalicek, W., O'Reilly, M., Chan, J., Lang, R., Rispoli, M., Davis, T., Shogren, K., Sigafoos, J., Lancioni, G., Antonucci, M., Langthorne, P., Andrews, A., & Dkidden, R. (2009). Using videoconferencing to conduct functional analysis of challenging behavior and develop classroom behavioral support plans for students with autism. *Education and Training in Developmental Disabilities, 44*, 207–217. https://www.jstor.org/stable/24233495

Martin, R. (1978). Expert and referent power: A framework for understanding and maximizing consultation effectiveness. *Journal of School Psychology, 16*, 49–55. https://doi.org/10.1016/0022-4405(78)90022-5

Mayworm, A. M., Sharkey, J. D., Hunnicutt, K. L., & Schiedel, K. C. (2016). Teacher consultation to enhance implementation of school-based restorative justice. *Journal of Educational and Psychological Consultation, 26*, 385–412. https://doi.org/10.1080/10474412.2016.1196364

McIntyre, L. L., Neece, C. L., Sanner, C. M., Rodriguez, G., & Safer-Lichtenstein, J. (2022). Telehealth delivery of a behavioral parent training program to Spanish-speaking Latinx parents of young children with developmental delay: Applying an implementation framework approach. *School Psychology Review, 51*(2), 206–220. https://doi.org/10.1080/2372966X.2021.1902749

National Association of School Psychologists. (2020). *Model for comprehensive and integrated school psychological services (NASP Practice Model)*. Author.

Newman, D. S., & Ingraham, C. L. (2017). Consultee-centered consultation: Contemporary perspectives and a framework for the future. *Journal of Educational and Psychological Consultation, 27*, 1–13. https://doi.org/10.1080/10474412.2016.1175307

Newman, D. S., & Morrison, J. Q. (2019). Giving expertise away through consultation: A framework for school psychology. In M. K. Burns (Ed.), *Introduction to school psychology: Controversies and current practice* (pp. 52–70). Oxford University Press.

Nickerson, A. B., & Sulkowski, M. L. (2021). Perspectives on COVID-19: Impacts on children, youth, families, and educators and the roles of human services professionals addressing diverse needs [Special issue]. *School Psychology, 36*(5).

Noell, G. H., & Gansle, K. A. (2014). Research examining the relationships between consultation procedures, treatment integrity, and outcomes. In W. P. Erchul & S. M. Sheridan (Eds.), *Handbook of research in school consultation* (2nd ed., pp. 386–408). Routledge.

Owens, J. S., Schwartz, M. E., Erchul, W. P., Himawan, L., Coles, E. K., Evans, S. W., & Schulte, A. C. (2017). Teacher perceptions of school consultants' social influence: Replication and expansion. *Journal of Educational and Psychological Consultation, 27*(4), 411–436. https://doi.org/10.1080/10474412.2016.1275649

Parker, J. S., Castillo, J. M., Sabnis, S., Daye, J., & Hanson, P. (2020). Culturally responsive consultation among practicing school psychologists. *Journal of Educational and Psychological Consultation, 30*, 119–155. https://doi.org/10.1080/10474412.2019.1680293

Proctor, E., Silmere, H., Raghavan, R., Hovmand, P., Aarons, G., Bunger, A., Griffey, R., & Hensley, M. (2011). Outcomes for implementation research: Conceptual distinctions, measurement challenges, and research agenda. *Administration and Policy in Mental Health, 38*(2), 65–76. https://doi.org/10.1007/s10488-010-0319-7

Raven, B. H. (1993). The bases of power: Origins and recent developments. *Journal of Social Issues, 49*, 227–251. https://doi.org/10.1111/j.1540-4560.1993.tb01191.x

Sanetti, L. M. H., Fallon, L. M., & Collier-Meek, M. A. (2013). Increasing teacher treatment integrity though performance feedback provided by school personnel. *Psychology in the Schools, 50*, 134–150. https://doi.org/10.1002/pits.21664

Sanetti, L. M. H., & Kratochwill, T. R. (Eds.). (2014). *Treatment integrity: A foundation for evidence-based practice in applied psychology*. American Psychological Association.

Sheridan, S. M., & Kratochwill, T. R. (2008). *Conjoint behavioral consultation: Promoting family–school connections and intervention* (2nd ed.). Springer.

Sheridan, S. M., Welch, M., & Orme, S. F. (1996). Is consultation effective? A review of outcome research. *Remedial and Special Education, 17*, 341–354. https://doi.org/10.1177/074193259601700605

Sheridan, S. M., Witte, A. L., Holmes, S. R., Coutts, M. J., Dent, A. L., Kunz, G. M., & Wu, C. (2017). A randomized trial examining the effects of conjoint behavioral consultation in rural schools: Student outcomes and the mediating role of the teacher–parent relationship. *Journal of School Psychology, 61*, 33–53. https://doi.org/10.1016/j.jsp.2016.12.002

Sibley, S. (1986). *A meta-analysis of school consultation research* [Unpublished doctoral dissertation]. Texas Woman's University, Denton, Texas.

Smith, T. E., Holmes, S. R., Sheridan, S. M., Cooper, J. M., Bloomfield, B. S., & Preast, J. L. (2021). The effects of consultation-based family-school engagement on student and parent outcomes: A meta-analysis. *Journal of Educational and Psychological Consultation, 31*(3), 278–306. https://doi.org/10.1080/10474412.2020.1749062

Song, S. Y., & Swearer, S. M. (2016). The cart before the horse: The challenge and promise of restorative social justice consultation in schools. *Journal of Educational and Psychological Consultation, 26*, 313–324. https://doi.org/10.1080/10474412.2016.1246972

Truscott, S. D., Kreskey, D., Bolling, M., Psimas, L., Graybill, E., Albritton, K., & Schwartz, A. (2012). Creating consultee change: A theory-based approach to learning and behavior change processes in school-based consultation. *Consulting Psychology Journal: Practice and Research, 64*, 63–82. https://doi.org/10.1037/a0027997

von Bertalanffy, L. (1968). *General systems theory*. Braziller.

Webster-Stratton, C. (2001). *The incredible years: Parents, teachers, and children training series, leader's guide*. Author.

What Works Clearinghouse. (2017). *Procedures and standards handbook* (3rd ed.). Author.

Zins, J. E., & Erchul, W. P. (2002). Best practices in school consultation. In A. Thomas & J. Grimes (Eds.), *Best practices in school psychology IV* (pp. 625–643). National Association of School Psychologists.

CHAPTER 13

School Violence and Crisis Prevention and Intervention

AMANDA B. NICKERSON

CHAPTER OBJECTIVES

After reading this chapter, you will be able to:

- Define *school violence* and *school crisis*.
- Describe how schools balance physical and psychological safety.
- Describe comprehensive planning for preventing targeted school violence.
- Identify the multitiered crisis intervention approach in the PREPaRE model of crisis prevention and intervention.
- Describe effective approaches for promoting equity in violence and crisis prevention and intervention.

NATIONAL ASSOCIATION OF SCHOOL PSYCHOLOGISTS PRACTICE MODEL CONNECTIONS

Domain 6: Services to Promote Safe and Supportive Schools
Domain 8: Equitable Practices for Diverse Student Populations
Domain 9: Research and Evidence-Based Practice

INTRODUCTION

In order to learn and thrive, students must feel safe in their schools and communities. This chapter begins by defining the concepts of school violence and crisis and situating them under the larger umbrella of school safety. Evidence-based practices in prevention and protection, including the need to balance physical and psychological safety and implement a rational, empirically based threat assessment process to assess and manage threats, are described. The importance of multidisciplinary crisis teams and comprehensive emergency operations plans, and mitigation, response, and recovery from crisis events is explicated, drawing on the National Association of School Psychologists' (NASP's) *PREPaRE* model (Brock et al., 2009, 2016). Notably, PREPaRE is a comprehensive, national training curriculum that trains school-employed mental health professionals and other educators in school crisis prevention and intervention. The PREPaRE acronym refers to the hierarchical and sequential activities involved in crisis prevention and intervention: **P**revent/Prepare for psychological trauma; **R**eaffirm physical health, security, and safety; **E**valuate psychological trauma; **P**rovide interventions (**a**nd) **R**espond to psychological needs; and **E**xamine the effectiveness of prevention and intervention efforts. Approaches that attend to equity are incorporated, as are areas in need of further attention in order to ensure that our schools are safe, welcoming, and inclusive for all students.

DEFINING SCHOOL VIOLENCE AND CRISIS

School violence and *school crisis* are broad, multifaceted terms. The World Health Organization (Krug et al., 2002) has defined *violence* as the intentional use of threatened or actual physical force or power, which results in or is highly likely to result in injury, death, psychological harm, or deprivation. According to the Centers for Disease Control and Prevention (CDC; 2016), **school violence** is youth violence (although it may also involve adults) that occurs at school, including at school-sponsored events as well as on the way to or from school or school-sponsored events. Acts of school violence include physical fights or assault, harassment, bullying, threats of violence or injury, gang violence, weapons and gun violence, or other deliberate means of causing harm to the staff and students (CDC, 2016; NASP, 2015).

School crises are defined as extremely negative events that have the potential to cause physical and/or emotional pain and generate feelings of powerlessness or entrapment; moreover, these events are often unpredictable in terms of how they unfold (Brock et al., 2009, 2016). These include but are not limited to war and terrorism, death (particularly violent or unexpected deaths), natural or human-caused disasters (e.g., earthquakes, chemical spills), severe illness or injury, and threatened death or injury (Brock et al., 2009, 2016).

Comprehensive school safety can be considered the umbrella that encompasses a multilayered approach to preventing, responding to, and recovering from school crises and school violence. Detailing the different areas in which schools must prepare for crisis situations, the U.S. Department of Education (2013) advocates for (a) prevention (capabilities put in place to avoid or stop a threat before an event starts); (b) protection, or efforts to secure against violence and other crises (e.g., supervision of students, locking exterior doors); (c) mitigation to reduce the impact of threats (e.g., lockdown and other emergency protocols); (d) response, which involves saving lives and property as well as meeting basic needs immediately after an event; and (e) recovery to assist schools and communities in rebuilding and restoring physical, health, social, and cultural resources and services.

EVIDENCE-BASED PRACTICE IN SCHOOL VIOLENCE AND CRISIS PREVENTION AND INTERVENTION

Prevention and Protection

Due in part to sensationalized media and reactive political responses to high-profile and tragic violent incidents in schools, a common approach to protecting our nation's schools from violence and crises focuses primarily on target hardening, or enhancing physical security by restricting access, employing more police and security, installing metal detectors, and preparing students and staff to deal directly with armed assailants (Cornell et al., 2021). Over the past two decades, public schools have greatly increased their use of security cameras (19% in 1999–2000 compared to 81% in 2015–2016) and active shooter school plans (79% in 2003–2004 compared to 92% in 2015–2016; Musu et al., 2019). Although physical safety in and around school buildings is important, empirical evidence has found that students, particularly those from racially/ethnically minoritized (REM) backgrounds, may feel less safe when there are more security cameras in the building (Lindstrom Johnson et al., 2018) and a greater presence of school resource officers (Pentek & Eisenberg, 2018; Theriot & Orme, 2016). In addition, schools that use more security are more likely to have students from economically disadvantaged and REM backgrounds, regardless of level of crime in the surrounding neighborhood (Nickerson & Spears, 2007; Servoss, 2017). Thus, from an evidence-based and socially just perspective, best practice in comprehensive prevention and protection efforts necessitates balancing physical and psychological safety (Nickerson et al., 2021).

PREVENTION AND PROTECTION: BALANCING PHYSICAL AND PSYCHOLOGY SAFETY

Crime Prevention Through Environmental Design (CPTED), which emphasizes natural surveillance (e.g., awareness of what is happening in school through adult supervision and monitoring, cameras, and communication), natural access control (e.g., screening visitors and only allowing access to authorized individuals), and territoriality (e.g., shared ownership of schools and grounds by creating and maintaining a clean, welcoming, and positive environment), is a widely recommended approach for schools to guide planning for *physical safety*, or focusing on physical structures and security of the school environment (Sprague & Walker, 2005; U.S. Department of Education, 2013). Research has shown that there is less violent behavior in schools where students perceive the environment as clean and comfortable (Lindstrom Johnson et al., 2017). Schools designed with CPTED principles are also perceived by students to be safer than those without these elements (Lamoreaux & Sulkowski, 2020).

Psychological safety refers to a focus on the emotional and behavioral well-being of students and staff in a school. Of primary concern are school climate and the use of multitiered systems of support (MTSS) as a framework for meeting students' academic, behavioral, and social–emotional needs (Cowan et al., 2013). In relation to behavioral and social–emotional needs, Positive Behavioral Interventions and Supports (PBIS; Sugai & Horner, 2006) and Social and Emotional Learning (SEL; Collaborative for Academic, Social, and Emotional Learning, 2012) are the most widely used and studied approaches. The implementation of PBIS is associated with decreased aggression and related discipline problems, improved school climate (Bradshaw et al., 2010; Caldarella et al., 2011), and reduced discipline referrals and suspensions (Noltemeyer et al., 2019). Schools that implement SEL also have improved student social competence and academic outcomes and decreased disruptive behavior (Durlak et al., 2011; Taylor et al., 2017). Combined PBIS and SEL approaches have been shown to lead to reduced externalizing behaviors and improved mental health outcomes compared to either approach implemented alone (Cook et al., 2015).

THREAT ASSESSMENT

Targeted school violence is preventable through a multidisciplinary threat assessment process that identifies, assesses, and intervenes with students who pose a threat (National Threat Assessment Center [NTAC], 2018, 2021). Table 13.1 provides details about

TABLE 13.1 Comprehensive Planning for Preventing Targeted Violence

Component
Support a positive school climate
Create a multidisciplinary threat assessment team <ul><li>Include administrator, school psychologist, school resource officer, and others (e.g., teachers, counselors, coaches)</li></ul>
Define behaviors that are concerning and prohibited <ul><li>Concerning behaviors occur on a continuum and may require intervention but do not necessarily indicate violence (e.g., withdrawal, grade decline)</li><li>Prohibited behaviors warrant immediate attention (e.g., threatening or engaging in violence, weapon carrying, bullying, criminal behavior)</li></ul>
Establish a central reporting mechanism <ul><li>Mechanism(s) (e.g., online form, dedicated email/phone number; anonymous option) should be monitored for immediate response</li></ul>
Determine criteria for involvement of law enforcement <ul><li>Weapons, violent threats, physical violence, or safety concerns should be reported to law enforcement to support or lead the assessment</li></ul>
Establish threat assessment procedures <ul><li>Clear processes and procedures should guide the threat assessment</li><li>Documents should include report source and contents; information gathered (e.g., interviews with student of concern, potential target(s), witnesses, school records, social media pages, locker search); student of concern behaviors and context; and intervention strategies used</li><li>The threat should be evaluated attending to:<ul><li>Motives and goals of student</li><li>Concerning/threatening communications (written, verbal, electronic)</li><li>Inappropriate interest in school shootings, mass violence, or weapons</li><li>Access to weapons (firearms, explosives, bladed weapons)</li><li>Stressful life events (e.g., losses, setbacks, bullying, breakups)</li><li>Impact of emotional and developmental issues (diagnosed disabilities must be taken into account for context and baseline behavior)</li><li>Hopelessness, desperation, suicidal ideation, and coping strategies</li><li>View of violence as acceptable or necessary to solve problems</li><li>Others' concern about student's statements or behaviors</li><li>Capacity to carry out an attack (e.g., organized thinking, behavior, and resources to plan and execute an attack)</li><li>Planning for an attack (e.g., identified target(s); research on timing, locations, and tactics; acquisition of and practice with weapon)</li><li>Consistency between statements and actions of student</li><li>Protective factors (e.g., positive, trusting relationships)</li></ul></li></ul>
Develop options for managing risk <ul><li>Individualized management plans are based on resources and supports needed depending on results of threat assessment:<ul><li>Monitoring, guidance, and/or counseling</li><li>Disciplinary consequences (recognizing that suspension or expulsion does not eliminate risk and may increase isolation)</li><li>Law enforcement notification</li><li>Improved security for target(s)</li><li>Modification of conditions to reduce likelihood of violence (e.g., remove means, connect student to prosocial mentors and peers)</li><li>Redirection of motives through behavioral intervention, counseling, bullying prevention, or other strategies</li><li>Reduced impact of stressors with resources and supports for coping</li></ul></li></ul>
Train all vested partners (school faculty, staff, and administrators; students; parents; school resource officers; and law enforcement) on the process and their roles

Source: Adapted from National Threat Assessment Center. (2018). *Enhancing school safety using a threat assessment model: An operational guide for preventing targeted school violence.* U.S. Secret Service, Department of Homeland Security. https://www.secretservice.gov/node/4464

comprehensive planning and the threat assessment process for preventing targeted violence. This requires a team approach, including an administrator, a school psychologist, and a school resource officer or other law enforcement professional, with others (e.g., counselor, social worker, general or special education teacher, coach, nurse) included as needed (Louvar Reeves & Brock, 2018). *Threat assessment* is one part of a more comprehensive approach to supporting a positive school climate in which students, teachers, and other community members are trained how to identify risk factors and warning signs and to report these concerns (Louvar Reeves & Brock, 2018; NTAC, 2018). There are multiple protocols for threat assessment, including but not limited to the Structured Assessment of Violence Risk in Youth (SAVRY; Borum et al., 2006); the Comprehensive School Threat Assessment Guidelines (CSTAG), originally known as the Virginia Student Threat Assessment Guidelines (Cornell & Sheras, 2006); and the U.S. Secret Service Model (Vossekuil et al., 2004). None of these are standardized rating scales; rather, they are protocols for gathering information about the level of concern or the extent to which a student poses a threat based on a number of themes (see Table 13.1), such as motives, capability, access, risk factors, and protective factors (NTAC, 2018).

Based on the determination of the threat in terms of severity or level of concern, the team develops a plan to intervene and manage the risk, which includes but is not limited to monitoring, guidance and skill-building (e.g., anger management, conflict resolution, problem-solving), behavioral interventions, notification of law enforcement, and disciplinary consequences (Louvar Reeves & Brock, 2018; NTAC, 2018). In relation to discipline, it is important to note that extreme or exclusionary discipline (e.g., out-of-school suspension, expulsion) does not eliminate the risk to the school and community and may increase isolation and disengagement; therefore, discipline should be on a continuum, ranging from actions such as having the student of concern issue an apology, developing a behavioral contract, and removing privileges to more intensive approaches such as detention, suspension, and expulsion (Cornell et al., 2012; Louvar Reeves & Brock, 2018; NTAC, 2018).

Threat assessment and management processes are supported by research, including field tests indicating that school staff trained in CSTAG showed reduced fears of school violence, decreased support for zero tolerance, and greater willingness to use threat assessment (Allen et al., 2008; Cornell et al., 2012) and that threat assessment teams were able to carry out the process practically, efficiently, and without violent outcomes (Cornell et al., 2004; Strong & Cornell, 2008). Studies on CSTAG have also found that schools using this model had less aggression, less bullying, reduced suspension rates, and greater willingness on the part of students to seek help for violent threats (Cornell et al., 2009, 2011). In addition, a randomized controlled trial of 40 schools revealed that students in schools using CSTAG were more likely to receive counseling services and parent conferences and less likely to be suspended or transferred compared to wait-list control schools (Cornell et al., 2012). Importantly, Cornell et al. (2018) found that schools using the threat assessment process had no significant racial disparities in exclusionary discipline (e.g., out-of-school suspensions, expulsions), criminal charges, and arrests compared to control schools.

Crisis Teams and Plans

A collaborative, multidisciplinary safety team should engage in careful planning to prepare for multiple threats and hazards across all settings and times (e.g., school-sponsored activities on and off school grounds, breaks and weekends) while attending to issues of accessibility and functional needs of students, staff, and the school community (U.S. Department of Education, 2013). The U.S. Department of Education's (2013) guide for emergency operations plans (EOPs) details the components that should be included in a comprehensive plan. For example, functional annexes, including but not limited to lockdown, evacuation, shelter-in-place, accounting for all persons, communications, family reunification, and continuity of operations, are critical operations and courses of action schools implement in crisis situations. Threat- and hazard-specific annexes complement the functional annexes but also provide unique procedures and responsibilities for a number of specific situations (e.g., bomb threat, suicide, chemical spill). These crisis teams and plans span all aspects of preparedness, from prevention through response and recovery.

Mitigation, Response, and Recovery

Having a well-developed crisis plan that school professionals are familiar with and that has been practiced through drills and exercises is associated with perceived readiness to respond to crises (Steeves et al., 2017; Werner, 2015). Training school staff and students in emergency response protocols (e.g., lockdown, evacuation) and practicing through drills allows them to implement the steps of the protocol and increases their perceptions of preparedness for responding to crises (Schildkraut et al., 2021; Schildkraut & Nickerson, 2020). This advance planning, practice, and coordination are essential for mitigating the impact of the event.

Mitigation and Response

Depending on the severity of the crisis (based on its impact, intensity, predictability, and duration), determinations are made about whether the crisis response should (a) be minimal or individual (usually one or two school professionals handling it as part of their routine duties); (b) be handled by the school building crisis team; (c) involve professionals from the district or more than one school in the district; or (d) utilize community- or regional-level resources (Brock et al., 2016). The crisis team also conducts psychological triage to evaluate the risk for psychological trauma based on individuals' physical proximity (i.e., seeing or hearing the crisis event), emotional proximity (relationship to individuals directly impacted by the crisis), prior risk and protective factors, perceptions of threat related to the event, and reactions to the crisis (Brock et al., 2016).

Universal, or Tier 1, crisis interventions include immediate action to ensure physical safety of all involved, which is accomplished by using the emergency response protocols and providing any medical care needed. Because children's perceptions of threat are closely associated with how adults react (DeVoe et al., 2011), it is important for teachers and other school staff members to model calm and accurate reassurance, to reunify students with their natural support systems (e.g., parents or primary caregivers, peers), and to maintain established routines to the extent possible (Brock et al., 2016). *Psychoeducation*, or providing information about the facts of the crisis event, how the school is responding, what reactions are expected, how caregivers can care for themselves and children, and where to seek additional support, is associated with improved coping (Gelkopf & Berger, 2009). Guidance and specific steps for providing psychoeducation to caregivers (parents, primary caregivers, school faculty and staff) and students in the form of brief classroom meetings are included in PREPaRE (Brock et al., 2016).

For students who may need more targeted (Tier 2) support, trained school crisis team members can facilitate a student psychoeducational lesson in classes, or, for those who share similar crisis experiences, a group-based crisis intervention may be indicated (Brock et al., 2016). The psychoeducational lesson includes sharing facts about the crisis event, answering questions and dispelling rumors, and teaching about common crisis reactions and coping strategies. The group-based crisis intervention is similar; however, it is a psychological (as opposed to psychoeducational) intervention, involving direct exploration of individuals' crisis experiences and reactions as well as the identification of strategies to help each person help themselves or others with coping (Brock et al., 2016). Students who are more severely traumatized may need intensive and sustained treatment. An evidence-based treatment for decreasing posttraumatic stress disorder (PTSD) and related symptoms (Jaycox et al., 2009; Morsette et al., 2009; Rolfsnes & Idsoe, 2011) that can be implemented in schools is the Cognitive Behavioral Intervention for Trauma in Schools (CBITS; Jaycox, 2003). CBITS is a skills-based intervention that includes group and individual components to reduce PTSD, depression, and behavior problems and to improve coping, support, and academic functioning for students in grades 5–12 who have experienced trauma (Jaycox, 2003). For the most severely traumatized, or if the school does not have the resources to provide intensive support, students and families can be referred to community mental health providers for evidence-based interventions, such as individual and group cognitive behavioral therapies (CBTs) and Eye Movement Desensitization and Reprocessing (see Dorsey et al., 2017).

PROMOTING EQUITY THROUGH PREVENTION AND INTERVENTION

NASP's (2016) *Resolution on Affirming the Rights to Safe and Supportive Schools and Communities for All Students* places an emphasis on safe, supportive, and inclusive schools that are free from all forms of violence (including but not limited to threats, bullying, and hate crimes). The resolution also explicitly addresses the need for school psychologists to engage in and advocate for culturally competent practices and to promote safe, inclusive, and socially just environments for all persons regardless of actual or perceived characteristics, including but not limited to race, ethnicity, immigration status, socioeconomic status, gender, gender identity, sexual orientation, and disability.

There is still much work to be done to address persistent and ongoing inequalities with respect to school safety, and the field of school psychology has begun to attend to these issues in a more systematic way. Researchers have called attention to the persistent problem of exclusionary discipline practices that disproportionately impact students of color as well as the ineffectiveness of current approaches (e.g., PBIS) in reducing this inequity without specific and explicit inclusion of culturally responsive practices (Fallon et al., 2021; McIntosh et al., 2021; Zakszeski et al., 2021). Even when data about inequities in school discipline practices are reviewed routinely (e.g., monthly), this in itself does not lead to changes or improvements in practice (McIntosh et al., 2020).

There is increasing evidence, however, that practices that center cultural responsiveness and racial equity in specific and intentional ways can reduce disproportionality in school discipline (McIntosh et al., 2021; Tobin & Vincent, 2011). Strategies that can help reduce these disparities involve ensuring (a) consistent and positive acknowledgment of student behavior; (b) active collection and use of data on problem behavior (disaggregated by race and ethnicity) to make decisions; (c) ongoing training on cultural responsiveness and function-based positive behavior interventions for teams; and (d) resources to conduct functional behavioral assessments and develop behavior support plans (Tobin & Vincent, 2011). In a 2021 randomized controlled trial, professional development that included a focus on collecting and analyzing data to systematically understand the causes of inequitable discipline practices, teaching about and neutralizing implicit bias, and implementation of strategies most likely to reduce inequities (e.g., improving student–teacher relationships, learning about family values, and teaching desired behaviors) resulted in significant decreases in disproportionate school discipline practices compared to the control schools (McIntosh et al., 2021).

As noted previously, there is also some evidence that schools that use threat assessment and management, as compared to control schools, do not have significant racial disparities in exclusionary discipline and arrests (Cornell et al., 2018). Despite this promising finding, O'Malley et al.'s (2018) review of the threat assessment literature indicated a general absence of content related to systemic discrimination, minoritized student stress, diverse family constellations, and implications for conceptualizing and intervening with threats. O'Malley et al. (2018) provided helpful guidance for incorporating cultural competence considerations in the threat assessment process, emphasizing practices such as the careful selection and training of threat assessment teams to attend to sources of implicit bias and discrimination, to identify cultural brokers and culturally adapted interventions, and to consider historical experiences and distrust of law enforcement.

Crisis prevention and intervention is another area where improvements are needed. In a review of state crisis planning materials, Annandale and colleagues (2011) found a lack of explicit mention of cultural competence training, the use of community resources to enhance efforts to reach diverse cultural groups, and the evaluation of crisis plans for cultural competence. For diverse students exposed to trauma and crises, there is evidence that some of the aforementioned intensive services, such as highly structured CBT tailored to students' culture and experiences, demonstrate positive effects (Sullivan & Simonson, 2016). In addition, CBITS (described earlier in this chapter) was developed specifically to be implemented in diverse schools where students experience trauma (Jaycox et al., 2009). This intervention has been adapted for Native American children through the incorporation of local stories and history, with sustained reductions in PTSD symptoms observed for children receiving this treatment (Morsette et al., 2009).

SOCIAL JUSTICE CONNECTIONS

How does social justice intersect with school violence and crisis prevention and intervention?

School-based practices that promote socially just violence and crisis prevention and intervention are sorely needed. This chapter has provided a review of the literature in this area. In sum, the following are key conclusions and implications from the violence and crisis literature in regard to promoting social justice for youth from traditionally marginalized backgrounds:

- School safety must be conceptualized in relation to systemic inequities and historical trauma that have excluded students of color from safe, welcoming, and inclusive school environments.
- Reducing disproportionality in exclusionary discipline must go beyond examining data about the problem to systematically understanding the causes of inequitable discipline practices, actively neutralizing implicit bias, and implementing strategies most likely to reduce inequities (e.g., improving student–teacher relationships through positive interactions and teaching desired behaviors within the context of family values).
- Threat assessment has shown some promise in reducing disparities in discipline, although more attention is needed to explicitly address cultural competence in all aspects of the process.
- School crisis planning and preparedness efforts would benefit from more systematic efforts to meet the needs of students and families from diverse cultural backgrounds.
- Intensive treatments for students exposed to traumatic experiences (e.g., CBT, CBITS) that are tailored to meet cultural needs have been found to be effective in reducing the negative impact of trauma.

SUMMARY AND CONCLUSIONS

Promoting safe, welcoming, and inclusive school environments for all students is imperative for the field of school psychology (NASP, 2016). This involves systematic efforts spanning from preventing violence and crises to recovering from traumatic experiences, with an emphasis on culturally responsive practices. Evidence-based practices in violence and crisis prevention and intervention are imperative. Moreover, continued attention and commitment to promoting equity through socially just crisis and violence prevention and intervention practices are sorely needed.

DISCUSSION QUESTIONS

1. What is school violence? What is a school crisis?
2. What are implications for schools that prioritize physical safety over psychological safety?
3. What are the central tenets of a comprehensive approach to assessing threats and preventing acts of targeted school violence?
4. How can schools best determine how to respond to student and staff needs after a crisis event?
5. In your opinion, what should school psychologists' highest priorities be in regard to ensuring cultural competence and socially just practice in violence and crisis prevention and intervention?

RECOMMENDED READINGS

Brock, S. E., Nickerson, A. B., Reeves, M. A., Conolly, C., Jimerson, S. R., Pesce, R. C., & Lazzaro, B. (2016). *School crisis prevention and intervention: The PREPaRE model* (2nd ed.). National Association of School Psychologists.

National Association of School Psychologists. (2016). *Resolution: Affirming the rights to safe and supportive schools and communities for all students.* https://www.nasponline.org/x37560.xml

National Threat Assessment Center. (2018). *Enhancing school safety using a threat assessment model: An operational guide for preventing targeted school violence.* U.S. Secret Service, Department of Homeland Security. https://www.cisa.gov/sites/default/files/publications/18_0711_USSS_NTAC-Enhancing-School-Safety-Guide.pdf

Nickerson, A. B., Randa, R., Jimerson, S., & Guerra, N. (2021). Safe places to learn: Advances in school safety research and practice. *School Psychology Review, 50*(2–3), 158–171. https://doi.org/10.1080/2372966X.2021.1871948

U.S. Department of Education, Office of Elementary and Secondary Education, Office of Safe and Healthy Students. (2013). *Guide for developing high-quality school emergency operations plans.* https://www.dhs.gov/sites/default/files/publications/REMS%20K-12%20Guide%20508_0.pdf

A robust set of instructor resources designed to supplement this text is located at http://connect.springerpub.com/content/book/978-0-8261-6344-8. Qualifying instructors may request access by emailing textbook@springerpub.com.

REFERENCES

Allen, K., Cornell, D., Lorek, E., & Sheras, P. (2008). Response of school personnel to student threat assessment training. *School Effectiveness and School Improvement, 19*, 319–332. https://doi.org/10.1080/09243450802332184

Annandale, N. O., Heath, M. A., Dean, B., Kemple, A., & Takino, Y. (2011). Assessing cultural competency in school crisis plans. *Journal of School Violence, 10*(1), 16–33. https://doi.org/10.1080/15388220.2010.519263

Borum, R., Bartel, P., & Forth, A. (2006). *Manual for the Structured Assessment for Violence Risk in Youth (SAVRY)*. Psychological Assessment Resources.

Bradshaw, C. P., Mitchell, M. M., & Leaf, P. L. (2010). Examining the effects of schoolwide positive behavioral interventions and supports on student outcomes: Results from a randomized controlled effectiveness trial in elementary schools. *Journal of Positive Behavior Interventions, 12*, 133–148. https://doi.org/10.1177/1098300709334798

Brock, S. E., Nickerson, A. B., Reeves, M. A., Conolly, C., Jimerson, S. R., Pesce, R. C., & Lazzaro, B. (2016). *School crisis prevention and intervention: The PREPaRE model* (2nd ed.). National Association of School Psychologists.

Brock, S. E., Nickerson, A. B., Reeves, M. A., Jimerson, S. R., Lieberman, R. A., & Feinberg, T. A. (2009). *School crisis prevention and intervention: The PREPaRE model*. National Association of School Psychologists.

Caldarella, P., Shatzer, R. H., Gray, K. M., Young, R. K., & Young, E. L. (2011). The effects of School-wide Positive Behavior Support on middle school climate and student outcomes. *Research in Middle Level Education Online, 35*, 1–14. https://doi.org/10.1080/19404476.2011.11462087

Centers for Disease Control and Prevention. (2016). *Understanding school violence*. Author. https://www.cdc.gov/violenceprevention/pdf/school_violence_fact_sheet-a.pdf

Collaborative for Academic, Social, and Emotional Learning. (2012). *CASEL program guide*. Author. https://pg.casel.org/

Cook, C. R., Frye, M., Slemrod, T., Lyon, A. R., Renshaw, T. L., & Zhang, Y. (2015). An integrated approach to universal prevention: Independent and combined effects of PBIS and SEL on youths' mental health. *School Psychology Quarterly, 30*, 166–183. https://doi.org/10.1037/spq0000102

Cornell, D. G., Allen, K., & Fan, X. (2012). A randomized controlled study of the Virginia Student Threat Assessment Guidelines in kindergarten through grade 12. *School Psychology Review, 41*(1), 100–115. https://doi.org/10.1080/02796015.2012.12087378

Cornell, D. G., Gregory, A., & Fan, X. (2011). Reductions in long-term suspensions following adoption of the Virginia Student Threat Assessment Guidelines. *Bulletin of the National Association of Secondary School Principals, 95*, 175–194. https://doi.org/10.1177/0192636511415255

Cornell, D. G., Maeng, J., Huang, F., Shukla, K., & Konold, T. (2018). Racial/ethnic parity in disciplinary consequences using student threat assessment. *School Psychology Review, 47*(2), 183–195. https://doi.org/10.17105/SPR-2017-0030.V47-2

Cornell, D. G., Mayer, M. J., & Sulkowski, M. L. (2021). History and future of school safety research. *School Psychology Review, 50*(2–3), 143–157. https://doi.org/10.1080/2372966X.2020.1857212

Cornell, D. G., & Sheras, P. (2006). *Guidelines for responding to student threats of violence*. Sopris West.

Cornell, D. G., Sheras, P., Gregory, A., & Fan, X. (2009). A retrospective study of school safety conditions in high schools using the Virginia Threat Assessment Guidelines versus alternative approaches. *School Psychology Quarterly, 24*, 119–129. https://doi.org/10.1037/a0016182

Cornell, D. G., Sheras, P., Kaplan, S., McConville, D., Douglass, J., Elkon, A., McKnight, L., Branson, C., & Cole, J. (2004). Guidelines for student threat assessment: Field-test findings. *School Psychology Review, 33*, 527–546. https://doi.org/10.1080/02796015.2004.12086266

Cowan, K. C., Vaillancourt, K., Rossen, E., & Pollitt, K. (2013). *A framework for safe and successful schools* [Brief]. National Association of School Psychologists. https://www.nasponline.org/resources-and-publications/resources-and-podcasts/school-safety-and-crisis/systems-level-prevention/a-framework-for-safe-and-successful-schools

DeVoe, E. R., Klein, T. P., Bannon, W., Jr., & Miranda-Julian, C. (2011). Young children in the aftermath of the World Trade Center attacks. *Psychological Trauma: Theory, Research, Practice, and Policy, 3*, 1–7. https://doi.org/10.1037/a0020567

Dorsey, S., McLaughlin, K. A., Kerns, S. E. U., Harrison, J. P., Lambert, H. K., Briggs, E. C., Cox, J. R., & Amaya-Jackson, L. (2017). Evidence base update for psychosocial treatments for children and adolescents exposed to traumatic events. *Journal of Clinical Child & Adolescent Psychology, 46*(3), 303–330. https://doi.org/10.1080/15374416.2016.1220309

Durlak, J. A., Weissberg, R. P., Dymniki, A. B., Taylor, R. D., & Schellinger, K. B. (2011). The impact on enhancing students' social emotional learning: A meta-analysis of school-based universal interventions. *Child Development*, 82, 405–432. https://doi.org/10.1111/j.1467-8624.2010.01564.x

Fallon, L. M., Veiga, M., & Sugai, G. (2021). Strengthening MTSS for behavior (MTSS-B) to promote racial equity. *School Psychology Review*. https://doi.org/10.1080/2372966x.2021.1972333

Gelkopf, M., & Berger, R. (2009). A school-based, teacher-mediated prevention program (ERASE-Stress) for reducing terror-related traumatic reactions in Israeli youth: A quasi-randomized controlled trial. *Journal of Child Psychology and Psychiatry*, 50, 962–971. https://doi.org/10.1111/j.1469-7610.2008.02021.x

Jaycox, L. (2003). *Cognitive-behavioral intervention for trauma in schools*. Sopris West.

Jaycox, L. H., Langley, A. K., Stein, B. D., Wong, M., Sharma, P., Scott, M., & Schonlau, M. (2009). Support for students exposed to trauma: A pilot study. *School Mental Health*, 1, 49–60. https://doi.org/10.1007/s12310-009-9007-8

Krug, E. G., Dahlberg, L. L., Mercy, J. A., Zwi, A. B., & Lozano, R. (2002). *World report on violence and health*. World Health Organization. https://www.who.int/violence_injury_prevention/violence/world_report/en/summary_en.pdf

Lamoreaux, D., & Sulkowski, M. L. (2020). An alternative to fortified schools: Using crime prevention through environmental design (CPTED) to balance student safety and psychological well-being. *Psychology in the Schools*, 57, 152–165. https://doi.org/10.1002/pits.22301

Lindstrom Johnson, S., Bottiani, J., Waasdorp, T. E., & Bradshaw, C. P. (2018). Surveillance or safekeeping? How school security officer and camera presence influence students' perceptions of safety, equity, and support. *Journal of Adolescent Health*, 63, 732–738. https://doi.org/10.1016/j.jadohealth.2018.06.008

Lindstrom Johnson, S., Waasdorp, T. E., Cash, A. H., Debnam, K. J., Milam, A. J., & Bradshaw, C. P. (2017). Assessing the association between observed school disorganization and school violence: Implications for school climate interventions. *Psychology of Violence*, 7, 181–191. https://doi.org/10.1037/vio0000045

Louvar Reeves, M. A., & Brock, S. E. (2018). School behavioral threat assessment and management. *Contemporary School Psychology*, 22(2), 148–162. https://doi.org/10.1007/s40688-017-0158-6

McIntosh, K., Girvan, E. J., Fairbanks Falcon, S., McDaniel, S. C., Smolkowski, K., Bastable, E., Santiago-Rosario, M. R., Izzard, S., Austin, S. C., Nese, R. N., & Baldy, T. S. (2021). Equity-focused PBIS approach reduces racial inequities in school discipline: A randomized controlled trial. *School Psychology*, 36(6), 433–444. https://doi.org/10.1037/spq0000466

McIntosh, K., Smolkowski, K., Gion, C. M., Witherspoon, L., Bastable, E., & Girvan, E. J. (2020). Awareness is not enough: A double-blind randomized controlled trial of the effects of providing discipline disproportionality data reports to school administrators. *Educational Researcher*, 49(7), 533–537. https://doi.org/10.3102/0013189X20939937

Morsette, A., Swaney, G., Stolle, D., Schuldberg, D., van den Pol, R., & Young, M. (2009). Cognitive Behavioral Intervention for Trauma in Schools (CBITS): School-based treatment on a rural American Indian reservation. *Journal of Behavior Therapy and Experimental Psychiatry*, 40, 169–178. https://doi.org/10.1016/j.jbtep.2008.07.006

Musu, L., Zhang, A., Wang, K., Zhang, J., & Oudekerk, B. A. (2019). *Indicators of School Crime and Safety: 2018* (NCES 2019-047/NCJ 252571). National Center for Education Statistics, U.S. Department of Education, and Bureau of Justice Statistics, Office of Justice Programs, U.S. Department of Justice.

National Association of School Psychologists. (2015). *School violence prevention* (Position Statement). https://www.nasponline.org/x26831.xml

National Association of School Psychologists. (2016). *Resolution: Affirming the rights to safe and supportive schools and communities for all students*. https://www.nasponline.org/x37560.xml

National Threat Assessment Center. (2018). *Enhancing school safety using a threat assessment model: An operational guide for preventing targeted school violence*. U.S. Secret Service, Department of Homeland Security. https://www.secretservice.gov/node/4464

National Threat Assessment Center. (2021). *Averting targeted school violence: A U.S. Secret Service analysis of plots against schools*. U.S. Secret Service, Department of Homeland Security. https://www.secretservice.gov/sites/default/files/reports/2021-03/USSS%20Averting%20Targeted%20School%20Violence.2021.03.pdf

Nickerson, A. B., Randa, R., Jimerson, S., & Guerra, N. (2021). Safe places to learn: Advances in school safety research and practice. *School Psychology Review*, 50(2–3), 158–171. https://doi.org/10.1080/2372966X.2021.1871948

Nickerson, A. B., & Spears, W. H. (2007). Influences on authoritarian and educational/therapeutic approaches to school violence prevention. *Journal of School Violence, 6*, 3–31. https://do.org/10.1300/J202v06n04_02

Noltemeyer, A., Palmer, K., James, A. G., & Wiechman, S. (2019). School-Wide Positive Behavioral Interventions and Supports (SW-PBIS): A synthesis of existing research. *International Journal of School & Educational Psychology, 7*(4), 253–262. https://doi.org/10.1080/21683603.2018.1425169

O'Malley, M. D., Wolf-Prusan, L., Lima Rodriguez, C., Xiong, R., & Swarts, M. R. (2018). Cultural-competence considerations for contemporary school-based threat assessment. *Psychology in the Schools, 56*(2), 255–275. https://doi.org/10.1002/pits.22197

Pentek, D., & Eisenberg, M. E. (2018). School resource officers, safety, and discipline: Perceptions and experiences across racial/ethnic groups in Minnesota secondary schools. *Children and Youth Services Review, 88*, 141–148. https://doi.org/10.1016/j.childyouth.2018.03.008

Rolfsnes, E. S., & Idsoe, T. (2011). School-based intervention programs for PTSD symptoms: A review and meta-analysis. *Journal of Traumatic Stress, 24*, 155–165. https://doi.org/10.1002/jts.20622

Schildkraut, J., & Nickerson, A. B. (2020). Ready to respond: Effects of lockdown drills and training on school emergency preparedness. *Victims and Offenders, 15*, 619–638. https://doi.org/10.1080/15564886.2020.1749199

Schildkraut, J., Nickerson, A. B., & Klingman, K. (2021). Reading, writing, responding: Faculty and staff perceptions of school safety and emergency preparedness in the context of lockdown drills. *Educational Policy, 36*(7). https://doi.org/10.1177/08959048211015617

Servoss, T. J. (2017). School security and student misbehavior. *Youth & Society, 49*, 755–778. https://doi.org/10.1177/0044118X14561007

Sprague, J. R., & Walker, H. M. (2005). *Safe and healthy schools: Practical prevention strategies*. Guilford Press.

Steeves, R. M. O., Metallo, S. A., Byrd, S. M., Erickson, M. R., Gresham, F. M. (2017). Crisis preparedness in schools: Evaluating staff perspectives and providing recommendations for best practice. *Psychology in the Schools, 54*(6), 563–580. https://doi.org/10.1002/pits.22017

Strong, K., & Cornell, D. (2008). Student threat assessment in Memphis City Schools: A descriptive report. *Behavioral Disorders, 34*, 42–54. https://doi.org/10.1177/019874290803400104

Sugai, G. M., & Horner, R. R. (2006). A promising approach for expanding and sustaining school-wide positive behavior support. *School Psychology Review, 35*, 245–259. https://doi.org/10.1080/02796015.2006.12087989

Sullivan, A. L., & Simonson, G. R. (2016). A systematic review of school-based social-emotional interventions for refugee and war-traumatized youth. *Review of Educational Research, 86*(2), 503–530. https://doi.org/10.3102/0034654315609419

Taylor, R. D., Oberle, E., Durlak, J. A., & Weissberg, R. P. (2017). Promoting positive youth development through school-based social and emotional learning interventions: A meta-analysis of follow-up effects. *Child Development, 88*, 1156–1171. https://doi.org/10.1111/cdev.12864

Theriot, M. T., & Orme, J. G. (2016). School resource officers and students' feelings of safety at school. *Youth Violence and Juvenile Justice, 14*(2), 130–146. https://doi.org/10.1177/1541204014564472

Tobin, T. J., & Vincent, C. G. (2011). Strategies for preventing disproportion ate exclusions of African American students. *Preventing School Failure, 55*(4), 192–201. https://doi.org/10.1080/1045988X.2010.532520

U.S. Department of Education. (2013). *Guide for developing high-quality school emergency operations plans*. Office of Elementary and Secondary Education, Office of Safe and Healthy Students. https://www.dhs.gov/sites/default/files/publications/REMS%20K-12%20Guide%20508_0.pdf

Vossekuil, B., Fein, R. A., Reddy, M., Borum, R., & Modzeleski, W. (2004, June). *The final report and findings of the Safe School Initiative: Implications for the prevention of school attacks in the United States*. U.S. Secret Service and U.S. Department of Education. https://www2.ed.gov/admins/lead/safety/preventingattacksreport.pdf

Werner, D. (2015). Are school social workers prepared for a major school crisis? Indicators of individual and school environment preparedness. *Children & Schools, 37*(1), 28–35. https://doi.org/10.1093/cs/cdu031

Zakszeski, B., Rutherford, L., Heidelburg, K., & Thomas, L. (2021). In pursuit of equity: Discipline disproportionality and SWPBIS implementation in urban schools. *School Psychology, 36*(2), 122–130. https://doi.org/10.1037/spq0000428

CHAPTER 14

Family, School, and Community Collaboration

JANISE S. PARKER ■ TIFFANY C. HORNSBY ■ ANGELINA NORTEY ■ AYANNA TROUTMAN ■ ALANA M. PARKER

CHAPTER OBJECTIVES

After reading this chapter, you will be able to:

- Define family, school, and community collaboration.
- Describe how schools can collaborate with families and community partners.
- Describe benefits of collaborative partnerships with families and communities.
- Describe how to engage in equity and social justice–oriented family and community partnerships.

NATIONAL ASSOCIATION OF SCHOOL PSYCHOLOGISTS PRACTICE MODEL CONNECTIONS

Domain 2: Consultation and Collaboration
Domain 7: Family, School, and Community Collaboration
Domain 8: Equitable Practices for Diverse Student Populations

INTRODUCTION

Bronfenbrenner's Ecological Systems Theory is widely known for its emphasis on the influence of various social environments on human development. Moreover, Epstein's (1995) model of overlapping spheres of influence recognizes that students learn and grow through their connection to three major contexts: school, family, and community. *Family* refers to a group of people who are connected by birth, marriage, adoption, or close relational and extended ties. *Community* can be conceptualized as a group of people living in a centralized area or a group of people who come together through a common interest. For this chapter, we discuss the idea of *community* through the lens of the first definition. Though some practices are expected to occur separately within the respective contexts of school, family, and community, other efforts for supporting youth development require much-needed collaboration between and among these contexts.

Partnership between schools and community organizations is one of six types of joint involvement efforts emphasized in Epstein's (1995) model. The focus on school–community partnerships has garnered much attention in research and practice across various disciplines of study. To date, school psychology scholars have primarily discussed general recommendations for partnering with various community-based organizations (Eagle & Dowd-Eagle, 2014) and specific considerations for partnering with clinical-based settings in the community (e.g., Bradley-Klug et al., 2013; Griffiths et al., 2022). Building upon prior scholarship in school psychology and related fields (e.g., school counseling; Bryan et al., 2019), this chapter is situated within an equity- and social justice–oriented perspective, with a focus on how school psychologists can center and channel marginalized communities' strengths and needs through youth- and family-centered collaboration within their professional practice.

DEFINING SCHOOL, FAMILY, AND COMMUNITY PARTNERSHIPS

As described in Chapter 1, the National Association of School Psychologist's (NASP's; 2020) Practice Model underscores the importance of school psychologists understanding practices and research related to family systems and influences as well as facilitating family–school–community partnerships to enhance youth outcomes. According to NASP (2020), school–community partnerships may entail school psychologists (a) fostering linkages and collaboration among schools, families, students, and community providers and (b) coordinating services when children are involved with multiple agencies. Indeed, the professional school psychology literature suggests that school psychologists play a vital role in developing and sustaining partnerships with community-based organizations (Doll et al., 2014; Eagle & Dowd-Eagle, 2014; Haupt et al., 2020). Broadly, *partnerships* refer to collaborative associations between two or more entities focused on a shared goal.

Eagle and Dowd-Eagle (2014), for example, coauthored a single chapter devoted to school partnerships in the sixth edition of NASP's *Best Practice in School Psychology* book series. One point of consideration in their chapter included the importance of school psychologists understanding the different types of organizations that may be available for partnerships (including services they may offer) and how such partnerships may manifest in practice. Regarding the former, a range of national and grassroots organizations exist in local communities, including civic organizations (e.g., Black fraternities and sororities), youth-centered programs, local businesses, civic groups, faith-based organizations, health and human services agencies, recreational centers, and regional libraries (Eagle & Dowd-Eagle, 2014; Griffin & Farris, 2010; Moore-Thomas & Day-Vines, 2010). Accordingly, community organizations have varying purposes that aim to engage different aspects of youths' academic, social, emotional, and behavioral development such as mentoring, tutoring, information sharing, parent/family support, classroom assistance, and business partnerships (Moore-Thomas & Day-Vines, 2010; Sanders, 2001).

To engage in this work, school psychologists must learn to embrace the unique and valuable contributions of multiple organizations, as research shows that some readily available *community agencies* (i.e., organizations in the local area that are developed to address one or more needs) are underutilized by school systems (Anderson-Butcher et al., 2006; Sanders, 2001). For example, though educators may frequently partner with local businesses (Sanders, 2001), school personnel may be less inclined to pursue partnerships with other local programs, especially those that serve a high number of marginalized youth (Anderson-Butcher et al., 2006). School psychologists may also negate partnership work with specific groups due to a limited appreciation for and knowledge of various community-based organizations. Because members and leaders in community organizations may be perceived as "natural helpers" who are better equipped to serve the cultural needs of families in the community (Power, 2003), assuming a socially just, culturally responsive stance involves checking biases to ensure that all students have access to meaningful resources in and outside of school.

It is also important to understand how school, family, and community partnerships may be realized through various configurations, recognizing that a "one size fits all" approach may be insufficient for meeting all students' needs. In this regard, Eagle and Dowd-Eagle (2014) explained that school–community partnerships may involve *school-linked* or *school-based* support. **School-based partnerships** typically involve services that occur within the physical structure of the school, such as after-school programming. Although school-based partnerships provide better student access to facilities and resources (by removing transportation barriers, for example), they can be limiting if funding and space are not available to support various initiatives and student confidentiality cannot be guaranteed (Eagle & Dowd-Eagle, 2014). In contrast, **school-linked partnerships** typically involve connecting families to community organizations outside of the school context. This approach does not require complete implementation in school settings, as school personnel may connect families to existing resources within the broader community. Nevertheless, school-linked partnerships can also be limited in scope if families cannot access the support due to structural and systemic barriers (e.g., cost and location of services).

Expanding upon the idea of school-linked and school-based partnerships, Valli et al. (2016) conducted a systematic literature review to develop a typology of school–community partnerships, with the goal of detailing the philosophical foundations and necessary conditions (e.g., time, funding, human capacity) required for each type. Valli and colleagues described *Family and Interagency Collaboration* as the most basic form of sustained partnership. Aligned with the idea of school-linked partnerships (Eagle & Dowd-Eagle, 2014), this model involves schools "coordinating the delivery of other services" (Valli et al., 2016, p. 729) and connecting families to outside agencies. This approach can be beneficial when school personnel cannot offer a full range of comprehensive services. However, one limitation of family and interagency collaboration is that partnerships are likely student-focused rather than family-focused. In contrast, *full-service schools* are designed to break down silos between schools and partnering organizations to serve the whole child and their family by integrating wraparound support during the school day within the school building. One limitation of this model includes difficulty sustaining funding, organization, and leadership to support in-school programming. *Full-service community schools* are implemented as "democratic schools by opening them . . . to greater decision making on the part of the neighborhood community" (Valli et al., 2016, p. 732). In this type of collaboration, the goal is to promote family engagement whereby families are viewed as essential and vocal partners in decision-making as the school offers a full range of services to students, families, and communities. Like full-service schools, the success of full-service community schools relies on sustained funding, organization, and leadership. It is also incumbent upon school personnel to remove cultural and power gaps between caregivers and educators to facilitate ongoing trusting relationships. The *Community Development Model* is the most expansive *and* inclusive model that aims to transform schools and whole communities by focusing on economic development, the creation of jobs, and community advocacy and leadership development. Schools, then, become the "points of contact for community members to deal with pressing political, economic, and cultural matters" (Valli et al., 2016, p. 736). In addition to ideal conditions for change (e.g., leadership and trusting relationship), this model requires schools to invest in a broad array of services to promote thriving, sustainable communities.

BENEFITS OF COLLABORATIVE PARTNERSHIPS WITH COMMUNITIES AND FAMILIES

Community-based programs serving school-age youth have been around for more than 100 years, with many early organizations located in church basements, storefronts, or settlement houses (Hirsch, 2011). In more recent history, community-based youth organizations sprang out of the New Deal and the Great Society, particularly in large, economically impoverished cities such as New Orleans (Ginwright, 2007; Kantor & Lowe, 1995). Though community organizations exist in the same economic, social, and political context as schools, Baldridge et al. (2017) argued that community organizations may have more flexibility to support marginalized youth because they do not possess the same bureaucratic constraints or hierarchical structures. As such, organizations that share proximity to students and schools are well positioned to supplement educational, social, and cultural experiences by targeting a plethora of student and family needs.

This section primarily summarizes how community-based involvement can benefit school-age youth. However, school, community, and family partnerships can benefit families and communities at large through adult-centered programming and the provision of social, financial, and informational support (Valli et al., 2016). In fact, it is incumbent upon school personnel to refrain from negating the importance of supporting students' families within partnership work. Family collaboration is critical for providing culturally responsive care (Jones & Hazuka, 2013), yet school and community partnerships are all too often youth-centered at the expense of ignoring larger family needs that contribute to adaptive or maladaptive development (Jones & Hazuka, 2013). If environmental constraints within the home preclude a student from experiencing healthy growth, partnership efforts should solicit assistance from community agencies to benefit students *and* their respective families.

Relative to direct benefits for school-age youth, community-based collaboration can foster positive youth development across various domains of functioning. Returning to the focus on promoting equitable outcomes, examples of positive outcomes for marginalized youth who are connected to community organizations can be found across disciplines. For example, researchers found that marginalized youth who participated in community-based programs were (a) less likely to be absent from school and receive a suspension or expulsion; (b) more likely to experience improved school grades and increased academic skill growth (e.g., in reading, math, and science); (c) more frequently enrolled in postsecondary educational institutions compared to their peers; and (d) less likely to experience diminished mental health (e.g., Bailey & Bradbury-Bailey, 2010; Eisenberg et al., 2020; Jenson et al., 2018). Other researchers found that community-based programs had a positive effect on youth's self-concept. Black youth participants, as an example, indicated that they were more inclined to (a) view themselves as agents of change; (b) see themselves in predominantly white career fields (i.e., STEM); (c) gain a sense of responsibility for their community; (d) develop a positive racial identity; and (e) be involved in civic and political engagement activities, including those aimed at challenging systemic oppression (Brittian Loyd & Williams, 2017; Ginwright, 2007; King & Pringle, 2019; Schwartz & Suyemoto, 2013). Likewise, LGBTQ+ youth participants in Gamarel et al.'s (2014) study experienced identity-based affirmation and safety through their connection to community-based organizations.

Baldridge et al. (2011) posit that community-based youth organizations are also uniquely positioned to support marginalized youth because they have the capacity to disrupt educational inequities by creating spaces that keep youth engaged, welcomed, and healed rather than excluded, alienated, and disenfranchised. A consistent finding in community-based youth organization research is the supportive role of positive relationships, both peer and intergenerational, for marginalized youth who are served (Baldridge et al., 2011; Fish et al., 2019; Gamarel et al., 2014; Ginwright, 2007, 2015; Jackson et al., 2014;

Woodland et al., 2009). Notably, the fostering of intergenerational ties is important for marginalized youths' healthy development because such ties create an expectation and opportunity to engage in social change within the community (Ginwright, 2007, 2015). There also is an opportunity to understand and appreciate shared struggle while learning about the importance of interconnectedness for the benefit of the community (Ginwright, 2007; Jackson et al., 2014).

The development of healthy relationships and provision of resources through community-based organizations supports the notion that these organizations can offer social and cultural capital for youth participants. According to Bourdieu et al. (1977), *cultural capital* refers to an accumulation of cultural knowledge, skills, and abilities, and *social capital* entails networks and connections possessed and inherited by groups in society. The traditional understanding of cultural and social capital has led to valuing select knowledge and social networks at the expense of marginalizing ways of being for people of color. Thus, Yosso (2005) presented the model of community cultural wealth as an array of knowledge, skills, abilities, and contacts possessed and utilized by people of color to survive and resist macro- and microforms of oppression. The model consists of six components that simultaneously co-occur: aspirational capital, navigational capital, linguistic capital, social capital, familial capital, and resistance capital (Yosso, 2005).

According to Yosso (2005), *aspirational capital* refers to one's ability to maintain hopes and dreams for the future, despite encountering real and perceived barriers. *Linguistic capital* is defined as the intellectual and social skills one attains through their communication experiences in more than one language or style. *Familial capital* refers to cultural knowledge one gains from immediate and extended kin, such as lessons of caring, coping, and providing for one's family. *Social capital* reflects the network of people (e.g., peers and community members) who may provide instrumental and emotional support to help one navigate social institutions. Consequently, *navigational capital* refers to one's capacity to navigate social institutions, which relies on the interaction between personal agency and connections with individuals in one's social networks. Finally, *resistance capital* includes the knowledge and skills one possesses to oppose inequality and systems of oppression.

Yosso's (2005) model of community cultural wealth asserts that marginalized people have historically had and continue to have resources that allow them to persist in their already abundant communities. Rather than viewing cultural and social capital as perfunctory relationships and connections to select resources, critical cultural/social capital helps youth understand oppressive structural conditions, build a strong racial identity, develop political optimism, and cultivate expectations about community change. Ginwright (2007) even characterized these adult–youth relationships as political acts because they encourage youth to heal from trauma, including institutional trauma experienced at school.

EQUITY AND SOCIAL JUSTICE–ORIENTED COMMUNITY AND FAMILY PARTNERSHIPS

School psychologists should not take for granted the internal and external work that must ensue to create and execute robust and justice-oriented community and family partnerships. In addition to recognizing and challenging one's own biases and attitudes (a necessary task for engaging in authentic collaboration), successful partnerships are likely to materialize through a team-based, systematic process (Bryan & Henry, 2012; Valli et al., 2016). Consequently, Sanders (2001) summarized key steps for forging and sustaining partnerships, which reflect the traditional problem-solving model: (a) identify issues or goals; (b) define the focus of the partnership; (c) identify community assets; (d) select partners; (e) monitor progress; (f) evaluate activities; and (g) share success. From the school counseling literature, Bryan and

Henry's (2012) equity-focused partnership process model may be particularly applicable for social justice–oriented school psychologists. Bryan and Henry (2012) presented a seven-stage model for partnership leadership teams (PLTs; which may include school psychologists) "to build partnerships that enhance educational resilience and academic success, and create equity and access for students, especially students from low-income and culturally diverse backgrounds" (Bryan et al., 2019, p. 277). This model is described in further detail later in this chapter.

Coupled with Bryan and Henry's (2012) model, Griffiths et al. (2022) synthesized the literature on school-based collaboration published over a 25-year period (1992–2017) to develop a framework comprising nine characteristics of successful collaboration in schools. The authors described these characteristics as "building blocks," emphasizing the need for some blocks to be developed and set in stone before moving forward to the next level. At the first and foundational level of their model is *relationship building* through (1) communication, (2) trust, and (3) mutual respect. The second level represents *shared values* and includes (4) developing shared goals and (5) common understanding. At level three, *active engagement* is a product of (6) shared responsibility and (7) active participation. Finally, at the fourth level, *collaboration* is achieved through (8) shared decision-making and (9) implementation. In sum, Griffiths et al. (2022) lay out the elements of effective collaboration and the role that school psychologists may have in establishing these relationships. Taken together, Griffiths et al.'s (2022) and Bryan and Henry's (2012) frameworks offer a guide for developing equity-focused school–community partnerships. The following steps integrate key aspects of their work to demonstrate how school psychologists can help facilitate equity-centered and social justice–oriented partnerships among schools, families, and communities.

Step 1: Preparing to Partner

The first step of Bryan and Henry's (2012) model is intended to lay the groundwork for school–community partnerships. In this stage, school psychologists are challenged to become familiar with culturally diverse families, work to understand students' cultural backgrounds, and recognize and interrogate their own biases about the students and families they serve. The fields of education and psychology have long been criticized as largely influenced by white-dominated ideals and narratives (Ladson-Billings, 2014; Paris, 2012; Yosso, 2005). This establishes the dominant narrative as the standard, and any other perspective is then described as "deviating" from the norm. Thus, school psychologists may initially struggle with identifying the cultural strengths that are to be celebrated, integrated, and built upon to support marginalized students. For example, school personnel may assume that impoverished neighborhoods lack resources within the community instead of identifying the various sources of support and protective factors that often exist in low socioeconomic status (low-SES) communities (Washington, 2010).

Similarly, racially/ethnically marginalized (REM) students have historically been viewed from a deficit viewpoint, wherein labels such as "at-risk" and "culturally disadvantaged" have been erroneously applied to groups of students who possess a culture-driven, nonwhite value system. As a result, school personnel may miss critical opportunities to reinforce the cultural wealth that REM students can and should access through community-based organizations. An essential belief that drives one's preparation to engage in partnership work should largely align with Paris's (2012) emphasis on culturally sustaining pedagogy. Culturally sustaining pedagogy provides a framework for how educators can be responsive to the pluralistic society in and surrounding schools—specifically, by encouraging REM students to maintain their cultural and linguistic competence while simultaneously providing them "access to dominant cultural competence" (Paris, 2012, p. 93). PLTs can be intentional about utilizing these aspects of cultural wealth to respond to identified needs.

Building cultural awareness, including bringing forth and challenging personal biases and assumptions, is a major goal at this stage. Based on Ford's (2004) review of self-reflective activities to prepare for culturally responsive school–community partnerships, questions to answer during this stage include: (a) *What are my beliefs and assumptions about the needs and strengths in the surrounding community?* (b) *How are my beliefs and assumptions influenced by my own power, pride, and prejudice?* and (c) *How are my beliefs and assumptions influenced by my knowledge of diverse populations, or lack thereof?* Most importantly, educators and school psychologists should ask, "How can I take active steps to address beliefs and assumptions that reflect biased, stereotypical, and ill-informed assumptions?" This work takes place long before interacting with members of the community, as it is the necessary self-work that allows school psychologists and other school personnel to identify extraneous variables as potential threats to collaboration.

As equity and social justice are lenses through which individuals view the world, recognizing and removing blinders allows for a change in perspective and a clear vision. Establishing and communicating a clear vision for a mutually beneficial partnership can help establish administrative buy-in (Bryan & Henry, 2012). It should be noted that although this step does not yet require community engagement, the foundational blocks for relationship building (as described by Griffiths et al., 2022) are being laid here and continue through Step 3 of Bryan and Henry's (2012) model (see below). Clarity yields open communication—the first building block—which Griffiths et al. (2022) describe as the ability to share ideas comfortably and effectively.

Bryan and Henry (2012) further emphasize the importance of disaggregating student data to reveal disparities and cultivate buy-in from school personnel during this stage of preparation. As experts in data-based decision-making, school psychologists could lead the charge to examine and leverage that information. For example, school psychologists can help identify patterns of demographic disparities in various indicators of student development, including differences in achievement, behavioral referrals, social–emotional functioning, and other markers of positive youth development. After identifying the areas of need, PLTs can move on to Step 2.

Step 2: Assessing Needs and Strengths

The second step of Bryan and Henry's (2012) model includes assessing the needs and strengths of the school and community to identify the goals of the partnership. Again, examining disaggregated data will elucidate areas of need and disparities between students in the school context. Additionally, educators should seek input from multiple vested partners to better understand the needs and strengths of students, families, and communities. Including families' perspectives is vital for reinforcing the notion that family members are valuable contributors and experts in their children's lives. It also helps establish trust (the second building block of Griffiths et al.'s [2022] framework) and promote shared leadership among families that are often disempowered and marginalized. Data collection methods at this stage may include the use of electronic surveys, focus groups, interviews, and social media posts to solicit feedback from families and community members. In collaboration with school counselors, school psychologists can then use these data to map resources in and out of the school to identify relevant members for the PLT.

When seeking insight about resources in the surrounding community, PLTs should probe various organizations to ensure that minority-serving/minority-led groups are not ignored. Drawing from Yosso's (2005) theory of community cultural wealth, PLTs should be intentional about identifying exemplars of cultural and social capital that are provided by different organizations during this stage of the partnership process. For example, data aggregation in Step 1 may reveal that REM students feel disempowered due to being immersed in an unsupportive school and community environment (e.g., one that is underfunded due to local policies). PLTs can partner with community-based organizations that have experience in helping youth develop a positive racial identity, including cultivating their involvement in civic and political engagement activities (e.g., Brittian Loyd & Williams, 2017; Ginwright, 2007; King & Pringle, 2019; Schwartz & Suyemoto, 2013), a form of *resistance capital*. As another example, data may show that marginalized students have limited access to social–emotional support in and out of school. Understanding that social–emotional support is not limited to intense mental health services, PLTs may collaborate with mentoring organizations to help students maintain hope for the future (*aspirational capital*) and develop a caring relationship with adults who will likely share similar values, beliefs, and/or experiences (*social capital*).

It is also important to note that marginalized families may lack trust in the school community and other white-dominated institutions such as the mental health field, due to the historical mistreatment and misconception of these families (Jones & Hazuka, 2013; Whaley, 2001). Thus, practitioners should identify cultural brokers in the school and surrounding community, as these individuals can help school personnel understand where the family is coming from and gain the trust of the family and community members (Griffin & Farris, 2010). Still, because members of marginalized groups are often overtaxed and overburdened when colleagues treat them as "spokespeople" for their entire group (e.g., Truscott et al., 2014), school psychologists and other members of the PLT must be committed to learning from cultural brokers through the use of relational competencies that enable them to understand and interact effectively with communities of color and other marginalized groups (see Eagle & Dowd-Eagle, 2014, for a description of desired relational attributes).

Step 3: Coming Together

After the goals of the partnership have been identified, the next step is to come together as a team. First, practitioners should reach out to members of the team and community as indicated by previous stages of the model. Again, it is important to be intentional about inviting and involving families and community members from marginalized backgrounds to ensure that they are heard throughout the process. Depending on their needs, this will require additional advocacy and collaboration with community agencies to provide child care and transportation. Logistically, the school contact person should also be cautious of scheduling meeting times primarily based on school personnel availability during the school day (Bryan & Henry, 2012). Demonstrating that the needs of traditionally marginalized families are a priority, even in the planning stages, can begin to create an inviting atmosphere for the partnership.

According to Bryan and Henry (2012), during the initial meetings the team should focus on reviewing and synthesizing data collected during previous steps, brainstorming how to meet the identified needs, and developing goals and an action plan for moving forward. The building block from Griffiths et al.'s (2022) model that corresponds to this step is mutual respect, which entails valuing each vested partner's skills, knowledge, and competence. With so many vested partners representing varied interests, conflict is likely to occur (Kim, 2019). However, Griffiths et al. (2022) suggest that open communication, trust, and mutual respect will yield productive resolutions while maintaining and even strengthening the relationship.

Step 4: Creating Shared Vision and Plan

The primary role of the PLT in Step 4 is to create a shared vision and plan. In Griffiths et al.'s (2022) framework, this level is similarly called shared values, for which shared goals and a common understanding are necessary building blocks. During this step, school psychologists can use their collaboration skills to make sure that people with less power are heard, given the importance of prioritizing empowerment and shared power over the hierarchical power dynamics inherent in school–community interactions (Jones & Hazuka, 2013; Valli et al., 2016). School psychologists can also use their problem-solving skills to assist the team in developing a partnership plan. This plan should include short- and long-term goals based on the data collected. Given their familiarity with principles of systems change, school psychologists are encouraged to start by identifying small, direct solutions to address disparities before scaling up (Moore-Thomas & Day-Vines, 2010). Bryan and Henry (2012) suggest that short-term goals should focus on activities occurring in a 1-year timeframe, while long-term goals may have a 3- or 5-year timeframe. Considering that one of the obstacles to collaboration is differing expectations, it may be necessary to compromise and find mutual goals on which the team can agree (Bryan & Henry, 2012; Eagle & Dowd-Eagle, 2014). The partnership plan should also include which outcomes will be measured and how, as well as with whom the team will communicate the plan. Specific considerations at this stage may also include identifying how the partnership will be funded (see examples listed by Sherman et al., 2007), how the partnership will be executed (consider the typologies described by Valli et al., 2016), and how long the partnership is expected to last.

Step 5: Taking Action

In the fifth stage of the model, the team's objective is to delegate roles and responsibilities to develop and implement partner activities. The school psychologist can assist with these efforts by providing examples of culturally responsive practices and evidence-based activities that members of the team could implement. As in previous steps, partners should be involved in coordinating, planning, and implementing practices (Bryan & Henry, 2012). Active engagement by each team member is key at this step and is built with shared responsibility and active participation (Griffiths et al., 2022). Not only are roles established, the onus is on each team member to fulfill their respective role(s). This promotes the importance of shared leadership and shared work, which consequently aids in maintaining trust and buy-in among community partners (Valli et al., 2016).

SOCIAL JUSTICE CONNECTIONS

What are some foundations of strong, justice-oriented school, family, and community partnerships?

This chapter has described approaches to school, family, and community partnerships that are grounded in principles of social justice. Such approaches implore school psychologists to (a) move beyond culturally responsive practices to emphasize justice-oriented practices; (b) implement a team-based approach; and (c) strive to realize distributive justice. The following are key considerations for addressing these goals.

Beyond Culturally Responsive Practices

- Culturally competent practice entails having the awareness, knowledge, and skills to serve diverse populations, whereas social justice–oriented practices involve a more expansive focus that includes advocacy for equitable service delivery at both the individual and systems level (Grapin, 2016).

(continued)

> **SOCIAL JUSTICE CONNECTIONS (*continued*)**
>
> - Traditional notions of supporting marginalized students have centered on culturally competent or responsive practices; however, such a focus may be insufficient. Through community partnership work, school psychologists can leverage the resources community agencies may offer to promote youth and family access to various sources of support that serve to dismantle inequitable student outcomes.
>
> **A Team-Based Approach**
>
> - It is impractical to believe that schools can meet all students' needs independently. The necessary resources are simply beyond the scope of what schools have available to them (Eagle & Dowd-Eagle, 2014). To optimize resource allocation and usage, school personnel should take a team approach by drawing from the contributions of multiple agencies.
> - School personnel must demonstrate respect for multiple perspectives (e.g., welcoming all vested partners to engage in decision-making). Oppressive and exclusionary practices aimed toward families and different agencies can disrupt healthy partnerships and further marginalize groups of students.
>
> **Distributive Justice**
>
> - ***Distributive justice*** focuses on how and to what extent resources are allocated in society (Shriberg, 2016).
> - Successful school–community partnerships may require sustained funding. Yet, students of color are most likely to attend schools with significant funding constraints that hamper their ability to thrive (Edbuild, 2019). School psychologists must advocate for equitable funding at the federal, state, and local levels to change the way resources are allocated to public schools so that all students can benefit from school–community partnerships.

Step 6: Evaluating and Celebrating Progress

Next, the team should evaluate student outcomes and celebrate progress. Data collection should be a collaborative process whereby the team decides which tools will be used, who will collect the data, and when it will be collected. The team should review quantitative and qualitative data to answer several questions: "Were the needs identified by the needs assessment met? What difference did the partnership activity make in helping the team reach the program's goals? What were the strengths and weaknesses of the process used to implement the program? How are students, families, the school, and the community different as a result of the partnerships?" (Bryan & Henry, 2012, p. 417). In addition to assessing student outcome data, the team should examine whether core characteristics of effective collaboration were present. Griffiths et al. (2022), for example, provide a checklist that can be used to identify any of the characteristics of successful partnerships that the team observed. Griffiths et al. (2022) suggest that each team member anonymously complete the checklist and that results be aggregated and reported to the group. From a social justice lens, the team would also evaluate whether equity and regard for all members manifested within the team's dynamic. For example, Kim (2019) developed a validated measure of transformative school–community collaboration that can be used to determine the extent to which school–community partnership efforts are equity-centered and empowering for all parties involved.

Finally, the team should develop a plan to share the results publicly, celebrate positive outcomes, and document challenges for future planning. Additionally, all vested partners should be recognized and celebrated for their participation and collaborative efforts. This is especially true for family members and community partners.

Step 7: Maintaining Momentum

Bryan and Henry (2012) warn that the final step of maintaining momentum is imperative yet difficult. To sustain school–community partnership initiatives, PLTs must plan for ongoing partnerships from the beginning. The hope is that the initial investment, relationship building, and shared leadership will result in buy-in and enthusiasm by school personnel, families, and community members. Additionally, public acknowledgements and celebration of successful partnerships can reinforce commitment and energize vested partners. In some respects, then, when the infrastructure is built well, sustainability is a byproduct. However, efforts to ensure lasting success should not stop there. PLTs should plan ongoing outreach efforts to expand partnerships, if warranted, and adjust based on data.

SUMMARY AND CONCLUSIONS

Focusing on community collaboration is not intended to absolve school leaders and other school personnel from their obligation to dismantle oppressive and biased practices that have long marginalized various groups of students. Instead, conversations centered on school, community, and family partnerships within the field should occur in conjunction with efforts to promote equitable outcomes and socially just practices for marginalized students. Schools cannot address all student needs alone (Eagle & Dowd-Eagle, 2014), and collaborative efforts between schools and community agencies can provide students and families with the capital they need to realize academic, social, emotional, behavioral, and financial success. School psychologists with expertise in data-based decision-making, consultation/collaboration, and problem-solving are well-positioned to serve on family and community partnership teams. In this role, school psychologists may help teams identify the most appropriate mode of partnership work (Valli et al., 2016). School psychologists can also apply Bryan and Henry's (2012) equity-focused partnership process model to ensure that all voices are honored and that students and families are well supported. The time is long overdue for school psychologists to move beyond the silos of their professional work and to connect with a range of community agencies to give marginalized youth a chance to realize their full potential.

DISCUSSION QUESTIONS

1. Describe the different approaches to school, community, and family partnerships. Which of these approaches may be more suitable for promoting long-term gains among youth and families served?
2. Describe why youth-centered partnerships alone may be insufficient for supporting the youth served.
3. How are school, community, and family partnerships beneficial for marginalized students?
4. Provide an example of each facet of cultural/social capital, as described by Yosso (2005), that school personnel may look for when identifying the strengths of local agencies.
5. How can schools ensure that all voices are heard and honored across each stage of Bryan and Henry's (2012) partnership model?

RECOMMENDED READINGS

Bryan, J., & Henry, L. (2012). A model for building school-family-community partnerships: Principles and process. *Journal of Counseling & Development, 90*(4), 408–420. https://doi.org/10.1002/j.1556-6676.2012.00052.x

Eagle, J. W., & Dowd-Eagle, S. E. (2014). Best practices in school-community partnerships. In P. Harrison & A. Thomas (Eds.), *Best practices in school psychology: Foundations* (pp. 197–210). National Association of School Psychologists.

Ginwright, S. (2015). *Hope and healing in urban education: How urban activists and teachers are reclaiming matters of the heart.* Routledge.

Griffiths, A. J., Alsip, J., Hart, S. R., Round, R. L., & Brady, J. (2021). Together we can do so much: A systematic review and conceptual framework of collaboration in schools. *Canadian Journal of School Psychology, 36*(1), 59–85. https://doi.org/10.1177/0829573520915368

Washington, A. R., Goings, R. B., & Henfield, M. S. (Eds.). (2020). *Creating and sustaining effective K–12 school partnerships: Firsthand accounts of promising practices.* Information Age Publishing.

A robust set of instructor resources designed to supplement this text is located at http://connect.springerpub.com/content/book/978-0-8261-6344-8. Qualifying instructors may request access by emailing textbook@springerpub.com.

REFERENCES

Anderson-Butcher, D., Stetler, E. G., & Midle, T. (2006). A case for expanded school–community partnerships in support of positive youth development. *Children & Schools, 28*(3), 155–163. https://doi.org/10.1093/cs/28.3.155

Bailey, D. F., & Bradbury-Bailey, M. E. (2010). Empowered youth programs: Partnerships for enhancing postsecondary outcomes of African American adolescents. *Professional School Counseling, 14*(1). https://doi.org/10.1177/2156759X1001400107

Baldridge, B., Hill, M., & Davis, J. (2011). New possibilities: (Re)engaging Black male youth within community-based educational spaces. *Race Ethnicity and Education, 14*(1), 121–136. https://doi.org/10.1080/13613324.2011.531984

Baldridge, B. J., Beck, N., Medina, J. C., & Reeves, M. A. (2017). Toward a new understanding of community-based education: The role of community-based educational spaces in disrupting inequality for minoritized youth. *Review of Research in Education, 41*(1), 381–402. https://doi.org/10.3102/0091732X16688622

Bourdieu, P., Passeron, J. C., & Nice, R. (1977). *Education, society, and culture* (R. Nice, Trans.). Sage.

Bradley-Klug, K. L., Jeffries-DeLoatche, K. L., Walsh, A. S. J., Bateman, L. P., Nadeau, J., Powers, D. J., & Cunningham, J. (2013). School psychologists' perceptions of primary care partnerships: Implications for building the collaborative bridge. *Advances in School Mental Health Promotion, 6*(1), 51–67. https://doi.org/10.1080/1754730X.2012.760921

Brittian Loyd, A., & Williams, B. V. (2017). The potential for youth programs to promote African American youth's development of ethnic and racial identity. *Child Development Perspectives, 11*(1), 29–38. https://doi.org/10.1111/cdep.12204

Bryan, J., Griffin, D., Kim, J., Griffin, D. M., & Young, A. (2019). School counselor leadership in school-family-community partnerships: An equity-focused partnership process model for moving the field forward. In S. B. Sheldon & T. A. Turner-Vorbeck (Eds.), *The Wiley handbook of family, school, and community relationships in education* (pp. 265–287). John Wiley & Sons. https://doi.org/10.1002/9781119083054.ch13

Bryan, J., & Henry, L. (2012). A model for building school-family-community partnerships: Principles and process. *Journal of Counseling & Development, 90*(4), 408–420. https://doi.org/10.1002/j.1556-6676.2012.00052.x

Doll, B., Cummings, J. A., & Chapla, B. A. (2014). Best practices in population-based school mental health services. In P. Harrison & A. Thomas (Eds.), *Best practices in school psychology* (pp. 149–163). National Association of School Psychologists.

Eagle, J. W., Dowd-Eagle, S. E. (2014). Best practices in school-community partnerships. In P. Harrison & A. Thomas (Eds.), *Best practices in school psychology: Foundations* (pp. 197–210). National Association of School Psychologists.

Edbuild. (2019). *$23 billion*. https://edbuild.org/content/23-billion/full-report.pdf

Eisenberg, M. E., Gower, A. L., Watson, R. J., Porta, C. M., & Saewyc, E. M. (2020). LGBTQ youth-serving organizations: What do they offer and do they protect against emotional distress? *Annals of LGBTQ Public and Population Health, 1*(1), 63–79. https://doi.org/10.1891/LGBTQ.2019-0008

Epstein, J. L. (1995). School/family/community partnerships. *Phi Delta Kappan, 76*(9), 701–712. https://jreadingclass.files.wordpress.com/2014/08/school-family-community-partnerships.pdf

Fish, J. N., Moody, R. L., Grossman, A. H., & Russell, S. T. (2019). LGBTQ youth-serving community-based organizations: Who participates and what difference does it make? *Journal of Youth and Adolescence, 48*(12), 2418–2431. https://doi.org/10.1007/s10964-019-01129-5

Ford, B. A. (2004). Preparing special educators for culturally responsive school-community partnerships. *Teacher Education and Special Education, 27*(3), 224–230. https://doi.org/10.1177/088840640402700302

Gamarel, K. E., Walker, J. N. J., Rivera, L., & Golub, S. A. (2014). Identity safety and relational health in youth spaces: A needs assessment with LGBTQ youth of color. *Journal of LGBT Youth, 11*(3), 289–315. https://doi.org/10.1080/19361653.2013.879464

Ginwright, S. (2007). Black youth activism and the role of critical social capital in Black community organizations. *American Behavioral Scientist, 51*(3), 403–418. https://doi.org/10.1177/0002764207306068

Ginwright, S. (2015). *Hope and healing in urban education: How urban activists and teachers are reclaiming matters of the heart*. Routledge.

Grapin, S. L. (2016). Social justice in school psychology: Applying principles of organizational consultation to facilitate change in graduate programs. *Journal of Educational and Psychological Consultation, 27*(2), 173–202. https://doi.org/10.1080/10474412.2016.1217489

Griffin, D., & Farris, A. (2010). School counselors and collaboration: Finding resources through community asset mapping. *Professional School Counseling, 13*, 248–256. https://www.jstor.org/stable/42732958

Griffiths, A. J., Alsip, J., Kennedy, K., Diamond, E. L., Palma, C., Abdou, A. S., Wiegand, R., & Brady, J. (2022). Families and schools together: Designing a model for university-community partnerships to support home-school collaborations. *Contemporary School Psychology, 26*, 422-434. https://doi.org/10.1007/s40688-021-00358-5

Haupt, R. L., Smith, N. D. W., Jones, P. C., Marks, L. C., Bradley-Klug, K. L., & Hermetet-Lindsay, K. D. (2020). Forming effective partnerships between school and community service providers. *Communiqué, 49*(1), 17–19.

Hirsch, B. (2011). Learning and development in after-school programs: Educators need to learn how best to work with after-school programs and use their contributions to young people. *Phi Delta Kappan, 92*(5), 66–69. https://doi.org/10.1177/003172171109200516

Jackson, I., Sealey-Ruiz, Y., & Watson, W. (2014). Reciprocal love: Mentoring Black and Latino males through an ethos of care. *Urban Education, 49*(4), 394–417. https://doi.org/10.1177/0042085913519336

Jenson, J. M., Veeh, C., Anyon, Y., Mary, J. S., Calhoun, M., Tejada, J., & Lechuga-Peña, S. (2018). Effects of an afterschool program on the academic outcomes of children and youth residing in public housing neighborhoods: A quasi-experimental study. *Children and Youth Services Review, 88*, 211–217. https://doi.org/10.1016/j.childyouth.2018.03.014

Jones, J. M., & Hazuka, H. L. (2013). Family, school, and community partnerships. In D. Shriberg, S. Y. Song, A. H. Miranda, & K. Radliff (Eds.), *School psychology and social justice: Conceptual foundations and tools for practice* (pp. 270–293). Routledge.

Kantor, H., & Lowe, R. (1995). Class, race, and the emergence of federal education policy: From the New Deal to the Great Society. *Educational Researcher, 24*(3), 4–21. https://doi.org/10.3102/0013189X024003004

Kim, J. (2019). Exploring the multidimensional constructs of transformative school–community collaboration from a critical paradigm. *Child & Family Social Work, 24*(2), 238–246. https://doi.org/10.1111/cfs.12608

King, N. S., & Pringle, R. M. (2019). Black girls speak STEM: Counterstories of informal and formal learning experiences. *Journal of Research in Science Teaching, 56*(5), 539–569. https://doi.org/10.1002/tea.21513

Ladson-Billings, G. (2014). Culturally relevant pedagogy 2.0: Aka the remix. *Harvard Educational Review, 84*(1), 74–84. https://doi.org/10.17763/haer.84.1.p2rj131485484751

Moore-Thomas, C., & Day-Vines, N. L. (2010). Culturally competent collaboration: School counselor collaboration with African American families and communities. *Professional School Counseling, 14*(1), 53–63. https://doi.org/10.1177/2156759X1001400106

National Association of School Psychologists. (2020). *The professional standards of the National Association of School Psychologists.* https://www.nasponline.org/standards-and-certification

Paris, D. (2012). Culturally sustaining pedagogy: A needed change in stance, terminology, and practice. *Educational Researcher, 41*(3), 93–97. https://doi.org/10.3102/0013189X12441244

Power, T. J. (2003). Promoting children's mental health: Reform through interdisciplinary and community partnerships. *School Psychology Review, 32*(1), 3–16. https://doi.org/10.1080/02796015.2003.12086177

Sanders, M. G. (2001). The role of "community" in comprehensive school, family, and community partnership programs. *The Elementary School Journal, 102*(1), 19–34. https://doi.org/10.1086/499691

Schwartz, S., & Suyemoto, K. (2013). Creating change from the inside: Youth development within a youth community organizing program. *Journal of Community Psychology, 41*(3), 341–358. https://doi.org/10.1002/jcop.21541

Sherman, R. H., Deich, S. G., & Langford, B. H. (2007). *Creating dedicated local and state revenue sources for youth programs.* https://files.eric.ed.gov/fulltext/ED499568.pdf

Shriberg, D. (2016). Commentary: School psychologists as advocates for racial justice and social justice: Some proposed steps. *School Psychology Forum, 10*(3), 337–339. https://ecommons.luc.edu/cgi/viewcontent.cgi?article=1134&context=education_facpubs

Truscott, S. D., Proctor, S. L., Albritton, K., Matthews, Y., & Daniel, K. (2014). African American school psychologists' perceptions of the opportunities and challenges of practicing in southeastern united states. *Psychology in the Schools, 51*(4), 366–383. https://doi.org/10.1002/pits.21753

Valli, L., Stefanski, A., & Jacobson, R. (2016). Typologizing school–community partnerships: A framework for analysis and action. *Urban Education, 51*(7), 719–747. https://doi.org/10.1177/0042085914549366

Washington, A. R. (2010). Professional school counselors and African American males: Using school/community collaboration to enhance academic performance. *Journal of African American Males in Education, 1*(1), 26–39. https://www.researchgate.net/publication/45534838_Professional_School_Counselors_and_African_American_Males_Using_SchoolCommunity_Collaboration_to_Enhance_Academic_Performance

Whaley, A. L. (2001). Cultural mistrust and mental health services for African Americans: A review and meta-analysis. *The Counseling Psychologist, 29*, 513–531. https://doi.org/10.1177/0011000001294003

Woodland, M. H., Martin, J. F., Hill, R. L., & Worrell, F. C. (2009). The most blessed room in the city: The influence of a youth development program on three young Black males. *Journal of Negro Education, 78*(3), 233–245. https://www.jstor.org/stable/25608743

Yosso, T. J. (2005). Whose culture has capital? A critical race theory discussion of community cultural wealth. *Race Ethnicity and Education, 8*(1), 69–91. https://doi.org/10.1080/1361332052000341006

CHAPTER 15

Systems Change and Program Evaluation

AMITY L. NOLTEMEYER ■ ERIN A. HARPER

CHAPTER OBJECTIVES

After reading this chapter, you will be able to:

- Identify the school psychologist's role within the systems change process.
- Describe the primary stages of the systems change process.
- Identify skills practitioners need to maximize success in the systems change process.
- Define and describe program evaluation.
- Describe how systems change and program evaluation can advance a social justice agenda.

NATIONAL ASSOCIATION OF SCHOOL PSYCHOLOGISTS PRACTICE MODEL CONNECTIONS

Domain 2: Consultation and Collaboration
Domain 5: School-Wide Practices to Promote Learning
Domain 8: Equitable Practices for Diverse Student Populations

INTRODUCTION

The field of school psychology has broadened its focus over time, gradually moving toward a systems-focused prevention and intervention orientation. The National Association of School Psychologists (NASP) Practice Model (2020) explicitly recognizes systems-level services as critical to the role of the school psychologist. Moreover, legislation such as the Every Student Succeeds Act (2015) further emphasizes the need for systemic approaches to prevention and intervention so as to create effective and equitable learning environments.

Despite these and other calls for effective systems-level change, research regarding perceptions of school psychologists' competence in this area is equivocal. In a study by Maki et al. (2019), school psychologists reported feelings of competence and confidence in implementing *systems change*. However, a survey study by Noltemeyer and McLaughlin (2011) found that school psychologists reported less expertise in systems-based service delivery than in other domains of practice. Furthermore, Wood and Hampton (2022) found that school principals would like school psychologists to spend more time in systems-level consultation but may not perceive them as having the necessary knowledge and skills to do so. Nevertheless, school psychologists are uniquely poised to advocate for, plan, and deliver systems-level services, and further developing their capacity and skills to do so should be a priority.

This chapter seeks to provide school psychologists with information on systems change and the practitioner leader's role within it. We begin by introducing the value of systems change, factors that influence the change process, and prominent systems change frameworks. Next, we outline considerations for leading systems change and educational reform efforts, including necessary skills for practitioners and considerations for maximizing success. Finally, we define *program evaluation* and describe how school psychologists can engage in process and outcome evaluation of their systems change efforts to inform further improvements. Throughout the chapter, we assume a social justice perspective in which school psychologists are viewed as advocates for equitable service delivery for all children and families.

SYSTEMS-LEVEL CHANGE IN THE SCHOOLS

Castillo and Curtis (2014) define a *system* as "an orderly combination of two or more individuals whose interaction is intended to produce a desired outcome" (p. 13). In an educational context, examples of systems include school districts, schools, grade-level teams, leadership teams, classrooms, professional learning committees, and disciplinary teams. Thus, the term *system* is a relative one and may refer to any one of a number of organizational levels. The goal of systems-level change is to increase the capacity of one or more systems to effectively address problems (Castillo & Curtis, 2014) and enhance outcomes.

A myriad of academic and behavioral indicators suggest that systems-level change is warranted to improve student and school outcomes in a meaningful way. Regarding the academic realm, recall the National Assessment of Educational Progress (NAEP) results described in Chapter 9. These data indicated that only 41% of fourth-graders, 34% of eighth-graders, and 24% of 12th-graders performed at or above the criteria for proficiency in mathematics on this assessment in 2019 (U.S. Department of Education et al., 2020). In the same year, scores for reading on the same assessment were similarly troubling, with 35% of fourth-graders, 34% of eighth-graders, and 37% of 12th-graders performing at or above the proficiency criteria (U.S. Department of Education et al., 2020). With numbers like these, it is clear that efforts to improve achievement at only the individual student level would be inefficient. Rather, system-wide changes to curricula design and delivery are needed to efficiently reach a larger number of students, thereby reducing the need for more individualized support.

Mental and behavioral health challenges are also common among youth in U.S. schools. For example, within the year prior to completing the 2017 High School Youth Risk Behavior Survey, 19% of high school students reported being bullied on school property, 31.5% felt sad or hopeless almost every day for at least 2 weeks in a row, and 17.2% seriously considered suicide within the past year (Centers for Disease Control and Prevention [CDC], 2017). Furthermore, approximately 2.8 million U.S. students received out-of-school suspensions in the 2013 to 2014 school year (Executive Office of the President, 2016). School climate may also be an important target for systems-level improvement in some settings;

for example, of 94,000 staff in 4,844 California schools, only 46% strongly agreed that their school was a supportive and inviting place to learn (WestEd, 2011). Moreover, only 39% of these respondents strongly agreed that their schools were supportive and inviting places to work (WestEd, 2011). These risks (i.e., those related to mental health challenges, school discipline, poor school climate) can be associated with a variety of negative outcomes for students, including conduct problems, increased absenteeism, poor academic achievement, and even school dropout (Fekkes et al., 2004; Noltemeyer et al., 2015; Thapa et al., 2013). Ultimately, a systems-level approach to prevention and intervention is warranted.

Importantly, any systems-level approach must consider the impact of privilege, oppression, discrimination, and power differentials pervasive in our society and schools that can impact access to effective services and outcomes. Particularly troubling are data revealing disparate trends for marginalized populations. For example, despite overall decreases in suicidal ideation and suicide plans from 1991 to 2017, Black adolescents experienced an increase in rates for suicide attempts, and Black adolescent boys experienced an increase in rates of injury caused by suicide attempts (Lindsey et al., 2019). Furthermore, Black, Latine, and Native American students are significantly more likely to be suspended from school, despite the fact that they do not commit more disciplinary offenses than their peers (e.g., U.S. Commission on Civil Rights, 2019). Students with disabilities are also substantially more likely to be suspended than their peers (e.g., U.S. Commission on Civil Rights, 2019). Systems-level reform is critical for eliminating these disparities among diverse groups and promoting equity and fairness for all students. Such systems-level efforts should be guided by a social justice agenda, which involves treating all individuals and groups with fairness and respect, ensuring the protection of educational rights and well-being of all children, recognizing and addressing inequities, and ensuring equal access to resources and opportunities offered in schools (NASP, 2017; North, 2006; Shriberg & Fenning, 2009; Shriberg et al., 2021).

RESEARCH ON SYSTEMS CHANGE AND EDUCATIONAL REFORM

Complex and pervasive challenges in schools require solutions that address entire systems, such as classrooms, grade levels, schools, and/or school districts. Furthermore, successful adoption and implementation of multitiered systems of support (MTSS) often require extensive changes in structures, practices, and personal beliefs. Therefore, it is important to consider the research on systems change and education reform, including factors that influence the change process and its key partners.

Education reform refers to the process of enacting fundamental, deep-rooted changes in the way educators conceptualize and implement school-based services. Not all changes to school practices constitute reform. For example, a school's decision to purchase new technology for its classrooms may increase the range and quality of resources available to students and teachers; however, in and of itself, this change may not constitute deep reform. Rather, this may instead represent a change that alters school procedures and/or practices that is not necessarily guided by a shared vision. As described by Fullan (2007), *shared vision* refers to the collective insights, values, goals, and understandings that are synthesized by participants in the change process to guide fundamental shifts in service delivery. In the present example, the introduction of technology into the classroom may not be guided by a mutually agreed-upon, underlying rationale for meaningfully influencing student learning. If this technology were being integrated in learning environments to fundamentally alter the way instruction or curriculum is conceptualized and delivered, however, it might be considered part of a reform process.

The literature on educational reform suggests that schools have historically faced challenges in implementing and sustaining systems changes. For example, Datnow and Stringfield (2000) found that only seven of 13 schools implementing a particular school reform initiative were continuing to implement it by the third year of the initiative. Similarly, in a study of comprehensive school reform, Vernez et al. (2006) found that none of the participating 350 schools had fully implemented system-wide change. These findings suggest that implementation of systems change is challenging and that it requires intentional planning, implementation, and sustainability methods to support long-term success.

Despite these disappointing findings, research suggests that the outlook for schools seeking to implement systems change is not entirely bleak. First, implementation can be facilitated through systematic efforts to cultivate environments and circumstances that enable change. For example, prior research on implementing Positive Behavioral Interventions and Supports (PBIS; described in Chapter 10) suggests that facilitators of successful systems change include factors such as vested partner buy-in, a shared vision for the change, administrative leadership, school psychologists as leaders, financial resources, district support, school-level or team-level professional development, and organizational restructuring (George et al., 2007; Kincaid et al., 2007). Furthermore, when implementation of systems change processes *is* strong, results can be powerful. As one example, Durlak and DuPre (2008) conducted a systematic review of more than 500 implementation studies on youth prevention and health promotion programs and found that well-implemented programs were associated with more beneficial outcomes. Overall, research in this area suggests that, although systems change can be challenging, high levels of implementation fidelity can be achieved and are associated with improvements in student outcomes.

FRAMEWORKS FOR SYSTEMS CHANGE

Several frameworks for planning and implementing systems change have been described in the literature (e.g., Adelman & Taylor, 1997; Fixsen et al., 2005; Fullan, 2007). A fundamental assumption of each of these frameworks is that implementation of systems change is a complex process; thus, although a framework may include identifiable phases, those phases may not always occur in a perfectly linear or nonrecursive fashion. Furthermore, an implementation science approach to systems change assumes that positive student outcomes are the product of "effective instruction supported by effective implementation conducted within organization and system contexts that enable (not hinder) the use of effective instruction and implementation supports" (Fixsen et al., 2015, p. 10). In this section, we focus on the Active Implementation Frameworks (AIF), developed based on earlier work by Fixsen et al. (2005) and the National Implementation Research Network.

The AIF highlights five ingredients that can contribute to the effective implementation of systems change: (a) usable innovations, (b) implementation drivers, (c) implementation teams, (d) implementation stages, and (e) improvement cycles (see Table 15.1). When planning for and implementing systems-level change, school psychologists should incorporate best practices from each of these areas. When doing so, it is important to consider how these ingredients can be embedded within and support each of the implementation stages (see Figure 15.1). As described by Fixsen et al. (2005), the *exploration* stage involves determining whether there is a match between the targeted systems change and the needs of the organization or its members. This stage ends with a decision to proceed with the change (if, in fact, the change is deemed to meet organizational needs). The *installation* stage, which commences following the decision to implement the change, includes several tasks that must be accomplished prior to implementation—for example, ensuring adequate funding

TABLE 15.1 Active Implementation Frameworks

Framework	Description/Key Components
Usable innovations	The change or program (as well as its components) should be clearly defined, able to be taught and learned, and able to be assessed.
Implementation teams	Diverse and representative groups that provide the support and structure to move the change forward toward full implementation.
Implementation drivers	Factors that enable the success of a change, by ensuring that the necessary competency and organizational supports are in place.
Implementation stages	Implementation of the change occurs in stages, which overlap to some degree. The four primary stages are Exploration, Installation, Initial Implementation, and Full Implementation. Planning for sustainability should occur across these stages.
Improvement cycles	Implementation teams should use rapid-cycle problem-solving (e.g., Plan, Do, Study, Act process) to inform positive improvements (in conjunction and addition to longer-term program evaluation processes).

Source: Adapted from National Implementation Research Network. (n.d.). *The active implementation frameworks*. Retrieved January 1, 2022, from https://nirn.fpg.unc.edu/sites/nirn.fpg.unc.edu/files/resources/AIHub%20Handout%201%20Active%20Implementation%20Frameworks.pdf

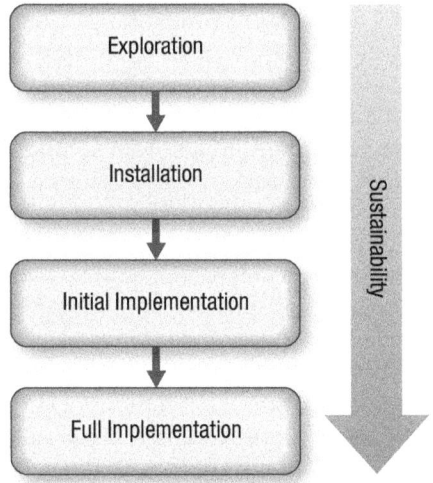

FIGURE 15.1 SYSTEMS CHANGE FRAMEWORK.

Source: Adapted from Fixsen, D. L., Naoom, S. F., Blase, K. A., Friedman, R. M., & Wallace, F. (2005). *Implementation research: A synthesis of the literature* (FMHI Publication #231). University of South Florida, Louis de la Parte Florida Mental Health Institute, The National Implementation Research Network.

and staffing, developing policy and evaluation strategies, planning for equitable implementation, and clarifying outcome goals. After these foundations have been established, the *initial implementation* stage begins. This stage constitutes the organization's first attempts at putting the change into practice. During initial implementation, changes may not occur evenly or simultaneously across the entire system and will warrant ongoing refinement through practice opportunities, professional development, and coaching. *Full implementation* occurs when the change becomes completely integrated into the system's practices and procedures, and implementation becomes more skillful and routine. Finally, an often overlooked but critical aspect of the change process is *sustainability* (also described in Chapter 8), which should be incorporated into the work of each of the prior stages. Sustainability involves planning for issues that could affect the continued implementation of the change, such as staff turnover, funding changes, and competing initiatives. According to Fixsen et al. (2005), the goal of this stage is "long-term survival and continued effectiveness of the implementation site in the context of a changing world" (p. 17).

School personnel and leadership teams engaged in systems-level work may use these stages as a framework for guiding the planning and implementation of their efforts, thereby ensuring that they do not overlook important considerations. For example, it is not uncommon for schools to rush through the exploration stage or to fail to plan for sustainability, both of which may diminish the impact and longevity of the initiative. Additionally, throughout these stages it is important to ensure that the perspectives and needs of diverse vested partners are incorporated and to strive for equitable access and outcomes in the implementation and sustainability phases.

CONSIDERATIONS FOR LEADING SYSTEMS CHANGE

As already noted, systems-level prevention and intervention are important components of the school psychologist's work. Properly trained and skilled school psychologists are well positioned to collaborate with other vested partners to initiate and implement change efforts that can enhance school and student functioning. This section reviews key considerations for implementing systems change, with a primary focus on the roles and skills necessary for school psychologists.

As discussed in Chapter 12, a primary role of school psychologists engaged in systems change is that of collaborative consultant. In a school setting, systems-level collaborative consultation is a process whereby a trained school consultant enters into a nonhierarchical relationship with a team of consultees to help lead efforts to develop, implement, and evaluate systems-level plans to support student success (Kampwirth & Powers, 2016). Collaborative consultants operate from the perspective that all team members contribute valuable input and expertise to team-based problem-solving and decision-making based on their previous experiences and skills.

To work successfully with other members of planning and/or implementation teams, collaborative consultants first need effective communication and interpersonal skills (Ysseldyke et al., 2006). In the context of school-based consultation, communication often involves an exchange of information between two or more individuals. Critical communication skills include attending, active listening, reframing, and empathy (Baillie, 2016; Kampwirth & Powers, 2016). Other skills necessary for successful communication include the ability to ask clarifying questions in a nonthreatening manner and the ability to maintain a goal-oriented mindset (Kampwirth & Powers, 2016). Strong interpersonal skills facilitate the effective transmission of information and help team members with diverse experiences and backgrounds form positive relationships, which effectively position them to work in concert toward meeting organizational goals. Examples of interpersonal skills include the ability to adapt, tolerate ambiguity, and be patient in difficult situations (Ysseldyke et al., 2006).

When implementing systems change in educational settings, consultants contribute content knowledge and intervention skills, as well as process knowledge during team problem-solving. Content knowledge refers to knowledge of the programs and changes to be implemented, whereas process knowledge refers to expertise in communication, consultation, and systems change processes necessary to support program implementation. Although it is impossible for school psychologists who lead systems change to know everything about each problem they may confront, systems change leaders should have foundational knowledge (i.e., *content knowledge*) of a range of evidence-based strategies and interventions to address various types of student and school issues. As described in

Chapter 8, school psychologists should be aware of resources for identifying appropriate evidence-based interventions, such as the What Works Clearinghouse (Institute of Education Sciences, n.d.; www.ies.ed.gov/ncee/WWC), the Evidence-Based Practices Resource Center (www.samhsa.gov/resource-search/ebp), and the Connecticut Clearinghouse (www.ctclearinghouse.org). Moreover, practitioners must be knowledgeable about principles and research related to resilience and risk factors in learning and mental health, multi-tiered prevention and intervention, home–school–community collaboration, and equitable service delivery for diverse populations.

Also critical for collaborative consultants engaged in systems change and educational reform is *process knowledge,* such as knowledge of systems change frameworks and facilitators of successful reform. As mentioned in Table 15.1, factors that contribute to successful systems change are referred to as ***implementation drivers*** and can be organized into three categories: competency supports, organization supports, and leadership supports (Fixsen et al., 2005). Competency supports include the selection, training, and coaching of team members who will implement the systems change. Organization supports, which are developed by system administrators, facilitate positive and productive organizational practices and a positive organizational climate. An example of an organization support is the use of high-quality data systems to assure smooth implementation of the intervention over time. Leadership supports include supports that help to resolve both technical and adaptive issues related to factors such as time, funding, and motivation. The National Implementation Research Network (https://nirn.fpg.unc.edu) provides a detailed description of each implementation driver and additional implementation resources.

Evaluating School and Student Outcomes Associated With the Change Process

As complex as the change process can be, it is important to realize that implementation is not the end of the process. A critical, but sometimes overlooked, aspect of the systems change process is program evaluation. ***Program evaluation*** is a "systematic process for planning, documenting, and assessing the implementation and outcomes of a program" (Stewart et al., 2021, p. 1). Evaluating the implementation and outcomes of a systems change initiative is critical, as the information that emerges can suggest whether the organization should continue, intensify, discontinue, or alter the program implementation. More specifically, program evaluation can inform both formative and summative decisions. (Recall from Chapter 7 that *formative* evaluation occurs during the course of program implementation, whereas *summative* evaluation takes place following implementation.) In formative decision-making, ongoing progress monitoring data on fidelity of implementation as well as student outcomes relevant to the particular systems change initiative can be used to drive continuous improvement (Castillo, 2014). For example, as highlighted in Table 15.1, implementation teams can use rapid-cycle problem-solving to inform improvements to systems change implementation. In regard to summative decision-making, larger spans of periodic data collection can be used to determine whether the outcomes of the systems change initiative justify its continuation (Castillo, 2014).

As an example of the formative–summative distinction, a school implementing PBIS may review weekly data on student office disciplinary referrals (ODRs), positive office referrals, and adult implementation and then make changes in PBIS practices based on areas of need identified through this evaluation. For instance, trends in when and where ODRs are occurring may reveal a need for more modeling, reinforcement, or supervision in those areas or at those times. Furthermore, an examination of ODR data disaggregated by race may reveal disparities indicating the need for a root cause analysis (Osher et al., 2015) to understand and address these trends. However, this same school may also perform a more comprehensive annual evaluation that summarizes outcomes over the course of the entire school year, which may be shared with district administrators who make decisions about funding and other supports for PBIS initiatives.

There are multiple program evaluation frameworks that school psychologists can use when conducting effective evaluations of systems-level change. For example, the CDC (1999) Framework for Program Evaluation in Public Health includes practical steps and standards that can be embedded within school practices to assess and improve systems-level interventions. As shown in Figure 15.2, the steps include engaging partners, describing the program, focusing the evaluation design, gathering credible evidence, justifying conclusions, and ensuring that the lessons learned are used and shared. These steps should be implemented while adhering to the following standards for quality evaluation activities: utility, feasibility, propriety, and accuracy. The Institute of Education Sciences' (IES's; 2021) Program Evaluation Toolkit provides another helpful framework for planning and implementing a successful evaluation. This framework includes planning for a logic model, evaluation questions, evaluation design, sampling, data quality, data collection, data analysis, and dissemination approaches (see Table 15.2). IES (2021) provides a variety of free online modules and training resources that walk through each of these processes.

When conducting a program evaluation, there are several important considerations for maximizing the validity and usefulness of the results. For example, evaluators should strive to use multimethod data collection strategies that incorporate data from multiple and diverse informants. To continue the PBIS example highlighted earlier, multimethod data collection might be operationalized as collecting several sources of quantitative (e.g., number of ODRs, number of positive office referrals) and qualitative (e.g., partner interviews) information. Multiple informants could be operationalized as collecting information from students, staff, and families, so as to comprehensively understand the impact on diverse groups.

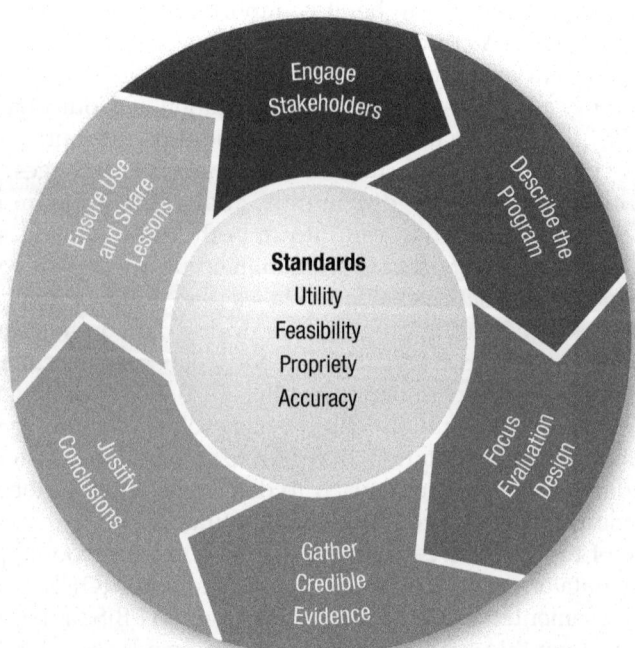

FIGURE 15.2 THE CDC FRAMEWORK FOR PROGRAM EVALUATION IN PUBLIC HEALTH.

Source: Centers for Disease Control and Prevention. (1999). *Program Performance and Evaluation Office.* Image reproduced with permission from https://www.cdc.gov/eval/framework/index.htm

TABLE 15.2 Institute of Education Sciences (IES) Toolkit Program Evaluation Considerations

Consideration	Example Question to Answer
Logic models	How do the parts of the program (e.g., resources, activities, outputs) relate to its expected outcomes?
Evaluation questions	What process and outcome questions related to my logic model am I trying to answer?
Evaluation design	What methods and processes can I use to answer my evaluation questions?
Evaluation samples	How can I ensure that my sample is representative and generalizable?
Data quality	What types of data will allow me to most thoroughly answer my research questions?
Data collection	What data collection tools and procedures are ideal for answering my research questions?
Data analysis	How should I prepare the data for analysis, analyze the data, and make recommendations based on the analyses?
Dissemination approaches	Who is the audience for the findings, and what is the best method of communicating the findings to them?

Source: Data from the Institute of Education Sciences. (2021). *Program evaluation toolkit: A module based toolkit for professional development and program evaluation.* https://ies.ed.gov/ncee/edlabs/regions/central/resources/pemtoolkit/index.asp

SOCIAL JUSTICE CONNECTIONS

How can program evaluation advance a social justice agenda?

Program evaluation offers important opportunities to advance a social justice agenda. Over the past few decades, scholars have underscored the integral link between program evaluation methodology and social justice (Cooper & Christie, 2005; Greene, 2006; House, 1991). These scholars have contended that because program evaluation is designed to serve the interests of society, it must advance the interests of all constituent groups, especially those that have been traditionally marginalized (e.g., Greene, 2006; Sirotnik, 1990). Miranda and Radliff (2016) refer to these inclusive program evaluation efforts as essential to delivering systems-level and individual-level services with a "social justice mind-set" (p. 20). As stated by Thomas and Madison (2010), "Respect for the rights of others is important to conducting fair and valid evaluations and in engaging in meaningful public discourse" (p. 572).

Based on this literature, the following recommendations may assist school psychologists in undertaking evaluations that are grounded in social justice principles and promote equity in service delivery.

1. Recognize that no evaluation process is entirely value neutral. Evaluators must be mindful of the values, assumptions, biases, and beliefs that impact their methodologies and approaches (Greene, 2006). Moreover, they must account for the cultural, social, economic, and political environments that enshroud the evaluation process. Evaluators should move away from efforts to stress objectivity and instead recognize the importance of acknowledging constituents' multiple perspectives and realities (Thomas & Madison, 2010).
2. Develop and employ high-quality communication skills (e.g., verbal expression and listening skills) as well as interpersonal skills (e.g., conflict resolution and group facilitation skills; Thomas & Madison, 2010). Building trust with partners is essential for obtaining honest input.

(continued)

> **SOCIAL JUSTICE CONNECTIONS (*continued*)**
>
> 3. Make it a priority to identify and engage the most disenfranchised partners in the evaluation process. These parties may include families who are recipients of program services or outside groups that are inadvertently affected or marginalized by the implementation process. Evaluators should seek not only to capture the perspectives of these individuals, but also to empower them to participate in the evaluation process (Cooper & Christie, 2005).
> 4. Ask the important and difficult questions, even when their answers raise difficult and uncomfortable considerations. These questions may include:
>   a. Who is accessing program services? In other words, are the intended recipients of services the ones who are benefiting from them? What might be some potential barriers to access?
>   b. Are the program's core values and delivery consistent with the cultural values of the populations it is designed to serve?
>   c. Are the various subgroups who are accessing the program receiving comparable benefits? Especially among traditionally marginalized groups, are there other needs that could and should be met but have not yet been addressed through program initiatives?
>
> One way to capture the perspectives of diverse partners is to use mixed methods evaluation designs. Mixed methods designs incorporate both quantitative data (e.g., numerical data) and qualitative data (e.g., field notes, interview transcripts, photographs). Collecting both quantitative and qualitative data can yield a much more comprehensive picture of the perspectives, needs, and values of diverse groups.

Another particularly important consideration related to the evaluation of systems change initiatives concerns the assessment of intervention fidelity (also referred to as implementation fidelity, treatment fidelity, implementation integrity, and treatment integrity). Recall from Chapter 8 that *intervention fidelity* refers to the degree to which an intervention or program is implemented as designed or intended. Inherently, systems change initiatives in schools tend to be complex and to require considerable effort, support, and collaborative teamwork from a variety of partners. Thus, many variables can influence program outcomes. To determine whether the outcomes observed are truly related to the systems change itself, it is first necessary to determine whether the systems change was implemented as intended. Widely used methods for assessing implementation integrity include direct observation of implementation, self-report checklists documenting the degree to which key implementation features were put into practice, and review of permanent products from implementation (e.g., student work samples). Ideally, implementation integrity should be assessed using multiple methods (Goss et al., 2007).

Notably, using program evaluation to demonstrate initial successes can facilitate the leveraging of resources to scale up implementation (Horner et al., 2019). For example, Horner et al. (2019, p. 71) discuss a framework in which initial investments in smaller implementation efforts provide "proof of concept" (e.g., using data on fidelity, outcomes, and reasonable cost), which in turn can be used to secure more funding, drive policy shifts, and encourage the reallocation of existing resources to support larger-scale implementation. Thus, when resources and capacity do not exist to support widespread systems change initially, school psychologists can gather data on smaller pilot projects (e.g., implementing the change in a grade level or classroom) and use those data to scale up adoption.

Overall, given their training in systems-level service delivery, school psychologists are uniquely qualified to facilitate the planning and implementation of the program evaluation processes outlined in the preceding text. Notably, *Research and Evidence-Based Practice* is one of the 10 domains in the NASP Practice Model (2020), which specifically states that "school psychologists, in collaboration with others, collect, analyze, and interpret program evaluation data in applied settings" (p. 9). Furthermore, school psychologists can approach program evaluation with a social justice orientation, carefully examining the degree to which access, implementation, and outcomes of systems change initiatives are equitable across student populations.

CASE EXAMPLE
Implementing Systems Change in School Districts

The following case example illustrates the applications of the systems change process in a fictitious school district.

Rushmore Independent School District (RISD) is a rural public school system located near a town that has been impacted by a natural disaster. Although no students in RISD were personally affected, the close proximity of the natural disaster prompted the new superintendent of RISD to explore the district's current policies and procedures for crisis preparedness, response, and recovery. The new superintendent discovered that although the school district had a crisis response plan, the plan was not comprehensive and had not been updated in more than a decade. Moreover, many of the school administrators, teachers, and support staff in the district were unaware that the plan existed.

Realizing the need to develop and implement a more comprehensive plan for crisis preparedness, response, and recovery, the superintendent requested a meeting with the district's director of student support services "to explore the enhancement of crisis response efforts in the district." The superintendent encouraged the support services director to invite others to the meeting who might be good candidates for a district-level planning team devoted to this issue. The support services director then invited the lead school psychologist, social worker, counselor, and nurse to attend the meeting with her.

During the initial meeting, the lead school psychologist shared information about PREPaRE, a crisis prevention and intervention model and training program developed by the National Association of School Psychologists (NASP). PREPaRE helps organizations better prepare for and respond to crisis events and takes into account the diverse needs of marginalized populations (Reeves et al., 2011). Interested in learning more about the program, the superintendent and other team members asked the school psychologist if she would develop a presentation about NASP's PREPaRE program for other members of the team and present it during a follow-up meeting. After the presentation, each team member was invited to ask questions and was given additional information about the program to review before the next meeting. At the third meeting, all team members reported that they supported implementation of the program, and the superintendent reported that funding was available for training. The team then decided to develop a survey to obtain feedback from other partners, including parents and students. After ensuring that they had responses from diverse and representative partners, survey results were presented to the district's Board of Education, and the board voted unanimously in favor of PREPaRE program training. The district-level planning team worked to develop a systematic plan for initial implementation, informed by local needs and resources. Furthermore, team members met quarterly thereafter to plan for and monitor the degree to which the resulting crisis prevention and intervention strategies were being effectively and equitably embedded into school practices, to plan for improvement and sustainability of efforts, and to evaluate outcomes.

SUMMARY AND CONCLUSIONS

As the role of the school psychologist has evolved, systems-level service provision has become an integral aspect of comprehensive school psychology service delivery. This chapter presented an overview of systems change and program evaluation and described the role of school psychologists in these dynamic processes. When implemented from a social justice perspective, systems change and program evaluation may contribute to equitable academic and social outcomes for children and youth.

DISCUSSION QUESTIONS

1. Not all schools that decide to implement systems change initiatives are successful in doing so. Based on the research presented in this chapter, what primary pieces of advice would you give to a school team that is thinking about undertaking systems change to help the team avoid failures in implementation and sustainability?
2. Consider the roles and skills that are important for school psychologists as they engage in systems-level work. Which of those discussed in the chapter are your personal strengths? Which are areas for continued growth, and how will you develop those over the next 5 years?
3. Why are both content knowledge and process knowledge important to systems-level consultation?
4. What is program evaluation and why is it a critical consideration when implementing systems change?
5. Why is a social justice perspective important when considering systems-level work? What are some concrete ways that you can infuse a social justice perspective into your systems-level work?

RECOMMENDED READINGS

Castillo, J. M., & Curtis, M. J. (2014). Best practices in systems-level change. In P. L. Harrison & A. Thomas (Eds.), *Best practices in school psychology: Systems-level services* (pp. 11–28). National Association of School Psychologists.

Fixsen, D. L., Naoom, S. F., Blase, K. A., Friedman, R. M., & Wallace, F. (2005). *Implementation research: A synthesis of the literature.* FMHI Publication #231. University of South Florida, Louis de la Parte Florida Mental Health Institute, The National Implementation Research Network.

Institute of Education Sciences. (2021). *Program evaluation toolkit: A module based toolkit for professional development and program evaluation.* https://ies.ed.gov/ncee/edlabs/regions/central/resources/pemtoolkit/index.asp

Miranda, A. H., & Radliff, K. M. (2016). Consulting with a social justice mind-set. In A. Miranda (Ed.), *Consultation across cultural contexts: Consultee-centered case studies* (pp. 13–22). Routledge.

National Association of School Psychologists. (n.d.). *Systems-level prevention.* https://www.nasponline.org/resources-and-publications/resources/school-safety-and-crisis/prevention-resources

 A robust set of instructor resources designed to supplement this text is located at http://connect.springerpub.com/content/book/978-0-8261-6344-8. Qualifying instructors may request access by emailing textbook@springerpub.com.

REFERENCES

Adelman, H. S., & Taylor, L. (1997). Toward a scale-up model for replicating new approaches to schooling. *Journal of Educational and Psychological Consultation, 8(2)*, 197–230. https://doi.org/10.1207/s1532768xjepc0802_6

Baillie, A. (2016). Cultural understanding and communication: Keys to successful multicultural school consultation. In A. Miranda (Ed.), *Consultation across cultural contexts: Consultee-centered case studies* (pp. 139–150). Routledge.

Castillo, J. M. (2014). Best practices in program evaluation. In P. L. Harrison & A. Thomas (Eds.), *Best practices in school psychology: Foundations* (pp. 11–28). National Association of School Psychologists.

Castillo, J. M., & Curtis, M. J. (2014). Best practices in systems-level change. In P. L. Harrison & A. Thomas (Eds.), *Best practices in school psychology: Systems-level services* (pp. 11–28). National Association of School Psychologists.

Centers for Disease Control and Prevention. (1999). Framework for program evaluation in public health. *MMWR, 48*(RR-11), 1–40. https://www.cdc.gov/mmwr/PDF/rr/rr4811.pdf

Centers for Disease Control and Prevention. (2017). *Youth risk behavior survey data.* https://www.cdc.gov/yrbs

Cooper, C. W., & Christie, C. A. (2005). Evaluating parent empowerment: A look at the potential of social justice evaluation in education. *Teachers College Record, 107*, 2248–2274. https://doi.org/10.1111/j.1467-9620.2005.00591.x

Datnow, A., & Stringfield, S. (2000). Working together for reliable school reform. *Journal of Education for Students Placed at Risk, 5*, 183–204. https://doi.org/10.1080/10824669.2000.9671386

Durlak, J. A., & DuPre, E. P. (2008). Implementation matters: A review of research on the influence of implementation on program outcomes and the factors affecting implementation. *American Journal of Community Psychology, 41*, 327–350. https://doi.org/10.1007/s10464-008-9165-0

Every Student Succeeds Act. (2015). Every Student Succeeds Act. Pub. L. No. 114-95, § 1177.

Executive Office of the President. (2016, December). *Report: The continuing need to rethink discipline.* https://www.ed.gov/news/press-releases/white-house-report-continuing-need-rethink-discipline

Fekkes, M., Pijpers, F., & Verloove-Vanhorick, S. (2004). Bullying behavior and associations with psychosomatic complaints and depression in victims. *Journal of Pediatrics, 144(1)*, 17–22. https://doi.org/10.1016/j.jpeds.2003.09.025

Fixsen, D., Blase, K., Van Dyke, M., Duda, M., Sims, B., & Ward, C. (2015). *Systemic changes in state education systems.* The State Implementation and Scaling-up of Evidence-based Practices Center. https://www.activeimplementation.org/wp-content/uploads/2021/06/SISEP-SystemsChangesInStateEducationSystems.pdf

Fixsen, D. L., Naoom, S. F., Blase, K. A., Friedman, R. M., & Wallace, F. (2005). *Implementation research: A synthesis of the literature.* FMHI Publication #231. University of South Florida, Louis de la Parte Florida Mental Health Institute, The National Implementation Research Network.

Fullan, M. (2007). *The new meaning of educational change* (4th ed.). Teacher's College Press.

George, M. P., White, G. P., & Schlaffer, J. J. (2007). Implementing school-wide behavior change: Lessons from the field. *Psychology in the Schools, 44*, 41–51. https://doi.org/10.1002/pits.20204

Goss, S., Noltemeyer, A., & Devore, H. (2007). Treatment integrity: A necessary component of response-to-intervention. *School Psychologist, 61(2)*, 34–38. https://apadivision16.org/wp-content/uploads/2015/12/TSP-Vol.-61-No.-2-April-2007.pdf

Greene, J. C. (2006). Evaluation, democracy, and social change. In I. F. Shaw, J. C. Greene, & M. M. Mark (Eds.), *The Sage handbook of evaluation* (pp. 118–140). Sage.

Horner, R. H., Ward, C. S., Fixsen, D. L., Sugai, G., McIntosh, K., Putnam, R., & Little, H. D. (2019). Resource leveraging to achieve large-scale implementation of effective educational practices. *Journal of Positive Behavior Interventions, 21(2)*, 67–76. https://doi.org/10.1177/1098300718783754

House, E. R. (1991). Evaluation and social justice: Where are we? In M. McLaughlin & D. Phillips (Eds.), *Evaluation and education at quarter century: National Society for the Study of Education yearbook* (pp. 233–246). University of Chicago Press.

Institute of Education Sciences. (n.d.). *What Works Clearinghouse*. U.S. Department of Education. http://ies.ed.gov/ncee/WWC

Institute of Education Sciences. (2021). *Program evaluation toolkit: A module based toolkit for professional development and program evaluation*. https://ies.ed.gov/ncee/edlabs/regions/central/resources/pemtoolkit/index.asp

Kampwirth, T. J., & Powers, K. M. (2016). *Collaborative consultation in the schools: Effective practices for students with learning and behavior problems* (5th ed.). Pearson Education.

Kincaid, D., Childs, K., Blaise, K. A., & Wallace, F. (2007). Identifying barriers and facilitators in implementing schoolwide positive behavior support. *Journal of Positive Behavior Interventions, 9*, 174–184. https://doi.org/10.1177/10983007070090030501

Lindsey, M. A., Sheftall, A. H., Xiao, Y., & Joe, S. (2019). Trends of suicidal behaviors among high school students in the United States: 1991–2017. *Pediatrics, 144*(5), Article e20191187. https://doi.org/10.1542/peds.2019-1187

Maki, E. D., Sheppard, A. V., James, J., Mueller, M., Broadhead, S., Brodsky, L., Couse, A., & Pearrow, M. (2019). School psychologists' perceptions of systems change: A case study. *School Psychology Forum, 13*(1), 16–28. https://www.nasponline.org/publications/periodicals/spf/volume-13/volume-13-issue-1-(spring-2019)/school-psychologists-perceptions-of-systems-change-a-case-study

Miranda, A. H., & Radliff, K. M. (2016). Consulting with a social justice mind-set. In A. Miranda (Ed.), *Consultation across cultural contexts: Consultee-centered case studies* (pp. 13–22). Routledge.

National Association of School Psychologists. (2017). *Social justice*. Author. https://www.nasponline.org/social-justice

National Association of School Psychologists. (2020). *The professional standards of the National Association of School Psychologists*. Author. https://www.nasponline.org/x55315.xml

Noltemeyer, A., & McLaughlin, C. L. (2011). School psychology's blueprint III: Knowledge, use, and competence. *School Psychology Forum, 5*, 74–86. https://www.researchgate.net/publication/259930809_School_Psychology's_Blueprint_III_A_Survey_of_Knowledge_Use_and_Competence

Noltemeyer, A., Ward, R. M., & Mcloughlin, C. S. (2015). Relationship between school suspension and student outcomes: A meta-analysis. *School Psychology Review, 44*, 224–240. https://edsource.org/wp-content/uploads/2018/09/Noltemeyer_Ward_2015_Meta-Analysis.pdf

North, C. E. (2006). More than words? Delving into the substantive meaning(s) of "social justice" in education. *Review of Educational Research, 76*, 507–536. https://journals.sagepub.com/doi/pdf/10.1177/0011000014548900

Osher, D., Fisher, D., Amos, L., Katz, J., Dwyer, K., Duffey, T., & Colombi, G. D. (2015). *Addressing the root causes of disparities in school discipline: An educator's action planning guide*. National Center on Safe Supportive Learning Environments. https://safesupportivelearning.ed.gov/sites/default/files/15-1547%20NCSSLE%20Root%20Causes%20Guide%20FINAL02%20mb.pdf

Reeves, M. A., Nickerson, A. B., Connolly-Wilson, C. N., Susan, M. K., Lazzaro, B. R., Jimerson, S. R., & Pesce, R. C. (2011). *PREPaRE: Crisis prevention and preparedness: Comprehensive school safety planning* (2nd ed.). National Association of School Psychologists.

Shriberg, D., & Fenning, P. A. (2009). School consultants as agents of social justice: Implications for practice: Introduction to the special issue. *Journal of Educational and Psychological Consultation, 19*, 1–7. https://doi.org/10.1080/10474410802462751

Shriberg, D., Harper, E. A., & McPherson, A. C. (2021). Fighting for social justice. In R. G. Floyd & T. L. Eckert (Eds.), *Handbook of university and professional careers in school psychology* (pp. 468–481). Routledge.

Sirotnik, E. A. (Ed.). (1990). *Evaluation and social justice: Issues in public education (New Directions for Program Evaluation, 45)*. Jossey-Bass.

Stewart, J., Joyce, J., Haines, M., Yanoski, D., Gagnon, D., Luke, K., Rhoads, C., & Germeroth, C. (2021, October). *Program evaluation toolkit: Quick start guide*. Institute of Education Sciences. https://ies.ed.gov/ncee/edlabs/regions/central/pdf/REL_2021112.pdf

Thapa, A., Cohen, J., Guffey, S., & Higgins-D'Alessandro, A. (2013). A review of school climate research. *Review of Educational Research, 83*(3), 357–385. https://doi.org/10.3102/0034654313483907

Thomas, V. G., & Madison, A. (2010). Integration of social justice into the teaching of evaluation. *American Journal of Evaluation, 31*, 570–583. https://doi.org/10.1177/1098214010368426

U.S. Commission on Civil Rights. (2019). *Beyond suspensions: Examining school discipline policies and connections to the school-to-prison pipeline for students of color with disabilities.* https://www.usccr.gov/files/pubs/2019/07-23-Beyond-Suspensions.pdf

U.S. Department of Education, Institute of Education Sciences, & National Center for Education Statistics. (2020). *The nation's report card.* http://www.nationsreportcard.gov

Vernez, G., Karam, R., Mariano, L. T., & DeMartini, C. (2006). *Evaluating comprehensive school reform models at scale: Focus on implementation.* https://www.rand.org/pubs/monographs/MG546.html

WestEd. (2011). *California school climate survey: Statewide results, 2008–2010.* Report 1. What teachers and other staff tell us about our schools. WestEd Health & Human Development Program for the California Department of Education. http://surveydata.wested.org/resources/CSCS_State0810_Main.pdf

Wood, B. J., & Hampton, E. (2022). An initial investigation of school principal perspectives on school psychologists as systems-level consultants. *Contemporary School Psychology, 26,* 173–181. https://doi.org/10.1007/s40688-020-00303-y

Ysseldyke, J. E., Burns, M., Dawson, P., Kelley, B., Morrison, D., Ortiz, S., & Telzrow, K. (2006). *School psychology: A blueprint for training and practice III.* National Association of School Psychologists.

CHAPTER 16

Research in School Psychology

TAI A. COLLINS ■ ALEXIS BLACKMON ■ JOSEPH S. WANG

CHAPTER OBJECTIVES

After reading this chapter, you will be able to:

- Discuss the importance of research to the field of school psychology.
- Identify research contributions within each of the 10 National Association of School Psychologists Practice Model domains, with a focus on social justice research.
- Describe the various research methodologies used in school psychology research.
- Describe the peer review process.
- Identify ways in which school psychologists are producers, consumers, and disseminators of research.

NATIONAL ASSOCIATION OF SCHOOL PSYCHOLOGISTS PRACTICE MODEL CONNECTIONS

Domain 9: Research and Evidence-Based Practice

INTRODUCTION

As a profession that utilizes a collaborative, problem-solving approach, school psychologists often engage in some form of research, including conducting, consuming, and disseminating research. Whether conducting observations or interpreting school-wide data, school psychologists use various research techniques and technologies to better understand the applied contexts in which they work. The importance of research is emphasized in Domain 9 of the National Association of School Psychologists (NASP; 2020) Practice Model. *Research* can be described as a systematic process of asking questions, collecting and analyzing data, and forming conclusions and future directions based on those data. School psychologists also have skills in program evaluation, and their role in implementing programs and interventions can ensure that research is informed by practice. From a social justice perspective, school psychologists may use their critical lens to examine how programs, policies, and educational services may disadvantage students who are marginalized and underserved in schools and broader society, as well as to engage in advocacy to create equitable educational spaces (Parris et al., 2019).

OVERVIEW OF RESEARCH IN SCHOOL PSYCHOLOGY

In this section, we provide a brief overview of research in the field of school psychology. It would be impossible to comprehensively review this broad topic within one chapter. As such, the purpose of this discussion is to point readers in the direction of relevant research in the field for further reading. We utilize the NASP (2020) Practice Model to frame this section, as we discuss research within the 10 domains of school psychological services. As noted in Chapter 1, the Practice Model lays out the scope of school psychologists' work and is critical for their professional identity, ethical practice, and advocacy on behalf of the field. Within each domain, we intentionally highlight social justice research, as well as some of the women and racially/ethnically minoritized (REM) scholars who have contributed to our epistemology.

Domain 1: Data-Based Decision-Making

Data-based decision-making is a pillar of school psychology practice because it is necessary for us to collect data to determine whether interventions and supports are working and how individuals are functioning within educational contexts. If a school were to implement a new reading curriculum, we would not be able to make decisions about its effectiveness without collecting data via assessment. As described in Chapter 7, *assessment* refers to the variety of methods used to collect data (e.g., direct observation, surveys, interviews, standardized tests). Much of the school psychology research literature has focused on assessment and using data to make decisions, such as in the areas of behavioral assessment (e.g., Eklund & Dowdy, 2014), academic assessment (e.g., Kilgus et al., 2014), and mental health assessment (e.g., von der Embse et al., 2018), among many others. Researchers have also focused on bias and equity within school psychology assessment and decision-making, such as the use of data to disrupt racial inequities in discipline (e.g., Blake et al., 2018) and special education decision-making (e.g., Sullivan, 2011).

Domain 2: Consultation and Collaboration

School psychologists work on teams to support students, families, and educators. This often requires engaging in consultation and collaboration with teachers, other school staff, and caregivers to promote the effective implementation of interventions and supports. Thus, school psychology researchers have conducted studies on effective ways to consult with partners to best support children in schools. The *Journal of Educational and Psychological Consultation* (*JEPC*) publishes research on consultation methods and theories (e.g., behavioral consultation, consultee-centered consultation, instructional consultation). Some research in the area of consultation and collaboration has explored methods for promoting teacher implementation of interventions (e.g., Fallon et al., 2015); the use of technology to consult with teachers and staff via teleconsultation (e.g., Fischer et al., 2017); and various models of consultation (e.g., Newman & Ingraham, 2017). Much of the recent literature has focused on social justice frameworks for consulting, such as utilizing culturally relevant consultation practices with REM populations (e.g., Jones et al., 2016; Miranda & Radliff, 2016) and restorative consultation practices designed to repair relationships as an alternative to exclusionary discipline (e.g., Song et al., 2020).

Domain 3: Academic Interventions and Instructional Supports

Improving students' academic skills is one of the primary purposes of education, and school psychologists are tasked with supporting teachers' academic instruction and students' academic skill development. School psychologists have developed interventions to improve students' reading skills, such as incremental rehearsal (e.g., Burns et al., 2012) and flash card drill (Volpe et al., 2011). In the area of math, researchers have focused on computational skills (e.g., Codding et al., 2009), generalization of math skills (e.g., Miller et al., 2011), and comparisons of different math interventions (e.g., Poncy et al., 2007), among other areas. A growing body of literature has also focused on writing and spelling intervention (e.g., Hier & Eckert, 2014). Social justice approaches to academic intervention have included strategies to improve the cultural relevance of math interventions (e.g., Luevano & Collins, 2020) and the utilization of peers to implement academic interventions for emerging bilingual students (e.g., Klingbeil, Moeyaert, et al., 2017).

Domain 4: Mental and Behavioral Health Services and Interventions

Schools have increasingly become sites of mental health support for youth, as mental health concerns are related to students' academic, behavioral, and social functioning; moreover, school variables can affect children's mental health. School psychologists have produced research at the forefront of school-based mental health (e.g., Suldo & Shaffer, 2008), mindfulness-based interventions (e.g., Klingbeil, Renshaw, et al., 2017), social–emotional learning (e.g., Eklund et al., 2018), and behavioral interventions (e.g., Radley & Dart, 2019). Culturally relevant approaches to mental health and behavioral interventions include cultural adaptations of interventions (e.g., Castro-Olivo et al., 2018); Afrocentric interventions (e.g., Heidelburg & Collins, 2022); approaches to mental health focused on improving youth well-being rather than only reducing risk (e.g., Lazarus et al., 2021); and examinations of the effectiveness of interventions with various minoritized populations (e.g., Long et al., 2019).

Domain 5: School-Wide Practices to Promote Learning

The work of school psychologists extends beyond working with individual teachers and students to supporting educational systems (e.g., classrooms, school buildings, districts) in providing effective services. In this area, the school psychology literature includes research focusing on effective implementation of multitiered systems of support (MTSS; e.g., Jimerson et al., 2016; Keller-Margulis, 2012). Researchers have also pushed the field forward regarding the infusion of equity, identity, and antiracism into MTSS, arguing for a culturally responsive version of this model that would intentionally reduce disparities, promote all students' well-being (e.g., Fallon et al., 2021; Proctor et al., 2012), and integrate trauma-informed services (von der Embse et al., 2019).

Domain 6: Services to Promote Safe and Supportive Schools

If we are to expect children to function well in schools, they must experience their educational settings as safe and supportive spaces. School psychologists address issues of school climate (i.e., individuals' school-based experiences) and school safety. Researchers have focused on strategies to build relationships between students and teachers (e.g., Cook et al., 2018) as well as the connections between students' school climate and bullying (Wang et al., 2013) and between school-based relationships and academic achievement (Vega et al., 2015). Research has also examined school climate at the intersections of race, gender, and dis/ability (e.g., Collins et al., 2022; La Salle et al., 2019). Moreover, it has explored the promotion of school safety for Black students following the murders of George Floyd and other unarmed Black people at the hands of the police (e.g., Heidelburg et al., 2022).

Domain 7: Family, School, and Community Collaboration

It is imperative that school psychologists facilitate connections between the family, school, and community, as positive student outcomes are best achieved when youth are surrounded by a consistent continuum of support. School psychologists are tasked with ensuring that the family and community are treated as valuable partners in students' education (e.g., Manz et al., 2009). For example, conjoint behavioral consultation (also described in Chapter 12) provides a framework for facilitating partnerships between schools and families by including families in decisions about interventions and supports (e.g., Garbacz et al., 2020). From a social justice perspective, school psychologists must demonstrate cultural humility in working with families from a variety of backgrounds to ensure that all members of the school community are invited to be valued and vested partners and that any historical and current barriers to the educational participation of minoritized families are removed (Marti et al., 2007).

Domain 8: Equitable Practices for Diverse Student Populations

As discussed throughout this chapter and book, a social justice framework is an essential component of all aspects of school psychologists' responsibilities. American educational systems do not treat all students equitably, as evidenced by disparities in academic achievement opportunities, discipline, mental health, and various other outcomes along lines of race, gender, ability, and the intersections of multiple identities. Within the literature, researchers have focused on topics such as the role of school psychologists in addressing educational disparities (e.g., Sullivan et al., 2013), culturally relevant consultation (e.g., Miranda & Radliff, 2016), and interventions intended to reduce disparities (e.g., Gion et al., 2020). Recent advancements in the social justice literature have integrated critical theories (e.g., critical race theory; intersectionality; dis/ability critical race studies) into school psychology practice. These advancements have focused on (a) examining issues of racism, power, oppression, and marginalization; (b) centering the voices and experiences of minoritized populations; and (c) engaging in advocacy to dismantle inequitable systems in schools (e.g., Proctor & Rivera, 2022; Sabnis & Proctor, 2021).

> **SOCIAL JUSTICE CONNECTIONS**
>
> *Who is and who is not included in school psychology research?*
>
> The school psychology research literature has traditionally centered white participants and researchers, excluding the experiences and epistemology of minoritized populations. ***Epistemology*** refers to the study and philosophy of knowledge construction, determining what is considered knowledge and what is excluded. A series of reviews of publications

(continued)

SOCIAL JUSTICE CONNECTIONS (*continued*)

in school psychology (discussed in Collins and colleagues [under review]) have detailed trends in diversity representation in research from 1975 to 2019 as well as research specific to social justice in the field from 2008 to 2019. These studies indicate that school psychology research has not regularly centered REM populations (especially Latinx and multiracial students), LGBTQ+ populations, and students experiencing economic marginalization, and few studies have critically examined these and other identities at the intersection of systemic oppression and marginalization in schools. Graves and colleagues (2020) identified a practice-to-research gap regarding social justice, as school psychology organizations and practitioners are outpacing school psychology researchers in regard to integrating social justice into their work. This poses potential problems for engaging in evidence-based practice, intensifying the need for school psychology research centering social justice. Recent advances in the field, such as Proctor and Rivera's (2022) book on critical theories in school psychology and counseling, are propelling the field forward in terms of dismantling the enduring effects of white supremacy on research and practice.

Domain 9: Research and Evidence-Based Practice

School psychologists serve as producers, consumers, and disseminators of research (Keith, 2008), as it is important for research to inform practice and for practice to inform research. School psychologists have published work to facilitate the use of strong research methodology (which we define and discuss later in this chapter) for the purposes of informing future research and school-based practice (e.g., Dart et al., 2021; Pendergast et al., 2017). In addition to the research on social justice publication trends described in this chapter's *Social Justice Connections*, researchers have also examined for whom and in which contexts interventions can be considered evidence-based (e.g., Ingraham & Oka, 2006). This scholarship is critical for informing school psychologists' decision-making about when and how to implement culturally relevant interventions.

Domain 10: Legal, Ethical, and Professional Practice

School psychologists must adhere to federal, state, and local laws governing their practice, as well as to the ethical codes that detail the scope of their work and principles of conduct. Researchers have discussed various ethical codes from professional organizations (e.g., the American Psychological Association, NASP) and their importance for school psychology practice in specific situations, such as in implementing MTSS (e.g., Burns et al., 2008). As school psychologists are ethically mandated to ensure the educational rights and opportunities of all students, researchers have discussed socially just and antiracist practice as an ethical imperative for all school psychologists (e.g., García-Vázquez et al., 2020; Pham et al., 2021).

RESEARCH METHODOLOGIES

School psychologists employ a variety of techniques to find answers to their research questions. This system of techniques to collect, process, and analyze phenomena can be broadly described as ***research methodology***. It is impossible to discuss research methodology, or the "how" of research, without acknowledging the quantitative–qualitative divide.

The topic of methodology often brings up philosophical differences among researchers, distinguishing those who use statistically driven methods (i.e., quantitative) from those who opt for more participant-driven methods of understanding (i.e., qualitative). This dichotomy is harmful to the future of research, although the philosophical differences underlying it are beyond the scope of this chapter. Fortunately, there is a growing movement to embrace mixed methods or an alternating approach to investigate areas of interest. This paradigm of diversifying methods is needed as the field attempts to answer increasingly complex questions and engage in non-Western ways of knowing (Bartholomew & Brown, 2012). The following describes major approaches to research, including specific examples of their subtypes. It also discusses program evaluation as a form of applied research that may include a variety of quantitative and qualitative methods.

Quantitative

Our overview of research methodologies begins with *quantitative research*, as the natural sciences (e.g., biology, chemistry) have traditionally relied on numerical approaches to understand the natural world. The historical influence of the quantitative approach extends to the social sciences as well. The quantitative approach focuses on *quantifying* variables and using statistical analyses to understand the relations between two or more variables. Researchers who use quantitative methods may be interested in how two or more variables are correlated, how one variable may reliably predict another, or how one variable may cause another to change. In short, the quantitative approach is useful for making generalizations about the relationship between variables by means of statistical analysis. The following describes major methods used within the quantitative approach and examples of each.

Survey designs are used to describe the current condition of a given phenomenon using numerical data. Researchers conducting surveys commonly use interviews and/or questionnaires to collect data from their participants. Researchers who choose this design may be interested in learning about the characteristics of a particular group. For example, the 2020 NASP Membership Survey collected demographic data from 1,308 randomly selected school psychologists and found that more than 80% of respondents identified as white (Goforth et al., 2021). Based on these results, the authors reiterated NASP's mission to investigate efforts to recruit and retain REM school psychologists. Survey designs can offer immediate takeaways and generate knowledge that encourages more in-depth inquiry into a given phenomenon.

Correlational designs seek to describe the relationships between two or more variables without directly manipulating the independent variable. Beyond description, correlational designs allow researchers to examine how closely related two or more variables are within a given phenomenon. It is important here to invoke the adage "correlation is not causation," as a reminder that just because two variables are correlated does not necessarily mean one causes the other. Despite this, correlational designs still have much utility to researchers. In healthcare, for example, correlational research can be used to determine which client factors, such as socioeconomic status, are correlated most strongly with a particular health attribute or health-related outcome (Curtis et al., 2016). Correlational designs can also help researchers generate new research questions and hypotheses for their field of study.

Causal-comparative designs examine the causal relationship between two or more distinct groups when it is not feasible or ethical to manipulate the independent variable. The key difference between causal-comparative and correlational designs is that causal-comparative designs attempt to understand causal relationships. Causal-comparative designs assume that cause-and-effect has already occurred and involve the nonrandom selection of two or more different groups (e.g., gender, setting). These designs can also examine the effects of two existing intervention programs when participants cannot be randomly assigned to an experimental or control group for various reasons (e.g., scheduling constraints of participants; Fuchs & Malone, 2021).

Experimental designs analyze the cause-and-effect relationship between two or more variables by manipulating the independent variable, controlling for confounding variables, and employing randomization. A randomized controlled trial (RCT; discussed in Chapter 8) is an example of an experimental design wherein participants are randomly assigned to an experimental or control group and an outcome measure is used to detect a potentially significant difference between the two groups. Although considered the most robust and rigorous quantitative method for determining cause-and-effect links, RCTs should be conducted only if they are ethically appropriate and clinically meaningful (Bhide et al., 2018). An equally strong but distinct method for determining causal relationships when large group studies are not possible—single-case designs—is discussed next.

Single-case design is a quantitative approach used to rigorously test research questions that may not be able to be answered with other research designs. Instead of randomly assigning participants to two or more groups, each participant (or group) serves as their own comparison group, and a dependent variable is repeatedly measured across time and intervention phases. Traditionally, single-case design is analyzed through visual analysis of the data paths, but statistical methods are also used to determine intervention effectiveness. Single-case research can demonstrate strong internal validity while also being economically feasible and easily conveyed to laypeople. Thus, single-case studies can be a viable alternative to large group studies such as RCTs (Lobo et al., 2017).

By quantifying phenomena into measurable variables, quantitative researchers test their hypotheses with statistical analysis and seek to measure the objective reality that purportedly exists independent of the researchers' experience. The value of quantitative methods cannot be overstated, given that so much of what we consider scientific fact was founded on quantitative traditions. Although we do not discuss at length the epistemological underpinnings of these methods, it is sufficient to state that quantitative methods often operate from a positivist paradigm. *Positivism* asserts that empirical facts exist apart from personal ideas or thoughts and that facts are governed by the law of cause and effect (Tuli, 2010).

One potential weakness of quantitative research is the way complex variables get reduced to numbers, which often does not paint a comprehensive picture of social phenomena. Within the social sciences in particular, quantitative methods have proven insufficient to fully describe the nature of structures and processes that underlie human behavior (Toomela, 2010). The quantitative approach has also been criticized as being used to justify and perpetuate longstanding social prejudices and oppression, although some researchers have reclaimed quantitative methods as a tool for social justice (Cokley & Awad, 2013). Qualitative research, in contrast but no less empirical, seeks to interpret the objective reality while also uncovering the relative truths that can be found within individuals, organizations, and various other social contexts.

Qualitative

Qualitative research relies on the narrative analysis of data rather than the use of numerical and statistical methods. The medium of choice for qualitative research is verbal. Researchers who use qualitative methods have a variety of techniques for collecting rich data from the social event or phenomenon being studied (e.g., semistructured focus groups; Moy et al., 2014). The qualitative approach utilizes the scientific method to interpret the phenomena that surround the research topic. Researchers may be interested in the perceptions of their participants regarding a particular experience or a specific topic about which they are knowledgeable (e.g., school psychology trainers' perspectives on evidence-based practices; Gonzalez et al., 2019). Whereas quantitative research examines the relations between predetermined variables, qualitative methods question the nature of the variables themselves and allow for variables to change over the course of the research process (Aspers & Corte, 2019). Thus, the epistemological underpinning of the qualitative approach (e.g., *interactionist–constructivist*, or the perspective that reality is subjective and that knowledge is actively constructed by people as they make sense of their world) is fundamentally different from quantitative methods. Although there is growing interest in qualitative methods, school psychology training programs continue to drag their feet in preparing students for this type of research. In general, students in psychology training programs often perceive qualitative methods as something other than, and in opposition to, quantitative methods (Roberts & Castell, 2016). The following paragraphs describe types of qualitative methods and, we hope, shed light on the legitimacy and immense power of the qualitative approach.

Case studies, from a qualitative perspective, are in-depth explorations of a particular case of interest, which could include persons, processes, and other social phenomena. In contrast to group research, case studies incorporate a variety of techniques to explore a single unit with rich detail and comprehensiveness. This intensive focus on an individual case also allows researchers to study how the case evolves over time and how it exists within its environment (Flyvbjerg, 2011).

Ethnography seeks to understand a particular group in their environment by observing and interviewing those in the group. Whereas case studies focus on the depth of inquiry, ethnographies have a broader approach to understanding social phenomena, focusing on a particular group's cultural patterns and perspectives. Auto-ethnographies incorporate the researchers' self-reflection and analysis in the understanding of a cultural group. For example, Knotek (2012) used audiotaped interviews of participants, direct observations, and the review of permanent products to illuminate the process of culturally responsive consultation in the implementation of an innovative problem-solving team.

Grounded theory utilizes induction and the triangulation of data to develop theories about a particular social phenomenon. Through a recursive coding process and critical reflection, a conceptual understanding (e.g., themes) of the social phenomenon begins to emerge from the data. Researchers who utilize grounded theory as an approach to qualitative research get close to their field of study. *Getting close* involves physically being in the space where the data are collected and being absorbed in the data. Aspers and Corte (2019) describe closeness as a requirement for identifying questions, developing new concepts, or making further distinctions about old concepts.

Phenomenology involves seeking to understand the lived experience of participants to generate a broader understanding of a specific phenomenon. Simply put, researchers want to learn about a certain social experience from individuals who went through it. Phenomenological studies can include the use of questionnaires with open-ended questions to ask experts about the state of their field of study (e.g., scientific research in school psychology; McIntosh et al., 2013). The philosophical roots of phenomenology include different traditions with different techniques for answering the "what" and "how" of human experience (Neubauer et al., 2019). Incorporating phenomenological methods allows researchers to provide a richer and more comprehensive description of human behavior and experience.

Narrative inquiry seeks to learn from the individual's or group's perspective on a certain experience or phenomenon; here the story (i.e., narrative) shared is the data. Researchers involved in narrative inquiry may discuss their biases and identities as part of the narrative analysis. The strength of narrative inquiry is its ability to amplify the voice of participants. Stories can be created by individuals or groups and facilitated by the researcher when co-construction is needed to give voice to certain groups. For example, in addition to in-depth interviews, O'Leary and Moloney (2020) asked parent participants of autistic children to document their children's sensory expressions (e.g., excitedly hand flapping or anxiously covering ears) and nonverbal responses as a way to authentically include their voices.

The strengths of qualitative methods lie in their ability to provide a detailed and complete picture of the social phenomena being studied. In addition, qualitative methods may reveal new variables to be studied as well as offer new insights as to how current variables can be understood in future studies. From a social justice perspective, qualitative research invites multiple perspectives and incorporates the human experience into the scientific process. The emphasis on giving voice to marginalized and underrepresented groups is a strength of qualitative methods. For example, through in-depth interviews and a rigorous coding process, Proctor and Truscott (2013) analyzed the perspectives of Black school psychologists on the factors important to them when selecting a school psychology graduate program. One area that may be lacking in qualitative research is its generalizability, although there are many techniques for applying results from qualitative research to other contexts (e.g., transferability; Maxwell, 2021). Overall, there has been increased advocacy for improving graduate training in qualitative methods as well as greater advocacy for the methodology's credibility in general.

Mixed Methods

As we have discussed, qualitative methods may be less well-suited to demonstrating causal relationships but can lead to the formulation of new theories to be examined via quantitative methods. Likewise, quantitative methods, with their emphasis on statistical significance, are somewhat incomplete in their ability to provide a comprehensive description of phenomena, particularly in the social sciences. One might suggest the combining or alternating of these methodologies to complement each other's deficiencies—a *mixed methods* approach. There are various mixed methods designs; one example is an *explanatory design*, in which an initial quantitative phase of a study is followed by a qualitative phase. For example, in a study examining student stress in elementary schools, Sotardi (2016) analyzed student data from a self-report daily school stress instrument for 8 weeks and followed up with individual interviews with each student regarding their coping skills.

Mixed methods have been increasingly popular, but the percentage of training programs that require qualitative or mixed methods coursework is still starkly low (i.e., 3%; Powell et al., 2008). To embrace this approach, researchers need to break from the traditions of old. The pragmatic approach suggests that researchers focus on the research problem itself and employ whichever method is best suited to answer their research questions. Mixed methods allow researchers in the social sciences to do "what works" in collecting a variety of data to answer their research questions and in utilizing different forms of data to compensate for any shortcomings (Bartholomew & Brown, 2012).

Program Evaluation

We conclude this section on research methodology with a specific example of applied research that is particularly relevant to the field of school psychology. The NASP (2020) Practice Model asserts that school psychologists understand program evaluation and apply their knowledge to support other school leaders in the development, implementation, and monitoring of school programs. As introduced in Chapter 15, program evaluation focuses on the assessment of a program's effectiveness within a system of data-based decision-making. As members of systems-level teams, school psychologists should be well-versed in program evaluation to ensure that programs are working to improve outcomes for all children.

It is imperative that school psychologists be skilled in program evaluation to uncover how some programs and policies may be disproportionately benefiting some students while disadvantaging others. Program evaluation can utilize quantitative, qualitative, or mixed methods. Overall, the field of school psychology must embrace a variety of approaches to understanding and redressing the inequities and systemic injustices that exist in educational settings (Parris et al., 2019).

PEER REVIEW

When authors submit a manuscript for publication in a research journal, the manuscript often undergoes a peer review process. *Peer review* is a quality control process wherein experts on a topic examine manuscripts, provide feedback to authors, and make recommendations for potential publication. Peer review is intended to serve as a filter to ensure that only high-quality research is published. During the peer review process, the validity, significance, and originality of the study is evaluated. Peer reviewers also help improve quality by providing suggestions to authors and correcting any errors before publication. This process excludes work that does not meet the research community's standards for research publication.

The Process

The peer review process begins when a research manuscript is submitted. A manuscript describes the purpose, methods, results, and conclusions of a research study. The manuscript is submitted to a journal that specializes in a relevant research field. An editor is assigned to the manuscript and monitors the peer review process to ensure that the reviews are conducted fairly and in an effective and timely manner. In the peer review stage, the editor sends the manuscript to reviewers who have the content and/or methodological expertise to properly evaluate it. The peer reviewers then evaluate many aspects of the manuscript, including the validity of findings, theoretical foundations of the work, appropriateness of the methods used, quality of experimental design, and the significance of the research. At the end of the review, reviewers are asked to recommend an editorial decision for the manuscript, such as acceptance for publication, rejection, or a request for revision. The editor (often an associate editor of the journal) then conducts their own review of the manuscript and reads the reviewers' feedback. At that point, the editor decides the status of the manuscript and communicates the decision and feedback to authors, who can then decide their next steps. If a manuscript is rejected with resubmission encouraged, authors can review the feedback and resubmit an edited version of the manuscript to undergo the peer review process again. If the paper is rejected, authors can use the feedback to edit and submit the manuscript to another journal. If the manuscript is accepted, the manuscript goes through a copyediting process to prepare it for publication in the journal.

Types of Reviews

The peer review process is generally conducted in one of three ways: open review, single-blind review, or double-blind review. In an *open review*, both the authors of the paper and the peer reviewers know each other's identities. Alternatively, in a *single-blind review*, the reviewers' identities are kept confidential, but the authors' identities are revealed to the reviewers. In a *double-blind review*, the identities of both the reviewers and authors are kept confidential. All three methods have advantages and disadvantages.

Open peer review has the advantage of holding reviewers accountable for giving timely and relevant reviews, since their identities are known; however, this may also cause reviewers to feel uncomfortable in providing critical feedback or to alter their feedback due to social pressure. Editors often find that completely open reviewing decreases the number of people willing to participate and leads to reviews of little value.

Single-blind and double-blind peer review are advantageous because reviewers are more likely to provide honest feedback when their identities are concealed. Moreover, one advantage double-blind reviews have over single-blind reviews is that they prevent any reputational biases from affecting reviewers' evaluation of manuscripts. Masking both the authors' and peer reviewers' identities is generally thought to minimize bias and maintain review quality. However, in all types of review processes, steps must be taken to ensure just and equitable review processes.

BECOMING A GOOD CONSUMER OF RESEARCH

School psychologists, as scientist practitioners, are consumers, producers, and disseminators of research. Applying research findings to practice is critical for effective service delivery, so school psychologists must regularly consume research to inform their work and skill development. School psychologists in a variety of settings also serve as producers of research, as they conduct the high-quality and relevant research described in this chapter. They are also disseminators of research, as they share the knowledge and skills they learn from research with teachers, school staff, families, and the community to ensure that all members of the educational community are using research evidence to best inform their support of youth.

Consuming research with a critical eye is important, as not all published research is relevant for every context or applicable to every situation. Part of a school psychologist's job is to review and interpret research findings to aid in their own decision-making. They cannot just blindly accept all research findings as truth and expect them to translate well to their own practices. No research study is perfect, so school psychologists must look at each one critically and ask questions about its limitations and applications to practice.

It is always important to consider the external validity of research findings. *External validity* refers to the extent to which study findings can be generalized to other populations and settings. For example, a study conducted with third-grade boys in Arizona may not be applicable to fifth-grade girls in Florida. As school psychologists read studies, they should consider how similar study participants are to the populations they serve, as this may allow them to determine how relevant the findings are for their own contexts. Another important factor to consider is whether the procedures can be replicated in their specific contexts. Do they have the resources, training, and time to replicate the procedures in the study? Not all interventions and assessments are feasible in all settings, and not all research findings will be generalizable to all populations and settings.

School psychologists should also critically evaluate the contributions of the study. Are the unique contributions of the study clear? This relates to the study's *internal validity*, or the extent to which its methodological design permitted the researchers to rule out alternative explanations for study findings. Other questions to ask when looking at research include its limitations, such as sample size and makeup, resources, and methodological concerns. Understanding these limitations and the impact they can have on study results is very important, as these matters can point to areas for future research and must be considered when adopting practices in schools.

School psychologists are responsible for implementing evidence-based practices based on research supporting their use. Using evidence-based practices increases the likelihood that interventions will be effective. Good consumers of research must also be disseminators, educating others on these evidence-based practices and advocating for changes in policies and practices.

SUMMARY AND CONCLUSIONS

Research is essential to the profession and practice of school psychology. School psychologists can engage in many different forms of research as producers, consumers, and disseminators. The school psychology research literature includes a wide range of research in all areas of school psychology practice, including quantitative, qualitative, and mixed methods approaches. School psychologists must critically review research to determine its relevance for their particular contexts and decide whether to use findings of various studies in their work. They must also be careful to center social justice in their practice and research so that they are most effectively advocating for equitable policies and practices for children and families.

DISCUSSION QUESTIONS

1. If school psychologists did not have research to inform their practice, what problems would arise?
2. In what ways can school psychology research more meaningfully include minoritized populations and voices?
3. How can we promote more mixed methods research in the field? How do we determine which research methodology (or methodologies) is (are) most appropriate to answer our research questions?
4. How can we determine if a research study's results are relevant in the contexts in which we work?
5. As you grow in your understanding and training in research methodologies, what can you do to ensure that you center social justice in your research?

RECOMMENDED READINGS

Bartholomew, T. T., & Brown, J. R. (2012). Mixed methods, culture, and psychology: A review of mixed methods in culture-specific psychological research. *International Perspectives in Psychology: Research, Practice, Consultation, 1*(3), 177–190. https://doi.org/10.1037/a0029219

Graves, S. L., Phillips, S., Johnson, K., Jones, M. A., & Thornton, D. (2020). Pseudoscience, an emerging field, or just a framework without outcomes? A bibliometric analysis and case study presentation of social justice research. *Contemporary School Psychology, 25*, 358–366. https://doi.org/10.1007/s40688-020-00310-z

Harrison, P., & Thomas, A. (Eds.). (2014). *Best practices in school psychology.* National Association of School Psychologists.

Proctor, S. L., & Rivera, D. P. (2022). *Critical theories for school psychology and counseling.* Routledge.

Sabnis, S. V., & Proctor, S. K. (2021). Use of critical theory to develop a conceptual framework for critical school psychology. *School Psychology Review, 51*(6), 661–675. https://doi.org/10.1080/2372966X.2021.1949248

 A robust set of instructor resources designed to supplement this text is located at http://connect.springerpub.com/content/book/978-0-8261-6344-8. Qualifying instructors may request access by emailing textbook@springerpub.com.

REFERENCES

Aspers, P., & Corte, U. (2019). What is qualitative in qualitative research. *Qualitative Sociology, 42*(2), 139–160. https://doi.org/10.1007/s11133-019-9413-7

Bartholomew, T. T., & Brown, J. R. (2012). Mixed methods, culture, and psychology: A review of mixed methods in culture-specific psychological research. *International Perspectives in Psychology: Research, Practice, Consultation, 1*(3), 177–190. https://doi.org/10.1037/a0029219

Bhide, A., Shah, P. S., & Acharya, G. (2018). A simplified guide to randomized controlled trials. *Acta Obstetricia et Gynecologica Scandinavica, 97*(4), 380–387. https://doi.org/10.1111/aogs.13309

Blake, J. J., Gregory, A., James, M., & Hasan, G. W. (2018). Early warning signs: Identifying opportunities to disrupt racial inequities in school discipline through data-based decision making. *School Psychology Forum: Research in Practice, 10*(3), 289–306. https://www.nasponline.org/publications/periodicals/spf/volume-10/volume-10-issue-3-(fall-2016)/early-warning-signs-identifying-opportunities-to-disrupt-racial-inequities-in-school-discipline-through-data-based-decision-making

Burns, M. K., Jacob, S., & Wagner, A. R. (2008). Ethical and legal issues associated with using response-to-intervention to assess learning disabilities. *Journal of School Psychology, 46*(3), 263–279. https://doi.org/10.1016/j.jsp.2007.06.001

Burns, M. K., Zaslofsky, A. F., Kanive, R., & Parker, D. C. (2012). Meta-analysis of incremental rehearsal using phi coefficients to compare single-case and group designs. *Journal of Behavioral Education, 21*, 185–202. https://doi.org/10.1007/s10864-012-9160-2

Castro-Olivo, S., Preciado, J., Le, L., Marciante, M., & Garcia, M. (2018). The effects of culturally adapted version of *First Steps to Success* for Latino English language learners: Preliminary pilot study. *Psychology in the Schools, 55*, 36–49. https://doi.org/10.1002/pits.22092

Codding, R. S., Hilt-Panahon, A., Panahon, C. J., & Benson, J. L. (2009). Addressing mathematics computation problems: A review of simple and moderate intensity interventions. *Education and Treatment of Children, 32*(2), 278–312. https://doi.org/10.1353/etc.0.0053

Cokley, K., & Awad, G. H. (2013). In defense of quantitative methods: Using the "master's tools" to promote social justice. *Journal for Social Action in Counseling & Psychology, 5*(2), 26–41. https://doi.org/10.33043/JSACP.5.2.26-41

Collins, T. A., La Salle, T. P., Rocha Neves, J., Foster, J. A., & Scott, M. N. (2022). No safe space: School climate experiences of Black boys with and without emotional and behavioral disorders. *School Psychology Review*. https://doi.org/10.1080/2372966x.2021.2021783

Collins, T. A., Newman, D. S., Endres, B. E., McIntire, H., Newman, C. L., Scott, M. N., Villarreal, J. N., & Gerrard, M. K. (under review). Social justice research in school psychology: Awakening the slumbering giant.

Cook, C. R., Duong, M. T., McIntosh, K., Fiat, A. E., Larson, M., Pullmann, M. D., & McGinnis, J. (2018). Addressing discipline disparities for Black male students: Linking malleable root causes to feasible and effective practices. *School Psychology Review, 47*(2), 135–152. https://doi.org/10.17105/SPR-2017-0026.V47-2

Curtis, E. A., Comiskey, C., & Dempsey, O. (2016). Importance and use of correlational research. *Nurse Researcher, 23*(6), 20–25. https://doi.org/10.7748/nr.2016.e1382

Dart, E. H., Van Norman, E. R., Klingbeil, D. A., & Radley, K. C. (2021). Graph construction and visual analysis: A comparison of curriculum-based measurement vendors. *Journal of Behavioral Education, 32*, 90–108. https://doi.org/10.1007/s10864-021-09440-7

Eklund, K., & Dowdy, E. (2014). Screening for behavioral and emotional risk versus traditional school identification methods. *School Mental Health: A Multidisciplinary Research and Practice Journal, 6*(1), 40–49. https://doi.org/10.1007/s12310-013-9109-1

Eklund, K., Kilpatrick, K. D., Kilgus, S. P., & Haider, A. (2018). A systematic review of state-level social-emotional learning standards: Implications for practice and research. *School Psychology Review, 47*(3), 316–326. https://doi.org/10.17105/SPR-2017.0116.V47-3

Fallon, L. M., Collier-Meek, M. A., Maggin, D. M., Sanetti, L. M. H., & Johnson, A. J. (2015). Is performance feedback for educators an evidence-based practice? A systematic review and evaluation based on single-case research. *Exceptional Children, 81*(2), 227–246. https://doi.org/10.1177/0014402914551738

Fallon, L. M., Velga, M., & Sugai, G. (2021). Strengthening MTSS for behavior (MTSS-B) to promote racial equity. *School Psychology Review.* https://doi.org/10.1080/2372966X.2021.1972333

Fischer, A. J., Dart, E. H., Radley, K. C., Richardson, D., Clark, R., & Wimberly, J. (2017). An evaluation of the effectiveness and acceptability of teleconsultation. *Journal of Educational & Psychological Consultation, 27*(4), 437–458. https://doi.org/10.1080/10474412.2016.1235978

Flyvbjerg, B. (2011). Case study. In N. K. Denzin & Y. S. Lincoln (Eds.), *The Sage handbook of qualitative research* (4th ed., pp. 301–316). Sage.

Fuchs, L. S., & Malone, A. S. (2021). Can teaching fractions improve teachers' fraction understanding?: Insights from a causal-comparative study. *The Elementary School Journal, 121*(4). https://doi.org/10.1086/713975

Garbacz, S. A., Beattie, T., Novotnak, T., Kurtz-Nelson, E., Zahn, M., Yim-Dockery, H., Cohenour, J., & Jordan, P. (2020). Examining the efficacy of conjoint behavioral consultation for middle school students with externalizing behavior problems. *Behavioral Disorders, 46*(1), 3–17. https://doi.org/10.1177/0198742919888844

García-Vázquez, E., Reddy, L., Arora, P., Crepeau-Hobson, F., Fenning, P., Hatt, C., Hughes, T., Jimerson, S., Malone, C., Minke, K., Radliff, K., Raines, T., Song, S., & Vaillancourt Strobach, K. (2020). School psychology unified antiracism statement and call to action. *School Psychology Review, 49*(3), 209–211. https://doi.org/10.1080/2372966X.2020.1809941

Gion, C., McIntosh, K., & Falcon, S. (2020). Effects of a multifaceted classroom intervention on racial disproportionality. *School Psychology Review, 51*(1), 67–83. https://doi.org/10.1080/2372966X.2020.1788906

Graves, S. L., Phillips, S., Johnson, K., Jones, M. A., & Thornton, D. (2020). Pseudoscience, an emerging field, or just a framework without outcomes? A bibliometric analysis and case study presentation of social justice research. *Contemporary School Psychology, 25*, 358–366. https://doi.org/10.1007/s40688-020-00310-z

Goforth, A. N., Farmer, R. L., Kim, S. Y., Naser, S. C., Lockwood, A. B., & Affrunti, N. W. (2021). Status of school psychology in 2020: Part 1, Demographics of the NASP Membership Survey. *NASP Research Reports, 5*(2). https://www.nasponline.org/Documents/Research%20and%20Policy/Research%20Center/NRR_2020-Membership-Survey-P1.pdf

Gonzalez, J. E., Stoiber, K. C., Clayton, R. J., Keller-Margulis, M., Reddy, L. A., & Forman, S. G. (2019) A qualitative analysis of school psychology trainers' perspectives on evidence-based practices. *International Journal of School & Educational Psychology, 9*(2), 132–147. https://doi.org/10.1080/21683603.2019.1668317

Heidelburg, K., & Collins, T. A. (2022). Development of *Black to Success*: A culturally enriched social skills program for Black adolescent males. *School Psychology Review.* https://doi.org/10.1080/2372966X.2021.2001691

Heidelburg, K., Phelps, C., & Collins, T. A. (2022). Reconceptualizing school safety for Black students. *School Psychology International, 43*(6), 591–612. https://doi.org/10.1177/01430343221074770

Hier, B. O., & Eckert, T. L. (2014). Evaluating elementary-aged students' abilities to generalize and maintain fluency gains of a performance feedback writing intervention. *School Psychology Quarterly, 29*(4), 488–502. https://doi.org/10.1037/spq0000040

Ingraham, C. L., & Oka, E. R. (2006). Multicultural issues in evidence-based interventions. *Journal of Applied School Psychology, 22*(2), 127–149. https://doi.org/10.1300/J370v22n02_07

Jimerson, S. R., Burns, M. K., & VanDerHeyden, A. M. (2016). *Handbook of response to intervention: The science and practice of multi-tiered systems of support* (2nd ed.). Springer.

Jones, J. M., Begay, K. K., Nakagawa, Y., Cevasco, M., & Sit, J. (2016). Multicultural counseling competence training: Adding value with multicultural consultation. *Journal of Educational & Psychological Consultation, 26*(3), 241–265. https://doi.org/10.1080/10474412.2015.1012671

Keith, T. Z. (2008). Best practices in using and conducting research in applied settings. In A. Thomas & J. Grimes (Eds.), *Best practices in school psychology V* (pp. 2165–2176). National Association of School Psychologists.

Keller-Margulis, M. A. (2012). Fidelity of implementation framework: A critical need for response to intervention models. *Psychology in the Schools, 49*(4), 342–352. https://doi.org/10.1002/pits.21602

Kilgus, S. P., Methe, S. A., Maggin, D. M., & Tomasula, J. L. (2014). Curriculum-based measurement of oral reading (R-CBM): A diagnostic test accuracy meta-analysis of evidence supporting use in universal screening. *Journal of School Psychology, 52*(4), 377–405. https://doi.org/10.1016/jsp.2014.06.002

Klingbeil, D. A., Moeyaert, M., Archer, C. T., Chimboza, T. M., & Zwolski, S. A., Jr. (2017). Efficacy of peer-mediated incremental rehearsal for English language learners. *School Psychology Review, 46*(1), 122–140. https://doi.org/10.17105/SPR46-1.122-140

Klingbeil, D. A., Renshaw, T. L., Willenbrick, J. B., Copek, R. A., Chan, K. T., Haddock, A., Yassine, J., & Clifton, J. (2017). Mindfulness-based interventions with youth: A comprehensive meta-analysis of group-design studies. *Journal of School Psychology, 63*, 77–103. https://doi.org/10.1016/j.jsp.2017.03.006

Knotek, S. E. (2012). Utilizing culturally responsive consultation to support innovation implementation in a rural school. *Consulting Psychology Journal: Practice and Research, 64*(1), 46–62. https://doi-org.uc.idm.oclc.org/10.1037/a0027993

La Salle, T. P., Wang, C., Wu, C., & Rocha Neves, J. (2019). Racial mismatch among minoritized students and white teachers: Implications and recommendations for moving forward. *Journal of Educational and Psychological Consultation, 30*(3), 314–343. https://doi.org/10.1080/10474412.2019.1673759

Lazarus, P. J., Doll, B., Song, S. Y., & Radliff, K. (2021). Transforming school mental health services based on a culturally responsible dual-factor model. *School Psychology Review, 51*(6), 755–770. https://doi.org/10.1080/2372966X.2021.1968282

Lobo, M. A., Moeyaert, M., Baraldi Cunha, A., & Babik, I. (2017). Single-case design, analysis, and quality assessment for intervention research. *Journal of Neurologic Physical Therapy, 41*(3), 187–197. https://doi.org/10.1097/NPT.0000000000000187

Long, A. C. J., Miller, F. G., & Upright, J. J. (2019). Classroom management for ethnic-racial minority students. *School Psychology, 34*(1). https://doi.org/10.1037/spq0000305

Luevano, C., & Collins, T. A. (2020). Culturally appropriate math problem solving instruction with English language learners. *School Psychology Review, 49*(2), 144–160. https://doi.org/10.1080/2372966X.2020.1717243

Manz, P. H., Mautone, J. A., & Martin, S. D. (2009). School psychologists' collaborations with families: An exploratory study of the interrelationships of their perceptions of professional efficacy and school climate, and demographic and training variables. *Journal of Applied School Psychology, 25*(1), 47–70. https://doi.org/10.1080/15377900802484158

Marti, D. C., Burt, J. D., & Sheridan, S. M. (2007). Conjoint behavioral consultation in practice: Working with diverse families. In S. M. Sheridan & T. R. Kratochwill (Eds.), *Conjoint behavioral consultation: Promoting family-school connections and interventions* (2nd ed., pp. 77–96). Springer.

Maxwell, J. A. (2021). Why qualitative methods are necessary for generalization. *Qualitative Psychology, 8*(1), 111–118. https://doi.org/10.1037/qup0000173

McIntosh, K., Martinez, R. S., Ty, S. V., & McClain, M. B. (2013). Scientific research in school psychology: Leading researchers weigh in on its past, present, and future. *Journal of School Psychology, 51*(3), 267–318. https://doi.org/10.1016/j.jsp.2013.04.003

Miller, K. C., Skinner, C. H., Gibby, L., Galyon, C. E., & Meadows-Allen, S. (2011). Evaluating generalization of addition-fact fluency using the taped-problems procedure in a second-grade classroom. *Journal of Behavioral Education, 20*, 203–220. https://doi.org/10.1007/s10864-011-9126-9

Miranda, A. H., & Radliff, K. M. (2016). Consulting with a social justice mind-set. In A. H. Miranda (Ed.), *Consultation across cultural contexts* (pp. 13–22). Routledge.

Moy, G. E., Briggs, A., Shriberg, D., Furrey, K. J., Smith, P., & Tompkins, N. (2014). Developing school psychologists as agents of social justice: A qualitative analysis of student understanding across three years. *Journal of School Psychology, 52*(3), 323–341. https://doi.org/10.1016/j.jsp.2014.03.001

National Association of School Psychologists. (2020). *The professional standards of the National Association of School Psychologists*. https://www.nasponline.org/standards-and-certification/nasp-2020-professional-standards-adopted

Neubauer, B. E., Witkop, C. T., & Varpio, L. (2019). How phenomenology can help us learn from the experiences of others. *Perspectives on Medical Education, 8*(2), 90–97. https://doi.org/10.1007/s40037-019-0509-2

Newman, D. S., & Ingraham, C. L. (2017). Consultee-centered consultation: Contemporary perspectives and a framework for the future. *Journal of Educational & Psychological Consultation, 27*(1), 1–12. https://doi.org/10.1080/10474412.2016.1175307

O'Leary, S., & Moloney, M. (2020). Understanding the experiences of young children on the autism spectrum as they navigate the Irish early years' education system: Valuing voices in child-centered narratives. *International Journal of Qualitative Methods, 19.* https://doi.org/10.1177/1609406920914696

Parris, L., Sabnis, S., Shriberg, D., Sullivan, A., Proctor, S. L., & Savage, T. (2019). Bringing social justice principles into school psychology research. *Communiqué, 48*(2), 6–8. https://www.nasponline.org/publications/periodicals/communique/issues/volume-48-issue-2

Pendergast, L. L., von der Embse, N., Kilgus, S. P., & Eklund, K. R. (2017). Measurement equivalence: A non-technical primer on categorical multi-group confirmatory factor analysis in school psychology. *Journal of School Psychology, 60,* 65–82. https://doi.org/10.1016/j.jsp.2016.11.002

Pham, A. V., Goforth, A. N., Agular, L. N., Burt, I., Bastian, R., & Diakow, D. M. (2021). Dismantling systemic inequities in school psychology: Cultural humility as a foundational approach to social justice. *School Psychology Review, 51*(6), 692–709. https://doi.org/10.1080/2372966X.2021.1941245

Poncy, B. C., Skinner, C. H., & Jaspers, K. E. (2007). Evaluating and comparing interventions designed to enhance math fact accuracy and fluency: Cover, copy and compare versus taped problems. *Journal of Behavioral Education, 16,* 27–37. https://doi.org/10.1007/s10864-006-9025-7

Powell, H., Mihalas, S., Onwuegbuzie, A. J., Suldo, S., & Daley, C. E. (2008). Mixed methods research in school psychology: A mixed methods investigation of trends in the literature. *Psychology in the Schools, 45*(4), 291–309. https://doi.org/10.1002/pits.20296

Proctor, S. L., Graves, S. L., Jr., & Esch, R. C. (2012). Assessing African American students for specific learning disabilities: The promises and perils of response to intervention. *The Journal of Negro Education, 81*(3), 268–282. https://doi.org/10.7709/jnegroeducation.81.3.0268

Proctor, S. L., & Rivera, D. P. (2022). *Critical theories for school psychology and counseling.* Routledge.

Proctor, S. L., & Truscott, S. D. (2013). Missing voices: African American school psychologists' perspectives on increasing professional diversity. *The Urban Review, 45,* 355–375. https://doi.org/10.1007/s11256-012-0232-3

Radley, K. C., & Dart, E. H. (Eds.). (2019). *Handbook of behavioral interventions in schools: Multi-tiered systems of support.* Oxford University Press.

Roberts, L. D., & Castell, E. (2016). "Having to shift everything we've learned to the side": Expanding research methods taught in psychology to incorporate qualitative methods. *Frontiers In Psychology, 7,* Article 688. https://doi.org/10.3389/fpsyg.2016.00688

Sabnis, S. V., & Proctor, S. K. (2021). Use of critical theory to develop a conceptual framework for critical school psychology. *School Psychology Review, 51*(6), 661–675. https://doi.org/10.1080/2372966X.2021.1949248

Song, S. Y., Eddy, J. M., Thompson, H. M., Adams, B., & Beskow, J. (2020). Restorative consultation in schools: A systematic review and call for restorative justice science to promote anti-racism and social justice. *Journal of Educational and Psychological Consultation, 30*(4), 462–476. https://doi.org/10.1080/10474412.2020.1819298

Sotardi, V. A. (2016). Understanding student stress and coping in elementary school: A mixed-method, longitudinal study. *Psychology in the Schools, 53*(7), 705–721. https://doi.org/10.1002/pits.21938

Suldo, S. M., & Shaffer, E. J. (2008). Looking beyond psychopathology: The dual-factor model of mental health in youth. *School Psychology Review, 37*(1), 52–68. https://doi.org/10.1080/02796015.2008.12087908

Sullivan, A. L. (2011). Disproportionality in special education identification and placement of English language learners. *Exceptional Children, 77*(3), 317–334. https://doi.org/10.1177/001440291107700304

Sullivan, A. L., Klingbeil, D. A., & Van Norman, E. R. (2013). Beyond behavior: Multilevel analysis of the influence of sociodemographics and school characteristics on students' risk of suspension. *School Psychology Review, 42*(1), 99–114. https://doi.org/10.1080/02796015.2013.12087493

Toomela, A. (2010). Quantitative methods in psychology: Inevitable and useless. *Frontiers in Psychology, 1,* Article 29. https://doi.org/10.3389/fpsyg.2010.00029

Tuli, F. (2010). The basis of distinction between qualitative and quantitative research in social science: Reflection on ontological, epistemological and methodological perspectives. *Ethiopian Journal of Education and Sciences, 6*(1), 97–108. https://doi.org/10.4314/ejesc.v6i1.65384

Vega, D., Moore III, J. L., & Miranda, A. H. (2015). In their own words: Perceived barriers to achievement by African American and Latino high school students. *American Secondary Education, 43*(3), 36–59. https://www.researchgate.net/publication/282095620_In_Their_Own_Words_Perceived_Barriers_To_Achievement_By_African_American_and_Latino_High_School_Students

Volpe, R. J., Mulé, C. M., Briesch, A. M., Joseph, L. M., & Burns, M. K. (2011). A comparison of two flashcard drill methods targeting word recognition. *Journal of Behavioral Education, 20*, 117–137. https://doi.org/10.1007/s10864-011-9124-y

von der Embse, N., Jester, D., Roy, D., & Post, J. (2018). Test anxiety effects, predictors, and correlates: A 30-year meta-analytic review. *Journal of Affective Disorders, 227*, 483–493. https://doi.org/10.1016/j.jad.2017.11.048

von der Embse, N., Rutherford, L., Mankin, A., & Jenkins, A. (2019). Demonstration of a trauma-informed assessment to intervention model in a large urban school district. *School Mental Health, 11*, 276–289. https://doi.org/10.1007/s12310-018-9294-z

Wang, C., Berry, B., & Swearer, S. M. (2013). The critical role of school climate in effective bullying prevention. *Theory Into Practice, 52*, 296–302. https://doi.org/10.1080/00405841.2013.829735

SECTION III
Looking Ahead

CHAPTER 17

Internationality of School and Educational Psychology

JOHN C. BEGENY ▪ EUI KYUNG KIM ▪ JIAYI WANG
▪ RAHMA HIDA ▪ KEAYSIA JACKSON ▪ KEVIN HAN

CHAPTER OBJECTIVES

After reading this chapter, you will be able to:

- Describe general characteristics of school and educational psychology (SAEP) from an international perspective.
- Describe key concepts and differences between internationalization and internationality in SAEP.
- Describe academic neocolonialism and how it relates to social justice issues in SAEP.
- Summarize key characteristics that are currently known about SAEP as an international profession, such as its international presence and the representation of international scholarship.
- Understand several challenges, barriers, and opportunities for promoting internationalization in SAEP as an equity-focused initiative.

NATIONAL ASSOCIATION OF SCHOOL PSYCHOLOGISTS PRACTICE MODEL CONNECTIONS

Domain 6: Services to Promote Safe and Supportive Schools
Domain 8: Equitable Practices for Diverse Student Populations
Domain 9: Research and Evidence-Based Practice

INTRODUCTION

This chapter describes school psychology from an international perspective. As discussed later, a focus on internationality within the profession also influences why this chapter intentionally refers to the discipline as *school and educational psychology*, rather than simply *school psychology*. In describing the internationality of the field, we discuss key concepts and definitions, relevant professional characteristics and statistics, and what it means to promote internationalization—rather than simply understanding or achieving internationality.

Additionally, we summarize some contemporary scholarship that is culturally informed, represents researchers and participants living in various parts of the world, and aims to address one or more social justice issues relevant to a particular geographic location. We conclude with a summary of challenges and opportunities that influence internationalization within the profession, which reflects another social justice imperative. The overall goal of this chapter is to inform readers about international topics connected to this discipline and, we hope, to inspire greater interest, learning, and participation in the internationality of school and educational psychology.

KEY CONCEPTS AND DEFINITIONS RELATED TO THE INTERNATIONALITY OF SCHOOL AND EDUCATIONAL PSYCHOLOGY

This section introduces key concepts and definitions related to the internationality of school and educational psychology as a field and discipline. Specifically, we describe what school and educational psychology means as a scholarly discipline in different countries around the world. We also discuss the meaning of terms such as *internationality*, *globalization*, and *internationalization* in the context of school and educational psychology. Furthermore, we discuss the concept of academic neocolonialism as a commonality of international disciplines and a barrier to internationalization. Potential variations in definitions of social justice will then be discussed, as we highlight how efforts to advance social justice should acknowledge cultural contexts and differences at both local and global levels.

Conceptualizing School and Educational Psychology

One approach to conceptualizing school and educational psychology is to consider the definition provided by the **International School Psychology Association** (ISPA). Among its five key objectives, ISPA aims to "promote the use of sound psychological principles within the context of education all over the world [and] promote communication between professionals who are committed to the improvement of the mental health of children in the world's schools" (ISPA, n.d.-a, para. 3). The definition of *school psychology* provided by ISPA (n.d.-b) states,

> the term school psychology is used in a general form to refer to professionals prepared in psychology and education and who are recognized as specialists in the provision of psychological services to children and youth within the contexts of schools, families, and other settings that impact their growth and development. As such, the term also refers to and is meant to include educational psychologists and others who display qualities this [ISPA] document associates with school psychology. (para. 1)

Therefore, this chapter addresses both *school and educational psychology* (SAEP), as they are commonly used terms to describe the subdiscipline of psychology that predominantly focuses on the learning and experience of individuals in K–12 educational settings (Begeny, 2018a).

The ISPA definition of school psychology provides a broad description of the discipline by specifying *individuals of interest* and *general goals* (e.g., promoting the growth and development of children and youth). However, this definition does not fully describe the diverse nature and scope of the discipline across all countries and global regions. Although there are approximately 83 countries that have at least some evidence of the presence of school psychology (Jimerson et al., 2008), definitions of SAEP across these countries are not always synonymous and may reflect diverse roles, services, epistemologies, and settings of practice unique to their countries and cultures. For example, depending on cultural perceptions of the roles of educational settings, psychologists may not be readily placed in schools, but rather provide similar services and practices in noneducational settings. Furthermore, school psychologists in other countries may engage in more diverse roles than do those in the United States; in Nigeria, for example, it has been reported that school psychologists serve broader roles, including school guidance counseling and special education services. Additional discussion is provided in Begeny et al. (2021) from this chapter's Recommended Readings.

Considering the potential variability in conceptualizations of SAEP across the globe, continued dialogue regarding culture- or country-specific terms and definitions is warranted. This dialogue can guide us to develop a more informed and context-based understanding of SAEP practice and scholarship; for example, the current needs of students, expectations of the roles and practices of school and educational psychologists, and the appropriateness of existing systems and supports should be understood within localized contexts and cultures. Thus, contributors to and consumers of SAEP scholarship should always be mindful of cultural and geographic diversity within the field to advance both internationality and internationalization.

Internationality, Globalization, and Internationalization

Internationality is not synonymous with *internationalization* (e.g., Begeny et al., 2019; Bernardo et al., 2018), as the former simply indicates relating to, affecting, or having members from more than one country. For example, SAEP can be considered international (or having internationality) by virtue of SAEP professionals being present in multiple countries or SAEP research being conducted in multiple countries. Internationalization, however, goes beyond securing international presence by emphasizing processes and values that attend to social justice and equity within international contexts. Although there is no one accepted definition of *internationalization* in psychology or in other disciplines (see Begeny, 2018a, for an extended discussion), work within counseling psychology has grappled with concepts and goals related to internationalization for more than 15 years (e.g., Gerstein et al., 2009; Marsella & Pedersen, 2004; Ng et al., 2012). The definition offered by Leung et al. (2009) captures some core aspects of internationalization, which they describe as "a continuous process of synthesizing knowledge generated through research, scholarship, and practice from different cultures and using this knowledge to solve problems in local and global communities" (p. 115). Leung and colleagues also highlight how internationalization processes should (a) aim to indigenize the profession to ensure that theories and practices are developed and rooted in local cultures and (b) emphasize values such as cultural sensitivity and reciprocal collaboration practices.

Across many disciplines, internationalization is often discussed within the context of globalization. Knight (1997) described the relationships between globalization and internationalization within higher education, stating, "Globalization is the flow of technology, economy, knowledge, people, values, and ideas . . . across borders. Internationalization of higher education is one of the ways a country responds to the impact of Globalization . . . Thus, internationalization and Globalization are seen as different but dynamically linked concepts" (p. 6). Similarly, globalization has influenced the internationalization of SAEP scholarship, theory, and practice. For example, multiple studies discuss best educational or psychoeducational practices with immigrant students and families (e.g., Walick & Sullivan, 2015) and how to synthesize exchanged values, theories, and/or methods to become more culturally informed and to promote inclusive practices and scholarship (e.g., Scharrón-del Río & Aja, 2020). Further discussion on the definitions, goals, and advantages of internationalization in SAEP appears later in this chapter.

Academic Neocolonialism and Social Justice

One potential barrier to the internationalization of SAEP is *academic neocolonialism*, or "the West's monopolistic control of and influence over the nature and flows of social scientific knowledge" (Alatas, 2003, p. 602). Academic neocolonialism has contributed to how knowledge is generated, transmitted, analyzed, and interpreted (Fumagalli, 2018; Mäki, 2013). Academic neocolonialism creates disproportionality in scholarly publications across countries, with scholars working in high-income countries usually overrepresented in scholarship compared to scholars working in low- and middle-income countries (e.g., Barrot, 2021; Begeny, Levy, Hida, Norwalk, Field, et al., 2018; O'Gorman et al., 2012; Thalmayer et al., 2021). Alatas (2003) noted that these "contemporary social science powers" generally favoring North America and Europe are accomplished through: (a) overrepresenting North American and European scholars in publication outlets such as peer-reviewed journals and books, (b) disseminating these scholars' work through such outlets, (c) influencing scholars who mainly work outside of North America and Europe to consume their work through these outlets, and (d) commanding domestic and international scholarly recognition and reputation.

As academic neocolonialism has thrived in the past decades, the internationalization of SAEP and other fields of psychology suffers from the suppression of innovative and culturally informed exploration, development, and transportation of knowledge (Begeny et al., 2021; Bernardo et al., 2018; Leung et al., 2009). In academic neocolonialism, greater value is placed on scholarship produced in high-income global regions, and the transportation of knowledge often flows from high-income areas to low- and middle-income regions, neglecting the unique context of the "receiving" geographic region. To counter the negative impact of academic neocolonialism, Bernardo et al. (2018) suggested that internationalization work should align with a set of values and perspectives, including "cultural humility, social justice, advocacy, multicultural competence, critical intercultural consciousness, equity, and complementarity and integration of local perspectives" (p. 988). The authors warned that internationalization work not based on the above-mentioned values has a risk of confirming power differences across nations. For example, SAEP scholars in Western Europe and North America may prejudge or undervalue others' work based on their geographic regions or cultures and take a quick stance to "help" and "teach others" to absorb and replicate what they define as best practice.

Promoting international work within a theoretical model of social justice also requires dialogue around what social justice means across the globe. Broad definitions of social justice may be universal, emphasizing the need for equal rights and opportunities for all individuals, regardless of their identities and backgrounds. However, aspects of social justice relevant to a particular country or culture may vary significantly (e.g., racism, poverty, violence, or other forms of oppression toward marginalized groups or individuals). More specific to justice-focused work in SAEP, there are geographically and culturally unique injustices that children and youth face in their daily lives; at the same time, there are globally similar injustices (e.g., racism) that SAEP professionals need to understand and seek to dismantle as well. Relatedly, even if two countries are affected by a common injustice (e.g., poverty), the country's or region's contextual, historical, sociopolitical, and cultural factors will influence specific definitions, manifestations, understandings, and solutions to that injustice. In describing the education debt, Ladson-Billings (2006) provides an example of this within the context of the United States.

Overall, having a social justice lens based only on Western-world cultural values and contexts may ultimately be a form of ethnocentrism and may distract one's attention from the contextual, historical, sociopolitical, and cultural factors that influence social justice issues in specific geographic locations. Later in this chapter, we elucidate some of these ideas when discussing internationalization, international examples of social justice issues reported in SAEP scholarship, and challenges and opportunities for SAEP as an international discipline.

CURRENT STATUS OF SCHOOL AND EDUCATIONAL PSYCHOLOGY AS AN INTERNATIONAL PROFESSION

Although a complete "status" of SAEP would be impossible to summarize in a single book chapter, this section highlights important characteristics of the discipline around the globe. Additionally, we introduce some contemporary topics to help readers get a deeper understanding of international issues of equity and social justice.

Characteristics and Statistics of School and Educational Psychology Internationally

Over the past few decades, there has generally been an increase in the presence of professionals around the world who identify as school and educational psychologists (in the ways defined earlier in this chapter). For example, Catterall (1982) estimated there were roughly 40,000 psychologists around the world working with school students and school-age children. Approximately 10 years later, this estimate rose to 87,000 based on survey data from respondents with expertise in SAEP across 54 countries (Oakland & Cunningham, 1992). In the 21st century, Jimerson and Colleagues (2008) conducted a search (e.g., through existing publications, the internet, relevant associations, and outreach to colleagues) and identified evidence of school psychology in 83 out of the 192 member states of the United Nations. In a follow-up study, Jimerson et al. (2009) conducted an internet search with country names and profession labels, examined existing publications, and contacted colleagues in each country who may have had additional information about the prevalence of SEAP professionals globally. Results of this work suggested that there were 76,122 school and educational psychologists across 48 countries as of 2007. A subsequent global estimate was reported by Brown and Jimerson (2015) based on personal communication between the authors and Thomas Oakland in 2013; accordingly, it was estimated that there were approximately 100,000 SAEP professionals around the world.

Despite what appears to be an increasing trend in the presence of SAEP professionals around the world, it is not surprising that geographic representation varies widely. For example, Jimerson et al. (2009) reported that the United States had the most professionals working within the discipline (N = 32,300), followed by Turkey (N = 11,327) and Spain (N = 3,600). Conversely, Trinidad and Tobago (N = 4), Tanzania (N = 3), and Jamaica (N = 1) reportedly had the fewest school and educational psychologists. Studies have also shown mixed results when exploring factors that might influence the presence of SAEP across countries. For example, gross domestic product (GDP; Cook et al., 2010; Oakland & Jimerson, 2014), public support for education (e.g., Oakland & Jimerson, 2007), and cultural modernity (e.g., a society's support for marginalized populations; Cook et al., 2010) were identified as significant predictors. However, other studies did not find significant results of GDP or public support for education in predicting the status of SAEP or the ratio of psychologists to students (e.g., Brown & Jimerson, 2015).

Also considering the presence of SAEP internationally, Begeny, Levy, Hida, Norwalk, Field, et al. (2018) examined 4,456 articles published from 2002 to 2016 among eight SAEP international journals. Among several findings, one was that authors' work affiliations reflected 109 different countries and territories. Notably, these results do not suggest that

SAEP is formally recognized as a discipline in all 109 countries and territories, nor do they imply that all authors contributing to SAEP journals identify as school or educational psychologists. Instead, these data indicate that scholarly work relevant to SAEP is quite ubiquitous, and the presence of SAEP (as assessed via scholarship) is relatively consistent with prior descriptions and estimates.

Collectively, the aforementioned estimates and statistics provide helpful insights regarding the presence of SAEP internationally; however, one large caveat in interpreting them is that different methods were used across studies, all of which had important limitations. It is unlikely that any research team will ever obtain an exact count of working school and educational psychologists around the world, but this should not deter researchers from continuing to explore and update information about the presence of SAEP internationally. Such data can serve as a basis for a better understanding of where and how SAEP professionals conduct their work or may assist in identifying key variables influencing the presence or development of SAEP in different countries—all of which contribute to an understanding of SAEP internationally.

SCHOOL AND EDUCATIONAL PSYCHOLOGY ORGANIZATIONS

With thousands of SAEP professionals around the world, international organizations can play a leadership role in the development of SAEP globally by promoting communication and advocacy among stakeholders, high standards for training and practice, and quality research.[1] For example, ISPA, established in 1982, has members representing more than 50 countries (Nastasi, 2018). It is one of the most influential organizations to promote SAEP worldwide through its annual conference and its official journal, the *International Journal of School and Education Psychology* (established in 2013 and currently publishing four volumes per year). Both provide platforms for professionals in the field to share information about research, theory, and practice in SAEP internationally and, ideally, to increase each other's understanding of culturally informed theories and concepts in psychology or education. ISPA also developed (Oakland et al., 1997) and later updated (ISPA, 2021) its international code of ethics for SAEP professionals, which aims to capture commonalities in acceptable professional standards across national boundaries while at the same time allowing for adaptations to countries' unique codes. The international code infuses global perspectives into SAEP practice; however, critical perspectives exist, and some argue that Western values and experiences still dominate the code of ethics and other core characteristics of ISPA (e.g., Begeny, Levy, Hida, & Norwalk, 2018; Mendes et al., 2016; Nastasi et al., 2020).

In addition to identifying ISPA as the leading international organization for the field, some (e.g., Jimerson et al., 2008; Kim et al., 2018) have documented national associations specifically for SAEP professionals in as many as 39 different countries. Examples of such organizations include Australian Psychologists and Counselors in Schools, Association of Educational Psychologists in the United Kingdom, Associação Brasileira de Psicologia Escolar e Educacional in Brazil, Canadian Association of School Psychologists, Greek Association of School Psychologists, Indian School Psychology Association, Jamaican Psychological Society, School Psychology Association of China, and Turkish Psychological Counseling and Guidance Association.

---

[1] We are aware of the conversation about using the term *stakeholders*, and note here that this term is used throughout this chapter to refer to individuals, groups, or organizations that can affect or are affected by a process, its goals, and/or its outcomes. This definition is consistent with its usage in fields such as psychology and evaluation, and it is adapted from the information and definitions shared by Bryson et al. (2011).

Training in School and Educational Psychology

Training and licensing are essential to SAEP, given the many technical skills required for the profession and the potential risk of harming students in the absence of appropriate standards. However, standards for training and licensing vary considerably across countries (Jimerson et al., 2007). Jimerson et al. (2008) found regulations related to licensing and credentialing of school psychologists in 29 countries, university programs for preparing school psychologists in 56 countries, and doctoral-level training programs in 19 countries. In a more recent study, Kim et al. (2018) identified 288 university faculty members affiliated with doctoral SAEP programs from 16 countries outside of the United States, including Australia, Canada, China, Ghana, Greece, Hong Kong from China, Iran, Japan, Jordan, Kenya, Philippines, South Africa, South Korea, Spain, Ukraine, and the United Kingdom. The small discrepancy between Jimerson et al.'s (2008) and Kim et al.'s (2018) findings could be due to slightly different search methods, the emergence of new programs, or the discontinuation of previously identified programs over the 10-year gap between the two studies (Kim et al., 2018).

It is also worth noting that professional training programs for SAEP are eligible for international accreditation. ISPA developed the *International Guidelines for the Preparation of School Psychologists* (Cunningham & Oakland, 1998) and has accredited eight programs in four countries (Cyprus, Hong Kong, The Netherlands, and the United States) as of 2022. This international accreditation not only acknowledges programs that have international commitment and demonstrated effort to impact students locally and globally, but also promotes international partnership and exchange. However, this accreditation opportunity should also be assessed from a critical and equity-focused lens. For example, its standards and requirements may pose challenges for programs in countries not accustomed to the accreditation process and the English language (Farrell et al., 2014). Additionally, the accreditation process and requirements may not reflect sufficient input from geographically diverse training program faculty and directors in SAEP. Considering the limited number of programs currently accredited by ISPA, more attention to the opportunities, challenges, value, and feasibility of international accreditation is warranted. Indeed, current standards could potentially serve as a meaningful starting point and, with greater attention from relevant and more representative stakeholders, have the potential for improvement and wider adoption by SAEP programs internationally.

Scholarly Journal Outlets Focused on School and Educational Psychology

Characteristics related to the development and dissemination of international scholarship in SAEP are important to understand for several reasons. For example, written scholarship offers opportunities for global communication and collaboration, and the production and dissemination of scholarship are intricately entwined with advancing internationalization in the discipline (as discussed later). Accordingly, some scholars have explored the structure, processes, and content of academic journals devoted to SAEP from an international perspective.

For example, Begeny and colleagues (2019) searched for and analyzed peer-reviewed scholarly outlets devoted to SAEP and identified 45 journals meeting their criteria. Among these 45 journals, 93% allowed free access to abstracts and 40% provided free access to all full-length articles. Additionally, 49% were affiliated with a national organization. Regarding geographic representation, the 45 journals represented 16 countries; however, this representation was disproportionate. For instance, only two journals were published in Eastern Europe (both from Romania), only one journal in Latin America (from Brazil), and none were published in Africa. On the contrary, the vast majority of journals were affiliated with Western World countries (N = 29). The study also found that English was the most common language of publication, with 81% of the journals publishing all or some articles in English. However, depending on the journal, full-length articles were available in several other languages, including Arabic, Chinese, Farsi, German, Japanese, Korean, Portuguese, and Spanish. Based on the 45 journals identified by Begeny et al. (2019), Wang and colleagues (2019) examined the geographic representation of editorial boards for those journals. Results showed that editorial board members represented 17 countries but that, again, the majority (80%) were affiliated with Western world countries, with 16% from Asian-Pacific countries and 2% or less from other global regions.

Overall, previous literature examining SAEP internationally has provided helpful information for understanding the development of the profession globally. However, one limitation of these data is that they may not accurately reflect the present status of the field, due to its ever-evolving nature. As an example, a few of the SAEP-focused journals identified by Begeny et al. (2019) have since been discontinued, and at least one new journal has emerged. Thus, the status data and organizational characteristics summarized in this chapter can only reflect the most recent, publicly available information.

Internationalization Within School and Educational Psychology

Some scholars have also explicitly considered concepts and research pertaining to the *internationalization* of SAEP. A brief description of internationalization was provided earlier in this chapter; however, this section will elaborate on what is meant by internationalization within the discipline and summarize some of the existing SAEP scholarship on this topic. It is important to note that efforts to better understand internationalization—and foster positive change from processes and values associated with internationalization—require a critical and equity-focused framework for approaching SAEP as an international discipline as well as a commitment to growing one's intercultural consciousness (Begeny, 2018b; Begeny et al., 2021).

What Is Internationalization and Why Is It Important?

Although there is no consensus on a single definition or description of *internationalization* in psychology or other disciplines, several scholars have described it as being an approach, framework, or process that includes an organizational emphasis, a representational emphasis, or a combination of the two (Arfken, 2012; Begeny, 2018a; Leung et al., 2009; van de Vijver, 2013). For example, in conveying an organizational emphasis, van de Vijver (2013) suggested that internationalization is "the approach in which existing or new psychological theories, methods, procedures, or data across cultures are synthesized so as to create a more culture-informed, inclusive, and globally applicable science and profession" (p. 761). In other words, psychologists may use values and processes of internationalization to expand psychology research, theory, or practice beyond a respective nation, global region, or culture.

A representational emphasis for internationalization arguably captures more of its ethical and social justice dimensions (Arfken, 2012; Begeny et al., 2021) and reflects the need for a discipline to better represent the global population. As one example, scholars within psychology and SAEP have advocated for efforts to improve geographic proportionality of study participants and/or authors represented in academic journals (e.g., Bajwa & König, 2019; Begeny, Levy, Hida, Norwalk, Field, et al., 2018; Hida et al., 2020; Thalmayer et al., 2021). A representational emphasis also attends to values commonly described as aligning with internationalization (see, for example, Begeny, 2018b; Bernardo et al., 2018; Leung et al., 2009; Ng et al., 2012). Examples of values include exhibiting cultural sensitivity, focusing on reciprocity during scholarly collaboration, and working to ensure that a discipline's research and practice are grounded in local cultures rather than "exported" from the global West (Marsella & Pedersen, 2004; Thalmayer et al., 2021).

With respect to SAEP more specifically, Begeny (2018b) offered one idea for a conceptual model of internationalization for the field (see Figure 17.1, reproduced from Begeny, 2018b) along with a working definition that utilized both organizational and representational emphases. More work and dialogue are needed to enhance definitions of *internationalization* for SAEP, but in the meantime, the following definition and description are one relatively comprehensive example:

> Internationalization within school and educational psychology [is] an intentional, intercultural, collaborative, and ongoing process involving transparent communication, representative stakeholders, a commitment to social justice, and various forms of data to inform decisions and strategic actions aimed at achieving context-relevant, equitable support and opportunities for professionals in the discipline. As an essential part of this definition and collaborative process, practices should also reflect cultural respect, reciprocity, inclusivity, value for all contributions, and co-creation of knowledge. In addition, the ongoing process should, at minimum, involve the following: (1) periodically identifying strengths and needs (e.g., by completing needs assessments) that are culturally relevant and relate directly to determining or achieving specified goals; (2) identifying representative stakeholders that align with the assessments and/or goals; and (3) articulating clear and stated benefits for stakeholders, including but not limited to school and educational psychology professionals. (Begeny, 2018b, p. 927)

The conceptual model in Figure 17.1 expands on this description, and Begeny (2018b) likewise describes and aligns nine unique internationalization goals and potential benefits with the conceptual model and definition. Examples of the goals and benefits of internationalization include (a) improving professionals' training and development, including but not limited to growth in areas such as critical intercultural consciousness; (b) identifying SAEP-relevant solutions to both local and global needs (e.g., developing and evaluating culturally appropriate assessments and interventions that also have culturally meaningful evidence of effectiveness); and (c) enhancing the international representation of individuals working within SAEP, such as by having geographically representative leadership reflected within international organizations as well as representative scholarship in discipline-specific journals.

Summary of Empirical Research Pertaining to Goals of Internationalization

This section focuses primarily on Goal 1 (summarized in Figure 17.1)—that is, the goal of enhancing internationally representative, culturally informed, and accessible scholarship that helps to improve local, national, and/or global research, practice, or theory. As shown in Figure 17.1, this goal has relevance to all other goals or benefits, and it is the area of internationalization that currently has the most published empirical work. As acknowledged in recent years (e.g., Begeny, 2018a), the topic of internationalization in SAEP is relatively new and (by definition) extends beyond an understanding of *internationality*. Therefore, it may not be surprising that the body of empirical work that has specifically explored topics, goals, or characteristics directly pertaining to internationalization in SAEP is relatively small. To our knowledge, existing research directly considering internationalization

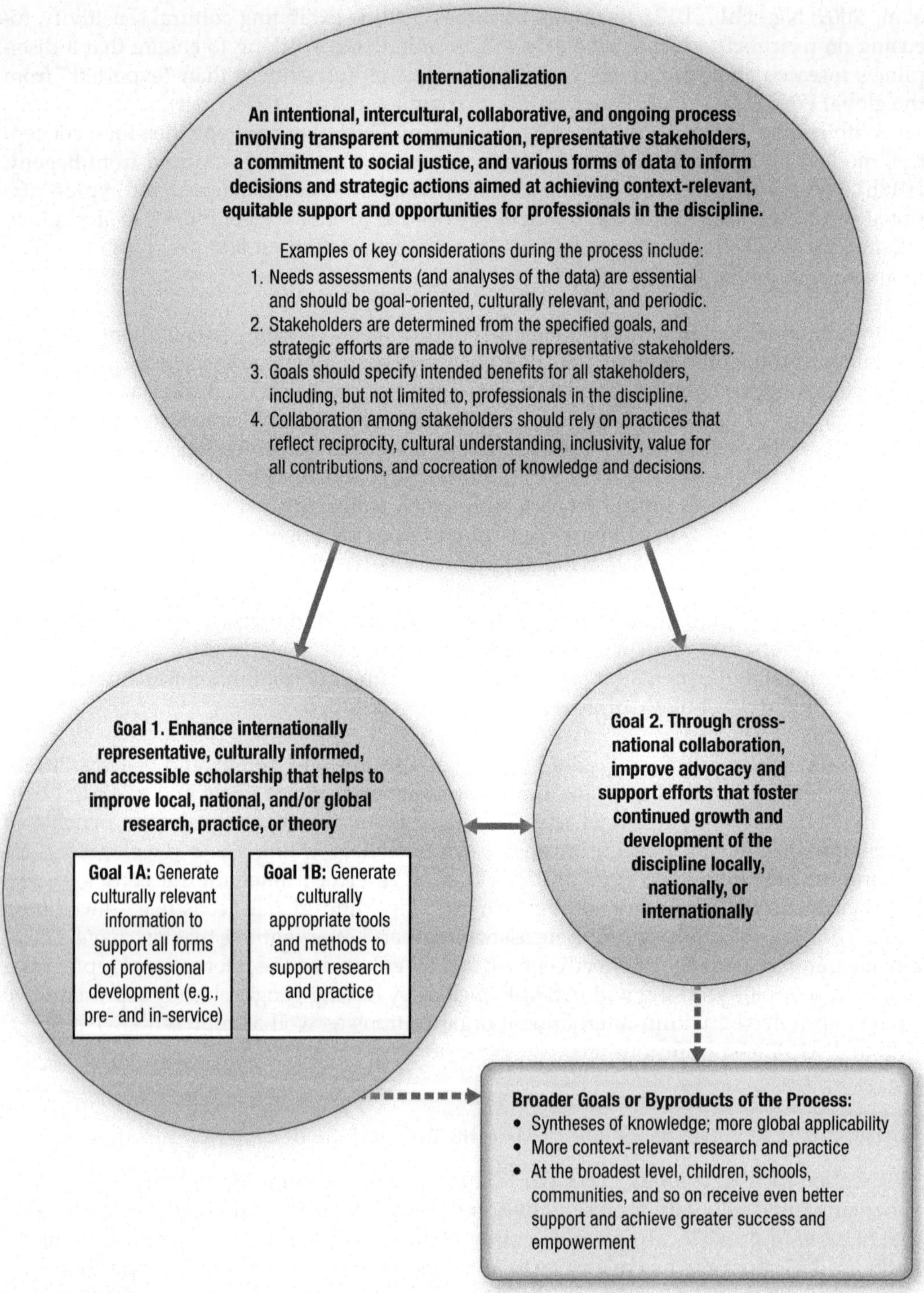

Internationalization

An intentional, intercultural, collaborative, and ongoing process involving transparent communication, representative stakeholders, a commitment to social justice, and various forms of data to inform decisions and strategic actions aimed at achieving context-relevant, equitable support and opportunities for professionals in the discipline.

Examples of key considerations during the process include:
1. Needs assessments (and analyses of the data) are essential and should be goal-oriented, culturally relevant, and periodic.
2. Stakeholders are determined from the specified goals, and strategic efforts are made to involve representative stakeholders.
3. Goals should specify intended benefits for all stakeholders, including, but not limited to, professionals in the discipline.
4. Collaboration among stakeholders should rely on practices that reflect reciprocity, cultural understanding, inclusivity, value for all contributions, and cocreation of knowledge and decisions.

Goal 1. Enhance internationally representative, culturally informed, and accessible scholarship that helps to improve local, national, and/or global research, practice, or theory

Goal 1A: Generate culturally relevant information to support all forms of professional development (e.g., pre- and in-service)

Goal 1B: Generate culturally appropriate tools and methods to support research and practice

Goal 2. Through cross-national collaboration, improve advocacy and support efforts that foster continued growth and development of the discipline locally, nationally, or internationally

Broader Goals or Byproducts of the Process:
- Syntheses of knowledge; more global applicability
- More context-relevant research and practice
- At the broadest level, children, schools, communities, and so on receive even better support and achieve greater success and empowerment

FIGURE 17.1 A CONCEPTUAL MODEL OF INTERNATIONALIZATION RELEVANT TO SCHOOL AND EDUCATIONAL PSYCHOLOGY.

Source: Begeny, J. C. (2018). A working definition and conceptual model of internationalization for school and educational psychology. *Psychology in the Schools, 55*(8), 924–940. https://doi.org/10.1002/pits.22157

in SAEP (a total of six published studies) can be summarized as follows: (a) three studies have sought to assess and understand internationally representative scholarship in the field; (b) two studies explored journal and editorial board characteristics to enhance understanding about representative scholarship; and (c) one study used qualitative methods to examine international SAEP professionals' perspectives about internationalization, including but not limited to issues of representative scholarship. Clearly, a theme of existing empirical work is internationally representative scholarship.

Before summarizing the six aforementioned studies, we want to highlight that reflecting on the processes, values, and goals of internationalization is important for understanding and fostering dialogue about SAEP as an international discipline. This is because engaging internationally to produce scholarship has the potential to yield negative consequences, even if unintended. For example, as Begeny and colleagues (2021) recently emphasized, "exploitation, paternalism, neoliberalism, language differences, and inequitable resources have all been described as barriers or negative impacts resulting from international work that does not strive to integrate internationalization processes and values" (p. 215).

As evidenced in the empirical work to date, SAEP still has considerable room for growth and improvement in regard to representative scholarship and related metrics associated with Goal 1 (summarized in Figure 17.1). For example, in examining the international representation of prevention and intervention research, one study (Begeny, Levy, Hida, & Norwalk, 2018) assessed articles across eight SAEP journals from 2002 to 2016 and found a disproportionately low number of articles representing authors or participants from countries outside of North America and Western Europe. Even more concerning, 85% of the experimental studies published within the eight journals reported on participants living in the United States, despite the estimate that only approximately 38% of employed school psychologists around the globe work in the United States. In an evaluation of a different set of eight SAEP journals aiming to publish international scholarship, Begeny, Levy, Hida, Norwalk, Field, et al. (2018) similarly found that the majority had authors (94%) and study participants (90%) that were affiliated with Western Europe as well as countries such as Australia, Canada, and the United States.

Following those two studies, Kim et al. (2018) specifically investigated publication patterns (e.g., journal outlets, language of publication) for scholars not affiliated with the United States. A systematic global search identifying more than 250 researchers affiliated with SAEP doctoral programs indicated that the large majority of these scholars published frequently in SAEP journals and published their articles in English, even if their work affiliation was in a country where English was not an official language. In essence, the findings by Kim and colleagues reveal that, even though scholars around the world publish in English and often in SAEP journals, they are collectively still underrepresented compared to scholars working in the United States or other Western world countries.

Work by Begeny et al. (2019) and Wang et al. (2019) helped to comprehensively document journal and editorial board characteristics of 45 journal outlets published around the world that focused on SAEP; collectively, these studies also highlighted limitations related to representation aspects of internationalization (e.g., underrepresentation of editorial board members from Africa, Eastern Europe, and Latin America). In a qualitative analysis of international SAEP scholars, including professionals who collectively worked in all global regions and more than 20 different countries, concerns were raised about advancing internationalization in SAEP along three primary themes: (a) issues associated with power, paternalism, and neoliberalism (including but not limited to scientific imperialism); (b) lack of critical dialogue and research related to internationalization; and (c) financial and linguistic barriers that undermined efforts to advance internationalization (Bernardo et al., 2018). Some of these concerns will be discussed in more detail later in this chapter.

SOCIAL JUSTICE CONNECTIONS

How are social justice issues addressed in contemporary and international scholarship within SAEP?

There are numerous areas of work and activity in the profession aiming to promote equity and social justice. To identify culturally informed, internationally representative scholarship that addresses contemporary social justice issues, we referenced the list of 45 SAEP journals identified by Begeny et al. (2019) and reviewed the 13 still in existence that (a) published all of their articles in English; and (b) had a mission statement with explicit interest in publishing international scholarship. We then utilized a defined set of key words (e.g., *diversity*, *multicultural*, *equity/inequity*, and *social justice*) to locate relevant articles published from 2018 to early 2022 in these journals. A total of 40 articles met our inclusion criteria.

To identify themes specific to geographic regions, we coded the 40 identified articles according to the country (or countries) in which study participants resided (if applicable). All articles were then grouped into geographic regions using the United Nations Regional Groups of Members States (2022) classification list, which provides an internationally recognized way to organize 193 countries into five distinct geopolitical regional groups. The following summarizes major themes in scholarship for each of these regions. Due to space limitations within this chapter, we could only provide a very broad summary of the 40 identified articles. For additional details, refer to Kim et al. (2023).

- *Western European and Others Group (WEOG)*
  Approximately half of the identified articles including contemporary issues of social justice in SAEP journals were affiliated with the WEOG region. Identified themes ranged from socio-economic status (SES), migrant/immigrant students, gender gaps in STEM, and promoting cultural diversity (e.g., different indigenous, ethnic, linguistic, and cultural backgrounds) in educational contexts. Additionally, articles from this region specified goals or suggestions for improving practices through a social justice lens.
- *Asia Pacific Group (APG)*
  Several studies from the APG highlighted the disadvantages that students with a lower SES face in terms of academic achievement and overall mental well-being. Another contemporary issue from the AP region was students' mental health in educational settings.
- *African Group (AG)*
  Several studies in the AG region highlighted the need for practitioners to recognize and accommodate the unique needs of orphans and vulnerable children (OVCs), who are often affected by depression, anxiety, stress, and lack of feelings of safety and security. Another prevalent issue reflected in scholarship represented in this region was the impact of HIV/AIDS on education. Finally, research represented within the AG highlighted how children exposed to multiple forms of violence face unique challenges and needs.
- *Eastern European Group (EEG)*
  Studies in the EEG region examined diversity in students' academic motivation and bullying victimization. Identified studies showed, for example, that there were distinct effects of socialization on mental health across gender groups and that there were higher levels of bullying in Eastern European countries than in Western European countries.

(continued)

> **SOCIAL JUSTICE CONNECTIONS (*continued*)**
>
> - ***Latin American and the Caribbean Group (GRULAC)***
>   Studies included in the GRULAC group explored issues encompassing SES and mental health complications, such as suicide. For instance, some studies showed key differences in linguistic experiences for toddlers from lower SES backgrounds and higher suicide rates of students categorized as low-income and Guyanese of East Indian descent.
>
> This study shows that there are both differences and similarities (e.g., examining impacts of SES) reflected in SAEP-related work around the globe. The summarized findings from Kim et al. (2023) identified at least a subset of this scholarship, although they certainly do not reflect all justice-focused work published in journals devoted to SAEP. Although this work has some methodological limitations (e.g., only recently published articles across a relatively limited subset of journals were reviewed; not all study authors who produced scholarship on social justice issues used the key words applied in our search), the review illuminates the prevalence, type, and internationality of SAEP-related scholarship, and we hope it encourages readers to further explore this type of work.

CHALLENGES AND OPPORTUNITIES FOR INTERNATIONAL SCHOOL AND EDUCATIONAL PSYCHOLOGY

Promoting the international applicability and global inclusivity of SAEP is associated with challenges and barriers as well as significant benefits and opportunities. This section discusses notable challenges within the broader context of academic neocolonialism, including social and political turmoil, linguistic barriers, and other key systemic barriers. Then, we discuss advantages and opportunities of internationalization, including moral, intellectual, and professional benefits; cultural humility; and ways in which school and educational psychologists can uniquely apply their role to promote values of internationalization and social justice.

Challenges and Barriers to Promoting Internationalization or Other Social Justice Initiatives

Academic Neocolonialism

As previously discussed, academic neocolonialism poses a significant threat to the advancement of goals of internationalization. In fact, many of the challenges associated with promoting internationalization can be understood within the broader context of the effects of academic neocolonialism. Issues at the heart of academic neocolonialism—such as power, privilege, and paternalism—often challenge ideals of internationalization, including values of equity, inclusivity, critical intercultural consciousness, and social justice (Begeny et al., 2021; Bernardo et al., 2018). It is important to emphasize that ideals, processes, and values of internationalization are applicable in nationally focused or internationally focused research and practice (Arfken, 2012; Begeny, 2018b); thus, we next turn to examples of challenges within national and international contexts.

Social and Political Turmoil Around the World

Sociopolitical climates can uniquely impact the extent to which certain issues relevant to SAEP research or practice are prioritized. As an example, the United States—where authors of this chapter currently reside—has a unique history of slavery, racism, and xenophobia. At the time this chapter was written in 2022, issues relevant to the sociopolitical climate in the United States included (a) mass incarceration and the ongoing school-to-prison pipeline targeting Black and Brown males and students with disabilities (Flannery, 2015); (b) a surge in the popularity of the White[2] nationalist movement (Southern Poverty Law Center, n.d.); (c) an uptick in school shootings described as a "uniquely American crisis" (World Population Review, 2022); (d) a record number of filing of antitransgender bills (American Civil Liberties Union, 2022); (e) an introduction of antiabortion bans seeking to undermine constitutionally protected reproductive rights (Guttmacher Institute, 2022); and (f) an introduction of new policies aiming to ban critical race theory in schools (Stout & Wilburn, 2022). The current sociopolitical climate influences the training, practice, and research of SAEP in many ways. For example, schools that employ school resource officers could be facilitating arrests of students for behaviors that would otherwise have resulted in school discipline. The rise in White nationalist rhetoric poses concerns for the safety and well-being of students of color. Fears about school shootings have been associated with negative mental health outcomes in adolescents (Riehm et al., 2021)—never mind the invaluable instructional time lost to participation in lockdown drills, despite limited evidence of their impact on students' mental health and minimal to no evaluation of whether they ultimately make students feel less safe (Saggers et al., 2021). Moreover, how can we most effectively support transgender students within a school that has discriminatory policies about the restrooms students are allowed to use or the sports they are allowed to play? How can we offer counseling services to problem-solve issues of unwanted pregnancies in states with abortion bans? How can we promote issues of social justice and racial equity when frameworks such as critical race theory are under scrutiny by school districts?

In the same way racist and discriminatory rhetoric has seen a rise in the United States, xenophobia has grown around the globe. Persistent challenges and dilemmas around the world pose a threat to the full realization of social justice and the advancement of children's rights. Such dilemmas include climate change, war, hunger, sexual exploitation, unemployment, intolerance and discrimination, migration, escape from persecution, forcible displacements, limited access to education, and abusive labor conditions (Cook, 2020). Such dilemmas also impact the extent to which researchers can fully realize their scholarly capabilities, ultimately impeding one objective of internationalization. For example, scholars in the Arab world cited issues related to political instability, warfare, and occupation as factors contributing to the underrepresentation of the Arab world in international SAEP scholarship; these issues played out in a variety of ways (e.g., travel bans preventing conference attendance, political instability resulting in power outages that thwarted completion of research manuscripts; Hida, 2021). These issues demonstrate how social and political turmoil can influence SAEP in research and practice, thereby creating unique challenges or barriers to promoting social justice nationally and internationally.

---

[2] We intentionally use an uppercase "W" for the term *White* for at least a few key reasons (in no particular order): (a) it is in accordance with current recommendations by the National Association of Black Journalists; (b) the capitalization of "White" challenges the privilege of racial invisibility granted to White people and also challenges White people to grapple with their racial identity and history, just as people of other races must continuously do; and (c) with race being a socially derived construct, we prefer consistency in capitalization for all such artificially constructed racial categories. There has been rich conversation on this topic and we share the following sources as examples of articles that in many ways align with our perspectives on capitalizing "White": https://tinyurl.com/yu54z7v5; https://tinyurl.com/yttuzfwf; and https://tinyurl.com/36pffzcd.

Linguistic Barriers

Language barriers represent a number of challenges for advancing the goals of internationalization and can impede progress toward values of social justice and equity. Linguistic barriers include the difficulty of translating concepts and theories in cross-cultural exchange efforts; practical and financial difficulties for scholars for whom English is not their first language (e.g., cost-prohibitive translation services); and unspoken rules of writing psychological papers (Begeny et al., 2021; van de Vijver, 2013).

Other Key Factors

A barrier to internationalization includes lack of geographic representation of editorial board members, with scholars from Western Europe and North America overrepresented on editorial boards of international SAEP journals (Wang et al., 2019). Additional factors affecting international research production and collaboration include graduate education (e.g., limited training in graduate school to collaborate internationally); mobility (e.g., scholars' ability to engage in travel and collaboration); disciplinary differences (e.g., the extent to which practices specific to one's discipline influence international research and collaboration); changes in international research communication (e.g., the growing role of technology and its potential to facilitate collaboration); funding (e.g., financial support to specifically foster international collaboration); regional initiatives (e.g., the extent to which certain geographic regions prioritize and support international collaboration); and multilateral and independent organizations (e.g., missions and values of international organizations; Begeny, Levy, Hida, & Norwalk, 2018; Begeny, Levy, Hida, Norwalk, Field, et al., 2018; Bernardo et al., 2018; van de Vijver, 2013; Woldegiyorgis et al., 2018). These factors can be barriers depending on an individual scholar's circumstances; therefore, those interested in collaborating internationally and engaging in research aligned with values of internationalization and social justice must be aware of and work to address these barriers.

Some Advantages and Opportunities for Promoting Internationalization

In light of the important challenges discussed in this chapter, there are numerous advantages and opportunities for promoting internationalization. Examples are as follows.

Moral, Intellectual, and Professional Advantages

van de Vijver (2013) outlined three imperatives of internationalization: *moral* (because internationalization makes the field more inclusive); *intellectual* (because internationalization makes psychology a better science); and *professional* (because internationalization makes for better practice). These imperatives represent significant benefits not only for our field overall but also for ourselves as researchers and practitioners and for the children, families, and schools and communities with whom we work and serve.

Cultural Humility

To understand opportunities for promoting internationalization, it is important to consider the ways in which populations living in the United States and other high-income countries differ from the **Majority World**, a term used in lieu of ones such as *developing world* and *third world* to remind us that most humans live in societies in Asia, Africa, Latin America, and the Caribbean (Kagitcibasi, 2002). We cannot assume that theories, measures, and interventions based on empirical evidence from Western countries can be generalized to the rest of the world (Thalmayer et al., 2021). With this in mind, *cultural humility*—defined as the "ability to maintain an interpersonal stance that is other-oriented (or open to the other) in relation to aspects of cultural identity that are most important to the person" (Hook et al., 2013, p. 2)—can be an asset for school and educational psychologists' processing of their work toward social justice and internationalization. Cultural humility challenges school and educational psychologists to be self-evaluative and self-critical, alleviate power imbalances, constantly learn, and serve as leaders and role models for students (Adelson & Brachfeld, 2020). It involves recognizing that cultures are neither siloed nor stagnant; rather, they are interactive, dynamic, and ever-evolving. It also involves understanding culture as a catalyst for human development (Cook, 2020).

APPLICATIONS OF SCHOOL AND EDUCATIONAL PSYCHOLOGY IN ADVANCING GOALS OF INTERNATIONALIZATION AND SOCIAL JUSTICE

SAEP professionals have unique opportunities to advance goals of internationalization and social justice in their research and practice. Opportunities include partnering with families to reach mutual goals of promoting a child's best interests and healthy development. Other opportunities include creating or adapting culturally responsive and context-specific assessment tools and interventions; promoting sensitivity to diversity in communication styles (e.g., lack of eye contact between children and adults, varying degrees of tolerance to interruptions between people in a conversation, use of cultural metaphor or somatic descriptions to explain and understand psychological conditions, differing gender roles); and understanding diversity in kinship patterns, familial ties, and the roles of key adults (e.g., religious leaders, indigenous healers, and community members; Cook, 2020). Promoting values of internationalization can be challenging and arduous as we face the insidious byproducts of academic neocolonialism and systemic oppression. Despite these challenges, advancing internationalization can help us achieve progress in social justice and can help us be better school and educational psychologists, better global citizens, and ultimately better people.

SUMMARY AND CONCLUSIONS

Although not easily defined, SAEP is clearly an international discipline that involves thousands of researchers and practitioners working hard to promote justice and equity for the students, families, educators, and communities whom they serve. However, the prevalence of injustice and systems of oppression around the globe—at local, national, and global-region levels—continues to undermine opportunities for far too many individuals and communities to learn and reach their full potential. These injustices call for even more SAEP professionals to double down and do their part in supporting all students while also working to dismantle oppressive systems that foster discrimination and inequity. Advancing internationalization within the profession—with both its values and processes—illustrates only one way to think about and positively influence systems or contexts that can promote equity and opportunity for those supported by SAEP professionals. At a minimum, we hope readers will continue to reflect upon and grow in their critical intercultural consciousness, whether they work locally or internationally.

DISCUSSION QUESTIONS

1. A variety of research methods have been used to examine the presence and characteristics of SAEP around the world. What are the relative benefits and limitations of these methods for understanding SAEP internationally? If you were to conduct a study to learn more about the field from an international perspective, what research questions would you ask and which methods would you use to address them?
2. What are some possible advantages and disadvantages for training programs of seeking accreditation from ISPA? What factors should be considered to ensure that such accreditation is culturally informed and equitable for all programs globally?
3. In what ways can or do processes and values of internationalization apply to your work? In what ways could such values and processes potentially help to advance the social justice initiatives you are most focused on or interested in?
4. Think about how you would describe and identify contemporary social justice issues that impact school-age youth. In what ways does the content in this chapter align (or not align) with your description? What are some ways you could go about identifying contemporary social justice issues in countries or global regions you are less familiar with?
5. What are some features that you have observed of oppressive systems that (a) have international relevance and (b) impact students, families, and/or school personnel within the school-based settings you are most familiar with?

RECOMMENDED READINGS

Arfken, M. (2012). Scratching the surface: Internationalization, cultural diversity and the politics of recognition. *Social and Personality Psychology Compass, 6*(6), 428–437. https://doi.org/10.1111/j.1751-9004.2012.00440.x

Begeny, J. C. (2018). A working definition and conceptual model of internationalization for school and educational psychology. *Psychology in the Schools, 55*, 924–940. https://doi.org/10.1002/pits.22157

Begeny, J. C., van Schalkwyk, G. J., Kim, E. K., Datu, J. A., Hida, R. M., Wang, J., & Grazioso, M. P. (2021). Engaging internationally to produce scholarship in school and educational psychology: A critical perspective. In R. G. Floyd & T. L. Eckert (Eds.), *Handbook of university and professional careers in school psychology* (pp. 212–228). Taylor & Francis.

Cook, P. (2020). Influences and opportunities of culture. In B. K. Nastasi, S. N. Hart, & S. C. Naser (Eds.), *International handbook on child rights and school psychology* (pp. 293–304). Springer.

Thalmayer, A. G., Toscanelli, C., & Arnett, J. J. (2021). The neglected 95% revisited: Is American psychology becoming less American? *American Psychologist, 76*(1), 116–129. https://doi.org/10.1037/amp0000622

A robust set of instructor resources designed to supplement this text is located at http://connect.springerpub.com/content/book/978-0-8261-6344-8. Qualifying instructors may request access by emailing textbook@springerpub.com.

REFERENCES

Adelson, E., & Brachfeld, M. (2020). Promoting and protecting child rights in the daily practice of school psychology. In B. K. Nastasi, S. N. Hart, & S. C. Naser (Eds.), *International handbook on child rights and school psychology* (pp. 293–304). Springer.

Alatas, S. F. (2003). Academic dependency and the global division of labour in the social sciences. *Current Sociology, 51*(6), 599–613. https://doi.org/10.1177/00113921030516003

American Civil Liberties Union. (2022, April 8). *Legislation affecting LGBTQ rights across the country.* https://www.aclu.org/legislation-affecting-lgbtq-rights-across-country

Arfken, M. (2012). Scratching the surface: Internationalization, cultural diversity and the politics of recognition. *Social and Personality Psychology Compass, 6*(6), 428–437. https://doi.org/10.1111/j.1751-9004.2012.00440.x

Bajwa, N. ul H., & König, C. J. (2019). How much is research in the top journals of industrial/organizational psychology dominated by authors from the U.S.? *Scientometrics, 120*(3), 1147–1161. https://doi.org/10.1007/s11192-019-03180-2

Barrot, J. S. (2021). Research on education in Southeast Asia (1996–2019): A bibliometric review. *Educational Review, 75*(2), 348–368. https://doi.org/10.1080/00131911.2021.1907313

Begeny, J. C. (2018a). An overview of internationalization and its relevance for school and educational psychology. *Psychology in the Schools, 55*(8), 897–907. https://doi.org/10.1002/pits.22161

Begeny, J. C. (2018b). A working definition and conceptual model of internationalization for school and educational psychology. *Psychology in the Schools, 55*(8), 924–940. https://doi.org/10.1002/pits.22157

Begeny, J., Levy, R. A., Hida, R., & Norwalk, K. (2018). Experimental research in school psychology internationally: An assessment of journal publications and implications for internationalization. *Psychology in the Schools, 55*(2), 120–136. https://doi.org/10.1002/pits.22070

Begeny, J. C., Levy, R. A., Hida, R., Norwalk, K., Field, S., Suzuki, H., Soriano-Ferrer, M., Scheunemann, A., Guerrant, M., Clinton, A., & Burneo, A. C. (2018). Geographically representative scholarship and internationalization in school and educational psychology: A bibliometric analysis of eight journals from 2002-2016. *Journal of School Psychology, 70,* 44–63. https://doi.org/10.1016/j.jsp.2018.07.001

Begeny, J. C., van Schalkwyk, G. J., Kim, E. K., Datu, J. A., Hida, R. M., Wang, J., & Grazioso, M. P. (2021). Engaging internationally to produce scholarship in school and educational psychology: A critical perspective. In R. G. Floyd & T. L. Eckert (Eds.), *Handbook of university and professional careers in school psychology.* (pp. 212–228). Taylor & Francis.

Begeny, J. C., Wang, J., Hida, R. M., Oluokun, H. O., & Jones, R. A. (2019). A global examination of peer-reviewed, scholarly journal outlets devoted to school and educational psychology. *School Psychology International, 40,* 547–580. https://doi.org/10.1177/0143034319881474

Bernardo, A. B. I., Begeny, J. C., Earle, O. B., Ginns, D. S., Grazioso, M. P., Soriano-Ferrer, M., Suzuki, H., & Zapata, R. (2018). Internationalization within school and educational psychology: Perspectives about positive indicators, critical considerations, and needs. *Psychology in the Schools, 55,* 982–992. https://doi.org/10.1002/pits.22160

Brown, J. A., & Jimerson, S. R. (2015). Toward understanding school psychology around the globe: Economical, educational, and professional factors. *International Journal of School & Educational Psychology, 3,* 73–84. https://doi.org/10.1080/21683603.2014.983212

Bryson, J. M., Patton, M. Q., & Bowman, R. A. (2011). Working with evaluation stakeholders: A rational, step-wise approach and toolkit. *Evaluation and Program Planning, 34,* 1–12. https://doi.org/10.1016/j.evalprogplan.2010.07.001

Catterall, C. (1982). International school psychology: Problems and promises. In C. R. Reynolds & T. B. Gutkin (Eds.), *The handbook of school psychology* (pp. 1103–1128). Wiley.

Cook, C. R., Jimerson, S. R., & Begeny, J. C. (2010). A model for predicting the presence of school psychology: An international examination of sociocultural, sociopolitical and socioeconomic influences. *School Psychology International, 31,* 438–461. https://doi.org/10.1177/0143034310377580

Cook, P. (2020). Influences and opportunities of culture. In B. K. Nastasi, S. N. Hart, & S. C. Naser (Eds.), *International handbook on child rights and school psychology.* (pp. 293–304). Springer.

Cunningham, J., & Oakland, T. (1998). International School Psychology Association guidelines for the preparation of school psychologists. *School Psychology International, 19*, 19–30. https://doi.org/10.1177/0143034398191002

Farrell, P., McFarland, M., Gonzalez, R., Hass, M., & Stiles, D. A. (2014). The role of international accreditation in promoting academic and professional preparation in school psychology. *International Journal of School & Educational Psychology, 2*, 205–213. https://doi.org/10.1080/21683603.2014.934621

Flannery, M. E. (2015, January 5). *The school-to-prison pipeline: Time to shut it down*. National Education Association. https://www.nea.org/advocating-for-change/new-from-nea/school-prison-pipeline-time-shut-it-down

Fumagalli, R. (2018). Who is afraid of scientific imperialism? *Synthese, 195*, 4125–4146. https://doi.org/10.1007/s11229-017-1411-2

Gerstein, L. H., Heppner, P. P., Ægisdóttir, S., Leung, S.-M. A., & Norsworthy, K. L. (2009). *International handbook of cross-cultural counseling: Cultural assumptions and practices worldwide*. Sage.

Guttmacher Institute. (2022, April 4). *2022 state legislative sessions: Abortion bans and restrictions on medication abortion dominate*. https://www.guttmacher.org/article/2022/03/2022-state-legislative-sessions-abortion-bans-and-restrictions-medication-abortion

Hida, R. M. (2021). *School and educational psychology in the Arab World: A mixed methods study examining publication trends and research practices of Arab scholars* [Doctoral dissertation]. NC State Repository of Theses and Dissertations, North Carolina State University.

Hida, R. M., Begeny, J. C., Oluokun, H. O., Bancroft, T. E., Fields-Turner, F. L., Ford, B. D., Jones, C. K., Ratliff, C. B., & Smith, A.Y. (2020). Internationalization and geographically representative scholarship in journals devoted to behavior analysis: An assessment of 10 journals across 15 years. *Scientometrics, 122*, 719–740. https://doi.org/10.1007/s11192-019-03289-4

Hook, J., Davis, D., Owen, J., Worthington, E., & Utsey, S. (2013). Cultural humility: Measuring openness to culturally diverse clients. *Journal of Counseling Psychology, 60*, 353–366. https://doi.org/10.1037/a0032595

International School Psychology Association. (n.d.-a). *About ISPA*. Retrieved April 24, 2023, from https://ispaweb.org/about-ispa

International School Psychology Association. (n.d.-b). *A definition of school psychology*. Retrieved April 24, 2023, from https://ispaweb.org/a-definition-of-school-psychology

International School Psychology Association. (2021, July 15). *Code of ethics*. https://www.ispaweb.org/wp-content/uploads/2021/07/ISPA-Code-of-Ethics-2021.pdf

Jimerson, S. R., Oakland, T. D., & Farrell, P. T. (Eds.). (2007). *The handbook of international school psychology*. Sage Publications.

Jimerson, S. R., Skokut, M., Cardenas, S., Malone, H., & Stewart, K. (2008). Where in the world is school psychology? Examining evidence of school psychology around the globe. *School Psychology International, 29*, 131–144. https://doi.org/10.1177/0143034308090056

Jimerson, S. R., Stewart, K., Skokut, M., Cardenas, S., & Malone, H. (2009). How many school psychologists are there in each country of the world?: International estimates of school psychologists and school psychologist-to-student ratios. *School Psychology International, 30*, 555–567. https://doi.org/10.1177/0143034309107077

Kagitcibasi, C. (2002). A model of family change in cultural context. *Online Readings in Psychology and Culture, 6*(3). https://doi.org/10.9707/2307-0919.1059

Kim, E. K., Begeny, J. C., Hida, R. M., Wang, J., Jones, R. A., & Oluokun, H. H. (2018). Publication characteristics and outlets of school and educational psychology scholars around the globe. *Psychology in the Schools, 55*, 955–968. https://doi.org/10.1002/pits.22158

Kim, E. K., Han, K., Jackson, K., Begeny, J. C., Hida, R. M., & Wang, J. (2023). A preliminary examination of how equity and justice topics are addressed in contemporary and international scholarship within school and educational psychology. Manuscript in preparation.

Knight, J. (1997). Internationalisation of higher education: A conceptual framework. In J. Knight & H. de Wit (Eds.), *Internationalisation of higher education in Asia Pacific countries* (pp. 5–19). European Association for International Education.

Ladson-Billings, G. (2006). From the achievement gap to the education debt: Understanding achievement in U.S. schools. *Educational Researcher, 35*, 3–12. https://doi.org/10.3102/0013189X035007003

Leung, S. A., Clawson, T., Norsworthy, K. L., Tena, A., Szilagyi, A., & Rogers, J. (2009). Internationalization of professional counseling: an indigenous perspective. In L. Gerstein, P. Heppner, S. Ægisdóttir, S.-M. Leung, & K. Norsworthy (Eds.), *International handbook of cross-cultural counseling: Cultural assumptions and practices worldwide* (pp. 111–123). Sage.

Mäki, U. (2013). Scientific imperialism: Difficulties in definition, identification, and assessment. *International Studies in the Philosophy of Science, 27*, 325–339. https://doi.org/10.1080/02698595.2013.825496

Marsella, A. J., & Pedersen, P. (2004). Internationalizing the counseling psychology curriculum: Toward new values, competencies, and directions. *Counselling Psychology Quarterly, 17*, 413–423. https://doi.org/10.1080/09515070412331331246

Mendes, S., Nascimento, I., Abreu-Lima, I., & Almeida, L. (2016). A study of the ethical dilemmas experienced by school psychologists in Portugal. *Ethics & Behavior, 26*, 395–414. https://doi.org/10.1080/10508422.2015.1029047

Nastasi, B. K. (2018). International School Psychology Association (ISPA). In M. Burns (Ed.), *Introduction to school psychology: Controversies and current practice* (pp. 106–116). Oxford University Press.

Nastasi, B. K., Chittooran, M. R. M., Arora, P., & Song, S. (2020). Infusing global and intercultural perspectives to transform school psychology and school psychologists. *School Psychology, 35*, 440–450. https://doi.org/10.1037/spq0000403

Ng, K. M., Choudhuri, D. D., Noonan, B. M., & Ceballos, P. (2012). An internationalization competency checklist for American counseling training programs. *International Journal for the Advancement of Counseling, 34*, 19–38. https://doi.org/10.1007/s10447-011-9141-5

Oakland, T. D., & Cunningham, J. L. (1992). A survey of school psychology in developed and developing countries. *School Psychology International, 13*, 99–129. https://doi.org/10.1177/0143034392132001

Oakland, T., Goldman, S., & Bischoff, H. (1997). Code of ethics of the International School Psychology Association. *School Psychology International, 18*, 291–298. https://doi.org/10.1177/0143034397184001

Oakland, T. D., & Jimerson, S. R. (2007). School psychology internationally: A retrospective view and influential conditions. In S. R. Jimerson, T. D. Oakland, & P. T. Farrell (Eds.), *The handbook of international school psychology* (pp. 453–462). Sage.

Oakland, T. D., & Jimerson, S. R. (2014). History and current status of school psychology internationally. In P. L. Harrison & A. Thomas (Eds.), *Best practices in school psychology VI: Foundations* (pp. 401–419). National Association of School Psychologists.

O'Gorman, J., Shum, D., Halford, K.W., & Ogilvie, J. (2012). World trends in psychological research output and impact. *International Perspectives in Psychology: Research, Practice, Consultation, 1*, 268–283. https://doi.org/10.1037/a0030520

Riehm, M. R., Adams, L. B., Krueger, E. A., Mattingly, D. T., Nestadt, P. S., & Leventhal, A. M. (2021). Adolescents' concerns about school violence or shootings and association with depressive, anxiety, and panic symptoms. *JAMA Network Open, 4*(11), Article e2132131. https://doi.org/10.1001/jamanetworkopen.2021.32131

Saggers, B., Campbell, M. A., Kelly, A. B., & Killingly, C. (2021). Are schools' lockdown drills really beneficial?—A commentary. *The Journal of School Health, 91*, 451–453. https://doi.org/10.1111/josh.13020

Scharrón-del Río, M. R., & Aja, A. A. (2020). Latinx: Inclusive language as liberation praxis. *Journal of Latinx Psychology, 8*, 7–20. https://doi.org/10.1037/lat0000140

Southern Poverty Law Center. (n.d.). *White nationalist*. https://www.splcenter.org/fighting-hate/extremist-files/ideology/white-nationalist

Stout, C., & Wilburn, T. (2022, February 1). *CRT map: Efforts to restrict teaching racism and bias have multiplied across the U.S*. Chalkbeat. https://www.chalkbeat.org/22525983/map-critical-race-theory-legislation-teaching-racism

Thalmayer, A. G., Toscanelli, C., & Arnett, J. J. (2021). The neglected 95% revisited: Is American psychology becoming less American? *American Psychologist, 76*, 116–129. https://doi.org/10.1037/amp0000622

United Nations. (n.d.). *Regional groups of member states*. Retrieved April 11, 2022, from https://www.un.org/dgacm/en/content/regional-groups

van de Vijver, F. J. R. (2013). Contributions of internationalization to psychology: Toward a global and inclusive discipline. *American Psychologist, 68*, 761–770. https://doi.org/10.1037/a0033762

Walick, C. M., & Sullivan, A. L. (2015). Educating somali immigrant and refugee students: A review of cultural-historical issues and related psychoeducational supports. *Journal of Applied School Psychology, 31*, 347–368. https://doi.org/10.1080/15377903.2015.1056921

Wang, J., Begeny, J. C., Hida, R. M., & Oluokun, H. H. (2019). Editorial boards of 45 journals devoted to school and educational psychology: International characteristics and publication patterns. *School Psychology International, 41*, 110–136. https://doi.org/10.1177/0143034319887522

Woldegiyorgis, A. A., Proctor, D., & de Wit, H. (2018). Internationalization of research: Key considerations and concerns. *Journal of Studies in International Education, 22*, 161–176. https://doi.org/10.1177/1028315318762804

World Population Review. (2022). *School shootings by country 2022.* https://worldpopulationreview.com/country-rankings/school-shootings-by-country

CHAPTER 18

Future of School Psychology

LORI E. UNRUH ■ KATHLEEN M. MINKE ■ ERIC ROSSEN

CHAPTER OBJECTIVES

After reading this chapter, you will be able to:

- Consider future directions of school psychology through a review of historical trends and contexts.
- Identify likely responses of school psychology professional organizations to current challenges, including shortages, implementation of standards revisions, and the evolution of professional roles.
- Discuss urgent challenges as we move into the future, including diversity, social justice, mental behavioral health, and technology.
- Describe specific action steps for individual school psychologists in creating a robust future for the field.

NATIONAL ASSOCIATION OF SCHOOL PSYCHOLOGISTS PRACTICE MODEL CONNECTIONS

Domain 8: Equitable Practices for Diverse Student Populations
Domain 9: Research and Evidence-Based Practice
Domain 10: Legal, Ethical, and Professional Practice

INTRODUCTION

Predicting the future is an intriguing task, but one that is fraught with pitfalls and potential for error. History is replete with failed predictions, such as from those who saw no potential in the possibility of a telephone ("Well-informed people know it is impossible to transmit the voice over wires and that were it possible to do so, the thing would be of no practical value"; *The Boston Post*, 1865) or an airplane ("Heavier-than-air flying machines are fantasy. Simple laws of physics make them impossible"; Lord Kelvin, president, British Royal Society, 1895). Even within more recent history, industry visionaries can be spectacularly wrong in forecasting advancements ("640 K [of computer memory] ought to be enough for anybody"; Bill Gates, founder and CEO of Microsoft, 1981). Therefore, it is with great humility and caution that we undertake the task of discussing the likely future of school psychology.

The purpose of this chapter is to offer predictions regarding future directions for the field. In particular, these predictions pertain to the composition of the workforce, the roles of school psychologists, and professional practices. Recommendations for contributing to the future of school psychology are offered at the end the chapter.

PAST PREDICTIONS OF THE FUTURE

School psychology has a long history of self-examination and looking toward a more positive future. Beginning with the Thayer Conference in 1954 and continuing through the most recent Futures of School Psychology Conference in 2012, leaders have come together periodically in efforts not just to predict but also to influence future directions in the field. Throughout the years, some issues have been discussed recurrently (e.g., credentialing and scope of practice), while others have become more prominent over time (e.g., multicultural competency, technology, and advocacy).

Returning briefly to Chapter 2, recall the Thayer Conference of 1954, in which some of the first organized discussions about the roles and preparation of school psychologists took place (Fagan, 2005). One of the outcomes of this conference was a broad vision of school psychologists as professionals who serve all children in educational settings. Two levels of training were recommended (i.e., the doctoral and "sub-doctoral" levels), with those practicing at the "sub-doctoral" level envisioned as having a separate title, narrower role, and supervision by doctoral-level school psychologists. Although the two levels of training persisted in the field's subsequent development, visions regarding title and practice did not come to pass. Indeed, later predictions that the field would naturally evolve into a profession centered on doctoral-level preparation and practice were similarly incorrect (e.g., Brown & Minke, 1986).

Several decades later, the Spring Hill (1981) and Olympia (1982) conferences were held jointly by the National Association of School Psychologists (NASP) and the American Psychological Association's (APA's) Division 16 (School Psychology) to provide follow-up to the Thayer Conference and to set directions and strategies for the field. At the time of these conferences, the field was still adjusting to the passage of Pub. L. No. 94-142 (the Education for All Handicapped Children Act of 1975; described in Chapters 2 and 5) and considering the impact of large-scale federal intervention in special education. The keynote address, delivered by William Bevan (1981), identified issues that are not terribly different from those we continue to face, such as austerity in government funding, the role of the federal government in education, and the potentially negative effects of far-reaching regulations. The need to define the core identity of school psychology was mentioned repeatedly (Lambert, 1981; Trachtman, 1981). Moreover, there was recognition that remediating the difficulties of one child at a time was not a viable approach to effectively reaching all children (Grimes, 1981; Shaffer, 1982). Nevertheless, practice continued to follow an individualized, deficit model of intervention, which emphasized identifying and remediating problems within children rather than building on strengths (Graden, 2004) and preventing children's learning and behavioral health issues through a more systems-oriented approach (Conoley et al., 2020).

Although change has been slow, there are signs that, as a field, we are beginning to embrace the skills and practices needed to function more proactively in the service of children, families, and schools. The 2002 Future of School Psychology Conference highlighted the need to move toward a population-based strategy of service delivery that emphasizes a continuum of services from the universal, preventive level through the intensive, highly individualized level, as embodied by multitiered systems of support (MTSS; Dawson et al., 2004). In addition, this conference urged the field to assume a problem-solving approach to school psychological services. As described in Chapter 8, this model emphasizes evidence-based practice and the gathering of data to guide the identification of appropriate interventions and evaluate their effectiveness. Finally, the 2002 conference recognized the need to integrate technology in practice and graduate preparation in ways that enhance service delivery.

The 2012 Futures Conference was very different from its predecessors because it was conducted virtually (in an effort to actualize the technology goals outlined in 2002). Notably, participants in that conference focused less on defining the profession and more on advancing it through skill development, leadership, and advocacy. As of the writing of this chapter, plans are being finalized for the 2023–2024 Futures Conference, which will shift the focus again with an emphasis, this time, on equity, diversity, and inclusion across all school psychological practices. This conference will be a year-long event with multiple virtual activities available at an international level.

PREDICTIONS FOR SCHOOL PSYCHOLOGY'S FUTURE

The real difficulty in changing the course of any enterprise lies not in developing new ideas but in escaping old ones.

—John Maynard Keynes

Forecasting the future of the field is a difficult and elusive task. Nevertheless, knowledge of past predictions, the field's evolution to date, and emerging trends in the field allow for tentative predictions of future directions.

Priorities of School Psychology's Professional Organizations Will Evolve

Several initiatives from APA and NASP likely will affect the field in the immediate future and beyond. In 2013, APA began exploring a move away from a focus on the traditional specialty areas (e.g., clinical, counseling, and school) and toward a more unified **health service psychologist** (HSP) designation through the publication *Professional Psychology in Health Care Services: A Blueprint for Education and Training* (Health Service Psychology Education Collaborative, 2013). In 2018, APA began work on the development of a plan for the accreditation of master's-level programs in health service psychology including clinical, counseling, and school (APA, 2021). The impact of this master's-level accreditation will not be known until it has been fully approved and implemented.

Considering these changes from APA, it is important to remember that although schools are increasingly likely to serve as venues for mental health service delivery, it is less clear that the larger community of psychologists understands how the school context differs from other community and clinical settings. Specifically, school psychological services (a) are situated within a different regulatory structure (e.g., credentialing usually through state departments of education rather than boards of psychology; federal and state laws and regulations that apply specifically to schools); (b) are provided to all students, not as "fee for service"; and (c) must address the educational impact of students' concerns, not just the mental health impact (Hughes & Minke, 2014). As such, school psychology practice emphasizes prevention, early intervention, and cross-system collaboration to a larger degree than other specialties do. As the HSP designation becomes more accepted across states, school psychologists will need to be sure that the distinctive aspects of school-based practice are addressed in graduate preparation programs and in state regulations. Because there is far greater need for mental health supports than is currently provided (e.g., Murphey et al., 2013; NASP, 2021a), the development of the HSP designation represents a great opportunity for collaboration among providers of psychological services to better serve all children, provided that school psychologists are integrally involved in shaping the implementation of school-based services.

NASP's focus as an organization is best represented through its strategic plan. Goals identified in the 2017–2022 NASP (2017a) strategic plan included: (a) workforce shortages (i.e., addressing the shortage of school psychologists); (b) the NASP Practice Model (i.e., advancing and implementing the *Model for Comprehensive and Integrated School Psychological Services* [NASP, 2010]); (c) leadership development (i.e., developing school psychologists' leadership skills to facilitate local, state, and national change); (d) mental/behavioral health providers (i.e., improving school psychologists' capacity to provide culturally competent and comprehensive mental and behavioral health services); and (e) social justice (i.e., ensuring that all youth are valued and that their rights are protected). Importantly, the fifth goal was added to address social justice more explicitly than in the past. As part of this effort, NASP adopted a definition of *social justice* that has been and will be the center of its efforts in this area going forward (NASP, 2017b). In addition, NASP established a Social Justice Committee to assist school psychologists in becoming more skilled in implementing nondiscriminatory practices in their work and advocating for equity at the district, state, and national levels.

The 2017–2022 NASP strategic goals were ambitious, and their significance has become increasingly apparent in light of recent educational challenges related to the coronavirus 2019 (COVID-19) pandemic, racial and other societal injustices, and increased gun violence, all of which have led to greater mental and behavioral health needs in children. In 2022, a new NASP strategic plan was developed for the years 2022–2027. This new plan includes three of the five previous strategic goals, namely: Goal A: Practice Model; Goal B: Workforce Shortages Solutions; and Goal C: Social Justice (NASP, 2022). Notably, new goal definitions were developed for each. The other two previous strategic goals (i.e., those related to leadership and mental and behavioral health providers, respectively) took on an operational rather than a strategic focus, and aspects of both were incorporated in the three 2022–2027 strategic goals. Achieving these goals will require an ongoing commitment from all NASP members—indeed, all school psychologists—to engage in lifelong professional development and targeted action to improve practice and outcomes for all children and youth.

School Psychology Will Continue to Experience Shortages (Though the Situation Will Improve)

School psychology has never experienced a period in which the supply of practitioners has met the demand (Fagan, 2004), and signs point to the continuation of that trend into the foreseeable future (Castillo et al., 2014; NASP, 2021f). Despite the longstanding impact of shortages on the history of the profession, it was not until 2015 that NASP first identified the remediation of shortages in school psychology as one of its strategic goals. This declaration by NASP leadership provided both a means for enacting coordinated efforts to reduce shortages and a mandate to better understand the mechanisms that have sustained these shortages over time.

Traditionally, the term *school psychology shortages* refers to an imbalance in supply and demand or, more specifically, to a lack of sufficient numbers of practitioners to fill available vacancies. However, shortages constitute a much more complex and nuanced issue than previously thought (see Bocanegra, Grapin, et al., 2017). In fact, the field has experienced shortages of school psychology practitioners, job openings, graduate preparation programs, graduate educators, internships, internship supervisors, cultural and linguistic diversity, program applicants, and respecialization opportunities. To further complicate this issue, the nature and extent of such shortages depends on geographic location as well as current social and economic influences.

Practitioner Shortages

Practitioner shortages tend to be the most conspicuous and significant type of shortages, as they pose the most immediate obstacles to service delivery and the main mission of school psychologists' work. The primary method of measuring shortages has been to examine ratios of students per school psychologist. National estimates of student-to-school psychologist ratios, obtained through NASP member surveys, generally have remained steady over the past 15 years, being 1,482:1 in 2004–2005 (Charvat, 2011); 1,383 in 2009–2010 (Charvat, 2011); 1,381 in 2014–2015 (Walcott et al., 2018); and 1,233 in 2019–2020 (Goforth et al., 2021). By comparison, the recommended student-to-practitioner ratio changed in 2010 from 1,000:1 to 500–700:1 (NASP, 2010) and then again in 2020 to 500:1 (NASP, 2020e). While the observed student-to-practitioner ratio has improved marginally over the past decade, its distance from NASP's recommended ratio has worsened.

Another source of school psychologist-to-student ratio data was made available for the first time in 2021. These data were provided by the U.S. Department of Education's National Center for Education Statistics (NCES) in what is known as the Common Core of Data. In the past, the NCES has provided data for teachers and other school personnel but not school psychologists. After much advocacy by NASP, school psychologists were included in this data set for the first time during the 2019–2020 school year. Calculations for the ratio data were based on information provided by state departments of education regarding the number of students served and the number of school psychologists employed in each state (NASP, 2021e). The initial data were recognized as provisional, with some state ratio data missing and other state ratio data not matching state reports. However, overall these data appeared consistent with other estimates in that they indicated significantly higher school psychologist-to-student ratios than the recommended 1:500.

Another way to measure practitioner shortages is to examine vacancies and job placement rates. Unfortunately, despite some available data from the U.S. Bureau of Labor Statistics (n.d.) on job openings and labor turnover, data specific to school psychology positions have not been collected systematically throughout the United States. However, the American Association for Employment in Education (AAEE) releases an annual estimate for the supply and demand of numerous education professions, including school psychology. These estimates are based on a survey conducted by the AAEE across both universities and school systems in which numbers of applicants and positions are compared. A numerical estimate of demand is created and placed into one of five categories: (a) *considerable shortage*, (b) *some shortage*, (c) *balanced*, (d) *some surplus*, and (e) *considerable surplus*. NASP (2021g) provided a summary of the data collected for the 2020–2021 academic year. This summary indicated that, since 2015, the school psychology staffing level has been rated annually at the *some shortage* level, and in 2021, all U.S. regions were at the *some shortage* level with the exception of two rated at the *considerable shortage* level. Looking regionally over time, it is clear that staffing levels in all regions generally vary from year to year, vacillating between the *some shortage* and *considerable shortage* levels.

NASP has undertaken several efforts to remediate school psychology shortages. For example, it developed and disseminated the *Shortages in School Psychology Resource Guide* (NASP, 2016b), which provides a range of recommendations for recruiting and retaining school psychologists. Another resource was developed to assist school psychologists in advocating for the need for more school psychologists (see NASP, 2021c). This resource highlights how school psychologists are critical to improving student positive mental health and learning outcomes, how shortages impede that work, and how these shortages can be addressed.

Social influences certainly play a role in the potential outlook for practitioner shortages, such as an increased recognition of integral links between mental health and academic success; federal, state, and local funding priorities; and the oscillation of educational control between federal and local governments. Additionally, it is unclear whether gradual increases in the number of school psychologist practitioners will be able to keep pace with growing enrollments in the U.S. public school system and the increased need for mental and behavioral health services, particularly in the aftermath of the COVID-19 pandemic. In any event, practitioner shortages are likely to continue, though based on graduate student enrollment trends (as described in the next section), it is unlikely that they will worsen significantly.

Graduate Student Enrollment Shortages

Though it has experienced only modest growth, enrollment in school psychology programs has increased over the past 20 years. In 1997, there were a reported 8,587 total students enrolled (including students working in internships); in 2013, that figure rose to 9,663 students (Rossen & von der Embse, 2014). In 2016, an estimated 9,797 total students were enrolled in school psychology programs (Gadke et al., 2017). In the same year, the number of new graduates entering the workforce was 2,581 (Gadke et al., 2017), as compared with an estimated 1,900 graduates in 2000 (Curtis et al., 2004). In 2020, the estimated number of students enrolled in school psychology programs rose to 11,728, and approximately 3,394 new graduates entered the workforce (Gadke et al., 2022).

Further, despite many reports of the "graying of the field" (i.e., projections that large cohorts of practitioners will retire, leaving significant numbers of job vacancies), data collected in 2016 suggested that school psychologists, at that time, had an average of 17.3 years until retirement. It was also noted that there had been a *decrease* in the average age of school psychologists (42.4 years) for the first time since 1990 (Walcott et al., 2016). However, the average age of school psychologists increased again in 2020 to 44 years (Goforth et al., 2021). Overall, more data are needed to determine whether increases in graduate student enrollment will be sufficient for serving the growing K–12 student population as well as filling anticipated job vacancies related to the retirement of school psychologists.

Graduate Program and Faculty Shortages

During the 2019–2020 academic year, there were 267 known institutions in the United States offering a graduate education program in school psychology (Gadke et al., 2022). By comparison, approximately 240 institutions offered school psychology programs in 2014 (Rossen & von der Embse, 2014). In 2014, the number of institutions offering training programs represented an 8% increase over the previous 35 years. Generally, while there has been some additional growth in program availability, it has been minimal, and many programs are currently reporting threats to their continued existence. Many factors may be contributing to this limited program growth, including the high costs of program development and maintenance and the considerable challenges associated with achieving program accreditation. Unfortunately, the lack of growth in programs has capped the number of new practitioners who are entering the field each year.

One potential barrier to increasing graduate student enrollment may concern the accessibility of programs to working professionals. Nearly 43% of school psychology graduate students report having been in the workforce during the year prior to entering a school psychology program (Bocanegra, Rossen, et al., 2017). The challenges associated with relocating and forfeiting a salary to attend school for several years have prompted programs to consider alternative methods for instruction. For example, programs catering to working professionals (i.e., programs that offer primarily weekend and evening courses) as well as distance education programs may emerge as one potential solution to this problem. In 2017, nearly one third of school psychology programs reported the use of some form of distance education technology (Hendricker et al., 2017), and in 2020 it was reported that the majority of programs reported using some form of distance education (Fischer et al., 2020). The use of distance education has likely increased further since the start of the COVID-19 pandemic, which forced many programs to expand their use of virtual services. There will likely be an ongoing increase in the implementation of distance education technology and/or the development of substantially or completely online programs. The success of these online programs likely will be contingent on their ability to meet accreditation standards regarding adequate knowledge and skill development (NASP, 2021b).

Another potential challenge may concern the accessibility of school psychology graduate training to professionals from other related fields. To address this issue, changes were made to the NASP (2020e) Professional Standards to provide specific definitions and guidance for addressing "respecialization and professional retraining" (p. 35). As described in Chapter 6, *respecialization and professional retraining* refers to a process by which candidates receive an individualized program of study leading to credentialing as a school psychologist without receiving a degree in school psychology. While NASP continues to support the specialist-level degree as the entry-level standard for the preparation of school psychologists, it was decided that further guidance was needed for those states creating alternative credentialing pathways. Subsequently, NASP developed a resource to assist programs interested in pursuing this possibility (NASP, 2020d).

In a related trend, shortages in the number of available school psychology graduate educators may continue to limit the availability of graduate programs. Graduate educators typically hold doctoral degrees; thus, monitoring enrollment trends in school psychology doctoral programs is key for determining the number of potential faculty members entering the field. In 2014, it was reported that enrollment in doctoral programs had increased over time (Rossen & von der Embse, 2014). However, a drop in enrollment was reported from 2016–2017 ($n = 3,091$) to 2017–2018 ($n = 2,791$), although it increased again during the 2018–2019 ($n = 2,852$) and 2019–2020 ($n = 2,925$) academic years, respectively (Gadke et al., 2021, 2022). Data for the 2019–2020 academic year noted that, on average, doctoral-level programs graduated 0.2 students who went on to obtain employment as university faculty (Gadke et al., 2022). (Other graduates from these doctoral programs generally sought employment in K–12 schools and other settings.) Given the small number of potential candidates for graduate educator positions, developing and sustaining new programs is likely to be difficult, particularly in rural areas that may have trouble recruiting new faculty.

The Specialist-Level Degree Will Remain the Entry-Level Degree for School Psychology

The specialist-level degree, currently defined by NASP as requiring a minimum of 60 graduate semester hours (including internship), has been and remains the entry-level degree for the profession. The availability of doctoral-level programs has grown more rapidly in recent years than that of specialist-level programs (Gadke et al., 2021; Rossen & von der Embse, 2014), with approximately one third of all programs offering degrees at the doctoral level. However, as noted in Chapter 6, no state agency currently requires a doctoral degree to work as a school psychologist, and no evidence supports the notion that doctoral-level practitioners provide higher quality services than specialist-level practitioners. Requiring a doctoral degree for school-based practice would essentially decrease an already insufficient workforce by 75% (Walcott et al., 2016), making such a change highly unlikely in the foreseeable future.

School Psychology Will Continue to Diversify (Though at a Slower Pace Than the United States Population)

As part of its periodic Membership Survey, NASP collects data on the racial and ethnic backgrounds of its members. Data from these surveys reflect a slow yet steady increase in the diversity of the profession from 1990 through 2020 (Curtis et al., 2012; Goforth et al., 2021; Walcott et al., 2016). Specifically, 94% of respondents identified as white in 1990, 87% in 2015, and 86% in 2020 (Goforth et al., 2021). The remaining respondents in the 2020 survey identified as Black and/or African American (4%), Asian (1%), American Indian/Alaska Native (3%), or more than one race (3%), and 3% of respondents did not provide information about their race or ethnicity. In addition, about 1% of respondents reported being of Arab, Middle Eastern, or North African (AMENA) origin, and 7.6% reported being of Hispanic or Latinx origin. Table 18.1 displays a history of racial and ethnic representation in school psychology.

Despite relatively slow growth in the representation of minoritized groups, data suggest that the future school psychology workforce may be more diverse than the current one. Approximately 25% of all school psychology graduate students during the 2015–2016 school year identified as members of racial and/or ethnic minoritized groups (Gadke et al., 2017). Moreover, during the 2019–2020 academic year, racially and ethnically minoritized students comprised approximately 33% of the total graduate student enrollment (Gadke et al., 2022). These data appear to suggest an increasing trend toward a more diverse student population, especially in comparison to practitioners represented in NASP member surveys.

TABLE 18.1 Racial/Ethnic Representation of School Psychologists Over Time

Ethnicity	Years of Data Collection						
	1980–1981	1989–1990	1999–2000	2004–2005	2009–2010	2014–2015	2019–2020
Black/African American	1.5	1.9	1.9	1.9	3.0	5.0	4.0
Caucasian	96.0	93.9	92.8	92.6	90.7	87.0	86.0
American Indian/Alaska Native	<1.0	1.1	0.6	0.8	0.6		1.0
Asian/Pacific Islander	<1.0	0.8	0.6	0.9	1.3	2.8	3.0
Hispanic	1.5	1.5	3.1	3.0	3.4	6.0	7.6
Other	<1.0	0.9	0.9	0.8	1.0		3.0

Sources: Curtis, M. J., Castillo, J. M., & Gelley, C. (2012, May). School psychology 2010: Demographics, employment, and the context for professional practices: Part 1, Table 1. Communiqué, 40, 1, 28–30. https://www.nasponline.org/publications/periodicals/communique/issues/volume-40-issue-1; Walcott, C. M., Charvat, J., McNamara, K. M., & Hyson, D. (2016). School psychology at a glance 2015: Member survey results. Paper presented at the Annual Convention of the National Association of School Psychologists, New Orleans, Louisiana. https://www.nasponline.org/Documents/Research%20and%20Policy/Research%20Center/Membership%20 Survey%202015%20Handout.pdf; Goforth, A. N., Farmer, R. L., Kim, S. Y., Naser, S. C., Lockwood, A. B., & Affrunti, N. W. (2021). Status of school psychology in 2020: Part 1, Demographics of the NASP Membership Survey. NASP Research Reports, 5(2). https://www.nasponline.org/Documents/Research%20and%20Policy/Research%20Center/NRR_2020-Membership-Survey-P1.pdf. Copyright 2012 by the National Association of School Psychologists, Bethesda, Maryland. Reprinted with permission of the publisher. www.nasponline.org.

As described in Chapter 3, the diversification of the school psychology workforce has been far outpaced by that of the student and family populations served in U.S. public schools. To illustrate this discrepancy, the white population as a percentage of the total U.S. population declined from 80% to 66% from 1980 to 2008 (Aud et al., 2010). Some estimates suggest that whites will account for less than half of the population by 2044, and more than half of all children will identify as members of minoritized groups by as early as 2020 (Colby & Ortman, 2015). The 2020 census further highlighted the increased racial and ethnic diversity of the country as defined by the representation and relative size of different racial and ethnic groups within a population (U.S. Census Bureau, 2021). There was a particularly large increase in the multiracial (two or more races) population, with a 276% increase in comparison to 2010; at the same time, the white population declined by 8.6%. These trends are expected to continue into the future.

Similarly, in 2015 only 14% of school psychologists reported fluency in a language other than English (Walcott et al., 2016), and in 2020 that number dropped to 8% (Goforth et al., 2021). In 2015, only approximately 8% of those who identified as multilingual also reported providing multilingual school psychological services, with that number decreasing to 7% in 2020. Current trends suggest that there has not been any improvement in the linguistic diversity of school psychologists and that the chasm between the diversity of school psychologists and that of the populations they serve will continue to widen.

It is also worth noting that school psychology has increasingly become a female-majority profession. In 1990, 65% of NASP members identified as female. This percentage increased with each successive survey through the year 2020, in which 87% of NASP members identified as female (Goforth et al., 2021). Similarly, approximately 87% of school psychology graduate students in 2019–2020 identified as female (Gadke et al., 2022). Notably, this trend is not unique to school psychology; related professions in psychology (75% female), social work (81.5% female), and elementary and middle school teachers (79.7% female) demonstrate a similar gender imbalance (U.S. Bureau of Labor Statistics, 2023). Unfortunately, gender pay gaps persist. In 2020, women had median weekly earnings that were 82% of those of male workers (U.S. Bureau of Labor Statistics, 2021). More equity in pay will likely lead to an overall increase in the average salary, thereby improving recruitment and retention of high-quality professionals in the field.

SOCIAL JUSTICE CONNECTIONS

Why is it essential to increase the representation of individuals from racial, ethnic, and linguistic (REL) minoritized backgrounds in the field?

The field of school psychology has experienced longstanding shortages of school psychologists from REL minoritized backgrounds. In a 2016 position statement, the National Association of School Psychologists (NASP; 2016a) recognized the need to increase cultural and linguistic diversity in the school psychology workforce. Ultimately, advocacy for initiatives that promote the diversification of school psychology is necessary at the local, state, and national levels. The following discussion provides several of the many possible and important answers to the question posed in this box.

1. As described in Chapter 3, the U.S. public school student body is rapidly diversifying. For example, there are approximately 350 languages spoken in the United States (U.S. Census Bureau, 2015). In the New York City (NYC) public schools alone, students

(continued)

SOCIAL JUSTICE CONNECTIONS (*continued*)

speak approximately 151 languages other than English (NYC Department of Education, Division of Multilingual Learners, 2021). However, among surveyed NASP members, only 24 different languages were reported (Goforth et al., 2021). Increasing diversity among school psychologists will be necessary to provide culturally responsive services (e.g., bilingual assessment services) to an increasingly diverse student clientele.

2. Individuals from REL minoritized backgrounds make critical contributions to identifying, investigating, and meeting the needs of students from these groups. For example, educators from REL minoritized backgrounds bring unique insights to discussions of racism and ethnocentrism, among other issues that may impact the lives of minoritized students (Quiocho & Rios, 2000; Villegas et al., 2012). Moreover, research suggests that matching service providers and clients based on language, race, and ethnicity confers a number of benefits for clients when psychological services are adapted to account for clients' culture and context (Bernal et al., 2009; Griner & Smith, 2006). (This does not mean that practitioners from REL privileged backgrounds cannot be effective service providers to minoritized youth. All school psychologists must strive for cultural competence to meet the needs of youth in schools.)

3. REL minoritized scholars have been essential to advancing a multicultural agenda in psychology. For example, Hartmann et al. (2013) estimated that nearly half of authors who contributed the most journal articles in ethnic minoritized psychology between 2003 and 2009 were ethnic minoritized scholars themselves. Given that racial and ethnic minoritized psychologists account for only approximately one fifth of the psychology workforce (APA, 2015), it is clear that scholars from these backgrounds have borne a disproportionate amount of responsibility for advancing this research. Notably, writing about issues relevant to REL minoritized populations should not be the sole responsibility of minoritized scholars, although these scholars have certainly been critical champions of psychology's multicultural agenda. Continuing to make sure their voices are heard will be essential for promoting equity in psychological service delivery.

4. School psychologists from REL minoritized backgrounds are important role models for all students and, in particular, for minoritized youth. For example, Covarrubias and Fryberg (2015) found that exposure to self-relevant models increased self-reported school belonging among Native American middle school students.

5. Increasing cultural and linguistic diversity in the workplace confers a number of positive benefits for school faculty and staff. For example, research indicates that intergroup contact (i.e., contact between individuals from different racial and ethnic backgrounds) may significantly reduce prejudice among individuals across diverse backgrounds (Pettigrew & Tropp, 2006). Specifically, Pettigrew and Tropp (2006) found that intergroup contact that met Allport's (1954) four optimal conditions was generally most impactful in facilitating prejudice reduction: (a) common goals; (b) equal status; (c) intergroup cooperation; and (d) support from authorities and societal customs. This research suggests that when essential conditions are met, increasing diversity among faculty and staff in school settings may contribute to the establishment of more positive, equitable, and productive work environments.

Professional Standards Will Continue to Evolve (Though at a Significantly Slower Rate Than the Profession)

As described in Chapter 6, professional standards define contemporary practices, promote effective and professional service delivery, and provide a foundation for the future of a field. In addition to NASP, which provides the most relevant standards for school psychology in the United States, APA and the International School Psychology Association (ISPA) also provide standards to help guide the profession.

Professional standards typically go through a significant review, revision, feedback, and approval process on an infrequent basis (e.g., every 10 years). Such infrequency allows for completion of the time-consuming development and implementation process, which can often take several years. However, this infrequency also makes standards less nimble and responsive to the frequent and ongoing changes in society, culture, and the field. As a result, standards typically are written in a way that allows for the profession to evolve without excessive restrictions or specificity. As an example, virtual service delivery methods (e.g., telepsychology and virtual assessments) have emerged in recent years, yet these services were addressed only minimally in the 2020 NASP Standards (NASP, 2020e). In developing these standards, it was recognized that addressing these issues more specifically would have run the risk of the standards becoming quickly obsolete given how swiftly the field changes. In addition to standards, the field typically relies on other tools, such as ongoing research, guidance documents, and shifting best practices, to support school psychologists with more specific, emerging trends.

Standards around practice have changed over time, though slightly. NASP's (1984) *Standards for the Provision of School Psychological Services* described the need for comprehensive services, including assessment, research, program planning and evaluation, and direct and indirect services to individuals, groups, and organizations. The most recent iteration of the practice standards from NASP (2020e), known as the *Model for Comprehensive and Integrated School Psychological Services* (i.e., the NASP Practice Model), includes many of the same concepts outlined in 1984, though they have been restructured to highlight different elements and expanded from earlier versions incrementally over time.

Despite the general stability of standards, some changes were seen in the development of the NASP 2020 standards. For example, standards related to program accreditation more directly addressed **distance education**. In the *Standards for the Graduate Preparation of School Psychologists* (NASP, 2020e), the use of distance education is not prohibited; however, there are no unique criteria established for distance education. Instead, as with all other programs, distance education programs have to demonstrate that candidates achieve adequate competencies in each domain of practice through the assessment of knowledge and skills. These standards also provide a description of how to use videoconferencing for face-to-face supervision requirements. In the NASP (2020e) Practice Model, the domain of *Diversity in Development and Learning* was changed to *Equitable Practices for Diverse Student Populations*, indicating a heightened awareness of the importance of equity, diversity, and inclusion in all school psychology practices. In NASP's (2020e) *Principles for Professional Ethics*, more guidance was provided regarding social media and other electronic communication. Future changes in these standards will most likely continue to occur on a slow, incremental basis.

The Role of the School Psychologist Will Evolve

Dating back to the early 1980s, school psychologists have struggled to identify a role that balances a focus on the traditional, individualized approach to special education service delivery with the broader range of preventive and early intervention services within a public health model of service delivery (as described in models such as MTSS). Although each successive revision of the NASP standards has further emphasized the delivery of a comprehensive range of prevention and intervention services, special education compliance tends to dominate the school psychologist's role. In 2004–2005, school psychologists reported that they spent more than 80% of their work time engaged in special education activities (Curtis et al., 2008). A decade later (2014–2015), individual evaluations for special education eligibility and participation in Individualized Education Program (IEP) development represented the two most frequent activities of school psychologists (Walcott et al., 2016). The average number of reported special education evaluations dropped slightly during that same time period, from 69 (34.7 initial evaluations, 34.3 reevaluations; Curtis et al., 2008) to 60 (28 initial evaluations, 32 reevaluations; Walcott et al., 2016).

Little has changed in the primary role of school psychologists since 2014. In the 2020 NASP member survey, 88% of school psychologists reported spending a great deal of their time completing special education evaluations, and 78% reported being involved in related special education work such as IEP meetings (Farmer et al., 2021). In addition, school psychologists reported an average of 50 evaluations (initial and reevaluations) completed annually and an increase in the number of school psychologists completing more than 50 reevaluations annually. It is clear that a focus on special education service delivery remains an integral, if not primary, component of the school psychologist's role. However, this same member survey also noted that many but not all school psychologists reported being involved in mental and behavioral health services (MBHS). Specifically, 88% reported that they were at least moderately capable of providing MBHS services, with 24% reporting that they sometimes provided MBHS services and 28% reporting that they often provide these services. In addition, most respondents who reported providing MBHS services indicated that they provided individual or group counseling services. A much smaller percentage of school psychologists reported providing individual or group services for academic or other type of concerns. The final conclusion from this survey was that practitioners in schools with the highest ratio of school psychologists to students were generally engaged in more assessment activities and fewer MBHS or other nonassessment services (Farmer et al., 2021).

Several factors may help support a more noticeable trend toward comprehensive service delivery models. One particularly notable factor is the continued evolution of the NASP (2020e) Practice Model. Although NASP has long advocated for comprehensive services, the adoption of the 2010 *Standards* represented the first time that a model of service delivery was specified. Updated and continued in the 2020 *Standards*, this model is designed, in part, to improve the consistent implementation of school psychological services. Additionally, the Practice Model "delineates what services might reasonably be expected to be available from most school psychologists and, thus, further defines the field" (NASP, 2020e, p. 1). Certainly, gaps continue to exist between the Practice Model and actual service delivery in schools. However, the Practice Model provides important benchmarks and avenues for advocacy to improve services and may serve as a critical tool in moving the needle.

In order to support school psychologists in implementing the Practice Model, NASP established the Excellence in School Psychological Services (ESPS) recognition program in 2019 (Cowan, 2021). The goal of this program is to provide recognition to school districts throughout the country where work is being done to implement the NASP Practice Model. This recognition focuses on districts' implementation of the Practice Model's six Organizational Principles, which are critical to enabling school psychologists to practice their comprehensive roles. Districts submit applications that are reviewed for recognition at one of five levels: *No Recognition*, *Emerging*, *Promising*, *Proficient*, and *Exemplary*. Incentives and benefits are provided to districts based on the level of recognition earned.

Every Student Succeeds Act

The Every Student Succeeds Act (ESSA), which took effect during the 2017–2018 school year, is a federal law that has provided some unique opportunities for school psychologists. Some of the major changes most relevant to the field of school psychology include a focus on improved assessment and accountability systems, improved mechanisms for identifying and providing support to struggling schools, and an emphasis on improving students' access to comprehensive learning supports and safe and supportive school climates. Within each of these major areas, the law authorizes the utilization of practices that promote a more comprehensive role for school psychologists. Despite the promise of ESSA for expanding student supports, the law also returns a great deal of control to state and local jurisdictions, which may lead to inconsistency in how school psychologists are utilized across states. Maintaining a consistent set of practices across the United States is important for establishing a professional identity in schools and within the broader fields of psychology and education. Ultimately, assuming that opportunities for role expansion are available in local jurisdictions, school psychologists will need to embrace a more comprehensive repertoire of service delivery activities that expands beyond their traditional focus on assessment. To assist in meeting this goal, NASP created (and updated in November 2021) a guidance document for school psychologists titled *Leveraging Essential School Practices, ESSA, MTSS, and the NASP Practice Model: A Crosswalk to Help Every School and Student Succeed* (NASP, 2021d). This document provides clear links between the ESSA policy provisions and MTSS practices as well as examples of school psychological services relevant to those provisions and practices.

Contract Services

In a similar vein, the use of contract services to meet special education compliance will likely continue. **Contract services** are those provided by a third-party agency that is external to and hired by a school district. Typically, such services are limited to discrete, reimbursable, short-term tasks such as special education evaluations or counseling. These services typically do not include more expansive, long-term activities such as systems-level prevention and intervention, program evaluation, ongoing consultation, or crisis planning and response. Some school systems may rely on contract services to compensate for shortages in available school psychologists or to avoid hiring full-time employees. Regardless of schools' reasons for utilizing contract services, the most likely outcome of their continued use is a reduction in the quantity and quality of comprehensive services provided to students and families. Nevertheless, until school psychology shortages are ameliorated, the use of contract services is likely to continue, and perhaps even increase, in the near future. To assist school psychologists and school districts in making decisions about contract services, NASP developed a resource titled *Considerations for Contract Services in School Psychology* (NASP, 2020a). This resource includes information regarding what contract services look like, what must be considered for state credentialing, various logistical considerations, the use of telehealth services, and ethical considerations.

Technology-Oriented Service Delivery

The COVID-19 pandemic has ultimately led to a need to better understand how technology can and should be used to support academic instruction as well as the work of school psychologists. Prior to the pandemic, state-led virtual school settings had been growing exponentially in the United States (see Tysinger et al., 2013), with all 50 states and the District of Columbia providing some form of virtual learning opportunities to their students (Watson et al., 2011). The challenge of providing school psychological services to students within virtual schools was already being recognized. Most school psychologists have had little experience or training in applying skills within a virtual setting. More specifically, they often know little about the tools available to support this type of work or how to navigate credentialing issues when providing services across state lines (Tysinger et al., 2013). In the past, these roles were often filled by contracting school psychologists or those specially assigned to independent online programs (Kennedy et al., 2012).

The pandemic led most schools either to go fully virtual for academic instruction or to develop some type of hybrid instructional approach, and school psychologists had to quickly adjust and develop skills for providing virtual school psychology services. Prior to this, there had already been some efforts to develop *telepsychology* practices, which have been defined by APA (2013) as the delivery of psychological services via telecommunication technologies, which include, but are not limited to, telephone, mobile devices, videoconferencing, texting, and other internet-based modalities. Research had already indicated that telephone- and video-based therapy services were effective in reducing symptoms of anxiety, depression, insomnia, and substance abuse (Lichstein et al., 2013; Rose et al., 2012; Silberbogen et al., 2012). These services were also identified as a potentially good option for individuals who faced barriers to accessing services due to their location (e.g., rural settings; Bischoff et al., 2004). This initial research led APA (2013) to develop its *Guidelines for the Practice of Telepsychology*. These guidelines addressed issues related to competence, consent, confidentiality, secure data and record keeping, assessment, and practice across jurisdictions. NASP followed suit in 2017 with the development of its *Considerations for Delivery of School Psychological Telehealth Services* (NASP, 2017c). However, most school psychologists had paid little attention to the initial research on telepsychology and pertinent guidelines because they had not anticipated needing to engage in virtual service delivery. Once it became clear that the COVID-19 pandemic would persist and thus shape new norms for virtual service delivery, many new resources for virtual school psychology practices were developed by both NASP and APA. This included an update to the 2017 NASP *Considerations for Delivery of School Psychological Telehealth Services* (NASP, 2020b) and a resource document titled *Virtual Service Delivery in Response to COVID-19 Disruptions* (NASP, 2020c). Moreover, both NASP and APA developed COVID-19 resource webpages. In addition, APA's Division 16 developed a document titled *APA's Guide to Schooling and Distance Learning During COVID-19* (APA, 2020). The long-term impact of these resources and broader shifts in service delivery is still to be discovered.

Social Justice: Equity, Diversity, and Inclusion

There has been increased recognition that engaging in social justice activities is an important component of school psychology work (Pham et al., 2021). The NASP (2020e) Professional Standards encourage proactive advocacy for social justice, and the APA (2017) *Multicultural Guidelines* underscore the need to understand and accommodate individual contexts, ecological systems, and intersectionality. In 2019, the NASP position statement on *Prejudice, Discrimination, and Racism* was adopted, stating that:

> Positive educational and social outcomes for all children and youth are possible, only in a society—and schools within it—that guarantees equitable treatment for all people, regardless of race, class, culture, language, gender, gender identity, religion, sexual orientation, nationality, citizenship, ability, and other dimensions of different. NASP firmly believes that all students are entitled to an education that affirms and validates the diversity of their cultural and individual differences, fosters resilience, and facilitates well-being and positive academic and mental health outcomes. (NASP, 2019, p. 1)

The need for school psychologists to be proactively involved in advancing social justice was further highlighted in the 2020 *School Psychology Unified Anti-Racism Statement and Call to Action* (García-Vázquez et al., 2020). Moreover, the 2020 NASP Membership Survey was the first to ask school psychologists about their knowledge of and engagement in social justice activities. Specifically, two questions were posed; the first asked members to indicate whether they had adequate knowledge about social justice issues in school psychology. Only 11% of survey participants reported that they were "knowledgeable" or "very knowledgeable" of social justice as part of school psychology practice. Those trained more recently reported being more knowledgeable. The second question probed the frequency with which members engaged in social justice activities in their respective work settings. Approximately one third of respondents reported that they "often" or "very often" engaged in social justice activities, with another third reporting "sometimes" and the last third indicating "never" or "rarely." Moreover, survey findings revealed that engagement with social justice was positively correlated with knowledge in this area. Presently, there appears to be significant momentum for advancing social justice-oriented practice and training, including opportunities for cultural self-reflection; justice-focused research; new approaches for addressing social justice concerns; improved graduate education in diversity, equity, and inclusion; and additional resources for practitioners. In sum, many school psychologists need more training, self-work, and guidance before they can fully engage in this important work.

MAKE THE FUTURE: DON'T WAIT FOR IT!

Clearly, school psychology faces many potential challenges and opportunities as it seeks to move forward as a field. School psychologists often fail to recognize them, however, and sometimes feel constrained by current practices. Indeed, change may seem daunting, yet it is possible and often necessary. For example, consider that the 30-semester-hour master's degree was once regarded as the entry-level degree in school psychology. Over the course of merely a decade (beginning in the 1980s), regulations were changed in nearly all states to require the specialist level of training (i.e., approximately 60 semester-hour credits) to enter the field. Clearly, change can happen, and when it does, the ripple effects of those changes can be abrupt and far-reaching.

The change process should be given careful attention. Although change is inevitable, positive changes can lose momentum when we take them for granted or fail to nurture them. School psychologists must seek continuous improvement in their practices, tools, and professional standards to maintain their stake in educational decision-making and service delivery. Moreover, they must take measures to embrace positive change while also maintaining practices that have proved effective and relevant over time. Ultimately, the future of our profession will be shaped by the actions (and inactions) of individuals both within and outside of school psychology. Although many of the predicted influences discussed in the preceding text may seem beyond the influence of individuals, the actions of individual school psychologists will significantly influence outcomes for school-age youth and the profession itself. The following recommendations are made to support school psychologists in shaping the future of the field.

1. **Start the year with specific goals for change.**
   At the beginning of each school year, develop at least one professional development goal and one systems-level goal. For example, you might decide to improve your knowledge of single-case designs for documenting student progress, increase your group counseling knowledge and skills, or update your knowledge of the

science of reading disorders. Accomplishing these kinds of goals will invigorate your practice and keep your skills fresh. At the systems level, you might choose to increase the visibility of school psychology services on your school's website, develop a presentation to the Parent–Teacher Association or school board about a contemporary mental health issue (e.g., suicide prevention), or volunteer to coordinate a community group's school-based activities. You might also want to increase your knowledge of implementation science to assist in meeting your systems-level goals. Such activities increase the positive visibility of the profession within the district and the community, especially when local decision makers are aware of them. They also may increase your professional competence and career satisfaction.

2. **Stop doing things that don't make sense.**
Solution-oriented counseling approaches adhere to a basic guideline: *If it is working, do it more. If it is not working, do something else* (e.g., Murphy, 2015). At times, school psychologists may find themselves caught in patterns of behavior that are not the most effective or efficient; however, institutional pressures and momentum may deter them from changing. For example, under Delaware regulations for special education, triennial reevaluation procedures do not require school psychologists to perform additional testing unless the IEP team determines that insufficient information is available to make relevant educational decisions. Likewise, in other states, regulations regarding the use of MTSS practices for learning disability identification no longer require the use of cognitive assessments. Nevertheless, many school psychologists continue to administer them, even though such assessments may add little value to the final eligibility decision. Overall, in many cases, reevaluations that involve extensive cognitive and achievement testing are not necessary, yet they often are undertaken (almost as a professional reflex).

Alternatively, reevaluations could serve as important opportunities to move away from extensive testing and toward more responsive, problem-solving procedures. Making changes like this requires school psychologists to be highly aware of their practice habits and the driving forces underlying those habits. School psychologists can scrutinize many practices and habits in their daily work. For instance, they might ask themselves:

> How "user-friendly" are my psychological reports? Do parents really understand "informed consent" documents? Are my team meetings genuinely directed toward problem-solving, or are they simply a vehicle for compliance with regulations? How is my school actively engaging families, especially those who experience the greatest barriers to participating?

Individual school psychologists can and should examine their work with an eye toward improvement and innovation. Such self-examination is an ethical responsibility and may lead to annual goals for change, as already discussed. Taking these steps may not be easy. By its very nature, advocacy requires individuals to voice their concerns when staying silent may be easier or more comfortable. Advocating for change may be less daunting, however, when undertaken with colleagues, including school psychologists, related professionals (e.g., school counselors, school social workers), and other vested partners (e.g., parents).

3. **Build alliances with colleagues.**
Many practitioners find that they are the only school psychologists in their building, or even in their district. This does not mean that they are without allies. Once you have a goal in mind, find out who in the school might share that goal. For example, teachers of students with disabilities, speech pathologists, and school social

workers are natural allies in prevention and early intervention. Enlisting support from building and district administrators (e.g., principals) is important as well, given that these individuals have the greatest control over funding streams and resource allocation. Build a problem-solving team and then evaluate its success (e.g., through fewer referrals for evaluation, improved attendance, or reduced retentions). Using your knowledge of program evaluation and single-case design, you can both implement evidence-based practices and build practice-based evidence for their success. Align your goals with the interests and goals of those around you, and find common ground. These are the kinds of activities that will demonstrate your worth to administrators and allow you to shape your role in ways that are consistent with the NASP Practice Model.

Becoming active in local, state, and national associations is also essential. There is an oft-repeated saying of unknown source: *If you are not at the table, you are on the menu*. Professional organizations provide a pathway to the proverbial *table* by alerting members to legislative and regulatory initiatives and providing them with opportunities to influence these initiatives before they become law. Similarly, local associations may alert members to important school board meetings and other activities. Staying connected to colleagues through professional associations can build leadership skills, professional knowledge, and support networks. Perhaps most importantly, involvement in professional organizations provides opportunities to directly influence the future of school psychology and the futures of students and families.

4. **Incorporate social justice into your work.**
An important goal for all school psychologists is to be committed to fairness and justice for all and to respect the dignity of all individuals and communities with whom they engage. This should include working to reduce and prevent prejudice and discrimination. Such work will require persistent efforts over the course of your career. As a first step, you might consider engaging in professional learning that will enable you to: (a) increase your understanding of and respect for diversity; (b) engage in critical reflection regarding your own biases; (c) encourage your colleagues in the same critical reflection; (d) provide supervision or consultation when encountering forces of oppression and privilege; and (e) identify resources regarding evidence-based practice and cultural responsiveness. In addition, taking steps to meaningfully and intentionally change your professional practices is critical; such steps may include: (a) calling attention to the impact of systemic factors such as racism, prejudice, and discrimination on students, families, schools, and communities; (b) intervening when you are a bystander to discrimination and harassment; (c) partnering with others to better understand population needs and lived experiences; (d) grounding your practices in an evidence-based framework; (e) establishing positive, productive, and collaborative alliances and relationships; (f) working with others to interrogate current practices, policies, and procedures; and (g) promoting systems change and equitable alternatives. Finally, engagement in the three aforementioned recommendations described herein can also assist in meeting these goals.

SUMMARY AND CONCLUSIONS

School psychology has a rich history of professional self-examination and planning for the future. The field has made great strides in identifying a professional identity, developing and implementing standards which support that identity, and establishing the importance of school psychological services in producing positive outcomes for students. Many changes in school psychology's history can be traced to federal and state legislation (e.g., the Individuals With Disabilities Education Act, state credentialing requirements), changing social and cultural contexts (e.g., increased awareness of the impact of mental health on academic performance), and the evolution of professional standards and best practices. Notably, all of those factors remain interconnected and are likely to continually influence the future. Looking ahead, challenges remain with respect to shortages, adequate diversity among practitioners, and emerging technologies. Individual school psychologists, when working collaboratively with allied professionals and guided by the field's professional organizations, can be effective change agents who facilitate positive outcomes for children, families, and schools.

DISCUSSION QUESTIONS

1. What are some potential barriers to promoting positive change in the field of school psychology? What steps might be necessary to address those barriers?
2. Which components of school psychology practice should *not* be subject to change in the future? In other words, what should stay the same?
3. Shortages have remained a central threat to the school psychology field for decades. What do you see as the most critical step toward alleviating these shortages in the next five years?
4. How has your use of technology changed in recent years? In what ways do you see technology affecting your future practice?
5. Identify one professional development goal and one systems-level goal for your future practice (or graduate preparation). What steps do you need to take to begin realizing these goals? How will you know you are making progress?

RECOMMENDED READINGS

Conoley, J. C., Powers, K., & Gutkin, T. B. (2020, November). How is school psychology doing: Why hasn't school psychology realized its promise? *School Psychology, 35*(6), 367–374. https://doi.org/10.1037/spq0000404

García-Vázquez, E., Reddy, L., Arora, P., Crepeau-Hobson F., Fenning, P., Hatt, C., Hughes, T., Jimerson, S., Malone, C., Minke, K., Radliff, K., Raines, T., Song, S., & Strobach, K .V. (2020). School psychology unified antiracism statement and call to action. *School Psychology Review, 49*(3), 209–211. https://doi.org/10.1080/2372966X.2020.1809941

National Association of School Psychologists. (2019). *Prejudice, discrimination, and racism* [Position statement]. https://www.nasponline.org/x26830.xml.

National Association of School Psychologists. (2020). *The professional standards of the National Association of School Psychologists.* https://www.nasponline.org/standards-and-certification/nasp-2020-professional-standards-adopted

National Association of School Psychologists. (2021, November). *Leveraging essential school practices, ESSA, MTSS, and the NASP Practice Model: A crosswalk to help every school and student succeed* [Policy brief]. https://www.nasponline.org/Documents/Research%20and%20Policy/ESSA/ESSA%20PM%20Crosswalk.Nov.2021.pdf

 A robust set of instructor resources designed to supplement this text is located at http://connect.springerpub.com/content/book/978-0-8261-6344-8. Qualifying instructors may request access by emailing textbook@springerpub.com.

REFERENCES

Allport, G. W. (1954). *The nature of prejudice*. Addison-Wesley.
American Psychological Association. (2013). Guidelines for the practice of telepsychology. *American Psychologist, 68,* 791–800. https://doi.org/10.1037/a0035001
American Psychological Association. (2015). *Demographics of the U.S. psychology workforce: Findings from the American Community Survey*. Author.
American Psychological Association. (2017). *Multicultural guidelines: An ecological approach to context, identity, and intersectionality.* http://www.apa.org/about/policy/multicultural-guidelines.pdf
American Psychological Association. (2020, September). *APA's guide to schooling and distance learning during COVID-19.* https://www.apa.org/ed/schools/teaching-learning/recommendations-starting-school-covid-19.pdf
American Psychological Association. (2021, October). *BEA/BPA Master's HSP competencies task force.* https://www.apa.org/ed/governance/bea/health-service-psychology-masters-competencies
Aud, S., Fox, M., & Kewal Ramani, A. (2010). *Status and trends in the education of racial and ethnic groups* (NCES 2010–2015). U.S. Department of Education. https://nces.ed.gov/pubs2010/2010015.pdf
Bernal, G., Jimenez-Chafey, M. I., & Domenech Rodriguez, M. M. (2009). Cultural adaptation of treatments: A resource for considering culture in evidence-based practice. *Professional Psychology: Research and Practice, 40,* 361–368. https://doi.org/10.1037/a0016401
Bevan, W. (1981). On coming of age among the professions. *School Psychology Review, 10,* 127–137.
Bischoff, R. J., Hollist, C. S., Smith, C. W., & Flack, P. (2004). Addressing the mental health needs of the underserved: Findings from a multiple case study of a behavioral telehealth project. *Contemporary Family Therapy, 26,* 179–198. https://doi.org/10.1023/B:COFT.0000031242.83259.fa
Bocanegra, J. O., Grapin, S. L., Nellis, L., M., & Rossen, E. (2017). A resource guide to remediating the school psychology shortages crisis. *Communiqué, 45,* 16–18. https://www.nasponline.org/publications/periodicals/communique/issues/volume-45
Bocanegra, J., Rossen, E., & Grapin, S. L. (2017). *Factors associated with graduate students' decisions to enter school psychology* [Research report]. National Association of School Psychologists. https://www.nasponline.org/Documents/Research%20and%20Policy/Research%20Center/NRR_Graduate_Students_Decisions_Bocanegra_et_al_2017.pdf
Brown, D. T., & Minke, K. M. (1986). School psychology graduate training: A comprehensive analysis. *American Psychologist, 41,* 1328–1338. https://doi.org/10.1037/0003-066X.41.12.1328
Castillo, J. M., Curtis, M. J., & Tan. S. Y. (2014). Personnel needs in school psychology: A 10-year follow-up study on predicted personnel shortages. *Psychology in the Schools, 51,* 832–849. https://doi.org/10.1002/pits.21786
Charvat, J. L. (2011). *Ratio of students per school psychologist by state: Data from the 2009–10 and 2004–05 NASP Membership Surveys*. National Association of School Psychologists. https://www.nasponline.org/Documents/Research%20and%20Policy/Research%20Center/Ratios_by_State_2005_and_2010.pdf
Colby, S. L., & Ortman, J. M. (2015). *Projections of the size and composition of the U.S. population: 2014 to 2060*. U.S. Department of Commerce, U.S. Census Bureau. https://www.census.gov/content/dam/Census/library/publications/2015/demo/p25-1143.pdf
Conoley, J. C., Powers, K., & Gutkin, T. B. (2020, November). How is school psychology doing: Why hasn't school psychology realized its promise? *School Psychology, 35, 6,* 367–374. https://doi.org/10.1037/spq0000404
Covarrubias, R., & Fryberg, S. A. (2015). The impact of self-relevant representations on school belonging for Native American students. *Cultural Diversity and Ethnic Minority Psychology, 21,* 10–18. https://doi.org/10.1037/a0037819
Cowan, K. C. (2021). 2021 ESPS recognition program designees. *Communiqué, 49,* 8, 20–21. https://www.nasponline.org/publications/periodicals/communique/issues/volume-49-issue-8
Curtis, M. J., Castillo, J. M., & Gelley, C. (2012, May). School psychology 2010: Demographics, employment, and the context for professional practices: Part 1. *Communiqué, 40,* 1, 28–30. https://www.nasponline.org/publications/periodicals/communique/issues/volume-40-issue-1

Curtis, M. J., Grier, J. E. C., & Hunley, S. A. (2004). The changing face of school psychology: Trends in data and projections for the future. *School Psychology Review, 33*, 49–66. https://doi.org/10.1080/02796015.2004.12086230

Curtis, M. J., Lopez, A. D., Castillo, J. M., Batsche, G. M., Minch, D., & Smith, J. C. (2008). The status of school psychology: Demographic characteristics, employment conditions, professional practices, and continuing professional development. *Communiqué, 36*, 27–29. https://www.nasponline.org/publications/periodicals/communique/issues/volume-36

Dawson, M., Cummings, J. A., Harrison, P. L., Short, R. J., Gorin, S., & Palomares, R. (2004). The 2002 multisite conference on the future of school psychology: Next steps. *School Psychology Review, 33*, 115–125. https://doi.org/10.1080/02796015.2004.12086235

Fagan, T. K. (2004). School psychology's significant discrepancy: Historical perspectives on personnel shortages. *Psychology in the Schools, 41*, 419–430. https://doi.org/10.1002/pits.10185

Fagan, T. K. (2005). The 50th anniversary of the Thayer Conference: Historical perspectives and accomplishments. *School Psychology Quarterly, 20*, 224–251. https://doi.org/10.1521/scpq.2005.20.3.224

Farmer, R. L., Goforth, A. N., Kim, S. Y., Naser, S. C., Lockwood, A. B., & Affrunti, N. W. (2021). Status of school psychology in 2020, Part 2: Professional practices in the NASP Membership Survey. *NASP Research Reports, 5*(3). https://www.nasponline.org/Documents/Research%20and%20Policy/Research%20Center/RR_NASP-2020-Membership-Survey-part-2.pdf

Fischer, A. J., Moy, G., Bloomfield, B. S., Whitcomb, S., & Florell, D. (2020). Faculty perceptions of distance education in school psychology training. *Trainer's Forum: Journal of the Trainers of School Psychologists, 37*(1), 34–43.

Gadke, D. L., Valley-Gray, S., & Rossen, E. (2017). NASP annual report of graduate education in school psychology: 2015–2016. *NASP Research Reports, 5*(2). https://www.nasponline.org/Documents/Research%20and%20Policy/Research%20Center/NRR_SP_Grad_Ed_2015-2016_Gadke_et_al_2017.pdf

Gadke, D. L., Valley-Gray, S., & Rossen, E. (2021). *NASP report of graduate education in school psychology: 2018–2019. NASP Research Reports, 5*(1). https://www.nasponline.org/Documents/Research%20and%20Policy/Research%20Center/NRR_SP_Grad_Ed_Report_2018-2019.pdf

Gadke, D. L., Valley-Gray, S., & Rossen, E. (2022). NASP report of graduate education in school psychology: 2019–2020. *NASP Research Reports, 6*(3). https://www.nasponline.org/Documents/Research%20and%20Policy/Research%20Center/RR_Grad-Ed-Report_2019-2020.pdf

García-Vázquez, E., Reddy, L., Arora, P., Crepeau-Hobson, F., Fenning, P., Hatt, C., Huges, T., Jimerson, S., Malone, C., Minke, K., Radliff, K., Raines, T., Song, S., & Strobach, K. V. (2020). School psychology unified antiracism statement and call to action. *School Psychology Review, 49*(3), 209–211. https://doi.org/10.1080/2372966X.2020.1809941

Goforth, N. A., Farmer, R. L., Kim, S. Y., Naser, S. C., Lockwood, A. B., & Affrunti, N. W. (2021). Status of school psychology in 2020: Part 1, Demographics of the NASP Membership Survey. *NASP Research Reports, 5*(2). https://www.nasponline.org/Documents/Research%20and%20Policy/Research%20Center/NRR_2020-Membership-Survey-P1.pdf

Graden, J. L. (2004). Synthesis and commentary: Arguments for change to consultation, prevention, and intervention: Will school psychology every achieve this promise? *Journal of Educational and Psychological Consultation, 154*, 345–359. https://doi.org/10.1080/10474412.2004.9669522

Grimes, J. (1981). Shaping the future of school psychology. *School Psychology Review, 10*(2), 206–231. https://doi.org/10.1080/02796015.1981.12084899

Griner, D., & Smith, T. (2006). Culturally adapted mental health interventions: A meta-analytic review. *Psychotherapy: Theory, Research, Practice, Training, 43*, 531–548. https://doi.org/10.1037/0033-3204.43.4.531

Hartmann, W. E., Kim, E. S., Kim, J. H. J., Nguyen, T. U., Wendt, D. C., Nagata, D. K., & Gone, J. P. (2013). In search of cultural diversity, revisited: Recent publication trends in cross-cultural and ethnic minority psychology. *Review of General Psychology, 17*(3), 243–254. https://doi.org/10.1037/a0032260

Health Service Psychology Education Collaborative. (2013). Professional psychology in health care services: A blueprint for education and training. *American Psychologist, 68*, 411–426. https://doi.org/10.1037/a0033265

Hendricker, E., Saeki, E., & Viola, S. (2017). Trends and perceptions of distance learning in school psychology. *Trainers' Forum: Journal of the Trainers of School Psychologists, 34*(2), 36–68.

Hughes, T. L., & Minke, K. M. (2014). Blueprint for health service psychology education and training: School psychology's response. *Training and Education in Professional Psychology, 8*, 26–30. https://doi.org/10.1037/tep0000019

Kennedy, K., Tysinger, D., LaFrance, J., & Bailey, C. (2012). Preparing education professionals for K–12 online learning. In M. Orey, S. A. Jones, & R. M. Branch (Eds.), *Educational media and technology yearbook*. Springer.

Lambert, N. (1981). School psychology training for the decades ahead, or rivers, streams, and creeks: Currents and tributaries to the sea. *School Psychology Review, 10*(2), 194–205. https://doi.org/10.1080/02796015.1981.12084898

Lichstein, K. L., Scogin, F., Thomas, S. J., DiNapoli, E. A., Dillon, H. R., & McFadden, A. (2013). Telehealth cognitive behavior therapy for co-occurring insomnia and depression symptoms in older adults. *Journal of Clinical Psychology, 69*, 1056–1065. https://doi.org/10.1002/jclp.22030

Murphey, D., Vaughn, B., & Barry, M. (2013). *Adolescent health highlight: Access to mental health care*. https://www.childtrends.org/wp-content/uploads/2013/04/Child_Trends-2013_01_01_AHH_MHAccessl.pdf

Murphy, J. J. (2015). *Solution-focused counseling in schools* (3rd ed.). American Counseling Association.

National Association of School Psychologists. (1984). *Standards for the provision of school psychological services*. Author.

National Association of School Psychologists. (2010). *Model for comprehensive and integrated school psychological services*. Author.

National Association of School Psychologists. (2016a). *Recruitment and retention of culturally and linguistically diverse school psychologists in graduate education programs* [Position statement]. https://www.nasponline.org/x36852.xml.

National Association of School Psychologists. (2016b). *Shortages in school psychology resource guide*. https://www.nasponline.org/resources-and-publications/resources/school-psychology/shortages-in-school-psychology-resource-guide

National Association of School Psychologists. (2017a). *Strategic plan: 2017-2022*. https://www.nasponline.org/assets/Documents/About%20School%20Psychology/NASP%202017-2022%20Strategic%20Plan_FINAL%20for%20Web.pdf

National Association of School Psychologists. (2017b, April). *Social justice*. http://www.nasponline.org/resources-and-publications/resources/diversity/social-justice

National Association of School Psychologists. (2017c, September). *Considerations for delivery of school psychological telehealth services* [Brief]. https://www.nasponline.org/x39099.xml

National Association of School Psychologists. (2019). *Prejudice, discrimination, and racism* [Position statement]. https://www.nasponline.org/x26830.xml

National Association of School Psychologists. (2020a). *Considerations for contract services in school psychology* [Brief]. https://www.nasponline.org/Documents/Resources%20and%20Publications/Considerations_Contract_Services.pdf

National Association of School Psychologists. (2020b). *Telehealth: Virtual service delivery updated recommendations*. COVID-19 Resources. https://www.nasponline.org/resources-and-publications/resources-and-podcasts/covid-19-resource-center/special-education-resources/telehealth-virtual-service-delivery-updated-recommendations

National Association of School Psychologists. (2020c). *Virtual service delivery in response to COVID-19 disruptions*. COVID-19 Resources. https://www.nasponline.org/resources-and-publications/resources-and-podcasts/school-safety-and-crisis/health-crisis-resources/virtual-service-delivery-in-response-to-covid-19-disruptions

National Association of School Psychologists. (2020d). *Guidance for respecialization and professional retraining*. https://www.nasponline.org/resources-and-publications/resources-and-podcasts/school-psychology/shortages-in-school-psychology-resource-guide/recruitment/recruiting-practitioners/respecialization-and-professional-retraining

National Association of School Psychologists. (2020e). *The professional standards of the National Association of School Psychologists: 2020*. https://www.nasponline.org/standards-and-certification/nasp-2020-professional-standards-adopted

National Association of School Psychologists. (2021a). *Comprehensive school-based mental and behavioural health services and school psychologists* [Handout]. https://www.nasponline.org/resources-and-publications/resources-and-podcasts/mental-and-behavioral-health/additional-resources/comprehensive-school-based-mental-and-behavioral-health-services-and-school-psychologists

National Association of School Psychologists. (2021b). *Considerations for distance education in school psychology* [Brief]. https://www.nasponline.org/Documents/Resources%20and%20Publications/Resources/NASP%20Considerations%20for%20Distance%20Education.pdf

National Association of School Psychologists. (2021c). *Improving school and student outcomes: The importance of addressing the shortages in school psychology* [Handout]. https://www.nasponline.org/x57447.xml

National Association of School Psychologists. (2021d). *Leveraging essential school practices, ESSA, MTSS, and the NASP practice model: A crosswalk to help every school and student succeed* [Policy brief]. https://www.nasponline.org/Documents/Research%20and%20Policy/ESSA/ESSA%20PM%20Crosswalk.Nov.2021.pdf

National Association of School Psychologists. (2021e). *School psychologist staffing supply and demand*. School Psychology. https://www.nasponline.org/resources-and-publications/resources-and-podcasts/school-psychology

National Association of School Psychologists. (2021f). *Shortages in school psychology: Challenges to meeting the growing needs of U.S. students and schools* [Research summary]. https://www.nasponline.org/x43315.xml

National Association of School Psychologists. (2021g). *Shortage of school psychologists: Student to school psychologist ratio 2019-2020*. https://www.nasponline.org/research-and-policy/policy-priorities/critical-policy-issues/shortage-of-school-psychologists

National Association of School Psychologists. (2022). *Strategic plan: 2022–2027*. https://www.nasponline.org/utility/about-nasp/vision-core-purpose-core-values-and-strategic-goals

New York City Department of Education, Division of Multilingual Learners. (2021, December). *2020–2021 ELL demographics: At-a-glance*. https://infohub.nyced.org/docs/default-source/default-document-library/sy-2020-21-ell-demographics-at-a-glance.pdf#:~:text=the%202020-2021%20school%20year%2C%20ELLs%20in%20NYC%20public,Uzbek%2C%20French%2C%20and%20Tadzhik.%20ELL%20Programs%20and%20Services

Pettigrew, T. F., & Tropp, L. R. (2006). A meta-analytic test of intergroup contact theory. *Journal of Personality and Social Psychology, 90*, 751–783. https://doi.org/10.1037/0022-3514.90.5.751

Pham, A. V., Goforth, A. N., Aguila, L. N., Burt, I., Bastian, R., & Diakow, D. M. (2021). Dismantling systemic inequities in school psychology: Cultural humility as a foundational approach to social to justice. *School Psychology Review, 15*(6), 692–709. https://doi.org/10.1080/2372966X.2021.1941245

Quiocho, A., & Rios, F. (2000). The power of their presence: Minority group teachers and schooling. *Review of Educational Research, 70*, 485–528. https://doi.org/10.2307/1170779

Rose, G. L., Skelly, J. M., Badger, G. J., Naylor, M. R., & Helzer, J. E. (2012). Interactive voice response for relapse prevention following cognitive-behavioral therapy for alcohol use disorders: A pilot study. *Psychological Services, 9*, 174–184. https://doi.org/10.1037/a0027606

Rossen, E., & von der Embse, N. (2014). Status of school psychology graduate education in the United States. In A. Thomas & P. Harrison (Eds.), *Best practices in school psychology: Foundations* (pp. 503–512). National Association of School Psychologists.

Shaffer, M. B. (1982). Improving the shape of school psychology: A practitioner's viewpoint. *School Psychology Review, 11*(2), 132–135. https://doi.org/10.1080/02796015.1982.12087326

Silberbogen, A. K., Ulloa, E., Mori, D. L., & Brown, K. (2012). A telehealth intervention for veterans on antiviral treatment for the hepatitis C virus. *Psychological Services, 9*, 163–173. https://doi.org/10.1037/a0026821

Trachtman, G. M. (1981). On such a full sea. *School Psychology Review, 10*(2), 138–181. https://doi.org/10.1080/02796015.1981.12084896

Tysinger, P. D., Tysinger, J. A., Diamanduros, T. D., & Kennedy, K. (2013). K–12 online learning and the training needs for school psychology practitioners. *School Psychology Forum: Research to Practice, 7*, 76–88. https://www.nasponline.org/publications/periodicals/spf/volume-7/volume-7-issue-3-(fall-2013)/k-12-online-learning-and-the-training-needs-for-school-psychology-practitioners

U.S. Bureau of Labor Statistics. (n.d.). *Job openings and labor turnover survey.* Retrieved May 25, 2023, from https://www.bls.gov/jlt

U.S. Bureau of Labor Statistics. (2021, September). *Highlights of women's earnings in 2020.* https://www.bls.gov/opub/reports/womens-earnings/2020/pdf/home.pdf

U.S. Bureau of Labor Statistics. (2023, January 25). *Labor force statistics from the current population survey.* https://www.bls.gov/cps/cpsaat11.htm

U.S. Census Bureau. (2015, November 3). *Census Bureau reports at least 350 languages spoken in U.S. homes* (Release Number: CB15-185). U.S. Department of Commerce. https://www.census.gov/newsroom/archives/2015-pr/cb15-185.html

U.S. Census Bureau. (2021, August). *Improved race and ethnicity measures reveal U.S. population is much more multi-racial.* U.S. Department of Commerce. https://www.census.gov/library/stories/2021/08/improved-race-ethnicity-measures-reveal-united-states-population-much-more-multiracial.html

Villegas, A. M., Strom, K., & Lucas, T. (2012). Closing the racial/ethnic gap between students of color and their teachers: An elusive goal. *Equity and Excellence in Education, 45,* 283–301. https://doi.org/10.1080/10665684.2012.656541

Walcott, C. M., Charvat, J., McNamara, K. M., & Hyson, D. (2016). *School psychology at a glance 2015: Member survey results.* Paper presented at the Annual Convention of the National Association of School Psychologists, New Orleans, LA. https://www.nasponline.org/Documents/Research%20and%20Policy/Research%20Center/Membership%20Survey%202015%20Handout.pdf

Walcott, C. M., Hyson D., McNamara, K., & Charvat, J. L. (2018). *Results from the NASP 2015 Membership Survey: Part one: Demographics and employment conditions.* [Research report]. National Association of School Psychologists Research Reports. https://www.nasponline.org/research-and-policy/research-center/nasp-research-reports

Watson, J., Murin, A., Vashaw, L., Gemin, B., & Rapp, C. (2011). *Keeping pace with K–12 online learning: An annual review of policy and practice.* Evergreen Consulting. https://files.eric.ed.gov/fulltext/ED535912.pdf

CHAPTER 19

Preparing for a Career in School Psychology

SARAH VALLEY-GRAY ■ DIANA JOYCE-BEAULIEU

CHAPTER OBJECTIVES

After reading this chapter, you will be able to:

- Delineate the range of career options in school psychology.
- Review considerations in selecting graduate training programs and degree tracks.
- Identify strategies for optimizing specialized coursework and supervised clinical experiences aligned with career goals.
- Discuss considerations for mentorship that enhances professional skills and scholarly productivity to facilitate acquisition of competitive internships and jobs.
- Provide guidance on acquiring preservice social justice advocacy knowledge and skills.

NATIONAL ASSOCIATION OF SCHOOL PSYCHOLOGISTS PRACTICE MODEL CONNECTIONS

Domain 9: Research and Evidence-Based Practice
Domain 10: Legal, Ethical, and Professional Practice

INTRODUCTION

As described throughout the preceding chapters, there are several diverse career options within the field of school psychology. Some of these career options involve working in pre-K–12 schools, whereas others involve working in hospitals, private practice, postsecondary institutions, and other settings. Awareness of employment options in school psychology early on allows preservice professionals to prepare themselves for the jobs of their choosing. This chapter reviews career opportunities in school psychology as well as considerations for choosing a graduate education program, coursework, field experiences, and other training experiences that are aligned with these paths. Additionally, it presents strategies for representing one's professional qualifications and experiences (i.e., through the development of a résumé or curriculum vitae [CV; plural: curricula vitae]).

CHOOSING A CAREER PATH IN SCHOOL PSYCHOLOGY: GENERAL CONSIDERATIONS

Recall from Chapter 1 that most school psychology practitioners are employed in public school settings. Results from the most recent Membership Survey of the National Association of School Psychologists (NASP) indicated that 82% of members are practitioners in schools (Goforth et al., 2021). Moreover, in a survey polling NASP members ($N = 993$), 96% identified as school-based practitioners working in traditional public schools, public charter schools, or private schools (including private charter; Goforth et al., 2021). In addition, school psychologists may work in colleges and universities to provide assessment and educational planning services to students with disabilities (Sulkowski & Joyce, 2012). They also may be employed in schools on armed forces' military bases, which serve children of personnel. In these roles, they may provide a wide range of services consistent with those provided in other pre-K–12 settings.

In addition, professionals with school psychology degrees may have opportunities to work in a variety of nonschool settings (NASP, n.d.). These opportunities typically are available to school psychologists with doctoral-level training and who are eligible for licensure as a psychologist (although, as noted in Chapter 6, nondoctoral practitioners in some states are permitted to provide a specified scope of services in private practice settings). The psychologist's license offers broader career opportunities within public health agencies, clinics, hospitals, community agencies, juvenile justice facilities, psychological test companies, research settings, and academia. Community agencies employing psychologists can include mental health centers, initiatives for at-risk youth, and some adjudicated youth programs. Positions within hospitals more often involve psychiatric diagnosis and crisis intervention, with an emphasis on short-term service provision, whereas outpatient clinics are treatment oriented and extend services over a longer period of time. Psychologists in private practice may offer a broader range of assessment and intervention services or specialized care for specific populations (e.g., children with autism spectrum disorders and children with chronic and severe medical conditions). Individuals with doctoral training also may hold faculty positions in college and university settings, which focus on teaching, supervision, and service as well as conducting research in school psychology and related disciplines. For additional information regarding licensure requirements as a psychologist, as well as licensure specifically as a school psychologist (where applicable) for each state and jurisdiction, please refer to the Association of State and Provincial Psychology Boards website (www.asppb.net/page/psybook).

Individuals who are interested in a career in school psychology should consider their personal interests, goals, values, and even personality characteristics. Some individuals may gravitate toward more direct service provision roles (i.e., applied practice), whereas others may prefer the more theoretical orientation of research discovery. Alternatively, some individuals may choose to blend research and practice roles, and many change areas of specialization and professional positions throughout their career. Given the compelling need for high-quality educational and psychological service providers and innovators, school psychologists take on a wide range of roles across many different types of settings.

FIELD-BASED PRACTITIONER CAREERS

General Considerations

As discussed previously, school psychologists who hold the specialist degree or its equivalent typically work in pre-K–12 school-based settings. Although there are many similarities among the roles and job characteristics of school psychologists employed nationwide, there is also considerable variability. For example, school psychologists employed in schools exclusively for students with emotional and behavioral disabilities may spend more time implementing school-wide behavioral intervention programs and delivering counseling services than conducting special education eligibility assessments. Conversely, some school psychologists spend a considerable amount of time engaged in special education eligibility activities (although this excessive focus on assessment at the cost of intervention delivery may suggest a need for systems-level reform; Walcott et al., 2016).

Moreover, some school psychologists may work for the duration of the academic year (e.g., 10 months), whereas others may work year-round (e.g., 12 months). In a survey of school-based practitioners, approximately 65% held a 10-month contract, 24% held an 11-month contract, and the remaining 12% held a 12-month contract (Goforth et al., 2021). Since public school systems generally follow a 10-month schedule, school psychologists with 11- or 12-month contracts are likely to have additional administrative roles (e.g., professional development preparation, special district initiatives/projects, and district policy advisement) or engage in scheduled assessment activities during the summer months. These may be important considerations for selecting job opportunities.

Like contract length, the type of contract that school psychologists hold may differ across districts. In some districts, school psychologists work under a teacher union contract; in others, they are employed under an administrative contract. Although seemingly a minor detail, the type of contract may affect the school psychologist's roles, responsibilities, and salary. Generally, school psychologists employed under union contracts have more formalized daily hour expectations. Conversely, school psychologists employed under a district's administrative contract may be expected to work more hours and to remain available for meetings during nontraditional hours (e.g., for on-call emergencies and evening school board meetings). Practitioners employed through administrative contracts also may be more likely to participate in district policy decision-making and, ultimately, are better positioned to advance to higher-level district administrative positions.

Considerations for Degree Types and Credentials

As described in Chapter 6, school psychologists can practice in pre-K–12 settings at the specialist (or its equivalent) or doctoral level; however, in most states, a doctoral degree is needed to practice outside of primary and secondary school settings (NASP, n.d.). In all states, school psychologists with specialist (or its equivalent) degrees are permitted to provide services in pre-K–12 schools, and in some states they are permitted to work in private practice, pending the completion of required postdegree work experiences (e.g., Florida). However, individuals who wish to work in hospitals, clinics, and other nonschool settings may need to obtain a doctoral degree and subsequently pursue licensure as a psychologist or work under the supervision of a licensed psychologist. In many cases, degree requirements are determined by the setting in which the practitioner provides services. While many programs offer a specialist degree (EdS. or PsyS.), due to different state and university policies, other degrees and certificates (e.g., MA, MS, Certificate of Advanced Study [CAS], Certificate of Advanced Graduate Study [CAGS], Master's Degree plus 30) may be conferred.

Considerations for Selecting Graduate Training and Specialized Coursework

When choosing a graduate program, awareness of the resources available through universities and graduate programs is critical. Applicants should consider the applied field experiences, the areas of expertise of the faculty, opportunities for engaging in research and service activities, the availability of faculty for mentorship, and any unique prospects for training offered by the program. Some programs may allow students to select a specialty from a list of approved areas and then select course offerings within those areas. Alternatively, some programs allow students to create their own specializations (which are subject to approval by academic advisors). In these cases, students may synthesize a program of study from course offerings across departments, schools, or colleges within their institutions. Other programs may have specialized practica options (e.g., autism spectrum disorder [ASD] clinic, university counseling center). Opportunities for specialization of coursework and practica are typically more abundant at the doctoral level as compared to the specialist level, given the extended program duration. As students plan their coursework and specialization areas, it is strongly advised that they keep their career goals in mind. For example, students who are interested in working with a specific population (e.g., early childhood or ethnically and racially diverse populations) should pursue a graduate program which has coursework relevant to serving these populations (e.g., preschool child development, multiculturalism, and social justice).

Likewise, if a student desires to work with clients in specific age groups or grade levels, having knowledge of developmental factors, contextual and environmental factors, and risk factors relevant to those groups is important. For example, practitioners who wish to work primarily with middle and high school students should be knowledgeable about important life events and developmental milestones relevant to adolescents. Such milestones may include the onset of puberty and the transition from elementary school (i.e., typically a highly structured environment) to middle and high school (typically less structured environments that afford students greater independence). During this transition, students face new social demands, academic expectations, and daily routines, among other changes. Additionally, half of all lifetime mental health syndromes emerge during childhood or adolescence, and three-fourths emerge prior to adulthood (American Psychiatric Association, 2013). Each syndrome has very specific developmental windows (e.g., preschool, early childhood, adolescence). Thus, it is important for practitioners working with adolescents to be highly familiar with the prevalent diagnoses and early symptom indicators for this age range.

In addition to familiarizing themselves with the unique developmental issues that adolescents face, practitioners must be knowledgeable about the legal, ethical, professional, administrative, and systems-level issues that impact middle and high school settings. These issues include matters related to accountability, state testing practices, academic standards and curricula, and postsecondary transition planning. For instance, educational law requires that school personnel develop postsecondary transition plans for adolescents with disabilities—something that is not required for younger children. Overall, aligning field-based training, extracurricular experiences, and coursework with career aspirations can better prepare individuals to be highly competitive for selective internships and job opportunities.

Considerations for Specialized Field Placements

In addition to coursework, field experiences are critical for preparing students for future employment. Recall from Chapter 6 that students generally complete two types of field experiences: *practica* (early to middle part of graduate preparation) and *internship* (end of graduate preparation). Graduate students typically complete practica within communities surrounding their graduate programs. Through these practica, school psychology graduate students have opportunities to serve children and adolescents across a range of ages and grade levels in the local schools and other settings (e.g., private practices, outpatient counseling centers, juvenile justice settings, alternative education programs, and community clinics).

Although field-based training sites ultimately are assigned by program faculty and/or practicum coordinators, students may benefit from researching the university's surrounding communities and populations as well as specific training sites to ensure that the program can provide an ideal match for their professional interests. For example, surrounding schools may serve a variety of populations (e.g., racially and ethnically diverse populations) and communities (e.g., urban, rural, and suburban communities) and, therefore, may offer different types of training opportunities (e.g., opportunities for bilingual assessment). When students complete their practica in settings with unique characteristics and training experiences, they have opportunities to develop more specialized competencies beyond the range of core competencies required of generalist practitioners.

In addition to considering differences between graduate education programs and communities, school psychology graduate students should consider unique opportunities offered within school districts. For example, some districts offer highly specialized educational programs for specific populations of students (e.g., early childhood populations and students with low-incidence disabilities). Additionally, resources within the district should be considered. For example, some districts have strong partnerships with community agencies and clinics—which also may open doors to valuable training opportunities.

Typically, graduate students have even more options for internship sites than for practicum sites, as they often leave the university's immediate surroundings to complete this experience. If communities surrounding the university are homogeneous or offer few opportunities to achieve the desired training, students can seek these types of experiences during their internship. Students may also consider seeking sites in the states in which they ultimately intend to become employed so that they can gain familiarity with state-specific practices and requirements. In addition, this provides an opportunity for students to develop relationships with supervisors and other practitioners in the district who can serve as mentors early in their careers. In sum, graduate students should strive to identify field experiences that facilitate their achievement of specific career goals.

Considerations for Identifying Mentors and Supervisors

Mentors can provide invaluable supports to school psychology graduate students. ***Mentorship*** can be formal or informal and can be provided by a variety of individuals. Some graduate training programs will assign students a peer mentor (typically an advanced graduate student) who offers guidance or advice on a variety of topics, such as program acclimation, socialization opportunities, potential training routes, and school–life balance. In addition to formally assigned peer mentors, students may seek informal peer mentors. When selecting peer mentors, students should identify individuals who share their interests or professional aspirations. Opportunities for peer mentorship in school psychology may also be found through NASP's online communities, which provide spaces for connecting with graduate students as well as school psychology professionals from across the country. While these relationships should not replace those with academic advisors and other faculty mentors, they can help support graduate students in many aspects of professional development (Joyce-Beaulieu & Rossen, 2016).

Mentoring relationships with faculty also are important for fostering successful training outcomes. Faculty members are well versed in program requirements and progress expectations, and they often have the resources to connect students to opportunities for professional development as well as other important career opportunities. Faculty members also can guide students in navigating the institution's deadlines, formal processes, and resources, such as on-campus career centers. These centers typically offer interview recording and coaching, résumé/curriculum vitae (CV) development and review, access to a wide range of employment listservs and resources, and guidance on professional interactions.

Sometimes faculty mentors are assigned by programs; however, students may be encouraged to change advisors as their professional interests evolve. Inquiring about faculty specializations and projects may help inform students' selection of potential mentors. Moreover, most program websites house considerable information about faculty members, such as CVs and brief biographies, which can help students to determine their potential "fit" with a particular mentor. Additionally, it is feasible to connect with faculty mentors both within and outside of the graduate program. Opportunities to network with other faculty and practitioners can be facilitated through professional association memberships, online special-interest groups, and professional conferences. For example, each year at the NASP Annual Convention, students and professionals can sign up for the Convention Mentor Program. In addition, there are a variety of opportunities for connecting with faculty, practitioners, and students through Division 16 of the American Psychological Association (APA). Individuals contacted through these venues can help students build specialized skills and knowledge, particularly if they have expertise in a desirable area. Furthermore, they may be able to provide letters of recommendation, access to early career opportunities, and information about training sites. Ultimately, synthesizing networks of diverse mentors may afford students access to valuable information and expertise.

Additionally, mentorship may be fostered through professional relationships with practica site supervisors, administrators, or other personnel. Throughout the completion of practica experiences, these individuals can offer both informal and formal mentorship and supervision. High-quality supervision is essential for professional development, and NASP (2018) encourages school psychologists at all levels, including trainee, early career, and expert levels, to seek supervision. More specifically, NASP (2018) outlines two types of supervision: *clinical* and *administrative*. **Clinical supervision** focuses on developing knowledge and skills in providing professional services (e.g., psychological and educational service delivery to children and families), while ***administrative supervision*** emphasizes developing skills in maintaining the organizational unit, such as personnel, legal, contractual, and other systems-level issues (NASP, 2018). It is recommended that students in school psychology graduate programs receive both types of supervision from more senior faculty and practitioners in their practicum settings (NASP, 2018).

In general, supervision should include ongoing, formative feedback supported by direct observation to ensure the development of supervisees' skills as well as the safety of the clients served (NASP, 2018). Supervisors should have competency in providing developmentally responsive supervision within the context of a strong relationship founded on trust (Guiney, 2019). Students who are seeking supervision for licensing purposes should secure a supervisor who has the appropriate credentials (e.g., doctoral degree and licensure) and who can provide the requisite number of hours for individual and/or group supervision, as delineated by state licensure and credentialing requirements. To ensure that both the supervisee and the supervisor have a clear understanding of expectations, a written supervision contract should clearly delineate the roles and responsibilities of both parties at the outset of the relationship (NASP, 2018). During graduate training, a formalized agreement typically occurs between the field-based training site and the university.

ACADEMIC CAREERS

General Considerations

Only a small percentage of school psychologists pursue employment in academia. In fact, during the 2019–2020 academic year, only 4% of doctoral school psychology program (SPP) graduates went on to obtain employment as faculty members (Gadke et al., 2022).

Although recent estimates are not available, an article published by Castillo et al. (2014) predicted that half of all faculty members would retire by 2025. This prediction has been supported by regular job announcements across the country advertising for faculty positions and suggests that there may be substantial opportunities for school psychologists seeking positions in academia.

The job responsibilities of most academics comprise three primary activities: teaching/supervision, research, and service (e.g., activities that support the academic program, the university functioning, and the profession). A variety of factors may influence the amount of time that faculty members devote to each of these activities. For example, faculty in tenure-track positions typically are expected to devote more time to research activities than non–tenure-track faculty. Conversely, many non–tenure-track faculty or tenure-track faculty in teaching institutions often are expected to devote greater amounts of time to teaching and program coordination activities.

The percentage of time that faculty members spend engaged in research, teaching/supervision, and service activities also varies by institution type. For example, faculty in doctoral-granting, research-intensive universities often spend large portions of time engaged in research activities. This is, in part, because doctoral students must engage in supervised research activity to meet their degree requirements. Conversely, faculty employed in institutions that emphasize teaching or offer only specialist-level degrees are likely to teach more courses, and teaching activities are weighted more heavily in the tenure and promotion process. Increasingly, higher education institutions are employing research faculty or clinical faculty (whose roles are primarily supervisory and/or teaching in nature) and program administrators to address the multitude of needs of the organization.

To fulfill their teaching obligations, faculty may teach using a variety of modalities, including traditional lecture, group discussion, and online or other remote formats. In fact, some SPPs offer significant portions of their curricula through distance education classes, which are often supplemented by in-person residential institutes allowing for faculty and students to meet face to face. Faculty who teach school psychology courses must possess effective communication skills, in-depth knowledge of the content they are teaching, and a firm command of pedagogical techniques. In SPPs, teaching activities also include supervisory responsibilities, wherein the faculty member oversees students' completion of practica or internship experiences. This involves collaborating with field placement supervisors to foster students' skill development in a variety of practice areas. Individuals who aspire to local or national recognition for their teaching may apply for training grants, develop innovative curricula, assume leadership roles in training policy or program accreditation, or produce scholarship (publications and conference presentations) related to best practices in graduate education.

Research also is a major activity for many faculty, particularly for those faculty whose job performance is evaluated based on scholarly productivity. The goal of many of these faculty members is to build a program of research that generates innovative knowledge, scholarship, and applications for practice. The type of research done by faculty members varies, with some pursuing more theoretical agendas while others pursue more applied agendas. (Applied agendas generally involve research that has more immediate and direct applications to school psychology practice.) Research-active faculty members are expected to mentor undergraduate and graduate students (frequently doctoral students), who serve as research assistants and facilitate the implementation of research activities. Individuals who wish to develop national recognition for their research may engage in designing and implementing multifaceted or cross-disciplinary research projects, acquiring grants to fund research teams, and publishing journal articles, conference proceedings, books, book chapters, and other scholarly materials.

The third component of academic appointments is service. Faculty members may engage in service both within their institutions as well as at the state, national, or international levels. Within the institution, faculty members may engage in service activities at the program level, department level, college/school level, and university level. Service within institutions typically involves serving as a member or leader on various committees at one or more organizational levels (e.g., college curriculum, faculty policy counsel, university senate and presidential committees). Program-level service may involve revising curricula, engaging in academic advising, and preparing for accreditation processes. Individuals who engage in service on a national level may serve in advocacy or policy development roles for national or international professional associations, such as NASP, APA, or the International School Psychology Association (ISPA). Examples of this type of service include significant contributions to the development of national standards, policy position papers, accreditation regulations, and state and national educational or mental health provision law. Other types of service include engaging in editorial work for school psychology journals, such as serving as an editor or reviewing articles. Overall, there is considerable variation in the roles and responsibilities of faculty members, all of which are important for sustaining the future of research and graduate preparation in school psychology.

Considerations for Degree Types and Credentials

Most university academic positions will require the highest terminal degree for the discipline. In school psychology, this is the doctoral degree, including designations such as PhD, EdD, or PsyD. Moreover, program faculty with clinical supervision roles typically are required to hold licensure for practice. If one's career goal is to obtain an academic position at a research-intensive institution, it is advantageous to pursue a doctoral degree from a university with a strong research emphasis and considerable grant activity.

Considerations for Specialized Coursework

As for all school psychologists, foundational coursework in the practice and profession of school psychology is critical for aspiring academics (and will be provided in any NASP-approved or APA-accredited program). Regarding specialized coursework, advance consideration of the type of academic position desired (e.g., predominantly teaching or research-intensive position) may be helpful to students in selecting their courses. Generally, for all types of positions, knowledge of adult teaching strategies, clinical supervision skills, statistical and research design methodologies, and writing skills is essential. Moreover, courses that prepare one for licensure (e.g., psychopharmacology, assessment, and counseling) and passing the national psychologist's exam (i.e., Examination for Professional Practice in Psychology [EPPP]) may be beneficial for students seeking academic roles that include direct clinical supervision. For individuals with a strong interest in pursuing research or student training grants, a course on grant writing or mentorship by a faculty member with this expertise is useful. Of course, students who plan to pursue research-intensive positions may wish to complete specialized coursework and practical experience in their anticipated areas of research. Additionally, students who wish to pursue academic positions specific to research and practice with specific populations (e.g., intellectual disabilities, early childhood), academic needs (e.g., learning disabilities), or mental health and behavioral needs (e.g., attention deficit hyperactivity disorder [ADHD]) should consider completing specialized coursework and continuing education in these areas. In addition, common areas for specialization include school neuropsychology and applied behavioral analysis, each of which require specialized training and supervision.

Considerations for Specialized Field Placements

Seeking appropriate practicum experiences also can strengthen an applicant's résumé (or CV) for competitive internships and career positions. Similar to specialized coursework, practica may allow students to explore service delivery in relation to specific populations, diagnoses, settings, or educational delivery models. Additionally, practicum sites may be an ideal source of research data (e.g., dissertation data), especially when the student's clinical and research interests are interrelated. A collaborative discussion with program faculty and field placement supervisors regarding individual training needs may help facilitate practicum placements that support the student's career goals. Field placement supervisors also can serve as highly qualified references for internship and job applications.

Considerations for Identifying Mentors and Supervisors

Graduate students who aspire to become faculty members should select their mentors carefully. In particular, they should consider the research, teaching, and clinical skills of potential mentors. For students who wish to pursue research-intensive positions, receiving close mentorship in research design, methods, data analysis, publication, and grant writing is especially important. For individuals interested in pursuing teaching-oriented faculty positions, opportunities for supervised teaching experience and mentorship by highly regarded instructors will be critical. Students who desire faculty positions with clinical supervision responsibilities should seek mentorship from field-based professionals who can foster the development of specialized practice competencies, provide guidance on the pursuit of essential credentials (e.g., licensure), and offer direct supervision in supervising others. For all students interested in faculty positions (regardless of position type), opportunities to copublish scholarship, copresent at conferences, and collaborate on service activities can be beneficial for preparing for future leadership in the field. Faculty mentors also can provide guidance on locating job listings, corresponding with search committees, and preparing for on- and off-campus interviews. Faculty members with strong professional networks may be able to assist students in connecting with other scholars and practitioners in the field who can advance their careers. Moreover, students who are highly involved in professional organizations and interest groups may be able to seek multiple mentors through these venues (e.g., Trainers of School Psychologists).

Research, Publishing, and Conference Presentations

Regardless of the specific type of academic position desired, research, publishing, and conference presentations are likely to play a major role in acquiring that first faculty position and building toward national recognition. Thus, building experience in conducting research, publishing, and presenting during graduate school is important. In strong mentorship relationships, the graduate student's advisor or supervisor is mindful of facilitating these experiences through a scaffolding process. Initially, the graduate student may assist with journal article or presentation development (e.g., through data collection and literature reviews), with the goal of eventually serving as first author on these types of scholarship. Thus, choosing mentors who are open to collaboration with students is essential.

Faculty members may produce a variety of scholarship, including journal articles, books and book chapters, conference presentations, technical reports, and treatment manuals, among other works. Generally, scholarship that undergoes peer review (as described in Chapter 16) is more highly regarded than work that is not peer reviewed. The number of research projects, publications, and presentations that students must complete during graduate school to be competitive for an academic position is not concretely defined and varies by discipline. Relatively little is known about the average number of publications produced by candidates seeking their first job as a school psychology faculty member; however, there are normative data on faculty productivity in the field. For example, Johnson and colleagues (2017) investigated publication rates of faculty from NASP-approved programs. During the 6-year period from 2010 to 2015, faculty published an average of 4.9 articles (i.e., approximately 0.82 articles per year).

Conference presentations also are an important form of scholarship in the field of school psychology. From the perspective of a faculty search committee, the perceived value of conference presentations likely will vary by the breadth of the target audience (e.g., national conferences versus state conferences), the presentation content (original research versus literature review), and the rigor of the conference's review process (e.g., double blind, single blind, or open review). Given the emphasis on research, publishing, and conference presentations as benchmarks for faculty achievement, acquiring experience in developing this type of scholarship during one's graduate education can provide the candidate with a significant advantage during job searches.

Involvement in research and other forms of scholarship requires a considerable amount of work, especially given that graduate students also are expected to balance the demands of practica and coursework at the same time. What can graduate students do to ensure that they are sufficiently prepared to enter the professoriate? In general, strong skills in research and publishing are essential. Thus, it is important to complete methodology coursework (e.g., courses on quantitative and qualitative methods) and to select a highly productive mentor who can provide essential scaffolding for building scholarly productivity.

ADDITIONAL CAREER OPTIONS

This chapter has noted that the most common career path for school psychologists leads toward the role of practitioner. Practitioners are mostly likely to work in schools, hospitals/clinics, community agencies/programs, or private practice. Additionally, a smaller proportion of school psychologists pursue faculty positions in graduate programs. However, there are other career opportunities within the profession, such as employment in military base schools (i.e., positions acquired through the U.S. Department of Defense), international schools (www.iss.edu; www.internationalschooljobs.com), and incarcerated youth programs through the state prison systems. Additionally, national psychology organizations, such as NASP and APA, offer advocacy and administrative positions within their institutions. Individuals who are interested in these types of employment should seek mentors with similar backgrounds and/or reach out to these organizations for more information about job roles and opportunities.

SOCIAL JUSTICE CONNECTIONS

How can preservice school psychologists prepare to become social justice agents?

Social justice advocacy requires strong foundational knowledge of school-based social issues as well as skills in coordinating systems change. Graduate preparation programs and professional organizations in school psychology offer many opportunities for developing knowledge and skills in social justice principles and advocacy. The following provides suggestions for graduate students who aspire to increase their knowledge and skills in this area.

(continued)

> **SOCIAL JUSTICE CONNECTIONS (*continued*)**
>
> 1. Seek faculty mentors who conduct research designed to identify and meet the needs of traditionally disenfranchised groups. When working with faculty mentors whose scholarship does not directly align with a social justice agenda, consider how social justice principles may be incorporated in this line of work as a direction for future research (e.g., possibly dissertation research).
> 2. Seek specialized coursework that advances knowledge and skills in social justice advocacy (e.g., courses on multiculturalism, law and ethics, and systems change).
> 3. Become involved with student groups that promote inclusion and multiculturalism on campus and within surrounding communities (e.g., multicultural groups; lesbian, gay, bisexual, transgender, and queer [LGBTQ] advocacy groups; community service organizations). If groups are not available, consider forming one on campus.
> 4. Seek training opportunities or volunteer to assist in supporting workgroups offered by local and state school psychology organizations. For example, some state school psychology associations offer opportunities for students to visit legislatures, assist with preparing advocacy statements, or organize outreach efforts across similar organizations (e.g., counseling associations).
> 5. Join special-interest groups in national associations that offer opportunities to network with advocacy leaders (e.g., NASP's Social Justice Interest Group, APA Special Interest Group Initiatives).
> 6. Seek applied training experiences (e.g., practica, internships, and postdoctoral training) that afford opportunities to work with traditionally marginalized youth and families. When pursuing this training, bear in mind that it is important to engage in ongoing reflection regarding personal beliefs, values, attitudes, and biases. Such reflection can be supported by and facilitated through the formal supervision process.

DEVELOPING A RÉSUMÉ OR CURRICULUM VITAE IN SCHOOL PSYCHOLOGY

Representing one's professional qualifications is an important part of securing training and employment opportunities. One way that professionals and students summarize their experiences and achievements is to develop a *résumé* or *curriculum vitae* (CV). One common question that many people ask is, *What is the difference between a résumé and CV, and which one should I have?*

Both résumés and CVs accomplish a similar goal: to outline and highlight an individual's education, experiences, and accolades. More specifically, both delineate education, professional qualifications, practica and internship experiences, research positions, publications, conference presentations, work experience, service, and extracurricular activities. Honors, achievements, and awards as well as special skills also may be highlighted (Williams-Nickelson et al., 2019). Additionally, both CVs and résumés begin with the individual's most recent information and move backward chronologically. One of the primary differences between a CV and a résumé, however, pertains to length. CVs typically are lengthier than résumés because they contain greater detail. Because CVs generally are discussed less frequently than résumés, they will be the focus of this section.

The first few lines of the CV should provide updated contact information. Next, educational information typically is displayed, including the names of the institutions attended, the dates attended, the degree(s) received, and major or concentrated areas of study. For degrees not yet awarded, it is acceptable to note an expected date of graduation. Grade-point average (GPA) also may be included with the education information (especially if it is high and augments the candidate's qualifications).

In sections describing research experiences, it is important to include project titles, supervising faculty, and a concise, detailed description of roles and responsibilities. Under practicum, employment, and internship experiences, a bulleted list of responsibilities will help the reader conceptualize the depth and breadth of skills acquired. These roles and responsibilities should be presented as action items. In this style, verbs such as "aided" or "provided" are used rather than "I statements" (e.g., "I was in charge of. . ."). Examples are provided in Table 19.1. It is important to avoid making vague statements and instead to use specific examples of job responsibilities.

One of the most important considerations in constructing a CV is to think about how it will be received by the target audience. Descriptions of experiences in CVs should use more sophisticated language rather than conversational phrases or terms. For example, using terms such as "assessment" instead of "testing" is likely to give the CV a more professional appearance. While representing oneself in a professional manner is important, it is also important to avoid exaggerating or inflating job responsibilities and experiences. For example, if an individual is only conversationally fluent in a language, the CV should not suggest that the individual is bilingual. Nevertheless, one should not minimize experiences. Overall, the individual should strive to develop relevant, compelling descriptions of work and educational experiences that also are accurate and informative.

One particularly effective strategy for constructing a CV is to emphasize only those experiences most relevant to the position desired. When developing a CV in response to a written internship or job announcement, mirroring the language in the announcement can be helpful. For example, if an internship site describes itself as having a behavioral orientation and a significant emphasis on applied research training, it may be beneficial for the applicant to list all coursework and research experiences with behavioral applications

TABLE 19.1 Sample Curriculum Vitae Entries Describing Professional Roles

Professional Experience	
May 2020–December 2021	**Graduate Research Assistant** **Success University** *Supervisor: Faculty L. Member, PhD, NCSP* • Conducted research and literature reviews • Assisted with development of study design and hypotheses • Presented research findings at national and state conferences
September 2018–April 2019	**School-Based Practica** **Achievement School District** *Supervisor: Samuel P. Sample, EdS* • Provided group counseling services to middle school students with disabilities • Conducted psychoeducational assessments to inform intervention development • Developed psychoeducational reports for planning of special education services

TABLE 19.2 Checklist for Curriculum Vitae Development

Curriculum Vitae Checklist (Bennett, 2014)
1. Demographic information: Name, two or more forms of contact information
2. Educational background: Degrees, institution, date obtained or anticipated, minors or areas of concentration, grade-point average (GPA), thesis or honors projects, and practica/internship experiences
3. Teaching or research assistantships: Dates, project or course titles, supervisors, role descriptions
4. Publications, professional presentations, grant writing: Related to career goals
5. Work experience: Relevant to graduate school or career goals
6. Extracurricular activities: Leadership roles, clubs/organizations related to professional goals, volunteer experiences related to goals
7. Honors, awards, scholarships: Relevant to career goals
8. Professional organization memberships and leadership activities: Relevant to career goals
9. Specialized skills: Computer/statistical software, language fluency, certifications
10. Writing style: Checked grammar, use of action verbs, sophistication of language

Source: Data from Bennett, S. (2014). *The elements of résumé style: Essential rules for writing résumés and cover letters that work* (2nd ed.). American Management Association.

in their CV. Including some volunteer or extracurricular activities may be helpful if the activities are related to the individual's professional goals. For example, serving as a youth camp counselor, participating in honor societies in psychology, and sponsoring community activities for children are all relevant to careers in serving youth. Additionally, it may be valuable to include experiences in philanthropic work, leadership positions, or educational service delivery (e.g., peer tutoring or mentoring), as they demonstrate skills in leadership and advocacy.

In summary, preparing a CV is an important way to share professional experiences and achievements with others. Seeking feedback from trusted peers and mentors can facilitate refinement and improvement of the CV. Individuals who are enrolled in postsecondary institutions may have access to career development centers and other institutional services that can assist with CV development. Program advisors, supervisors, and other mentors may also provide valuable guidance in this area. Table 19.2 provides a checklist for CV development.

SUMMARY AND CONCLUSIONS

The field of school psychology offers a wide range of rewarding career trajectories that serve the academic and mental health needs of children and youth. Most professionals practice within the pre-K–12 public school systems; however, professional opportunities also abound within public agencies, clinics, hospitals, juvenile justice, private practice, and academia. Early consideration of graduate training programs, degree tracks, and training components aligned with career goals can maximize an individual's preparedness for acquiring a competitive internship and job. Thus, graduate programs' coursework rigor (as mandated by accreditation and credentialing standards), opportunities for diverse practica/internship training, and faculty mentorship are pivotal considerations. This chapter has offered guidance on each of these key factors. To support future planning, a Graduate Program Worksheet is provided.

Graduate Program Worksheet

Career Goal:							
	Action Plan	Specialization Coursework	Specialized Practica	Teaching, Research Goals	Publications, Presentations	Mentorship Needs	Licensure or Credential
Specialist (or equivalent) and Doctoral Degree	Year 1						
	Year 2						
	Year 3						
Doctoral Degree Only	Year 4						
	Year 5						
	Year 6						

Although many of the essential elements of preparing for a career in school psychology will be supported by the existing training program infrastructure, graduate students may also utilize some strategies to enhance their education and networking options. These strategies include seeking specialized coursework and applied training experiences (e.g., applied behavioral analysis, school neuropsychology), participating in local and national interest groups, and becoming involved in state and national school psychology associations. Additionally, fostering strong mentoring relationships with faculty who are active in advocacy efforts, educational practice reform, and research addressing the needs of specific populations can provide valuable connections for pursuing those areas of interest. Ultimately, a career in school psychology offers significant opportunity for implementing principles of social justice and serving a wide range of youth and families.

DISCUSSION QUESTIONS

1. Compare and contrast the school psychology practitioner and academic faculty roles. List considerations for selecting a graduate education program.
2. What are some factors to consider in seeking a mentor or supervisor? Which factors are most important to you?
3. How might you go about researching the populations and communities surrounding your university? Which individuals or resources might you consult? How might you better understand the nature of practicum training in your institution?
4. Which types of employment settings and professional roles interest you most? What steps will you take to realize these goals?
5. How might you customize your professional preparation to emphasize a social justice perspective?

RECOMMENDED READINGS

Barraclough, C., & Machek, G. (2010). School psychologist's role concerning children with chronic illnesses in schools. *Journal of Applied School Psychology, 26*(2), 132–148. https://doi.org/10.1080/15377901003712694

Blake, J. J., Graves, S., Jimerson, S., & Newell, M. (2016). Diversification of school psychology: Developing an evidence base from current research and practice. *School Psychology Quarterly, 31*(3), 305–310. https://doi.org/10.1037/spq0000180

Farmer, R. L., Goforth, A. N., Kim, S. Y., Naser, S. C., Lockwood, A. B., & Affrunti, N. W. (2021). Status of school psychology in 2020, Part 2: Professional practices in the NASP Membership Survey. *NASP Research Reports, 5*(3), 1–17. https://www.nasponline.org/research-and-policy/research-center/nasp-research-reports

Gischlar, K. L. (2022). Why (not) school psychology?: A survey of undergraduate psychology majors' preferences. *Contemporary School Psychology, 26*, 4–13. https://doi.org/10.1007/s40688-020-00350-5

Eklund, K., Embse, N., & Oyen, K. (2020). The landscape of advocacy in public schools: The role of school psychologists. *Psychological Services, 17*(S1), 81–85. https://doi.org/10.1037/ser0000373

A robust set of instructor resources designed to supplement this text is located at http://connect.springerpub.com/content/book/978-0-8261-6344-8. Qualifying instructors may request access by emailing textbook@springerpub.com.

REFERENCES

American Psychiatric Association. (2013). *Diagnostic and statistical manual of mental disorders* (5th ed.). https://doi.org/10.1176/appi.books.9780890425596

Bennett, S. (2014). *The elements of résumé style: Essential rules for writing résumés and cover letters that work* (2nd ed.). American Management Association.

Castillo, J. M., Curtis, M. J., & Tan, S. Y. (2014). Personnel needs in school psychology: A 10-year follow-up study of predicted personnel shortages. *Psychology in the Schools, 51*, 832–849. https://doi.org/10.1002/pits.21786

Gadke, D. L., Valley-Gray, S., & Rossen, E. (2022). NASP report of graduate education in school psychology: 2019–2020. *NASP Research Reports, 6*(3), 1–10. https://www.nasponline.org/research-and-policy/research-center/nasp-research-reports

Goforth, A. N., Farmer, R. L., Kim, S. Y., Naser, S. C., Lockwood, A. B., & Affrunti, N. W. (2021). Status of school psychology in 2020: Part 1, Demographics of the NASP Membership Survey. *NASP Research Reports, 5*(2). https://www.nasponline.org/research-and-policy/research-center/nasp-research-reports

Guiney, M. C. (2019). *The school psychology supervisor's toolkit*. Routledge.

Johnson, N. D., Hulac, D., Schneider, M. M., & Ushijima, S. C. (2017). Scholarly productivity of school psychology faculty: 2010–2015. *Trainers' Forum, 34*(3), 15–33. https://www.sptpjournal.org/archival-issues

Joyce-Beaulieu, D., & Rossen, E. (2016). *The school psychology practicum and internship handbook*. Springer Publishing Company.

National Association of School Psychologists. (n.d.). *A career in school psychology: Frequently asked questions*. https://www.nasponline.org/about-school-psychology/becoming-a-school-psychologist/a-career-in-school-psychology-frequently-asked-questions#where

National Association of School Psychologists. (2018). *Supervision in school psychology* [Position statement]. https://www.nasponline.org/assets/Documents/Research%20and%20Policy/Position%20Statements/Supervision_in_School.pdf

Sulkowski, M., & Joyce, D. (2012). School psychology goes to college: The emerging role of school psychology in college communities. *Psychology in the Schools, 49,* 809–815. https://doi.org/10.1002/pits.21634

Walcott, C. M., Charvat, J., McNamara, K. M., & Hyson, D. M. (2016). *School psychology at a glance: 2015 member survey results* [PowerPoint slides]. https://www.nasponline.org/Documents/Research%20and%20Policy/Research%20Center/Membership%20Survey%202015%20Handout.pdf

Williams-Nickelson, C., Prinstein, M., & Keilin, G. (2019). *Internships in psychology: The APAGS workbook for writing successful applications and finding the right fit* (4th ed.). American Psychological Association.

Glossary

academic neocolonialism—the imposition of Western values and perspectives on the development and dissemination of knowledge in various areas of study, including the social sciences

accreditation—a voluntary system by which institutions of higher education or programs in those institutions are peer-reviewed and subsequently recognized (if judged to be meeting particular standards)

accuracy intervention—intervention designed to increase students' correct use of a skill

administrative supervision—an evaluative relationship in which a more experienced professional (i.e., supervisor) works with a more novice one (i.e., supervisee) to develop the latter's knowledge and skill in managing service delivery, including personnel, legal, contractual, and other systems-level issues

advocacy—the practice of proactively representing and supporting a cause or group of individuals

advocacy consultation—a cooperative partnership in which a consultant partners with individuals or groups from historically or systemically disenfranchised backgrounds in order to deconstruct barriers to client success and/or promote social and organizational change

American Psychological Association—professional organization that represents many different types of psychologists, such as social, clinical, health, counseling, cognitive, forensic, and school psychologists

antecedent—stimulus that precedes a target behavior

antecedent strategy—intervention approach that involves altering the environment in which a problem behavior typically occurs in order to prevent it from occurring

antiracism—active countering of racism as a system of privilege, inequality, and oppression based on perceived categorical differences

applied professional ethics—the application of broad ethical principles and specific rules of conduct to problems that arise in the professional practice of school psychology

assessment—a methodical process that involves the collection, evaluation, integration, and application of data to guide decision-making and to achieve professional objectives

autonomy—the ability to self-govern and assert responsible control over one's life, including the freedom of choice and action

behavior intervention plan (BIP)—an individualized plan for both preventing challenging behaviors and teaching students more appropriate responses

behavioral consultation—a cooperative partnership in which a consultant works with a consultee to facilitate change in observable client problems; now often referred to as problem-solving consultation

beneficence—the obligation to act for the benefit of those in one's care and to protect and defend the rights of others; to prevent harm and to act to remove conditions that will cause harm to others; responsible caring

brief experimental analysis—the systematic process of quickly assessing the relative effects of two or more interventions on a target behavior so as to determine which approach is likely to be most successful

Brown et al. v. Board of Education of Topeka—landmark court case in which the U.S. Supreme Court ruled that state laws establishing segregated schools for white and African American students were unconstitutional

case study—a research method involving the in-depth explorations of a particular case or exemplar of interest, which could include persons, processes, and other social phenomena

causal-comparative design—a research method used to examine the causal relationship between two or more distinct, nonrandomly selected groups when it is not feasible or ethical to manipulate the independent variable

child study bureau—units prevalent in the early 1900's that were associated with school districts and devoted to conducting research on students in order to establish typical development and identify atypically developing students

client—in consultation, the recipient of services delivered by a consultee

clinical supervision—an evaluative relationship in which a more experienced professional (i.e., supervisor) works with a more novice one (i.e., supervisee) to develop the latter's knowledge and skill in providing psychological and educational services

code of ethics—a body of principles and guidelines, typically developed and endorsed by a professional organization or other entities, for engaging in equitable and morally sound professional behaviors that ensure the well-being of affected parties

community—groups of individuals in a localized area

community agency—organization in the local area that is developed to address one or more needs

compulsory schooling—legal requirement that children of particular ages attend school for a designated period of time

computer adaptive interim test—computer-administered assessment designed to obtain a precise, real-time estimate of an individual's skills by presenting them with test items matched to their skill level (as determined by their responses to previous test items)

conjoint behavioral consultation—a strengths-based partnership in which caregivers, teachers, and other personnel engage in a collaborative problem-solving process over time and across settings to facilitate positive, observable change in a student's behaviors and outcomes

consequence—behavior or event that occurs subsequent to a target behavior

consequence strategy—intervention approach that addresses a problem behavior by targeting outcomes and responses to the problem behavior and replacement behavior(s)

construct—conceptual abstraction of a phenomenon that is not directly observable but is theorized to influence observable behaviors

consultant—an individual who provides professional guidance and expertise to another individual, group, or system (i.e., consultee)

consultation—a cooperative partnership in which a consultant and consultee engage in a reciprocal problem-solving process to support the well-being of a third party (i.e., client)

consultee—the person or entity that implements an action plan resulting from consultation in order to directly deliver the recommended services to a third party (i.e., client)

contract services—psychological and educational services provided by a third-party agency that is external to and hired by a school district

coronavirus 2019 (COVID-19) pandemic—global epidemic beginning in 2019 caused by the spread of the severe acute respiratory syndrome coronavirus 2 (SARS-CoV-2), leading to millions of infections, deaths, hospitalizations, and major disruptions in schooling and other daily life activities

correlational design—a research method used to describe the relationships between two or more variables without needing to directly manipulate the independent variable

credentialing—a process, typically at the state level, of establishing qualifications and authorizing individuals to practice professionally

criterion-referenced test—standardized assessment in which a student's performance is interpreted relative to a predetermined benchmark (e.g., grade-level standard)

critical consciousness—the ability and commitment to recognize, analyze, and act against systems of inequality

cultural adaptation—the process of modifying an intervention to ensure that it is congruent with the patterns, meanings, and values of a client's culture

cultural capital—an accumulation of cultural knowledge, skills, and abilities

cultural humility—orientation to continually reflecting on and acknowledging the limitations of one's cultural lens while also seeking to understand the cultural values of others on their terms

cultural responsiveness—the appreciation of assets and differences in regard to language, values, customs, and experiences and the implementation of practices that are sensitive to these differences

curriculum-based measurement—a standardized set of brief assessments that measure students' accuracy and speed (i.e., fluency) in performing various skills in reading, mathematics, writing, or spelling

curriculum vitae—a formal document that typically provides greater detail than a résumé and is primarily focused on describing an individual's academic credentials, including their education, professional experiences, qualifications, and accomplishments

data-based decision-making—the use of any number of assessment or data collection strategies to inform the design, implementation, and evaluation of services and programs

decoding—knowledge and skill in applying sound–letter correspondences when reading

Direct Behavior Ratings (DBRs)—teacher ratings of student behavior that are completed at the end of an instructional block or activity

direct observation—assessment technique in which the observer directly views and measures an individual's behaviors

direct service—professional activity in which the provider has firsthand contact with the client

distance education—instruction that occurs when the instructor and learners are in different physical locations

distributive justice—fairness with regard to how resources are allocated in society

diversity—a spectrum of individual differences related to factors such as age, disability status, gender or gender identity, race, ethnicity, national origin, religion, sexual orientation, language, and socioeconomic status

double-blind review—type of scholarly peer review in which the identities of both the reviewers and the authors are kept confidential

due process—a legal protection that requires government officials to afford all individuals fair and equal treatment through the judicial system

ecological model—approach to psychological service delivery that focuses on person–environment interactions that give rise to academic and behavioral problems

education reform—process of enacting fundamental, deep-rooted changes in the way educators conceptualize and implement school-based services

effect size—used in meta-analysis, a standardized measure of the magnitude of an effect

epistemology—the study and philosophy of knowledge construction

equal protection clause—component of the 14th Amendment to the U.S. Constitution that prohibits states from denying any individual in its territory equal protection under the law

equality—state in which all individuals or groups are afforded the same resources and opportunities

equity—state in which individuals or groups are afforded resources and opportunities in accordance with their unique needs and circumstances

ethics—a system of principles of conduct that guides the behavior of an individual and/or the execution of an activity

ethnography—a research method in which the researcher seeks to understand a particular group in their environment by observing and interviewing those in the group

eugenics—discriminatory practice or advocacy of controlled selective breeding of human populations that assumes the inferiority of ethnic and racial minoritized groups and people with disabilities

Every Student Succeeds Act—federal U.S. legislation that regulates state accountability systems in education and allocates support and resources to promote the educational success of all students

evidence-based interventions—interventions that are likely to produce positive outcomes for clients because they are supported by high-quality research indicating that such outcomes are probable

experimental design—a research method used to analyze the cause-and-effect relationship between two or more variables by manipulating the independent variable, controlling for confounding variables, and randomization

expert power—relationship dynamic in which a consultee perceives a consultant to possess great knowledge and expertise, resulting in a demonstrated change in the consultee's beliefs, attitudes, or behaviors

explanatory design—a mixed methods research design in which an initial quantitative phase of a study is followed by a qualitative phase

exploration—stage of the systems change process that involves determining whether there is a match between the targeted change and the needs of the organization or its members

externalizing behavior—challenging behaviors that are directed outward, such as aggression and hyperactivity

external validity—the extent to which study findings can be generalized to other populations and settings

family—group of people who are connected by birth, marriage, adoption, or close relational and extended ties

Family Educational Rights and Privacy Act—federal U.S. legislation that protects and safeguards the rights of parents by guaranteeing the privacy and confidentiality of student educational records

fidelity (ethics)—continuing faithfulness to the truth and to one's professional duties

504 Plan—a plan detailing the services and accommodations to which a student with a disability is entitled in school under the Rehabilitation Act of 1973

fluency intervention—intervention designed to increase a student's automaticity or speed in implementing a skill accurately

formative assessment—the collection and use of information to monitor students' progress over the course of intervention

full implementation—stage of the systems change process in which the change becomes completely integrated into the organization's practices and procedures and implementation becomes more skillful and routine

functional behavior assessment (FBA)—a method of collecting data to inform a hypothesis regarding why a behavior is occurring

gap analysis—method of describing needs and goals that quantifies the difference between current performance and targeted or desired performance

general outcome measure—assessment that requires the integration of several component skills that make up an academic task and thus can be used as a measure of student performance across an academic year

generalization—an individual's application of a new skill or behavior learned in one context to other, different contexts

grounded theory—a qualitative approach to research using induction and triangulation of data to develop theories about phenomena

health service psychologist—a doctoral-level psychologist who is trained to deliver prevention, intervention, and/or assessment services to support the mental and physical health of consumers

Hybrid Years—era (1896–1969) in school psychology's history in which the profession comprised a diverse range of practitioners in psychology and education who provided psychoeducational services to school-age youth

implementation—The process of incorporating a program or practice at the individual, group, or organizational level

implementation driver—a factor that enables successful systems change

indirect observation—assessment technique in which the assessor relies on others to view and report on an individual's behaviors

indirect service—professional activity in which the provider does not have firsthand contact with the client but instead supports the client's functioning through interaction with a third party, such as a caregiver or teacher

Individualized Education Program (IEP)—a comprehensive plan detailing the specific disability services to which a student is entitled (under the Individuals With Disabilities Education Improvement Act) to support their access to the curriculum and participation in the school community

Individuals With Disabilities Education Improvement Act (IDEIA)—federal U.S. legislation designed to protect the educational rights of students with disabilities ages 3 to 21

initial implementation—stage of the systems change process in which an organization makes its first attempts at putting the change into practice

installation—stage of the systems change process in which schools prepare to implement a change, such as by securing funding, ensuring appropriate staffing, and planning for equitable implementation

instructional environment—the location, items, people, and curriculum used wherein students' academic learning occurs

instructional intensity—the quality and/or quantity (e.g., duration) of academic instruction, often defined by the amount of intervention time provided to a student or the number of students per intervention group

intellectual disability—significantly below average cognitive functioning with deficits in adaptive behavior

intellectual giftedness—high achievement capability in areas such as intellectual, creative, artistic, or leadership capacity, or in specific academic domains

intelligence—the ability to reason abstractly, solve complex problems, and acquire new knowledge

intelligence test—a standardized measure of individual differences in general and specific cognitive abilities

interactionist–constructivist—the epistemological perspective that reality is subjective and that knowledge is actively constructed by people as they make sense of their world

internal validity—the extent to whether a study's methodological design permitted the researchers to rule out alternative explanations for study findings

internalized racism—the acceptance of negative stereotypes about one's own racial or ethnic group

internalizing behavior—challenging behavior that is directed inward, such as anxiety and depression

International School Psychology Association (ISPA)—an international organization that seeks to promote worldwide cooperation, networking, and preparation among school and educational psychologists

internationality—relating to, affecting, or having members from more than one country

internationalization—an intentional, reciprocal, and collaborative process that involves intercultural and fair integration of perspectives, values, and priorities from representative stakeholders to inform shared strategic goals that are context-relevant and focused on equitable opportunities

internship—a culminating field experience in school psychology graduate preparation that requires the integration of skills developed during practica and, in many cases, greater independence (although interns continue to be closely supervised by their appointed field-based and university-based supervisors)

interpersonal racism—racist interactions between individuals in day-to-day interpersonal experiences

interpersonal skills—verbal and nonverbal communication techniques and approaches that consultants use when interacting with consultees and clients

intersectionality—a theoretical framework for understanding how aspects of a person's social identities combine to create different modes of discrimination and privilege

intervention—services that address problems that have already become apparent

intervention fidelity—the extent to which an intervention is delivered as planned or conceptualized by its developers

interviews—purposeful and planned encounters intended to obtain information about a person's behaviors, preferences, experiences, strengths, and areas of need

introspection—observation of one's own mental state and conscious thought

law—system of rules of conduct enforced by a government or other authority

least restrictive environment—the environment, educational setting, or placement in which the child is educated with peers without disabilities to the maximum extent possible

Majority World—a term used to describe countries in Asia, Africa, Latin America, and the Caribbean, signaling that the preponderance of the world's population resides in these parts of the globe

manualized—term used to describe an intervention that is carried out according to detailed and structured procedures

medical model—approach to psychological service delivery that focuses on identifying inherent problems within children through extensive diagnostic and assessment procedures

mental health consultation—a cooperative partnership in which a consultant often targets consultee-related factors (e.g., consultee assumptions and behaviors) as the focus for change

mentorship—a relationship in which a more experienced professional (i.e., mentor) works with a more novice one (i.e., mentee) to develop the latter's career, knowledge, and skill, without the evaluative component found in supervisory relationships

meta-analysis—a study that employs a quantitative method for summarizing the effects of a treatment across large numbers of original research studies investigating that treatment

mixed methods research—a set of research methods in which quantitative and qualitative techniques are integrated

Model Licensure Act—the American Psychological Association's formal recommendations to states regarding requirements for licensure in psychology

multicultural competence—display of knowledge, attitudes, and behaviors that result in successful interactions with multicultural populations

multicultural consultation—the process of providing indirect services to support clients while carefully considering, recognizing, and understanding aspects of cultural diversity that impact communication, goals, and pathways toward those goals

multicultural education—a wide variety of programs and practices designed to facilitate educational equity for individuals of all genders, racial and ethnic groups, language backgrounds, social classes, exceptionalities, and cultures

multiculturalism—worldview that acknowledges and values the diverse cultural identities, values, and perspectives of others

multiple exemplars—different ways, settings, or formats in which a skill can be applied

multitiered systems of support—a comprehensive service delivery framework that provides a continuum of prevention and intervention services to meet the needs of all students

narrative inquiry—a research method in which the researcher seeks to learn from an individual's or group's perspective on a certain experience or phenomenon, wherein the story (i.e., narrative) shared constitutes the data

NASP Practice Model—official policy of the National Association of School Psychologists comprising 10 domains of practice and six organizational principles that describe comprehensive school psychological service delivery

National Association of School Psychologists (NASP)—U.S.-based organization that represents the professional interests of school psychologists

nonmaleficence—the obligation to act in a manner that does not inflict harm on others; as it relates to professional competence, providing a standard of care that minimizes or avoids risk

nonpractice credential—recognition issued by nongovernment agencies (e.g., professional organizations) that serves as a marker of quality or specialized training

norm-referenced test—standardized assessment in which a student's performance is interpreted relative to a peer group

nosology—the application of scientific inquiry to the systematic examination and classification of physical and psychological diseases and disorders

number sense—an individual's general facility with numerical concepts

objectivity—the perception of client problems in a manner that is free from judgment, bias, and other psychological interference

observation—assessment technique used to examine an individual's patterns of behavior

open review—type of scholarly peer review process in which both the authors of the paper and the peer reviewers know each other's identities

organization development consultation—a planned, systemic process in which a consultant works to introduce new principles and practices into an organization with the goal of effecting organizational improvement, effectiveness, and competence

outcome assessment—an evaluative assessment that takes place following an intervention

partnership—a collaborative association focused on a shared goal between two or more entities

peer review—a quality control process wherein experts provide feedback on a research article or other type of professional manuscript prior to its publication (or subsequent rejection)

permanent product—the material entities that result from a given action or task that provide insight into the processes associated with that task

phenomenology—a research method that involves exploring the lived experiences of participants in order to come up with a broader understanding of a particular phenomenon

phonological awareness—the understanding that words are composed of smaller units of sound

physical safety—a focus on physical structures and security of the school environment

Plessy v. Ferguson—landmark court case in which the U.S. Supreme Court ruled that state laws requiring the racial segregation of public facilities were constitutional on the basis that these facilities would be "separate but equal"

Positive Behavioral Interventions and Supports (PBIS)—a three-tiered problem-solving framework for providing behavioral supports to all students in a school system

positivism—the epistemological perspective that empirical facts exist apart from personal ideas or thoughts and that facts are governed by the law of cause and effect

practice credential—recognition awarded by a government agency (e.g., state education agency) that allows an individual to practice psychology legally in a specified range of settings (e.g., K–12 schools)

practicum—a field-based experience generally occurring during the early-to-middle years of school psychology graduate preparation that exposes students to professional settings and builds skills in psychological and educational service delivery through close supervision

PREPaRE—a comprehensive, national training curriculum developed by the National Association of School Psychologists (NASP) that trains school-employed mental health professionals and other educators in school crisis prevention and intervention

prevention—services that foster student competencies (e.g., academic and social skills) so as to promote healthy development and to avoid the onset of long-term problems

privilege—a set of unearned benefits, advantages, and opportunities that are afforded to an individual due to their membership in a particular social group

problem-solving—an approach used to gather and synthesize information in a logical manner and, subsequently, to make educational decisions that best serve students and school systems

professional standards—benchmarks that delineate expectations for preparation, practice, and/or continuing education for a group of professionals

program evaluation—a process for assessing the implementation and outcomes of an initiative

progress monitoring—the periodic assessment of student behaviors or skills to assess change and development over time

psychoeducation—the process of providing information about mental health issues, wellness, and treatment to students, families, and others

psychological safety—a focus on the emotional and behavioral well-being of students and staff in a school

psychometrics—the study of psychological measurement

public health model—population-based approach to addressing academic, health, and social problems that incorporates environmental factors as well as comprehensive, multilayered prevention and intervention efforts

punishment—consequence that leads to the decreased recurrence of a behavior

qualitative research—a set of research methods that rely on the narrative analysis of verbal data

quantitative research—a set of research methods that rely on numerical approaches to understand the natural world

racism—individual, structural, political, economic, and social forces that discriminate against and disadvantage people of color based on their race for the purpose of maintaining white supremacy

random assignment—the process of sorting research participants into treatment and comparison groups based on chance (i.e., each participant is equally likely to be assigned to any one particular group)

randomized controlled trial—experimental design in which two randomly assigned groups of participants are compared, namely: an experimental group (i.e., group of participants who receive the intervention under investigation) and a control group (i.e., comparison group of participants who do not receive the intervention)

reading comprehension—the construction of meaning from text

reading fluency—the rate, accuracy, and prosody of an individual's reading

reason for referral—questions regarding an individual's current functioning and behavior that are used to guide and inform the assessment process and are to be answered by assessment results

referent power—relationship dynamic in which a consultee perceives favorably or identifies with a consultant, resulting in a demonstrated change in the consultee's beliefs, attitudes, or behaviors

Rehabilitation Act of 1973—federal U.S. civil rights legislation that prohibits discrimination against individuals with disabilities

reinforcement—consequence that leads to the increased recurrence of a behavior

relationship skills—skills necessary for communicating, cooperating, and interacting appropriately with others

reliability—the extent to which measures yield consistent scores and are free from error

replacement behavior—behavior that serves the same or a similar function as a problem behavior but is considered to be a more appropriate alternative to the problem behavior

research—a systematic process of asking questions, collecting and analyzing data, and forming conclusions and future directions

research methodology—a system of techniques to collect, process, and analyze phenomena and answer research questions

respecialization and professional retraining—a process whereby institutions enroll students from related fields or backgrounds in a nondegree-seeking program that leads to state certification or licensure only

responsible decision-making—a process of balancing concerns regarding social norms, others' perspectives, ethical considerations, and personal goals to make choices about one's own actions

résumé—a formal document that summarizes one's education, experiences, and professional qualifications and accomplishments

school-based partnership—collaborative efforts occurring in school settings wherein students and families can receive support from local agencies within the school context

school-based restorative justice—a systemic approach to discipline that engages all parties affected by a behavioral incident in proactive conflict resolution

school crises—extremely negative events that are often unpredictable in regard to how they unfold and that have the potential to cause physical and emotional pain and to generate feelings of powerlessness or entrapment

school-linked partnership—collaborative efforts occurring through school settings wherein students and families are connected to local agencies

school psychology—profession that focuses primarily on providing psychological and educational services to children, families, schools, and other organizations to support the academic, social, emotional, and behavioral well-being of youth

school psychology preparation—the coursework and supervised field experiences required to earn a graduate degree in school psychology

school violence—intentional use of threatened or actual physical force or power, which results in or is highly likely to result in injury, death, psychological harm, or deprivation that occurs at school, including school-sponsored events or in transit to or from those events

scientist-practitioner model—approach to psychology training that emphasizes preparation in both research and clinical practice

self-awareness—an individual's skills in recognizing personal strengths, weaknesses, thoughts, and emotions

self-management—an individual's skills in regulating thoughts and emotions

shared vision—the collective insights, values, goals, and understandings that are synthesized by participants in the change process to guide fundamental shifts in service delivery

single-blind review—type of scholarly peer review in which the reviewers' identities are kept confidential but the authors' identities are revealed to the reviewers

single-case design—a quantitative approach to research typically using small samples where the participants serve as their own control

social awareness—an individual's recognition of the perspectives of others and social norms that dictate acceptable behaviors

social capital—networks and connections possessed and inherited by groups in society

social, emotional, and behavioral (SEB) skills—a broad range of interrelated skills in self-regulating emotion and behavior as well as in interacting with others

social and emotional learning (SEL)—the process by which individuals acquire the knowledge, attitudes, and skills necessary to recognize, regulate, and express emotions, set positive goals, and maintain positive relationships with others

social justice—the fair and equitable treatment of all individuals in the context of schools, communities, and other settings that are affirming of their identities, values, and perspectives

specialist-level degree—minimum level of education for school psychology practice that generally requires at least 3 years of full-time graduate study (or the equivalent) beyond the bachelor's degree, involving at least 60 graduate semester or 90 graduate quarter hours

specialty—defined area of psychological practice that requires advanced knowledge and skills acquired through an organized sequence of education and training

specific learning disability (SLD)—unexpected academic underachievement that is not primarily the result of inadequate opportunities for learning or of visual, hearing, motor, intellectual, emotional, or behavioral disabilities

stereotype threat—fear or anxiety of confirming a widely held yet inaccurate perception of one's own cultural group(s)

strengths-based assessment—process of evaluating personal competencies (e.g., emotional and behavioral skills) that enhance coping, allow individuals to set and accomplish goals, and promote development in domains such as academic achievement and social functioning

student-level services—professional activities that involve working with individuals or groups of children or adolescents

summative assessment—the collection and use of information to evaluate students' learning and attainment of instructional objectives after the curricular content addressing these objectives has been delivered

survey design—a research method used to describe the current condition of a given phenomenon using numerical data and that often involves the use of questionnaires

sustainability—stage of the systems change process that involves planning for issues that could affect the continued or long-term implementation of the change

system—multiple individuals or entities that interact to produce an outcome

systematic direct observation (SDO)—a form of direct behavioral observation that involves having a trained observer enter the classroom to examine and record in real time the occurrence of a small number of preselected student behaviors

systemic racism—racism that is deeply embedded in and throughout systems, laws, policies, and practices that perpetuate prejudice or discrimination and social inequities on a larger scale

systems change—a process aimed at improving outcomes through altering or transforming one or more systems

systems-level services—professional activities that involve working with organizations or specific organizational levels to impact client outcomes on a larger scale

task analysis—procedure for breaking down a multistep process (e.g., long division) into its individual parts to determine what the student needs to know and the actions they must take to accurately complete the task

team-based consultation—a cooperative partnership guided by a consultant who collaborates with individuals in various roles (e.g., teachers, administrators) to organize their efforts toward serving clients and/or facilitating systems change

teleconsultation—the process of conducting consultation services through technology, both synchronously through videoconferencing and asynchronously through various collaboration applications

telepsychology—the delivery of psychological services via telecommunication technologies, which include but are not limited to telephone, mobile devices, videoconferencing, texting, and other internet-based modalities

testing—a method used to measure human attributes and achievements that comprises standardized procedures for sampling and scoring behavior in specified domains

Thayer Conference—first professional gathering in the United States exclusively focused on the professional practice of school psychologists

Thoroughbred Years—era (1970–present) in school psychology's history in which the profession's identity became more cohesive and established

threat assessment—a process of assessment and violence prevention that involves evaluating individuals who engage in threatening behavior to determine whether they demonstrate serious intent to carry out a violent act

Tier 1—within the context of multitiered systems of support (MTSS), a level of prevention and intervention in which services are provided to all students at the classroom, school, or district level

Tier 2—within the context of multitiered systems of support (MTSS), a level of prevention and intervention in which services are provided to students deemed to be at risk for academic, social, emotional, or behavioral problems

Tier 3—within the context of multitiered systems of support (MTSS), a level of prevention and intervention in which services are provided to students with indicated academic, social, emotional, or behavioral problems

universal screening—administration of brief measures of target skills or behaviors to an entire population of students (e.g., all students within a grade level, school, or school district) to identify individuals in need of additional supports

validity—various sources of evidence that support the specific use of a measure and the interpretations of data it produces

vocabulary—knowledge of individual words in text

Youth Participatory Action Research—a process in which youth investigate social inequities to improve their lives, communities, and the institutions intended to serve them

Index

AAAP (American Association of Applied Psychologists), 25
AAEE (American Association for Employment in Education), 309
AASP (American Academy of School Psychology), 32
academic assessment and intervention, 155–167. *See also* curriculum-based measurement (CBM)
  accuracy interventions, 165
  addressing, through multitiered systems of support, 162–166
  computer adaptive interim tests, 160–161
  criterion-referenced tests (CRTs), 161
  environment, assessing, 157–158
  fluency interventions, 165
  instructional intensity, 165
  measuring academic skills, 158–162
  multiple exemplars, 165
  norm-referenced tests (NRTs), 161
  state-mandated tests, 161–162
academic careers, 334–338
academic interventions and supports, 7
academic neocolonialism, 295
  social justice and, 286–287
academic skill problems, 156–157
  definitions and prevalence of, 156–157
  mathematics, 156–157
  reading, 156
  written language, 157
acceptability, of intervention, 211
accreditation, 107
accuracy interventions, 165
achievement gap, 48
active engagement, 238
Active Implementation Frameworks (AIF), 250–252
adaptive behavior, 195
ADHD (attention deficit hyperactivity disorder) symptoms, 62
administrative supervision, 334

advocacy, 14, 34
  social justice, 55–56
AIF (Active Implementation Frameworks), 250–252
alternative credentialing, 112
American Academy of School Psychology (AASP), 32
American Association for Employment in Education (AAEE), 309
American Association of Applied Psychologists (AAAP), 25
American Psychological Association (APA), 4, 85
  code of ethics, 84, 85
  Standards of Accreditation (SoA) for Health Service Psychology, 102, 105, 107
Anger Coping Program, 177
antecedents, 130, 180, 182
antiracism and school psychology, 61–74. *See also* racism
APA (American Psychological Association), 4, 85
APPIC (Association of Psychology and Postdoctoral Internship Center), 113
applied professional ethics, 84
Army Alpha intelligence test, 22–23
Army Beta intelligence test, 22–23
aspirational capital, 237, 240
ASPPB (Association of State and Provincial Psychology Boards), 114
assessment, 15, 121–134
  behavioral observations, 129–130
  criterion-referenced comparisons (CRCs), 127–128
  during intervention, 126–127
  formative assessment, 124–125
  historical records, 128–129
  integrating and reporting assessment results, 131–132
  for intervention, 125–127
  interviews, 131

assessment *(continued)*
  multicultural considerations in, 132–133
  norm-referenced comparisons (NRCs), 127–128
  in practice of school psychology, importance of, 122
  progress monitoring, 126–127
  qualitative interpretations, 128
  rating scales, 130
  reliability, 124
  in schools, purposes of, 125–127
  strengths-based assessments, 129
  summative assessment, 124–125
  techniques, 127–131
  testing, 127–128
  tests, essential features of, 123–124
  validity, 123–124
Association of Psychology and Postdoctoral Internship Center (APPIC), 113
Association of State and Provincial Psychology Boards (ASPPB), 114
attention deficit hyperactivity disorder (ADHD) symptoms, 62
autonomy of clients, 86
awareness, multicultural competence, 132

BC (behavioral consultation), 206
Beckham, Albert Sidney, 23, 25
behavior intervention plan (BIP), 181–182
behavior rating scales, 176
behavioral consultation (BC), 206
behavioral health services, 7
behavioral observations, 129–130
behavioral skills, 172
beneficence, 87
biases, identifying and challenging, 54
Binet, Alfred, 22, 191
Binet-Simon Intelligence Scale, 22
biological intelligence, 190
BIP (behavior intervention plan), 181–182
Bond, Horace Mann, 23
brief experimental analysis, 211
Brown et al. v. Board of Education of Topeka, 26–27, 28
Buckley Amendment, 91. *See also* Family Educational Rights and Privacy Act

CA (chronological age), intelligence testing, 191–192
Canady, Herman, 23
Caplan, Gerald, 205
career in school psychology, preparing for, 329–342. *See also* field-based practitioner careers
  general considerations, 330
  résumé or curriculum vitae, developing, 339–341

case studies, 270
CASEL (Collaborative for Academic, Social, and Emotional Learning), 211
CATs (computer adaptive interim tests), 158, 160–161
Cattell-Horn-Carroll (CHC) theory, 191, 192
causal-comparative designs, 268–269
CBC (conjoint behavioral consultation), 206–207
CBM (curriculum-based measurement), 158–160
CBM-R (curriculum-based measures of oral reading), 158–159
CE (continuing education), 114
certification, 109
change agent, 149
CHC (Cattell-Horn-Carroll) theory, 191, 192
CHEA (Council for Higher Education Accreditation), 29
child clinical psychology, 13
child study movement, 21–23
chronological age (CA), intelligence testing, 191–192
civil rights movement, 26–27
Clark, Kenneth, 26
Clark, Mamie Phipps, 26
classroom and grade-level teams, multitiered systems of support, 208
class-wide behavioral interventions, 175
client, in consultation, 204
clinical supervision, 334
CLSs (correct letter sequences), 160
code of ethics, 84, 85
  of the American Psychological Association, 84, 85
  of the International School Psychology Association, 88–89
  of the National Association of School Psychologists, 30, 35, 85–88
cognitive assessment, 189–198. *See also* intelligence
  intellectual disability (ID), 195
  intellectual giftedness, 195
  intelligence and social justice, 196–197
  specific learning disability (SLD), 195–196
collaboration, 238
  family, school, and community, 8
Collaborative for Academic, Social, and Emotional Learning (CASEL), 211
communication process, 149
community, 233
  agencies, 234
  development model, 235
compatibility, intervention planning and implementation, 150
complexity, intervention planning and implementation, 150

Comprehensive School Threat Assessment
    Guidelines (CSTAG), 225
compulsory schooling, 21
computer adaptive interim tests (CATs),
    158, 160–161
conjoint behavioral consultation (CBC), 206–207
consequences, 130, 180
  strategies, 182
constructs, 123
consultant, 204
consultation, 203–216. *See also* problem-solving
    process, consultation as
  as a problem-solving process, 210
  behavioral consultation (BC), 206
  collaboration and, 5, 7
  conjoint behavioral consultation
    (CBC), 206–207
  defining, 204–205
  effectiveness of, 213–214
  major models/modalities of, 205–209
  mental health consultation (MHC), 205–206
  multicultural considerations, 214–215
  organization development consultation
    (ODC), 207–208
  relationship building/establishing a
    cooperative partnership, 210
  social justice in, 215–216
  team-based consultation, 208–209
  teleconsultation, 209
consultee, 204
continuing education (CE), 114
continuing professional development
    (CPD), 114
contract services, 317
Coping Cat, 183
coronavirus 2019 (COVID-19) pandemic, 34–35
correct letter sequences (CLSs), 160
correct word sequences (CWS), 160
correlational designs, 268
Council for Higher Education Accreditation
    (CHEA), 29
COVID-19 (coronavirus 2019) pandemic, 34–35
CPD (continuing professional
    development), 114
CPTED (Crime Prevention Through
    Environmental Design), 223
CRCs (criterion-referenced comparisons),
    127–128
credentialing in school psychology, 109–115.
    See also nonpractice credentials; practice
    credentials
  Nationally Certified School Psychologist
    (NCSP) credential, 115
  for practice in schools, 110–112
Crime Prevention Through Environmental
    Design (CPTED), 223

crisis intervention, 32
crisis teams and plans, 225–226
criterion-referenced comparisons (CRCs), 127–128
criterion-referenced tests (CRTs), 158, 161
critical skills, 34
CRTs (criterion-referenced tests), 158, 161
CSTAG (Comprehensive School Threat
    Assessment Guidelines), 225
cultural capital, 237
cultural humility, 297–298
cultural responsiveness, 44, 132
curriculum-based measurement
    (CBM), 158–160
  math CBM, 159–160
  reading CBM, 158–159
  spelling CBM, 160
  writing CBM, 160
curriculum-based measures of oral reading
    (CBM-R), 158–159
curriculum vitae (CV), developing, 339–341
CV (curriculum vitae), developing, 339–341
CWS (correct word sequences), 160

Daily Behavior Report Card (DBRC), 177
data-based decision-making, 5–6, 143, 264
DBRC (Daily Behavior Report Card), 177
DBRs (Direct Behavior Ratings), 179
degree types, 103–104
  credentials and, 331, 336
demographics of school psychologists, 45–46
diagnosis/eligibility determination, 125–126
differential diagnosis, 194
Direct Behavior Ratings (DBRs), 179
direct services, 7
disability, 33, 90
discipline, 49–50
disproportionality in special education, 64
distance education, 315
diversity, 43, 318
Doctor of Education (EdD), 104
Doctor of Philosophy (PhD), 104
Doctor of Psychology (PsyD), 104
doctoral degrees, 103, 104
doctoral practice, 113
double-blind review, 272
due process, 89

EAHCA (Education for All Handicapped
    Children Act), 28–29, 33, 89, 190, 194
EBIs (evidence-based interventions), 147–148,
    151, 206, 211, 212
ecological model, 32
Education for All Handicapped Children Act
    (EAHCA), 28–29, 33, 89, 190, 194
education reform, 249
educational diagnostician, 113

Educational Testing Service (ETS), 111
ELLs (English Language Learners), 47, 132–133
emergency operations plans (EOPs), 225–226
emerging profession, 23–24
English Language Learners (ELLs), 47, 132–133
environment, assessing, 157–158
EOPs (emergency operations plans), 225–226
EPPP (Examination for Professional Practice in Psychology), 111
equal protection clause, 89
equality, 9
equitable practices for diverse populations, 9
equity, 9, 318
equity-focused partnership process model, 237–243
ESPS (Excellence in School Psychological Services), 316
ESSA (Every Student Succeeds Act), 91, 127, 317
ETS (Educational Testing Service), 111
ethical and legal foundations, 83–97
  ethical violations, consequences of, 96–97
  Every Student Succeeds Act (ESSA), 91
  Individuals With Disabilities Education Improvement Act (IDEIA), 89–90
  law and ethics, defining, 84–85
  model for, 92–93
  No Child Left Behind (NCLB) Act, 91–92
  Principles for Professional Ethics, NASP, 30, 84, 85–88, 102, 315
  professional competence and responsibility, 87–88
  professional relationships, honesty and integrity in, 88
  public legislation relevant to, 89–92
  Rehabilitation Act of 1973, 90–91
  respecting the dignity and rights of all persons, 86–87
  schools, families, communities, the profession, and society, 88
Ethical Principles of Psychologists and Code of Conduct, 84, 85
Ethical Standards of Psychologists, 85
ethical violations, consequences of, 96–97
ethics, 84
ethnography, 270
eugenics, 23
Europe, psychology emergence in, 20
Every Student Succeeds Act (ESSA), 91, 127, 317
evidence-based interventions (EBIs), 147–148, 151, 206, 211, 212
Examination for Professional Practice in Psychology (EPPP), 111
Excellence in School Psychological Services (ESPS), 316
experimental designs, 269

expert power, 211
explanatory design, 271
exploration stage, systems change, 250
external validity, 273
externalizing behaviors, 176

factor analysis, 191
FACTS (Functional Assessment Checklist for Teachers and Staff), 180
familial capital, 237
Family Educational Rights and Privacy Act (FERPA), 91, 209
family, school, and community collaboration, 233–243
  assessing needs and strengths, 239–240
  collaborative partnerships, benefits of, 236–237
  coming together, 240
  creating shared vision and plan, 240–241
  defining, 234–235
  equity and social justice-oriented, 237–243
  evaluating and celebrating progress, 242–243
  maintaining momentum, 243
  preparing to partner, 238–239
  taking action, 241–242
FAPE (free and appropriate public education), 28, 89, 194–195
FBA (functional behavior assessment), 180–181
federally mandated special education services, emergence of, 28–29
FERPA (Family Educational Rights and Privacy Act), 91, 209
fidelity, 88, 151
field-based practitioner careers, 330–334
  degree types and credentials, 331, 336
  general considerations, 330–331
  graduate training and specialized coursework, 331–332
  mentors and supervisors, 333–334, 337
  specialized field placements, 332–333, 336
flexibility, intervention planning and implementation, 150
fluency interventions, 165
formative assessment, 124–125
formative evaluation, 253
free and appropriate public education (FAPE), 28, 89, 194–195
full-service schools, 235
Functional Assessment Checklist for Teachers and Staff (FACTS), 180
functional behavior assessment (FBA), 180–181
future of school psychology, 305–322
  contract services, 317
  diversifying, 312–313
  Every Student Succeeds Act (ESSA), 317

past predictions of the future, 306–307
predictions for, 307–319
professional standards will continue to evolve, 315
school psychologist role, 315–319
shortages, 308–311
social justice, equity, diversity, and inclusion, 318–319
specialist-level degree, 311–312
technology-oriented service delivery, 317–318

Galton, Francis, 23
gap analysis, 146
GBG (Good Behavior Game), 175
Gender and Sexuality Alliance (GSA) club, 55
general outcome measure, 158
generalization, 213
Gesell, Arnold, 24, 68
globalization, 284–285
Goddard, Henry, 22
Good Behavior Game (GBG), 175
graduate preparation, 101–116
　American Psychological Association (APA) standards for, 105
　content and structure, 104–106
　degree types, 103–104
　doctoral degrees, 103, 104
　graduate program accreditation, 107–109
　International School Psychology Association (ISPA) training standards, 105
　National Association of School Psychologists (NASP) graduate preparation standards, 105
　nondoctoral degrees, 103–104
　professional standards, 102–103
　program accreditation, competency areas, 104–106
graduate programs
　accreditation, 107–109
　faculty shortages and, 310–311
　professional accreditation and, 29–30
graduate student enrollment shortages, 310
graduate training and specialized coursework, 331–332
grounded theory, 270
GSA (Gender and Sexuality Alliance) club, 55
Guidelines for the Provision of School Psychological Services, 30

Hall, Granville Stanley, 21–22, 68
handicap, 33. *See also* disability
HBCUs (historically Black colleges and universities), 25
health service psychologist (HSP), 307, 308
Henri, Victor, 22
Hildreth, Gertrude, 24
Hines, Laura, 24, 25
historical records, 128–129
historically Black colleges and universities (HBCUs), 25
homogeneous workforce, challenges in, 46
Horn-Cattell's fluid and crystallized (Gf-Gc) theory, 191
HSP (health service psychologist), 307, 308
Hybrid Years, 20–28
　child study movement, 21–22
　civil rights movement, 26–27
　emerging profession, 23–24
　Europe and United States, psychology emergence in, 20
　growth of training, 24–25
　intelligence-testing movement, 22–23
　labor force and education, changing landscape of, 20–21
　professional organizations, 25, 27
　Thayer Conference, 27
　World War II, 25–26

ID (intellectual disability), 195
IDEA (Individuals With Disabilities Education Act), 29
IDEIA (Individuals With Disabilities Education Improvement Act), 33, 89–90, 126, 194
IEP (Individualized Education Program), 11, 28, 90
IES (Institute of Education Sciences) toolkit program, 254, 255
implementation, intervention, 149–151
　adoption, 150
　components and stages, 149–150
　dissemination, 150
　implementation, 150
　outcomes, evaluating, 151
　sustainability, 150
implementation drivers, 250, 251, 253
implementers, 149
inclusion, 318–319
indirect services, 8, 204
individual student-level and problem-solving teams, multitiered systems of support, 208
Individualized Education Program (IEP), 11, 28, 90
individuals of interest, 284
Individuals With Disabilities Education Act (IDEA), 29
Individuals With Disabilities Education Improvement Act (IDEIA), 33, 89–90, 126, 194
inequitable access to quality instruction, 64–65
innovation, 149

installation stage, systems change, 250
Institute of Education Sciences (IES) toolkit
    program, 254, 255
instructional environment, 158
instructional intensity, 165
intellectual disability (ID), 195
intellectual giftedness, 195
intellectual internationalization, 297
intelligence, 190
    biological, 190
    distribution of, 192–193
    intelligence quotient, 191
    psychometric, 190
    social, 190
    structure of, 191–192
    testing, in the schools, 194–196
    testing movement, 22–23
    tests, 190
        interpretation of, 193–194
interactionist–constructivist approach, 270
internal consistency, 124
internal validity, 273
internalized racism in K–12 schools, 66
internalized/intrapersonal racism, 62, 63
internalizing behaviors, 176
International School Psychology Association
    (ISPA), 88–89, 102, 284
    code of ethics of, 88–89
    training standards, 105
internationality of school and educational
    psychology, 283–298
    academic neocolonialism and social
        justice, 286–287
    challenges and opportunities for, 295–298
    characteristics and statistics, 287–290
    conceptualizing, 284–285
    current status of, 287–293
    globalization, internationalization and, 285
    goals of, 291–293
    key concepts and definitions, 284–287
    linguistic barriers, 297
    organizations, 288
    scholarly journal outlets focused
        on, 289–290
    social and political turmoil around the
        world, 296
    training in, 289
internationalization, 284–285, 297–298
    advantages and opportunities for
        promoting, 297–298
    cultural humility, 297–298
    intellectual advantages, 297
    moral advantages, 297
    professional advantages, 297
    within school and educational
        psychology, 290–293

internship, 111
interpersonal racism in K–12 schools, 66
interpersonal/individual/personally mediated
    racism, 62, 63
interpersonal skills, 210
intersectionality, 45
intersectionality and racism in
    schools, 66–67
intervention, 140
    assessment for, 125–126
    diagnosis/eligibility determination, 125–126
    screening, 125
intervention effectiveness and follow-up,
    evaluating, 212–213
intervention fidelity, 151, 212, 256
intervention planning and implementation,
    139–152. *See also* multitiered systems of
    support (MTSS)
    compatibility, 150
    complexity, 150
    flexibility, 150
    implementation, 149–151
    observability, 150
    problem-solving model, 145–146
    relative advantage, 150
    riskiness, 150
    selecting interventions, 147–148, 150
    task relevance, 150
    training and technical assistance,
        providing, 150–151
    trialability, 150
interviews, 131
introspection, 20
ipsative analyses, 193
ISPA (International School Psychology
    Association), 88–89, 102, 284

Jackson, John Henry, 24
Jenkins, Martin, 23
*Jones Intentional Multicultural Interview
    Schedule*, 131

K–12 education, racism in, 63–67
    disproportionality in special education, 64
    inequitable access to quality
        instruction, 64–65
    internalized racism, 66
    interpersonal racism, 66
    intersectionality in schools and, 66–67
    origins and early development, 67–68
    school psychology professional
        practices, 68–69
    school-to-prison pipeline, 65
    systemic racism, 63–65
knowledge, multicultural
    competence, 132

labor force and education, changing landscape of, 20–21
law and ethics, defining, 84–85
leadership, 34
least restrictive environment (LRE), 89
legal and ethical decision-making, model for, 92–93
legislation of the 1990s and 2000s, 33
Licensed (Clinical) Professional Counselor, 114
Licensed Educational Psychologist, 114
Licensed Mental Health Counselor/Therapist, 114
Licensed Psycho-Educational Specialist, 114
Licensed Specialist in School Psychology (LSSP), 111
licensure, 109
LIEM (low income and economic marginalization), 47, 51–52
Life Skills Training program, 149
linguistic barriers, 297
low income and economic marginalization (LIEM), 47, 51–52
LRE (least restrictive environment), 89
LSSP (Licensed Specialist in School Psychology), 111

MA (mental age), intelligence testing, 191
Majority World, 297
math curriculum-based measurement, 159–160
mathematics, 156–157
medical model, 32
mental age (MA), intelligence testing, 191
mental and behavioral health services, 7
mental health and behavioral interventions, 265
mental health consultation (MHC), 205–206
mentors, 333–334, 337
meta-analysis, 213
MHC (mental health consultation), 205–206
minoritized students, 54–55
 increasing knowledge of, 54–55
 share and improve skills related to, 55
minority-serving institutions (MSIs), 25
mitigation, response, and recovery, 226–227
mixed methods, 271
MLA (Model Licensure Act), 33–34
Model Licensure Act (MLA), 33–34
moral internationalization, 297
MSIs (minority-serving institutions), 25
MTSS (multitiered systems of support), 33, 92, 140–145, 162–166, 173–184
multicultural competence, 44
multicultural considerations in assessment, 132–133
multicultural education, 44
multicultural foundations, 43–56
 homogeneous workforce, challenges in, 46
 social justice, intersectionality foundations and, 44–45
 U.S. public school students, 46–48
multiculturalism and social justice in school psychology practice, 14–15, 53–56, 214
 biases, identifying and challenging, 54
 minoritized students, increasing knowledge of, 54–56
 personal awareness and knowledge of self as intersectional, developing, 53
 recommendations for enhancing, 53–56
 social justice advocacy, 55–56
multiple exemplars, 165
multitiered systems of support (MTSS), 33, 92, 140–145, 162–166, 173–184
 addressing academic skill problems through, 162–166
 assessment and intervention in, 141
 screening, assessment, and progress monitoring in, 143–145
 for social, emotional, and behavioral (SEB) functioning, 173–184
 Tier 1, 141–144, 162–163
 Tier 2, 142, 144–145, 163–166
 Tier 3, 142–145, 166

narrative inquiry, 270
NASP (National Association of School Psychologists), 4, 27, 46, 48, 101, 156, 222
NASP Practice Model, 5–10, 83, 234, 264–267, 271, 316
NASP's *Principles for Professional Ethics*, 30, 84, 85–88, 102, 315
National Association of School Psychologists (NASP), 4, 27, 46, 48, 101, 156, 222
 graduate preparation standards, 105
 Practice Model, 5–10, 83, 234, 264–267, 271, 316
 Principles for Professional Ethics, 30, 84, 85–88, 102, 315
 Professional Standards of the National Association of School Psychologists, 30
National Center for Education Statistics (NCES), 309
National Council for Accreditation of Teacher Education (NCATE), 29, 108
National Emergency Assistance Team (NEAT), 32
National School Psychology Certification System (NCSP), 30–31
National School Psychology Inservice Training Network (NSPITN), 29–30
Nationally Certified School Psychologist (NCSP), 96, 108, 109, 115
navigational capital, 237
NCATE (National Council for Accreditation of Teacher Education), 29, 108

NCES (National Center for Education Statistics), 309
NCLB (No Child Left Behind) Act, 33, 91–92
NCSP (Nationally Certified School Psychologist), 96, 108, 109, 115
NCSP (National School Psychology Certification System), 30–31
NEAT (National Emergency Assistance Team), 32
No Child Left Behind (NCLB) Act, 33, 91–92
nondegree-seeking programs, 112–113
nondoctoral degrees, 103–104
nondoctoral practice, 114
nonmaleficence, 87
nonpractice credentials, 109, 115
nonsense word fluency (NWF), 158
norm-referenced comparisons (NRCs), 127–128
norm-referenced tests (NRTs), 128, 158, 161
NRCs (norm-referenced comparisons), 127–128
NRTs (norm-referenced tests), 128, 158, 161
NSPITN (National School Psychology Inservice Training Network), 29–30
number sense, 157
NWF (nonsense word fluency), 158

objectivity, 215
observability, intervention planning and implementation, 150
observed score, 124
ODC (organization development consultation), 207–208
ODRs (office disciplinary referrals), 253
office disciplinary referrals (ODRs), 253
open review, 272
opportunity gap, 48–49
organization development consultation (ODC), 207–208
organizational conflict in the 21st century, 33–34
outcome assessment, 127

PARC (Pennsylvania Association for Retarded Children), 28
pattern of strengths and weaknesses (PSW) approach, 196
PBIS (Positive Behavioral Interventions and Supports), 174, 223, 250
PBQ (Problem Behavior Questionnaire), 180
peer review, 272–273
   process, 272
   types of, 272–273
Pennsylvania Association for Retarded Children (PARC), 28
permanent products, 179
personal awareness and knowledge of self as intersectional, developing, 53

phenomenology, 270
phonological awareness, 156
physical safety, 223
Plessy v. Ferguson, 26
Positive Behavioral Interventions and Supports (PBIS), 174, 223, 250
positivism, 269
Power/Interaction Model of Interpersonal Influence, 211–212
practice credentials, 109
   alternative, provisional, or temporary credentialing, 112
   doctoral practice, 113
   eligibility and education, 110
   examinations, 111
   maintenance and renewal of, 114
   nondoctoral practice, 114
   outside of schools, 113–114
   for practice in schools, 110–112
   related credentials, 113
   respecialization and professional retraining (RPR), 112–113
   setting and scope of services, 112
   at state level, 109–114
   supervised field experiences, 111
   title, 111
practicum, 111
practitioner shortages, 309–310
PREPaRE model, 32, 222, 257
prevention, 140
primary implementers, 149
Principles for Professional Ethics, NASP, 30, 84, 85–88, 102, 315
Principles of Psychology, The, 20
privilege, 53
Problem Behavior Questionnaire (PBQ), 180
problem-solving model, 145–146
   plan development and implementation, 146
   plan evaluation, 146
   problem analysis, 146
   problem identification, 146
problem-solving process, consultation as, 206, 210–213
   analyzing the problem, 211
   identifying and clarifying the problem, 210–212
   implementation procedures and responsibilities, clarifying, 212–213
   implementing the intervention, 212
   intervention effectiveness and follow-up, evaluating, 212–213
   relationship building/establishing a cooperative partnership, 210
   selecting an intervention, 211–212
professional competence and responsibility, 87–88

professional identity, 25–27
professional internationalization, 297
professional organizations, 25
professional relationships, honesty and integrity in, 88
professional standards, 102–103
Professional Standards of the National Association of School Psychologists, 30
program accreditation, competency areas, 104–106
program evaluation, 248, 253, 271–272
progress monitoring, 126–127, 144
provisional credentialing, 112
PSW (pattern of strengths and weaknesses) approach, 196
psychoeducation, 226
psychological safety, 223
Psychological Service for School Problems, 24
psychometric intelligence, 190
psychometrics, 123
psychometrist, 113
public health model, 33
public legislation relevant to school psychology, 89–92
punishment, 180

qualitative interpretations, 128
qualitative research, 269–271
quantitative research, 268–269

racism, 62–63. *See also* antiracism and school psychology; K–12 education, racism in
  internalized/intrapersonal racism, 62, 63
  interpersonal/individual/personally mediated racism, 62, 63
  levels of, 62–63
  school psychology and, 67–70
  systemic/structural/institutionalized racism, 62, 63
random assignment, 147
randomized controlled trial (RCT), 147, 214, 269
rating scales, 130, 178–179
raw score, intelligence testing, 192
RCT (randomized controlled trial), 147, 214, 269
reading, 156
  comprehension, 156
  fluency, 156
reason for referral, 122
referent power, 211
referral question, 122
Rehabilitation Act of 1973, 90–91
reinforcement, 180
relationship building, 175, 210, 238
relative advantage, intervention planning and implementation, 150

reliability, 124
replacement behaviors, 182
report writing, 15
research in school psychology, 263–274
  academic interventions and instructional supports, 265
  becoming a good consumer of, 273
  case studies, 270
  causal-comparative designs, 268
  consultation and collaboration, 264–265
  correlational designs, 268
  data-based decision-making, 264
  equitable practices for diverse student populations, 266
  ethnography, 270
  evidence-based practice and, 267
  experimental designs, 269
  family, school, and community collaboration, 266
  grounded theory, 270
  interactionist–constructivist, 270
  legal, ethical, and professional practice, 267
  mental health and behavioral interventions, 265
  methodologies, 267–272
  mixed methods, 271
  narrative inquiry, 270
  peer review, 272–273
  phenomenology, 270
  program evaluation, 271–272
  qualitative research, 269–271
  quantitative research, 268–269
  school-wide practices to promote learning, 265
  services to promote safe and supportive schools, 265–266
  single-case design, 269
  survey designs, 268
resistance capital, 237, 240
respecialization and professional retraining (RPR), 112–113
responsible decision-making, 175
restorative justice (RJ), 215–216
  school-based restorative justice (SBRJ), 50–51
résumé, developing, 339–341
reviews, 272–273
  double-blind review, 272
  open review, 272
  process, 272
  single-blind review, 272
  types of, 272–273
riskiness, intervention planning and implementation, 150
RJ (restorative justice), 215–216

RPR (respecialization and professional retraining), 112–113

SAEP (school and educational psychology), 284–293, 294–295, 296
Sanchez, George, 23
SAVRY (Structured Assessment of Violence Risk in Youth), 225
SBRJ (school-based restorative justice), 50–51
school and educational psychology (SAEP), 284–293, 294–295, 296
school-based partnerships, 235
school-based restorative justice (SBRJ), 50–51
school climate, 52
school district leadership teams, multitiered systems of support, 208
school leadership teams, multitiered systems of support, 208
school-linked partnerships, 235
school psychological professional practices, 5–10
　academic interventions and supports, 7
　consultation and collaboration, 5, 7
　data-based decision-making, 5–6
　direct services, 7
　equitable practices for diverse populations, 9
　family, school, and community collaboration, 8
　indirect services, 8
　legal, ethical, and professional practice, 10
　mental and behavioral health services, 7
　practices that permeate all services, 5–7
　and related professions, 12–13
　research and evidence-based practice, 9
　school-wide practices to promote learning, 8
　service delivery, foundations of, 9–10
　services to promote safe and supportive schools, 8
　student-level services, 7
school psychologists, 10–12, 45–46
　demographics of, 45–46
　full-time psychologists, professional practices of, 11
　NASP's *Principles for Professional Ethics*, 30, 84, 85–88, 102, 315
　professional activities and employment of, 10–12
school psychology, 3–17, 284
　child clinical psychology versus, 13
　defining, 4–5
　history, 20
　multiculturalism and, 14–15
　school counseling versus, 12
　social justice and, 13–16
school psychology preparation, 103

school psychology professional practices, 68–69
school psychology programs (SPPs), 103–104
school psychology research and graduate preparation, 69–70
School Psychology Specialist (SPS), 111
school-to-prison pipeline, 65
school violence and crisis, 221–229
　balancing physical and psychology safety, 223
　comprehensive planning for preventing, 223–225
　crisis teams and plans, 225–226
　defining, 222–227
　mitigation, response, and recovery, 226–227
　PREPaRE model, 222
　prevention and intervention, 221–229
　　evidence-based practice in, 222
　　promoting equity through, 227–228
　prevention and protection, 222–226
　threat assessment, 223–225
school-wide practices to promote learning, 8, 265
scientist-practitioner model, 27
screening, 125
SDO (systematic direct observation), 178
SEB (social, emotional, and behavioral) assessment and intervention, 171–184
secondary implementers, 149
Section 504 Plan, 90
SEL (social and emotional learning), 174–175, 223
self-awareness, 174
self-management, 174
self-monitoring, 177
semistructured interviews, 181
service delivery, foundations of, 9–10
shared values, 238
shared vision, 249
shortages, school psychology, 308–311
　balanced, 309
　considerable shortage, 309
　considerable surplus, 309
　graduate program and faculty shortages, 310–311
　graduate student enrollment shortages, 310
　practitioner shortages, 309–310
　some shortage, 309
　some surplus, 309
Simon, Théodore, 22, 191
single-blind review, 272
single-case design, 269
skill, multicultural competence, 132
SLD (specific learning disability), 195–196
SoA (Standards of Accreditation) for Health Service Psychology, 102, 105, 107

social capital, 237, 240
social and emotional learning (SEL), 174–175, 223
social, emotional, and behavioral (SEB) assessment and intervention, 171–184
  assessment, 175–179
  behavior intervention plan (BIP), 181–182
  class-wide behavioral interventions, 175
  definitions and prevalence, 172–173
  Direct Behavior Ratings (DBRs), 179
  functional behavior assessment (FBA), 180–181
  intervention, 181–183
  multitiered systems of support (MTSS) for, 173–184
  permanent products, 179
  Positive Behavioral Interventions and Supports (PBIS), 173–174
  rating scales, 178–179
  social and emotional learning (SEL), 174–175
  systematic direct observation (SDO), 178
  therapeutic interventions, 183
  Tier 1 interventions, 173–177
  Tier 2 interventions, 177–179
social intelligence, 190
social justice, 13–16, 214, 318
  advocacy, 55–56
  in consultation, 215–216
  defining, 13–14
  school psychology and, 13–16
Social Skills Intervention Guide, 177
social system, 149
Society for the Study of School Psychology (SSSP), 32, 71
Spearman, Charles, 191
special education, disproportionality in, 64
special programming, representation in, 49
specialist-level degree, 103
specialized field placements, 332–333, 336
specialty, 4
specific learning disability (SLD), 195–196
spelling curriculum-based measurement, 160
SPPs (school psychology programs), 103–104
Spring Hill Symposium and Olympia Conference, 29
SPS (School Psychology Specialist), 111
SSSP (Society for the Study of School Psychology), 32, 71
standard deviation, 192
Standards of Accreditation (SoA) for Health Service Psychology, 102, 105, 107
Stanford-Binet Scale, 68, 193
state-mandated tests, 161–162
state-wide assessments, 127
stereotype threat, 197
strengths-based assessments, 129

structural racism, 62–63
Structured Assessment of Violence Risk in Youth (SAVRY), 225
structured interview schedules, 181
student-level services, 7
summative assessment, 124–125
summative evaluation, 253
supervised field experiences, 111
supervisors, 333–334, 337
survey designs, 268
systematic direct observation (SDO), 178
systemic racism in K–12 schools, 62–65
systemic/structural/institutionalized racism, 62, 63
systems change, 247–258
  considerations for leading, 252–257
  and educational reform, research on, 249–250
  evaluating school and student outcomes in, 253–257
  exploration stage, 250
  frameworks for, 250–252
  full implementation, 251
  implementation drivers, 253
  initial implementation stage, 251
  installation stage, 250
  program evaluation and, 247–258
  in the schools, 248–249
  sustainability, 251
systems-level services, 8

task analysis, 164
task relevance, intervention planning and implementation, 150
team-based consultation, 208–209
technology-oriented service delivery, 317–318
teleconsultation, 209
telepsychology practices, 318
temporary credentialing, 112
Terman, Lewis, 22, 68
testing, 127–128
test–retest reliability, 124
tests, essential features of, 123–124
Thayer Conference, 27, 70, 306
therapeutic interventions, 183
Thorndike, Edward, 22
Thoroughbred Years (1970–present), 20, 28–35
  coronavirus 2019 pandemic, 34–35
  ecological model, 32
  evolving agenda, 32–33
  federally mandated special education services, emergence of, 28–29
  graduate programs and professional accreditation, 29–30
  legislation of the 1990s and 2000s, 33
  medical model, 32

Thoroughbred Years (1970–present) (*continued*)
    organizational conflict, 33–34
    past to the present, transition, 34
    professional regulation, 30–31
    public health model, 33
    Spring Hill Symposium and Olympia Conference, 29–30
    training and practice, advances in, 29–30
threat assessment, 223–225
three-stratum theory, 191
total words spelled correctly (WSC), 160
total words written (TWW), 160
total WSC (words spelled correctly), 160
trialability, intervention planning and implementation, 150
TWW (total words written), 160

United States, psychology emergence in, 20
universal screening, 125, 143
U.S. public school students, 46–52
    demographics of, 46–48
    discipline, 49–50
    low income and economic marginalization (LIEM), 47, 51–52
    minoritized students, challenges faced by, 48–52
    opportunity gap, 48–49
    school climate, 52
    special programming, representation in, 49

Vail Conference, 31
validity, 123–124
vested partners, intervention implementation, 149
vocabulary, 156

Wechsler Intelligence Scale for Children, Fifth Edition, 192
WIF (word identification fluency), 158
Witmer, Lightner, 22, 67–68
Woodcock-Johnson, Fourth Edition, Tests of Achievement, 128
Woodcock-Johnson IV Tests of Cognitive Abilities, 192
word identification fluency (WIF), 158
words read correctly per minute (WRCM), 59
World War II, impact on psychology, 25–26
WRCM (words read correctly per minute), 59
writing curriculum-based measurement, 160
written language, 157

Youth Participatory Action Research (YPAR), 73
YPAR (Youth Participatory Action Research), 73